Worship & Rejoice

Hope Publishing Company
CAROL STREAM IL 60188

WORSHIP & REJOICE

Hope Publishing Company
380 South Main Place
Carol Stream, IL 60188
800-323-1049
fax 630-665-2552
email hope@hopepublishing.com
www.hopepublishing.com

			code no.
ISBN:	0-916642-68-2	Blue Pew Edition	8020
ISBN:	0-916642-70-4	Red Pew Edition	8024
ISBN:	0-916642-69-0	Green Pew Edition	8025
ISBN:	0-916642-72-0	Accompaniment Edition (blue only)	8022

First Edition 2001

WORSHIP & REJOICE

FOREWORD

Founded in 1892, Hope Publishing Company is an independent, non-denominational publisher of church music. Our first publication was a collection of "advance pages" for a hymnal released in 1894. Throughout our history we have continued to produce new hymnals for the churches of North America. Being responsive to the scriptural imperative, "Sing a new song to the Lord," our mission is unmistakably clear: the high calling and privilege of providing new music resources to aid the church in worship. Today, churches are drawing their music from both traditional and contemporary sources, from near and far. *Worship & Rejoice* was conceived to meet all the worship needs of that church in this new day.

We have tried to open our hearts and our hands, to cast our nets wider, to be more inclusive in assembling the contents of this collection. Serious consideration has been given to multicultural expressions of faith through song. Many new contemporary resources have been tapped, including a number of hymns from Taizé as well as other songs of ecumenical origin. We have also included a wide selection of praise and worship, and contemporary Christian songs. The historic hymns, those passed down to us from generation to generation, have been carefully scrutinized to assure their clarity and relevance. In the same thoughtful manner, the selection of music features tunes that are both musically satisfying and singable.

We are indebted to a large number of people who helped in the preparation of this book. Every hymnal Hope produced from 1950 to 1990 was under the supervision of editor, Dr. Donald P. Hustad. His vision and expertise laid the groundwork for this project. Emeritus editor, Dr. Carlton R. Young, was an early enthusiast and served as a consultant. Scott A. Shorney served as project coordinator, and was assisted by Susan Gilbert, Angela Zajac, and the entire Hope staff. Andrew Parks of River Falls, Wisconsin, produced the clean note-setting displayed on these pages. Under the watchful eye of Roger Wagner, all of our hymnbooks are printed and bound by Bang Printing of Brainard, Minnesota. Larry Shackley of Columbia, South Carolina, provided the guitar chords found in the accompaniment edition. John Shorney was responible for design and layout. The title calligraphy was created by Arthur Modjeski of Bloomingdale, Illinois. Micah Marty of Chicago, Illinois, provided the photographs and Rosa + Wesley Design Associates in Winfield, Illinois, created the section division pages. For proofreading and indexes, gratitude is expressed for the excellent help provided by Dr. Austin C. Lovelace, James Clemens, and the Rev. Greg Asimakoupoulos.

The 20th century opened with the great hope that it would become the Christian century—that enlightened and thoughtful people would lead us into an age of peace and understanding. History proved otherwise as that century ushered in world wars, global conflicts and, at its close, a growing secular culture. Many in the Christian community are pondering whether this new millennium will truly become a post-Christian era. Yet, new beginnings are always filled with hope, and those of us who work for a company that claims that name have dedicated our time and effort to producing a book that we trust will encourage and support the faith community well into this new century. To quote poet Fred Pratt Green:

When in our music God is glorified,
And adoration leaves no room for pride,
It is as though the whole creation cried,
"Allcluia!"

May *Worship & Rejoice* fulfill the challenge we set for ourselves when this project began. Our prayer is that this hymnal will be used as an instrument of God's grace and peace, and serve today's church in the worship of Almighty God.

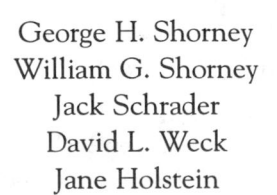

George H. Shorney
William G. Shorney
Jack Schrader
David L. Weck
Jane Holstein

CONTENTS

THE CHURCH PRAISING 1-151

- God 1-19
  - of Creation 20-40
  - of Majesty & Power 41-54
  - of Love & Mercy 55-68
  - of Providence & Care 69-86
- Jesus Christ 87-127
- The Holy Spirit 128-135
- The Trinity 136-151

THE CHURCH YEAR 152-342

- Advent 152-177
- Christmas 178-228
- Epiphany 229-249
- Lent 250-264
- Palm Sunday 265-271
- Holy Week 272-286
- Easter 287-316
- Ascension 317-324
- Pentecost 325-334
- Christ the King 335-342

THE CHURCH REDEEMED 343-540

- Call to Discipleship 343-354
- New Life in Christ 355-369
- Confession & Forgiveness 370-387
- Christian Community 388-396
- Love & Joy 397-403
- Faith & Hope 404-421
- Trust & Assurance 422-452
- Commitment & Renewal 453-468
- Prayer & Devotion 469-493
- Pilgrimage & Perseverance 494-506

Conflict & Victory 507-514
Death & Life Eternal 515-527
Communion of Saints 528-531
New Creation 532-540

THE CHURCH IN THE WORLD 541-645

Nature & Foundation 541-550
Witness & Mission 551-565
Ministry & Service 566-593
Christian Unity 594-604
Family & Relationships 605-613
Justice & Peace 614-627
Healing & Wholeness 628-640
Art & Science 641-645

THE CHURCH IN WORSHIP 646-749

Gathering 646-661
Word & Teaching 662-671
Affirmation of Faith 672-675
Baptism 676-680
Child Dedication 681-683
Stewardship & Giving 684-688
Holy Communion 689-707
Going Forth 708-719
Special Times & Seasons 720-731
Service Music 732-749

INDEXES

Index of Copyright Owners 790-804
Scriptural Index 805-816
Index of Hymn Tunes 817-819
Metrical Index 820-823
Index of Authors, Composers and Sources 824-830
Topical Index 831-855
Alphabetical Index 856-864

THE CHURCH PRAISING

1 God Is Here!

1 God is here! As we your peo - ple meet to of - fer
2 Here are sym - bols to re - mind us of our life - long
3 Here our chil - dren find a wel - come in the Shep - herd's
4 Lord of all, of church and king - dom, in an age of
praise and prayer, may we find in full - er mea - sure
need of grace; here are ta - ble, font, and pul - pit;
flock and fold; here as bread and wine are tak - en,
change and doubt, keep us faith - ful to the Gos - pel;
what it is in Christ we share. Here, as in the world a -
here the cross has cen - tral place. Here in hon - es - ty of
Christ sus - tains us as of old. Here the ser - vants of the
help us work your pur - pose out. Here, in this day's ded - i -
round us, all our var - ied skills and arts wait the
preach - ing, here in si - lence, as in speech, here, in
Ser - vant seek in wor - ship to ex - plore what it
ca - tion, all we have to give, re - ceive; we, who

WORDS: Fred Pratt Green (1903-2000)
MUSIC: Cyril V. Taylor (1907-1991)

ABBOT'S LEIGH
8.7.8.7.D.

com - ing of the Spir - it in - to o - pen minds and hearts.
new - ness and re - new - al, God the Spir - it comes to each.
means in dai - ly liv - ing to be - lieve and to a - dore.
can - not live with - out you, we a - dore you! We be - lieve!

O Worship the King 2

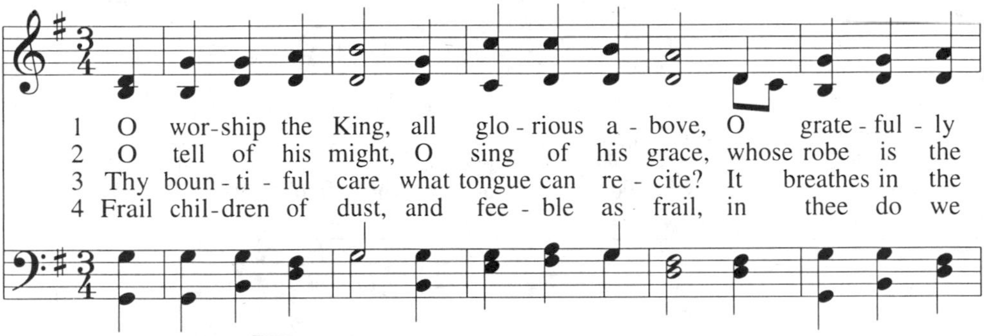
1 O wor-ship the King, all glo - rious a - bove, O grate - ful - ly
2 O tell of his might, O sing of his grace, whose robe is the
3 Thy boun - ti - ful care what tongue can re - cite? It breathes in the
4 Frail chil-dren of dust, and fee - ble as frail, in thee do we

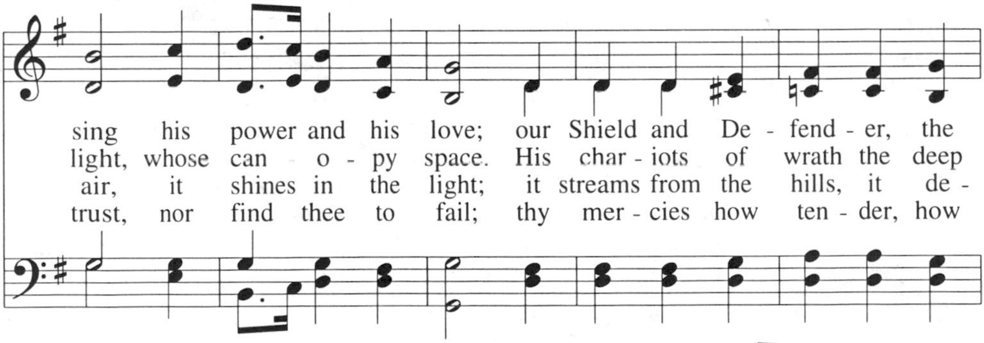
sing his power and his love; our Shield and De - fend - er, the
light, whose can o - py space. His char - iots of wrath the deep
air, it shines in the light; it streams from the hills, it de -
trust, nor find thee to fail; thy mer - cies how ten - der, how

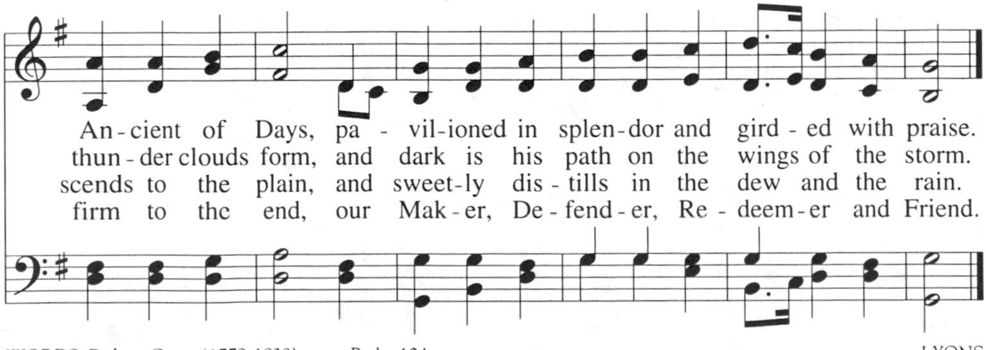
An - cient of Days, pa - vil-ioned in splen-dor and gird - ed with praise.
thun - der clouds form, and dark is his path on the wings of the storm.
scends to the plain, and sweet-ly dis - tills in the dew and the rain.
firm to the end, our Mak - er, De - fend - er, Re - deem - er and Friend.

WORDS: Robert Grant (1779-1838); para. Psalm 104
MUSIC: Attr. Johann M. Haydn (1737-1806); William Gardiner's *Sacred Melodies*, Vol. II, 1815

LYONS
10.10.11.11.

3 God, We Praise You!

1 God, we praise you! God, we bless you! God, we name you sov-ereign Lord!
2 True a - pos - tles, faith-ful proph-ets, saints who set the world a - blaze,
3 Je - sus Christ, the King of glo - ry, ev - er - last - ing Son of God,
4 Christ, at God's right hand vic - to - rious, you will judge the world you made;
Might - y King whom an - gels wor - ship, Fa - ther, by your church a - dored:
mar - tyrs, once un-known, un - heed - ed, join one grow - ing song of praise,
hum - ble was your vir - gin moth - er, hard the lone - ly path you trod.
Lord, in mer - cy help your ser - vants for whose free - dom you have paid.
all cre - a - tion shows your glo - ry, heaven and earth draw near your throne
while your church on earth con - fess - es one ma - jes - tic Trin - i - ty:
By your cross is sin de - feat - ed, hell con - front - ed face to face,
Raise us up from dust to glo - ry, guard us from all sin to - day;
sing - ing, "Ho - ly, ho - ly, ho - ly, Lord of hosts, and God a - lone."
Fa - ther, Son, and Ho - ly Spir - it, God, our hope e - ter - nal - ly.
heav - en o - pened to be - liev - ers, sin - ners jus - ti - fied by grace.
King en - throned a - bove all prais - es, save your peo - ple, God, we pray.

WORDS: Christopher Idle (1938-); para. *Te Deum Laudamus*
MUSIC: C. Hubert H. Parry (1848-1918)

RUSTINGTON
8.7.8.7.D.

Bless His Holy Name

4

Eb Bb7/F Bb7 Eb Bb7 Eb7 Ab Abm6
Bless the Lord, O my soul, and all that is with - in me, bless his
Eb/Bb Ebm6/Bb Bb Bb7 Eb Eb F7/C Bb
ho - ly name. He has done great things,
Cm7 Bb7/D Eb Eb7 Ab Abm6/F
he has done great things, he has done great things, bless his
Eb/Bb Bb7 Eb Eb Bb7/F Bb7
ho - ly name. Bless the Lord, O my soul, and
Eb Bb7 Eb7 Ab Abm6 Eb/Bb Ebm6/Bb Bb Bb7 Eb
all that is with - in me, bless his ho - ly name.

WORDS and MUSIC: Andraé Crouch (1945-); para. Psalm 103:1

5 Halle, Halle, Hallelujah

Refrain
Hal - le, hal - le, hal - le - lu - jah.
hal - le - lu - jah.
jah.
Hal - le, hal - le, hal - le - lu - jah.
hal - le - lu - jah.
jah.
Hal - le, hal - le, hal - le - lu - jah. Hal - le -
1, 2 (Second time to verse)
Last time
lu - jah, hal - le - lu - jah.
lu - jah, hal - le - lu, hal - le - lu - jah. jah.
lu - jah, hal - le - lu - jah.

WORDS: Caribbean; verses Hal H. Hopson (1933-); para. Psalm 150
MUSIC: Caribbean melody; original music and setting by Hal H. Hopson (1933-)

Verses (Optional Solo)
1 Praise God in this ho - ly place, ev - ery na - tion, ev - ery race.
2 Ev - ery-thing that breathes now praise; sing your songs, let voic - es raise.
Come, make joy - ful mu - sic to the Lord.
Sound the trum - pet, sound it clear. Sound it for the world to hear.
Play the cym - bals, play the lute; play the tim - brel, play the flute.
to Refrain
Come, make joy - ful mu - sic to the Lord.

6 Let the Whole Creation Cry

1 Let the whole cre - a - tion cry, "Glo - ry to the Lord on high!"
2 Chris-tians striv - ing for the Lord, proph-ets burn-ing with his Word,
3 Men and wom - en, young and old, raise the an - them loud and bold,

Heaven and earth, a - wake and sing, "Praise to our al - might-y King!"
those to whom the arts be - long add their voic - es to the song.
and let chil - dren's hap - py hearts in this wor-ship take their parts;

Praise him, an - gel hosts a - bove, ev - er bright and fair in love;
Those of knowl-edge and of law, to the glo - rious cir - cle draw;
from the north to south-ern pole let the might-y cho - rus roll:

sun and moon, lift up your voice; night and stars, in God re - joice.
all who work and all who wait, sing, "The Lord is good and great!"
"Ho - ly, Ho - ly, Ho - ly One, glo - ry be to God a - lone!"

WORDS: Stopford A. Brooke (1832-1916), alt.
MUSIC: Jakob Hintze (1622-1702); arr. J. S. Bach (1685-1750)

SALZBURG
7.7.7.7.D.

When in Our Music God Is Glorified 7

Unison
1 When in our mu - sic God is glo - ri - fied,
2 How of - ten, mak - ing mu - sic, we have found
3 So has the Church, in lit - ur - gy and song,
4 And did not Je - sus sing a psalm that night
5 Let ev - ery in - stru-ment be tuned for praise!
and ad - o - ra - tion leaves no room for pride,
a new di - men - sion in the world of sound,
in faith and love, through cen - tu - ries of wrong,
when ut - most e - vil strove a - gainst the light?
Let all re - joice who have a voice to raise!
it is as though the whole cre - a - tion cried:
as wor - ship moved us to a more pro - found
borne wit - ness to the truth in ev - ery tongue:
Then let us sing, for whom he won the fight:
And may God give us faith to sing al - ways:
1–4
5
1–4 Al - le - lu - ia!
5 Al - le - lu - ia!

WORDS: Fred Pratt Green (1903-2000)
MUSIC: Charles V. Stanford (1852-1924)

ENGELBERG
10.10.10.Alleluias

8 New Songs of Celebration

1 New songs of cel - e - bra - tion ren - der to God who
2 Joy - ful - ly, heart - i - ly re - sound - ing, let ev - ery
3 Riv - ers and seas and tor - rents roar - ing, hon - or the
has great won - ders done; love sits en - throned in age - less splen - dor;
in - stru - ment and voice peal out the praise of grace a - bound - ing,
Lord with wild ac - claim; moun-tains and stones, look up a - dor - ing,
come and a - dore the Might - y One. God has made known the great sal -
call - ing the whole world to re - joice. Trum - pets and or - gans, set in
and find a voice to praise God's name. Right - eous, com - mand - ing, ev - er
va - tion which all the saints with joy con - fess. God has re -
mo - tion such sounds as make the heav - ens ring; all things that
glo - rious, prais - es be sung that nev - er cease: just is our

WORDS: Erik Routley (1917-1982); para. Psalm 98
MUSIC: Louis Bourgeois (ca. 1510-1561), *Genevan Psalter*, 1551

RENDEZ À DIEU
9.8.9.8.D.

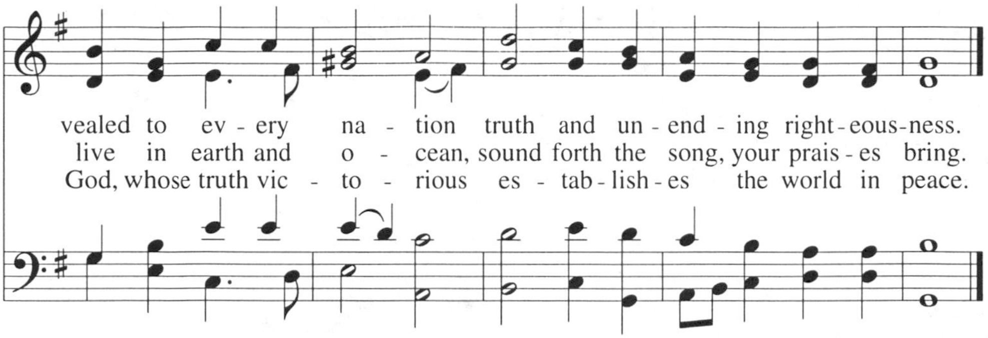
vealed to ev - ery na - tion truth and un - end - ing right - eous-ness.
live in earth and o - cean, sound forth the song, your prais - es bring.
God, whose truth vic - to - rious es - tab - lish - es the world in peace.

Come, Let Us Praise the Lord 9

1 Come, let us praise the Lord, with joy our God ac - claim, his
2 Our God of match-less worth, our King be - yond com - pare, the
3 In wor - ship bow the knee, our glo - rious God con - fess; the
4 Come, hear his voice to - day, re - ceive what love im - parts; his
great-ness tell a - broad and bless his sav - ing name. Lift high your
deep - est bounds of earth, the hills, are in his care. He all de -
great Cre - a - tor, he, the Lord of Right - eous - ness. He reigns un -
ho - ly will o - bey and hard - en not your hearts. His ways are
songs be - fore his throne to whom a - lone all praise be - longs.
crees, who by his hand pre - pared the land and formed the seas.
seen: his flock he feeds and gent - ly leads in pas - tures green.
best; and lead at last, all trou - bles past, to per - fect rest.

WORDS: Timothy Dudley-Smith (1926-); para. Psalm 95
MUSIC: John Darwall (1731-1789)

DARWALL'S 148th
6.6.6.6.4.4.8.

10 Sing a New Song

Refrain (Unison)
Sing a new song un - to the Lord; let your song be
sung from moun - tains high. Sing a new song
un - to the Lord, sing-ing, "Al - le - lu - ia."

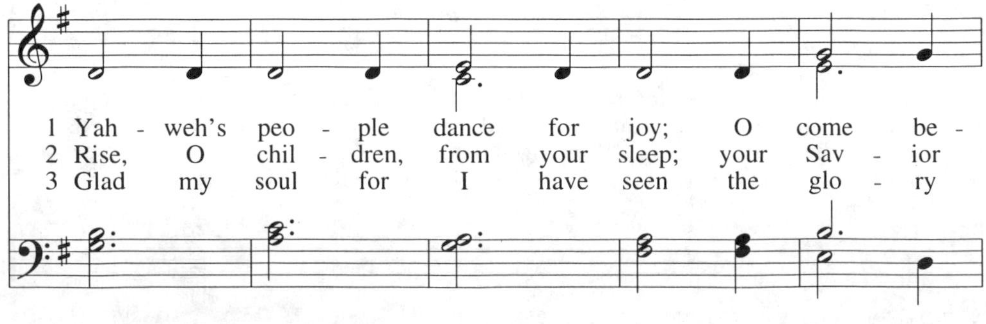
1 Yah - weh's peo - ple dance for joy; O come be -
2 Rise, O chil - dren, from your sleep; your Sav - ior
3 Glad my soul for I have seen the glo - ry

WORDS and MUSIC: Daniel L. Schutte (1947-)

fore the Lord. And play for him on
now has come. He has turned your
of the Lord. The trum - pet sounds; the
to Refrain
glad tam - bou-rines, and let your trum - pet sound.
sor - row to joy, and filled your soul with song.
dead shall be raised. I know my Sav - ior lives.

Stand Up and Bless the Lord 11

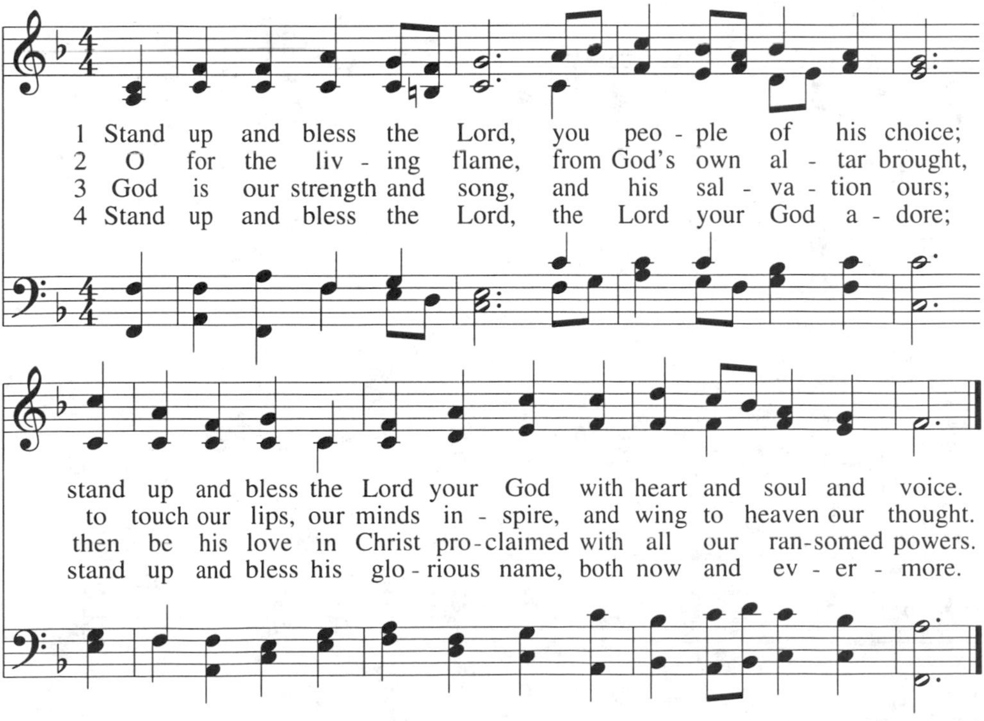
1 Stand up and bless the Lord, you peo - ple of his choice;
2 O for the liv - ing flame, from God's own al - tar brought,
3 God is our strength and song, and his sal - va - tion ours;
4 Stand up and bless the Lord, the Lord your God a - dore;
stand up and bless the Lord your God with heart and soul and voice.
to touch our lips, our minds in - spire, and wing to heaven our thought.
then be his love in Christ pro-claimed with all our ran-somed powers.
stand up and bless his glo - rious name, both now and ev - er - more.

WORDS: James Montgomery (1771-1854)
MUSIC: Aaron Williams' *New Universal Psalmodist*, 1770

ST. THOMAS
S.M.

12 Be Exalted, O God

Cm7 F7 Bb F7/C Bb/D Bb F/A C7/G F
Be ex - alt - ed, O God, a - bove the heav - ens;
Cm7 F Eb/F Bb Bdim7 F7/C
let thy glo - ry be o - ver all the earth.
Cm7 F7 Bb F7/C Bb/D Bb F/A C7/G F
Be ex - alt - ed, O God, a - bove the heav - ens;
Cm7 F Eb/F F7 Bb
let thy glo - ry be o - ver all the earth.

WORDS: Brent Chambers (1948-); para. Psalm 57:9-11
MUSIC: Brent Chambers (1948-)

Sing a New Song to the Lord 13

Unison
1 Sing a new song to the Lord, he to whom won-ders be-long; re-joice in his tri-umph and tell of his power, O sing to the Lord a new song!
2 Now to the ends of the earth see his sal-va-tion is shown; and still he re-mem-bers his mer-cy and truth, un-chang-ing in love to his own.
3 Sing a new song and re-joice, pub-lish his prais-es a-broad; let voic-es in cho-rus, with trum-pet and horn, re-sound for the joy of the Lord!
4 Join with the hills and the sea thun-ders of praise to pro-long; in judg-ment and jus-tice he comes to the earth, O sing to the Lord a new song!
1–3
4

WORDS: Timothy Dudley-Smith (1926-)
MUSIC: David G. Wilson (1940-)

ONSLOW SQUARE
7.7.11.8.

14 Now Thank We All Our God

1 Now thank we all our God with heart and hands and voic - es,
2 O may this boun - teous God through all our life be near us,
3 All praise and thanks to God the Fa - ther now be giv - en,
who won-drous things has done, in whom his world re - joic - es;
with ev - er joy - ful hearts and bless - ed peace to cheer us;
the Son, and him who reigns with them in high - est heav - en,
who, from our moth - er's arms, has blessed us on our way
and keep us in his grace and guide us when per - plexed,
the one e - ter - nal God whom earth and heaven a - dore;
with count - less gifts of love, and still is ours to - day.
and free us from all ills in this world and the next.
for thus it was, is now, and shall be ev - er - more.

WORDS: Martin Rinkart (1586-1649); tr. Catherine Winkworth (1827-1878), alt.
MUSIC: Johann Crüger (1598-1662); harm. Felix Mendelssohn (1809-1847)

NUN DANKET ALLE GOTT
6.7.6.7.6.6.6.6.

O, Sing to the Lord

Cantad al Señor

Unison
Em B B7
1 O, sing to the Lord, O, sing God a new song. O, sing to the
2 For God is the Lord, and God has done won-ders. For God is the
3 For Je - sus is Lord! A - men! Al - le - lu - ia! For Je - sus is
1 Can - tad al Se - ñor un cán - ti - co nue - vo. Can - tad al Se -
2 Pues nues-tro Se - ñor ha he - cho pro - di - gios. Pues nues-tro Se -
3 ¡Je - sús es Se - ñor! ¡A - mén! A - le - lu - ya! ¡Je - sús es Se -
B7 Em
Lord. O, sing God a new song. O, sing to the Lord, O,
Lord, and God has done won - ders. For God is the Lord, and
Lord! A - men! Al - le - lu - ia! For Je - sus is Lord! A -
ñor un cán - ti - co nue - vo. Can - tad al Se - ñor un
ñor ha he - cho pro - di - gios. Pues nues - tro Se - ñor ha
ñor! ¡A - mén! A - le - lu - ya! ¡Je - sús es Se - ñor! ¡A -
E7 Am Em B7 Em
sing God a new song. O, sing to our God. O, sing to our God.
God has done won-ders. O, sing to our God, O, sing to our God.
men! Al - le - lu - ia! O, sing to our God, O, sing to our God.
cán - ti - co nue - vo. ¡Can-tad al Se - ñor, can - tad al Se - ñor!
he - cho pro - di - gios. ¡Can-tad al Se - ñor, can - tad al Se - ñor!
mén! A - le - lu - ya! ¡Can-tad al Se - ñor, can - tad al Se - ñor!

WORDS: Brazilian folk song, "Cantai ao Senhor;"
Spanish and English translations from Portuguese by Gerhard Cartford (1923-)
MUSIC: Brazilian folk melody; arr. Jack Schrader (1942-)

CANTAD AL SEÑOR
Irregular

16 The God of Abraham Praise

1 The God of A-braham praise, who reigns en-throned a - bove;
2 Your Spir - it still flows free, high surg - ing where it will;
3 You have e - ter - nal life im - plant - ed in the soul;
the an - cient of e - ter - nal days, the God of love!
in proph-et's word you spoke of old and you speak still.
your love shall be our strength and stay, while a - ges roll.
The Lord, the great I Am, by earth and heaven con - fessed,
Es - tab-lished is your law, and change-less it shall stand,
We praise you, liv - ing God! We praise your ho - ly name;
we bow be - fore your ho - ly name, for - ev - er blest.
deep writ up - on the hu - man heart, on sea or land.
who was, and is, and is to be, for - e'er the same!

WORDS: Hebrew *Yigdal*, Daniel ben Judah, ca. 1400;
tr. Newton Mann (1836-1926) and Max Landsberg (1845-1928)
MUSIC: Hebrew melody; adapt. Thomas Olivers (1725-1799) and Meyer Lyon (1751-1797)

LEONI
6.6.8.4.D.

Praise the Lord! O Heavens, Adore Him 17

1 Praise the Lord! O heavens, a - dore him; praise him, an - gels in the height;
2 Praise the Lord, for he is gra - cious; nev - er shall his prom - ise fail;
sun and moon, bow down be - fore him; praise him, shin - ing stars of light.
God has made his saints vic - to - rious; sin and death shall not pre - vail.
Praise the Lord, for he hath spo - ken; worlds his might - y voice o - beyed;
Praise the God of our sal - va - tion; hosts on high, his power pro - claim;
laws which nev - er shall be bro - ken for their guid - ance he has made.
heaven and earth, and all cre - a - tion, laud and mag - ni - fy his name.

WORDS: *The Foundling Hospital Collection*, 1796, alt.; para. Psalm 148
MUSIC: Franz Joseph Haydn (1732-1809)

AUSTRIAN HYMN
8.7.8.7.D.

18 The Name of the Lord

Unison
F
Fmaj7 Bb/F
1 Bless-ed be the name of the Lord,
2 Glo - ry to the name of the Lord,
3 Ho - ly is the name of the Lord,
Bless-ed be the name of the Lord;
Glo-ry to the name of the Lord;
Ho-ly is the name of the Lord;
C/F F F/A Bb C Bb/C C
Bless-ed be the name of the Lord Most High!
Glo-ry to the name of the Lord Most High!
Ho-ly is the name of the Lord Most High!
Bb/C F Fmaj7 Bb/F
Bless-ed be the name of the Lord,
Glo - ry to the name of the Lord,
Ho - ly is the name of the Lord,
Bless-ed be the name of the Lord;
Glo - ry to the name of the Lord;
Ho - ly is the name of the Lord;
C/F F F/A Bb F/C C7 F
Bless-ed be the name of the Lord Most High!
Glo - ry to the name of the Lord Most High!
Ho - ly is the name of the Lord Most High!
Bb/F F F Bb/F
The name of the Lord is a strong tow-
F Gm/F F C C7sus
- er; the right-eous run in - to it,
F Bb/F F Bb/F
and they are saved. The name of the Lord is

WORDS and MUSIC: Clinton Utterbach (20th c.)

F Gm/F F
a strong tow - er; the right-eous run in -
C C7sus F Bb/F F
- to it, and they are saved.

Blessed Be the Lord God Almighty 19

Fsus F7 Bb Dm7 Bb/D F/Eb Eb Cm7
Bless - ed be the Lord God al - might - y, who
Eb/F F Eb/F F7sus F Bb F7sus F7
was, and is, and is to come; Bless - ed be the
Bb Dm7 Bb/D F/Eb Eb Cm7 Eb/F F Eb/F F Bb
Lord God al - might - y, who reigns for - ev - er - more.

WORDS and MUSIC: Bob Fitts (1955-)

20 Like a Mighty River Flowing

1 Like a might - y riv - er flow - ing,
2 Like the hills se - rene and e - ven,
3 Like the sum - mer breez - es play - ing,
4 Like the morn - ing sun as - cend - ed,
5 Like the a - zure o - cean swell - ing,
like a flower in beau - ty grow - ing,
like the cours - ing clouds of heav - en,
like the tall trees soft - ly sway - ing,
like the scents of eve - ning blend - ed,
like the jew - el all - ex - cell - ing,
far be - yond all hu - man know - ing
like the heart that's been for - giv - en
like the lips of si - lent pray - ing
like a friend - ship nev - er end - ed
far be - yond our hu - man tell - ing
is the per - fect peace of God.

WORDS: Michael Perry (1942-1996)
MUSIC: German melody, 14th c.; arr. Ralph Vaughan Williams (1872-1958)

QUEM PASTORES LAUDAVERE
8.8.8.7.

This Is My Father's World 21

1 This is my Fa-ther's world, and to my lis-tening ears all
2 This is our Fa-ther's world: O let us not for - get that
3 This is my Fa-ther's world: he shines in all that's fair; in the
na - ture sings, and round me rings the mu - sic of the spheres.
though the wrong is great and strong, God is the rul - er yet.
rus - tling grass I hear him pass, he speaks to me ev-ery-where.
This is my Fa - ther's world: I rest me in the thought of
He trusts us with his world, to keep it clean and fair— all
This is my Fa - ther's world: why should my heart be sad? The
rocks and trees, of skies and seas—his hand the won - ders wrought.
earth and trees, all skies and seas, all crea - tures ev - ery - where.
Lord is King, let heav - en ring! God reigns; let earth be glad!

WORDS: Maltbie D. Babcock (1858-1901), alt.; vs. 2 rev. Mary Babcock Crawford (1909-)
MUSIC: English melody; adapt. Franklin L. Sheppard (1852-1930)

TERRA BEATA
S.M.D.

22 Let All Things Now Living

1 Let all things now liv - ing a song of thanks - giv - ing to
2 His law he en - forc - es; the stars in their cours - es and
God the Cre - a - tor tri - um - phant - ly raise, who
sun in its or - bit o - be - dient - ly shine; the
fash - ioned and made us, pro - tect - ed and stayed us, who
hills and the moun - tains, the riv - ers and foun - tains, the
guides us and leads to the end of our days. His
deeps of the o - cean pro - claim him di - vine. We

WORDS: Katherine K. Davis (1892-1980)
MUSIC: Welsh melody

ASH GROVE
12.11.12.11.D.

ban - ners are o'er us, his light goes be - fore us, a
too should be voic - ing our love and re - joic - ing; with
pil - lar of fire shin - ing forth in the night, till
glad ad - o - ra - tion a song let us raise, till
shad - ows have van - ished and dark - ness is ban - ished, as
all things now liv - ing u - nite in thanks - giv - ing: to
for - ward we trav - el from light in - to light.
God in the high - est, ho - san - na and praise!

23 All Creatures of Our God and King

1 All crea-tures of our God and King, lift up your voice and with us
2 O rush-ing wind that art so strong, you clouds that sail in heaven a -
3 O flow-ing wa - ter, pure and clear, make mu - sic for your Lord to
4 All you who are of ten - der heart, for - giv - ing oth - ers, take your
5 Let all things their Cre - a - tor bless, and wor-ship him in hum - ble-
sing Al - le - lu - ia, Al - le - lu - ia! O burn-ing sun with gold - en
long, O praise him, Al - le - lu - ia! O ris - ing morn in praise re-
hear, Al - le - lu - ia, Al - le - lu - ia! O fire so mas-ter - ful and
part, sing prais - es, Al - le - lu - ia! All you who pain and sor-row
ness, O praise him, Al - le - lu - ia! Praise, praise the Fa-ther, praise the
beam, and sil - ver moon with soft - er gleam, O praise him, O
joice, O lights of eve-ning, find a voice, O praise him, O
bright, pro - vid - ing us with warmth and light, O praise him, O
bear, praise God and on him cast your care, O praise him, O
Son, and praise the Spir - it, Three in One, O praise him, O
praise him, Al - le - lu - ia, Al - le - lu - ia, Al - le - lu - ia!

WORDS: St. Francis of Assisi (1182-1226); tr. William H. Draper (1855-1933), alt.
MUSIC: *Geistliche Kirchengesäng*, Cologne, 1623; arr. Ralph Vaughan Williams (1872-1958)

LASST UNS ERFREUEN
L.M.Alleluias

God, You Spin the Whirling Planets 24

1 God, you spin the whirl-ing plan-ets, fill the seas and spread the plain,
2 You have called us to be faith-ful in our life and min-is-try.
3 God, your will is still cre-at-ing, call-ing us to life made new,
mold the moun-tains, fash-ion blos-soms, call forth sun-shine, wind, and rain.
We re-spond in grate-ful wor-ship, joined in one com-mun-i-ty.
now re-veal to us fresh vis-tas where there's work to dare and do.
We, cre-at-ed in your im-age, would a true re-flec-tion be
When we blur your gra-cious im-age, fo-cus us and make us whole,
Keep us clear of all dis-tor-tion, fash-ion us with lov-ing care,
of your jus-tice, grace, and mer-cy, and the truth that makes us free.
healed and strength-ened as your peo-ple, we move on-ward toward your goal.
thus, new crea-tures in your im-age, we'll pro-claim Christ ev-ery-where.

WORDS: Jane Parker Huber (1926-)
MUSIC: Ludwig van Beethoven (1770-1827)

HYMN TO JOY
8.7.8.7.D.

25 Let All Creation Bless the Lord

1 Let all cre - a - tion bless the Lord, till heaven with praise is
2 All liv - ing things up - on the earth, green fer - tile hills and
3 O men and wom - en ev - ery - where, lift up a hymn of
ring - ing. Sun, moon, and stars, peal out a chord, stir up the an -
moun - tains, sing to the God who gave you birth! Be joy - ful, springs
glo - ry. Let all who know God's stead - fast care tell out sal - va -
gels' sing - ing. Sing, wind and rain! Sing, snow and sleet! Make
and foun - tains, lithe wa - ter - life, bright air - borne birds, wild
tion's sto - ry. No tongue be si - lent— sing your part, you
mu - sic, day, night, cold, and heat!
rov - ing beasts, tame flocks and herds! Ex - alt the God who made you.
hum - ble souls and meek of heart!

WORDS: Carl P. Daw, Jr. (1944-); para. the *Benedicite*
MUSIC: Bohemian Brethren's *Kirchengesänge*, Berlin, 1566; harm. Heinrich Reimann (1850-1906)

MIT FREUDEN ZART
8.7.8.7.8.8.7.

Many and Great

Unison
1 Man - y and great, O God, are your works,
2 Grant un - to us com - mun - ion with you,
(Opt. Hand Drum)
Mak - er of earth and sky. Your hands have
O star - a - bid - ing One. Come un - to
set the heav - ens with stars; your fin - gers spread the
us and dwell with us; with you are found the
moun - tains and plains. Lo, at your word the
gifts of life. Bless us with life that
wa - ters were formed; deep seas o - bey your voice.
has no end, e - ter - nal life with you.

WORDS: Joseph R. Renville, 19th c.; para. Philip Frazier (1892-1964), alt.
MUSIC: Native American melody; arr. Jack Schrader (1942-)

LACQUIPARLE
Irregular

27 God of Creation, All-Powerful

Unison
1 God of cre - a - tion, all - power - ful, all - wise, Lord of the
2 God of the a - ges, through time's trou - bled years you are the
3 God of re - demp - tion, who wrought our re - birth, called out your
4 God of your peo - ple, your Word still stands fast; do for us
5 God of our now, all our trust is in you, Cov - e - nant
u - ni - verse rich with sur - prise, Mak - er, Sus - tain - er, and
one in whom his - tory co - heres; na - tions and em - pires your
church from the ends of the earth, still you are Sav - ior, put
now as you've done in the past! Yours is the king - dom, your
God, ev - er faith - ful and true; Sov - ereign Cre - a - tor, Re -
Rul - er of all, we are your chil - dren—you hear when we call.
pur - pose ful - fill, mov - ing in free - dom, yet work - ing your will.
dark - ness to flight; o - ver - come sin by sal - va - tion's pure light!
tri - umph we claim, chal - leng - ing e - vil in Je - sus' strong name.
deem - er, and Lord, now and for - ev - er your name be a - dored!

WORDS: Margaret Clarkson (1915-)
MUSIC: Irish melody; harm. Carlton R. Young (1926-)

SLANE
10.10.10.10.

For Beauty of Meadows

1 For beau - ty of mead - ows, for gran - deur of trees,
2 As stew - ards of beau - ty re - ceived at your hand,
3 Teach us once a - gain to be gar - deners in peace;
for flow - ers of wood - lands, for crea - tures of seas,
as crea - tures who hear your most ur - gent com - mand,
all na - ture a - round us is ours but on lease;
for all you cre - at - ed and gave us to share,
we turn from our waste - ful de - struc - tion of life,
your name we would hal - low in all that we do,
we praise you, Cre - a - tor, ex - tol - ling your care.
con - fess - ing our fail - ures, con - fess - ing our strife.
ful - fill - ing our call - ing, cre - at - ing with you.

WORDS: Walter H. Farquharson (1936-)
MUSIC: Welsh melody

ST. DENIO
11.11.11.11.

29 God of the Sparrow

Unison
G C Em Am Dm
1 God of the spar - row God of the whale
2 God of the earth-quake God of the storm
3 God of the rain - bow God of the cross
4 God of the hun - gry God of the sick
5 God of the neigh - bor God of the foe
6 God of the a - ges God near at hand
G C F E7 Am Em
God of the swirl - ing stars How does the crea - ture say
God of the trum - pet blast How does the crea - ture cry
God of the emp - ty grave How does the crea - ture say
God of the prod - i - gal How does the crea - ture say
God of the prun - ing hook How does the crea - ture say
God of the lov - ing heart How do your chil - dren say
1–5
6
F Em Am Dm Gsus G C
Awe How does the crea - ture say Praise
Woe How does the crea - ture cry Save
Grace How does the crea - ture say Thanks
Care How does the crea - ture say Life
Love How does the crea - ture say Peace
Joy How do your chil - dren say Home
*

*last time

WORDS: Jaroslav J. Vajda (1919-)
MUSIC: Carl F. Schalk (1929-)

ROEDER
5.4.6.7.7.

All Things Bright and Beautiful 30

Refrain (Unison)
All things bright and beau-ti - ful, all crea-tures great and small,
all things wise and won-der-ful: the Lord God made them all.
1 Each lit - tle flower that o - pens, each lit - tle bird that sings,
2 The pur - ple-head - ed moun-tains, the riv - er run - ning by,
3 The cold wind in the win - ter, the pleas-ant sum-mer sun,
4 God gave us eyes to see them, and lips that we might tell
God made their glow-ing col - ors, and made their ti - ny wings.
the sun - set and the morn - ing that bright-ens up the sky.
the ripe fruits in the gar - den: God made them ev - ery one.
how great is God Al - might - y, who has made all things well.
to Refrain

WORDS: Cecil F. Alexander (1818-1895)
MUSIC: English melody, 17th c.; arr. Martin Shaw (1875-1958)

ROYAL OAK
7.6.7.6.Ref.

31 I Sing the Almighty Power of God

1 I sing the almighty power of God that made the mountains rise,
that spread the flowing seas abroad and built the lofty skies.
I sing the wisdom that ordained the sun to rule the day;
the moon shines full at his command and all the stars obey.
2 I sing the goodness of the Lord that filled the earth with food;
he formed the creatures with his word and then pronounced them good.
Lord, how your wonders are displayed wher-e'er I turn my eye,
if I survey the ground I tread or gaze upon the sky!
3 There's not a plant or flower below but makes your glories known;
and clouds arise and tempests blow by order from your throne;
while all that borrows life from you is ever in your care,
and everywhere that I may be, you, God, are present there.

WORDS: Isaac Watts (1674-1748)
MUSIC: *Gesangbuch der H. W. K. Hofkapelle*, 1784

ELLACOMBE
C.M.D.

Creating God, Your Fingers Trace 32

1 Cre - at - ing God, your fin - gers trace the
2 Sus - tain - ing God, your hands up - hold earth's
3 Re - deem - ing God, your arms em - brace all
4 In - dwell - ing God, your gos - pel claims one

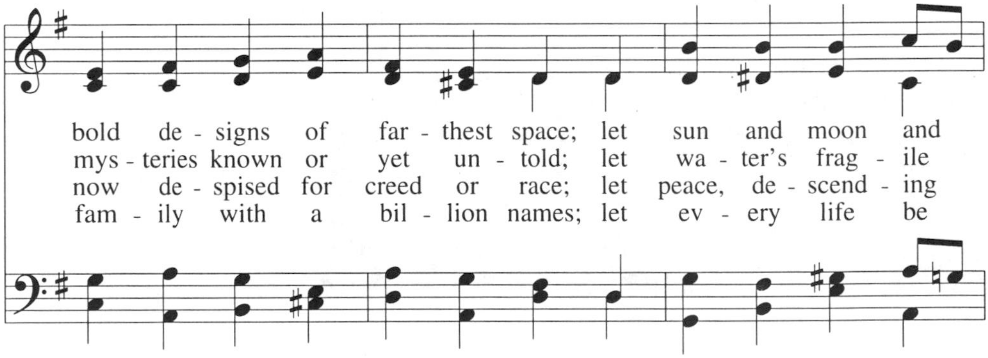
bold de - signs of far - thest space; let sun and moon and
mys - teries known or yet un - told; let wa - ter's frag - ile
now de - spised for creed or race; let peace, de - scend - ing
fam - ily with a bil - lion names; let ev - ery life be

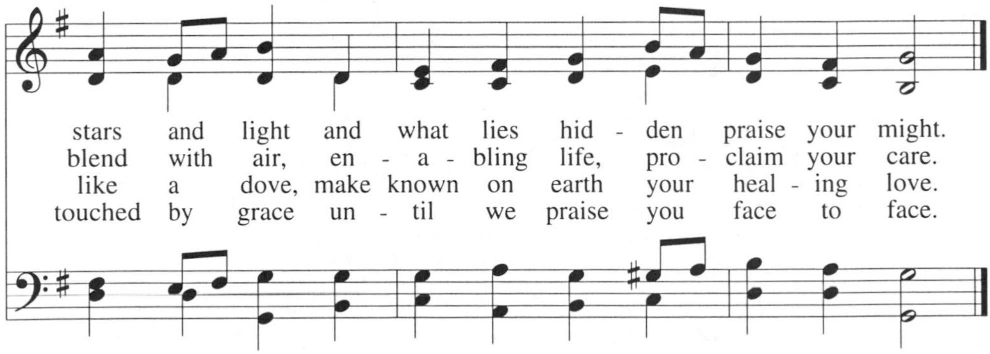
stars and light and what lies hid - den praise your might.
blend with air, en - a - bling life, pro - claim your care.
like a dove, make known on earth your heal - ing love.
touched by grace un - til we praise you face to face.

WORDS: Jeffery Rowthorn (1934-)
MUSIC: Robert A. Schumann (1810-1856)

CANONBURY
L.M.

33 Let's Sing unto the Lord

Cantemos al Señor

Unison
Dm
A7
1 Let's sing un-to the Lord a hymn of glad re - joic-ing.
2 Let's sing un-to the Lord a hymn of ad - o - ra-tion,
1 Can - te-mos al Se - ñor un him-no de a-le - grí-a,
2 Can - te-mos al Se - ñor un him-no de a-la - ban-za
Dm
Let's sing a hymn of love, at the new day's fresh be - gin-ning.
which shows our love and faith and the hope of all cre - a - tion.
un cán - ti - co de a - mor al na - cer el nue - vo dí - a.
que ex - pre - se nues-tro a - mor, nues-tra fe y nues-tra es-pe - ran-za.
A7
God made the sky a - bove, the stars, the sun, the o - ceans;
Through all that has been made, the Lord is praised for great-ness,
Él hi - zo el cie-lo, el mar, el sol y las es - tre - llas
En to - da la crea - ción pre - go - na su gran - de - za,
Dm
and God saw it was good, for those works were filled with beau-ty.
and so we sing to God, who be - stows such love - ly bless-ings.
y vio en e - llos bon - dad, pues sus o - bras e - ran be - llas.
a - sí nues-tro can - tar va a-nun - cian - do su be - lle - za.

WORDS: Carlos Rosas (20th c.); tr. Roberto Escamilla (1931-), Elise S. Eslinger (1942-), and George Lockwood (1946-)
MUSIC: Carlos Rosas (20th c.); arr. Raquel Mora Martínez (1940-)

ROSAS
6.7.6.8.D.Ref.

Refrain
C
Bb
A
Al - le - lu - ia! Al - le - lu - ia!
¡A - le - lu - ya! ¡A - le - lu - ya!
Gm
Dm
A7
Dm
Let's sing un - to the Lord. Al - le - lu - ia!
Can - te - mos al Se - ñor. ¡A - le - lu - ya!

Praise God from Whom All Blessings Flow 34

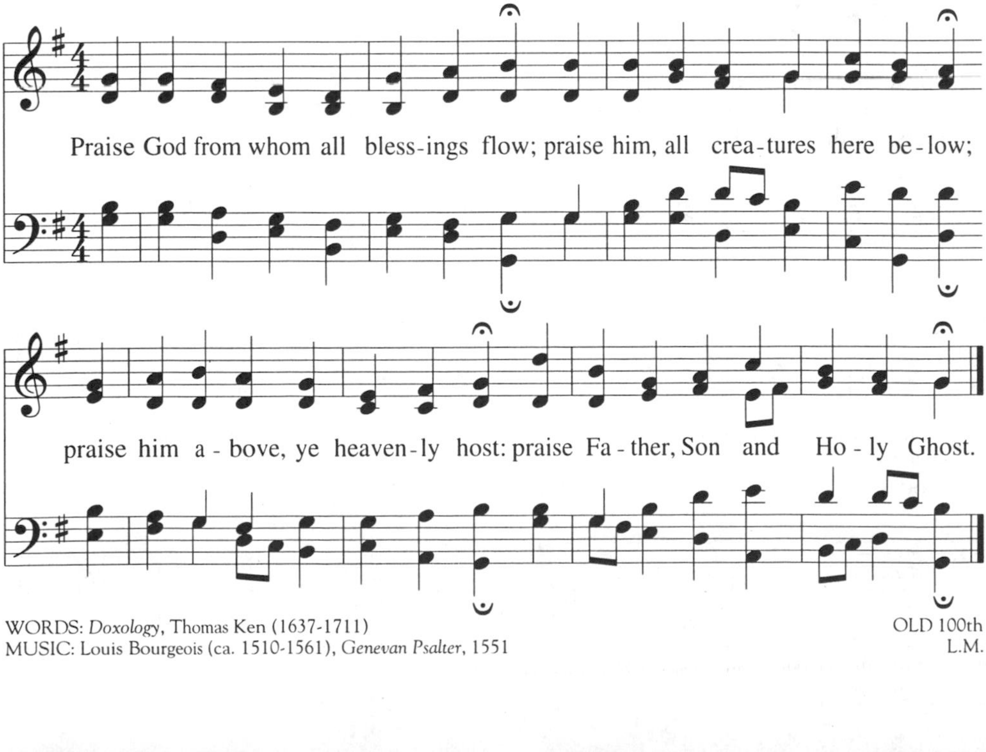
Praise God from whom all bless-ings flow; praise him, all crea-tures here be-low;
praise him a - bove, ye heaven-ly host: praise Fa - ther, Son and Ho - ly Ghost.

WORDS: *Doxology*, Thomas Ken (1637-1711)
MUSIC: Louis Bourgeois (ca. 1510-1561), *Genevan Psalter*, 1551

OLD 100th
L.M.

35 Morning Has Broken

Unison
1 Morn-ing has bro - ken like the first morn - ing,
2 Sweet the rain's new fall sun-lit from heav - en,
3 Mine is the sun - light! Mine is the morn - ing
black-bird has spo - ken like the first bird.
like the first dew - fall on the first grass.
born of the one light E - den saw play!
Praise for the sing - ing! Praise for the morn - ing!
Praise for the sweet - ness of the wet gar - den,
Praise with e - la - tion, praise ev - ery morn - ing,
Praise for them, spring - ing fresh from the Word!
sprung in com - plete - ness where his feet pass.
God's re - cre - a - tion of the new day!

WORDS: Eleanor Farjeon (1881-1965)
MUSIC: Gaelic melody; arr. David Evans (1874-1948)

BUNESSAN
5.5.5.4.D.

Thank You, God, for Water, Soil, and Air 36

1 Thank you, God, for wa - ter, soil, and air, large gifts sup-port-ing
2 Thank you, God, for min - er - als and ores, the ba - sis of all
3 Thank you, God, for price-less en - er - gy, stored in each at - om,
4 Thank you, God, for weav-ing na - ture's life in - to a seam-less
5 Thank you, God, for mak - ing plan - et earth a home for us and
ev - ery - thing that lives. For - give our spoil - ing and a - buse of
build-ing, wealth, and speed. For - give our reck - less plun-der - ing and
gath-ered from the sun. For - give our greed and care-less - ness of
robe, a frag - ile whole. For - give our haste that tam-pers un - a -
a - ges yet un - born. Help us to share, con - sid - er, save, and
them. Help us re - new the face of the earth.
waste. Help us re - new the face of the earth.
power. Help us re - new the face of the earth.
ware. Help us re - new the face of the earth.
store. Come and re - new the face of the earth.

WORDS: Brian Wren (1936-)
MUSIC: John Weaver (1937-)

AMSTEIN
9.10.10.9.

37 God in His Love for Us

1 God in his love for us lent us this plan - et,
2 Thanks be to God for its boun - ty and beau - ty,
3 Long have our hu - man wars ru - ined its har - vest;
4 Earth is the Lord's: it is ours to en - joy it,
gave it a pur - pose in time and in space:
life that sus - tains us in bod - y and mind:
long has earth bowed to the ter - ror of force;
ours, as his stew - ards, to farm and de - fend.
small as a spark from the fire of cre - a - tion,
plen - ty for all, if we learn how to share it,
long have we wast - ed what oth - ers have need of,
From its pol - lu - tion, mis - use, and de - struc - tion,
cra - dle of life and the home of our race.
rich - es un - dreamed of to fath - om and find.
poi - soned the foun - tain of life at its source.
good Lord, de - liv - er us, world with - out end!

WORDS: Fred Pratt Green (1903-2000)
MUSIC: James P. Harding (1850-1911)

MORNING STAR
11.10.11.10.

Touch the Earth Lightly

Unison
1 Touch the earth light - ly, use the earth gent - ly,
2 We who en - dan - ger, who cre - ate hun - ger,
3 Let there be green - ing, birth from the burn - ing,
4 God of all liv - ing, God of all lov - ing,
nour - ish the life of the world in our care:
a - gents of death for all crea-tures that live,
wa - ter that bless - es and air that is sweet,
God of the seed - ling, the snow and the sun,
gift of great won - der, ours to sur - ren - der,
we who would fos - ter clouds of dis - as - ter—
health in God's gar - den, hope in God's chil - dren,
teach us, de - flect us, Christ re - con - nect us,
1–3
4
trust for the chil - dren to - mor - row will bear.
God of our plan - et, fore - stall and for - give!
re - gen - er - a - tion that peace will com - plete.
us - ing us gent - ly, and mak - ing us one.

WORDS: Shirley Erena Murray (1931-)
MUSIC: Colin Gibson (1933-)

TENDERNESS
5.5.10.D.

39 All You Works of God, Bless the Lord!

Unison
1 All you works of God, bless the Lord!
2 Hills and moun - tains, now sing his worth,
3 Come hu - man - i - ty, sing a - long,
4 Bless the Lord, all you pure of heart;
All you an - gels, now bless the Lord;
all you green things that grow on earth;
sing, you peo - ple of God, a song;
all you hum - ble, his prais - es start;
come you heav - ens and powers that be,
seas and riv - ers, you springs and wells,
priests and serv - ants, your Lord now bless,
God the Fa - ther and Son a - dore,
praise the Lord and his maj - es - ty:
beasts and cat - tle, you birds and whales:
join, you spir - its and souls at rest.
bless the Spir - it for - ev - er - more!
Refrain
Raise your voic - es high,

WORDS: Stephen P. Starke (1955-)
MUSIC: Jamaican folk tune; adapt. Doreen Potter (1925-1980)

LINSTEAD
8.8.8.8.Ref.

praise and mag - ni - fy, all you works of God, bless the Lord!

For the Beauty of the Earth 40

1 For the beau - ty of the earth, for the glo - ry of the skies,
2 For the won - der of each hour of the day and of the night,
3 For the joy of hu - man love, broth - er, sis - ter, par - ent, child,
4 For the church that ev - er - more lift - eth ho - ly hands a - bove,
5 For thy - self, best gift di - vine, to our race so free - ly given;
for the love which from our birth o - ver and a - round us lies,
hill and vale and tree and flower, sun and moon and stars of light,
friends on earth and friends a - bove; for all gen - tle thoughts and mild,
of - fering up on ev - ery shore her pure sac - ri - fice of love,
for that great, great love of thine, peace on earth and joy in heaven,
Lord of all, to thee we raise this our hymn of grate - ful praise.

WORDS: Folliott S. Pierpoint (1835-1917), alt.
MUSIC: Conrad Kocher (1786-1872); arr. William H. Monk (1823-1889)

DIX
7.7.7.7.7.7.

41 Tell Out, My Soul

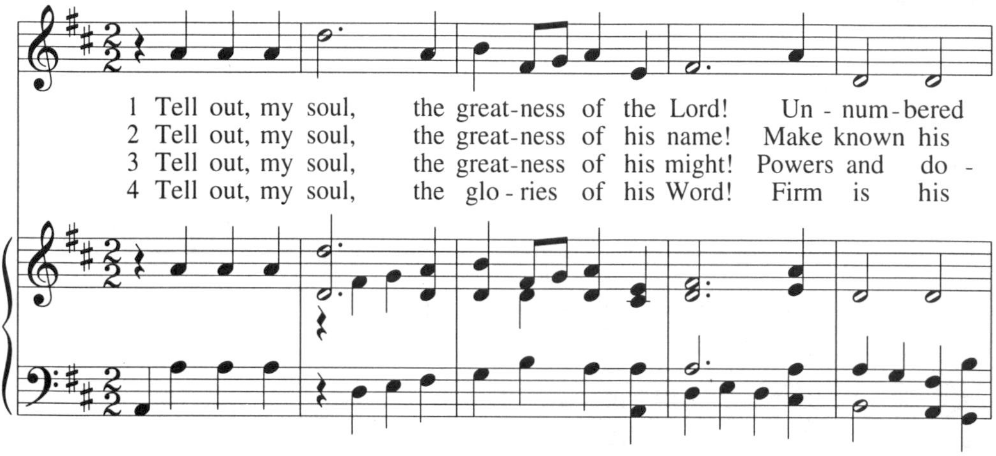
1 Tell out, my soul, the great-ness of the Lord! Un - num-bered
2 Tell out, my soul, the great-ness of his name! Make known his
3 Tell out, my soul, the great-ness of his might! Powers and do -
4 Tell out, my soul, the glo - ries of his Word! Firm is his

bless-ings give my spir - it voice; ten - der to me the
might, the deeds his arm has done; his mer - cy sure, from
min - ions lay their glo - ry by. Proud hearts and stub - born
prom - ise, and his mer - cy sure. Tell out, my soul, the

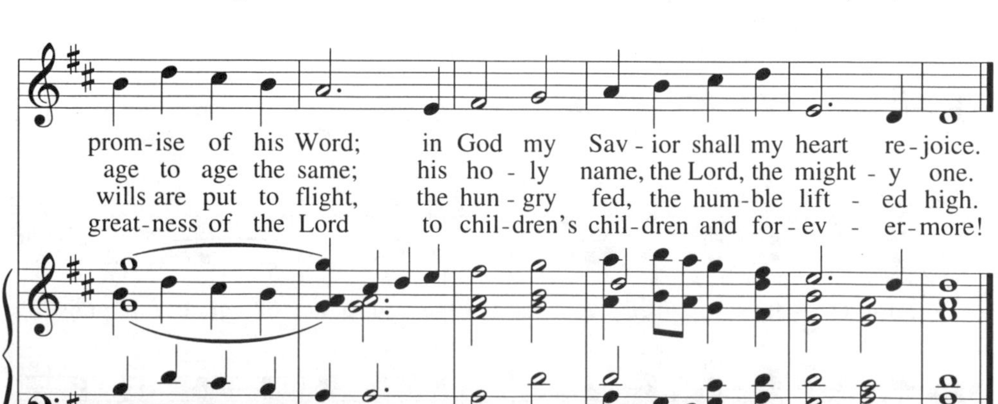
prom-ise of his Word; in God my Sav - ior shall my heart re - joice.
age to age the same; his ho - ly name, the Lord, the might - y one.
wills are put to flight, the hun - gry fed, the hum-ble lift - ed high.
great-ness of the Lord to chil-dren's chil-dren and for - ev - er-more!

WORDS: Timothy Dudley-Smith (1926-)
MUSIC: Walter Greatorex (1877-1949), alt.

WOODLANDS
10.10.10.10.

How Majestic Is Your Name

C C/E F Dm7 G C C/E C
O Lord, our Lord, how ma - jes - tic is your name in all the
1 2
G C G C/E F Dm7 G G7/B C C/E
earth. O earth. O Lord, we praise your name. O
F Dm7 G Am7 G7/B C B B7/D♯ Em D D7/F♯
Lord, we mag - ni - fy your name: Prince of Peace, Might - y
G G7/F C/E F Gsus G7 C
God, O Lord God Al - might - y.

WORDS and MUSIC: Michael W. Smith (1957-)

43 Majesty

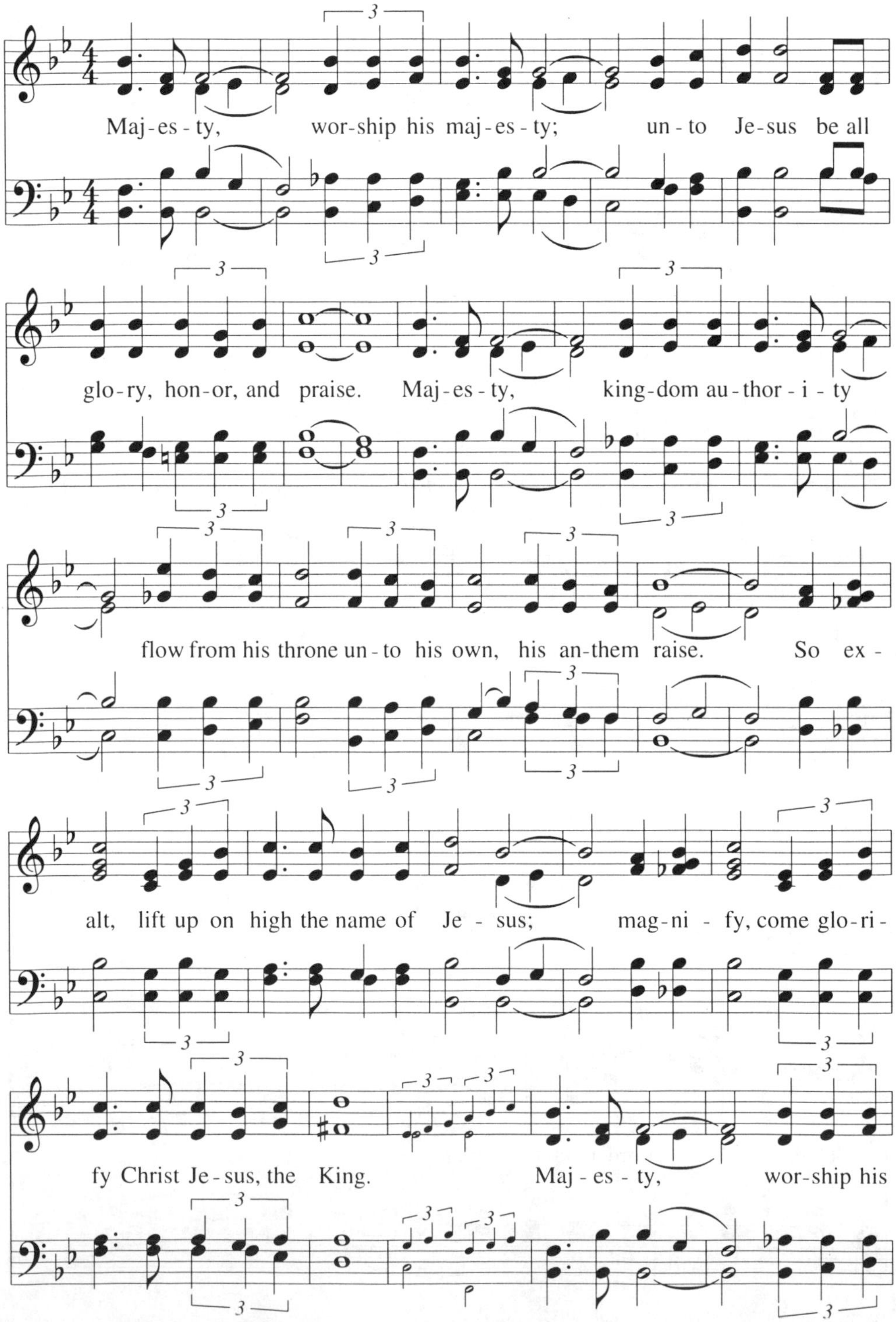
Maj-es-ty, wor-ship his maj-es-ty; un-to Je-sus be all
glo-ry, hon-or, and praise. Maj-es-ty, king-dom au-thor-i-ty
flow from his throne un-to his own, his an-them raise. So exalt, lift up on high the name of Je-sus; mag-ni-fy, come glo-ri-
fy Christ Je-sus, the King. Maj-es-ty, wor-ship his

WORDS and MUSIC: Jack W. Hayford (1934-); arr. Eugene Thomas (1941-)

3
maj - es - ty; Je - sus, who died, now glo - ri - fied, King of all kings.

Doxology

44

D F#m7 Gmaj7 F#m7 Bm7 Em7 Asus A
Praise God from whom all bless - ings flow, praise him all
Dmaj7 Bm7 Em7 A D G/A D F#m7 Gmaj7
crea - tures here be - low; praise him a - bove, you heav - en - ly
F#m7 Bm7 G D2/F# D/F# Bm7 Em7 Gmaj7/A A D
host, praise Fa - ther, Son and Ho - ly Ghost.

WORDS and MUSIC: Jimmy Owens (1930-)

45 Mighty Is Our God

Bb Dm7 Eb Eb/F F Bb Dm7 Eb Eb/F F
Might-y is our God, might-y is our King;
Glo - ry to our God, glo - ry to our King;
4th (last) time to CODA
Bb Dm7 Gm Gm7 Cm7 Eb/F F Bb
1, 3
might-y is our Lord, Rul-er of ev - ery - thing.
glo - ry to our Lord, Rul-er of ev - ery - thing.
2
Ab Ab2 Eb Eb/Bb
His name is high - er, high-er than an - y oth-
Bb Ab Ab2
- er name; his power is great - er, for
Eb/G Ebmaj7 F Eb/F
D.C.
he has cre - at - ed ev - ery - thing.
CODA
Cm7 Eb/F F Bb
Rul - er of ev - ery - thing.

WORDS and MUSIC: Eugene Greco (1960-), Gerrit Gustafson (1948-) and Don Moen (1950-)

Praise the Lord Who Reigns Above 46

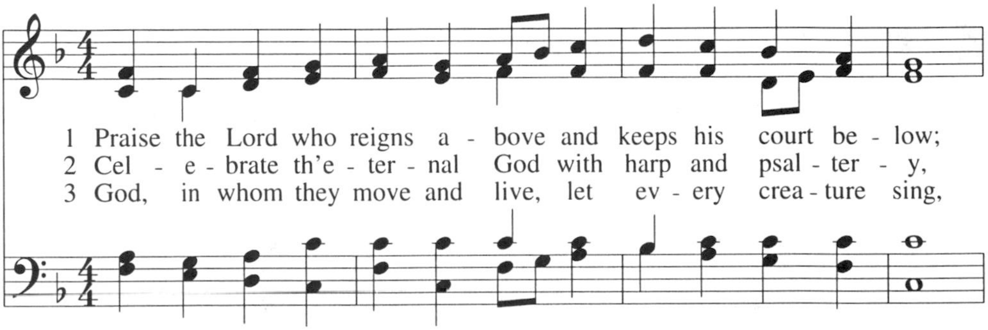
1 Praise the Lord who reigns a - bove and keeps his court be - low;
2 Cel - e - brate th'e - ter - nal God with harp and psal - ter - y,
3 God, in whom they move and live, let ev - ery crea - ture sing,

praise the ho - ly God of love, and all his great-ness show;
tim - brels soft and cym - bals loud in this high praise a - gree;
glo - ry to their Mak - er give, and hom - age to their King.

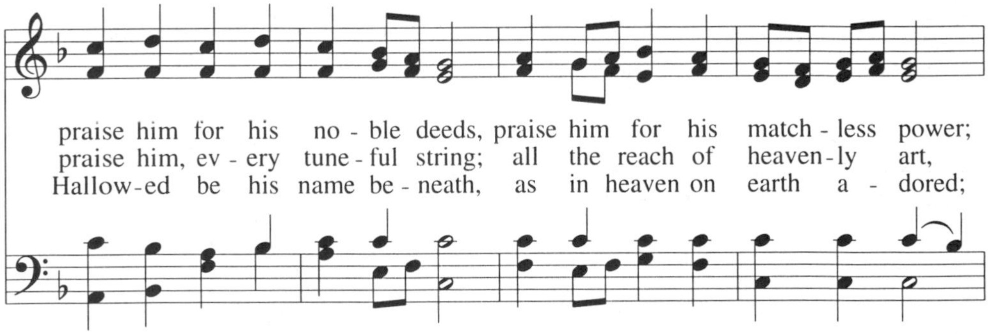
praise him for his no - ble deeds, praise him for his match - less power;
praise him, ev - ery tune - ful string; all the reach of heaven - ly art,
Hallow-ed be his name be - neath, as in heaven on earth a - dored;

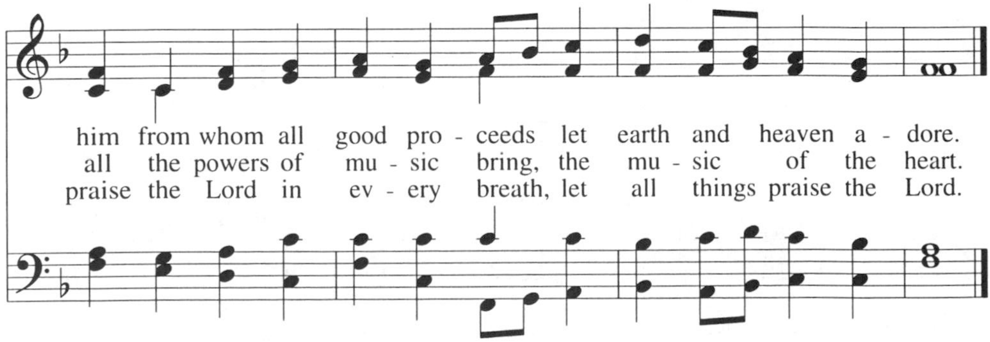
him from whom all good pro - ceeds let earth and heaven a - dore.
all the powers of mu - sic bring, the mu - sic of the heart.
praise the Lord in ev - ery breath, let all things praise the Lord.

WORDS: Charles Wesley (1707-1788); para. Psalm 150
MUSIC: *Foundery Collection*, 1742

AMSTERDAM
7.6.7.6.7.7.7.6.

47 We Exalt Thee

F F#dim7 Gm C7 3 F C/E
For thou, O Lord, art high a - bove all the earth;
Dm 3 Gm 1 C7 Bb/C F Bb2/F
thou art ex - alt - ed far a - bove all gods.
F F F#dim7 2 C7 Bb/C C F Bb/C
For thou, O
bove all gods.
Parts
C7 F2 F C/E
We ex - alt thee, we ex - alt thee, we ex -
Bb2/D Bb/D Bb/C 1 C7 F Bb2/C C7 2 Am/C C7 F
alt thee, O Lord. We ex -
O Lord.

WORDS and MUSIC: Pete Sanchez, Jr. (1948-); para. Psalm 97:9

Immortal, Invisible, God Only Wise 48

1 Im - mor - tal, in - vis - i - ble, God on - ly wise,
2 Un - rest - ing, un - hast - ing, and si - lent as light,
3 To all life thou giv - est, to both great and small;
4 Great Fa - ther of glo - ry, pure Fa - ther of light,
in light in - ac - ces - si - ble hid from our eyes,
nor want - ing, nor wast - ing, thou rul - est in might;
in all life thou liv - est, the true life of all;
thine an - gels a - dore thee, all veil - ing their sight;
most bless - ed, most glo - rious, the An - cient of Days,
thy jus - tice like moun - tains high soar - ing a - bove
we blos - som and flour - ish as leaves on the tree,
all praise we would ren - der, O help us to see
al - might - y, vic - to - rious, thy great name we praise.
thy clouds, which are foun - tains of good - ness and love.
and with - er and per - ish— but naught chang - eth thee.
'tis on - ly the splen - dor of light hid - eth thee.

WORDS: Walter Chalmers Smith (1824-1908), alt.
MUSIC: Welsh melody; harm. John Roberts (1822-1877)

ST. DENIO
11.11.11.11.

49 Let All the World

Unison
1 Let all the world in ev-ery cor-ner sing: my God and King! The heavens are not too high, his praise may thi - ther fly; the earth is not too low, his prais-es there may grow.
2 Let all the world in ev-ery cor-ner sing: my God and King! The church with psalms must shout, no door can keep them out; but, more than all, the heart must bear the long-est part.
Let all the world in ev-ery cor-ner sing: my God and King!
Let all the world in ev-ery cor-ner sing: my God and King!

WORDS: George Herbert (1593-1633)
MUSIC: Paul Liljestrand (1931-)

CONRAD
14.12.12.14.

Great Is the Lord

Unison
C F/C G/B C F G F C
Great is the Lord, he is ho-ly and just; by his pow-er we trust in his love.
Great is the Lord, he is faith-ful and true; by his mer-cy he proves he is love.
Parts Bb/C F/C Bb/C F C/F F6 C Bb/C F/C Bb/C F/C
1 Great is the Lord and wor-thy of glo-ry! Great is the Lord and
2 Great are you, Lord, and wor-thy of glo-ry! Great are you, Lord, and
G G7 C Bb/C F/C Bb/C D D/F# G Bm7(b5)/F E E/G# Am
wor-thy of praise. Great is the Lord; now lift up your voice, now lift up your voice:
wor-thy of praise. Great are you, Lord; I lift up my voice, I lift up my voice:
Dm7 G7sus G7 F/C G7 Am Am/G Dm7 G7sus G7 F/G G7 1 C 2 C
Great is the Lord! Great is the Lord!
Great are you, Lord! Great are you, Lord!

WORDS and MUSIC: Michael W. Smith (1957-) and Deborah D. Smith (1958-)

51 How Great Thou Art

1 O Lord my God, when I in awe-some won - der con - sid - er
2 When through the woods and for - est glades I wan - der and hear the
3 And when I think that God, his Son not spar - ing, sent him to
4 When Christ shall come with shout of ac - cla - ma - tion and take me
all the worlds thy hands have made, I see the stars, I hear the roll - ing
birds sing sweet - ly in the trees, when I look down from loft - y moun-tain
die, I scarce can take it in, that on the cross, my bur-den glad - ly
home, what joy shall fill my heart! Then I shall bow in hum-ble ad - o-
thun - der, thy power through-out the u - ni - verse dis - played.
gran - deur, and hear the brook and feel the gen - tle breeze.
bear - ing, he bled and died to take a - way my sin.
ra - tion, and there pro - claim, "My God, how great thou art."
Refrain
Then sings my soul, my Sav - ior God, to thee: how great thou

WORDS and MUSIC: Stuart K. Hine (1899-1989)

art, how great thou art! Then sings my soul, my Sav - ior God, to
thee: how great thou art, how great thou art!

You Are My God 52

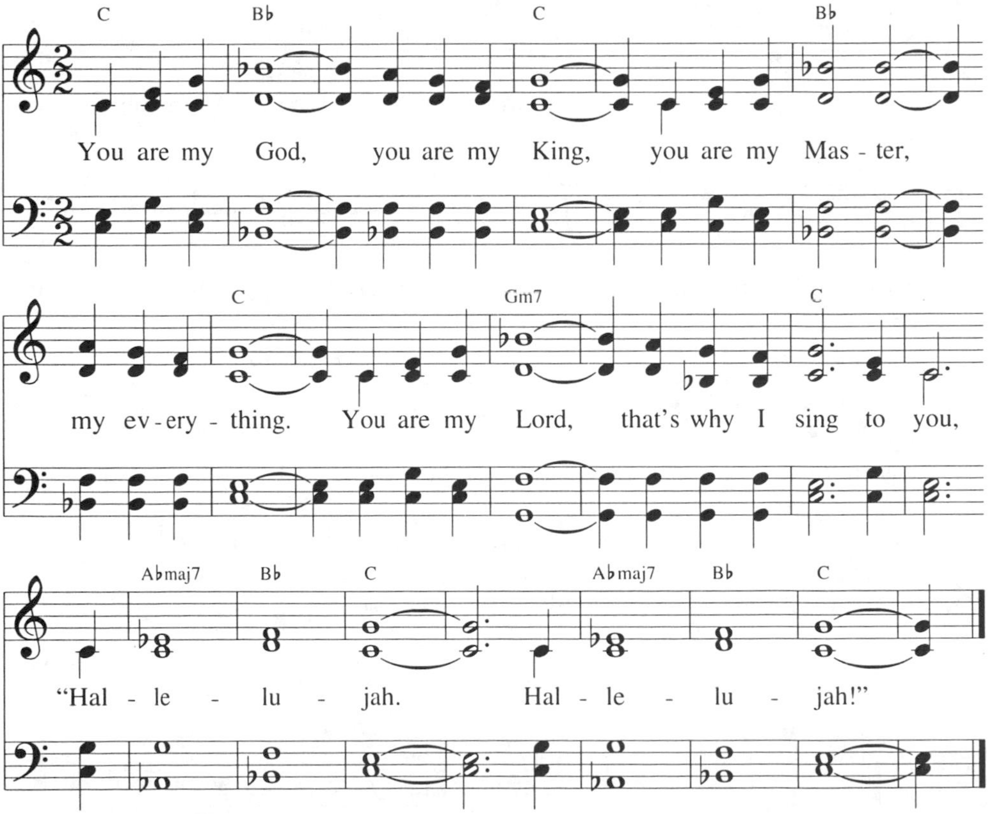
C Bb C Bb
You are my God, you are my King, you are my Mas - ter,
C Gm7 C
my ev - ery - thing. You are my Lord, that's why I sing to you,
Abmaj7 Bb C Abmaj7 Bb C
"Hal - le - lu - jah. Hal - le - lu - jah!"

WORDS and MUSIC: Macon Delavan (1932- 1995)

53 I Stand in Awe

Eb7 Ab2 Abmaj7
You are beau - ti - ful be - yond de - scrip - tion, too
Db/Ab Ab2 Db/Eb Eb Ab Db/Ab Ab
mar - vel - ous for words; too won - der - ful for com - pre -
Absus Ab Db Eb/Db Db Ebsus Eb C
hen - sion, like noth - ing ev - er seen or heard. Who can
Fm Bbsus Bb Db
grasp your in - fi - nite wis - dom? Who can fath - om the
Eb Eb7 Ab2
depth of your love? You are beau - ti - ful be - yond de -
Abmaj7 Db Eb7sus Eb7 Ab Db/Eb Eb7
scrip - tion, maj - es - ty en - throned a - bove. And I
Parts Ab Eb/Ab Eb/Db Db Db/Eb Ab Eb/Ab Eb/Db Db
stand, I stand in awe of you, I stand, I stand in awe of you; ho - ly

WORDS and MUSIC: Mark Altrogge (1950-)

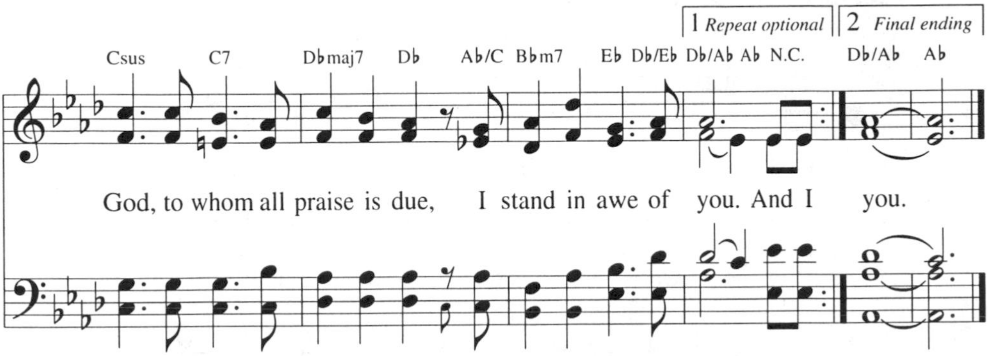
1 Repeat optional
2 Final ending
Csus C7 Dbmaj7 Db Ab/C Bbm7 Eb Db/Eb Db/Ab Ab N.C. Db/Ab Ab
God, to whom all praise is due, I stand in awe of you. And I you.

Let There Be Praise 54

Eb Bb/D Eb Cm Fm
1 Let there be praise, let there be joy in our
2 Let there be praise, let there be joy in our
Bb Gm Cm 1 Db2 Db
hearts. Sing to the Lord, give him the glo - ry;
hearts. For - ev - er - more let his love
Bbsus Bb 2 Fm Eb/G Ab Eb/Bb Bb7 Eb
(glo - ry;) fill the air, and let there be praise.

WORDS and MUSIC: Dick Tunney (1956-) and Melodie Tunney (1960-)

55 Great God, Your Love Has Called Us Here

1 Great God, your love has called us here, as we, by love, for love were made. Your liv - ing like - ness still we bear, though marred, dis - hon - ored, dis - o - beyed. We come, with all our heart and mind your call to hear, your love to find.
2 We come with self - in - flict - ed pains of brok-en trust and chos - en wrong, half - free, half - bound by in - ner chains, by so - cial forc - es swept a - long, by powers and sys - tems close con - fined, yet seek - ing hope for hu - man - kind.
3 Great God, in Christ you call our name and then re - ceive us as your own, not through some mer - it, right or claim, but by your gra - cious love a - lone. We strain to glimpse your mer - cy seat and find you kneel - ing at our feet.
4 Then take the towel, and break the bread, and hum-ble us, and call us friends. Suf - fer and serve till all are fed, and show how grand - ly love in - tends to work till all cre - a - tion sings, to fill all worlds, to crown all things.
5 Great God, in Christ you set us free your life to live, your joy to share. Give us your Spir - it's lib - er - ty to turn from guilt and dull de - spair and of - fer all that faith can do while love is mak - ing all things new.

WORDS: Brian Wren (1936-)
MUSIC: Erik Routley (1917-1982)

ABINGDON
8.8.8.8.8.8.

Sing Praise to God Who Reigns Above 56

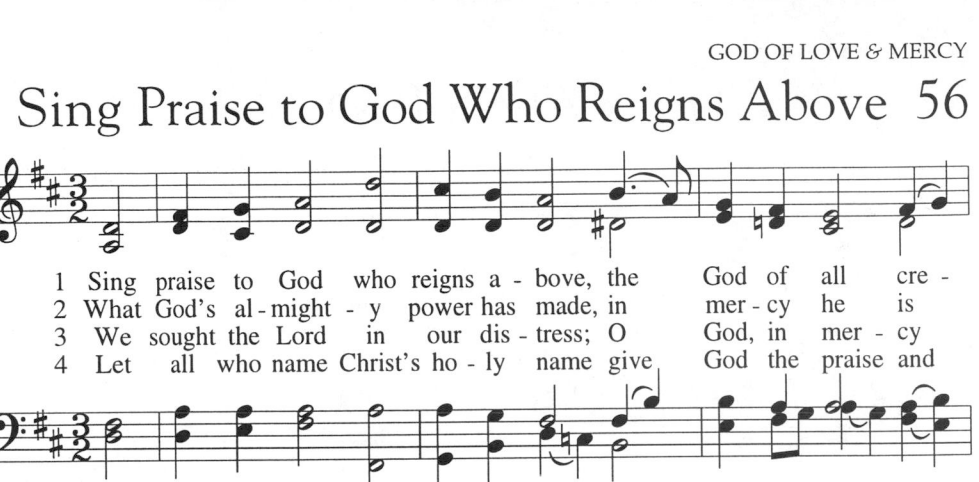

1 Sing praise to God who reigns a - bove, the God of all cre -
2 What God's al - might - y power has made, in mer - cy he is
3 We sought the Lord in our dis - tress; O God, in mer - cy
4 Let all who name Christ's ho - ly name give God the praise and
a - tion, the God of power, the God of love, the God of our
keep - ing; by morn - ing glow or eve - ning shade his eye is nev -
hear us. Our Sav - ior saw our help - less - ness and came with peace
glo - ry. Let all who know his power pro - claim a - loud the won -
sal - va - tion. My soul with com - fort rich he fills, and
er sleep - ing. And where he rules in king - ly might, there
to cheer us. For this we thank and praise the Lord, who
drous sto - ry. Cast ev - ery i - dol from its throne; the
ev - ery grief he gent - ly stills: to God all praise and glo - ry!
all is just and all is right: to God all praise and glo - ry!
is by one and all a - dored: to God all praise and glo - ry!
Lord is God, and he a - lone: to God all praise and glo - ry!

WORDS: Johann J. Schütz (1640-1690); tr. Frances Cox (1812-1897)
MUSIC: Bohemian Brethren's *Kirchengesänge*, Berlin, 1566; harm. Heinrich Reimann (1850-1906)

MIT FREUDEN ZART
8.7.8.7.8.8.7.

57 Think About His Love

Refrain
D
G
Think a-bout his love, think a-bout his good - ness,
D
Asus
A
F♯m/A
think a-bout his grace that's brought us through. For as
Gmaj7
F♯m7
D/F♯
Em7
high as the heav-ens a-bove, so great is the meas-ure of our Fa-ther's
Gmaj7/A
A
Gmaj7
G6
D
love. Great is the meas-ure of our Fa-ther's love.

WORDS and MUSIC: Walt Harrah (1948-)

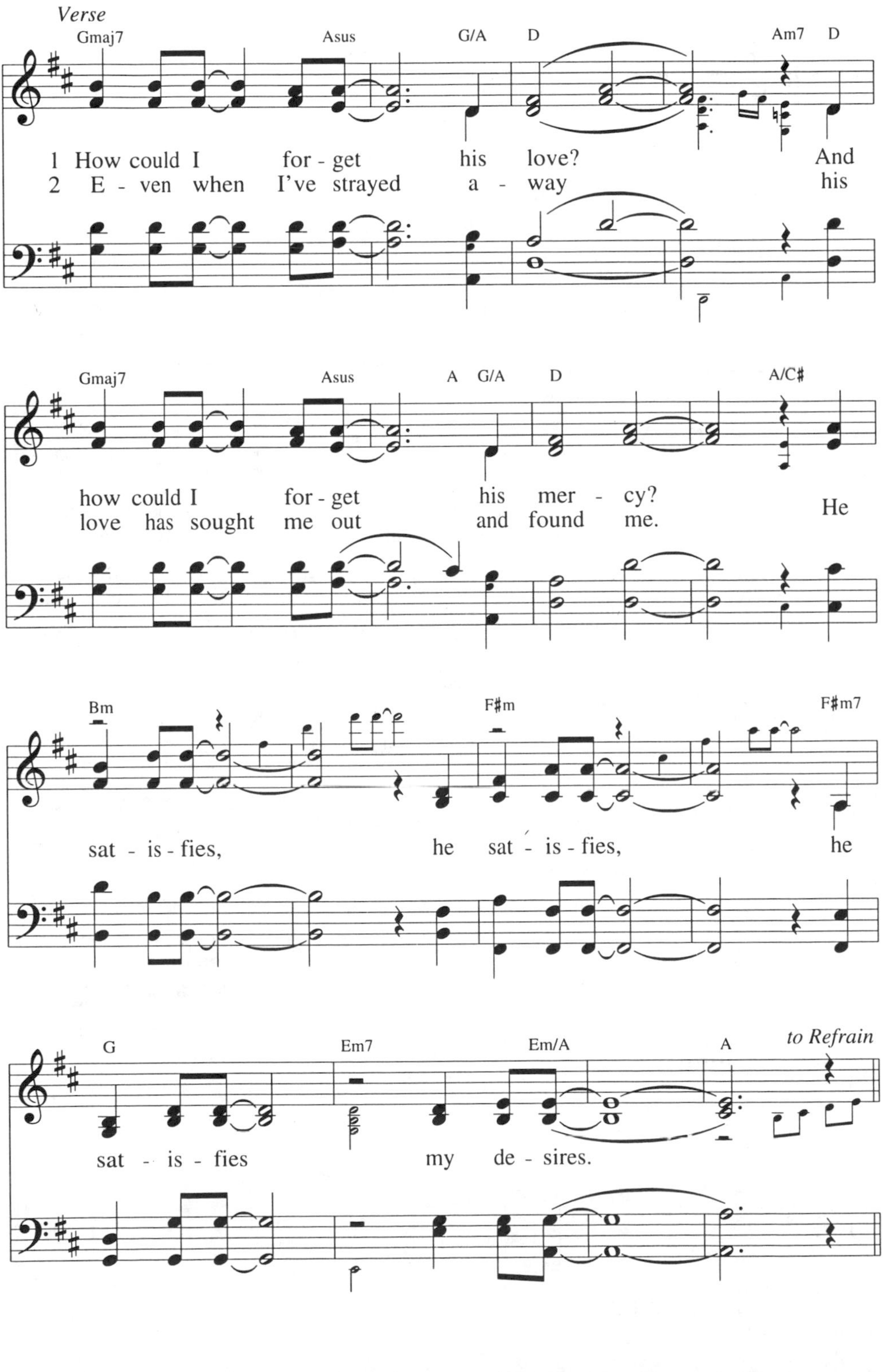
Verse
Gmaj7
Asus
G/A
D
Am7
D
1 How could I for - get his love? And
2 E - ven when I've strayed a - way his
Gmaj7
Asus
A
G/A
D
A/C#
how could I for - get his mer - cy?
love has sought me out and found me.
He
Bm
F#m
F#m7
sat - is - fies, he sat - is - fies, he
G
Em7
Em/A
A
to Refrain
sat - is - fies my de - sires.

58 God of Many Names

1 God of man - y names, gath - ered in - to One,
God of hov - ering wings, womb and birth of time,
2 God of Jew - ish faith, ex - o - dus and law,
God of Je - sus Christ, rab - bi of the poor,
3 God of wound - ed hands, web and loom of love,
God of man - y names, gath - ered in - to One,
in your glo - ry come and meet us, mov - ing, end - less - ly be - com - ing;
joy - ful - ly we sing your prais - es, breath of life in ev - ery peo - ple,
in your glo - ry come and meet us, joy of Mir - i - am and Mo - ses;
joy - ful - ly we sing your prais - es, cru - ci - fied, a - live for - ev - er,
in your glo - ry come and meet us, car - pen - ter of new cre - a - tion;
joy - ful - ly we sing your prais - es, mov - ing, end - less - ly be - com - ing,
Refrain
Hush, hush, hal - le - lu - jah, hal - le - lu - jah! Shout, shout, hal - le - lu - jah, hal - le - lu - jah!
1, 2
3
Sing, sing, hal - le - lu - jah, hal - le - lu - jah! Sing God is love, God is love! love!

WORDS: Brian Wren (1936-)
MUSIC: William P. Rowan (1951-)

MANY NAMES
5.5.8.8.Ref.

59 Joyful, Joyful, We Adore Thee

1 Joy - ful, joy - ful, we a - dore thee, God of glo - ry, Lord of love;
2 All thy works with joy sur-round thee, earth and heaven re - flect thy rays,
3 Thou art giv - ing and for - giv - ing, ev - er bless - ing, ev - er blest,
4 Mor - tals, join the hap - py cho - rus which the morn - ing stars be - gan;
hearts un - fold like flowers be - fore thee, open - ing to the sun a - bove.
stars and an - gels sing a - round thee, cen - ter of un - bro - ken praise.
well-spring of the joy of liv - ing, o - cean depth of hap - py rest!
love di - vine is reign - ing o'er us, join - ing all with - in its span.
Melt the clouds of sin and sad - ness, drive the dark of doubt a - way;
Field and for - est, vale and moun-tain, flow - ery mead-ow, flash - ing sea,
Thou our Fa - ther, Christ our Broth - er— all who live in love are thine;
Ev - er sing - ing, march we on - ward, vic - tors in the midst of strife;
giv - er of im - mor - tal glad - ness, fill us with the light of day!
chant - ing bird and flow - ing foun - tain call us to re - joice in thee.
teach us how to love each oth - er, lift us to the joy di - vine.
joy - ful mu - sic leads us sun - ward in the tri - umph song of life.

WORDS: Henry Van Dyke (1852-1933)
MUSIC: Ludwig van Beethoven (1770-1827)

HYMN TO JOY
8.7.8.7.D.

60 I Will Sing of the Mercies

G/A D A
1 I will sing of the mer-cies of the Lord for - ev - er, I will sing, I will
2 All the hosts of the an - gels sing God's praise for - ev - er for the things he has
D G/A D
sing. I will sing of the mer-cies of the Lord for - ev - er, I will
done. All the hosts of the an - gels sing God's praise for - ev - er, all the
A A7 D G D
sing of the mer-cies of the Lord. With my mouth will I make known your
hosts of the an - gels sing God's praise. Who can be com-pared to God in
A A7 G/D D G D
faith-ful-ness, your faith-ful-ness; with my mouth will I make known your
faith-ful-ness, in faith-ful-ness? Who can be com-pared to God in

WORDS: James H. Fillmore (1849-1936), alt.; vs. 2 Marie J. Post (1919-); para. Psalm 89:1, 5, 8 FILLMORE
MUSIC: James H. Fillmore (1849-1936) Irregular

A/E
E7sus E7 A G/A
D
faith-ful-ness to all gen-er - a - tions. I will sing of the mer-cies of the
faith-ful-ness to all gen-er - a - tions? I will sing of the mer-cies of the
A
A7
D
Lord for - ev - er, I will sing of the mer-cies of the Lord.
Lord for - ev - er, I will sing of the mer-cies of the Lord.

There's a Wideness in God's Mercy 61

1 There's a wide-ness in God's mer-cy like the wide-ness of the sea;
2 There is wel-come for the sin-ner and more grac-es for the good;
3 For the love of God is broad-er than the meas-ure of our mind;
4 If our love were but more sim-ple, we would take him at his word,
there's a kind-ness in his jus-tice which is more than lib-er-ty.
there is mer-cy with the Sav-ior; there is heal-ing in his blood.
and the heart of the E-ter-nal is most won-der-ful-ly kind.
and our lives would be il-lu-mined by the pres-ence of our Lord.

WORDS: Frederick W. Faber (1814-1863)
MUSIC: Lizzie S. Tourjée (1858-1913)

WELLESLEY
8.7.8.7.

62 In the Lord Alone

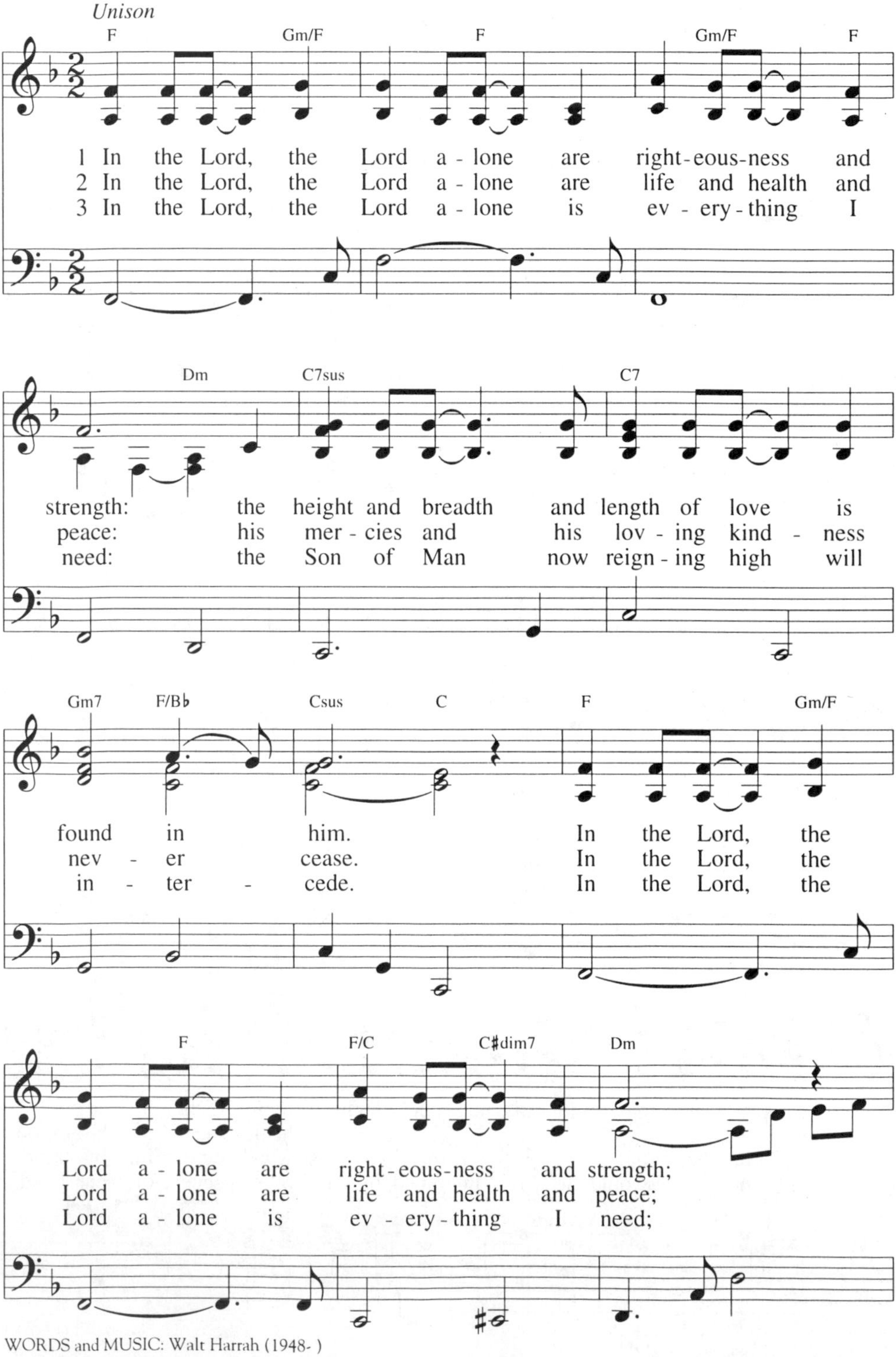
Unison
F Gm/F F Gm/F F
1 In the Lord, the Lord a - lone are right-eous-ness and
2 In the Lord, the Lord a - lone are life and health and
3 In the Lord, the Lord a - lone is ev - ery - thing I
Dm C7sus C7
strength: the height and breadth and length of love is
peace: his mer - cies and his lov - ing kind - ness
need: the Son of Man now reign - ing high will
Gm7 F/B♭ Csus C F Gm/F
found in him. In the Lord, the
nev - er cease. In the Lord, the
in - ter - cede. In the Lord, the
F F/C C♯dim7 Dm
Lord a - lone are right - eous - ness and strength;
Lord a - lone are life and health and peace;
Lord a - lone is ev - ery - thing I need;

WORDS and MUSIC: Walt Harrah (1948-)

B♭
F/C
C7
F
in the Lord, in the Lord a - lone.

Give to Our God Immortal Praise 63

1 Give to our God im - mor - tal praise; mer - cy and
2 He built the earth, he spread the sky, and fixed the
3 He fills the sun with morn - ing light; he bids the
4 He sent His Son with power to save from guilt and
5 Through this vast world he guides our feet, and leads us
truth are all his ways: won - ders of grace to
star - ry lights on high: won - ders of grace to
moon di - rect the night: his mer - cies ev - er
dark - ness and the grave: won - ders of grace to
to his heav - enly seat: his mer - cies ev - er
God be - long; re - peat his mer - cies in your song.
God be - long; re - peat his mer - cies in your song.
shall en - dure, when suns and moons shall shine no more.
God be - long; re - peat his mer - cies in your song.
shall en - dure, when this our world shall be no more.

WORDS: Isaac Watts (1674-1748)
MUSIC: John Hatton (ca. 1710-1793)

DUKE STREET
L.M.

64 O God Beyond All Praising

Unison
1 O God be-yond all prais - ing, we wor-ship you to - day
2 Then hear, O gra-cious Sav - ior, ac - cept the love we bring,
and sing the love a - maz - ing that songs can - not re - pay;
that we who know your fa - vor may serve you as our King;
for we can on - ly won - der at ev - ery gift you send,
and wheth - er our to - mor-rows be filled with good or ill,
at bless-ings with - out num - ber and mer-cies with - out end;
we'll tri-umph through our sor - rows and rise to bless you still:

WORDS: Michael Perry (1942-1996)
MUSIC: Gustav T. Holst (1874-1934)

THAXTED
13.13.13.13.13.13.

we lift our hearts be - fore you and wait up - on your Word,
to mar - vel at your beau - ty and glo - ry in your ways,
we hon - or and a - dore you, our great and might - y Lord.
and make a joy - ful du - ty our sac - ri - fice of praise.

God Moves in a Mysterious Way 65

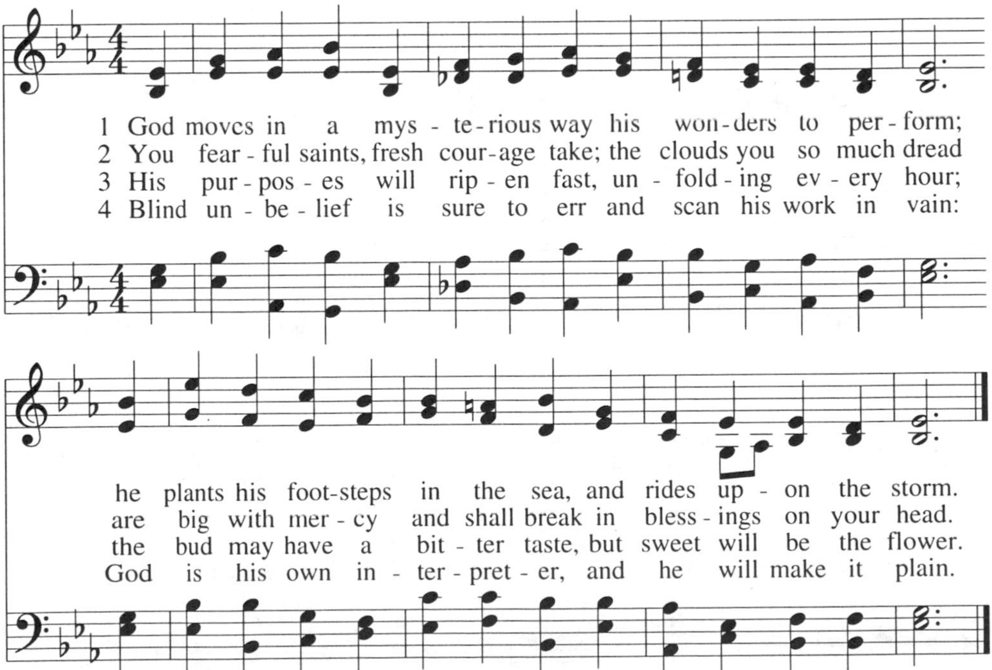
1 God moves in a mys - te - rious way his won - ders to per - form;
2 You fear - ful saints, fresh cour - age take; the clouds you so much dread
3 His pur - pos - es will rip - en fast, un - fold - ing ev - ery hour;
4 Blind un - be - lief is sure to err and scan his work in vain:
he plants his foot-steps in the sea, and rides up - on the storm.
are big with mer - cy and shall break in bless - ings on your head.
the bud may have a bit - ter taste, but sweet will be the flower.
God is his own in - ter - pret - er, and he will make it plain.

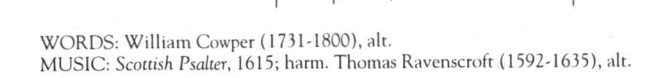

WORDS: William Cowper (1731-1800), alt.
MUSIC: *Scottish Psalter*, 1615; harm. Thomas Ravenscroft (1592-1635), alt.

DUNDEE
C.M.

66 To God Be the Glory

1 To God be the glo - ry, great things he hath done; so loved he the
2 O per - fect re - demp-tion, the pur-chase of blood, to ev - ery be -
3 Great things he hath taught us, great things he hath done, and great our re -
world that he gave us his Son, who yield - ed his life an a -
liev - er the prom - ise of God; the vil - est of - fend - er who
joic - ing through Je - sus the Son; but pur - er, and high - er and
tone-ment for sin, and o - pened the life - gate that all may go in.
tru - ly be - lieves, that mo - ment from Je - sus a par - don re - ceives.
great - er will be our won - der, our trans - port, when Je - sus we see.
Refrain
Praise the Lord, praise the Lord, let the earth hear his voice! Praise the Lord, praise the

WORDS: Fanny J. Crosby (1820-1915)
MUSIC: William H. Doane (1832-1915)

TO GOD BE THE GLORY
11.11.11.11.Ref.

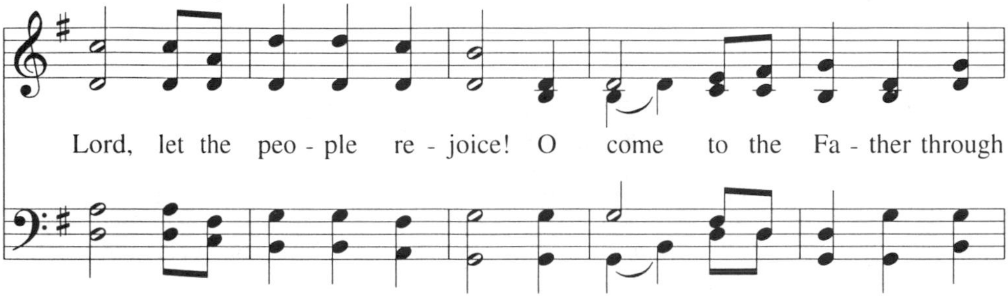
Lord, let the peo - ple re - joice! O come to the Fa - ther through

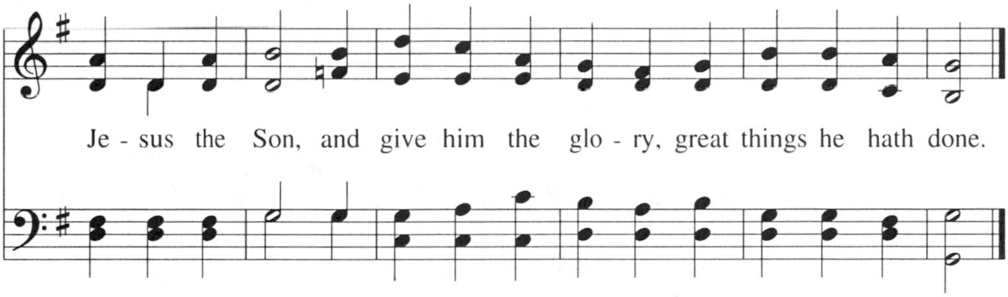
Je - sus the Son, and give him the glo - ry, great things he hath done.

Come, We That Love the Lord 67

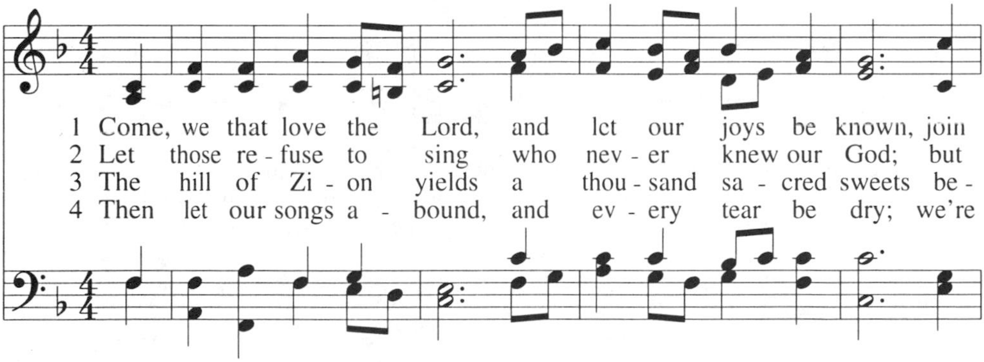
1 Come, we that love the Lord, and let our joys be known, join
2 Let those re - fuse to sing who nev - er knew our God; but
3 The hill of Zi - on yields a thou - sand sa - cred sweets be -
4 Then let our songs a - bound, and ev - ery tear be dry; we're

in a song with sweet ac - cord, and thus sur - round the throne.
chil - dren of the heaven - ly King may speak their joys a - broad.
fore we reach the heaven - ly fields, or walk the gold - en streets.
march - ing through Em - man - uel's ground to fair - er worlds on high.

WORDS: Isaac Watts (1674-1748)
MUSIC: Aaron Williams' *New Universal Psalmodist*, 1770

ST. THOMAS
S.M.

68 Come, Thou Fount of Every Blessing

1 Come, thou Fount of ev-ery bless-ing, tune my heart to sing thy grace;
2 Here I raise to thee an al-tar, hith-er by thy help I've come;
3 O to grace how great a debt-or dai-ly I'm con-strained to be!
streams of mer-cy, nev-er ceas-ing, call for songs of loud-est praise.
and I hope, by thy good plea-sure, safe-ly to ar-rive at home.
Let thy good-ness, like a fet-ter, bind my wan-dering heart to thee;
Teach me some me-lo-dious son-net, sung by flam-ing tongues a-bove;
Je-sus sought me when a stran-ger, wan-dering from the fold of God;
prone to wan-der, Lord, I feel it, prone to leave the God I love;
praise his name–I'm fixed up-on it—name of God's re-deem-ing love.
he, to res-cue me from dan-ger, bought me with his pre-cious blood.
here's my heart, O, take and seal it; seal it for thy courts a-bove.

WORDS: Robert Robinson (1735-1790)
MUSIC: John Wyeth's *Repository of Sacred Music*, 1813

NETTLETON
8.7.8.7.D.

I Worship You, Almighty God 69

Gsus G Em9 Em7 Am7 C/D G D7sus D
I wor-ship you, al-might-y God; there is none like you. I
Gsus G Em9 Em7 Am7 Am7/D D7
wor-ship you, O Prince of Peace; that is what I want to do. I
C/G G Em7 G/A Am7 D7
give you praise for you are my righ-teous-ness. I
Gsus G Em9 Em7 Am7 C/D D7 Gsus G
wor-ship you, al-might-y God; there is none like you.

WORDS and MUSIC: Sondra Corbett-Wood (1963-)

70 Lord, for the Years

1 Lord, for the years your love has kept and guid - ed,
urged and in - spired us, cheered us on our way,
sought us and saved us, par - doned and pro - vid - ed,
Lord of the years, we bring our thanks to - day.
2 Lord, for that word, the word of life which fires us,
speaks to our hearts and sets our souls a - blaze,
teach - es and trains, re - bukes us and in - spires us,
Lord of the word, re - ceive your peo - ple's praise.
3 Lord, for our land, in this our gen - er - a - tion,
spir - its op - pressed by pleas - ure, wealth and care;
for young and old, for this and ev - ery na - tion,
Lord of our land, be pleased to hear our prayer.
4 Lord, for our world; when we dis - own and doubt him,
love - less in strength, and com - fort - less in pain;
hun - gry and help - less, lost in - deed with - out him,
Lord of the world, we pray that Christ may reign.
5 Lord, for our - selves; in liv - ing power re - make us—
self on the cross and Christ up - on the throne;
past put be - hind us, for the fu - ture take us,
Lord of our lives, to live for Christ a - lone.

WORDS: Timothy Dudley-Smith (1926-)
MUSIC: Michael Baughen (1930-); arr. David Iliff (1939-)

LORD OF THE YEARS
11.10.11.10.

Praise to the Lord, the Almighty 71

1 Praise to the Lord, the Al - might - y, the King of cre - a -
2 Praise to the Lord, a - bove all things so won-drous - ly reign -
3 Praise to the Lord, who will pros - per your work and de - fend
4 Praise to the Lord! O let all that is in me a - dore

tion! O my soul, praise him, for he is your health and sal -
ing; shel - tering you un - der his wings, and so gent - ly sus -
you: sure - ly his good - ness and mer - cy shall dai - ly at -
him! All that has life and breath, come now with prais - es be -

va - tion! Come, all who hear; now to his
tain - ing! Have you not seen all that is
tend you. Pon - der a - new what the Al -
fore him. Let the A - men sound from his

tem - ple draw near, join me in glad ad - o - ra - tion!
need - ful has been sent by his gra-cious or - dain - ing?
might - y can do, if with his love he be - friends you.
peo - ple a - gain; glad - ly for - ev - er a - dore him.

WORDS: Joachim Neander (1650-1680); tr. Catherine Winkworth (1827-1878), alt.
MUSIC: *Stralsund Gesangbuch*, 1665

LOBE DEN HERREN
14.14.4.7.8.

72 Great Is Thy Faithfulness

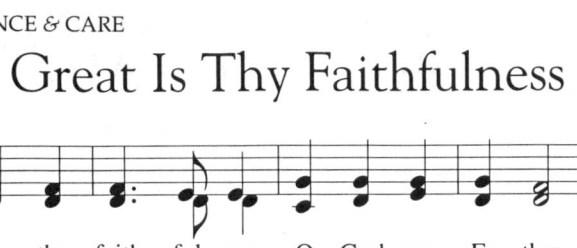

1 Great is thy faith - ful-ness, O God my Fa - ther, there is no
2 Sum - mer and win - ter, and spring-time and har - vest, sun, moon and
3 Par - don for sin and a peace that en - dur - eth, thy own dear
shad - ow of turn - ing with thee; thou chang - est not, thy com -
stars in their cours - es a - bove join with all na - ture in
pres - ence to cheer and to guide; strength for to - day and bright
pas-sions they fail not; as thou has been thou for - ev - er wilt be.
man - i - fold wit-ness to thy great faith - ful-ness, mer - cy and love.
hope for to - mor-row, bless-ings all mine, with ten thou-sand be - side!
Refrain
Great is thy faith - ful - ness! Great is thy faith - ful - ness!
Morn-ing by morn-ing new mer-cies I see; all I have need - ed thy

WORDS: Thomas O. Chisholm (1866-1960)
MUSIC: William M. Runyan (1870-1957)

FAITHFULNESS
11.10.11.10.Ref.

hand hath pro - vid - ed— great is thy faith - ful-ness, Lord, un - to me!

The Lord My Shepherd Guards Me Well 73

1 The Lord my Shep-herd guards me well, and all my wants are fed:
2 Though I should walk in dark - est ways through val - leys like the grave,
3 For me a ta - ble has been spread where all my foes can see;
4 Your stead-fast love will fol - low me to shield me all my days
a - mid green pas - tures made to lie, be - side still wa - ters led.
no e - vil shall I ev - er fear; your pres - ence makes me brave.
you bathe my head with fra-grant oil to soothe and hon - or me.
and bring me to your ho - ly house, re - deemed from er - ror's ways,
My care-worn soul grows strong and whole when God's true path I tread.
On my be - half your rod and staff as - sure me you will save.
My heart and cup are both filled up with joy - ful ec - sta - sy.
my whole life long to join the song of those who sing God's praise.

WORDS: Carl P. Daw, Jr. (1944-); para. Psalm 23
MUSIC: James L. Bain (1840-1925); arr. Gordon Jacob (1895-1984)

BROTHER JAMES' AIR
8.6.8.6.8.6.

74 Eternal Father, Strong to Save

1 E - ter - nal Fa - ther, strong to save, whose arm has bound the rest - less wave, who told the might - y o - cean deep its own ap - point - ed bounds to keep: O hear us when we cry to thee for those in per - il on the sea.
2 O Christ, whose voice the wa - ters heard and hushed their rag - ing at your word, who walked a - cross the surg - ing deep and in the storm lay calm in sleep: O hear us when we cry to thee for those in per - il on the sea.
3 Cre - a - tor Spir - it, by whose breath were fash - ioned sea and sky and earth; who made the storm - y cha - os cease and gave us life and light and peace: O hear us when we cry to thee for those in per - il on the sea.
4 O Trin - i - ty of love and power, pre - serve their lives in dan - ger's hour; from rock and tem - pest, flood and flame, pro - tect them by your ho - ly name, and to your glo - ry let there be glad hymns of praise from land and sea.

WORDS: William Whiting (1825-1878), alt.
MUSIC: John B. Dykes (1823-1876)

MELITA
8.8.8.8.8.8.

By Gracious Powers

1 By gra - cious pow'rs so won - der - ful - ly shel - tered,
2 Yet is this heart by its old foe tor - ment - ed,
3 And when this cup you give is filled to brim - ming
4 Yet when a - gain in this same world you give us
5 By gra - cious pow'rs so faith - ful - ly pro - tect - ed,
and con - fi - dent - ly wait - ing come what may,
still e - vil days bring bur - dens hard to bear;
with bit - ter suf - fering, hard to un - der - stand,
the joy we had, the bright - ness of your sun,
so qui - et - ly, so won - der - ful - ly near,
we know that God is with us night and morn - ing,
Oh, give our fright - ened souls the sure sal - va - tion,
we take it thank - ful - ly and with - out trem - bling
we shall re - mem - ber all the days we lived through
I'll live each day in hope, with you be - side me,
and nev - er fails to greet us each new day.
for which, O Lord, you taught us to pre - pare.
out of so good and so be - loved a hand.
and our whole life shall then be yours a - lone.
and go with you through ev - ery com - ing year.

WORDS: Dietrich Bonhöffer (1906-1945); tr. Fred Pratt Green (1903-2000)
MUSIC. *Paris Antiphoner*, 1681; harm. John B. Dykes (1823-1876)

O QUANTA QUALIA
11.10.11.10

76 We Are Singing, for the Lord Is Our Light

Siyahamba

Refrain
We are sing - ing,* for the Lord is our light,
Si - ya - hamb' e - ku - kha - ny - en' kwen - khos,'
we are sing - ing, for the Lord is our light.
si - ya - hamb' e - ku - kha - ny - en' kwen - khos'.
We are sing - ing,
Si - ya - ham ba,
Oh we are
Oo si - ya -
We are sing - ing, sing - ing, we are sing - ing, sing - ing, we are
Si - ya - ham - ba, ham - ba, si - ya - ham - ba, ham - ba, si - ya -
we are
si - ya -
1
2
sing - ing for the Lord is our light. We are our light.
hamb' e - ku - kha - ny - en kwen - khos. Si - ya - kwen - khos.
sing - ing for the Lord is, for the Lord is our light. We are our light.
hamb' e - ku - kha - ny - en' kwen, kha - ny - en' kwen - khos. Si - ya - kwen - khos.
sing - ing for the Lord is our light. We are our light.
hamb' e - ku - kha - ny - en kwen - khos. Si - ya - kwen - khos.

*marching/praying

WORDS: South African; tr. and original verses by Hal H. Hopson (1933-)
MUSIC: Zulu melody; adapted and original verses by Hal H. Hopson (1933-)

SIYAHAMBA
Irregular

Verses (Optional Solo)
1 The Lord is the strength of our lives; of whom shall we be a - fraid?
2 One thing have we asked of the Lord, yes, this is the thing we seek:
3 When bur - dens are heav - y to bear, our shel - ter is God a - lone.
4 We walk in the strength of the Lord, God's love is ev - er sure.
Though foes may be near to de - stroy, the
To dwell in the house of the Lord; to
Our feet are lift - ed high; yes,
We shout that the world may hear, we
Lord will be our light.
live with God for - ev - er. We are
high up - on a rock. Si - ya -
sing a joy - ful song.
D.S. (Refrain)

77 I Greet Thee, Who My Sure Redeemer Art

1 I greet thee, who my sure Re - deem - er art,
2 Thou art the King of mer - cy and of grace,
3 Thou art the life by which a - lone we live
4 Thou hast the true and per - fect gen - tle - ness,
5 Our hope is in no oth - er save in thee;
my on - ly trust and Sav - ior of my heart,
reign - ing om - ni - po - tent in ev - ery place:
and all our sub - stance and our strength re - ceive;
thou hast no harsh - ness and no bit - ter - ness:
our faith is built up - on thy prom - ise free;
who pain didst un - der - go for my poor sake;
so come, O King, and our whole be - ing sway;
com - fort us by thy faith and by thy power,
make us to taste the sweet grace found in thee
come, give us peace, make us so strong and sure,
I pray thee from our hearts all cares to take.
shine on us with the light of thy pure day.
nor daunt our hearts when comes the try - ing hour.
and ev - er stay in thy sweet u - ni - ty.
that we may con - querors be and ills en - dure.

WORDS: Attr. John Calvin (1509-1564); tr. Elizabeth I. Smith (1817-1898), alt.
MUSIC: *Genevan Psalter*, 1551

TOULON
10.10.10.10.

God of the Ages, History's Maker 78

Unison
1 God of the a - ges, his - to - ry's Mak - er,
2 God of this morn - ing, glad - ly your chil - dren
3 God of to - mor - row, strong o - ver - com - er,
4 Lord of past a - ges, Lord of this morn - ing,
plan - ning our path - way, hold - ing us fast,
wor - ship be - fore you, trust - ing - ly bow:
princ - es of dark - ness own your com - mand:
Lord of the fu - ture, help us, we pray:
shap - ing in mer - cy all that con - cerns us:
teach us to know you al - ways a - mong us,
what then can harm us? We are your peo - ple,
teach us to trust you, love and o - bey you,
Fa - ther, we praise you, Lord of the past.
qui - et - ly sov - ereign— Lord of our now.
now and for - ev - er kept by your hand.
crown you each mo - ment, Lord of to - day.

WORDS: Margaret Clarkson (1915-)
MUSIC: Gaelic melody

BUNESSAN
10.9.10.9.

79 I'll Praise My Maker While I've Breath

1 I'll praise my Mak - er while I've breath, and when my voice is lost in death, praise shall em - ploy my no - blest powers; my days of praise are nev - er past while life and thought and be - ing last or im - mor - tal - i - ty en - dures.
2 Hap - py are those whose hopes re - ly on God the Lord, who made the sky, and earth, the sea, the night and day; his truth for - ev - er stands se - cure, he keeps his prom - ise to the poor, and none who seeks is turned a - way.
3 The Lord gives eye - sight to the blind, he calms and heals the trou - bled mind; he sends the wound-ed con-science peace; he helps the strang - er in dis - tress, the wid - ow and the fa - ther - less, and grants the pris - oner glad re - lease.
4 I'll praise him while he lends me breath, and when my voice is lost in death, praise shall em - ploy my no - blest powers; my days of praise are nev - er past while life and thought and be - ing last or im - mor - tal - i - ty en - dures.

WORDS: Isaac Watts (1674-1748); adapt. John Wesley (1703-1791), alt.; para. Psalm 146 — OLD 113th

MUSIC: *Strasburger Kirchenamt*, 1525; attr. Matthaus Greiter (ca. 1500-1550); harm. V. Earle Copes (1921-) — 8.8.8.8.8.8.

He's Got the Whole World in His Hands 80

Unison
C7 F Gm7 F/A Gm7 F Gm7 Am
1 He's got the whole world in his hands, he's got the
2 He's got the wind and the rain in his hands, he's got the
3 He's got the ti - ny lit - tle ba - by in his hands, he's got the
4 He's got you and me, broth-er, in his hands, he's got
Gm7 Bb/C C7 F Gm7
whole world in his hands, he's got the whole
wind and the rain in his hands, he's got the wind and the
ti - ny lit - tle ba - by in his hands, he's got the ti - ny lit - tle
you and me, sis - ter, in his hands, he's got all of us to-
F/A Gm7 F Am7(b5)/Eb D7 Gm7 C7 F
world in his hands, he's got the whole world in his hands.
rain in his hands, he's got the whole world in his hands.
ba - by in his hands, he's got the whole world in his hands.
geth-er in his hands, he's got the whole world in his hands.

WORDS and MUSIC: African-American spiritual; arr. Eugene Thomas (1941-)

WHOLE WORLD
Irregular

81 We Gather Together

1 We gath - er to - geth - er to ask the Lord's bless - ing;
2 Be - side us to guide us, our God with us join - ing,
3 We all do ex - tol thee, our lead - er tri - um - phant,
he chas - tens and has - tens his will to make known;
or - dain - ing, main - tain - ing his king - dom di - vine;
and pray that thou still our de - fend - er wilt be;
the wick - ed op - press - ing now cease from dis - tress - ing,
so from the be - gin - ning the fight we were win - ning:
let thy con - gre - ga - tion es - cape trib - u - la - tion:
sing prais - es to his name: he for - gets not his own.
thou, Lord, wast at our side, all glo - ry be thine!
thy name be ev - er praised! O Lord, make us free!

WORDS: Netherlands folk hymn; tr. Theodore Baker (1851-1934)
MUSIC: *Nederlandtsch Gedenckclanck*, 1626; arr. Edward Kremser (1838-1914)

KREMSER
12.11.12.11.

Praise, My Soul, the King of Heaven 82

1 Praise, my soul, the King of heav - en, to his feet your trib - ute bring; ran - somed, healed, re - stored, for - giv - en, ev - er - more his prais - es sing. Al - le - lu - ia! Al - le - lu - ia! Praise the ev - er - last - ing King!
2 Praise him for his grace and fa - vor to all peo - ple in dis - tress. Praise him, still the same for - ev - er, slow to chide and swift to bless. Al - le - lu - ia! Al - le - lu - ia! Glo - rious in his faith - ful - ness!
3 Fa - ther - like, he tends and spares us; all our hopes and fears he knows. In his hands he gent - ly bears us, res - cues us from all our foes. Al - le - lu - ia! Al - le - lu - ia! Wide - ly as his mer - cy flows!
4 An - gels, help us to a - dore him, you be - hold him face to face. Sun and moon, bow down be - fore him; all who dwell in time and space. Al - le - lu - ia! Al - le - lu - ia! Praise with us the God of grace!

WORDS: Henry F. Lyte (1793-1847), alt; para. Psalm 103
MUSIC: John Goss (1800-1880)

LAUDA ANIMA
8.7.8.7.8.7.

83 Children of the Heavenly Father

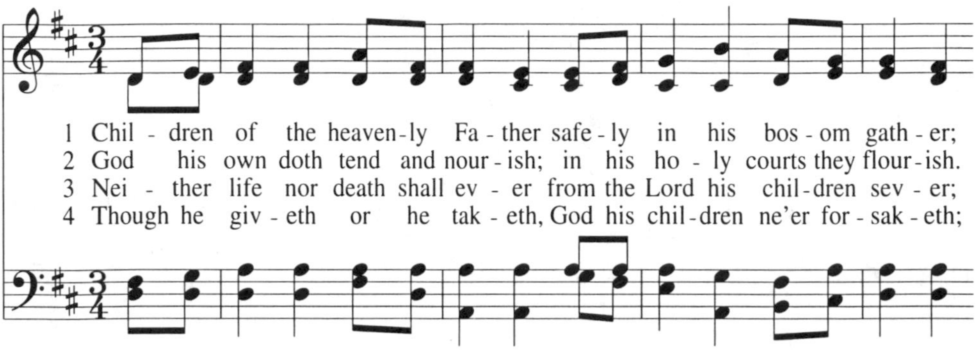
1 Chil - dren of the heaven-ly Fa - ther safe - ly in his bos - om gath - er;
2 God his own doth tend and nour - ish; in his ho - ly courts they flour - ish.
3 Nei - ther life nor death shall ev - er from the Lord his chil-dren sev - er;
4 Though he giv - eth or he tak - eth, God his chil-dren ne'er for - sak - eth;

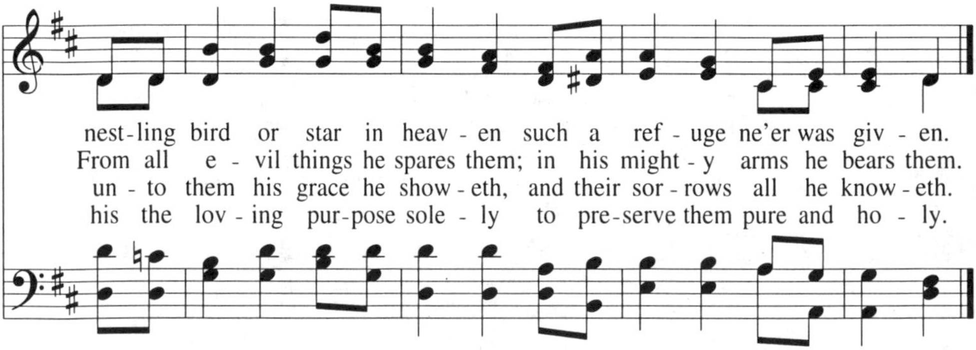
nest-ling bird or star in heav - en such a ref - uge ne'er was giv - en.
From all e - vil things he spares them; in his might - y arms he bears them.
un - to them his grace he show - eth, and their sor - rows all he know - eth.
his the lov - ing pur-pose sole - ly to pre-serve them pure and ho - ly.

WORDS: Carolina Sandell Berg (1832-1903); tr. Ernest W. Olson (1870-1958) — TRYGGARE KAN INGEN VARA
MUSIC: Swedish melody — L.M.

84 O God, Our Help in Ages Past

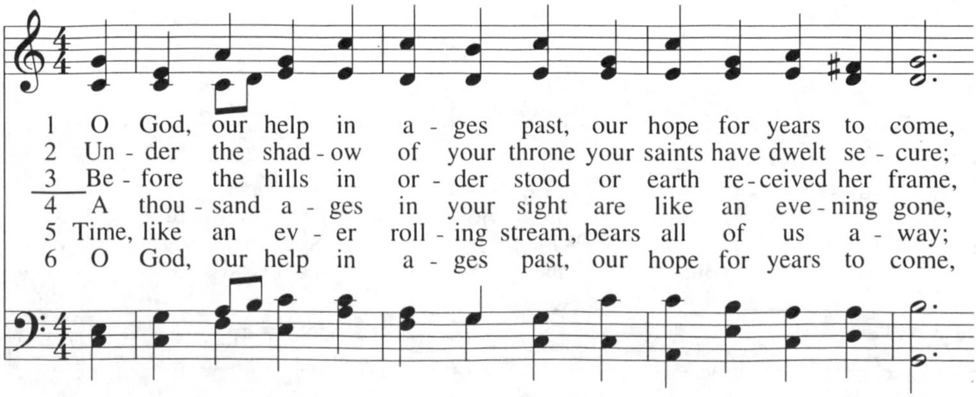
1 O God, our help in a - ges past, our hope for years to come,
2 Un - der the shad - ow of your throne your saints have dwelt se - cure;
3 Be - fore the hills in or - der stood or earth re-ceived her frame,
4 A thou - sand a - ges in your sight are like an eve - ning gone,
5 Time, like an ev - er roll - ing stream, bears all of us a - way;
6 O God, our help in a - ges past, our hope for years to come,

WORDS: Isaac Watts (1674-1748), alt.; para. Psalm 90 — ST. ANNE
MUSIC: Attr. William Croft (1678-1727) — C.M.

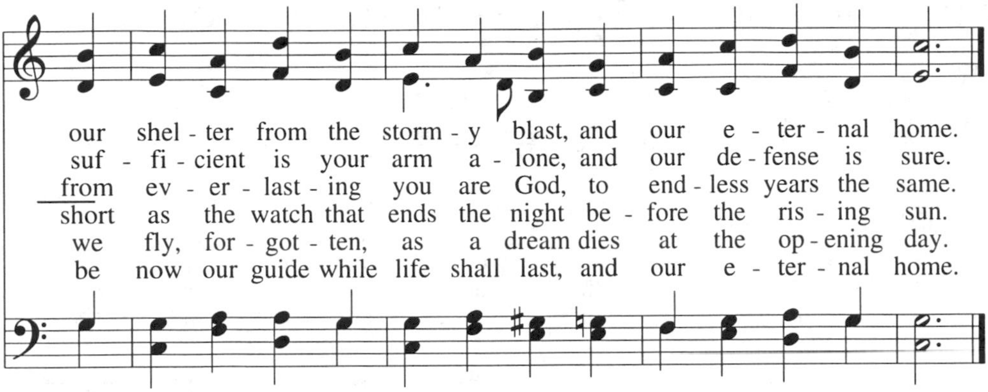
our shel - ter from the storm - y blast, and our e - ter - nal home.
suf - fi - cient is your arm a - lone, and our de - fense is sure.
from ev - er - last - ing you are God, to end - less years the same.
short as the watch that ends the night be - fore the ris - ing sun.
we fly, for - got - ten, as a dream dies at the op - ening day.
be now our guide while life shall last, and our e - ter - nal home.

I Love You, Lord 85

F Bb/F C7/G F/A C F F7/Eb Bb/D F/C
I love you, Lord, and I lift my voice to wor - ship
C7/Bb F/A C7sus/G Gm7 C7 N.C. F Bb/F C7/G F/A
you, O my soul, re - joice! Take joy, my King, in
C F F7/Eb Bb/D F/C C7sus/G C7 F Bb/F F
what you hear: may it be a sweet, sweet sound in your ear.

WORDS and MUSIC: Laurie Klein (1950-)

86 The Lord's My Shepherd, I'll Not Want

1 The Lord's my Shep - herd, I'll not want; he
2 My soul he doth re - store a - gain; and
3 Yea, though I walk through death's dark vale, yet
4 My ta - ble thou hast fur - nish - ed in
5 Good - ness and mer - cy all my life shall
makes me down to lie in pas - tures green; he
me to walk doth make with - in the paths of
will I fear no ill; for thou art with me,
pres - ence of my foes; my head thou dost with
sure - ly fol - low me; and in God's house for -
lead - eth me the qui - et wa - ters by.
right - eous - ness, e'en for his own name's sake.
and thy rod and staff me com - fort still.
oil a - noint, and my cup o - ver - flows.
ev - er - more my dwell - ing place shall be.

WORDS: *Scottish Psalter*, 1650; para. Psalm 23
MUSIC: Jessie S. Irvine (1836-1887); arr. David Grant (1833-1893)

CRIMOND
C.M.

Come, Christians, Join to Sing

1 Come, Chris-tians, join to sing Al - le - lu - ia! A - men!
2 Come, lift your hearts on high, Al - le - lu - ia! A - men!
3 Praise yet our Christ a - gain, Al - le - lu - ia! A - men!
loud praise to Christ our King; Al - le - lu - ia! A - men!
let prais - es fill the sky; Al - le - lu - ia! A - men!
life shall not end the strain; Al - le - lu - ia! A - men!
Let all, with heart and voice, be - fore his throne re - joice;
Christ is our Guide and Friend; to us he'll con - de - scend;
On heav - en's bliss - ful shore his good - ness we'll a - dore,
praise is his gra - cious choice: Al - le - lu - ia! A - men!
his love shall nev - er end: Al - le - lu - ia! A - men!
sing - ing for - ev - er - more, "Al - le - lu - ia! A - men!"

WORDS: Christian H. Bateman (1813-1889)
MUSIC: Spanish melody; arr. David Evans (1874-1948)

MADRID
6.6.6.6.D.

88 Lord, I Lift Your Name on High

Unison
G2 C D C G2 C
Lord, I lift your name on high, Lord, I love to sing your
D C G2 C D C
prais - es. I'm so glad you're in my life,
G2 C Dsus D G C
I'm so glad you came to save us. You came from heav-en to earth
D C G C D C
to show the way, from the earth to the cross, my debt to pay;
G C D Em7
from the cross to the grave, from the grave to the sky;

WORDS and MUSIC: Rick Founds (1954-)

Am7 Am7/D D7 G C/G G
Lord, I lift your name on high.

Rise, Shine, You People! 89

Unison
1 Rise, shine, you peo - ple! Christ the Lord has en - tered our
2 See how he sends the powers of e - vil reel - ing; and
3 Come, cel - e - brate; your ban - ners high un - furl - ing, your
4 Tell how the Fa - ther sent his Son to save us. Tell
hu - man sto - ry; God in him is cen - tered. Christ comes to
brings us free - dom, light, and life and heal - ing. All men and
songs and prayers a - gainst the dark-ness hurl - ing. To all the
of the Son, who life and free - dom gave us. Tell how the
us, by death and sin sur-round - ed, with grace un - bound - ed.
wom - en, who by guilt are driv - en, now are for - giv - en.
world go out and tell the sto - ry of Je - sus' glo - ry.
Spir - it calls from ev - ery na - tion his new cre - a - tion.

WORDS: Ronald A. Klug (1939-), alt.
MUSIC: Dale Wood (1934-)

WOJTKIEWIECZ
11.11.11.5.

90 Jesus! What a Friend for Sinners!

1 Je - sus! what a Friend for sin - ners! Je - sus! Lov - er of my soul; friends may fail me, foes as - sail me, he, my Sav - ior, makes me whole.
2 Je - sus! what a Strength in weak - ness! Let me hide my - self in him; tempt - ed, tried, and some - times fail - ing, he, my Strength, my vic - tory wins.
3 Je - sus! what a Help in sor - row! While the bil - lows o'er me roll, e - ven when my heart is break - ing, he, my Com - fort, helps my soul.
4 Je - sus! what a Guide and Keep - er! While the tem - pest still is high, storms a - bout me, night o'er - takes me, he, my Pi - lot, hears my cry.
5 Je - sus! I do now re - ceive him, more than all in him I find, he has grant - ed me for - give - ness, I am his, and he is mine.
Refrain
Hal - le - lu - jah! what a Sav - ior! Hal - le - lu - jah! what a Friend! Sav - ing,

WORDS: J. Wilbur Chapman (1859-1918)
MUSIC: Rowland H. Prichard (1811-1887)

HYFRYDOL
8.7.8.7.D.

help - ing, keep - ing, lov - ing, he is with me to the end.

Christ, Whose Glory Fills the Skies 91

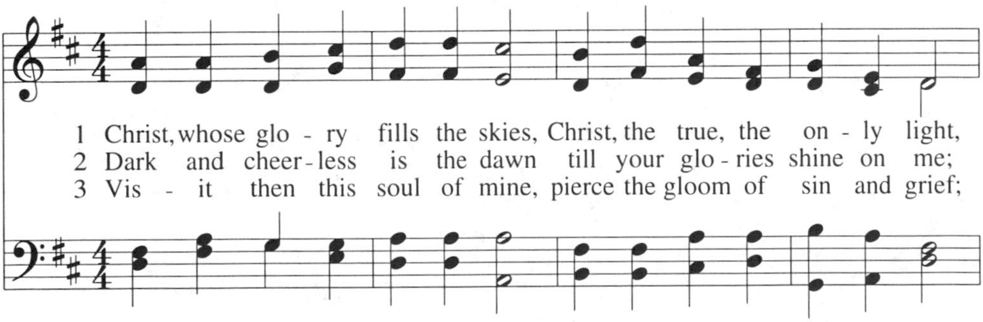
1 Christ, whose glo - ry fills the skies, Christ, the true, the on - ly light,
2 Dark and cheer - less is the dawn till your glo - ries shine on me;
3 Vis - it then this soul of mine, pierce the gloom of sin and grief;

Sun of right-eous - ness, a - rise, tri - umph o - ver shades of night:
joy - less is the day's re - turn till your mer - cy's beams I see:
fill me, ra - dian - cy di - vine, scat - ter all my un - be - lief:

Day-spring from on high, be near, Day - star, in my heart ap - pear!
as they in - ward light im - part, cheer my eyes and warm my heart.
more and more your - self dis - play, shin - ing to the per - fect day!

WORDS: Charles Wesley (1707-1788), alt.
MUSIC. J. G. Werner's *Choralbuch*, 1815; harm. William H. Havergal (1793-1870)

RATISBON
7.7.7.7.7.7.

92 All Hail King Jesus!

Unison
F/A C/G F C/E C C/E Bb/F F
All hail King Je - sus! All hail Em - man - u - el,
A/E Dm G9/B G9 Gm
King of kings, Lord of lords, Bright Morn-ing Star.
C Bb/C C F Fmaj7/E F/Eb Bb/D Bb
And through-out e - ter - ni - ty, I'll sing your prais - es;
Gm7(b5) F/C Dm7 Gm7 Bb/C C7 F Bb/F F
and I'll reign with you through-out e - ter - ni - ty.

WORDS and MUSIC: Dave Moody (1948-)

Praise the One Who Breaks the Darkness 93

1 Praise the One who breaks the dark-ness with a lib - er - at-ing light.
2 Praise the One who blessed the chil-dren with a strong yet gen-tle word.
3 Praise the one true love in - car - nate: Christ, who suf-fered in our place.
Praise the One who frees the pris-oners, turn-ing blind-ness in - to sight.
Praise the One who drove out de - mons with a pierc-ing two-edged sword.
Je - sus died and rose for man - y that we may know God by grace.
Praise the One who preached the gos - pel, heal-ing ev - ery dread dis-ease,
Praise the One who brings cool wa - ter to the des-ert's burn-ing sand.
Let us sing for joy and glad-ness, see-ing what our God has done.
calm-ing storms and feed-ing thou-sands with the ver - y bread of peace.
From this well comes liv - ing wa - ter quench-ing thirst in ev - ery land.
Praise the one re - deem-ing glo - ry; praise the One who makes us one.

WORDS: Rusty Edwards (1955-)
MUSIC: John Wyeth's *Repository of Sacred Music*, 1813

NETTLETON
8.7.8.7.D.

94 Shout to the Lord

Unison
Bb F Gm Dm/F Eb
1 My Je - sus, my Sav - ior, Lord, there is none like you.
2 My com-fort, my shel - ter, tow - er of ref - uge and strength.
Bb/F Eb
1
Bb/D Gm7 Ab Cm7/G
All of my days I want to praise the won-ders of your might - y
Let ev-ery breath, all that I am,
Fsus F
love.
2
Bb/D Gm Gm7 Ab F
nev-er cease to wor - ship you.
Refrain
Bb Gm Eb Eb/F F7 Bb Gm
Shout to the Lord, all the earth, let us sing; pow-er and maj-

WORDS and MUSIC: Darlene Zschech (1965-)

Ebmaj7 Fsus F Gm
- es - ty, praise to the King. Moun-tains bow down and the seas
Eb F Cm7 F
will roar at the sound of your name.
Bb Gm Eb Eb/F F
I sing for joy at the work of your hands; for -
Bb Gm Ebmaj7 Fsus F Gm
ev - er I'll love you, for - ev - er I'll stand. Noth-ing com-pares
Eb Eb/F F7 Bb
to the prom - ise I have in you.

95 Praise Him! Praise Him!

1 Praise him! Praise him! Je - sus, our bless-ed Re-deem - er! Sing, O
2 Praise him! Praise him! Je - sus, our bless-ed Re-deem - er! For our
3 Praise him! Praise him! Je - sus, our bless-ed Re-deem - er! Heaven-ly
earth, his won-der - ful love pro - claim! Hail him! Hail him!
sins he suf-fered, and bled, and died; he our rock, our
por - tals loud with ho - san - nas ring! Je - sus, Sav - ior,
High-est arch-an-gels in glo - ry; strength and hon - or give to his
hope of e - ter - nal sal - va - tion. Hail him, hail him, Je - sus the
reign-eth for - ev - er and ev - er. Crown him, crown him, Proph-et and
ho - ly name! Like a shep-herd Je-sus will guard his chil-dren,
cru - ci - fied. Sound his prais - es! Je-sus who bore our sor-rows;
Priest and King! Christ is com - ing, o - ver the world vic - to - rious,

WORDS: Fanny J. Crosby (1820-1915)
MUSIC: Chester G. Allen (1838-1878)

JOYFUL SONG
12.10.12.10.11.10.11.10.

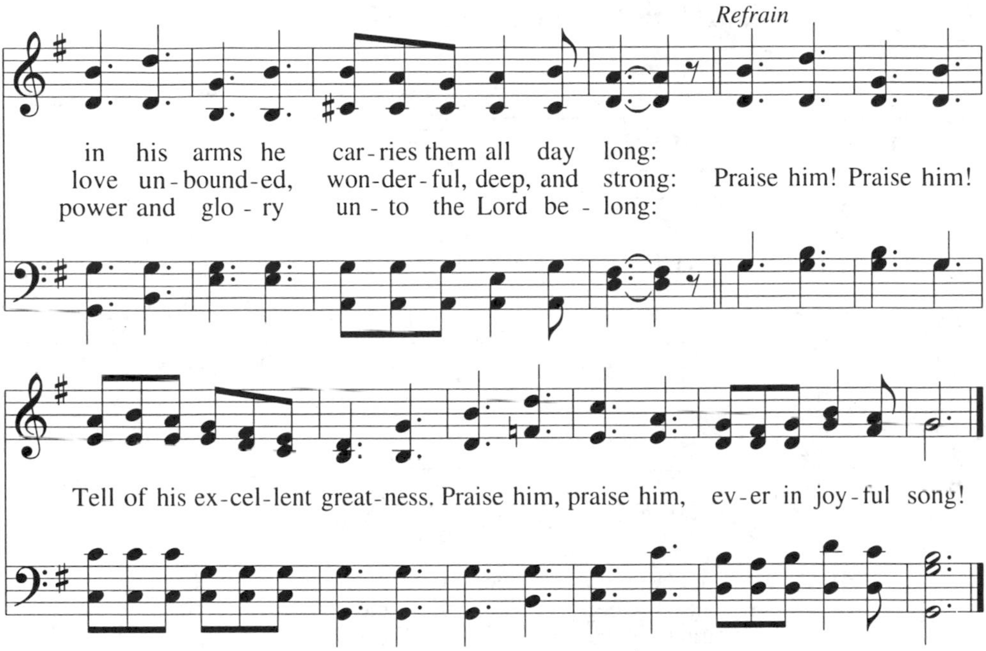
Refrain
in his arms he car-ries them all day long:
love un-bound-ed, won-der-ful, deep, and strong: Praise him! Praise him!
power and glo-ry un-to the Lord be-long:
Tell of his ex-cel-lent great-ness. Praise him, praise him, ev-er in joy-ful song!

O for a Thousand Tongues to Sing 96

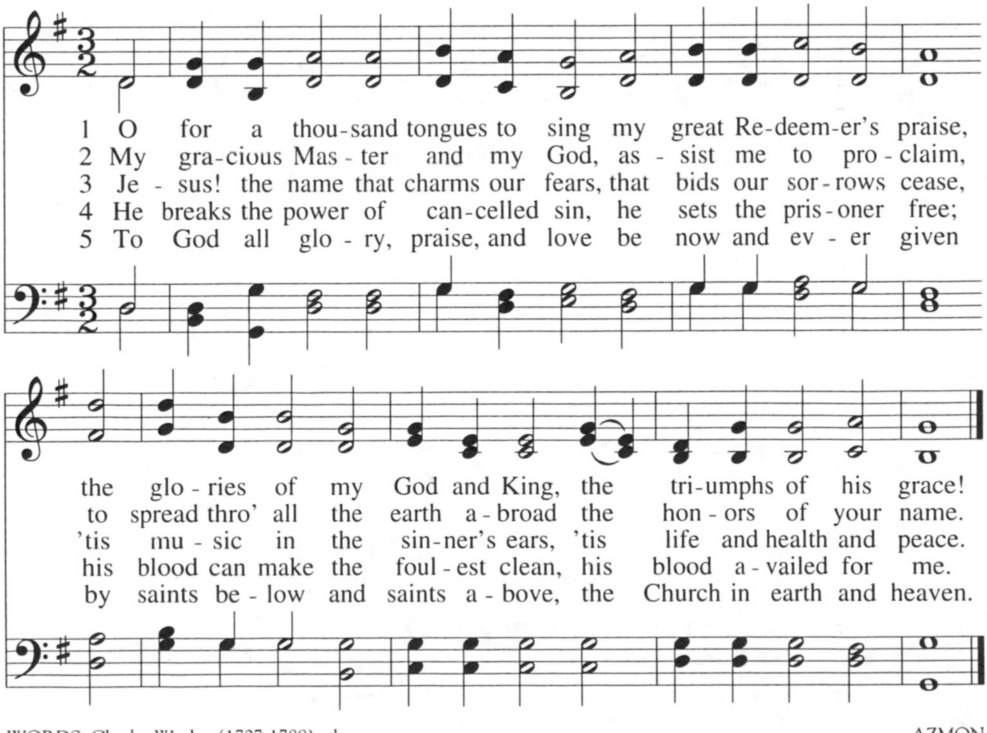
1 O for a thou-sand tongues to sing my great Re-deem-er's praise,
2 My gra-cious Mas-ter and my God, as-sist me to pro-claim,
3 Je-sus! the name that charms our fears, that bids our sor-rows cease,
4 He breaks the power of can-celled sin, he sets the pris-oner free;
5 To God all glo-ry, praise, and love be now and ev-er given
the glo-ries of my God and King, the tri-umphs of his grace!
to spread thro' all the earth a-broad the hon-ors of your name.
'tis mu-sic in the sin-ner's ears, 'tis life and health and peace.
his blood can make the foul-est clean, his blood a-vailed for me.
by saints be-low and saints a-bove, the Church in earth and heaven.

WORDS: Charles Wesley (1707-1788), alt.
MUSIC: Carl G. Gläser (1784-1829); arr. Lowell Mason (1792-1872)

AZMON
C.M.

97 Meekness and Majesty

Unison
C Am Em Am7
1 Meek - ness and maj - es - ty, hu - man and de - i - ty,
2 Fa - ther's pure ra - di - ance, per - fect in in - no - cence;
3 Wis - dom un - search - a - ble, God, the in - vis - i - ble;
C Am D7 Dm/G G7
in per - fect har - mo - ny, the One who is God.
yet learns o - be - di - ence to death on a cross.
love in - de - struct - i - ble in frail - ty ap - pears.
C C/B♭ F F♯dim7
Lord of e - ter - ni - ty, dwells in hu - man - i - ty;
Suf - fering to give us life, con - quering through sac - ri - fice;
Lord of in - fin - i - ty, stoop - ing so ten - der - ly;
Em Am7 Dm G7 C
kneels in hu - mil - i - ty and wash - es our feet.
and as they cru - ci - fy prays, "Fa - ther, for - give."
lifts our hu - man - i - ty to the heights of his throne.

WORDS and MUSIC: Graham Kendrick (1950-)

Dm7 F/G G G/F E7 G/A Am
O what a mys-ter - y, meek - ness and maj - es - ty;
F#dim7 C2/G Am7 Dm7 G7 Ab Bb C
bow down and wor - ship, for this is your God.

Hallelujah! Praise the Lamb! 98

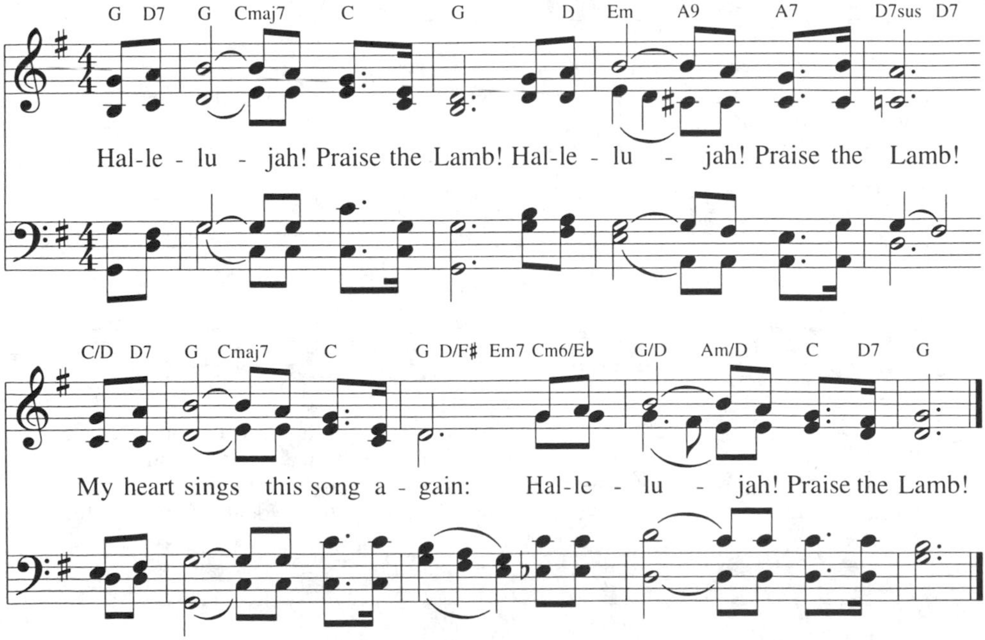
G D7 G Cmaj7 C G D Em A9 A7 D7sus D7
Hal-le - lu - jah! Praise the Lamb! Hal-le - lu - jah! Praise the Lamb!
C/D D7 G Cmaj7 C G D/F# Em7 Cm6/Eb G/D Am/D C D7 G
My heart sings this song a - gain: Hal-le - lu - jah! Praise the Lamb!

WORDS and MUSIC: Pam Thum (1961-), Constant Change (1964-) and Gary McSpadden (1943-)

99 You, Lord, Are Both Lamb and Shepherd

1 You, Lord, are both lamb and shep - herd. You, Lord, are both prince and slave. You, peace - mak - er and sword - bring - er of the way you took and gave. You, the ev - er - last - ing in - stant; you, whom we both scorn and crave.
2 Clothed in light up - on the moun - tain, stripped of might up - on the cross, shin - ing in e - ter - nal glo - ry, beg - gared by a sol - dier's toss, you, the ev - er - last - ing in - stant; you, who are both gift and cost.
3 You, who walk each day be - side us, sit in pow - er at God's side. You, who preach a way that's nar - row, have a love that reach - es wide. You, the ev - er - last - ing in - stant; you, who are our pil - grim guide.
4 Wor - thy is our earth - ly Je - sus! Wor - thy is our cos - mic Christ! Wor - thy your de - feat and vic - tory. Wor - thy still your peace and strife. You, the ev - er - last - ing in - stant; you, who are our death and life.

WORDS: Sylvia G. Dunstan (1955-1993), alt.
MUSIC: Henry T. Smart (1813-1879)

REGENT SQUARE
8.7.8.7.8.7.

All Hail the Power of Jesus' Name! 100

1 All hail the power of Je - sus' name! Let an - gels pros-trate
2 Ye cho - sen seed of Is - rael's race, ye ran-somed from the
3 Let ev - ery kin - dred, ev - ery tribe, on this ter - res - trial
4 O that with yon - der sa - cred throng we at his feet may
fall, let an - gels pros-trate fall; bring forth the roy - al di - a -
fall, ye ran-somed from the fall, hail him who saves you by his
ball, on this ter - res - trial ball, to him all maj - es - ty as -
fall, we at his feet may fall! We'll join the ev - er - last - ing
dem,
grace, and crown him, crown him,
cribe,
song, and crown him, crown him, crown him, crown him, crown him,
crown
crown him, crown him, and crown him Lord of all.
him, and crown him

WORDS: Edward Perronet (1726-1792); adapt. John Rippon (1751-1836)
MUSIC: James Ellor (1819-1899)

DIADEM
C.M. Repeats

101 Name of All Majesty

1 Name of all maj - es - ty, fath - om - less mys - ter - y,
2 Child of our des - ti - ny, God from e - ter - ni - ty,
3 Sav - ior of Cal - va - ry, cost - li - est vic - to - ry,
4 Source of all sov - ereign - ty, light, im - mor - tal - i - ty,
King of the a - ges by an - gels a - dored;
love of the Fa - ther on sin - ners out - poured;
dark - ness de - feat - ed and E - den re - stored;
life ev - er - last - ing and heav - en as - sured;
power and au - thor - i - ty, splen - dor and dig - ni - ty,
see now what God has done send - ing his on - ly Son,
born as a man to die, nailed to a cross on high,
so with the ran-somed, we praise him e - ter - nal - ly,
bow to his mas - ter - y— Je - sus is Lord!
Christ the be - lov - ed One— Je - sus is Lord!
cold in the grave to lie— Je - sus is Lord!
Christ in his maj - es - ty— Je - sus is Lord!

WORDS: Timothy Dudley-Smith (1926-)
MUSIC: Michael Baughen (1930-); arr. by Noël Tredinnick (1949-), alt.

MAJESTAS
6.6.5.5.6.6.6.4.

His Name Is Wonderful

102

F Gm/F F D D7/F♯ G$^4_2$ Gm C7 B♭/F F
His name is Won-der-ful, his name is Won-der-ful, his name is Won-der-ful,
G7 C7 F Gm/F F D D7/F♯ G$^4_2$ Gm
Je-sus, my Lord; he is the might-y King, Mas-ter of ev-ery-thing,
C7 B♭/F F C7 F C7 F/C C7
his name is Won-der-ful, Je-sus, my Lord. He's the great Shep-herd, the
F C7/G F/A F G7 F/G G7 C C7 F
Rock of all a-ges, Al-might-y God is he; bow down be-
Gm/F F D D7/F♯ G$^4_2$ Gm C7 B♭/F F C7 F
fore him, love and a-dore him, his name is Won-der-ful, Je-sus my Lord.

WORDS and MUSIC: Audrey Mieir (1916-1996)

MIEIR
Irregular

103 Glory to the Lamb

C G/B F/A Dm7 G7sus G7 C
1 Glo - ry, glo - ry, glo - ry to the Lamb. Glo - ry,
2 Wor - thy, wor - thy, wor - thy is the Lamb. Wor - thy,
3 Ho - ly, ho - ly, ho - ly is the Lamb. Ho - ly,
G/B G Dm7 G F/G Csus C
Refrain
Em7 F G/F
glo - ry, glo - ry to the Lamb.
wor - thy, wor - thy is the Lamb. For he is glo - ri - ous and
ho - ly, ho - ly is the Lamb.
Em7 Am7 Dm7 G Bb/C C Bb/D C/E
wor - thy to be praised, the Lamb up - on the throne; and
F G/F Em7 Am7 Dm7 G7sus G7 G7sus Csus C
un - to him we lift our voice in praise, the Lamb up - on the throne.

WORDS and MUSIC: Larry Dempsey (1946-1995)

Hidden Christ, Alive for Ever 104

1 Hid - den Christ, a - live for ev - er, Sav - ior, Ser - vant, Friend and Lord,
2 End - less or - bits by our plan - et spin - ning round its speed - ing star
3 Still your life and way of liv - ing, God - re - veal - ing, Spir - it - blown,
4 Who can tell, through earth - ly e - ons, all your lov - ing power has done,
5 Christ our hope, a - live a - mong us, take our love, our work, our prayer.

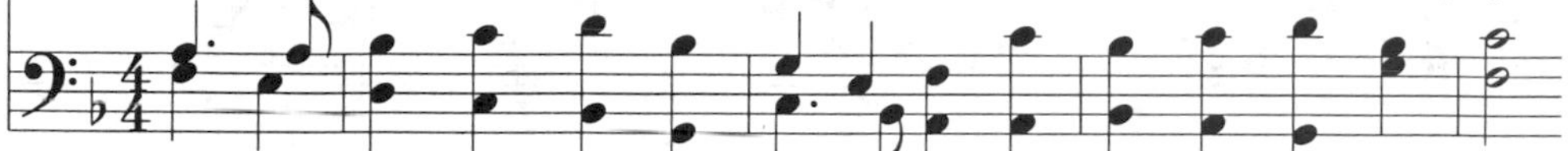

year by year, un - seen, you of - fer life un - dy - ing, love out - poured.
can - not trace cre - a - tion's se - cret: why we live and whose we are.
teach - ing, heal - ing, sins for - giv - ing, meas - ure and in - spire our own,
chang - ing hearts and shap - ing na - tions, seek - ing all, re - ject - ing none?
We will trust and tell your pur - pose, brav - ing e - vil and de - spair,

Day by day, you walk a - mong us, known and hon - ored, yet con - cealed,
Je - sus, you a - lone un - cov - er na - ture's rhy - thm, rea - son, rhyme,
lov - ing earth's de - spised, re - ject - ed, till with them you hang in pain,
Speech - es fail, but songs soar high - er, trac - ing how, in ev - ery place,
in your name be - friend - ing, mend - ing, mak - ing peace and set - ting free,

free - ing, chid - ing, lead - ing, guid - ing, till your glo - ry is re - vealed.
so your birth - day is our cen - ter: hinge of his - to - ry and time.
brok - en, bur - ied, res - ur - rec - ted, life laid down, our life to gain.
twice ten hun - dred years have num - bered count - less works of bound - less grace!
show - ing, giv - ing and ac - claim - ing signs of joy and ju - bi - lee.

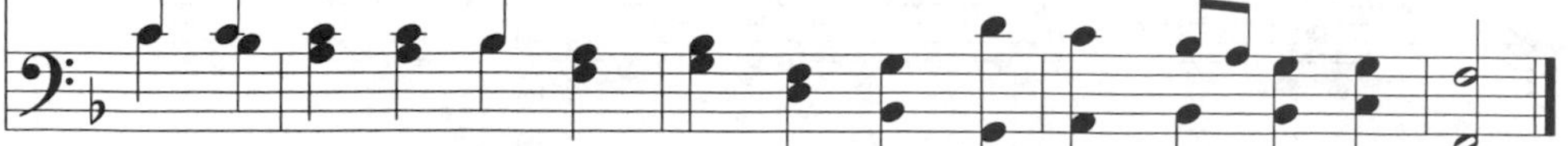

WORDS: Brian Wren (1936-)
MUSIC: C. Hubert H. Parry (1848-1918)

RUSTINGTON
8.7.8.7.D.

105 Beautiful Savior

Unison
C F/A Bb C C/E F
Beau-ti-ful Sav - ior, Won-der-ful Coun - sel - or, clothed in
Gm7 Gm/F C/E Dm7
maj - es-ty, Lord of his - to-ry, you're the Way, the Truth, the
C C/Bb F/A Bb C C/E
Life. Star of the Morn - ing, glo-rious in ho - li -
F Gm7 Gm/F
ness, you're the Ris - en One, heav-en's Cham-pi - on, and you

WORDS and MUSIC: Stuart Townend (20th c.)

C/E Bb/D C F Eb/Bb Bb F
reign, you reign o - ver all!

All Hail the Power of Jesus' Name! 106

1 All hail the power of Je - sus' name! Let an - gels pros - trate fall;
2 Ye cho - sen seed of Is - rael's race, ye ran - somed from the fall,
3 Let ev - ery kin - dred, ev - ery tribe on this ter - res - trial ball,
4 O that with yon - der sa - cred throng we at his feet may fall!
bring forth the roy - al di - a - dem, and crown him Lord of all;
hail him who saves you by his grace, and crown him Lord of all;
to him all maj - es - ty as - cribe, and crown him Lord of all;
We'll join the ev - er - last - ing song, and crown him Lord of all;
bring forth the roy - al di - a - dem, and crown him Lord of all!
hail him who saves you by his grace, and crown him Lord of all!
to him all maj - es - ty as - cribe, and crown him Lord of all!
we'll join the ev - er - last - ing song, and crown him Lord of all!

WORDS: Edward Perronet (1726-1792); adapt. John Rippon (1751-1836)
MUSIC: Oliver Holden (1765-1844)

CORONATION
8.6.8.6.8.6.

107 O Light Whose Splendor Thrills

1 O Light whose splen - dor thrills and glad - dens
2 As twi - light hov - ers near at sun - set,
3 In all life's bril - liant, time - less mo - ments,
with ra - diance bright - er than the sun,
and lamps are lit, and chil - dren nod,
let faith - ful voic - es sing your praise,
pure gleam of God's un - end - ing glo - ry,
in eve - ning hymns we lift our voic - es
O Son of God, our life - be - stow - er,
O Je - sus, blest A - noint - ed One:
to Fa - ther, Spir - it, Son, one God.
whose glo - ry light - ens end - less days.

WORDS: Greek hymn, 3rd c.; para. Carl P. Daw, Jr. (1944-)
MUSIC: Clement Scholefield (1839-1904)

ST. CLEMENT
9.8.9.8.

There's Something About That Name 108

Je - sus, Je - sus, Je - sus: there's just some-thing a - bout that
name! Mas - ter, Sav - ior, Je - sus, like the fra - grance
af - ter the rain; Je - sus, Je - sus, Je - sus, let all
heav-en and earth pro - claim: Kings and king-doms will
all pass a - way, but there's some-thing a - bout that name!

WORDS: Gloria Gaither (1942-) and William J. Gaither (1936-)
MUSIC: William J. Gaither (1936-)

THAT NAME
Irregular

109 O, How I Love Jesus

1 There is a name I love to hear, I love to sing its worth;
2 It tells me of a Sav - ior's love, who died to set me free;
3 It tells of One whose lov - ing heart can feel my deep - est woe,
it sounds like mu - sic in my ear, the sweet - est name on earth.
it tells me of his pre - cious blood, the sin - ner's per - fect plea.
who in each sor - row bears a part, that none can bear be - low.
Refrain
O, how I love Je - sus, O, how I love Je - sus,
O, how I love Je - sus, be - cause he first loved me!

WORDS: Frederick Whitfield (1829-1904); ref. anonymous
MUSIC: American melody

O, HOW I LOVE JESUS
C.M.Ref.

We Come, O Christ, to You 110

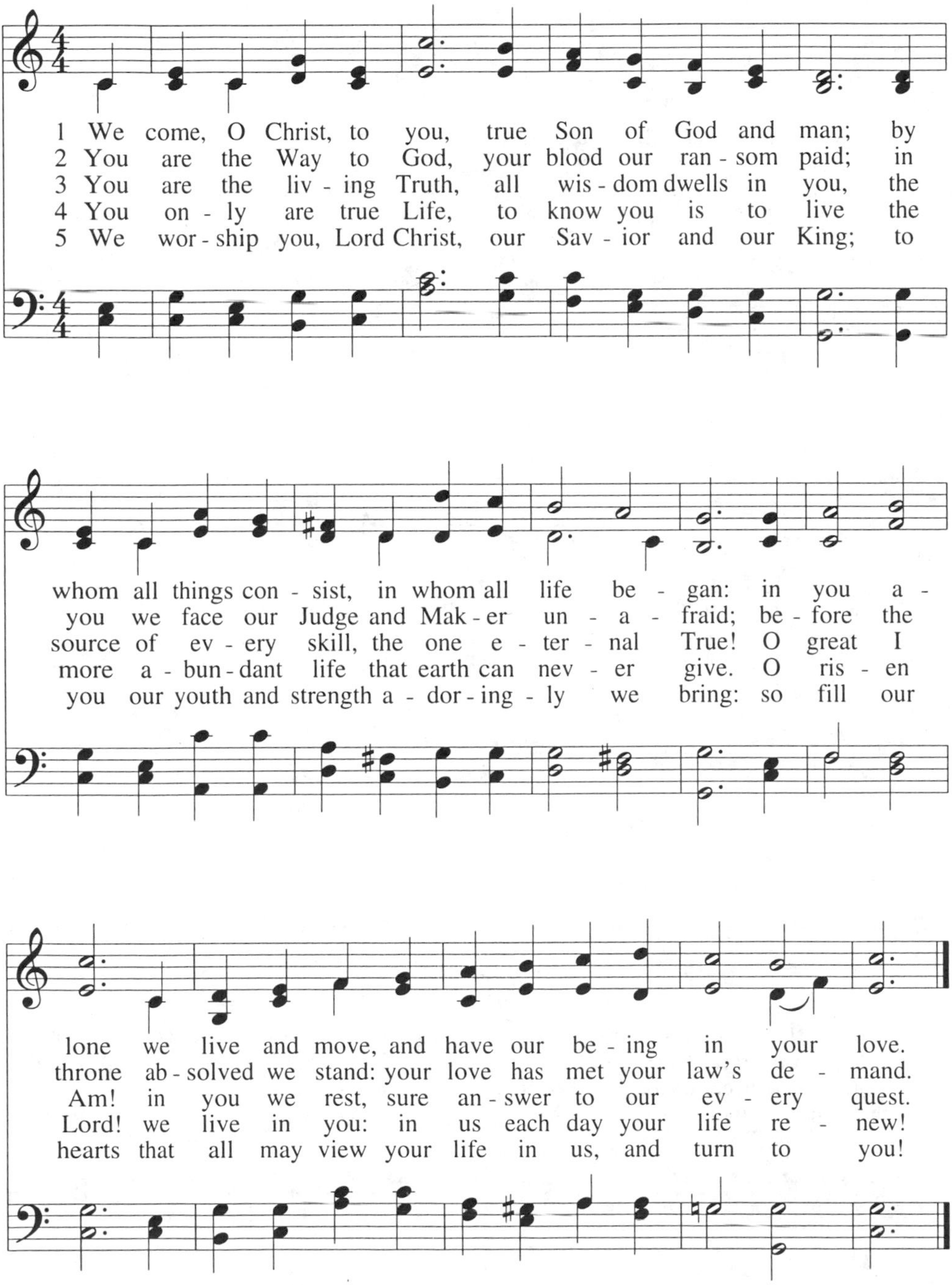
1 We come, O Christ, to you, true Son of God and man; by
2 You are the Way to God, your blood our ran - som paid; in
3 You are the liv - ing Truth, all wis - dom dwells in you, the
4 You on - ly are true Life, to know you is to live the
5 We wor - ship you, Lord Christ, our Sav - ior and our King; to
whom all things con - sist, in whom all life be - gan: in you a -
you we face our Judge and Mak - er un - a - fraid; be - fore the
source of ev - ery skill, the one e - ter - nal True! O great I
more a - bun - dant life that earth can nev - er give. O ris - en
you our youth and strength a - dor - ing - ly we bring: so fill our
lone we live and move, and have our be - ing in your love.
throne ab - solved we stand: your love has met your law's de - mand.
Am! in you we rest, sure an - swer to our ev - ery quest.
Lord! we live in you: in us each day your life re - new!
hearts that all may view your life in us, and turn to you!

WORDS: Margaret Clarkson (1915-)
MUSIC: John Darwall (1731-1789)

DARWALL'S 148th
6.6.6.6.4.4.8.

111 When Morning Gilds the Skies

1 When morn-ing gilds the skies, my heart a - wak - ing cries,
2 Does sad - ness fill my mind? A sol - ace here I find,
3 The night be-comes as day, when from the heart we say,
4 Be this, while life is mine, my can - ti - cle di - vine,
may Je - sus Christ be praised! A - like at work and prayer
may Je - sus Christ be praised! Or fades my earth - ly bliss?
may Je - sus Christ be praised! The powers of dark-ness fear
may Je - sus Christ be praised! Be this th'e - ter - nal song
to Je - sus I re - pair, may Je - sus Christ be praised!
My com - fort still is this, may Je - sus Christ be praised!
when this sweet chant they hear, may Je - sus Christ be praised!
through all the a - ges long, may Je - sus Christ be praised!

WORDS: *Katholisches Gesangbuch*, 1828; tr. Edward Caswall (1814-1878)
MUSIC: Joseph Barnby (1838-1896)

LAUDES DOMINI
6.6.6.6.6.6.

You Servants of God 112

1 You serv-ants of God, your Mas-ter pro-claim, and pub-lish a-broad his won-der-ful name; the name all-vic-to-rious of Je-sus ex-tol; his king-dom is glo-rious and rules o-ver all.
2 God rules in the heights, al-might-y to save; though hid from our sight, his pres-ence we have; the great con-gre-ga-tion his tri-umph shall sing, as-crib-ing sal-va-tion to Je-sus our King.
3 "Sal-va-tion to God who sits on the throne!" let all cry a-loud and hon-or the Son: the prais-es of Je-sus the an-gels pro-claim, fall down on their fac-es and wor-ship the Lamb.
4 Then let us a-dore and give him his right, all glo-ry and power, all wis-dom and might: all hon-or and bless-ing, with an-gels a-bove, and thanks nev-er ceas-ing, and in-fi-nite love.

WORDS: Charles Wesley (1707-1788), alt.
MUSIC: William Croft (1678-1727)

HANOVER
10.10.11.11.

113 Rejoice, Ye Pure in Heart

1 Re - joice, ye pure in heart, re - joice, give thanks and sing;
2 Bright youth and snow-crowned age, strong souls and spir - its meek,
3 With voice as full and strong as o - cean's surg - ing praise,
4 Yes, on through life's long path, still chant - ing as you go,
your fes - tal ban - ner wave on high, the cross of Christ your King.
raise high your free, ex - ult - ing song, God's won-drous prais-es speak.
send forth the hymns the saints have loved, the psalms of an - cient days.
from youth to age, by night and day, in glad-ness and in woe.
Refrain
Re - joice, re - joice, re - joice, give thanks and sing.
Re - joice, re - joice,

WORDS: Edward H. Plumptre (1821-1891), alt.
MUSIC: Arthur H. Messiter (1834-1916)

MARION
S.M.Ref.

114 O Come, Let Us Adore Him

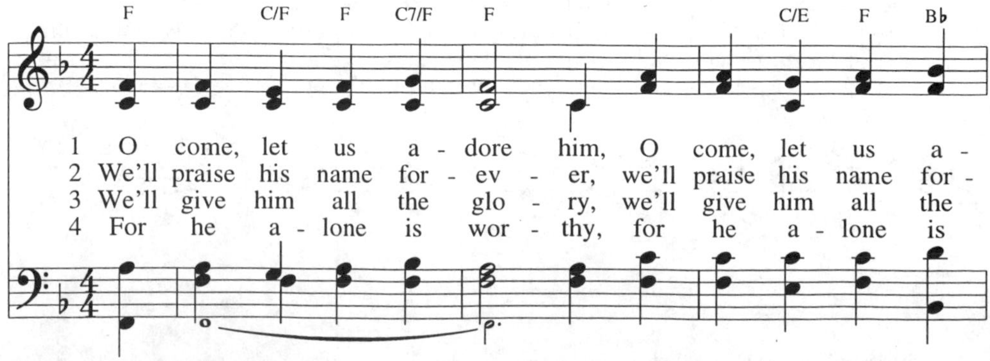
F C/F F C7/F F C/E F Bb
1 O come, let us a - dore him, O come, let us a -
2 We'll praise his name for - ev - er, we'll praise his name for -
3 We'll give him all the glo - ry, we'll give him all the
4 For he a - lone is wor - thy, for he a - lone is

WORDS: Attr. John F. Wade (1711-1786); tr. Frederick Oakeley (1802-1880); vss. 2-4 anonymous
MUSIC: John F. Wade's *Cantus Diversi*, 1751

ADESTE FIDELES
Irregular

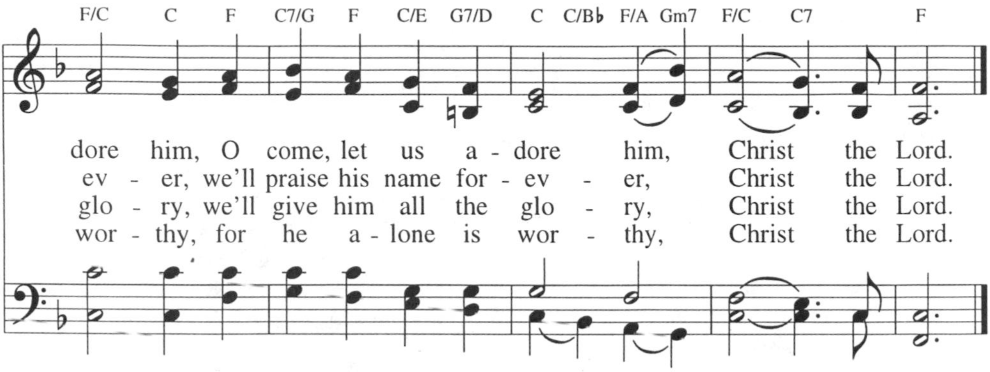
F/C C F C7/G F C/E G7/D C C/B♭ F/A Gm7 F/C C7 F
dore him, O come, let us a - dore him, Christ the Lord.
ev - er, we'll praise his name for - ev - er, Christ the Lord.
glo - ry, we'll give him all the glo - ry, Christ the Lord.
wor - thy, for he a - lone is wor - thy, Christ the Lord.

Praise the Name of Jesus 115

D G D G D
Praise the name of Je - sus, praise the name of Je - sus.
G D G D G D/F# A7/E D
He's my Rock, he's my For - tress, he's my De - liv - er - er, in
E7 A D Em/G D/A A7 D
him will I trust. Praise the name of Je - sus.

WORDS and MUSIC: Roy Hicks, Jr. (1943-); para. Psalm 18:1

116 Worthy Is the Lamb

Bb Cm/Bb Bb7 Eb Eb/D Cm Dm/C Cm7
Wor-thy is the Lamb that was slain, wor-thy is the Lamb that was
F F/Eb Bb/D Gm Gm/F Em7(b5) Fsus F
slain, wor-thy is the Lamb that was slain, to re-ceive
Bb Bb/D Cm Cm7 F7 Cm Dm/C Cm7
pow-er and rich-es and wis-dom and strength, hon-or and glo-ry and
F F/Eb Bb/D Bb+/D Eb Em7(b5)
bless-ing! Wor-thy is the Lamb, wor-thy is the Lamb,
Bb/F Em7(b5)/G Em7(b5) Fsus F F7sus/C F7 Bb
wor-thy is the Lamb that was slain, wor-thy is the Lamb!

WORDS and MUSIC: Don Wyrtzen (1942-); para. Revelation 5:12

There Is a Redeemer

D Em/D D G/D D A D G A D A7
1 There is a Re - deem - er— Je - sus, God's own Son;
2 Je - sus, my Re - deem - er, name a - bove all names;
3 When I stand in Glo - ry, I will see his face;
D Em/D D G/D D G Asus A G/A D
Pre-cious Lamb of God, Mes - si - ah, Ho - ly One.
Pre-cious Lamb of God, Mes - si - ah, Hope for sin - ners slain.
there I'll serve my King for - ev - er in that ho - ly place.
Refrain
D D/F# G D G A D A7
Thank you, O my Fa - ther, for giv-ing us your Son, and
D Em/D D G/D D Em/D D G Asus A G/A D
leav - ing your Spir - it till the work on earth is done.

WORDS and MUSIC: Melody Green (1946-)

118 Lord of the Dance

Unison
G
Em
Bm
Em
1 I danced in the morn-ing when the world was be - gun, and I
2 I danced for the scribe and the Phar - i - see, but they
3 I danced on the Sab-bath and I cured the lame, the
4 I danced on a Fri - day when the sky turned black; it's
5 They cut me down and I leapt up high,
Am
D7
danced in the moon and the stars and the sun, and I
would not dance and they would not fol - low me; I
ho - ly peo - ple said it was a shame; they
hard to dance with the dev - il on your back; they
I am the life that - 'll nev - er, nev - er die; I'll
G
Em
Bm
Em
came down from heav - en and I danced on the earth. At
danced for the fish - er - men, for James and John; they
whipped and they stripped and they hung me on high; and they
bur - ied my bod - y and they thought I'd gone, but
live in you if you'll live in me;
Am
D7
C/G
G
Refrain
G
Bm
Beth - le - hem I had my birth.
came with me and the Dance went on.
left me there on a cross to die. Dance, then, where -
I am the Dance and I still go on.
I am the Lord of the Dance, said he.

WORDS: Sydney Carter (1915-)
MUSIC: Shaker melody, 19th c.; adapt. Sydney Carter (1915-)

LORD OF THE DANCE
Irregular.Ref.

Em G
ever you may be; I am the Lord of the
Am/C D D7/C G C/G G/D D7/C
Dance, said he. And I'll lead you all where-ever you may
G/B Am/C Am D7 G C/G G
be, and I'll lead you all in the Dance, said he.

Come into His Presence 119

I II III IV
1 Come in-to his pres-ence sing-ing al-le-lu-ia, al-le-lu-ia, al-le-lu-ia.
2 Come in-to his pres-ence sing-ing Je-sus is Lord, Je-sus is Lord, Je-sus is Lord.
3 Praise the Lord to-geth-er sing-ing wor-thy the Lamb, wor-thy the Lamb, wor-thy the Lamb.
4 Praise the Lord to-geth-er sing-ing glo-ry to God, glo-ry to God, glo-ry to God.

WORDS and MUSIC: Anonymous

120 Sing Alleluia to the Lord

Descant
(Lord!)
1 Lift up your hearts un - to the Lord,
Unison
1 Lift up your hearts un - to the Lord,
lift up your
Sing al - le - lu - ia, al - le - lu - ia;
hearts un - to the Lord.
Sing al - le - lu - ia, sing al - le - lu - ia;
Final ending
lift up your hearts un - to the (Lord!)
Final ending
lift up your hearts un - to the Lord!

2 In Christ the world has been redeemed.
3 His resurrection sets us free.
4 Therefore we celebrate the feast.
5 Sing alleluia to the Lord!

WORDS: Early Christian liturgy; vs. 5, Linda Stassen (1951-)
MUSIC: Linda Stassen (1951-); harm. Dale Grotenhuis (1931-)

Christ Is the World's Light

Unison
1 Christ is the world's light, Christ and none
2 Christ is the world's peace, Christ and none
3 Christ is the world's life, Christ and none
4 Give God the glo - ry, God and none
oth - er; born in our dark - ness, he be - came our
oth - er; no one can serve him, and de - spise an -
oth - er; sold once for sil - ver, mur - dered here, our
oth - er; give God the glo - ry, Spir - it, Son and
broth - er— if we have seen him, we have seen the
oth - er. Who else u - nites us, one in God the
broth - er— he, who re - deems us, reigns with God the
Fa - ther; give God the glo - ry, God - with - us our
Fa - ther: Glo - ry to God on high!
Fa - ther? Glo - ry to God on high!
Fa - ther: Glo - ry to God on high!
broth - er: Glo - ry to God on high!

WORDS: Fred Pratt Green (1903-2000)
MUSIC: *Paris Antiphoner*, 1681

CHRISTE SANCTORUM
10.11.11.6.

122 He Is Exalted

F F/A Bb
He is ex - alt - ed, the King is ex - alt - ed on high; I will
Bb/C C7 F F/A Bb C/Bb
praise him. He is ex - alt - ed, for - ev - er ex - alt - ed, and I will
Bb/C C Dsus D Gm Dm/F C/E Bb/C
praise his name! He is the Lord; for -
F Am Bb F/A Gm Dm/F C/E Bb/C F Am
ev - er his truth shall reign. Heav - en and earth re - joice in his ho - ly
Bb F/A Gm7 Gm7/F Eb Bb/C F
name. He is ex - alt - ed, the King is ex - alt - ed on high.

WORDS and MUSIC: Twila Paris (1958-)

Fairest Lord Jesus

1 Fair - est Lord Je - sus, rul - er of all na - ture,
2 Fair are the mead - ows, fair - er still the wood - lands,
3 Fair is the sun - shine, fair - er still the moon - light,
4 Beau - ti - ful Sav - ior! Lord of the na - tions!
O thou of God and man the Son,
robed in the bloom - ing garb of spring:
and all the twin - kling, star - ry host:
Son of God and Son of man!
thee will I cher - ish, thee will I hon - or,
Je - sus is fair - er, Je - sus is pur - er,
Je - sus shines bright - er, Je - sus shines pur - er,
Glo - ry and hon - or, praise, ad - o - ra - tion,
thou, my soul's glo - ry, joy, and crown!
who makes the woe - ful heart to sing.
than all the an - gels heaven can boast.
now and for - ev - er - more be thine!

WORDS: *Gesangbuch*, Münster, 1677
MUSIC: *Schlesische Volkslieder*, 1842

CRUSADER'S HYMN
5.6.8.5.5.8.

124 Open Your Hearts

Unison
E
1 O - pen your hearts, all you who hear this, o - pen your
2 We have come to greet the Sav - ior, we have
3 Je - sus is here, we bow be - fore him, Je - sus is
F
E
hearts to know God's love, o - pen your hearts to
come to wor - ship him, we have come to
here with - in this place. Je - sus is here a -
Dm
E
hear his mes - sage: Je - sus makes us one.
sing God's prais - es; wor - thy is his name.
mong his peo - ple, chil - dren of his grace.
Refrain (faster)
Am
Praise the Lord for he has loved us, al - le - lu -

WORDS and MUSIC: Israeli folk song; tr. Carolyn Fritsch (20th c.)

YISRAEL V'ORAITA
9.8.9.5.Ref.

E
ia, and his love is come to free us.
1, 2
Am
3
Am
Al - le - lu - ia!
ia!

In the Name of the Lord

125

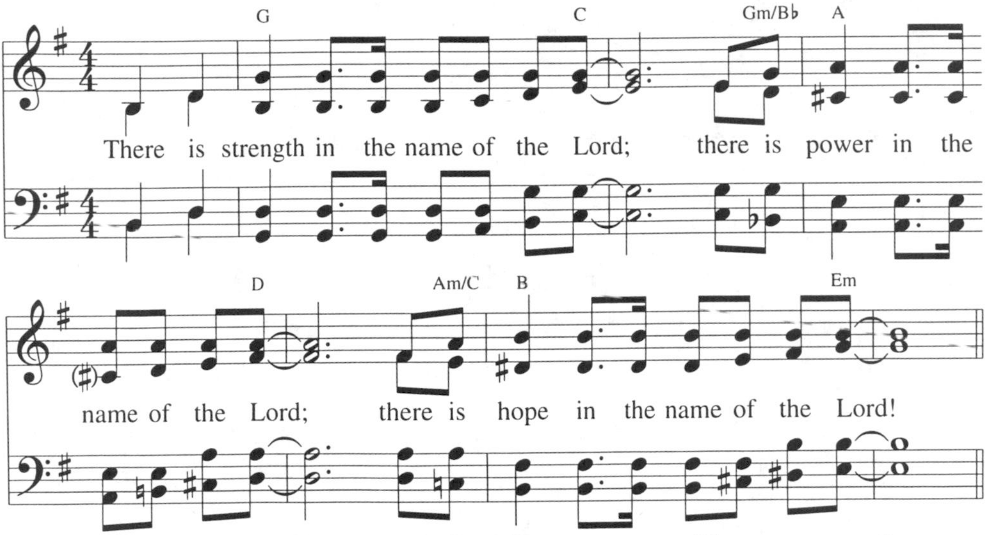
G
C
Gm/B♭
A
There is strength in the name of the Lord; there is power in the
D
Am/C
B
Em
name of the Lord; there is hope in the name of the Lord!
Am
G/B
Am/C
G/D
D7
3
G
Bless-ed is he who comes in the name of the Lord!
3

WORDS: Phill McHugh (1951-), Gloria Gaither (1942-) and Sandi Patty (1956-)
MUSIC: Sandi Patty (1956-); arr. Robert F. Douglas (1941-)

126 Thou Art Worthy

Bb Eb/Bb Bb Eb/Bb Bb
Thou art wor - thy, thou art wor - thy, thou art wor - thy, O
Fsus F Bb Eb/Bb Cm7 Bb/F
Lord, to re-ceive glo - ry, glo - ry and hon - or, glo - ry and
F7 Eb/F F7 Bb F Gm7/F F Bb
hon - or and power; for thou hast cre - at - ed, hast all things cre -
Cm7/Bb Bb F Gm7/F F Bb
at - ed, thou hast cre - at - ed all things, and for thy
Fm/Ab Bb/Ab Eb/G Ebm6/Gb Bb/F F7 Eb/F F7 Bb
pleas-ure they are cre - at - ed: for thou art wor-thy, O Lord!

WORDS: Pauline Michael Mills (1898-1992); para. Revelation 4:11, 5:9
MUSIC: Pauline Michael Mills (1898-1992); arr. Jack Schrader (1942-)

Come, Holy Spirit

I
C2
Come, Ho - ly Spir - it,
come, Ho - ly Spir - it.
II
Hear us call-ing,
hear us call-ing,
F6/9
Fmaj7
C2
Come, Ho - ly Spir-it,
come, Ho - ly Spir-it;
hear us call-ing to you.
Hear us call-ing;
Dm
G7sus
G7
C
F/C
hear us call - ing,
hear us call - ing to you.
hear us call - ing,
hear us call - ing to you.
C
Am7
Dm7
G
G7/F
Em
Come, give your gift,
come, bring your truth;
Ed - i - fy your church;
glo-ri - fy our
Am
Dm
G7
C
come, be our guide,
come walk be - side.
Lord;
point the way, come walk be - side.

WORDS and MUSIC: Mark Foreman (20th c.)

128 Spirit, Working in Creation

1 Spir - it, work-ing in cre - a - tion, bring-ing or - der out of strife:
2 Spir - it, o - ver - shad - owing Ma - ry as the Christ-child in her grew:
3 Spir - it, driv - ing to the des - ert e - ven God's A - noint - ed One:
4 Spir - it, wind and flame, em - power-ing fear - less wit - ness to the lost:
come a - round God's gath - ered peo - ple, giv - ing har - mo - ny and life.
come, so that the Christ with - in us may to - day be born a - new.
come to us in trial and test - ing that God's will in us be done.
come, u - nite, re - new your won-ders as of a new Pen - te - cost!"
Spir - it, speak-ing through the proph-ets so the voice of God was heard:
Spir - it, com - ing from the Fa - ther as a dove up - on our Lord:
Spir - it, breathed on the dis - ci - ples, giv - ing peace where there was fear:
Praise and glo - ry, Ho - ly Spir - it, for your love on us out - poured,
come, in - spire, a - lert your peo-ple to this day's pro - phet - ic word.
come up - on your fa - vored peo-ple, and your bless-ings be out-poured.
come a - mong us, touch us, send us, mak-ing Je - sus' pres - ence near.
giv - ing hon - or to the Fa - ther and pro - claim - ing Je - sus "Lord."

WORDS: John Richards (1939-)
MUSIC: Dutch melody, 18th c.; arr. Julius Röntgen (1855-1933)

IN BABILONE
8.7.8.7.D.

Be Still, for the Spirit of the Lord 129

Unison
D F#m7 Bm Em7 A
1 Be still, for the Spir-it of the Lord, the Ho - ly One, is here.
2 Be still, for the glo-ry of the Lord is shin-ing all a - round;
3 Be still, for the pow-er of the Lord is mov-ing in this place,
D F#m7 Bm Em7 Asus A
Come, bow be - fore him now, with rev-erence and with fear.
he burns with ho - ly fire, with splen-dor he is crowned.
he comes to cleanse and heal, to min - is - ter his grace.
G A/G D/F# G A/G D/F#
In him no sin is found, we stand on ho - ly ground.
How awe-some is the sight, our ra-diant King of light!
No work too hard for him, in faith re - ceive from him.
G A F#m7 Bm Em7 Asus A D
Be still, for the Spir-it of the Lord, the Ho - ly One, is here.
Be still, for the glo-ry of the Lord is shin-ing all a-round.
Be still, for the pow-er of the Lord is mov-ing in this place.

WORDS and MUSIC: David Evans (20th c.)

130 God Sends Us the Spirit

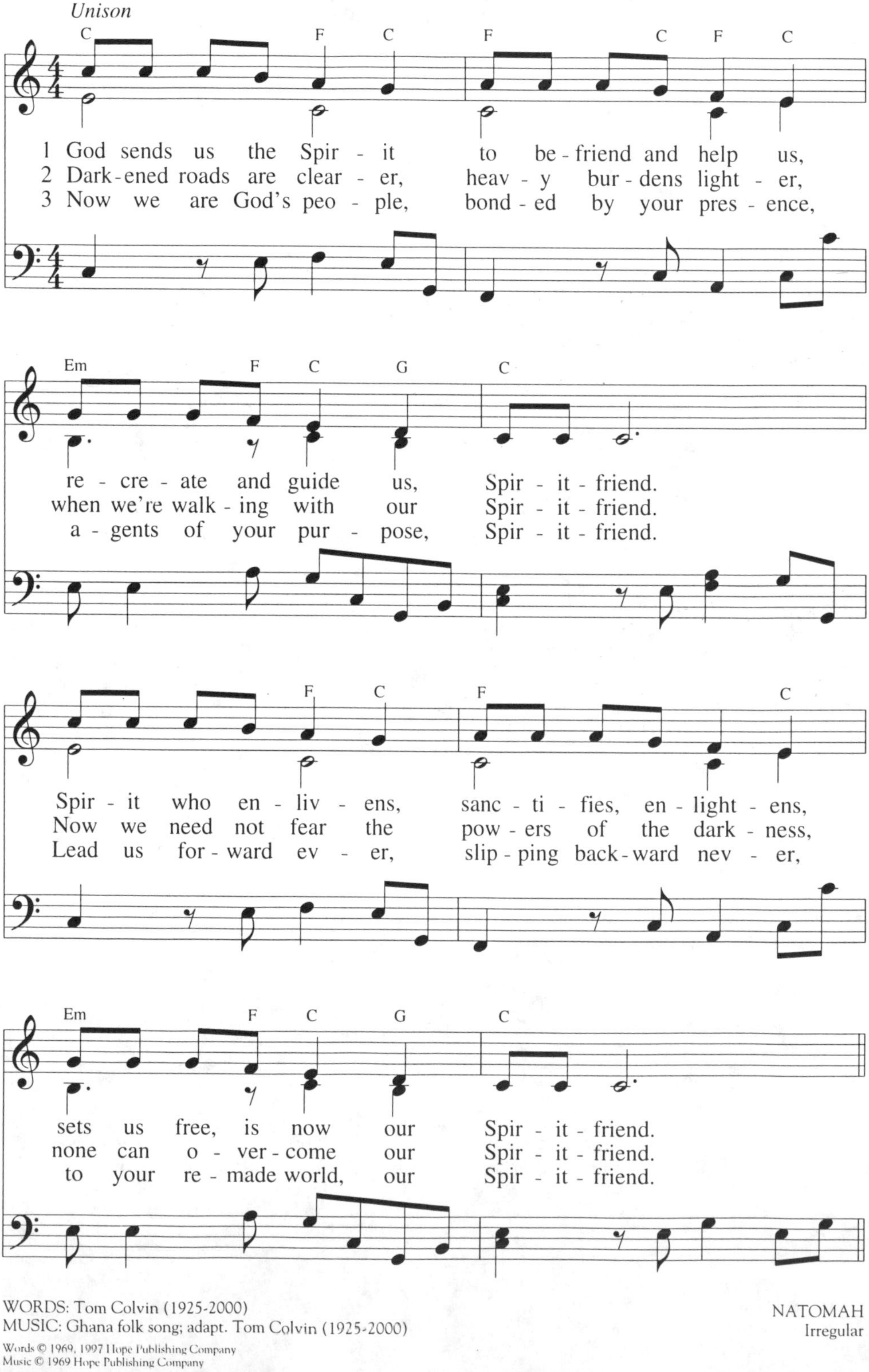
Unison
C F C F C F C
1 God sends us the Spir - it to be - friend and help us,
2 Dark - ened roads are clear - er, heav - y bur - dens light - er,
3 Now we are God's peo - ple, bond - ed by your pres - ence,
Em F C G C
re - cre - ate and guide us, Spir - it - friend.
when we're walk - ing with our Spir - it - friend.
a - gents of your pur - pose, Spir - it - friend.
F C F C
Spir - it who en - liv - ens, sanc - ti - fies, en - light - ens,
Now we need not fear the pow - ers of the dark - ness,
Lead us for - ward ev - er, slip - ping back - ward nev - er,
Em F C G C
sets us free, is now our Spir - it - friend.
none can o - ver - come our Spir - it - friend.
to your re - made world, our Spir - it - friend.

WORDS: Tom Colvin (1925-2000)
MUSIC: Ghana folk song; adapt. Tom Colvin (1925-2000)

NATOMAH
Irregular

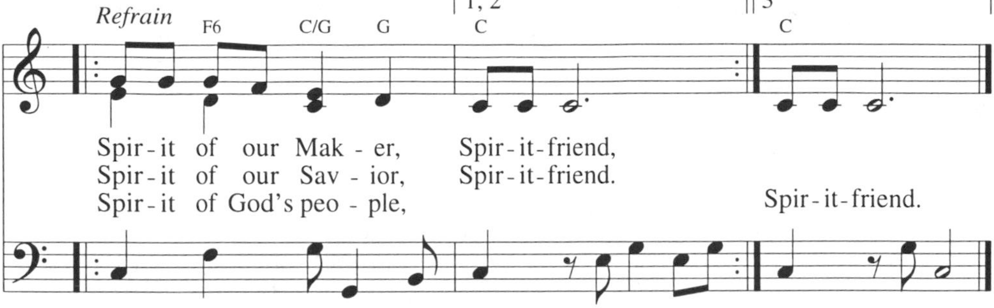
Refrain
F6 C/G G C C
1, 2
3
Spir-it of our Mak-er, Spir-it-friend,
Spir-it of our Sav-ior, Spir-it-friend.
Spir-it of God's peo-ple, Spir-it-friend.

Surely the Presence 131

D F#m7 Gmaj7 Em
Sure-ly the pres-ence of the Lord is in this place; I can
Em7 A7 D Em/D A7
feel his might-y pow-er and his grace. I can
D F#m7 Gmaj7 Em
hear the brush of an-gels' wings, I see glo-ry on each face;
Em7 A7 Em7 A7 D
sure-ly the pres-ence of the Lord is in this place.

WORDS and MUSIC: Lanny Wolfe (1942-)

132 Spirit of God, Descend upon My Heart

1 Spir - it of God, de - scend up - on my heart,
2 I ask no dream, no proph - et ec - sta - sies,
3 Did you not bid us love you, God and King,
4 Teach me to feel that you are al - ways nigh;
5 Teach me to love you as your an - gels love,
free it from sin, through all its puls - es move.
no sud - den rend - ing of the veil of clay,
love you with all our heart and strength and mind?
teach me the strug - gles of the soul to bear,
one ho - ly pas - sion fill - ing all my frame:
Stoop to my weak - ness, might - y as you are,
no an - gel vis - i - tant, no o - pening skies,
I see your cross— there teach my heart to cling.
to check the ris - ing doubt, the reb - el sigh;
the bap - tism of the heaven - de - scend - ed Dove,
and make me love you as I ought to love.
but take the dim - ness of my soul a - way.
O let me seek you and O let me find!
teach me the pa - tience of un - an - swered prayer.
my heart an al - tar, and your love the flame.

WORDS: George Croly (1780-1860), alt.
MUSIC: Frederick C. Atkinson (1841-1897)

MORECAMBE
10.10.10.10.

There's a Spirit in the Air

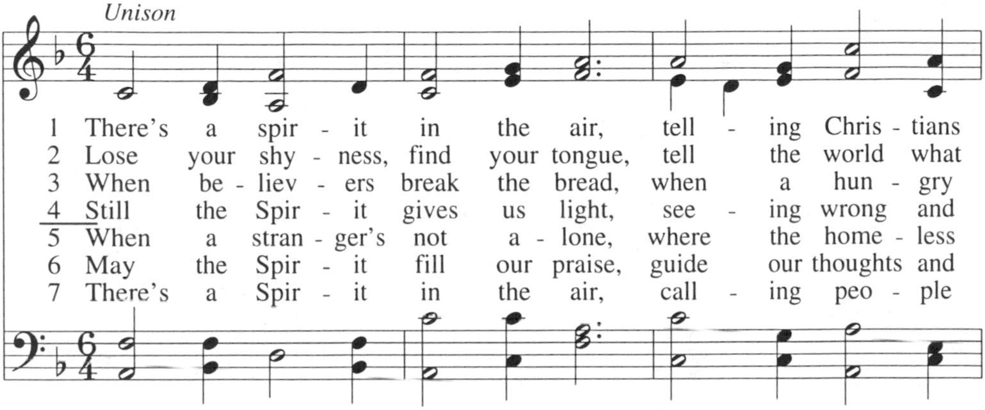
Unison
1 There's a spir - it in the air, tell - ing Chris - tians
2 Lose your shy - ness, find your tongue, tell the world what
3 When be - liev - ers break the bread, when a hun - gry
4 Still the Spir - it gives us light, see - ing wrong and
5 When a stran - ger's not a - lone, where the home - less
6 May the Spir - it fill our praise, guide our thoughts and
7 There's a Spir - it in the air, call - ing peo - ple

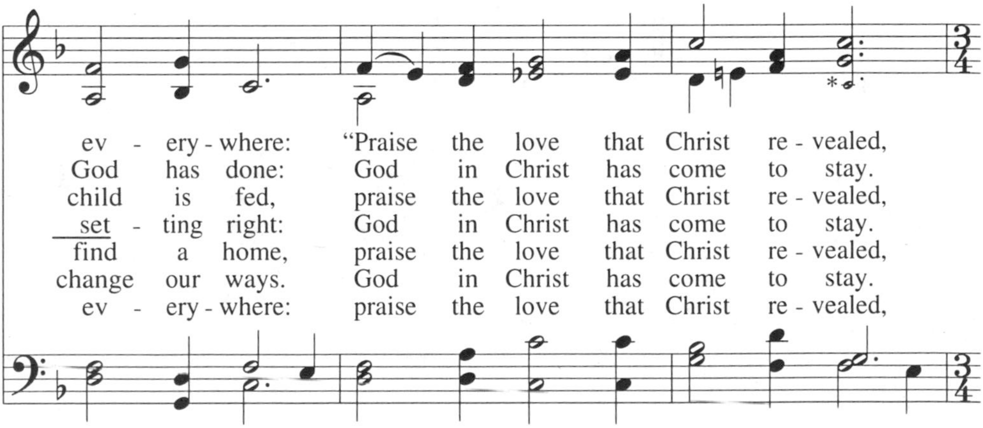
ev - ery - where: "Praise the love that Christ re - vealed,
God has done: God in Christ has come to stay.
child is fed, praise the love that Christ re - vealed,
set - ting right: God in Christ has come to stay.
find a home, praise the love that Christ re - vealed,
change our ways. God in Christ has come to stay.
ev - ery - where: praise the love that Christ re - vealed,
*

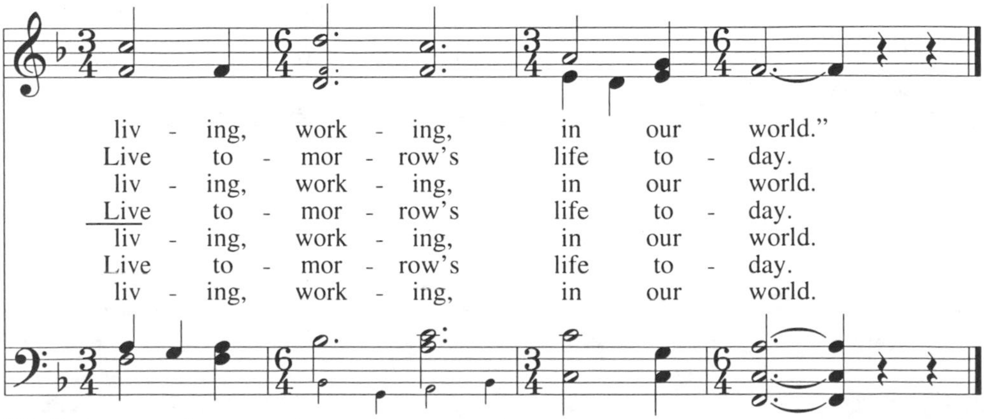
liv - ing, work - ing, in our world."
Live to - mor - row's life to - day.
liv - ing, work - ing, in our world.
Live to - mor - row's life to - day.
liv - ing, work - ing, in our world.
Live to - mor - row's life to - day.
liv - ing, work - ing, in our world.

*Small notes: organ only.

WORDS: Brian Wren (1936-)
MUSIC: John W. Wilson (1905-1992)

LAUDS
7.7.7.7.

134 Sweet, Sweet Spirit

There's a sweet, sweet Spir - it in this place, and I
know that it's the Spir - it of the Lord; there are
sweet ex - pres - sions on each face, and I
know they feel the pres - ence of the Lord.
Refrain
Sweet Ho - ly Spir - it, sweet heav-en - ly Dove, stay right here

WORDS and MUSIC: Doris Akers (1922-1995)

with us, fill - ing us with your love; and for these bless-ings
we lift our hearts in praise; with-out a doubt we'll know that
we have been re - vived when we shall leave this place.

Loving Spirit

135

1 Lov - ing Spir - it, lov-ing Spir - it, you have cho - sen me to be—
2 Like a moth-er you en-fold me, hold my life with-in your own,
3 Like a fa-ther you pro-tect me, teach me the dis-cern-ing eye,
4 Friend and lov - er, in your close-ness I am known and held and blessed:
5 Lov - ing Spir - it, lov-ing Spir - it, you have cho - sen me to be—
you have drawn me to your won - der, you have set your sign on me.
feed me with your ver - y bod - y, form me of your flesh and bone.
hoist me up up - on your shoul-der, let me see the world from high.
in your prom - ise is my com - fort, in your pres-ence I may rest.
you have drawn me to your won - der, you have set your sign on me.

WORDS: Shirley Erena Murray (1931-)
MUSIC: David Gregof Corner (1585-1648); arr. William Smith Rockstro (1823-1895)

OMNI DIE
8.7.8.7.

136 Holy, Holy, Holy! Lord God Almighty!

1 Ho - ly, ho - ly, ho - ly! Lord God Al - might - y!
2 Ho - ly, ho - ly, ho - ly! All the saints a - dore thee,
3 Ho - ly, ho - ly, ho - ly! though the dark-ness hide thee,
4 Ho - ly, ho - ly, ho - ly! Lord God Al - might - y!
Ear - ly in the morn - ing our song shall rise to thee.
cast - ing down their gold - en crowns a - round the glass - y sea;
though the eye made blind by sin thy glo - ry may not see,
All thy works shall praise thy name, in earth, and sky, and sea;
Ho - ly, ho - ly, ho - ly! Mer - ci - ful and might - y!
cher - u - bim and ser - a - phim fall - ing down be - fore thee,
on - ly thou art ho - ly; there is none be - side thee,
Ho - ly, ho - ly, ho - ly! Mer - ci - ful and might - y!
God in three per - sons, bless - ed Trin - i - ty!
which wert and art, and ev - er - more shalt be.
per - fect in power, in love and pu - ri - ty.
God in three per - sons, bless - ed Trin - i - ty!

WORDS: Reginald Heber (1783-1826)
MUSIC: John B. Dykes (1823-1876)

NICAEA
11.12.12.10.

Worthy of Worship

1 Wor-thy of wor-ship, wor-thy of praise, wor-thy of hon-or and glo - ry; wor-thy of all the glad songs we can sing, wor-thy of all of the off-erings we bring.
2 Wor-thy of rev-erence, wor-thy of fear, wor-thy of love and de-vo - tion; wor-thy of bow-ing and bend-ing of knees, wor-thy of all this and add-ed to these—
3 Al-might-y Fa-ther, Mas-ter and Lord, King of all kings and Re-deem - er, Won-der-ful Coun-se-lor, Com-fort-er, Friend, Sav-ior, and source of our life with-out end.
Refrain
You are wor - thy, Fa-ther, Cre-at-or. You are wor - thy, Sav-ior, Sus-tain-er. You are wor - thy, wor-thy and won-der-ful; wor-thy of wor-ship and praise.

WORDS: Terry W. York (1949-)
MUSIC: Mark Blankenship (1943-)

JUDSON
Irregular

138 Holy God, We Praise Your Name

1 Ho - ly God, we praise your name, Lord of all, we
2 Hark! the loud ce - les - tial hymn an - gel choirs a -
3 All a - pos - tles join the strain as your sa - cred
4 Ho - ly Fa - ther, Ho - ly Son, Ho - ly Spir - it,
bow be - fore you; all on earth your scep - ter claim,
bove are rais - ing; cher - u - bim and ser - a - phim
Name they hal - low; proph - ets swell the glad re - frain,
Three we name you; while in es - sence on - ly one,
all in heaven a - bove a - dore you; in - fi - nite your
in un - ceas - ing cho - rus prais - ing, fill the heavens with
and the white - robed mar - tyrs fol - low; and from morn to
un - di - vid - ed God we claim you, then, a - dor - ing,
vast do - main, ev - er - last - ing is your reign.
sweet ac - cord: ho - ly, ho - ly, ho - ly Lord.
set of sun, through the Church the song goes on.
bend the knee, while we own the mys - ter - y.

WORDS: Attr. Ignaz Franz (1719-1790); tr. Clarence A. Walworth (1820-1900), alt.; para. *Te Deum*
MUSIC: *Katholisches Gesangbuch*, 1774

GROSSER GOTT
7.8.7.8.7.7.

God Is One, Unique and Holy 139

1 God is One, u-nique and ho - ly, end-less dance of love and light,
2 God is One - ness-by-Com-mun-ion: nev - er dis-tant or a - lone,
3 Through the pain that lov-ing Wis-dom could fore-see, but not fore - stall,
on-ly source of mind and bod - y, star-cloud, at - om, day and night:
at the heart of all be-long - ing: loy-al freind-ship, lov-ing home,
God is One though torn and an-guished in the Christ's for-sak-en call,
ev - ery - thing that is or could be tells God's an-guish and de - light.
com-mon mind and shared a - gree - ment, com-mon loaf and sung Sha - lom.
One through death and res - ur - rec - tion, One in Spir - it, One for all.

WORDS: Brian Wren (1936-)
MUSIC: Peter Cutts (1937-)

TRINITY
8.7.8.7.8.7.

140 Praise and Thanksgiving Be to God

1 Praise and thanks - giv - ing be to God our mak - er,
2 Not our own ho - li - ness nor that we have striv - en
3 Come, Ho - ly Spir - it, come in vis - i - ta - tion;
4 Praise to the Fa - ther, Son, and Ho - ly Spir - it;
source of all bless - ing, prod - i - gal cre - a - tor.
brings us the peace which you, O Christ, have giv - en.
you are the truth, our hope, and our sal - va - tion.
one Lord, one faith, one source of ev - ery mer - it.
Bap - tized and made your own, now we come be -
Bap - tized and set a - part, strength - en us, O
Bap - tize with joy and power, give, O Dove de -
Here now re - new your church through this wa - ter
fore you, while we a - dore you.
Sav - ior, with grace and fa - vor.
scend - ing, life nev - er end - ing.
giv - en; grant peace from heav - en.

WORDS: H. Francis Yardley (1911-1990), alt.
MUSIC: *Paris Antiphoner*, 1681; harm. David Evans (1874-1948), alt.

CHRISTE SANCTORUM
11.11.11.5.

Sing of a God in Majestic Divinity 141

1 Sing of a God in ma - jes - tic di - vin - i - ty,
2 Sing of a child who was cra - dled so ten - der - ly,
3 Sing of a Spir - it who dai - ly ad - dress - ing us,
4 Sing of this God who in glo - ry and mys - ter - y
seed - ing the heav - ens with num - ber - less stars,
sing of a boy - hood by Gal - i - lee's lake;
lives in our sci - en - ces, na - ture and arts;
choos - es to lie in hu - man - i - ty's womb,
form - ing our dust and our dreams of in - fin - i - ty,
sing of a cross and a Sav - ior who won - drous - ly
mov - ing through all of cre - a - tion and bless - ing us,
en - ters the pris - on and pain of our his - to - ry,
God of our lives and the judge of our wars.
suf - fered and died for hu - man - i - ty's sake.
guid - ing our minds and en - gag - ing our hearts.
ris - es tri - um - phant and o - pens the tomb.

WORDS: Herbert O'Driscoll (1928-)
MUSIC: Johann H. Rheinhardt's *Choralbuch*, 1754

ÜTTINGEN
12.10.12.10.

142 Sing Praise to the Father

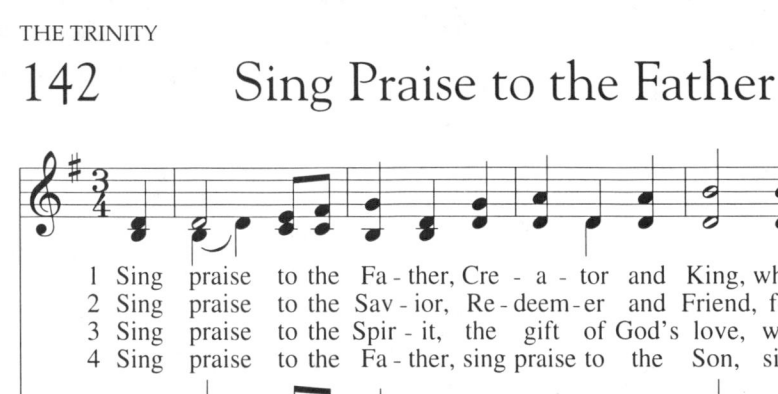

1 Sing praise to the Fa - ther, Cre - a - tor and King, whose mer - cy has taught us a new song to sing; who made us, and loved us tho' reb - els and lost, and planned our re - demp-tion at in - fi - nite cost.
2 Sing praise to the Sav - ior, Re - deem - er and Friend, for grace past all tell - ing, for love with - out end; who stripped off his glo - ry, put on mor - tal sin, and died in our stead, full a - tone-ment to win.
3 Sing praise to the Spir - it, the gift of God's love, who quick-ens our hearts with new life from a - bove, who woos us, sub - dues us, and seals us his own, and fault - less pre - sents us be - fore the White Throne.
4 Sing praise to the Fa - ther, sing praise to the Son, sing praise to the Spir - it, great God Three in One; the God of sal - va - tion, of glo - ry, of grace, who wrought our re - demp-tion—my soul, sing his praise!
Refrain
Bless the Lord, bless the Lord, bless the Lord, O my soul, for the grace that re-

WORDS: Margaret Clarkson (1915-)
MUSIC: William H. Doane (1832-1915)

TO GOD BE THE GLORY
11.11.11.11.Ref.

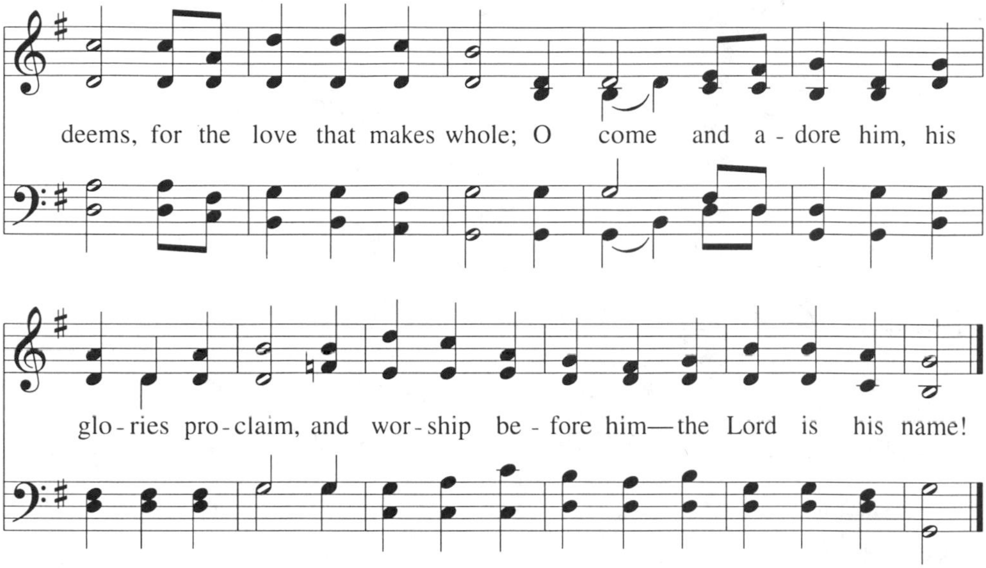
deems, for the love that makes whole; O come and a - dore him, his
glo - ries pro - claim, and wor - ship be - fore him—the Lord is his name!

Father, I Adore You

143

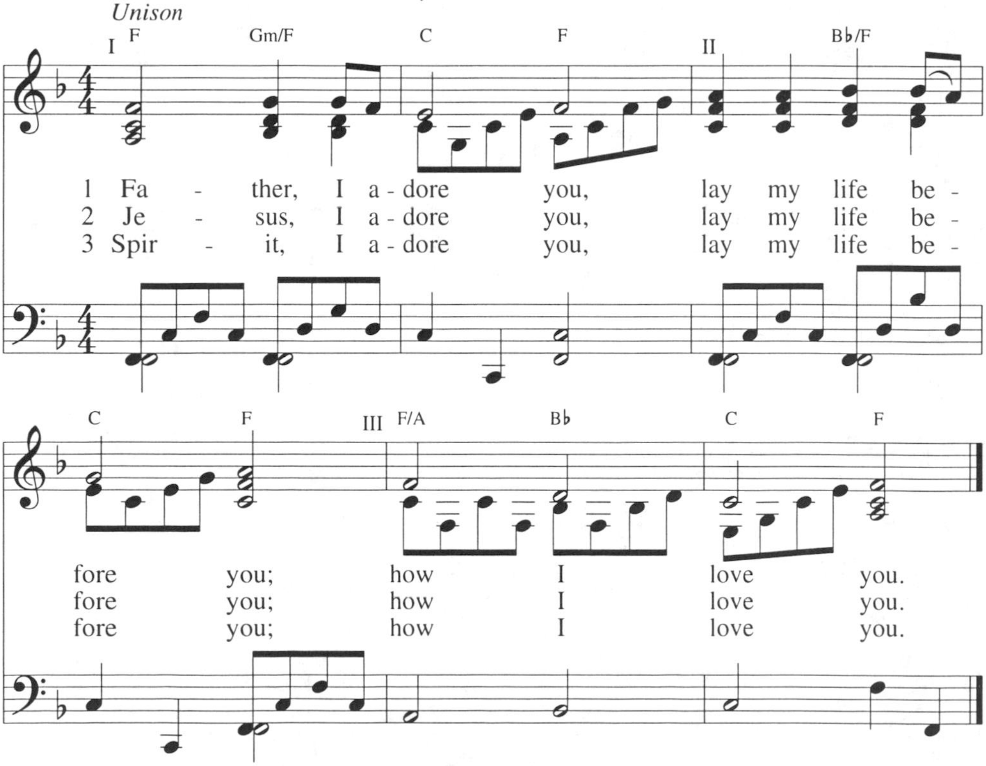
Unison
I F Gm/F C F II Bb/F
1 Fa - ther, I a - dore you, lay my life be -
2 Je - sus, I a - dore you, lay my life be -
3 Spir - it, I a - dore you, lay my life be -
C F III F/A Bb C F
fore you; how I love you.
fore you; how I love you.
fore you; how I love you.

WORDS and MUSIC: Terrye Coelho (1952-)

144 O Splendor of God's Glory Bright

1 O splen-dor of God's glo - ry bright, from light e - ter - nal bring-ing light,
2 Come, ver - y Sun of heav-en's love, in last - ing ra - diance from a - bove,
3 Con-firm our will to do the right, and keep our hearts from en - vy's blight;
4 All praise to God the Fa - ther be, all praise, e - ter - nal Son, to thee,
O Light of light, the foun-tain spring, O Day, all days il - lu - min - ing:
and pour the Ho - ly Spir - it's ray on all we think or do to - day.
let faith her ea - ger fires re - new, and hate the false, and love the true.
whom with the Spir - it we a - dore for - ev - er and for - ev - er-more.

WORDS: Ambrose of Milan, 4th c.; tr. composite
MUSIC: Trier manuscript, 15th c.; adapt. Michael Praetorius (1571-1621)

PUER NOBIS
L.M.

145 Glory Be to God, Creator

Unison
1 Glo-ry be to God, Cre - a - tor, glo-ry be to God the
(2) was in the be - gin-ning, it is now and so shall
(3) ho - ly God Al-might-y, ho-ly, ho - ly Prince of
Son, glo - ry be to God the Spir - it, known as
be in a world with-out an end - ing, glo - ry
Peace, ho - ly, ho - ly Wind of Pres - ence, ho - ly,

WORDS and MUSIC: Richard K. Carlson (1956-)

RENEWED
8.7.8.7.

1, 2
3
Three, yet God the One. 2 As it
through e - ter - ni - ty. 3 Ho-ly,
ho - ly, ho - ly. A - men.
8

Glorify Thy Name 146

C F/C C G7 F/G G7 C2 C Em7 C/E
1 Fa - ther, we love you, we wor-ship and a - dore you, glo - ri - fy thy
2 Je - sus, we love you, we wor-ship and a - dore you, glo - ri - fy thy
3 Spir - it, we love you, we wor-ship and a - dore you, glo - ri - fy thy
F C/G F/A Gsus G C F
name in all the earth; glo - ri - fy thy name,
E7sus D2/F# E7/G# Am F G/F F/A G7sus G7 F/A G7 F/C C
glo - ri - fy thy name, glo - ri - fy thy name in all the earth.

WORDS and MUSIC: Donna Adkins (1940-)

147 Praise God from Whom All Blessings Flow

Unison
Praise God from whom all bless-ings flow. Praise God, all crea-tures high and
low. Al-le-lu-ia, al-le-lu-ia! Praise God, in Je-sus ful-ly
known: Cre-a-tor, Word, and Spir-it one. Al-le-lu-ia, al-le-
lu-ia! Al-le-lu-ia, al-le-lu-ia, al-le-lu-ia!

WORDS: Brian Wren (1936-)
MUSIC: *Geistliche Kirchengesäng*, Cologne, 1623; harm. Hal H. Hopson (1933-)

LASST UNS ERFREUEN
L.M.Alleluias

Come, Thou Almighty King 148

1 Come, thou Al - might - y King, help us thy name to sing, help us to praise: Father, all glo - ri - ous, o'er all vic - to - ri - ous, come and reign o - ver us, An - cient of Days.
2 Come, thou In - car - nate Word, gird on thy might - y sword, our prayer at - tend: come, and thy peo - ple bless, and give thy word suc - cess: Spir - it of ho - li - ness, on us de - scend.
3 Come, Ho - ly Com - fort - er, thy sa - cred wit - ness bear in this glad hour: thou who al - might - y art, now rule in ev - ery heart, and ne'er from us de - part, Spir - it of power.
4 To thee, great One in Three, e - ter - nal prais - es be hence, ev - er - more! Thy sov - ereign maj - es - ty may we in glo - ry see, and to e - ter - ni - ty love and a - dore!

WORDS: Anonymous, ca. 1757
MUSIC: Felice de Giardini (1716-1796)

ITALIAN HYMN
6.6.4.6.6.6.4.

149 God the Spirit, Guide and Guardian

1 God the Spir - it, guide and guard - ian, wind - sped flame and
2 Christ our Sav - ior, sov - ereign, shep - herd, Word made flesh, Love
3 Great Cre - a - tor, life - be - stow - er, truth be - yond all
4 Tri - une God, mys - te - rious be - ing, un - di - vid - ed
hov - ering dove, breath of life and voice of proph - ets, sign of
cru - ci - fied, teach - er, heal - er, suf - fering ser - vant, friend of
thought's re - call, fount of wis - dom, womb of mer - cy, giv - ing
and di - verse, deep - er than our minds can fath - om, great - er
bless - ing, power of love: give to those who lead your peo - ple,
sin - ners, foe of pride: in your tend - ing may all pas - tors*
and for - giv - ing all: as you know our strength and weak - ness,
than our creeds re - hearse: help us in our var - ied call - ings
fresh a - noint - ing of your grace; send them forth as
learn and live a shep - herd's care; grant them cour - age
so may those the church ex - alts o - ver - see its
your full im - age to pro - claim, that our min - is -

*When appropriate, *ministers, leaders, elders,* or *deacons* may be substituted for *pastors.*

WORDS: Carl P. Daw, Jr. (1944-)
MUSIC: Rowland H. Prichard (1811-1887); arr. Ralph Vaughan Williams (1872-1958)

HYFRYDOL
8.7.8.7.D.

bold a - pos - tles to your church in ev - ery place.
and com - pas - sion shown through word and deed and prayer.
life stead - fast - ly yet not o - ver - look its faults.
tries u - nit - ing may give glo - ry to your name.

My Lord of Light 150

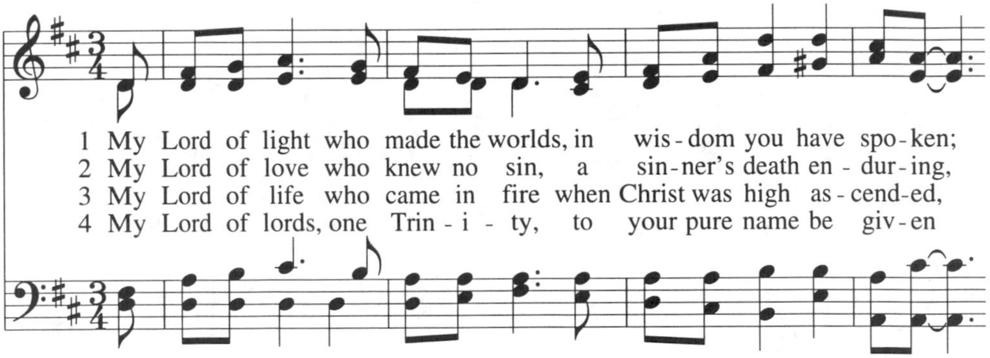
1 My Lord of light who made the worlds, in wis - dom you have spo - ken;
2 My Lord of love who knew no sin, a sin - ner's death en - dur - ing,
3 My Lord of life who came in fire when Christ was high as - cend - ed,
4 My Lord of lords, one Trin - i - ty, to your pure name be giv - en

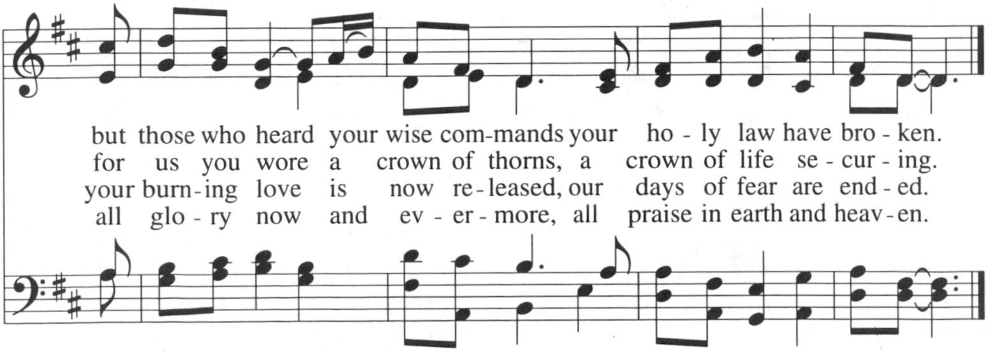
but those who heard your wise com - mands your ho - ly law have bro - ken.
for us you wore a crown of thorns, a crown of life se - cur - ing.
your burn - ing love is now re - leased, our days of fear are end - ed.
all glo - ry now and ev - er - more, all praise in earth and heav - en.

WORDS: Christopher Idle (1938-)
MUSIC: English folk tune; arr. Alice Parker (1925-)

BARBARA ALLEN
8.7.8.7.

151 Holy Is the Lord

Ho - ly, ho - ly, ho - ly, ho - ly is the Lord.
Ho - ly, ho - ly, ho - ly, ho - ly is the Lord.
Ho - ly is the Fa - ther, ho - ly is the Son,
ho - ly is the Spir - it: bless - ed Three - in - One.

WORDS: Para. Isaiah 6:3
MUSIC: Franz Schubert (1797-1828)

HOLY IS THE LORD
6.5.6.5.D.

THE CHURCH YEAR

152 Prepare the Way, O Zion

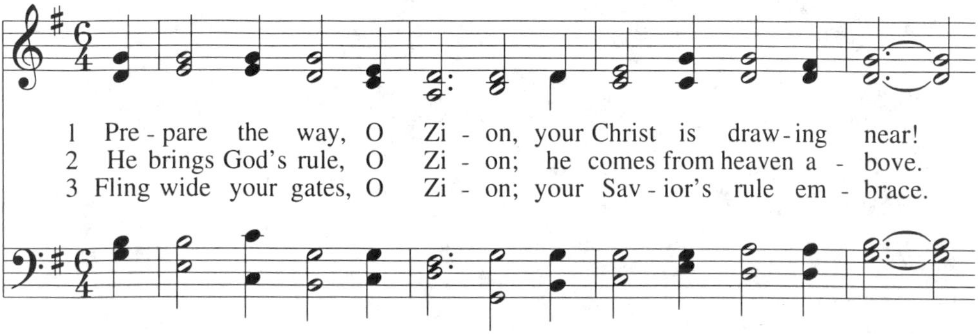
1 Pre - pare the way, O Zi - on, your Christ is draw - ing near!
2 He brings God's rule, O Zi - on; he comes from heaven a - bove.
3 Fling wide your gates, O Zi - on; your Sav - ior's rule em - brace.

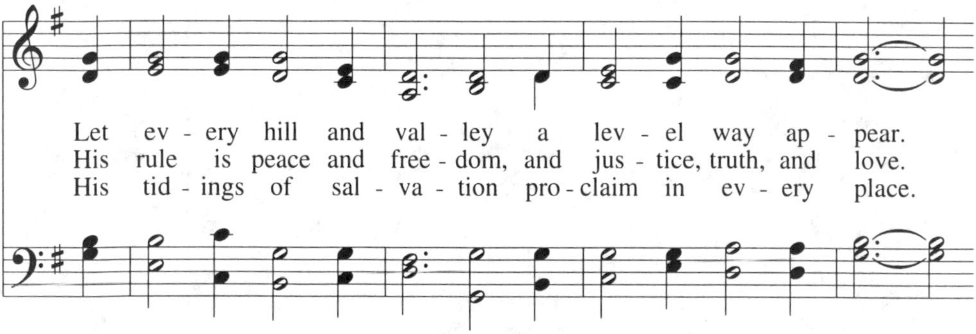
Let ev - ery hill and val - ley a lev - el way ap - pear.
His rule is peace and free - dom, and jus - tice, truth, and love.
His tid - ings of sal - va - tion pro - claim in ev - ery place.

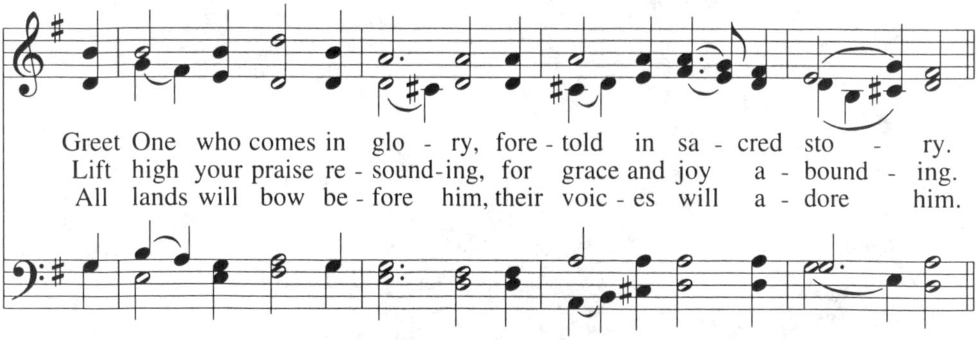
Greet One who comes in glo - ry, fore - told in sa - cred sto - ry.
Lift high your praise re - sound - ing, for grace and joy a - bound - ing.
All lands will bow be - fore him, their voic - es will a - dore him.

Refrain
Oh, blest is Christ that came in God's most ho - ly name.

WORDS: Frans Mikael Franzen (1772-1847); tr. composite;
adapt. Charles P. Price (1920-1999)
MUSIC: *Then Swenska Psalmboken*, 1697

BEREDEN VÄG FÖR HERRAN
7.6.7.6.7.7.Ref.

Come, Thou Long-Expected Jesus 153

1 Come, thou long - ex - pect-ed Je - sus, born to set thy peo-ple free;
2 Born thy peo - ple to de - liv - er, born a child and yet a king,
from our fears and sins re - lease us; let us find our rest in thee.
born to reign in us for - ev - er, now thy gra - cious king-dom bring.
Is - rael's strength and con - so - la - tion, hope of all the earth thou art;
By thine own e - ter - nal Spir - it rule in all our hearts a - lone;
dear De - sire of ev - ery na - tion, Joy of ev - ery long-ing heart.
by thine all - suf - fi - cient mer - it raise us to thy glo-rious throne.

WORDS: Charles Wesley (1707-1788)
MUSIC: Rowland H. Prichard (1811-1887); arr. Ralph Vaughan Williams (1872-1958)

HYFRYDOL
8.7.8.7.D.

154 O Come, O Come, Emmanuel

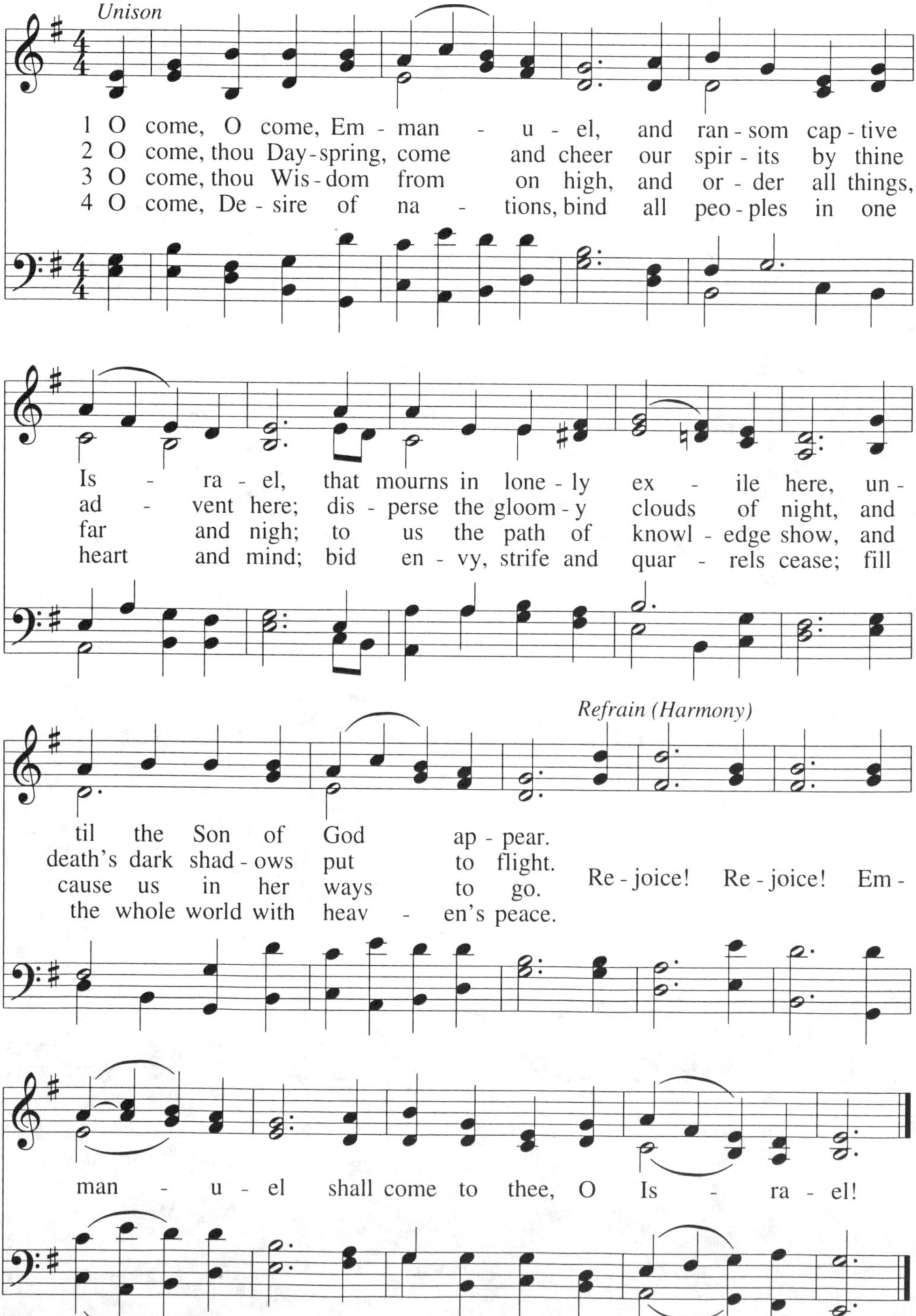
Unison
1 O come, O come, Em - man - u - el, and ran - som cap - tive
2 O come, thou Day - spring, come and cheer our spir - its by thine
3 O come, thou Wis - dom from on high, and or - der all things,
4 O come, De - sire of na - tions, bind all peo - ples in one
Is - ra - el, that mourns in lone - ly ex - ile here, un -
ad - vent here; dis - perse the gloom - y clouds of night, and
far and nigh; to us the path of knowl - edge show, and
heart and mind; bid en - vy, strife and quar - rels cease; fill
til the Son of God ap - pear.
death's dark shad - ows put to flight.
cause us in her ways to go.
the whole world with heav - en's peace.
Refrain (Harmony)
Re - joice! Re - joice! Em -
man - u - el shall come to thee, O Is - ra - el!

WORDS: Latin, 9th c.; tr. John M. Neale (1818-1866); vss. 3 and 4 tr. Henry S. Coffin (1877-1954)
MUSIC: French melody, 15th c.; harm. Thomas Helmore (1811-1890)

VENI EMMANUEL
L.M.Ref.

Comfort, Comfort Now My People 155

1 "Com - fort, com - fort now my peo - ple; tell of peace!" so says our God.
2 For the her - ald's voice is cry - ing in the des - ert far and near,
3 Straight shall be what long was crook - ed, and the rough - er plac - es plain!
Com - fort those who sit in dark - ness mourn-ing un - der sor - row's load.
call - ing us to true re - pent - ance since the King - dom now is here.
Let your hearts be true and hum - ble, as be - fits his ho - ly reign!
To God's peo - ple now pro-claim that God's par - don waits for them!
Oh, that warn - ing cry o - bey! Now pre - pare for God a way!
For the glo - ry of the Lord now on earth is shed a - broad,
Tell them that their war is o - ver; God will reign in peace for - ev - er!
Let the val - leys rise to meet him, and the hills bow down to greet him!
and all flesh shall see the to - ken that God's word is nev - er bro - ken.

WORDS: Johannes G. Olearius (1611-1684); tr. Catherine Winkworth (1827-1878), alt.; para. Isaiah 40:1-5
MUSIC: Louis Bourgeois (ca. 1510-1561), *Genevan Psalter*, 1551

GENEVAN 42
8.7.8.7.7.7.8.8.

156 On Jordan's Bank the Baptist's Cry

1 On Jor - dan's bank the Bap - tist's cry an - nounc - es
2 Let ev - ery heart be cleansed from sin, make straight the
3 For you are our sal - va - tion, Lord, our ref - uge
4 To heal the sick, stretch out your hand, and make the
5 To you, O Christ, all prais - es be, whose ad - vent
that the Lord is nigh: a - wake and lis - ten
way for God with - in, and so pre - pare to
and our great re - ward; with - out your grace we
fall - en sin - ner stand; shine out, and let your
sets your peo - ple free; whom with the Fa - ther
for he brings glad tid - ings of the King of kings.
be the home where such a might - y guest may come.
waste a - way like flowers that with - er and de - cay.
light re - store earth's own true love - li - ness once more.
we a - dore and Ho - ly Spir - it ev - er - more!

WORDS: Charles Coffin (1676-1749); tr. John Chandler (1806-1876)
MUSIC: Trier manuscript, 15th c.; adapt. Michael Praetorius (1571-1621); harm. George R. Woodward (1848-1934)

PUER NOBIS
L.M.

Come Now, O Prince of Peace 157

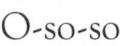

O-so-so

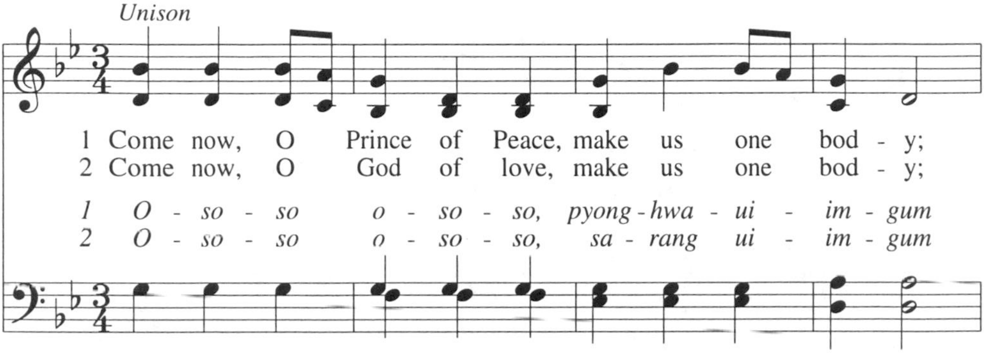
Unison
1 Come now, O Prince of Peace, make us one bod - y;
2 Come now, O God of love, make us one bod - y;
1 O - so - so o - so - so, pyong - hwa - ui - im - gum
2 O - so - so o - so - so, sa - rang ui - im - gum

come, O Lord Je - sus, re - con - cile your peo - ple.
come, O Lord Je - sus, re - con - cile your peo - ple.
u - ri - ga han - mon i - ru - ge ha so - so.
u - ri - ga han - mon i - ru - ge ha so - so.

3 Come now and set us free,
O God our Savior;
come, O Lord Jesus,
reconcile all nations.

4 Come, Hope of unity,
make us one body;
come, O Lord Jesus,
reconcile all nations.

3 O-so-so o-so-so
cha-yu ui-im-gumm
u-ri-ga han-mon
i-ru-ge ha-so-so.

4 O-so-so o-so-so
tong-il ui-im-gum,
u-ri-ga han-mon
i-ru-ge ha-so-so.

WORDS and MUSIC: Geonyong Lee (1947-); tr. Marion Pope (20th c.)

O-SO-SO
6.5.5.6.

158 Blessed Be the God of Israel

Unison
1 Blessed be the God of Is - rael, who comes to set us free,
2 Now from the house of Da - vid a child of grace has come,
3 On all by death im - pris - oned the sun be - gins to rise,
who vis - its and re - deems us, and grants us lib - er - ty.
a Sav - ior who will lead us to our e - ter - nal home.
the dawn - ing of for - give - ness up - on the sin - ner's eyes,
The proph - ets spoke of mer - cy, of free - dom and re - lease;
Be - fore him goes the her - ald, fore - run - ner in the way,
to guide the feet of pil - grims a - long the paths of peace;
God shall ful - fill the prom - ise to bring our peo - ple peace.
the proph - et of sal - va - tion, the har - bin - ger of day.
O bless our God and Sav - ior with songs that nev - er cease!

WORDS: Michael Perry (1942-1996)
MUSIC: Hal H. Hopson (1933-)

MERLE'S TUNE
7.6.7.6.D.

The King of Glory Comes

Refrain (Unison)
Em Bm7 Em Bm7 Em
The King of glo - ry comes, the na - tion re - joic - es.
1–4
Final ending
Em Bm7 Em Bm7 Em Em
O - pen the gates be - fore him, lift up your voic - es. voic - es.
sfz
Verses
G Am7 G/B C D7 Am/C G/B G
1 Who is the King of glo - ry: what shall we call him?
2 In all of Gal - i - lee, in cit - y or vil - lage,
3 He gave his life for us, the pledge of sal - va - tion,
4 He con - quered sin and death; he tru - ly has ris - en,
to Refrain
Em D Cmaj7 G/B Cmaj7 D G B7+5
He is Em - man - u - el, the prom - ised of a - ges.
he goes a - mong his peo - ple, cur - ing their ill - ness.
he took up - on him - self the sins of the na - tion.
and he will share with us his heav - en - ly vi - sion.

WORDS: Willard F. Jabusch (1930-)
MUSIC: Israeli folk song; arr. John Ferguson (1941-)

PROMISED ONE
12.12.Ref.

160 Awake! Awake, and Greet the New Morn

G Am7 G C D D7
1 A - wake! a - wake, and greet the new morn, for
2 To us, to all in sor - row and fear, Em -
3 In dark - est night his com - ing shall be, when
4 Re - joice, re - joice, take heart in the night, though
G C Am7 D7 G Am7
an - gels her - ald its dawn - ing. Sing out your joy, for
man - u - el comes a - sing - ing, his hum - ble song is
all the world is de - spair - ing, as morn - ing light so
dark the win - ter and cheer - less, the ris - ing sun shall
G C D G Am7 D C G
soon he is born, be - hold! the Child of our long - ing.
qui - et and near, yet fills the earth with its ring - ing;
qui - et and free, so warm and gen - tle and car - ing.
crown you with light, be strong and lov - ing and fear - less.

WORDS and MUSIC: Marty Haugen (1950-)

REJOICE, REJOICE
Irregular

D G D Em Am D
Come as a ba - by weak and poor, to bring all hearts to -
mu - sic to heal the bro - ken soul and hymns of lov - ing -
Then shall the mute break forth in song, the lame shall leap in
Love be our song and love our prayer and love our end - less
Em D7 G C B7 Em
geth - er, he o - pens wide the heaven - ly door and
kind - ness, the thun - der of his an - thems roll to
won - der, the weak be raised a - bove the strong, and
sto - ry; may God fill ev - ery day we share and
Am7 D7 G Am7 G
lives now in - side us for ev - er.
shat - ter all ha - tred and blind - ness.
weap - ons be bro - ken a - sun - der.
bring us at last in - to glo - ry.

161 People, Look East

1 Peo-ple, look east, the time is near of the crown-ing of the year. Make your house fair as you are a - ble, trim the hearth and set the ta - ble. Peo-ple, look east and sing to - day: Love, the Guest, is on the way.
2 Fur-rows, be glad. Though earth is bare, one more seed is plant - ed there. Give up your strength the seed to nour - ish, that in course the flow-er may flour-ish. Peo-ple, look east and sing to - day: Love, the Rose, is on the way.
3 Stars, keep the watch. When night is dim, one more light the bowl shall brim, shin - ing be - yond the frost - y weath - er, bright as sun and moon to - geth - er. Peo-ple, look east and sing to - day: Love, the Star, is on the way.
4 An - gels an-nounce with shouts of mirth him who brings new life to earth. Set ev - ery peak and val - ley hum - ming with the word, the Lord is com - ing. Peo-ple, look east and sing to - day: Love, the Lord, is on the way.

WORDS: Eleanor Farjeon (1881-1965)
MUSIC: French melody; arr. Martin Shaw (1875-1958)

BESANÇON
8.7.9.8.8.7.

like a child

Unison
Gm C Am Dm
1 like a child love would send to re - veal and to mend, like a
2 like a child we will meet, rag - ged clothes, dirt - y feet, like a
3 like a child born to pray and to show us the way, like a
Gm C F D7
child and a friend, Je - sus comes like a
child on the street, Je - sus comes like a
child here to stay, Je - sus comes like a
Gm7 C Am Dm7
child we may find claim - ing heart soul and mind, like a
child we once knew com - ing back in - to view, like a
child we re - ceive all that love can con - ceive, like a
Gm7 C11 F
child strong and kind, Je - sus comes
child born a - new, Je - sus comes
child we be - lieve Je - sus comes

WORDS and MUSIC: Daniel Charles Damon (1955-)

LIKE A CHILD
3.3.3.3.3.3.3.3.D.

163 All Earth Is Hopeful

Toda la Tierra

Unison
1 All earth is hope - ful, the Sav - ior comes at last!
2 Peo - ple of Is - rael, you heard the proph - et tell:
1 To - da la tier - ra es - per - ra al Sal - va - dor
2 Di - ce el pro - fe - ta al pueb - lo de Is - ra - el:
Fur - rows lie o - pen for God's cre - a - tive task: this, the
"A vir - gin moth - er will bear Em - man - u - el"; she con -
y el sur - co a - bier - to, la o - bra del Se - ñor; es el
"De ma - dre vir - gen ya vie - ne Em - man - u - el," se - rá
la - bor of peo - ple who strug - gle to see how
ceived him, "God with us," our broth - er, whose birth re -
mun - do que lu - cha por la li - ber - tad, re -
"Di - os con nos - tros," her - ma - no se - rá, con

TAULÉ
11.11.12.12.

WORDS: Alberto Taulé (1932-); tr. Madeleine Forell Marshall (1946-)
MUSIC: Alberto Taulé (1932-); arr. Skinner Chávez-Melo (1944-1992)

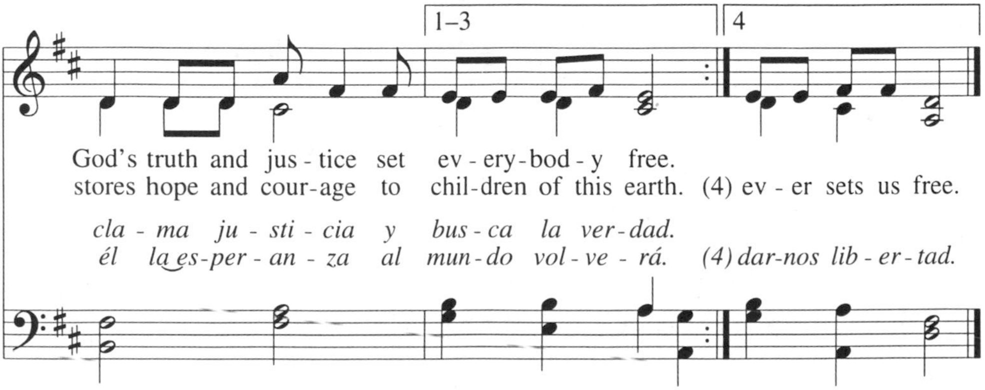
1–3
4
God's truth and jus - tice set ev - ery - bod - y free.
stores hope and cour-age to chil-dren of this earth. (4) ev - er sets us free.
cla - ma ju - sti - cia y bus - ca la ver - dad.
él la es-per - an - za al mun - do vol - ve - rá. (4) dar-nos lib - er - tad.

3 Mountains and valleys will have to be prepared;
new highways opened, new protocols declared.
Almost here! God is nearing, in beauty and grace!
All clear every gateway, in haste, come out in haste!

4 We first saw Jesus a baby in a crib.
This same Lord Jesus today has come to live
in our world; he is present, in neighbors we see
our Jesus is with us, and ever sets us free.

3 Montes y valles habrá que preparar;
nuevos caminos tenemos que trazar.
Él está ya muy cerca, venidlo a encontrar,
y todas las puertas abrid de par en par.

4 En una cueva Jesús apareció,
pero en el mundo está presente hoy.
Vive en nuestros hermanos, con ellos está;
y vuelve de nuevo a darnos libertad.

164 Wake, Awake, for Night Is Flying

1 Wake, a - wake, for night is fly - ing, the watch-men on the
2 Zi - on hears the watch - men sing - ing, and in her heart new
3 Now let all the heavens a - dore you, and saints and an - gels
heights are cry - ing; a - wake, Je - ru - sa - lem, at last.
joy is spring - ing. She wakes, she ris - es from her gloom,
sing be - fore you. The harps and cym-bals all u - nite.
Mid-night hears the wel - come voic - es, and at the thrill-ing
for her Lord comes down all - glo - rious, the strong in grace, in
Of one pearl each shin - ing por - tal, where, dwell - ing with the
cry re - joice - es: "Come forth, you maid - ens! Night is past.
truth vic - to - rious. Her star is risen; her light is come.
choir im - mor - tal, we gath - er round your daz - zling light.

WORDS: Philipp Nicolai (1556-1608); tr. Catherine Winkworth (1827-1878), alt.
MUSIC: Philipp Nicolai (1556-1608); harm. J. S. Bach (1685-1750)

WACHET AUF
Irregular

The bride - groom comes! A - wake; your lamps with glad - ness
O, come, you Bless - ed One, Lord Je - sus, God's own
No eye has seen, no ear has yet been trained to
take!" Al - le - lu - ia! Pre - pare your - selves to
Son. Sing ho - san - na! We go un - til the
hear what joy is ours! Cre - scen - dos rise; your
meet the Lord, whose light has stirred the wait - ing guard.
halls we view where you have bid us dine with you.
halls re - sound; ho - san - nas blend in cos - mic sound.

165 When God Is a Child

Refrain
When God is a child there's joy in our song. The last shall be first and the
a tempo
weak shall be strong, and none shall be a -
1–3
fraid.
4
fraid.
1 Hope is a star that
2 Peace is a rib - bon that
3 Joy is a song that
4 Love is a flame that
1–3
4

WORDS: Brian Wren (1936-)
MUSIC: John Carter (1930-)

GATES
Irregular

rit.
to Refrain
shines in the night, lead - ing us on till the morn - ing is bright. When
cir - cles the earth, giv - ing a prom - ise of safe - ty and worth. When
wel - comes the dawn, tell - ing the world that the Sav - ior is born. When
burns in our heart, Je - sus has come and will nev - er de - part. When
rit.

Wait for the Lord 166

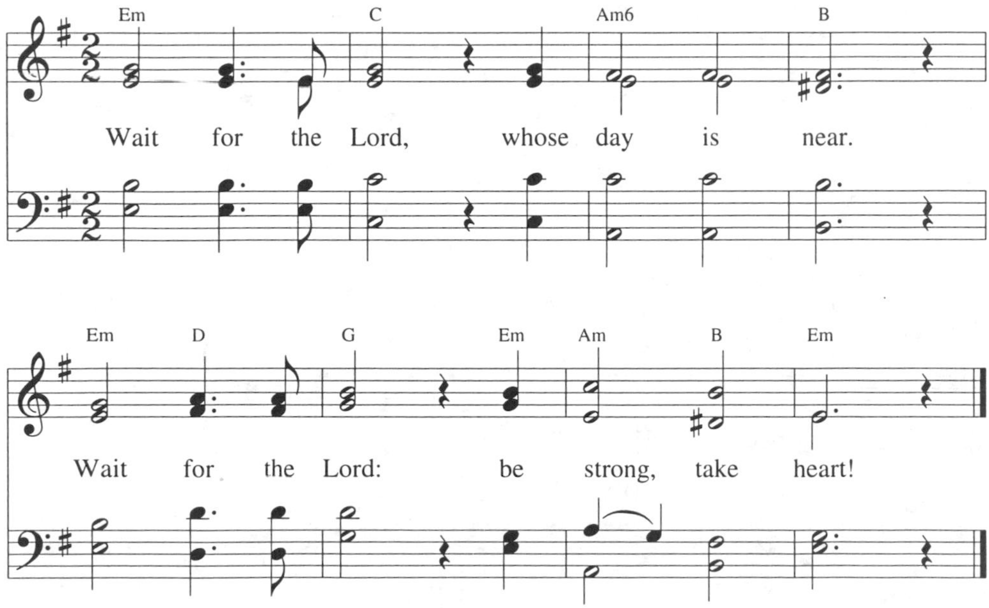
Em
C
Am6
B
Wait for the Lord, whose day is near.
Em
D
G
Em
Am
B
Em
Wait for the Lord: be strong, take heart!

WORDS and MUSIC: Taizé Community

167 Long Ago, Prophets Knew

1 Long a - go, proph-ets knew Christ would come, born a Jew, come to make all things new, bear his peo-ple's bur - den, free - ly love and par - don.
2 God in time, God in man, this is God's time-less plan: he will come, as a man, born him-self of wom - an, God di - vine - ly hu - man.
3 Ma - ry, hail! Though a - fraid, she be - lieved, she o - beyed. In her womb, God is laid till the time ex - pect - ed, nur-tured and pro - tect - ed.
4 Jour-ney ends! Where a - far Beth-lehem shines, like a star, sta - ble door stands a - jar: un - born Son of Ma - ry, Sav - ior, do not tar - ry!
Refrain
Ring, bells, ring, ring, ring! Sing, choirs, sing,
8vb
(8vb)
r.h.
l.h.

WORDS: Fred Pratt Green (1903-2000)
MUSIC: *Piae Cantiones*, 1582; arr. Gustav T. Holst (1874-1934)

PERSONENT HODIE
6.6.6.6.6.Ref.

sing, sing!
1–3 When he comes, when he comes, who will make him wel-come?
4 Je - sus comes, Je - sus comes, we will make him wel-come!
(8vb)

Savior of the Nations, Come 168

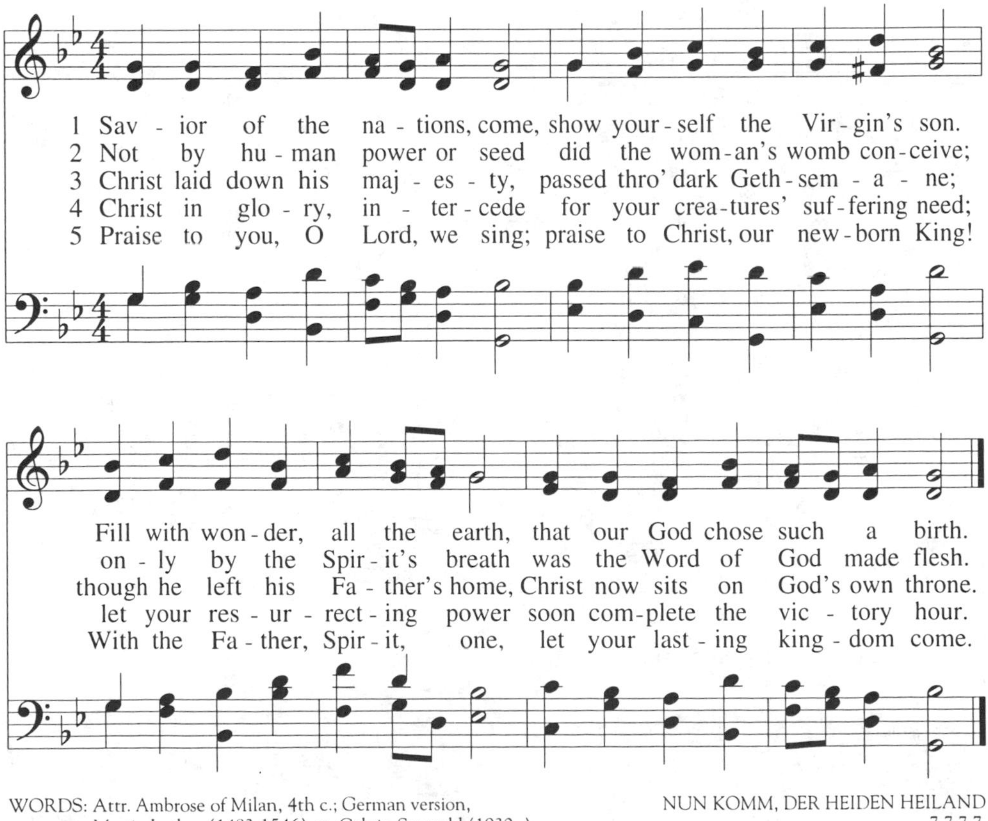
1 Sav - ior of the na - tions, come, show your - self the Vir - gin's son.
2 Not by hu - man power or seed did the wom-an's womb con-ceive;
3 Christ laid down his maj - es - ty, passed thro' dark Geth - sem - a - ne;
4 Christ in glo - ry, in - ter - cede for your crea-tures' suf-fering need;
5 Praise to you, O Lord, we sing; praise to Christ, our new - born King!
Fill with won - der, all the earth, that our God chose such a birth.
on - ly by the Spir - it's breath was the Word of God made flesh.
though he left his Fa - ther's home, Christ now sits on God's own throne.
let your res - ur - rect - ing power soon com-plete the vic - tory hour.
With the Fa - ther, Spir - it, one, let your last - ing king - dom come.

WORDS: Attr. Ambrose of Milan, 4th c.; German version, Martin Luther (1483-1546); tr. Calvin Seerveld (1930-)
MUSIC: *Enchiridia*, 1524; harm. Seth Calvisius (1556-1615)

NUN KOMM, DER HEIDEN HEILAND
7.7.7.7.

169 The Angel Gabriel from Heaven Came

1 The an - gel Ga - bri - el from heav - en came, his
2 "For know a bless - ed moth - er you shall be, all
3 Then gen - tle Ma - ry meek - ly bowed her head. "To
4 Of her, Em - man - u - el, the Christ, was born in
wings as drift - ed snow, his eyes as flame, "All
gen - er - a - tions praise con - tin - ual - ly, your
me be as it pleas - es God," she said. "My
Beth - le - hem, all on a Christ - mas morn, and
hail," said he, "O low - ly maid - en Ma - ry,"
Son shall be Em - man - u - el, by seers fore - told,"
soul shall laud and mag - ni - fy God's ho - ly name."
Chris - tian folk through-out the world will ev - er say:
Most high - ly fa - vored Ma - ry, glo - ri - a!

WORDS: Basque carol; para. Sabine Baring-Gould (1834-1924), alt.
MUSIC: Basque melody; arr. Edgar Pettman (1865-1943), John Wickham (20th c.)

GABRIEL'S MESSAGE
10.10.12.10.

My Soul Proclaims with Wonder 170

Refrain (Unison)
My soul pro-claims with won - der the great-ness of the Lord,
re - joic - ing in God's good - ness my spir - it is re - stored.
1 To me has God shown fa - vor, to one the world thought frail,
2 God's mer - cy shields the faith - ful and saves them from de - feat,
3 The might - y have been van-quished, the low - ly lift - ed up.
4 To A - bra-ham's de-scend - ants, the Lord will stead - fast prove,
to Refrain
and ev - ery age will ech - o the an - gel's first "All hail!"
with strength that turns to scat - ter the proud in their con - ceit.
The hun - gry find a - bun - dance, the rich, an emp - ty cup.
for God has made with Is - rael a cov - e - nant of love.

WORDS: Carl P. Daw, Jr. (1944-)
MUSIC: J. Harold Moyer (1927-)

WALNUT
7.6.7.6.D.

171 To a Maid Whose Name Was Mary

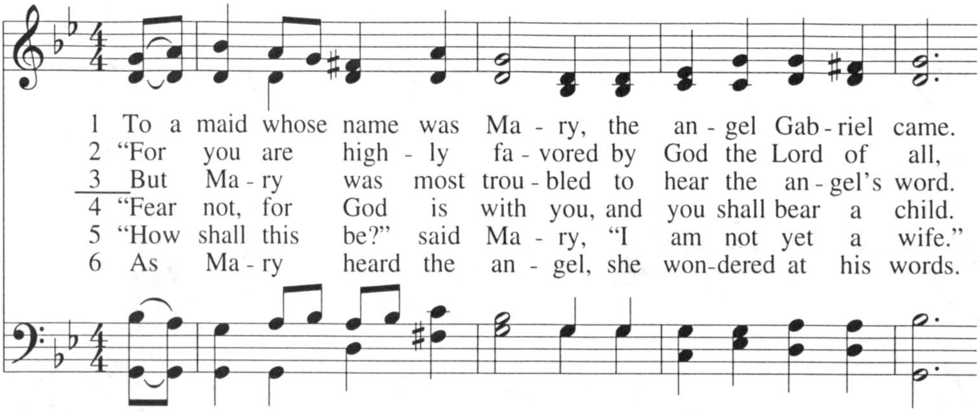
1 To a maid whose name was Ma - ry, the an - gel Gab - riel came.
2 "For you are high - ly fa - vored by God the Lord of all,
3 But Ma - ry was most trou - bled to hear the an - gel's word.
4 "Fear not, for God is with you, and you shall bear a child.
5 "How shall this be?" said Ma - ry, "I am not yet a wife."
6 As Ma - ry heard the an - gel, she won-dered at his words.

"Fear not," the an - gel told her, "I come to bring good news;
who ev - en now is with you. You are on earth most blest;
What was the an - gel say - ing? It trou - bled her to hear,
His name shall be called Je - sus, God's off - spring from on high.
The an - gel an - swered quick - ly, "The power of the Most High
"Be - hold, I am your hand - maid," she said un - to her God.

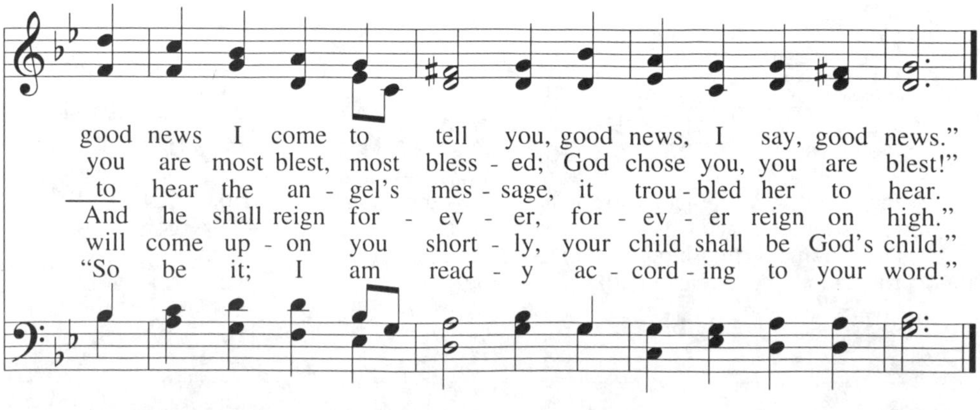
good news I come to tell you, good news, I say, good news."
you are most blest, most bless - ed; God chose you, you are blest!"
to hear the an - gel's mes - sage, it trou - bled her to hear.
And he shall reign for - ev - er, for - ev - er reign on high."
will come up - on you short - ly, your child shall be God's child."
"So be it; I am read - y ac - cord - ing to your word."

WORDS: Gracia Grindal (1943-)
MUSIC: Rusty Edwards (1955-)

ANNUNCIATION
7.6.7.6.7.6.

For Ages Women Hoped and Prayed 172

1 For ag-es wom-en hoped and prayed to bear th'a-noint-ed One,
2 Young Ma-ry did not think to hope for mir-a-cles of birth,
3 Our hearts re-joice as Ma-ry's song be-comes our hymn of praise.
both Is-rael's Sav-ior and the world's, the new day's shin-ing sun.
and God chose her to be the one to make Christ's home on earth.
For Christ has come, Em-man-u-el, to claim our years and days.
Did they not know? Did they not guess what pain would then be theirs,
So Ma-ry sang her heart-felt praise of God who sets things straight;
Both pres-ent now and com-ing still, ac-com-plished fact and dream,
if God's a-noint-ed graced their home in an-swer to their prayers?
the might-y fall, the weak are raised, the hun-gry fill their plate.
we join the song that Ma-ry sings, an earth-ly, heaven-ly theme.

WORDS: Jane Parker Huber (1926-) | NOEL
MUSIC: English melody; arr. Arthur S. Sullivan (1842-1900) | C.M.D.

173 Magnificat

Sing Out, My Soul

I G C D7 G
Ma - gni - fi - cat. Ma - gni - fi - cat.
Sing out, my soul. Sing out, my soul.
II
Ma - gni - fi - cat a - ni - ma me - a Do - mi - num.
Sing out and glo - ri - fy the Lord who sets us free.
III
Ma - gni - fi - cat. Ma - gni - fi - cat.
Sing out, my soul. Sing out, my soul.
IV
Ma - gni - fi - cat a - ni - ma me - a!
Sing out and glo - ri - fy the Lord God!

WORDS: Taizé Community, 1978; para. Luke 1:46
MUSIC: Jacques Berthier (1923-1994)

174 Prepare the Way of the Lord

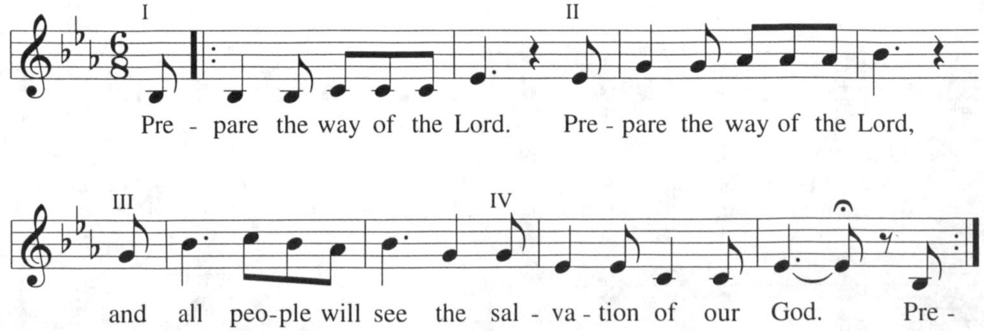
I II
Pre - pare the way of the Lord. Pre - pare the way of the Lord,
III IV
and all peo-ple will see the sal - va - tion of our God. Pre -

WORDS: Isaiah 40:3; 52:10
MUSIC: Jacques Berthier (1923-1994) and the Taizé Community, 1984

We Light the Advent Candles 175

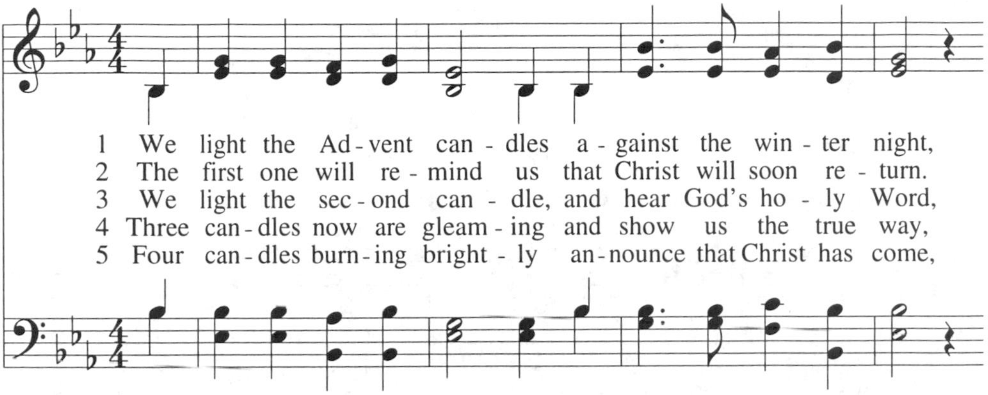
1 We light the Ad-vent can-dles a-gainst the win-ter night,
2 The first one will re-mind us that Christ will soon re-turn.
3 We light the sec-ond can-dle, and hear God's ho-ly Word,
4 Three can-dles now are gleam-ing and show us the true way,
5 Four can-dles burn-ing bright-ly an-nounce that Christ has come,

to wel-come our Lord Je-sus who is the world's True Light,
We light it in the dark-ness and watch it gleam and burn,
it tells us, cling to Je-sus, pre-pare to meet your Lord,
re-joice, the Bap-tist cries out, your Lord has come to-day,
pre-pare, my heart, be-lieve it, and give the Christ child room,

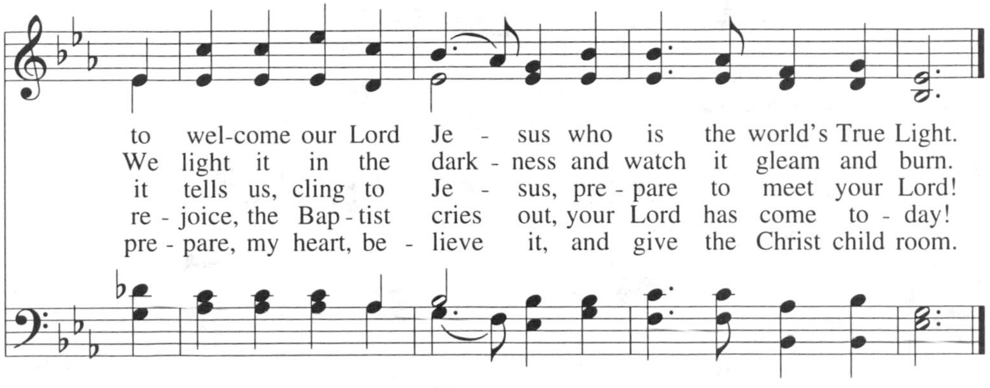
to wel-come our Lord Je-sus who is the world's True Light.
We light it in the dark-ness and watch it gleam and burn.
it tells us, cling to Je-sus, pre-pare to meet your Lord!
re-joice, the Bap-tist cries out, your Lord has come to-day!
pre-pare, my heart, be-lieve it, and give the Christ child room.

WORDS: Gracia Grindal (1943-)
MUSIC: German folk tune

WIR HATTEN GEBAUET
7.6.7.6.7.6.

176 Lift Up Your Heads, O Mighty Gates

1 Lift up your heads, O might - y gates: be - hold, the
2 Fling wide the por - tals of your heart: make it a
3 Re - deem - er, come! I o - pen wide my heart to
4 So come, my Sov - ereign, en - ter in! Let new and
King of glo - ry waits! The King of kings is
tem - ple set a - part from earth - ly use for
you: here, Lord, a - bide! Let me your in - ner
no - bler life be - gin! Your Ho - ly Spir - it
draw - ing near, the Sav - ior of the world is here.
heaven's em - ploy, a - dorned with prayer and love and joy.
pres - ence feel: your grace and love in me re - veal.
guide us on, un - til the glo - rious crown be won.
8

WORDS: George Weissel (1590-1635); tr. Catherine Winkworth (1827-1878); para. Psalm 24:7-10 — TRURO
MUSIC: Thomas Williams' *Psalmodia Evangelica*, 1789 — L.M.

177 Jesus, Name Above All Names

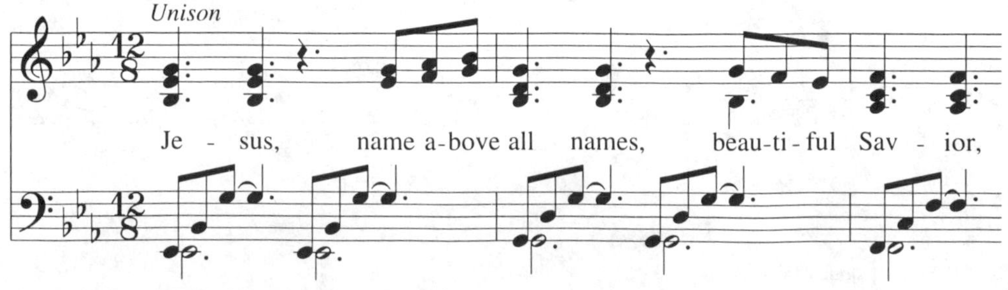
Unison
Je - sus, name a-bove all names, beau-ti-ful Sav - ior,

WORDS and MUSIC: Naida Hearn (1944-)

glo-ri-ous Lord. Em-man-u-el, God is
with us, bless-ed Re-deem - er, Liv-ing Word.

Emmanuel, Emmanuel 178

Unison
Em-man - u - el, Em-man - u - el, his name is
called Em-man - u - el. God with us,
re-vealed in us, his name is called Em-man-u - el.

WORDS and MUSIC: Bob McGee (1944-)

179 Joy to the World!

1 Joy to the world! the Lord is come; let earth re - ceive her King; let ev - ery heart pre - pare him room, and heaven and na - ture sing, and heaven and na - ture sing, and heaven, and heaven and na - ture sing.
2 Joy to the earth! the Sav - ior reigns; let all their songs em - ploy; while fields and floods, rocks, hills, and plains re - peat the sound - ing joy, re - peat the sound - ing joy, re - peat, re - peat the sound - ing joy.
3 No more let sins and sor - rows grow, nor thorns in - fest the ground; he comes to make his bless - ings flow far as the curse is found, far as the curse is found, far as, far as the curse is found.
4 He rules the world with truth and grace, and makes the na - tions prove the glo - ries of his right - eous - ness, and won - ders of his love, and won - ders of his love, and won - ders, won - ders of his love.
(1) and heaven and na - ture sing,
(1) and
heaven and na - ture sing,

WORDS: Isaac Watts (1674-1748)
MUSIC: George Frideric Handel (1685-1759); arr. Lowell Mason (1792-1872)

ANTIOCH
C.M.Repeats

O Little Town of Bethlehem 180

1 O lit - tle town of Beth - le - hem, how still we see thee lie!
2 For Christ is born of Ma - ry, and gath - ered all a - bove,
3 How si - lent - ly, how si - lent - ly the won - drous gift is given!
4 O ho - ly Child of Beth - le - hem, de - scend to us, we pray;
A - bove thy deep and dream-less sleep the si - lent stars go by.
while mor - tals sleep, the an - gels keep their watch of won-dering love,
So God im - parts to hu - man hearts the bless - ings of his heaven.
cast out our sin, and en - ter in; be born in us to - day.
Yet in thy dark streets shin - eth the ev - er - last - ing Light;
O morn - ing stars, to - geth - er pro - claim the ho - ly birth,
No ear may hear his com - ing, but in this world of sin,
We hear the Christ-mas an - gels the great glad ti - dings tell;
the hopes and fears of all the years are met in thee to - night.
and prais - es sing to God the King, and peace to all on earth.
where meek souls will re - ceive him still the dear Christ en - ters in.
O come to us, a - bide with us, our Lord Em - man - u - el.

WORDS: Phillips Brooks (1835-1893)
MUSIC: Lewis H. Redner (1831-1908)

ST. LOUIS
8.6.8.6.7.6.8.6.

181 Of the Father's Love Begotten

Unison
1 Of the Fa-ther's love be-got-ten, ere the world be-gan to be,
2 O that birth for-ev-er bless-ed, when a vir-gin, blest with grace,
3 Let the heights of heaven a-dore him; an-gel hosts his prais-es sing:
4 Christ, to thee, with God the Fa-ther, and, O Ho-ly Ghost, to thee,
he is Al-pha and O-me-ga, he the source, the end-ing he,
by the Ho-ly Ghost con-ceiv-ing, bore the Sav-ior of our race;
powers, do-min-ions, bow be-fore him, and ex-tol our God and King;
hymn and chant and high thanks-giv-ing and un-wea-ried prais-es be:
of the things that are, that have been, and that fu-ture
and the babe, the world's Re-deem-er, first re-vealed his
let no tongue on earth be si-lent, ev-ery voice in
hon-or, glo-ry, and do-min-ion, and e-ter-nal
years shall see, ev-er-more and ev-er-more!
sa-cred face, ev-er-more and ev-er-more!
con-cert ring, ev-er-more and ev-er-more!
vic-to-ry, ev-er-more and ev-er-more! A-men.

WORDS: Marcus Aurelius C. Prudentius, 4th c.; tr. John M. Neale (1818-1866) and Henry W. Baker (1821-1877)
MUSIC: Plainsong, 13th c.

DIVINUM MYSTERIUM
8.7.8.7.8.7.7.

O Come, All Ye Faithful

1 O come, all ye faith - ful, joy - ful and tri - um - phant, O
2 Sing, choirs of an - gels, sing in ex - ul - ta - tion,
3 Yea, Lord, we greet thee, born this hap - py morn - ing,
come ye, O come ye to Beth - le - hem;
sing, all ye cit - i - zens of heaven a - bove;
Je - sus, to thee be all glo - ry given;
come and be - hold him, born the King of an - gels;
glo - ry to God, all glo - ry in the high - est;
Word of the Fa - ther, now in flesh ap - pear - ing;
Refrain
O come, let us a - dore him, O come, let us a - dore him,
O come, let us a - dore him, Christ, the Lord.

WORDS: Attr. John F. Wade (1711-1786); tr. Frederick Oakeley (1802-1880)
MUSIC: John F. Wade's *Cantus Diversi*, 1751

ADESTE FIDELES
Irregular

183 Once in Royal David's City

1 Once in roy - al Da - vid's cit - y stood a low - ly cat - tle
2 He came down to earth from heav - en who is God and Lord of
3 Je - sus is our child - hood's pat - tern, day by day like us he
4 And our eyes at last shall see him, through his own re - deem-ing
shed, where a moth - er laid her ba - by in a
all, and his shel - ter was a sta - ble, and his
grew; he was lit - tle, weak, and help - less, tears and
love; for that child, so dear and gen - tle, is our
man - ger for his bed: Ma - ry was that moth - er
cra - dle was a stall: with the poor and meek and
smiles like us he knew: and he feels for all our
Lord in heaven a - bove: and he leads his chil - dren
mild, Je - sus Christ her lit - tle child.
low - ly lived on earth, our Sav - ior ho - ly.
sad - ness, and he shares in all our glad - ness.
on to the place where he has gone.

WORDS: Cecil F. Alexander (1818-1895)
MUSIC: Henry J. Gauntlett (1805-1876)

IRBY
8.7.8.7.7.7.

What Child Is This

Em D/F# G D Em Am/C B
1 What child is this, who, laid to rest, on Ma-ry's lap is sleep-ing?
2 Why lies he in such mean es - tate where ox and ass are feed-ing?
3 So bring him in - cense, gold, and myrrh, come peas-ant, king, to own him;
Em D/F# G D Em Am B Esus Em
Whom an - gels greet with an-thems sweet, while shep-herds watch are keep-ing?
Good Chris-tian, fear: for sin - ners here the si - lent Word is plead-ing.
the King of kings sal - va - tion brings, let lov - ing hearts en-throne him.
Refrain
Bm G D Em Am/C B
This, this is Christ the King, whom shep-herds guard and an - gels sing;
Nails, spear shall pierce him through, the cross be borne for me, for you;
Raise, raise the song on high, the Vir - gin sings her lul - la - by;
Bm G D Em Am B Esus Em
haste, haste to bring him laud, the babe, the son of Ma - ry!
hail, hail the Word made flesh, the babe, the son of Ma - ry!
joy, joy for Christ is born, the babe, the son of Ma - ry!

WORDS: William C. Dix (1837-1898)
MUSIC: English melody, 16th c.; arr. *Christmas Carols New and Old*, 1871

GREENSLEEVES
8.7.8.7.Ref.

185 Hark! the Herald Angels Sing

1 Hark! the her - ald an - gels sing, "Glo - ry to the new-born King:
2 Christ, by high - est heaven a - dored, Christ, the ev - er - last - ing Lord,
3 Hail the heaven-born Prince of Peace! Hail the Sun of Right-eous-ness!
peace on earth, and mer - cy mild, God and sin - ners rec - on - ciled!"
late in time be - hold him come, off-spring of the Vir-gin's womb:
Light and life to all he brings, risen with heal - ing in his wings.
Joy - ful, all ye na - tions, rise, join the tri - umph of the skies;
veiled in flesh the God-head see; hail th'in - car - nate De - i - ty,
Mild he lays his glo - ry by, born that we no more may die,
with th'an - gel - ic host pro-claim, "Christ is born in Beth - le - hem!"
pleased with us in flesh to dwell, Je - sus, our Em - man - u - el.
born to raise us from the earth, born to give us sec - ond birth.

WORDS: Charles Wesley (1707-1788), alt.
MUSIC: Felix Mendelssohn (1809-1847); adapt. William H. Cummings (1831-1915)

MENDELSSOHN
7.7.7.7.D.

Hark! the her - ald an - gels sing, "Glo - ry to the new-born King."

Silent Night! Holy Night! 186

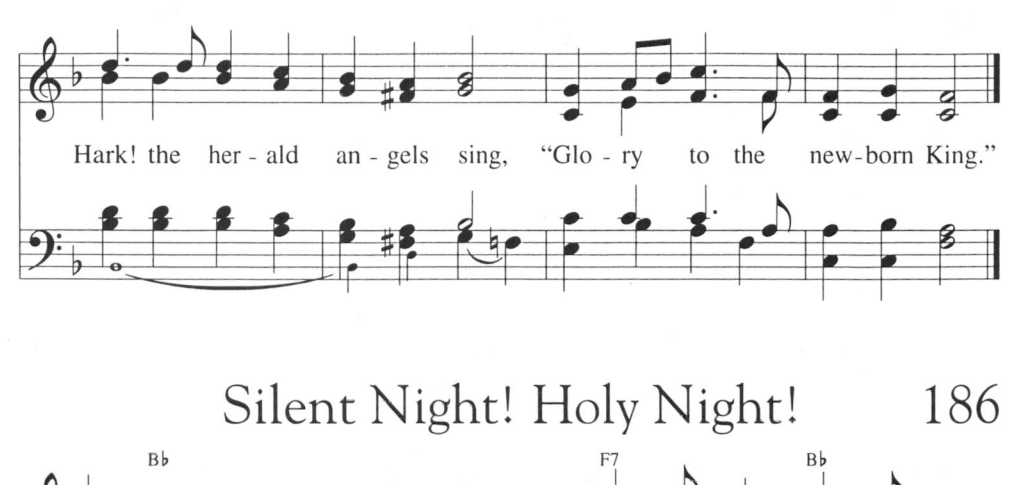

1 Si - lent night! ho - ly night! All is calm, all is bright
'round yon vir - gin moth-er and child; ho - ly in-fant, so ten-der and
mild, sleep in heav-en-ly peace, sleep in heav-en-ly peace.
2 Si - lent night! ho - ly night! Shep-herds quake at the sight,
glo - ries stream from heav-en a - far, heaven-ly hosts sing al - le - lu-
ia; Christ, the Sav - ior, is born! Christ, the Sav - ior, is born!
3 Si - lent night! ho - ly night! Son of God, love's pure light,
ra - diant beams from thy ho - ly face, with the dawn of re - deem - ing
grace, Je - sus, Lord, at thy birth, Je - sus, Lord, at thy birth.

WORDS: Joseph Mohr (1792-1848); tr. John F. Young (1820-1885)
MUSIC: Franz Gruber (1787-1863)

STILLE NACHT
Irregular

187 O Holy Night

Introduction/Interlude
1 O ho - ly night, the stars are bright - ly shin - ing, it is the night of the dear Sav - ior's birth.
2 Led by the light of faith se - rene - ly beam - ing, with glow - ing heart by his cra - dle we stand.
3 Tru - ly he taught us to love one an - oth - er; his law is love and his gos - pel is peace.
Long lay the world in sin and er - ror pin - ing, till he ap - peared and the soul felt its worth.
So led by light of a star sweet - ly gleam - ing, here came the wise men from the O - rient land.
Chains shall he break, for the slave is our broth - er, and in his name all op - pres - sion shall cease.
A thrill of hope the
The King of kings lay
Sweet hymns of joy in

WORDS: John S. Dwight (1813-1893)
MUSIC: Adolphe C. Adam (1803-1856); arr. Jack Schrader (1942-)

CANTIQUE DE NOEL
Irregular

wea - ry world re - joic - es, for yon - der breaks a new and glo - rious morn!
thus in low - ly man - ger, in all our tri - als born to be our friend;
grate - ful cho - rus rais - ing, let all with - in us praise his ho - ly name.
Fall on your knees! O hear the an - gel voic - es! O
he knows our need, he guards us from all dan - ger. Be -
Christ is the Lord! O praise his name for - ev - er! His
night di - vine! O night when Christ was born! O
hold your King; be - fore him low - ly bend! Be -
power and glo - ry ev - er - more pro - claim! His
1, 2
night di - vine! O night, O night di - vine!
hold your King; be - fore him low - ly bend!
power and
3
glo - ry ev - er - more pro - claim!

188 Angels We Have Heard on High

1 An - gels we have heard on high sweet - ly sing - ing o'er the plains,
2 Shep-herds, why this ju - bi - lee? Why your joy - ous strains pro - long?
3 Come to Beth - le - hem, and see him whose birth the an - gels sing;
and the moun-tains in re - ply ech - o back their joy - ous strains.
Say, what may the ti - dings be which in - spire your heaven-ly song?
come, a - dore on bend - ed knee Christ the Lord, the new - born King.
Refrain
Glo - - - - - - ri - a
in ex - cel - sis De - o! Glo - - - - -

WORDS and MUSIC: French carol, 18th c.

GLORIA
7.7.7.7.Ref.

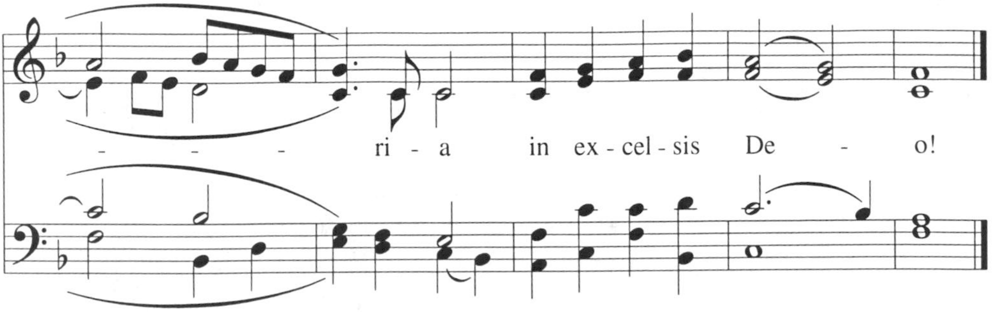
- - - - ri - a in ex - cel - sis De - o!

Angels, from the Realms of Glory 189

1 An - gels, from the realms of glo - ry, wing your flight o'er all the earth;
2 Shep-herds, in the fields a - bid - ing, watch-ing o'er your flocks by night,
3 Sag - es, leave your con - tem - pla - tions, bright - er vi - sions beam a - far;
4 Saints be - fore the al - tar bend - ing, watch-ing long in hope and fear,
you who sang cre - a - tion's sto - ry, now pro-claim Mes - si - ah's birth:
God with us is now re - sid - ing, yon - der shines the in - fant light:
seek the great De - sire of na - tions, you have seen the na - tal star:
sud - den - ly the Lord, de-scend-ing, in his tem - ple shall ap - pear:
Come and wor-ship, come and wor-ship, wor-ship Christ, the new-born King.

WORDS: James Montgomery (1771-1854)
MUSIC: Henry T. Smart (1813-1879)

REGENT SQUARE
8.7.8.7.8.7.

190 Lo, How a Rose E'er Blooming

1 Lo, how a Rose e'er bloom-ing from ten - der stem hath sprung,
2 I - sa - iah 'twas fore - told it, the Rose I have in mind;
3 This flower, whose fra-grance ten - der with sweet-ness fills the air,
of Jes - se's lin - eage com - ing as saints of old have sung.
with Mar - y we be - hold it, the vir - gin moth - er kind.
dis - pels with glo-rious splen - dor the dark-ness ev - ery - where.
It came, a flower - et bright, a - mid the cold of
To show God's love a - right she bore to us a
True man yet ver - y God, from sin and death he
win - ter, when half - spent was the night.
Sav - ior, when half - spent was the night.
saves us and light - ens ev - ery load.

WORDS: German, 16th c.; tr. Theodore Baker (1851-1934);
tr. vs. 3, Harriet Krauth Spaeth (1845-1925)
MUSIC: *Alte Catholische Geistliche Kirchengesäng*, 1599; arr. Michael Praetorius (1571-1621)

ES IST EIN ROS'
7.6.7.6.6.7.6.

It Came upon the Midnight Clear 191

1 It came up-on the mid-night clear, that glo-rious song of old,
2 Still through the clo-ven skies they come, with peace-ful wings un-furled,
3 For lo, the days are has-tening on, by proph-ets seen of old,
from an-gels bend-ing near the earth to touch their harps of gold:
and still their heaven-ly mu-sic floats o'er all the wea-ry world;
when, with the ev-er-cir-cling years, shall come the time fore-told,
"Peace on the earth, good-will to all, from heaven's all gra-cious King":
a-bove its sad and low-ly plains they bend on hov-ering wing,
when peace shall o-ver all the earth its an-cient splen-dors fling,
the world in sol-emn still-ness lay to hear the an-gels sing.
and ev-er o'er its Ba-bel sounds the bless-ed an-gels sing.
and all the world give back the song which now the an-gels sing.

WORDS: Edmund H. Sears (1810-1876)
MUSIC: Richard S. Willis (1819-1900)

CAROL
C.M.D.

192 Mary, Did You Know?

Unison
Cm Bb
1 Ma - ry, did you know that your ba - by boy would
2 Ma - ry, did you know that your ba - by boy would
Ab Cm G Gsus
some - day walk on wa - ter? Ma - ry, did you
give sight to a blind man? Ma - ry, did you
Cm Bb Ab Fm/G
know that your ba - by boy would save our sons and daugh-
know that your ba - by boy will calm a storm with his
G Gsus Ab Bb
- ters? Did you know that your ba - by boy has
hand? Did you know that your ba - by boy has
Eb Gm7/D Cm Fm7 Fm/Eb
come to make you new? This child that you de - liv -
walked where an - gels trod? When you kissed your lit - tle ba -
Fm6/D Cm/G 1 G 2 G
- ered, will soon de - liv - er you.
- by, then you kissed the face of God.

WORDS: Mark Lowry (20th c.)
MUSIC: Buddy Greene (20th c.); arr. Jack Schrader (1942-)

Harmony
Gsus Ab Bb Cm Cm/Bb Ab
The blind will see, the deaf will hear, the dead will live a - gain;
Eb/G Fm7 Bb Ab Gm7 Fm7 Fm/D Gsus G
the lame will leap, the dumb will speak the prais - es of the Lamb.
Unison
Gsus Cm Bb
Ma - ry, did you know that your ba - by boy is
Ab Cm G Gsus Cm Bb
Lord of all cre - a - tion? Ma - ry, did you know that your ba -
Ab Fm/G G Gsus Ab
- by boy will one day rule the na - tions? Did you know
Bb Eb Gm7/D Cm
that your ba - by boy was heav - en's per - fect Lamb? This
Fm Fm/Eb Fm6/D Cm/G G7 Cm
sleep - ing child you're hold - ing is the great "I AM!"

193 Sing We Now of Christmas

Unison
1 Sing we now of Christ - mas, No - el, sing we here!
2 An - gels called to shep - herds, "Leave your flocks at rest,
3 In Beth - le - hem they found him; Jo - seph and Ma - ry mild,
4 From the east - ern coun - try came the kings a - far,
5 Gold and myrrh they took there, gifts of great - est price;
Hear our grate - ful prais - es to the Babe so dear.
jour - ney forth to Beth - le - hem, find the lamb - kin blest."
seat - ed by the man - ger, watch - ing the ho - ly child.
bear - ing gifts to Beth - le - hem guid - ed by a star.
there was ne'er a place on earth so like par - a - dise.
Refrain
Sing we No - el, the King is born, No - el!
Sing we now of Christ - mas, sing we now No - el!

WORDS and MUSIC: French carol, 15th c.

NOËL NOUVELET
6.5.6.5.Ref.

Born in the Night, Mary's Child 194

Unison
3
1 Born in the night, Ma-ry's Child, a long way from your home;
2 Clear shin-ing light, Ma-ry's Child, your face lights up our way;
3 Truth of our life, Ma-ry's Child, you tell us God is good;
4 Hope of the world, Ma-ry's Child, you're com-ing soon to reign;
com - ing in need, Ma-ry's Child, born in a bor-rowed room.
light of the world, Ma-ry's Child, dawn on our dark-ened day.
prove it is true, Ma-ry's Child, go to your cross of wood.
Sav - ior of all, Ma-ry's Child, walk in our streets a - gain.

WORDS: Geoffrey Ainger (1925-)
MUSIC: Geoffrey Ainger (1925-); arr. Richard D. Wetzel (1935-)

MARY'S CHILD
7.6.7.6.

Gloria, Gloria, Gloria 195

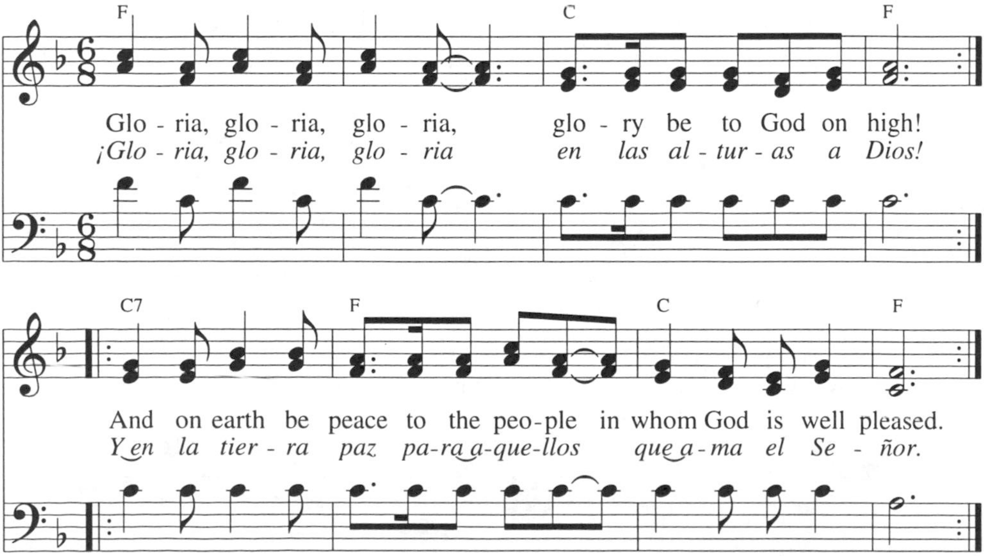
F C F
Glo - ria, glo - ria, glo - ria, glo - ry be to God on high!
¡Glo - ria, glo - ria, glo - ria en las al - tur - as a Dios!
C7 F C F
And on earth be peace to the peo-ple in whom God is well pleased.
Y en la tier - ra paz pa-ra a-que-llos que a-ma el Se - ñor.

WORDS: Luke 2:14
MUSIC: Pablo Sosa (1933-)

GLORIA CUECA
Irregular

196 In the Bleak Midwinter

1 In the bleak mid - win - ter, frost - y wind made moan,
2 Our God, heaven can - not hold him, nor earth sus - tain;
3 An - gels and arch - an - gels may have gath - ered there,
4 What can I give him, poor as I am?
earth stood hard as i - ron, wa - ter like a stone;
heaven and earth shall flee a - way when he comes to reign:
cher - u - bim and ser - a - phim thronged the air;
If I were a shep - herd, I would bring a lamb;
snow had fall - en, snow on snow, snow on snow,
in the bleak mid - win - ter a sta - ble - place suf - ficed
but his moth - er on - ly, in her maid - en bliss,
if I were a wise man, I would do my part;
in the bleak mid - win - ter, long a - go.
the Lord God in - car - nate, Je - sus Christ.
wor - shiped the Be - lov - ed with a kiss.
yet what I can I give him: give my heart.
8

WORDS: Christina Rossetti (1830-1894)
MUSIC: Gustav T. Holst (1874-1934)

CRANHAM
Irregular

Come and Hear the Joyful Singing 197

Unison
1 Come and hear the joy - ful sing - ing, Al - le - lu - ia, glo - ri - a,
2 An - gels of his birth are tell - ing, Al - le - lu - ia, glo - ri - a,
3 Choir and peo - ple, shout in won - der, Al - le - lu - ia, glo - ri - a,
set the bells of heav - en ring - ing; Al - le - lu - ia, glo - ri - a,
Prince of Peace all powers ex - cel - ling; Al - le - lu - ia, glo - ri - a,
let the might - y or - gan thun - der; Al - le - lu - ia, glo - ri - a,
God the Lord has shown us fav - or— Al - le - lu - ia, glo - ri - a,
death and hell can - not de - feat him: Al - le - lu - ia, glo - ri - a,
thank our God for love a - maz - ing, Al - le - lu - ia, glo - ri - a,
Christ is born to be our Sav - ior. Al - le - lu - ia, glo - ri - a!
go to Beth - le - hem and greet him. Al - le - lu - ia, glo - ri - a!
Fa - ther, Son and Spir - it prais - ing. Al - le - lu - ia, glo - ri - a!

WORDS: Michael Perry (1942-1996)
MUSIC: Hal H. Hopson (1933-)

JOYFUL SINGING
8.7.8.7.D.

198 Good Christian Friends, Rejoice

1 Good Chris-tian friends, re - joice with heart and soul and voice;
2 Good Chris-tian friends, re - joice with heart and soul and voice;
3 Good Chris-tian friends, re - joice with heart and soul and voice;
give ye heed to what we say: Je - sus Christ is born to - day;
now ye hear of end - less bliss; Je - sus Christ was born for this;
now ye need not fear the grave; Je - sus Christ was born to save;
ox and ass be - fore him bow, and he is in the man - ger now.
he has o - pened heav - en's door, and we are blest for - ev - er - more.
calls you one and calls you all to gain his ev - er - last - ing hall.
Christ is born to - day! Christ is born to - day!
Christ was born for this! Christ was born for this!
Christ was born to save! Christ was born to save!

WORDS: Latin carol, 14th c.; tr. John M. Neale (1818-1866), alt.
MUSIC: German melody, 14th c.

IN DULCI JUBILO
Irregular

Carol at the Manger

Unison
Eb Ab Eb Eb/G Cm Fm7 Bb
1 Ho-ly Child with-in the man-ger, long a-go yet ev-er near;
2 Once a-gain we tell the sto-ry—how your love for us was shown,
3 Ho-ly Child with-in the man-ger, lead us ev-er in your way,
Bb7 Cm Fm/Ab Bb Cm Eb/G Fm7 Bb7 Ebsus Eb
come as friend to ev-ery stran-ger, come as hope for ev-ery fear.
when the im-age of your glo-ry wore an im-age like our own.
so we see in ev-ery stran-ger how you come to us to-day.
Cm Ab Eb Bb Eb Ab Eb Bbsus Bb
As you lived to heal the bro-ken, greet the out-cast, free the bound,
Come, en-light-en with your wis-dom, come and fill us with your grace.
In our lives and in our liv-ing give us strength to live as you,
G7/B Cm Bb Fm Ab Eb Fm7 Bb7 Ab/Eb Eb
as you taught us love un-spo-ken, teach us now where you are found.
May the fire of your com-pas-sion kin-dle ev-ery land and race.
that our hearts might be for-giv-ing and our spir-its strong and true.

WORDS and MUSIC: Marty Haugen (1950-)

JOYOUS LIGHT
8.7.8.7.D.

200 While by the Sheep

1 While by the sheep we watched at night, glad tid - ings brought an an - gel bright.
2 There shall be born, so he did say, in Beth - le - hem a Child to - day.
3 There shall the Child lie in a stall, this Child who shall re - deem us all.
4 This gift of God we'll cher - ish well, that ev - er joy our hearts shall fill.
How great our joy! Great our joy!
Joy, joy, joy! Joy, joy, joy! Praise we the Lord in heaven on high! Praise we the Lord in heaven on high!
echo p
f

WORDS and MUSIC: German carol; arr. Hugo Jüngst (1853-1923)

JÜNGST
Irregular

He Is Born

Refrain (Unison)
He is born, the di-vine Christ child, play the o-boe and bag-pipes mer-ri-ly!
He is born, the ho-ly child, sing we all of the Sav-ior mild.
1 Through long a-ges of the past proph-ets have fore-told his com-ing;
2 Oh, how love-ly, oh, how pure is this per-fect child of heav-en;
3 Je-sus, Lord of all the world, com-ing as a child a-mong us;
through long a-ges of the past, now the time has come at last!
oh, how love-ly, oh, how pure, gra-cious gift of God sent down.
Je-sus, Lord of all the world, grant to us your heaven-ly peace.
to Refrain

WORDS: French carol; arr. Donald P. Hustad (1918-)

IL EST NÉ
Irregular

202 Break Forth, O Beauteous Heavenly Light

1 Break forth, O beau - teous heaven-ly light, and ush - er in the
2 Come, dear - est child, in - to our hearts, and leave your crib be -
morn - ing; O shep - herds, shud - der not in fright, but
hind you! Let this be where the new life starts for
hear the an - gel's warn - ing. This child, now weak in in - fan-
all who seek and find you. To you the hon - or, thanks, and
cy, our con - fi - dence and joy shall be, the power of
praise, for all your gifts this time of grace; come, con - quer

WORDS: Johann Rist (1607-1667); tr. John Troutbeck (1832-1899), alt;
vs. 2 Fred Pratt Green (1903-2000)
MUSIC: Johann Schop (1590-1664); harm. J. S. Bach (1685-1750)

ERMUNTRE DICH
8.7.8.7.8.8.7.7.

Sa - tan break - ing, our peace e - ter - nal mak - ing.
and de - liv - er this world, and us, for - ev - er.

Away in a Manger 203

Unison (or Duet)

1 A - way in a man-ger, no crib for a bed, the lit - tle Lord
2 The cat - tle are low-ing, the Ba - by a - wakes, but lit - tle Lord
3 Be near me, Lord Je - sus; I ask thee to stay close by me for -
Je - sus laid down his sweet head; the stars in the sky looked
Je - sus, no cry - ing he makes. I love thee, Lord Je - sus, look
ev - er, and love me, I pray. Bless all the dear chil - dren in
down where he lay, the lit - tle Lord Je - sus a - sleep on the hay.
down from the sky and stay by my side un - til morn-ing is nigh.
thy ten - der care, and fit us for heav - en, to live with thee there.

WORDS: Anonymous, 1885; vs. 3 John Thomas McFarland (1851-1913)
MUSIC: James R. Murray (1841-1905)

AWAY IN A MANGER
11.11.11.11.

204 Down to Earth, as a Dove

1 Down to earth, as a dove, came to light holy love: Jesus Christ from above bringing great salvation meant for every nation.
2 This is love come to light, now is fear put to flight. God defeats darkest night, giving for our sorrows hope of new tomorrows.
3 Christ the Lord comes to feed hungry people in need; in the house there is bread: Jesus in a stable, in the church a table.
Refrain
Let us sing, sing, sing, dance and spring,
r.h.
l.h.
8vb
(8vb)

WORDS: Fred Kaan (1929-)
MUSIC: *Piae Cantiones*, 1582; arr. Gustav T. Holst (1874-1934)

PERSONENT HODIE
6.6.6.6.6.Ref.

spring, spring, Christ is here, ev - er near! Glo - ria in ex - cel - sis.
(8vb)

Away in a Manger

205

Unison
1 A - way in a man - ger, no crib for a bed, the lit - tle Lord
2 The cat - tle are low - ing, the Ba - by a - wakes, but lit - tle Lord
3 Be near me, Lord Je - sus; I ask thee to stay close by me for -
Je - sus laid down his sweet head; the stars in the bright sky looked
Je - sus, no cry - ing he makes. I love thee, Lord Je - sus, look
ev - er, and love me, I pray. Bless all the dear chil - dren in
down where he lay, the lit - tle Lord Je - sus a - sleep on the hay.
down from the sky and stay by my side un - til morn - ing is nigh.
thy ten - der care, and fit us for heav - en, to live with thee there.

WORDS: Anonymous, 1885; vs. 3 John Thomas McFarland (1851-1913)
MUSIC: William J. Kirkpatrick (1838-1921)

CRADLE SONG
11.11.11.11.

206 A Stable Lamp Is Lighted

1 A sta - ble lamp is light - ed whose
(2) child through Da - vid's cit - y shall
(3) he shall be for - sak - en, and
(4) now, as at the end - ing, the
glow shall wake the sky; the stars shall bend their
ride in tri - umph by; the palm shall strew its
yield - ed up to die; the sky shall groan and
low is lift - ed high; the stars shall bend their
voic - es, and ev - ery stone shall cry. And
branch - es, and ev - ery stone shall cry. And
dark - en, and ev - ery stone shall cry. And
voic - es, and ev - ery stone shall cry. And

WORDS: Richard Wilbur (1921-), "A Christmas Hymn" from *Advice to a Prophet and Other Poems*
MUSIC: David Hurd (1950-)

ANDUJAR
7.6.7.6.6.6.7.6.

ev - ery stone shall cry, and straw like gold shall shine; a
ev - ery stone shall cry, though heav - y, dull, and dumb, and
ev - ery stone shall cry, for hearts made hard by sin: God's
ev - ery stone shall cry, in prais - es of the child by
barn shall har - bor heav - en, a stall be-come a shrine.
lie with-in the road - way to pave his king-dom come.
blood up-on the spear - head, God's love re-fused a - gain.
whose de-scent a-mong us the worlds are rec - on - ciled.
1–3
4
2 This
3 Yet
4 But

207 Oh, Sleep Now, Holy Baby

A La Ru

A7 D A7 D Bm G Bm F♯7
1 Oh, sleep now, ho - ly ba - by, with your head a - gainst my breast;
2 You need not fear King Her-od, he will bring no harm to you; so
1 Duér-me - te, Ni - ño lin - do, en los bra-zos del a - mor mien -
2 No te - mas al rey He - ro - des que na - da te ha de ha - cer; en
Bm F♯m/A Gmaj7 F♯ A7/G D/A G/A A7 D
mean-while the pangs of my sor - row are soothed and put to rest.
rest in the arms of your moth - er who sings you a la ru.
tras que duer-me y des - can - sa la pe - na de mi do - lor.
los bra - zos de tu ma - dre y ahi na - die te ha de o-fen - der.
Refrain
D7/F♯ G A7/E D/F♯ B7 Em A D
*A la ru, a la mé, a la ru, a la mé,

*These are lullaby words with no specific meaning.

WORDS and MUSIC: Hispanic folk song; tr. and arr. John Donald Robb (1892-1989)

A LA RU
Irregular

D7/F♯ G A7 B7 E7 D/A G/A A7 D
a la ru, a la mé, a la ru, a la ru, a la mé.

Oh, How Joyfully 208

Unison
1 Oh, how joy - ful - ly, oh, how hope - ful - ly,
2 Oh, how joy - ful - ly, oh, how peace - ful - ly,
3 Oh, how joy - ful - ly, oh, how thank - ful - ly,
waits the world on Christ - mas Eve! Love comes heal - ing,
sleeps the world on Christ - mas Night! Sins are cov - ered,
wakes the world on Christ - mas Morn! God has spo - ken,
God re - veal - ing. Friends, be joy - ful and be - lieve!
grace dis - cov - ered. In our dark - ness shines the light!
death is bro - ken. Al - le - lu - ia! Christ is born!

WORDS: Brian Wren (1936-)
MUSIC: Sicilian melody, 18th c.

SICILIAN MARINERS
5.5.7.4.4.7.

209 Rise Up, Shepherd, and Follow

1 There's a star in the east on Christ-mas morn.
2 If you take good heed to the an-gel's word,
Rise up, shep-herd, and fol-low. It will lead to the
rise up, shep-herd, and fol-low. You'll for-get your
place where the Sav-ior's born. Rise up, shep-herd, and
flock, you'll for-get your herd. Rise up, shep-herd, and
fol-low.
fol-low.
Refrain
Fol-low, fol-low;

WORDS and MUSIC: African-American spiritual; arr. Jack Schrader (1942-)

FOLLOW
Irregular

rise up, shep-herd and fol - low. Fol - low the star of

Beth - le - hem; rise up, shep - herd, and fol - low.

Love Came Down at Christmas 210

1 Love came down at Christ - mas, Love all love - ly, Love di - vine;
2 Wor - ship we the God - head, Love in - car - nate, Love di - vine;
3 Love shall be our to - ken; love be yours and love be mine;

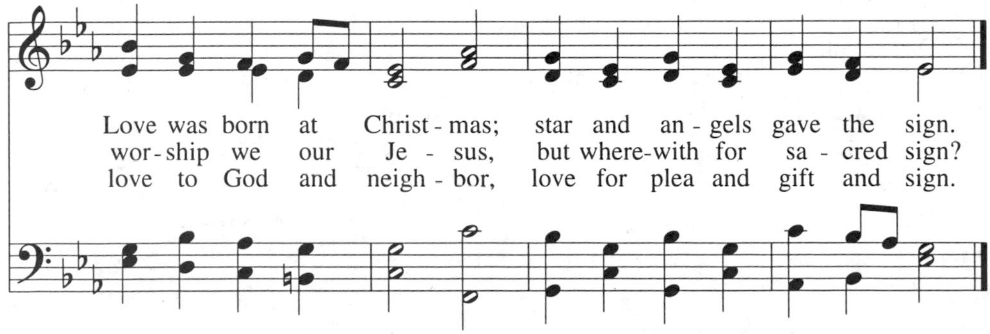
Love was born at Christ - mas; star and an - gels gave the sign.
wor - ship we our Je - sus, but where-with for sa - cred sign?
love to God and neigh - bor, love for plea and gift and sign.

WORDS: Christina Rossetti (1830-1894), alt.
MUSIC: Maurice C. Whitney (1909-1984)

WHITNEY
6.7.6.7.

211 That Boy-Child of Mary

Refrain
That boy-child of Ma - ry was born in a sta - ble,

a man-ger his cra - dle in Beth - le-hem.

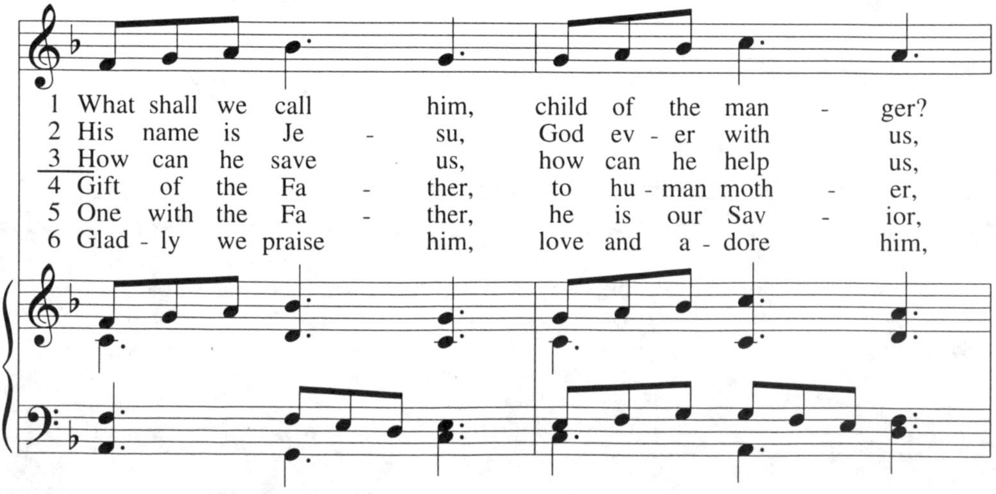
1 What shall we call him, child of the man - ger?
2 His name is Je - su, God ev - er with us,
3 How can he save us, how can he help us,
4 Gift of the Fa - ther, to hu - man moth - er,
5 One with the Fa - ther, he is our Sav - ior,
6 Glad - ly we praise him, love and a - dore him,

WORDS: Tom Colvin (1925-2000)
MUSIC: Malawi melody; adapt. Tom Colvin (1925-2000)

BLANTYRE
Irregular

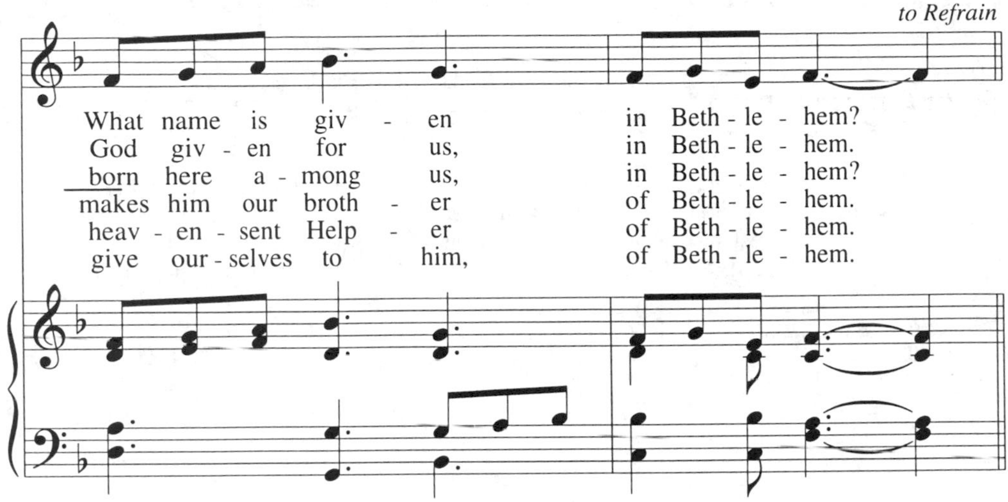
to Refrain
What name is giv - en in Beth - le - hem?
God giv - en for us, in Beth - le - hem.
born here a - mong us, in Beth - le - hem?
makes him our broth - er of Beth - le - hem.
heav - en - sent Help - er of Beth - le - hem.
give our - selves to him, of Beth - le - hem.

Raise a Song of Gladness 212

Jubilate Deo

I
II
Raise a song of glad - ness, peo - ples of the earth.
Ju - bi - la - te De - o om - nis ter - ra.
Christ has come, bring - ing peace, joy to ev - ery heart.
Ser - vi - te Do - mi - no in lae - ti - ti - a.
Al - le - lu - ia, al - le - lu - ia, joy to ev - ery heart!
Al - le - lu - ia, al - le - lu - ia, in lae - ti - ti - a.
Al - le - lu - ia, al - le - lu - ia, joy to ev - ery heart!
Al - le - lu - ia, al - le - lu - ia, in lae - ti - ti - a!

WORDS: Taizé Community, 1978; para. Psalm 100
MUSIC: Jacques Berthier (1923-1994)

213 'Twas in the Moon of Wintertime

Unison
1 'Twas in the moon of win - ter - time, when all the birds had fled,
2 With - in a lodge of bro - ken bark the ten - der babe was found,
3 The ear - liest moon of win - ter - time is not so round and fair
4 O chil - dren of the for - est free, O sons of Man - i - tou,
that might - y Git - chi Man - i - tou* sent an - gel choirs in -
a rag - ged robe of rab - bit skin en - wrapped his beau - ty
as was the ring of glo - ry on the help - less in - fant
the Ho - ly Child of earth and heaven is born to - day for
stead; be - fore their light the stars grew dim and wan - dering
'round; but as the hunt - er braves drew nigh the an - gel
there. The chiefs from far be - fore him knelt with gifts of
you. Come kneel be - fore the ra - diant boy who brings you
hunt - ers heard the hymn:
song rang loud and high:
fox and beav - er pelt.
beau - ty, peace and joy.
"Je - sus your King is born,

*Gitchi Manitou = Great God

WORDS: Jean de Brébeuf (1593-1649); tr. Jesse Edgar Middleton (1872-1960)
MUSIC: French carol, 16th c.

UNE JEUNE PUCELLE
8.6.8.6.8.8.Ref.

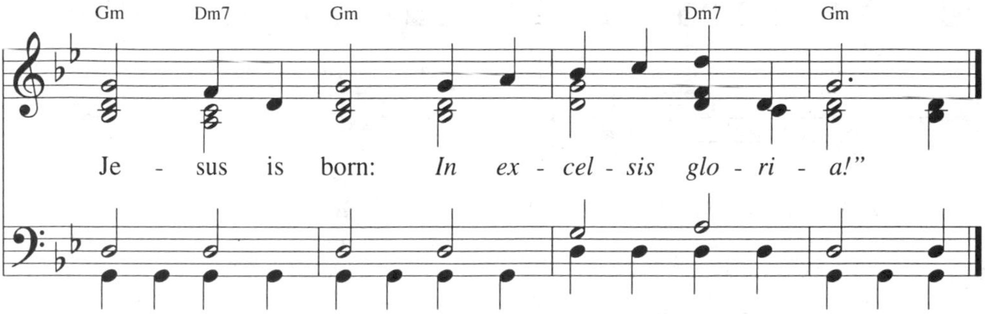
Gm Dm7 Gm Dm7 Gm
Je - sus is born: *In ex - cel - sis glo - ri - a!"*

Still, Still, Still 214

Eb Eb/D Cm Cm/Bb Fm/Ab Bb7 Eb Eb/Bb
1 Still, still, still, he sleeps this night so chill! The
2 Sleep, sleep, sleep, he lies in slum - ber deep while
Bb Bb7 Eb Bb Bb7 Eb
Vir - gin's ten - der arms en - fold - ing, warm and safe the Child are hold - ing.
an - gel hosts from heaven come wing - ing, sweet - est songs of joy are sing - ing.
Eb Eb/D Cm Cm/Bb Fm/Ab Bb7 Eb
Still, still, still, he sleeps this night so chill.
Sleep, sleep, sleep, he lies in slum - ber deep.
8

WORDS: Austrian carol; tr. George K. Evans (1917-)
MUSIC: Austrian melody; arr. Walter Ehret (1918-)

STILL, STILL, STILL
3.6.9.8.3.6.

215 Were You There on That Christmas Night

F Dm Gm Gm7/Bb C C/E
1 Were you there, were you there on that Christ - mas night, when the
2 Did you see, did you see how they hailed him King, with the
4 Did you know, did you know it was God's own Son, the sal -
F Am Am7 Bb Bbmaj7 C7 C/Bb Am Am/C
world was filled with a ho - ly light? Were you there to be -
gifts so rare that they chose to bring? Did you see how they
va - tion of the world be - gun? Did you know it was
Dm Gm Gm7 C7 Bb/C C7 F Bb/F F
(Fine)
hold when the won - der fore - told came to earth?
bowed, as they praised him a - loud at his birth?
love that was sent from a - bove to the earth?
F/A Bb C/Bb Am Am/C Dm
3 Did you hear how the choirs of an - gels sang at the

WORDS and MUSIC: Natalie Sleeth (1930-1992)

JUXTAPOSITION
Irregular

Gm Gm/F C7/E C F F/A B♭
glo - ry of the sight? Did you hear how the
C/B♭ Am Am/C Dm G7sus G7 Csus C
to verse 4
bells of heav - en rang all through the night?

Adoramus Te 216

We Adore You

Fine
1 A - do - ra - mus te, Je - su Chris - te, al-le - lu - ia, al-le - lu - ia!
1 We a - dore your name, Je-sus Sav - ior, al-le - lu - ia, al-le - lu - ia! *Et lau-*
2 You are born to - day, Je-sus Sav - ior, al-le - lu - ia, al-le - lu - ia! Praise and
3 We are born a - new, Je-sus Sav - ior, al-le - lu - ia, al-le - lu - ia!
D.C.
da - mus te, Je - su Chris - te, et lau - da - mus te, al-le - lu - ia!
bless your name, Je-sus Sav - ior, praise and bless your name, al-le - lu - ia!

WORDS and MUSIC: Taizé Community

217 No Obvious Angels

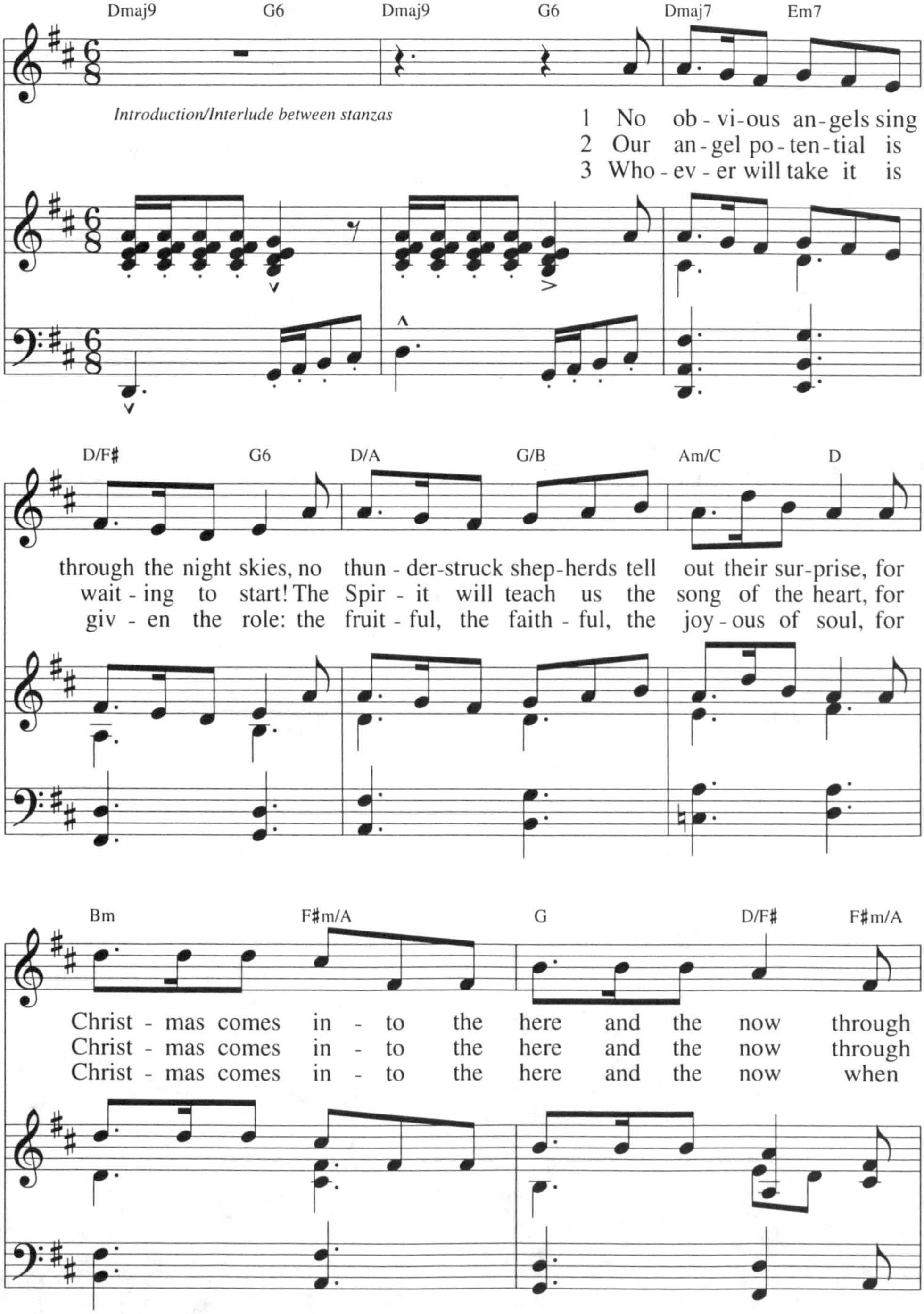
Dmaj9 G6 Dmaj9 G6 Dmaj7 Em7
Introduction/Interlude between stanzas
1 No ob - vi-ous an-gels sing
2 Our an-gel po-ten-tial is
3 Who-ev-er will take it is
D/F# G6 D/A G/B Am/C D
through the night skies, no thun - der-struck shep-herds tell out their sur-prise, for
wait - ing to start! The Spir - it will teach us the song of the heart, for
giv - en the role: the fruit - ful, the faith - ful, the joy - ous of soul, for
Bm F#m/A G D/F# F#m/A
Christ - mas comes in - to the here and the now through
Christ - mas comes in - to the here and the now through
Christ - mas comes in - to the here and the now when

WORDS: Shirley Erena Murray (1931-)
MUSIC: Carlton R. Young (1926-)

NEW WORLD CAROL
Irregular

Bm G/A Dmaj7 Em7/B D/C
star - sight-ed peo - ple, the watch - ful and hope - ful, who wake us to
peace-mak - er peo - ple, the just and the gen - tle, the stars who will
we are the an - gels who dream and de - liv - er, who rise and cre -
1, 2
Bm Gmaj7 Em7 A
see a new world.
light the new world.
3
Bm Gmaj7 Em7 D
ate this new world!
f

218 Go, Tell It on the Mountain

Refrain (Unison)
Go, tell it on the moun - tain, o-ver the hills and ev - ery-where;
go, tell it on the moun - tain that Je - sus Christ is born.
Parts
1 While shep-herds kept their watch-ing o'er si - lent flocks by night,
2 The shep-herds feared and trem-bled when, lo! a - bove the earth
3 Down in a low - ly man - ger the hum - ble Christ was born,
to Refrain
be - hold, through-out the heav-ens there shone a ho - ly light.
rang out the an - gel cho - rus that hailed our Sav - ior's birth.
and God sent us sal - va - tion that bless - ed Christ-mas morn.

WORDS: John W. Work (1872-1925)
MUSIC: African-American spiritual

GO, TELL IT
Irregular

Jesus, Oh, What a Wonderful Child 219

G Am/D G G9/B C C7 G
Je-sus, Je-sus, oh, what a won-der-ful Child.
G C/D G A7 A9 D
Je-sus, Je-sus, so ho-ly, meek, and mild; new
G Am/G Gm7 Am G C
life, new hope the Child will bring. Lis-ten to the
C#dim7 G/D D7 G Am/G G#dim7 Am A9/E D7 G
an-gels sing, "Glo-ry, glo-ry, glo - ry," let the heav-ens ring!

WORDS and MUSIC: African-American spiritual; arr. Jeffrey Radford (1953-)

WONDERFUL CHILD
Irregular

220 Mary Had a Baby

1 Ma - ry had a ba - by, my Lord;
2 What did she name him, my Lord?
3 She named him King Je - sus, my Lord. She
4 Where was he born, my Lord?
5 Born in a man - ger, my Lord.
Ma - ry had a ba - by, my Lord.
What did she name him, my Lord?
named him King Je - sus, my Lord. She
Where was he born, my Lord?
Born in a man - ger, my Lord.
Ma - ry had a ba - by, Ma - ry had a ba - by,
What did she name him, what did she name him,
named him King Je - sus, she named him King Je - sus, she
Where was he born, where was he born,
Born in a man - ger, born in a man - ger,
Ma - ry had a ba - by, my Lord.
what did she name him, my Lord?
named him King Je - sus, my Lord.
where was he born, my Lord?
born in a man - ger, my Lord.

WORDS and MUSIC: African-American spiritual

Infant Holy, Infant Lowly

1 In - fant ho - ly, in - fant low - ly, for his bed a cat - tle stall;
2 Flocks were sleep-ing: shep-herds keep-ing vig - il till the morn-ing new
ox - en low - ing, lit - tle know-ing Christ the babe is Lord of all.
saw the glo - ry, heard the sto - ry, ti - dings of the Gos-pel true.
Swift are wing - ing an-gels sing - ing, no - els ring - ing, tid - ings bring - ing:
Thus re - joic - ing, free from sor - row, prais-es voic - ing greet the mor - row:
Christ the babe is Lord of all. Christ the babe is Lord of all.
Christ the babe was born for you. Christ the babe was born for you.

WORDS: Polish carol; tr. Edith M. G. Reed (1885-1933)
MUSIC: Polish folk tune, adapt. A. E. Rusbridge (1917-1969)

W̦ ZLOBIE LEZY
8.7.8.7.8.7.7.

222 On Christmas Night All Christians Sing

Unison
1 On Christ-mas night all Chris - tians sing to hear the news the an - gels bring; on Christ - mas night all Chris - tians sing to hear the news the an - gels bring: news of great joy, news of great mirth, news of our mer - ci - ful King's birth.
2 Then why should we on earth be sad, since our Re - deem - er made us glad? Then why should we on earth be sad, since our Re - deem - er made us glad, when from our sin he set us free, all for to gain our lib - er - ty?
3 All out of dark - ness we have light, which made the an - gels sing this night; all out of dark - ness we have light, which made the an - gels sing this night: "Glo - ry to God and peace to men, now and for - ev - er - more. A - men."

WORDS and MUSIC: English carol; harm. Ralph Vaughan Williams (1872-1958)

SUSSEX CAROL
8.8.8.8.8.8.

Star-Child

1 Star - Child, earth - Child, go - be-tween of God, love Child,
2 Street child, beat child, no place left to go, hurt child,
3 Grown child, old child, mem-ory full of years, sad child,
4 Spared child, spoiled child, hav - ing, want - ing more, wise child,
5 Hope - for - peace Child, God's stu - pen - dous sign, down - to -
Christ Child, heav-en's light-ning rod:
used child no one wants to know:
lost child, sto - ry told in tears:
faith child know-ing joy in store:
earth Child, Star of stars that shine:
Refrain
This year, this year let the day ar -
rive when Christ-mas comes for ev - ery - one, ev - ery - one a - live!

WORDS: Shirley Erena Murray (1931-)
MUSIC: Carlton R. Young (1926-)

STAR-CHILD
4.5.4.5.Ref.

224 The Birthday of a King

Unison
1 In the lit - tle vil - lage of Beth - le - hem, there lay a Child one day, and the sky was bright with a ho - ly light o'er the place where Je - sus lay.
2 'Twas a hum - ble birth-place, but O how much God gave to us that day; from the man - ger bed what a path has led, what a per - fect, ho - ly way.
Refrain (harmony optional)
Al - le - lu - ia! O how the an - gels sang. Al - le - lu - ia! How it rang! And the sky was bright with a ho - ly light, 'twas the birth - day of a King.

WORDS and MUSIC: William Harold Neidlinger (1900-); arr. Robert F. Douglas (1941-)

I Wonder as I Wander

Unison
Gm Cm7 Gm7 Cm
1 I won - der as I wan - der, out un - der the sky, how
2 When Ma - ry birthed Je - sus, 'twas in a cow's stall, with
3 If Je - sus had want - ed for an - y wee thing, a
4 I won - der as I wan - der, out un - der the sky, how
Gm Cm7 Gm7 Gm
Je - sus the Sav - ior did come for to die for
wise men and farm - ers and shep - herds and all, but
star in the sky or a bird on the wing, or
Je - sus the Sav - ior did come for to die for
Gm Cm7 Gm7 G7
poor ordi - nary peo - ple like you and like I; I
high from God's heav - en a star's light did fall, the
all of God's an - gels in heaven for to sing, he
poor ordi - nary peo - ple like you and like I; I
Cm Gm/B♭ Am7(♭5) Gm7 Cm/G Optional Coda Gm Dm7 Gm
won - der as I wan - der, out un - der the sky.
prom - ise of a - ges it then did re - call.
sure - ly could have it, 'cause he was the King.
won - der as I wan - der, out un - der the sky. Out un - der the sky.

WORDS: Appalachian carol; coll. John Jacob Niles (1892-1980) — I WONDER AS I WANDER
MUSIC: Appalachian melody; coll. John Jacob Niles (1892-1980); arr. Donald P. Hustad (1918-) — Irregular

226 God's Love Made Visible!

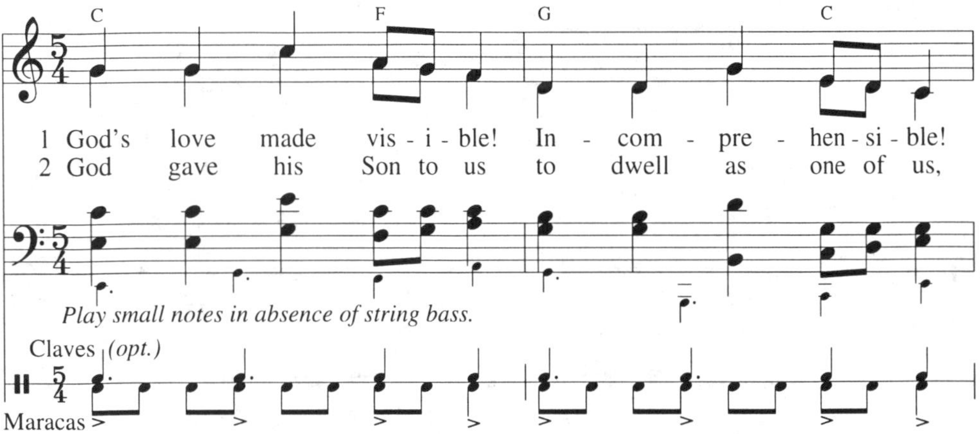
C F G C
1 God's love made vis - i - ble! In - com - pre - hen - si - ble!
2 God gave his Son to us to dwell as one of us,
Play small notes in absence of string bass.
Claves (opt.)
Maracas

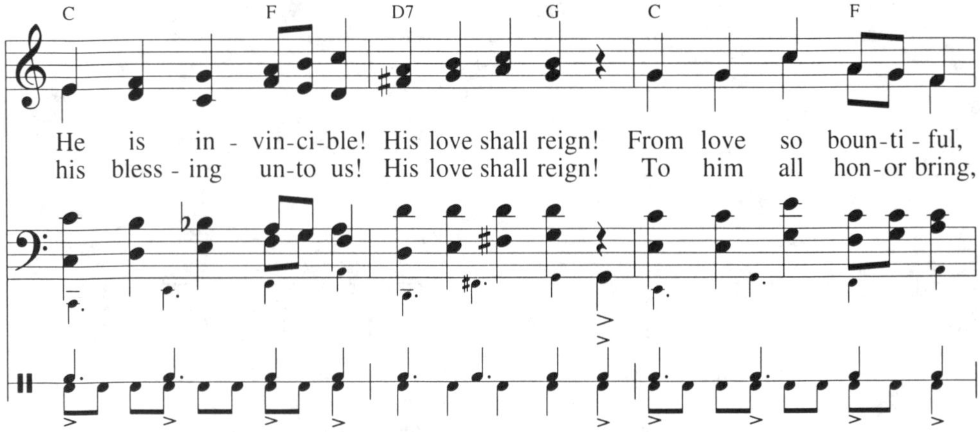
C F D7 G C F
He is in - vin-ci-ble! His love shall reign! From love so boun-ti - ful,
his bless - ing un-to us! His love shall reign! To him all hon-or bring,

G C C7 F Dm C/G G7 C
bless - ings un - count-a - ble make death sur-mount-a - ble! His love shall reign!
heav - en and earth will sing, prais - ing our Lord and King! His love shall reign!

WORDS: Iola Brubeck (1923-)
MUSIC: Dave Brubeck (1920-)

POSADA
Irregular

Ab Eb/Ab Ab Eb/Ab Ab Eb/Ab
Joy - ful - ly pray for peace and good will! All of our yearn-ing
O - pen all doors this day of his birth, all of good will in -
Ab G7 C F
he will ful - fill. Live in a lov - ing way!
her - it the earth. His star will al - ways be
G C C7 F Dm C/G G7 C
Praise him for ev - ery day! O - pen your hearts and pray! His love shall reign!
guid - ing hu - man - i - ty through-out e - ter - ni - ty! His love shall reign!

227 See Him Lying on a Bed of Straw

Unison
1 See him ly - ing on a bed of straw: a
2 Star of sil - ver, sweep a - cross the skies,
3 An - gels, sing a - gain the song you sang,
4 Mine are rich - es, from your pov - er - ty,
draft - y sta - ble with an o - pen door;
show where Je - sus in the man - ger lies;
sing the glo - ry of God's gra - cious plan;
from your in - no - cence, e - ter - ni - ty;
Ma - ry cra - dl - ing the babe she bore— the
shep - herds, swift - ly from your stu - por rise to
sing that Beth - l'em's lit - tle ba - by can
mine for - give - ness by your death for me,
Prince of glo - ry is his name.
see the Sav - ior of the world!
be the Sav - ior of us all.
child of sor - row for my joy.

WORDS and MUSIC: Michael Perry (1942-1996); arr. Stephen Coates (1952-) and others

CALYPSO CAROL
9.9.9.7.Ref.

Refrain
O now car - ry me to Beth - le - hem to
see the Lord of love a - gain:
just as poor as was the sta - ble then, the
Prince of glo - ry when he came.

228 While Shepherds Watched Their Flocks

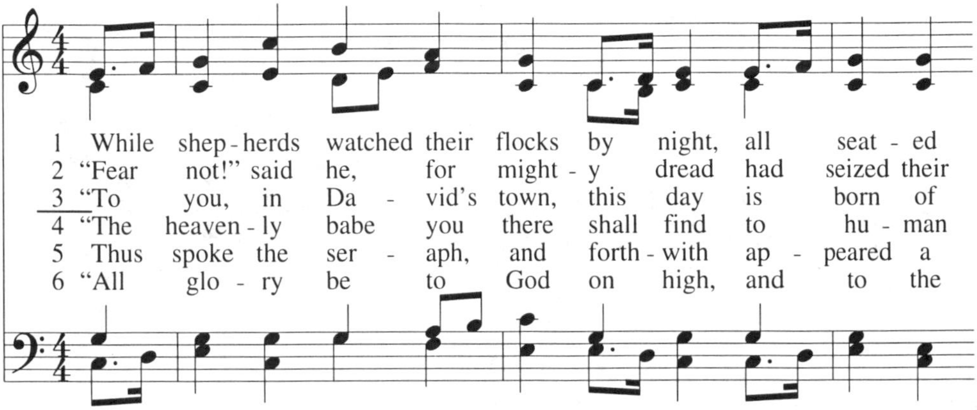
1 While shep-herds watched their flocks by night, all seat - ed
2 "Fear not!" said he, for might - y dread had seized their
3 "To you, in Da - vid's town, this day is born of
4 "The heaven - ly babe you there shall find to hu - man
5 Thus spoke the ser - aph, and forth - with ap - peared a
6 "All glo - ry be to God on high, and to the

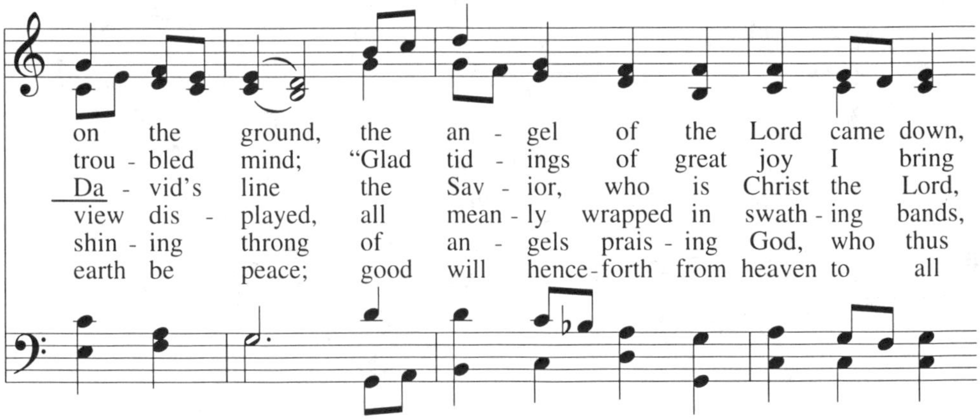
on the ground, the an - gel of the Lord came down,
trou - bled mind; "Glad tid - ings of great joy I bring
Da - vid's line the Sav - ior, who is Christ the Lord,
view dis - played, all mean - ly wrapped in swath - ing bands,
shin - ing throng of an - gels prais - ing God, who thus
earth be peace; good will hence-forth from heaven to all

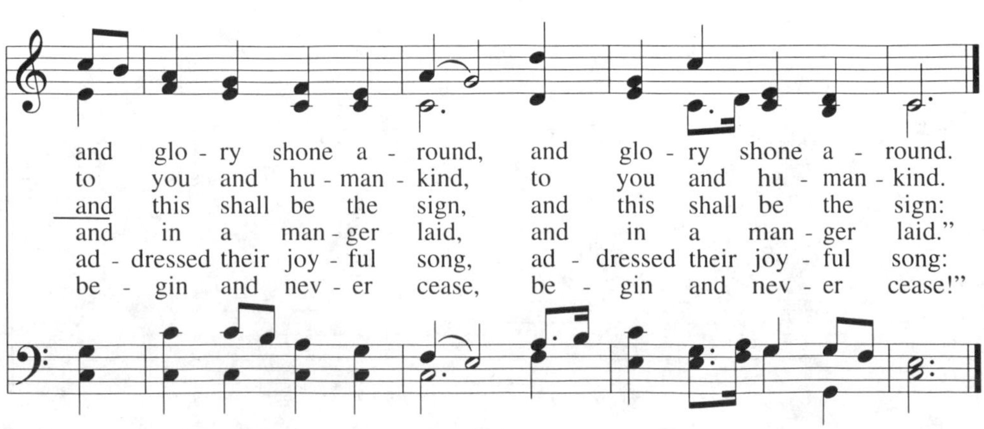
and glo - ry shone a - round, and glo - ry shone a - round.
to you and hu - man - kind, to you and hu - man - kind.
and this shall be the sign, and this shall be the sign:
and in a man - ger laid, and in a man - ger laid."
ad - dressed their joy - ful song, ad - dressed their joy - ful song:
be - gin and nev - er cease, be - gin and nev - er cease!"

WORDS: Nahum Tate (1652-1715); para. Luke 2:8-14, alt.
MUSIC: Weyman's *Melodia Sacra*, 1815; arr. George Frideric Handel (1685-1759)

CHRISTMAS
C.M.

The First Noel

1 The first No - el, the an - gel did say, was to cer - tain poor shep - herds in fields as they lay; in fields where they lay keep - ing their sheep, on a cold win - ter's night that was so deep.
2 They look - ed up and saw a star shin - ing in the east, be - yond them far, and to the earth it gave great light, and so it con - tin - ued both day and night.
3 And by the light of that same star three wise men came from coun - try far, to seek for a king was their in - tent, and to fol - low the star wher - ev - er it went.
4 This star drew nigh to the north - west, o'er Beth - le - hem it took its rest, and there it did both stop and stay, right o - ver the place where Je - sus lay.
5 Then en - tered in those wise men three, full rev - erent - ly up - on their knee, and of - fered there in his pres - sence their gold, and myrrh, and frank - in - cense.
6 Then let us all with one ac - cord sing prais - es to our heav - en - ly Lord, who hath made heaven and earth of naught, and with his blood our life hath bought.
Refrain
No - el, No - el, No - el, No - el, born is the King of Is - ra - el.

WORDS: English carol
MUSIC: W. Sandys' *Christmas Carols*, 1833; arr. John Stainer (1840-1901)

THE FIRST NOEL
Irregular

230 O Morning Star, How Fair and Bright!

1 O Morn - ing Star, how fair and bright! You shine with God's
2 Come, heaven - ly bride - groom, light di - vine, and deep with - in
3 What joy to know, when life is past, the Lord we love
own truth and light, a - glow with grace and mer - cy!
our hearts now shine; there light a flame un - dy - ing!
is first and last, the end and the be - gin - ning!
Of Ja - cob's race, King Da - vid's Son, our Lord and mas -
In your one bod - y let us be as liv - ing branch-
He will one day, O glo - rious grace, trans - port us to
ter, you have won our hearts to serve you on - ly!
es of a tree, your life our lives sup - ply - ing.
that hap - py place be - yond all tears and sin - ning!

WORDS: Philipp Nicolai (1556-1608); tr. *Lutheran Book of Worship*, 1978;
tr. vs. 3 Catherine Winkworth (1827-1878)
MUSIC: Philipp Nicolai (1556-1608); arr. J. S. Bach (1685-1750)

WIE SCHÖN LEUCHTET
Irregular

You are ho - ly— fair and glo - rious, all vic - to - rious,
Je - sus, Je - sus— now pos - sess us, turn and bless us!
A - men! A - men! Come, Lord Je - sus! Crown of glad - ness,
rich in bless - ing, rule and might o'er all pos - sess - ing!
Here in sad - ness eye and heart long for your glad - ness!
we are yearn - ing for the day of your re - turn - ing.

231 Arise, Your Light Is Come!

1 A - rise, your light is come! The Spir - it's call o - bey; show
2 A - rise, your light is come! Fling wide the pris - on door; pro -
3 A - rise, your light is come! All you in sor - row born, bind
4 A - rise, your light is come! The moun-tains burst in song! Rise
forth the glo - ry of your God which shines on you to - day.
claim the cap-tive's lib - er - ty, good ti - dings to the poor.
up the bro - ken - heart - ed ones and com - fort those who mourn.
up like ea - gles on the wing, God's power will make us strong.

WORDS: Ruth Duck (1947-)
MUSIC: William H. Walter (1825-1893)

FESTAL SONG
S.M.

232 Let All Mortal Flesh Keep Silence

Unison
1 Let all mor - tal flesh keep si - lence, and with fear and
2 King of kings, yet born of Ma - ry, as of old on
3 Rank on rank the host of heav - en spreads its van-guard
4 At his feet the six - winged ser - aph, cher - u - bim, with
trem - bling stand; pon - der noth - ing earth - ly mind - ed,
earth he stood, Lord of lords, in hu - man ves - ture,
on the way, as the Light of light de - scend - eth
sleep - less eye, veil their fac - es to the Pres - ence,
for with bless - ing in his hand Christ our God to earth de -
in the bod - y and the blood, he will give to all the
from the realms of end - less day, that the powers of hell may
as with cease-less voice they cry, "Al - le - lu - ia, al - le -
scend - eth, our full hom - age to de - mand.
faith - ful his own self for heaven - ly food.
van - ish as the dark - ness clears a - way.
lu - ia, al - le - lu - ia, Lord most high!"

WORDS: *Liturgy of St. James*, 4th c.; adapt. Gerard Moultrie (1829-1885)
MUSIC: French melody, 17th c.; harm. Ralph Vaughan Williams (1872-1958)

PICARDY
8.7.8.7.8.7.

We Three Kings of Orient Are 233

1 We three kings of O - ri - ent are, bear - ing gifts we trav-erse a - far,
2 Born a king on Beth - le-hem's plain, gold I bring to crown him a - gain,
3 Frank - in - cense to of - fer have I, in - cense owns a de - i - ty nigh;
4 Myrrh is mine; its bit - ter per - fume breathes a life of gath - er - ing gloom:
5 Glo-rious now be - hold him a - rise, King and God and Sac - ri - fice;
field and foun - tain, moor and moun - tain, fol - low - ing yon - der star.
King for - ev - er, ceas - ing nev - er o - ver us all to reign.
prayer and prais - ing, voic - es rais - ing, wor - ship - ing God on high.
sor - rowing, sigh - ing, bleed - ing, dy - ing, sealed in the stone - cold tomb.
Al - le - lu - ia! Al - le - lu - ia! sounds through the earth and skies.
Refrain
O star of won - der, star of night, star with roy - al beau - ty bright,
west - ward lead - ing, still pro - ceed - ing, guide us to thy per - fect light.

WORDS and MUSIC: John H. Hopkins, Jr. (1820-1891), alt.

KINGS OF ORIENT
8.8.8.6.Ref.

234 Wise Men, They Came to Look for Wisdom

1 Wise men, they came to look for wis-dom, find-ing one wis-er than they knew; rich men, they met with one yet rich-er— King of the kings, they knelt to you: Je-sus, our wis-dom from a-bove, wealth and re-demp-tion, life and love.
2 Pil-grims they were, from un-known coun-tries, search-ing for one who knows the world; lost are their names and strange their jour-neys, famed is their zeal to find the child: Je-sus, in you the lost are claimed, a-liens are found and known and named.
3 Ma-gi, they stooped to see your splen-dor, led by a star to light su-preme; prom-ised Mes-si-ah, Lord e-ter-nal, glo-ry and peace are in your name: Joy of each day, our song by night, shine on our path your ho-ly light.
4 Guests of their God, they o-pened treas-ures, in-cense and gold and sol-emn myrrh; wel-com-ing one too young to ques-tion how came these gifts, and what they were: Gift be-yond price of gold or gem, make a-mong us your Beth-le-hem.

WORDS: Christopher Idle (1938-)
MUSIC: Georg Neumark (1621-1681)

NEUMARK
9.8.9.8.8.8.

Brightest and Best of the Stars 235

1 Bright - est and best of the stars of the morn - ing,
2 What shall we give him, in cost - ly de - vo - tion?
3 Vain - ly we of - fer each lav - ish ob - la - tion,
4 Bright - est and best of the stars of the morn - ing,
dawn on our dark - ness and come to our aid;
Shall we bring in - cense and of - ferings di - vine,
vain - ly with gifts would his fa - vor se - cure;
dawn on our dark - ness and come to our aid;
star of the east, the ho - ri - zon a - dorn - ing,
gems of the moun - tain and pearls of the o - cean,
rich - er by far is the heart's ad - o - ra - tion,
star of the east, the ho - ri - zon a - dorn - ing,
guide where our in - fant Re - deem - er is laid.
myrrh from the for - est or gold from the mine?
dear - er to God are the prayers of the poor.
guide where our in - fant Re - deem - er is laid!

WORDS: Reginald Heber (1783-1826)
MUSIC: James P. Harding (1850-1911); adapt. *The Church Hymnal*, 1894

MORNING STAR
11.10.11.10.

236 As with Gladness

1 As with glad - ness men of old did the guid - ing star be - hold; as with joy they hailed its light, lead - ing on - ward, beam - ing bright, so, most gra - cious Lord, may we ev - er - more your splen - dor see.
2 As with joy - ful steps they sped to that low - ly man - ger bed, there to bend the knee be - fore him whom heaven and earth a - dore, so, may we with will - ing feet ev - er seek the mer - cy seat.
3 As they of - fered gifts most rare at that man - ger rude and bare, so may we with ho - ly joy, pure and free from sin's al - loy, all our cost - liest treas - ures bring, Christ, to you, our heaven - ly King.
4 Ho - ly Je - sus, ev - ery day keep us in the nar - row way; and when earth - ly things are past, bring our ran - somed souls at last where they need no star to guide, where no clouds thy glo - ry hide.

WORDS: William C. Dix (1837-1898), alt.
MUSIC: Conrad Kocher (1786-1872)

DIX
7.7.7.7.7.7.

The Hands That First Held Mary's Child 237

1 The hands that first held Ma - ry's child were hard from work - ing wood,
2 When Jo - seph mar-veled at the size of that small breath-ing frame,
3 "This child shall be Em - man - u - el, not God up - on the throne,
4 The tools that Jo - seph laid a - side a mob would lat - er lift
from boards they sawed and planed and filed and splin-ters they with - stood.
and gazed up - on those bright new eyes and spoke the in - fant's name,
but God with us, Em - man - u - el, as close as blood and bone."
and use with an - ger, fear, and pride to cru - ci - fy God's gift.
This day they gripped no tool of steel, they drove no i - ron nail,
the an-gel's words he once had dreamed poured down from heav-en's height,
The ti - ny form in Jo - seph's palms con - firmed what he had heard,
Let us, O Lord, not on - ly hold the child who's born to - day,
but cra - dled from the head to heel our Lord, new-born and frail.
and like the host of stars that beamed blessed earth with wel - come light.
and from his heart rose hymns and psalms for heav - en's hu - man word.
but charged with faith may we be bold to fol - low in his way.

WORDS: Thomas H. Troeger (1945-)
MUSIC: English melody; arr. Ralph Vaughan Williams (1872-1958), alt.

KINGSFOLD
C.M.D.

238 From a Distant Home

De Tierra Lejana Venimos

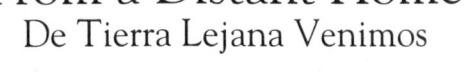

Unison
Dm
Gm
1 From a dis - tant home the Sav - ior we come seek - ing,
2 Glow - ing gold I bring the new-born babe so ho - ly,
1 De tie - rra le - ja - na ve - ni - mos a - ver - te,
2 Al re - cién na - ci - do que es Rey de los re - yes,
A/G
A
Dm
us - ing as our guide the star so bright - ly beam - ing.
to - ken of his power to reign a - bove in glo - ry.
nos sir - ve de gui - a la es - tre - lla de O - rien - te.
o - ro le re - ga - lo pa - ra or - nar sus sie - nes.
Refrain
E7/D
A/D
G
D
Gm/D
A7sus
A7
Love - ly east - ern star that tells us of God's morn - ing,
Glo - ry in the high - est to the Son of Heav - en,
Oh bri - llan - te es - tre - lla que a - nun - cias la au - ro - ra
Glo - ria en las al - tu - ras al Hi - jo de Dios,
Dm/A
1
heav - en's won - drous light, O nev - er cease your shin - ing!
and up - on the earth be
no nos fal - te nun - ca tu luz bien - he - cho - ra.
Glo - ria en las al - tu - ras

WORDS: Puerto Rican carol, tr. George K. Evans (1917-)
MUSIC: Puerto Rican melody; arr. Walter Ehret (1918-)

ISLA DEL ENCANTO
12.12.Ref.

2
A7
Dm
peace and love to all.
y en la tie - rra a - mor.

3 Frankincense I bring
the child of God's own choosing,
token of our prayers
to heaven ever rising.
Refrain

4 Bitter myrrh have I
to give the infant Jesus,
token of the pain
that he will bear to save us.
Refrain

3 Como es Dios el Niño
le regalo incienso,
perfume con alma
que sube hasta el cielo.
Estribillo

4 Al Niño del cielo
que bajó a la tierra,
le regalo mirra
que inspira tristeza.
Estribillo

239 When John Baptized by Jordan's River

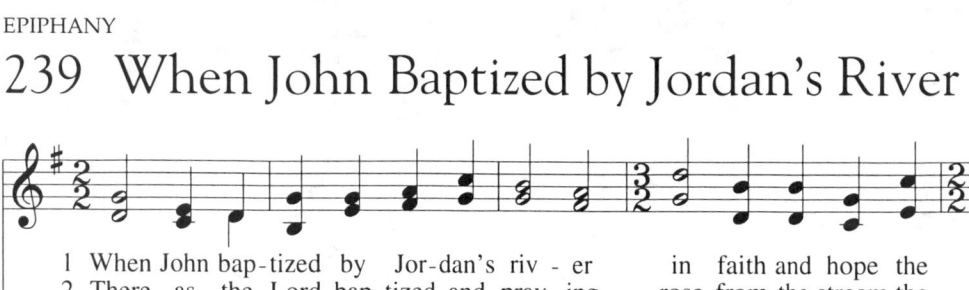

1 When John bap-tized by Jor-dan's riv - er in faith and hope the
2 There as the Lord, bap-tized and pray - ing, rose from the stream the
3 O Son of Man, our na - ture shar - ing, in whose o - be-dience
peo - ple came, that John and Jor - dan might de - liv - er
sin - less One, a voice was heard from heav - en say - ing,
all are blest, Sav - ior, our sins and sor - rows bear - ing,
their trou-bled souls from sin and shame. They came to seek a new be -
"This is my own be - lov - ed Son." There as the Fa - ther's word was
hear us and grant us this re - quest: dai - ly to grow, by grace de -
gin - ning, the hu - man spir - it's age - less quest, re - pent - ance
spo - ken, not in the power of wind and flame, but of his
fend - ed, filled with the Spir - it from a - bove; in Christ bap-

WORDS: Timothy Dudley-Smith (1926-)
MUSIC: Louis Bourgeois (ca. 1510-1561), *Genevan Psalter*, 1551; arr. Jack Schrader (1942-)

RENDEZ À DIEU
9.8.9.8.D.

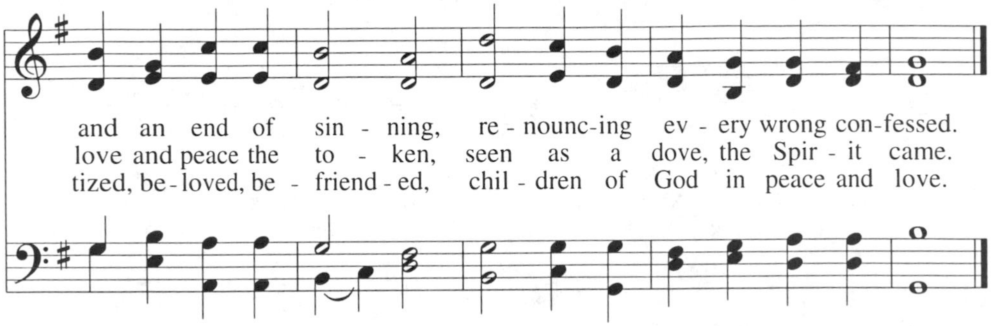
and an end of sin - ning, re - nounc-ing ev - ery wrong con-fessed.
love and peace the to - ken, seen as a dove, the Spir - it came.
tized, be-loved, be - friend-ed, chil - dren of God in peace and love.

Gloria, Gloria 240

Glory to God

I
II
Glo - ri - a, glo - ri - a in ex-cel - sis De - o!
Glo-ry to God, glo-ry to God, glo - ry in the high - est!

III
IV
Glo - ri - a, glo - ri - a, al - le - lu - ia, al - le - lu - ia!
Glo-ry to God, glo-ry to God, al - le - lu - ia, al - le - lu - ia!

WORDS: Traditional; adapt. Taizé Community, 1978
MUSIC: Jacques Berthier (1923-1994)

241 When Jesus Came to Jordan

1 When Je - sus came to Jor - dan to be bap - tized by John,
2 He came to share temp - ta - tion, our ut - most woe and loss,
3 Come, Ho - ly Spir - it, aid us to keep the vows we make;
he did not come for par - don but as the sin - less one.
for us and our sal - va - tion to die up - on the cross.
this ver - y day in - vade us, and ev - ery bond - age break.
He came to share re - pent - ance with all who mourn their sins,
So when the dove de - scend - ed on him, the Son of Man,
Come, give our lives di - rec - tion, the gift we cov - et most:
to speak the vi - tal sen - tence with which good news be - gins.
the hid - den years had end - ded, the age of grace be - gan.
to share the res - ur - rec - tion that leads to Pen - te - cost.

WORDS: Fred Pratt Green (1903-2000); para. Matthew 3:13-17, Mark 1:9-11, Luke 3:21-22
MUSIC: *Neuvermehrtes Gesangbuch*, 1693

MUNICH
7.6.7.6.D.

O Sing a Song of Bethlehem

242

1 O sing a song of Beth-le-hem, of shep-herds watch-ing there,
2 O sing a song of Naz-a-reth, of sun-ny days of joy,
3 O sing a song of Gal-i-lee, of lake and woods and hill,
4 O sing a song of Cal-va-ry, its glo-ry and dis-may;
and of the news that came to them from an-gels in the air:
O sing of fra-grant flow-ers' breath, and of the sin-less Boy:
of him who walked up-on the sea and bade the waves be still:
of him who hung up-on the tree, and took our sins a-way:
the light that shone on Beth-le-hem fills all the world to-day;
for now the flowers of Naz-a-reth in ev-ery heart may grow;
for though, like waves on Gal-i-lee, dark seas of trou-ble roll,
for he who died on Cal-va-ry is ris-en from the grave,
of Je-sus' birth and peace on earth the an-gels sing al-way.
now spreads the fame of his dear name on all the winds that blow.
when faith has heard the Mas-ter's word, falls peace up-on the soul.
and Christ, our Lord, by heaven a-dored, is might-y now to save.

WORDS: Louis F. Benson (1855-1930)
MUSIC: English melody; arr. Ralph Vaughan Williams (1872-1958)

KINGSFOLD
C.M.D.

243 Songs of Thankfulness and Praise

1 Songs of thank-ful-ness and praise, Je - sus, Lord, to you we raise;
2 God re-vealed at Jor-dan's stream, proph-et, priest and king su-preme;
3 God re-vealed in val - iant fight, con-quer-ing the dev - il's might;
4 Stars shall fall and heav-ens fade, sun and moon shall dark be made;
once re-vealed, when heav-en's star brought the wise men from a - far;
once re-vealed in power di - vine chang-ing wa - ter in - to wine;
sins for - giv - en, sick-ness healed, life re-stored and God re-vealed:
Christ will then like light-ning shine, all will see the glo-rious sign;
branch of roy - al Da-vid's stem in your birth at Beth - le - hem,
Ca - na's ho - ly wed-ding guest keep - ing to the last the best;
once re-vealed in gra-cious will ev - er bring-ing good from ill,
all will then the trum-pet hear, all will see the Son ap - pear,
Word be - fore the world be - gan, God re-vealed to us in man.

WORDS: Christopher Wordsworth (1807-1885); rev. Jubilate Hymns, 1982
MUSIC: George J. Elvey (1816-1893)

ST. GEORGE'S, WINDSOR
7.7.7.7.D.

O Love, How Deep, How Broad 244

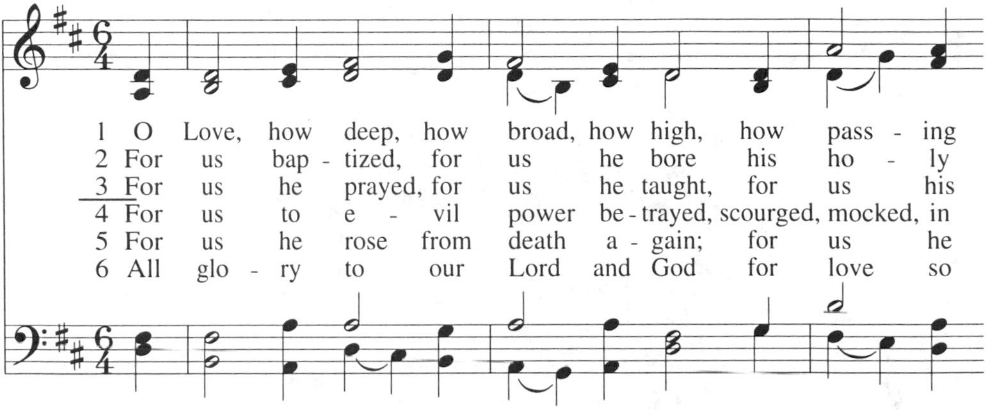
1 O Love, how deep, how broad, how high, how pass - ing
2 For us bap - tized, for us he bore his ho - ly
3 For us he prayed, for us he taught, for us his
4 For us to e - vil power be - trayed, scourged, mocked, in
5 For us he rose from death a - gain; for us he
6 All glo - ry to our Lord and God for love so

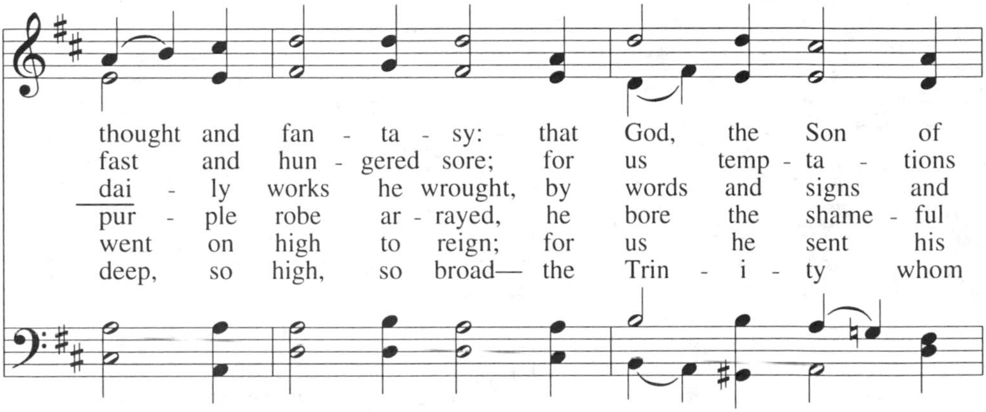
thought and fan - ta - sy: that God, the Son of
fast and hun - gered sore; for us temp - ta - tions
dai - ly works he wrought, by words and signs and
pur - ple robe ar - rayed, he bore the shame - ful
went on high to reign; for us he sent his
deep, so high, so broad— the Trin - i - ty whom

God, should take our mor - tal form for mor - tals' sake.
sharp he knew, for us the tempt - er o - ver - threw.
ac - tions, thus still seek - ing not him - self, but us.
cross and death, for us gave up his dy - ing breath.
Spir - it here to guide, to com - fort, and to cheer.
we a - dore for - ev - er and for - ev - er - more.

WORDS: Latin hymn, 15th c.; tr. Benjamin Webb (1819-1885), alt.
MUSIC: Trier manuscript, 15th c.; adapt. Michael Praetorius (1571-1621); harm. George R. Woodward (1848-1934)

PUER NOBIS
L.M.

245 We Have Come at Christ's Own Bidding

Unison
1 We have come at Christ's own bid - ding to this high and
2 Light breaks through our clouds and shad - ows, splen - dor bathes the
3 Strength-ened by this glimpse of glo - ry, fear - ful lest our
ho - ly place, where we wait with hope and long - ing for some
flesh -joined Word, Mo - ses and E - li - jah mar - vel as the
faith de - cline, we, like Pe - ter, find it tempt-ing to re -
to - ken of God's grace. Here we pray for new as - sur - ance
heav - enly voice is heard. Eyes and hearts be - hold with won - der
main and build a shrine. But true wor - ship gives us cour - age
that our faith is not in vain, search - ing like those
how the Law and Proph - ets meet: Christ with gar - ments
to pro - claim what we pro - fess, that our dai - ly

WORDS: Carl P. Daw, Jr. (1944-)
MUSIC: Leavitt's *The Christian Lyre*, 1830; arr. Jack Schrader (1942-)

PLEADING SAVIOR
8.7.8.7.D.

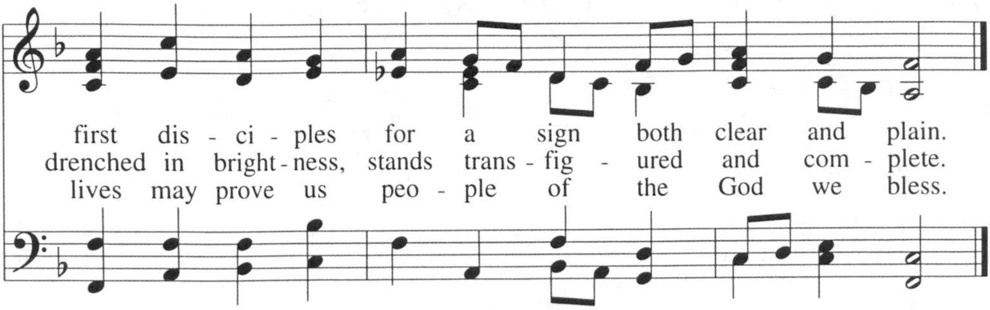
first dis - ci - ples for a sign both clear and plain.
drenched in bright - ness, stands trans - fig - ured and com - plete.
lives may prove us peo - ple of the God we bless.

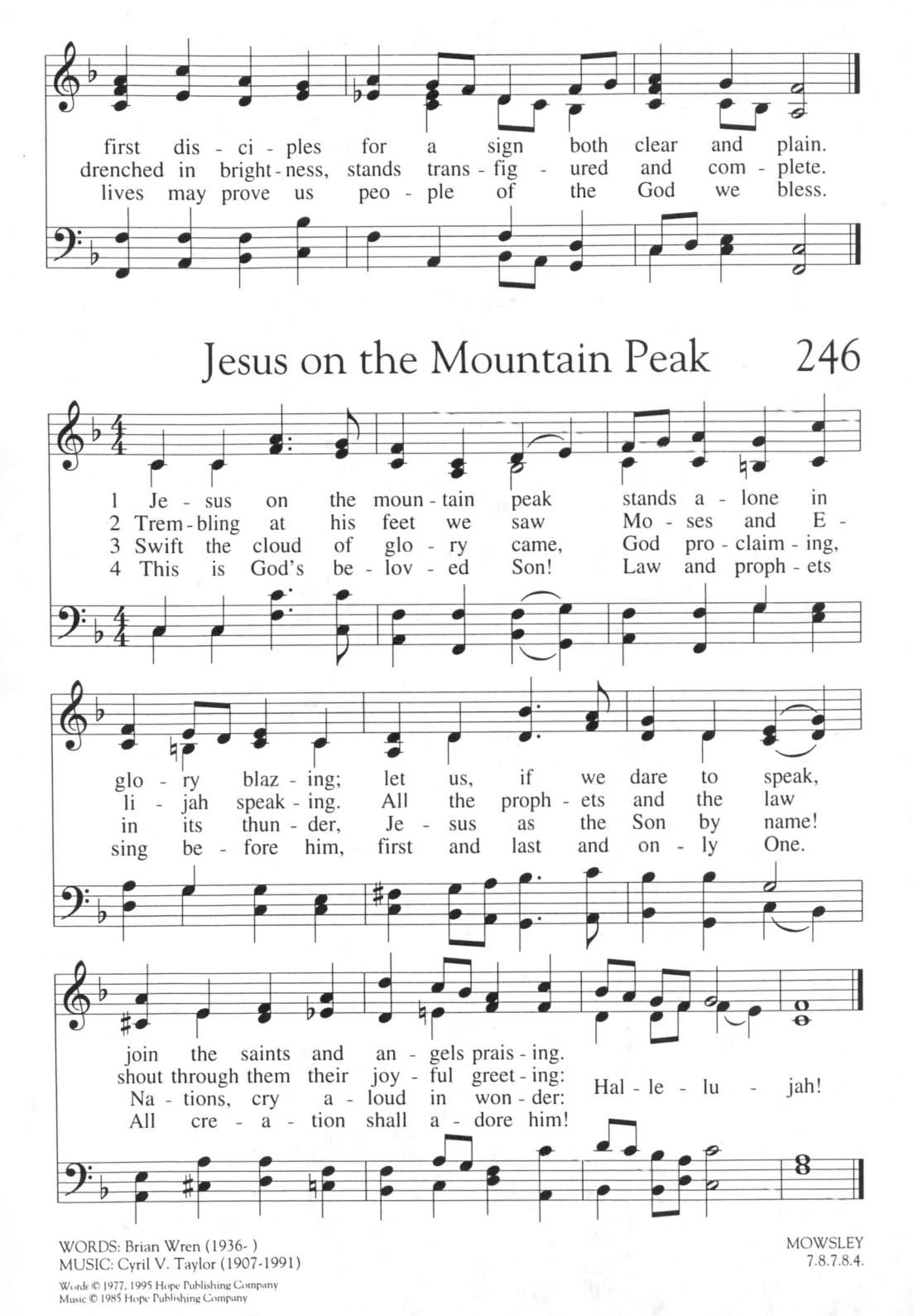

Jesus on the Mountain Peak 246

1 Je - sus on the moun - tain peak stands a - lone in glo - ry blaz - ing; let us, if we dare to speak, join the saints and an - gels prais - ing.
2 Trem - bling at his feet we saw Mo - ses and E - li - jah speak - ing. All the proph - ets and the law shout through them their joy - ful greet - ing:
3 Swift the cloud of glo - ry came, God pro - claim - ing, in its thun - der, Je - sus as the Son by name! Na - tions, cry a - loud in won - der:
4 This is God's be - lov - ed Son! Law and proph - ets sing be - fore him, first and last and on - ly One. All cre - a - tion shall a - dore him!
Hal - le - lu - jah!

WORDS: Brian Wren (1936-)
MUSIC: Cyril V. Taylor (1907-1991)

MOWSLEY
7.8.7.8.4.

247 Sing of God Made Manifest

1 Sing of God made man-i - fest in a child ro - bust and blest,
2 Sing of God made man-i - fest when at Jor - dan John con-fessed,
3 Sing of God made man-i - fest when Christ came as wed - ding guest
4 Sing of God made man-i - fest on the cloud-capped moun-tain's crest,
to whose home in Beth - le - hem where a star had guid-ed them,
"I should be bap - tized by you, but your bid - ding I will do."
and at Ca - na gave a sign, turn - ing wa - ter in - to wine;
where the law and proph - ets waned so that Christ a - lone re - mained:
Ma - gi came and gifts un-bound, signs mys - te - rious and pro-found:
Then from heaven a dou - ble sign—dove - like Spir - it, voice di - vine—
fur - ther still was love re - vealed as he taught, for - gave, and healed,
glimpse of glo - ry, pledge of grace, given as Je - sus set his face
myrrh and frank - in - cense and gold grave and God and King fore - told.
hailed the true A - noint - ed One: "This is my be - lov - ed Son."
bring - ing light and life to all who would lis - ten to God's call.
towards the wait - ing cross and grave, sign of hope that God would save.

WORDS: Carl P. Daw Jr. (1944-)
MUSIC: Jakob Hintze (1622-1702); arr. J. S. Bach (1685-1750)

SALZBURG
7.7.7.7.D.

I Want to Walk as a Child of the Light 248

1 I want to walk as a child of the light; I want to fol-low
2 I want to see the bright-ness of God; I want to look at
3 I'm look-ing for the com-ing of Christ; I want to be with
Je - sus. God set the stars to give light to the world; the
Je - sus. Clear Sun of right-eous-ness, shine on my path, and
Je - sus. When we have run with pa-tience the race, we
Refrain
star of my life is Je - sus.
show me the way to the Fa - ther. In him there is no dark-ness at
shall know the joy of Je - sus.
all; the night and the day are both a - like. The Lamb is the
light of the cit - y of God: Shine in my heart, Lord Je - sus.

WORDS and MUSIC: Kathleen Thomerson (1934-)

HOUSTON
10.7.10.8.Ref.

249 Amen, Amen

All
F Gm F/A Gm/B♭ F/C C7
A - men, a - men, a - men, a - men, a -
Leader
1 See the lit-tle ba-by ly-ing in a man-ger on Christ-mas morn-ing.
2 See him at the tem-ple talk-ing to the el-ders; how they mar-veled at his wis-dom.
3 See him at the sea-side preach-ing and heal-ing the blind and fee-ble.
4 See him in the gar-den pray-ing to his Fa-ther in deep-est sor-row.
5 Then they cru-ci-fied him, Je-sus our Sav-ior, and he rose on Eas-ter.
All
men. A - men, a - men, a - men, a - men, a - men.
Last time

WORDS and MUSIC: African-American spiritual; arr. Nelsie T. Johnson (1912-)

Throughout These Lenten Days and Nights 250

1 Through - out these Lent - en days and nights we
2 The pil - grim Christ, the Lamb of God, who
3 We bear the si - lence, cross and pain of
4 And though the road is hard and steep, the
5 So let us choose the path of One who
6 Re - joice, O sons and daugh - ters! Sing and
turn to walk the in - ward way, where, meet - ing Christ, our
found in weak - ness great - er power, em - brac - es us, though
hu - man bur - dens, hu - man strife, while sis - ters, broth - ers
Spir - it ev - er calls us on through Cal - vary's dy - ing,
wore, for us, the crown of thorn, and slept in death that
shout ho - san - nas! Raise the strain! For Christ, whose death Good
guide and light, we live in hope till Eas - ter Day.
lost and flawed, and leads us to his Ris - ing Hour.
help sus - tain our cour - age till the Feast of Life.
dark and deep, un - til we see the com - ing Dawn.
we might wake to life on Res - ur - rec - tion Morn!
Fri - day brings on Eas - ter Day will rise a - gain!

WORDS: James Gertmenian (1947-)
MUSIC: *Musikalisches Handbuch*, 1690; arr. William H. Havergal (1793-1870)

WINCHESTER NEW
8.8.8.8.

251 I Come to the Cross

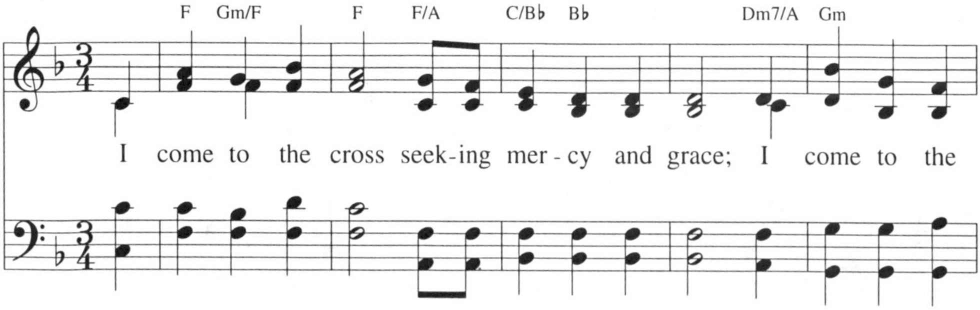
F Gm/F F F/A C/B♭ B♭ Dm7/A Gm
I come to the cross seek-ing mer - cy and grace; I come to the

C7 F G7/D C F Gm/F F
cross where you died in my place. Out of my weak - ness and

C/B♭ B♭ Dm7/A Gm C7 F 1 2
in - to your strength; hum-bly I come to the cross.

Am Dm Gm C7 F B♭ Dm/B G7/B
Your arms are o - pen, you call me by name, you wel-come this child that was

WORDS and MUSIC: Bill Batstone (20th c.) and Bob Somma (20th c.)

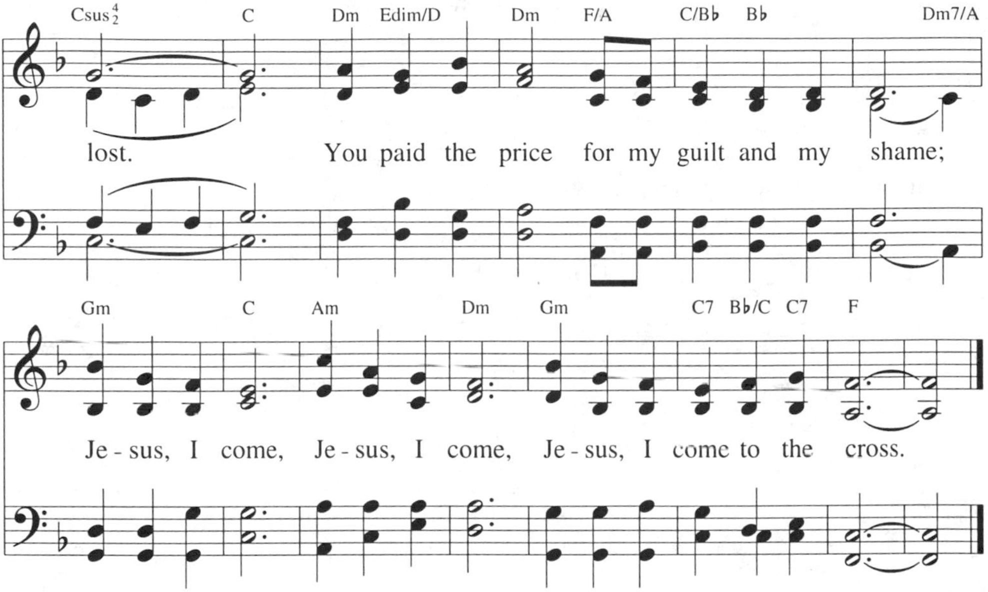
Csus4/2 C Dm Edim/D Dm F/A C/B♭ B♭ Dm7/A
lost. You paid the price for my guilt and my shame;
Gm C Am Dm Gm C7 B♭/C C7 F
Je - sus, I come, Je - sus, I come, Je - sus, I come to the cross.

Lord, Who Throughout These Forty Days 252

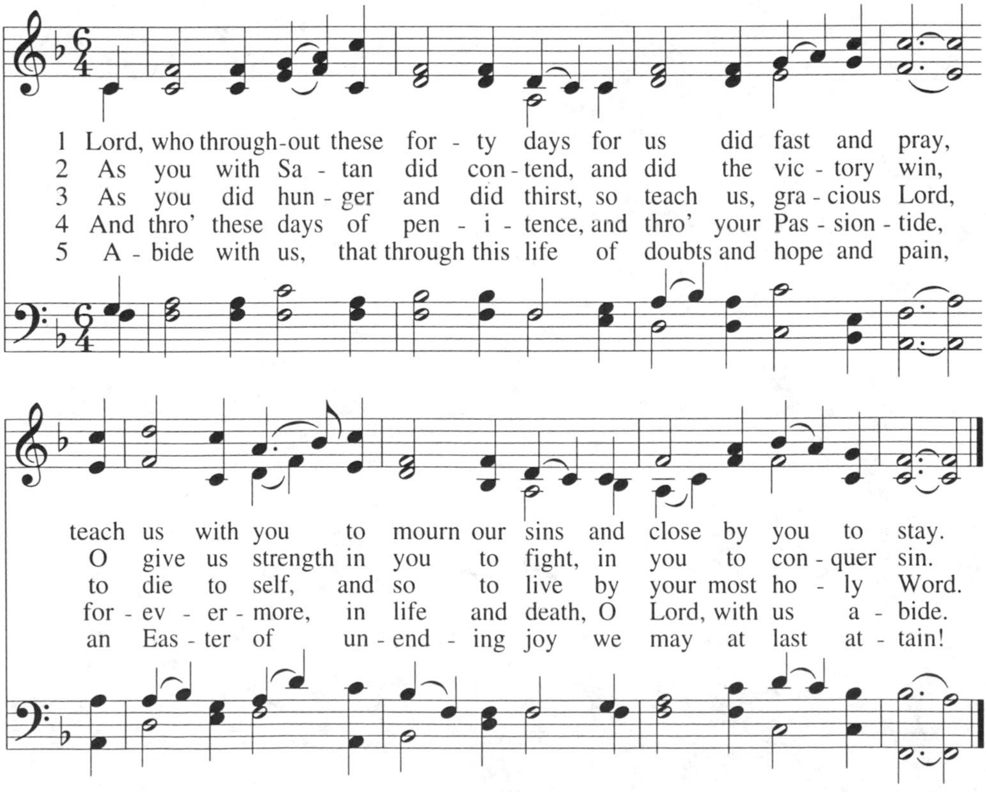
1 Lord, who through-out these for - ty days for us did fast and pray,
2 As you with Sa - tan did con - tend, and did the vic - tory win,
3 As you did hun - ger and did thirst, so teach us, gra - cious Lord,
4 And thro' these days of pen - i - tence, and thro' your Pas - sion - tide,
5 A - bide with us, that through this life of doubts and hope and pain,
teach us with you to mourn our sins and close by you to stay.
O give us strength in you to fight, in you to con - quer sin.
to die to self, and so to live by your most ho - ly Word.
for - ev - er - more, in life and death, O Lord, with us a - bide.
an Eas - ter of un - end - ing joy we may at last at - tain!

WORDS: Claudia F. Hernaman (1838-1898), alt.
MUSIC: American melody, adapt.; harm. Annabel Morris Buchanan (1889-1983)

LAND OF REST
C.M.

253 Lead Me to Calvary

1 King of my life, I crown thee now, thine shall the glo - ry be;
2 Show me the tomb where thou wast laid, ten - der - ly mourned and wept;
3 Let me, like Ma - ry through the gloom, come with a gift to thee;
4 May I be will - ing, Lord, to bear dai - ly my cross for thee;
lest I for - get thy thorn-crowned brow, lead me to Cal - va - ry.
an - gels in robes of light ar - rayed guard - ed thee while thou slept.
show to me now the emp - ty tomb, lead me to Cal - va - ry.
e - ven thy cup of grief to share, thou hast borne all for me.
Refrain
Lest I for-get Geth-sem - a - ne, lest I for-get thine ag - o - ny,
lest I for - get thy love for me, lead me to Cal - va - ry.

WORDS: Jennie E. Hussey (1874-1958)
MUSIC: William J. Kirkpatrick (1838-1921)

DUNCANNON
C.M.Ref.

Jesus Walked This Lonesome Valley 254

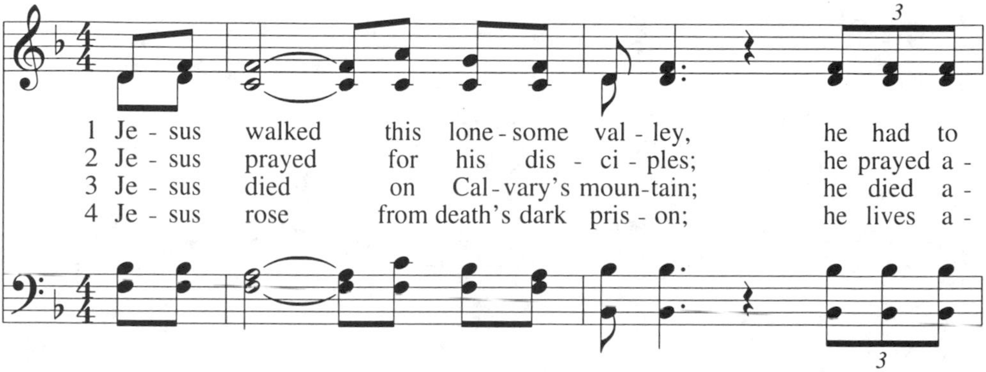
1 Je - sus walked this lone - some val - ley, he had to
2 Je - sus prayed for his dis - ci - ples; he prayed a -
3 Je - sus died on Cal - vary's moun - tain; he died a -
4 Je - sus rose from death's dark pris - on; he lives a -

walk it by him - self; O, no - bod - y else could walk it
lone for you and me. O, no - bod - y else could bear such
lone for you and me. O, no - bod - y else could die for
gain for you and me. O, no - bod - y else could bring us

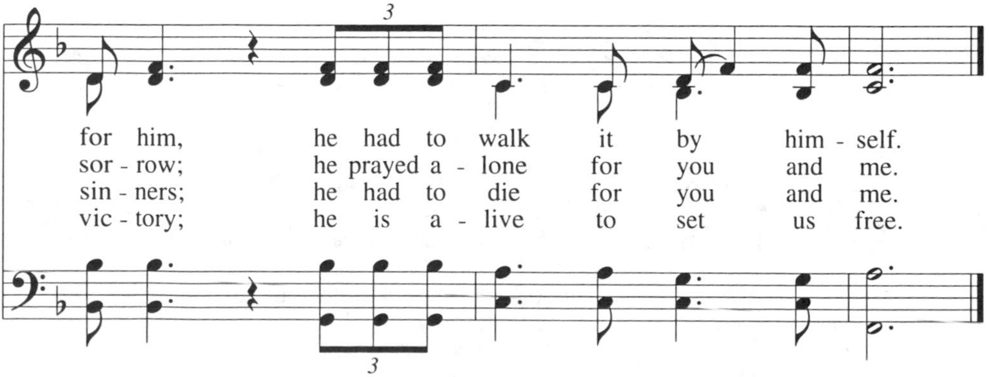
for him, he had to walk it by him - self.
sor - row; he prayed a - lone for you and me.
sin - ners; he had to die for you and me.
vic - tory; he is a - live to set us free.

WORDS and MUSIC: African-American spiritual; vss. 2-4 Jack Schrader (1942-)

LONESOME VALLEY
Irregular

255 Beneath the Cross of Jesus

1 Be - neath the cross of Je - sus I glad - ly take my stand—
2 Up - on that cross of Je - sus my eye at times can see
3 I take, O cross, your shad - ow for my a - bid - ing place;
the shad - ow of a might - y Rock with - in a wea - ry land,
the ver - y dy - ing form of One who suf - fered there for me;
I ask no oth - er sun-shine than the sun - shine of his face,
a home with - in the wil - der - ness, a rest up - on the way,
and from my smit - ten heart with tears two won - ders I con - fess—
con - tent to let the world go by, to know no gain nor loss,
from the burn - ing of the noon - tide heat, and the bur - den of the day.
the won - ders of re - deem - ing love and my un - wor - thi - ness.
my sin - ful self my on - ly shame, my glo - ry all the cross.

WORDS: Elizabeth C. Clephane (1830-1869), alt.
MUSIC: Frederick C. Maker (1844-1927)

ST. CHRISTOPHER
7.6.8.6.8.6.8.6.

There Is a Fountain Filled with Blood 256

1 There is a foun-tain filled with blood drawn from Im-man - uel's veins, and sin - ners, plunged be - neath that flood, lose all their guilt - y stains: lose all their guilt - y stains, lose all their guilt - y stains; and sin - ners, plunged be - neath that flood, lose all their guilt - y stains.
2 The dy - ing thief re - joiced to see that foun-tain in his day, and there may I, though vile as he, wash all my sins a - way: wash all my sins a - way, wash all my sins a - way; and there may I, though vile as he, wash all my sins a - way.
3 Dear dy - ing Lamb, thy pre - cious blood shall nev - er lose its power, till all the ran - somed Church of God be saved, to sin no more: be saved, to sin no more, be saved, to sin no more; till all the ran - somed Church of God be saved, to sin no more.
4 E'er since by faith I saw the stream thy flow-ing wounds sup - ply, re - deem-ing love has been my theme, and shall be till I die: and shall be till I die, and shall be till I die; re - deem-ing love has been my theme, and shall be till I die.
5 When this poor lisp - ing, stam-mering tongue lies si - lent in the grave, then in a no - bler, sweet - er song I'll sing thy power to save: I'll sing thy power to save, I'll sing thy power to save; then in a no - bler, sweet - er song I'll sing thy power to save.

WORDS: William Cowper (1731-1800)
MUSIC: American melody; arr. Lowell Mason (1792-1872)

CLEANSING FOUNTAIN
8.6.8.6.6.6.8.6.

257 What Wondrous Love Is This

1 What won-drous love is this, O my soul, O my soul, what
2 When I was sink - ing down, sink - ing down, sink - ing down, when
3 To God and to the Lamb I will sing, I will sing, to
4 And when from death I'm free, I'll sing on, I'll sing on, and
won - drous love is this, O my soul! What won-drous love is
I was sink-ing down, sink - ing down; when I was sink-ing
God and to the Lamb I will sing! To God and to the
when from death I'm free, I'll sing on! And when from death I'm
this that caused the Lord of bliss to bear the dread-ful curse for my
down be - neath God's right-eous frown, Christ laid a - side his crown for my
Lamb, who is the great "I AM," while mil-lions join the theme, I will
free, I'll sing and joy - ful be, and through e - ter - ni - ty I'll sing
soul, for my soul, to bear the dread-ful curse for my soul!
soul, for my soul, Christ laid a - side his crown for my soul!
sing, I will sing, while mil - lions join the theme, I will sing!
on, I'll sing on, and through e - ter - ni - ty I'll sing on!

WORDS: Appalachian folk hymn
MUSIC: *Southern Harmony*, 1835

WONDROUS LOVE
12.9.12.12.9.

At the Cross

Eb Eb/G Ab Eb/G Bb7/F Eb Bb
1 A - las! and did my Sav - ior bleed, and did my Sov-ereign die?
2 Was it for crimes that I have done, he groaned up - on the tree?
3 Well might the sun in dark-ness hide and shut its glo - ries in,
4 But drops of grief can ne'er re - pay the debt of love I owe;
Eb Ab/Eb Eb Fm/Ab Eb/Bb Bb7 Eb
Would he de - vote that sa - cred head for sin - ners such as I?
A - maz - ing pit - y! Grace un-known! And love be - yond de - gree!
when Christ, the might - y Mak - er, died for his own crea - ture's sin.
here, Lord, I give my - self a - way—'tis all that I can do!
Refrain
Eb Ab/Eb Eb Eb/Bb Bb
At the cross, at the cross where I first saw the light, and the
Bb7 Eb/Bb Bb7 Eb Ab
bur-den of my heart rolled a - way,
rolled a - way,
it was there by faith
Eb Fm/Ab Bb7 Eb
I re - ceived my sight, and now I am hap - py all the day!

WORDS: Isaac Watts (1674-1748); ref. Ralph E. Hudson (1843-1901)
MUSIC: Ralph E. Hudson(1843-1901); ref. melody John H. Hewitt (1801-1890)

HUDSON
C.M.Ref.

259 Amazing Love

A D Em7
1 My Lord, what love is this that
2 And so they watched him die, de -
3 And now this love of Christ shall
A7sus A7 G/D D N.C. D
pays so dear - ly; that I, the
spised, re - ject - ed; but O the
flow like riv - ers; come, wash your
Em7 G Asus A D
guilt - y one may go free?
blood he shed flowed for me.
guilt a - way, live a - gain.
Refrain
A -
Am7 D Fmaj7
maz - ing love, O what sac - ri - fice, the Son of God,

WORDS and MUSIC: Graham Kendrick (1950-)

A2(no3)
A
D
Am7
given for me; my debt he pays and my
D
Am7
death he dies, that I might
D
Am7
D
live, that I might live.

260 The Old Rugged Cross

1 On a hill far a - way stood an old rug - ged cross, the
2 O that old rug - ged cross, so de - spised by the world, has a
3 In the old rug - ged cross, stained with blood so di - vine, a
4 To the old rug - ged cross I will ev - er be true, its
em - blem of suf - fering and shame; and I love that old cross, where the
won - drous at - trac - tion for me; for the dear Lamb of God left his
won - drous beau - ty I see; for 'twas on that old cross Je - sus
shame and re - proach glad - ly bear; then he'll call me some day to my
dear - est and best for a world of lost sin - ners was slain.
glo - ry a - bove to bear it to dark Cal - va - ry.
suf - fered and died to par - don and sanc - ti - fy me.
home far a - way, where his glo - ry for - ev - er I'll share.
Refrain
So I'll cher - ish the
old rug - ged cross, till my tro - phies at last I lay down; I will
cross, the old rug - ged cross,

WORDS and MUSIC: George Bennard (1873-1958)

OLD RUGGED CROSS
Irregular

cling to the old rug-ged cross, and ex-change it some day for a crown.
cross, the old rug-ged cross,

When I Survey the Wondrous Cross 261

1 When I sur - vey the won - drous cross on which the Prince of glo - ry died, my rich - est gain I count but loss, and pour con - tempt on all my pride.
2 For - bid it, Lord, that I should boast, save in the death of Christ, my God; all the vain things that charm me most, I sac - ri - fice them to his blood.
3 See, from his head, his hands, his feet, sor - row and love flow min - gled down. Did e'er such love and sor - row meet, or thorns com - pose so rich a crown?
4 Were the whole realm of na - ture mine, that were an of - fering far too small; love so a - maz - ing, so di - vine, de - mands my soul, my life, my all.

WORDS: Isaac Watts (1674-1748)
MUSIC: Lowell Mason (1792-1872)

HAMBURG
L.M.

262 Ah, Holy Jesus

1 Ah, holy Jesus, how have you offended,
2 Who was the guilty? Who brought this upon you?
3 For me, kind Jesus, was your incarnation,
4 Therefore, dear Jesus, since I cannot pay you,
that mortal judgment has on you descended? By foes derided, by your own rejected, O most afflicted!
It is my treason, Lord, that has undone you. 'Twas I, Lord Jesus, I it was denied you; I crucified you.
your mortal sorrow, and your life's oblation, your death of anguish and your bitter passion, for my salvation.
I do adore you, and will ever pray you, think on your pity and your love unswerving, not my deserving.

WORDS: Johann Heermann (1585-1647); tr. Robert Bridges (1844-1930), alt.
MUSIC: Johann Crüger (1598-1662)

HERZLIEBSTER JESU
11.11.11.5.

263 Alas! and Did My Savior Bleed

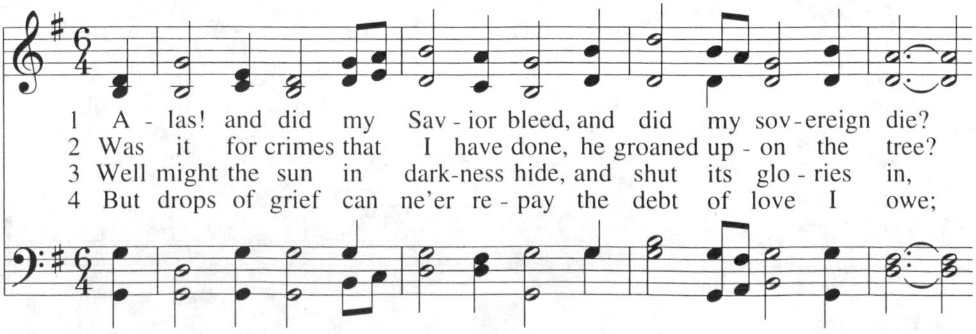
1 Alas! and did my Savior bleed, and did my sovereign die?
2 Was it for crimes that I have done, he groaned upon the tree?
3 Well might the sun in darkness hide, and shut its glories in,
4 But drops of grief can ne'er repay the debt of love I owe;

WORDS: Isaac Watts (1674-1748)
MUSIC: Hugh Wilson (1764-1824); adapt. Robert Smith (1780-1829)

MARTYRDOM
C.M.

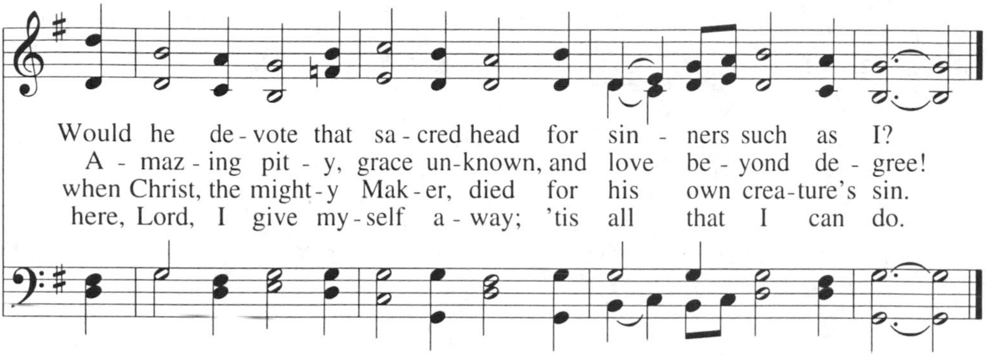
Would he de - vote that sa - cred head for sin - ners such as I?
A - maz - ing pit - y, grace un-known, and love be - yond de - gree!
when Christ, the might - y Mak - er, died for his own crea-ture's sin.
here, Lord, I give my - self a - way; 'tis all that I can do.

In the Cross of Christ I Glory 264

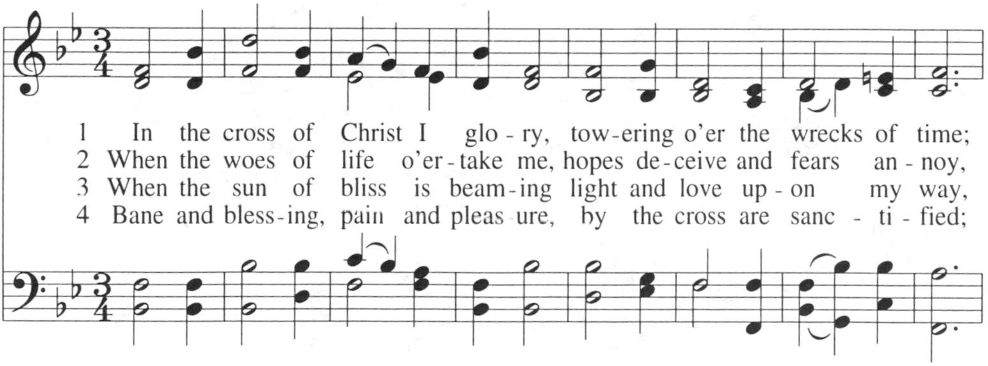
1 In the cross of Christ I glo - ry, tow-ering o'er the wrecks of time;
2 When the woes of life o'er - take me, hopes de - ceive and fears an - noy,
3 When the sun of bliss is beam - ing light and love up - on my way,
4 Bane and bless - ing, pain and pleas - ure, by the cross are sanc - ti - fied;

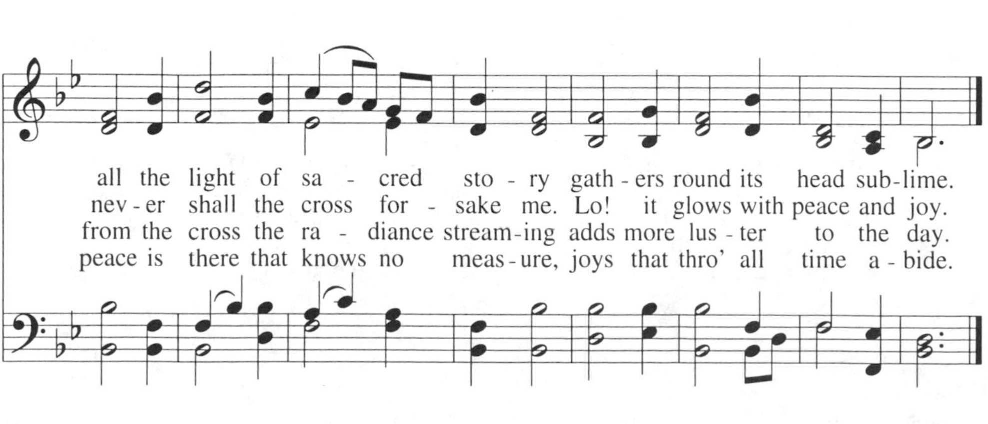
all the light of sa - cred sto - ry gath - ers round its head sub - lime.
nev - er shall the cross for - sake me. Lo! it glows with peace and joy.
from the cross the ra - diance stream - ing adds more lus - ter to the day.
peace is there that knows no meas - ure, joys that thro' all time a - bide.

WORDS: John Bowring (1792-1872)
MUSIC: Ithamar Conkey (1815-1867)

RATHBUN
8.7.8.7.

265 All Glory, Laud and Honor

Refrain
All glo - ry, laud and hon - or to you, Re-deem - er, King,
to whom the lips of chil - dren made sweet ho - san - nas ring.
1 You are the King of Is - rael, and Da-vid's roy - al Son,
2 The com-pa - ny of an - gels are prais-ing you on high,
3 The peo - ple of the He - brews with palms be - fore you went;
4 To you, be - fore your pas - sion, they sang their hymns of praise;
5 As you re - ceived their prais - es, ac - cept the prayers we bring,
to Refrain
now in the Lord's name com - ing, our King and bless - ed One!
cre - a - tion and all mor - tals in cho - rus make re - ply:
our praise and prayer and an - thems be - fore you we pre - sent:
to you, now high ex - alt - ed, our mel - o - dy we raise:
for you de - light in good - ness, O good and gra-cious King!

WORDS: Theodulph of Orleans (ca. 760-821); tr. John M. Neale (1818-1866), alt.
MUSIC: Melchior Teschner (1584-1635)

ST. THEODULPH
7.6.7.6.D.

Hosanna

Unison
G D Em C D
1 Ho - san - na, ho - san - na, ho - san-na in the high - est! Ho-
2 Glo - ry, glo - ry, glo-ry to the King of kings!
G D Em C D
san - na, ho - san - na, ho - san-na in the high - est!
Glo - ry, glo - ry, glo-ry to the King of kings!
C D G C D G
Lord, we lift up your name with hearts full of praise;
C D G D/F# Em C D G C/G G
be ex-alt-ed, oh Lord my God! Ho - san-na in the high - est!
Glo-ry to the King of kings!
8vb

WORDS and MUSIC: Carl Tuttle (1953-)

267 Hosanna, Loud Hosanna

1 Ho - san - na, loud ho - san - na, the lit - tle chil - dren sang;
2 From Ol - i - vet they fol - lowed 'mid an ex - ult - ant crowd,
3 "Ho - san - na in the high - est!" That an - cient song we sing,
through pil - lared court and tem - ple the love - ly an - them rang:
the vic - tor palm branch wav - ing, and chant - ing clear and loud;
for Christ is our Re - deem - er, the Lord of heaven our King.
to Je - sus, who had blessed them, close fold - ed to his breast,
the Lord of earth and heav - en rode on in low - ly state,
O may we ev - er praise him with heart and life and voice,
the chil - dren sang their prais - es, the sim - plest and the best.
nor scorned that lit - tle chil - dren should on his bid - ding wait.
and in his bliss - ful pres - ence e - ter - nal - ly re - joice!

WORDS: Jennette Threlfall (1821-1880); para. Matthew 21:1-11
MUSIC: *Gesangbuch der H. W. K. Hofkapelle*, 1784

ELLACOMBE
7.6.7.6.D.

Ride On, Ride On in Majesty! 268

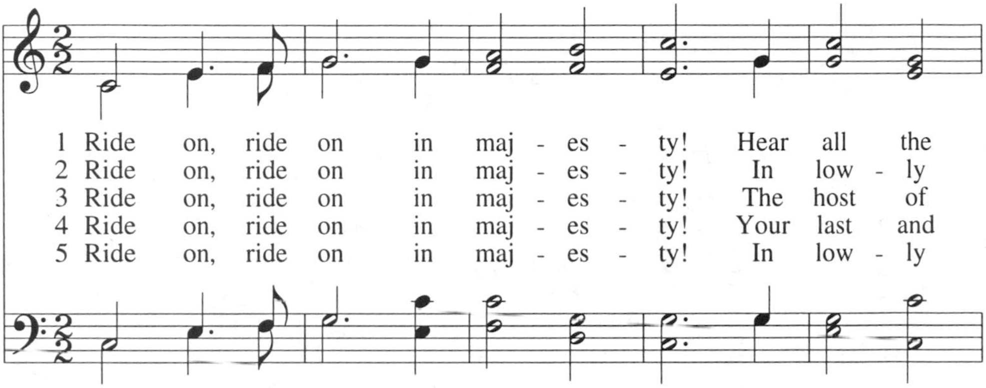
1 Ride on, ride on in maj - es - ty! Hear all the
2 Ride on, ride on in maj - es - ty! In low - ly
3 Ride on, ride on in maj - es - ty! The host of
4 Ride on, ride on in maj - es - ty! Your last and
5 Ride on, ride on in maj - es - ty! In low - ly

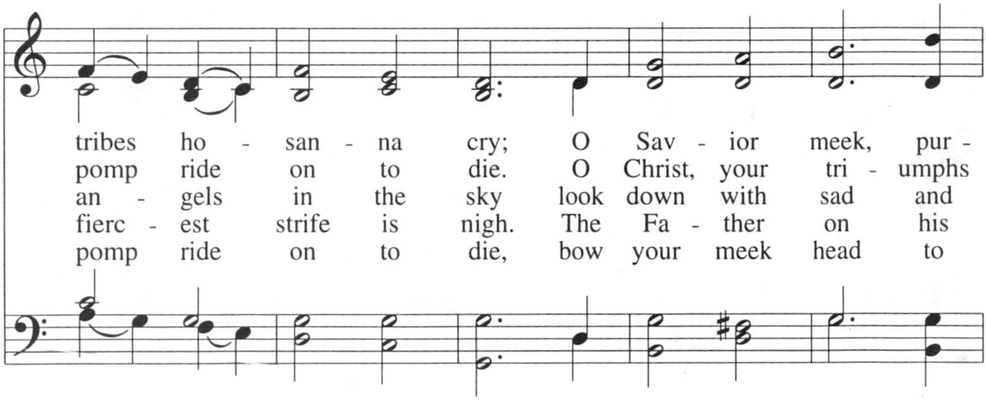
tribes ho - san - na cry; O Sav - ior meek, pur -
pomp ride on to die. O Christ, your tri - umphs
an - gels in the sky look down with sad and
fierc - est strife is nigh. The Fa - ther on his
pomp ride on to die, bow your meek head to

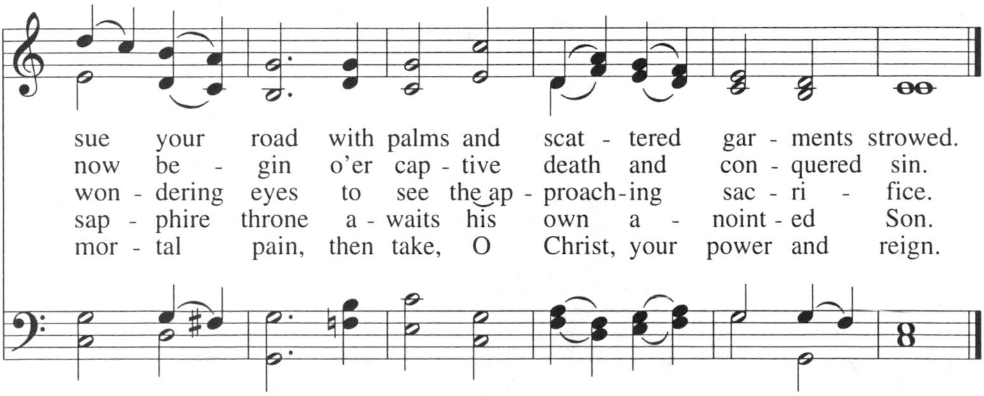
sue your road with palms and scat - tered gar - ments strowed.
now be - gin o'er cap - tive death and con - quered sin.
won - dering eyes to see the ap - proach-ing sac - ri - fice.
sap - phire throne a - waits his own a - noint - ed Son.
mor - tal pain, then take, O Christ, your power and reign.
8

WORDS: Henry H. Milman (1791-1868), alt.
MUSIC: Thomas Williams' *Psalmodia Evangelica*, 1789

TRURO
L.M.

269 Sanna, Sannanina

Hosanna

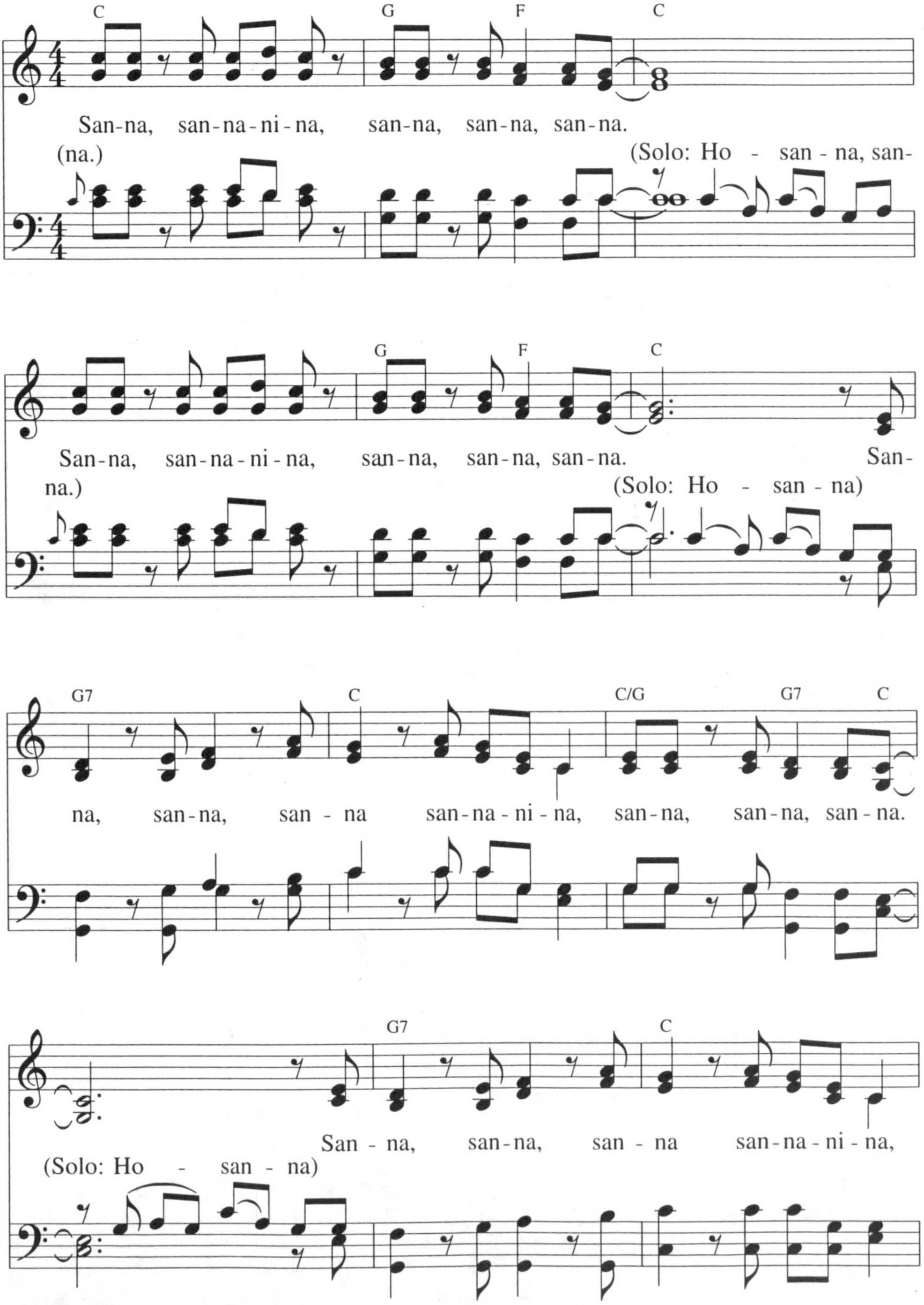
C G F C
San-na, san-na-ni-na, san-na, san-na, san-na.
(na.) (Solo: Ho - san - na, san-
G F C
San-na, san-na-ni-na, san-na, san-na, san-na. San-
na.) (Solo: Ho - san - na)
G7 C C/G G7 C
na, san-na, san - na san-na-ni-na, san-na, san-na, san-na.
G7 C
San - na, san-na, san - na san-na-ni-na,
(Solo: Ho - san - na)

WORDS and MUSIC: South African; arr. Geoff Weaver (1943-)

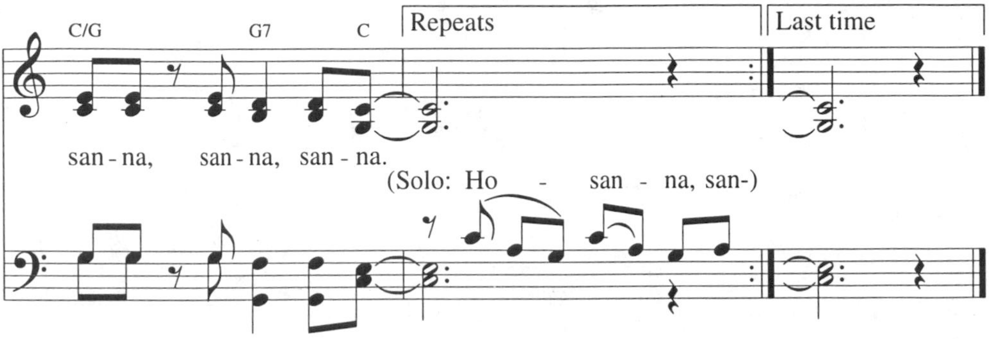
C/G
G7
C
Repeats
Last time
san - na, san - na, san - na.
(Solo: Ho - san - na, san-)

O How He Loves You and Me 270

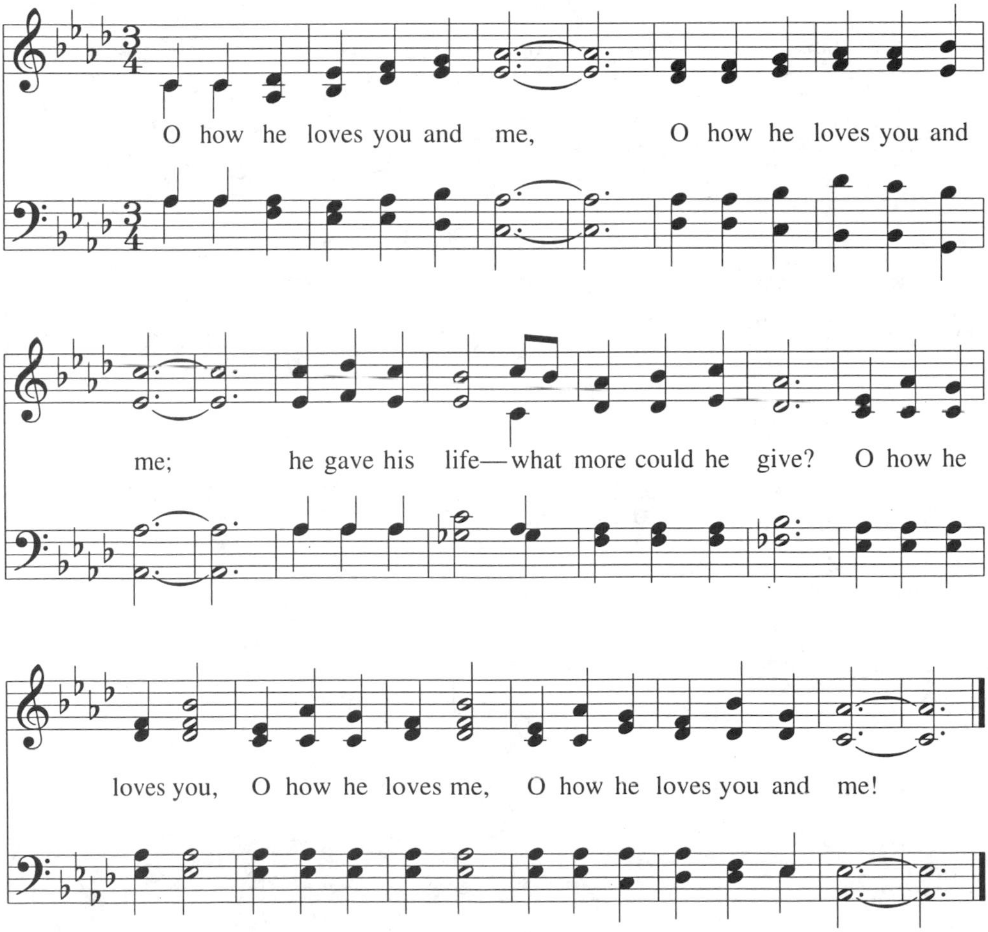
O how he loves you and me,
O how he loves you and me;
he gave his life—what more could he give?
O how he loves you,
O how he loves me,
O how he loves you and me!

WORDS and MUSIC: Kurt Kaiser (1934-)

271 Lift Up Your Heads

G D/A G/B C D7 C/D D7 G
Lift up your heads to the com - ing King.
F/G G7 C D/C G/B D7sus/A D7 C/D D7
Bow be - fore him and a - dore him, sing!
G D/A G/B C D7 C/D D7 G
To his maj - es - ty, let your prais - es be
F/G G7 C D/C G/B Am7 G/B D7sus D7 C/D G
pure and ho - ly, giv - ing glo - ry to the King of kings.

WORDS and MUSIC: Steve Fry (1954-)

Go to Dark Gethsemane

1 Go to dark Geth - sem - a - ne, you that feel the tempt - er's power; your Re - deem - er's con - flict see; watch with him one bit - ter hour; turn not from his griefs a - way; learn of Je - sus Christ to pray.
2 Fol - low to the judg - ment hall; view the Lord of life ar - raigned. O the worm - wood and the gall! O the pangs his soul sus - tained! Shun not suf - fering, shame, or loss; learn of him to bear the cross.
3 Cal - vary's mourn - ful moun - tain climb; there, a - dor - ing at his feet, mark that mir - a - cle of time, God's own sac - ri - fice com - plete: "It is fin - ished!" hear him cry; learn of Je - sus Christ to die.

WORDS: James Montgomery (1771-1854), alt.
MUSIC: Richard Redhead (1820-1901)

REDHEAD
7.7.7.7.7.7.

273 Jesu, Jesu, Fill Us with Your Love

Refrain (Unison)
D
A7/E
Je - su, Je - su, fill us with your love,
A A7/E A D
Em/G A7 D
show us how to serve the neigh-bors we have from you.
D Bm Em Em/G A7
1 Kneels at the feet of his friends, si - lent - ly wash - es their
2 Neigh-bors are wealth - y and poor, var - ied in col - or and
3 These are the ones we should serve, these are the ones we should
4 Lov - ing puts us on our knees, si - lent - ly wash-ing their
D D/F# Bm Em/G A7 D
to Refrain
feet, Mas - ter who acts as a slave to them.
race, neigh-bors are near us and far a - way.
love, all these are neigh-bors to us and you.
feet, this is the way we should live with you.

WORDS: Tom Colvin (1925-2000)
MUSIC: Ghana folk song; adapt. Tom Colvin (1925-2000); arr. Charles H. Webb (1933-)

CHEREPONI
Irregular

An Upper Room with Evening Lamps 274

1 An up - per room with eve - ning lamps a - shine,
2 We see by faith up - on the cross dis - played
3 Dead for our sins, yet reign - ing now a - bove,
4 So send us out, to love and serve and praise,
the twelve dis - ci - ples, and the ta - ble spread;
his bod - y bro - ken and his blood out - poured;
still to our hearts we find his pres - ence given;
filled with his Spir - it, as the Mas - ter said:
now in our turn Christ bids us pour the wine,
in that dread robe of maj - es - ty ar - rayed
take for our - selves the pledg - es of his love,
love, joy and peace the wine of all our days,
and in re - mem-brance bless and break the bread.
we gaze in wor - ship on the dy - ing Lord.
fore - taste and to - ken of that feast in heaven.
Christ and his life our true and liv - ing bread.

WORDS: Timothy Dudley-Smith (1926-)
MUSIC: William H. Monk (1823-1889)

EVENTIDE
10.10.10.10.

275 An Upper Room Did Our Lord Prepare

C/D D7 G Am Cmaj7 Dsus C/E Dsus D
1 An up - per room did our Lord pre - pare for those he
2 A last - ing gift Je - sus gave his own: to share his
3 And af - ter sup - per he washed their feet, for ser - vice,
4 No end there is! We de - part in peace, he loves be -
C G/B Am Am/E D Am/C G/B Am/C
loved un - til the end: and his dis - ci - ples still
bread, his lov - ing cup. What - ev - er bur - dens may
too, is sac - ra - ment. In Christ our joy shall be
yond the ut - ter - most: in ev - ery room in our
Bm/D Em G/B Am/C G/D D7 G
gath - er there to cel - e - brate their ris - en friend.
bow us down, he by his cross shall lift us up.
made com - plete: sent out to serve, as he was sent.
Fa - ther's house Christ will be there, as Lord and Host.

WORDS: Fred Pratt Green (1903-2000)
MUSIC: English melody; harm. John Weaver (1937-)

O WALY WALY
9.8.9.8.

Christ, Let Us Come with You 276

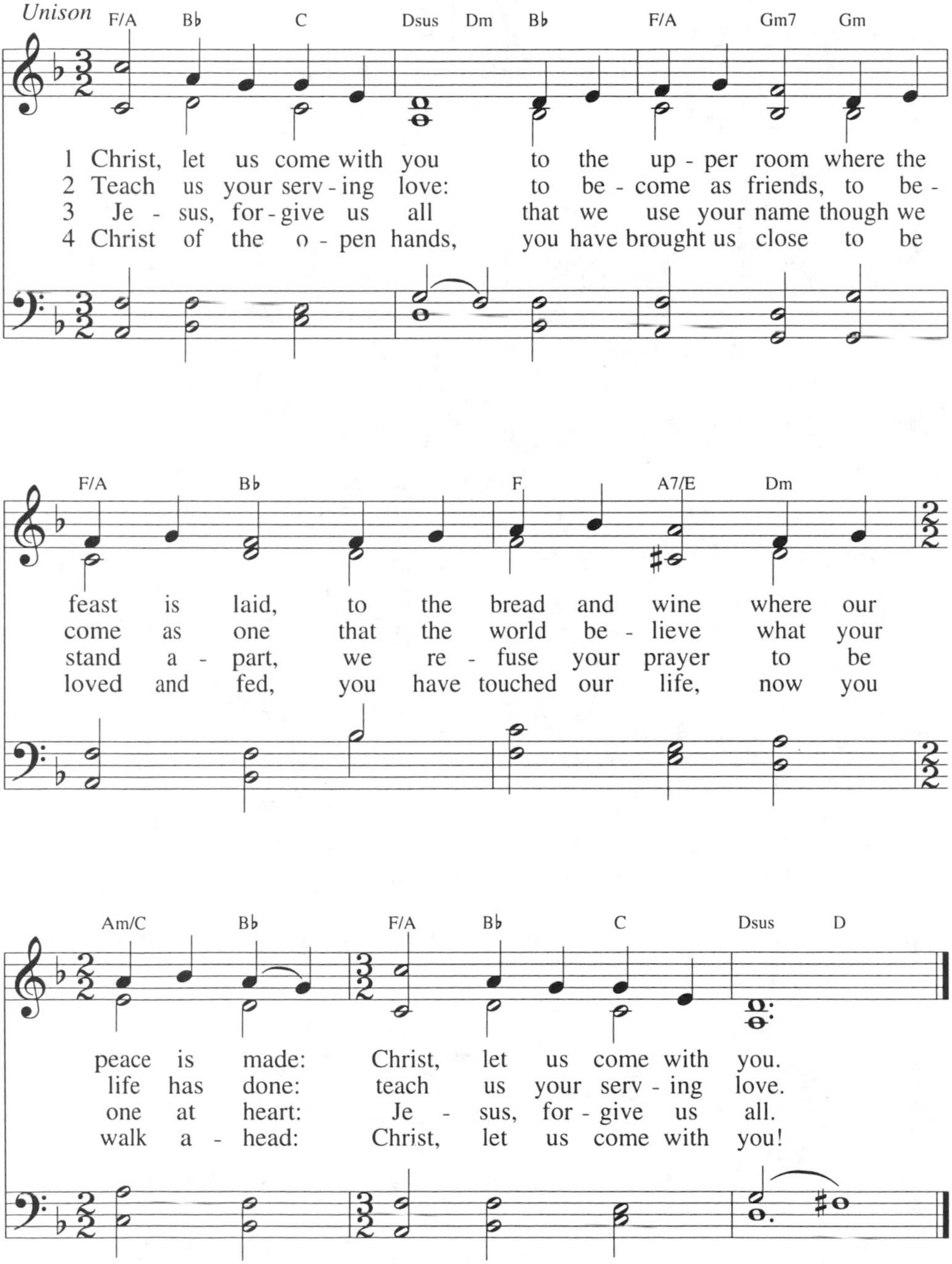
Unison
F/A Bb C Dsus Dm Bb F/A Gm7 Gm
1 Christ, let us come with you to the up - per room where the
2 Teach us your serv - ing love: to be - come as friends, to be -
3 Je - sus, for - give us all that we use your name though we
4 Christ of the o - pen hands, you have brought us close to be
F/A Bb F A7/E Dm
feast is laid, to the bread and wine where our
come as one that the world be - lieve what your
stand a - part, we re - fuse your prayer to be
loved and fed, you have touched our life, now you
Am/C Bb F/A Bb C Dsus D
peace is made: Christ, let us come with you.
life has done: teach us your serv - ing love.
one at heart: Je - sus, for - give us all.
walk a - head: Christ, let us come with you!

WORDS: Shirley Erena Murray (1931-)
MUSIC: Colin Gibson (1933-)

WROSLYN ROAD
6.5.5.5.5.6.

277 My Savior's Love

1 I stand a-mazed in the pres-ence of Je - sus the Naz - a - rene,
2 For me it was in the gar - den he prayed: "Not my will but thine."
3 He took my sins and my sor - rows, he made them his ver - y own;
4 When with the ran-somed in glo - ry his face I at last shall see,
and won-der how he could love me, a sin - ner, con-demned, un-clean.
He had no tears for his own griefs, but sweat drops of blood for mine.
he bore the bur - den to Cal - vary, and suf-fered, and died a - lone.
'twill be my joy through the a - ges to sing of his love for me.
Refrain
How mar-vel-ous, how won-der-ful! And my song shall ev - er be:
O how mar-vel-ous! O how won-der-ful!
How mar-vel-ous, how won-der-ful is my Sav-ior's love for me!
O how mar-vel-ous! O how won-der-ful!

WORDS and MUSIC: Charles H. Gabriel (1856-1932)

MY SAVIOR'S LOVE
8.7.8.7.Ref.

To Mock Your Reign

1 To mock your reign, O dear-est Lord, they made a crown of thorns;
2 In mock ac - claim, O gra-cious Lord, they snatched a pur - ple cloak;
3 A scep-tered reed, O pa-tient Lord, they thrust in-to your hand,
set you with taunts a - long that road from which no one re - turns.
your pas - sion turned, for all they cared, in - to a sol - dier's joke.
and act - ed out their grim cha-rade to its ap - point-ed end.
They could not know, as we do now, how glo - rious is that crown;
They could not know, as we do now, that though we mer-it blame,
They could not know, as we do now, though em - pires rise and fall,
that thorns would flower up - on your brow, your sor-rows heal our own.
you will your robe of mer - cy throw a - round our na - ked shame.
your king-dom shall not cease to grow till love em-brac-es all.

WORDS: Fred Pratt Green (1903-2000); para. Matthew 27:27-31, Mark 15:16-20, John 19:1-5
MUSIC: English melody; arr. Ralph Vaughan Williams (1872-1958)

KINGSFOLD
C.M.D.

279 A Purple Robe

Unison
1 A pur - ple robe, a crown of thorn, a reed in his right hand; be - fore the sol - diers' spite and scorn I see my Sav - ior stand. He bears be - tween the Ro - man guard the weight of all our woe; a stum - bling fig - ure, bowed and scarred, I see my Sav - ior go.
2 He hangs, by whom the world was made, be - neath the dark - ened sky; the ev - er - last - ing ran - som paid, I see my Sav - ior die. He shares on high his Fa - ther's throne, who once in mer - cy came; for all his love to sin - ners shown I sing my Sav - ior's name.

WORDS: Timothy Dudley-Smith (1926-)
MUSIC: David G. Wilson (1940-); arr. Noël Tredinnick (1949-)

A PURPLE ROBE
C.M.D.

He Never Said a Mumbalin' Word 280

1 They cru - ci - fied my Lord, and he nev - er said a mum - ba - lin' word; they cru - ci - fied my Lord, and he nev - er said a mum - ba - lin' word. Not a word, not a word, not a word.
2 They nailed him to a tree, and he nev - er said a mum - ba - lin' word; they nailed him to the tree, and he nev - er said a mum - ba - lin' word.
3 They pierced him in the side, and he nev - er said a mum - ba - lin' word; they pierced him in the side, and he nev - er said a mum - ba - lin' word.
4 He bowed his head and died, and he nev - er said a mum - ba - lin' word; he bowed his head and died, and he nev - er said a mum - ba - lin' word.

WORDS and MUSIC: African-American spiritual

SUFFERER
Irregular

281 Lamb of God

Unison
F/G C G7 C G/B
1 Your on - ly Son, no sin to hide, but you have
2 Your gift of love, they cru - ci - fied, they laughed and
3 I was so lost, I should have died, but you have
Am Fmaj9 Gsus G7 C/E F C/G
sent him from your side, to walk up - on this guilt - y
scorned him as he died, the hum - ble King they named a
brought me to your side, to be led by your staff and
Am Fmaj7 C/E Fmaj7 G7 C
Refrain
C/E
sod, and to be - come the Lamb of God.
fraud and sac - ri - ficed the Lamb of God. O Lamb of
rod, and to be called a lamb of God.
Am G/F C/E C G/B Am Fmaj9 Gsus G C/E
God, sweet Lamb of God, I love the ho - ly Lamb of God! O wash me

WORDS and MUSIC: Twila Paris (1958-)

LAMB OF GOD
L.M.Ref.

F Em/G Am Fm/A♭ C/G Fmaj7 G7 C G/C F/C C
in his pre-cious blood— my Je-sus Christ, the Lamb of God.

Behold the Lamb of God 282

A D/A E/A Bm/A D/A Esus E
Be - hold the Lamb of God, be - hold the Lamb of God
Be - hold the Lamb, the Lamb of God

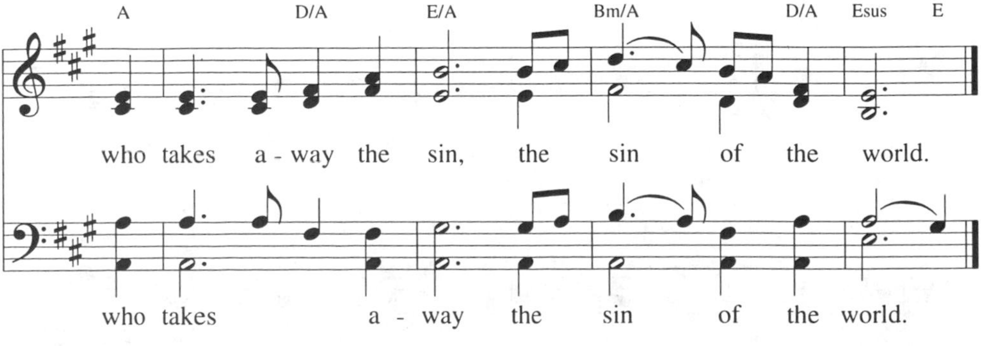
A D/A E/A Bm/A D/A Esus E
who takes a - way the sin, the sin of the world.
who takes a - way the sin of the world.

WORDS and MUSIC: John L. Bell (1949-)

283 Were You There

1 Were you there when they cru - ci - fied my Lord? Were you
2 Were you there when they nailed him to the tree? Were you
3 Were you there when they laid him in the tomb? Were you
there when they cru - ci - fied my Lord?
there when they nailed him to the tree? Oh!
there when they laid him in the tomb?
Some-times it caus - es me to trem-ble, trem-ble, trem - ble.
Were you there when they cru - ci - fied my Lord?
Were you there when they nailed him to the tree?
Were you there when they laid him in the tomb?

WORDS and MUSIC: African-American spiritual

WERE YOU THERE
Irregular

O Sacred Head, Now Wounded 284

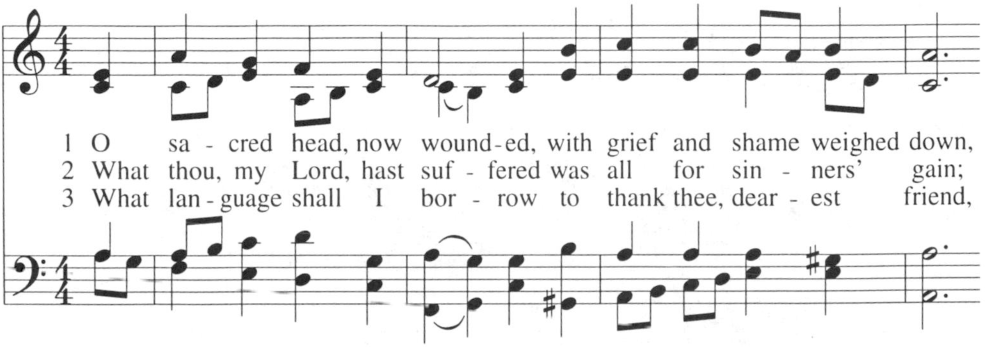
1 O sa - cred head, now wound-ed, with grief and shame weighed down,
2 What thou, my Lord, hast suf - fered was all for sin - ners' gain;
3 What lan - guage shall I bor - row to thank thee, dear - est friend,

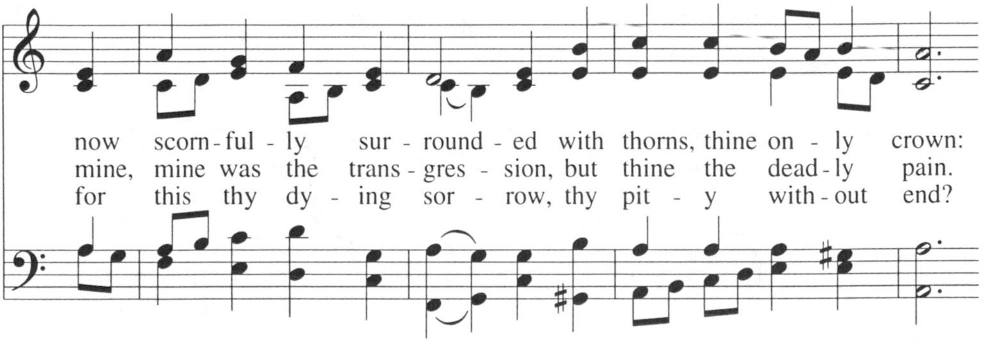
now scorn-ful - ly sur - round - ed with thorns, thine on - ly crown:
mine, mine was the trans - gres - sion, but thine the dead - ly pain.
for this thy dy - ing sor - row, thy pit - y with - out end?

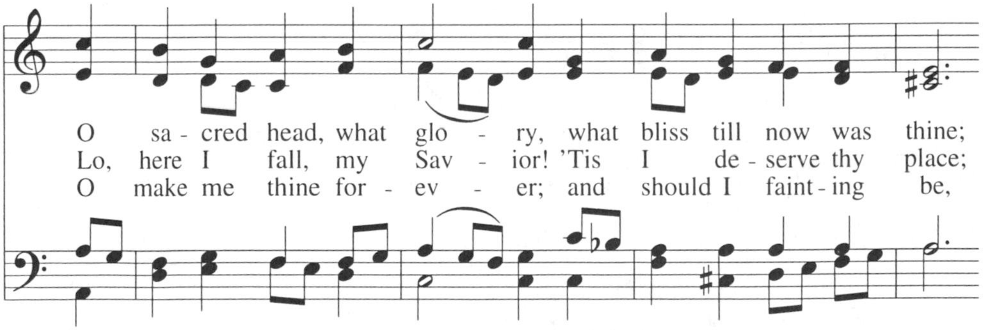
O sa - cred head, what glo - ry, what bliss till now was thine;
Lo, here I fall, my Sav - ior! 'Tis I de - serve thy place;
O make me thine for - ev - er; and should I faint - ing be,

yet, though de - spised and go - ry, I joy to call thee mine.
look on me with thy fa - vor, and grant to me thy grace.
Lord, let me nev - er, nev - er out - live my love to thee.

WORDS: Attr. Bernard of Clairvaux, 12th c.; tr. James W. Alexander (1804-1859)
MUSIC: Hans Leo Hassler (1564-1612); arr. J. S. Bach (1685-1750)

PASSION CHORALE
7.6.7.6.D.

285 Jesus, Remember Me

Je - sus, re - mem-ber me when you come in - to your King-dom.
Je - sus, re - mem-ber me when you come in - to your King-dom.

WORDS: Taizé Community, 1981; para. Luke 23:42
MUSIC: Jacques Berthier (1923-1994)

286 Stay with Me

Stay with me, re - main here with me. Watch and
pray, watch and pray.

WORDS: Taizé Community, 1978; para. Matthew 26:36-41
MUSIC: Jacques Berthier (1923-1994)

Lift High the Cross

Refrain (Unison)
Lift high the cross, the love of Christ pro - claim till
all the world a - dore his sa - cred name.
Verse (parts)
1 Come, Chris - tians, fol - low where our Sav - ior trod,
2 All new - born ser - vants of the Cru - ci - fied
3 O Lord, once lift - ed on the glo - rious tree,
4 So shall our song of tri - umph ev - er be:
to Refrain
our King vic - to - rious, Christ, the Son of God.
bear on their brow the seal of Christ who died.
your death has brought us life e - ter - nal - ly.
praise to the Cru - ci - fied for vic - to - ry.

WORDS: George W. Kitchin (1827-1912); rev. Michael R. Newbolt (1874-1956), alt.
MUSIC: Sydney H. Nicholson (1875-1947)

CRUCIFER
10.10.10.10.

288 Christ the Lord Is Risen Today

1 Christ the Lord is risen to - day, Al - le - lu - ia!
2 Love's re-deem-ing work is done, Al - le - lu - ia!
3 Lives a - gain our glo-rious King, Al - le - lu - ia!
4 Soar we now where Christ has led, Al - le - lu - ia!
All cre - a - tion, join to say Al - le - lu - ia!
Fought the fight, the bat - tle won, Al - le - lu - ia!
Where, O death, is now thy sting? Al - le - lu - ia!
Fol-lowing our ex - alt - ed Head, Al - le - lu - ia!
Raise your joys and tri-umphs high, Al - le - lu - ia!
Death in vain for - bids him rise, Al - le - lu - ia!
Once he died our souls to save, Al - le - lu - ia!
Made like him, like him we rise, Al - le - lu - ia!
Sing, ye heavens, and earth re - ply, Al - le - lu - ia!
Christ has o - pened par - a - dise. Al - le - lu - ia!
Where thy vic - to - ry, O grave? Al - le - lu - ia!
Ours the cross, the grave, the skies. Al - le - lu - ia!

WORDS: Charles Wesley (1707-1788), alt.
MUSIC: *Lyra Davidica*, 1708

EASTER HYMN
7.7.7.7.Alleluias

Alleluia, Alleluia! Hearts to Heaven 289

1 Al - le - lu - ia, al - le - lu - ia! Hearts to heaven and voic - es raise:
2 Al - le - lu - ia, Christ is ris - en! Death at last has met de - feat:
3 Christ is ris - en, we are ris - en! Set your hearts on things a - bove;
4 Al - le - lu - ia, al - le - lu - ia! Glo - ry be to God on high:
sing to God a hymn of glad-ness, sing to God a hymn of praise;
see the an - cient powers of e - vil in con - fu - sion and re - treat;
there in all the Fa - ther's glo - ry lives and reigns our King of love;
Al - le - lu - ia to the Sav - ior who has gained the vic - to - ry;
he who on the cross a vic - tim for the world's sal - va - tion bled—
once he died, and once was bur - ied: now he lives for - ev - er - more,
hear the word of peace he brings us, see his wound-ed hands and side!
Al - le - lu - ia to the Spir - it, fount of love and sanc - ti - ty!
Je - sus Christ, the King of Glo - ry, now is ris - en from the dead.
Je - sus Christ, the world's Re - deem - er, whom we wor - ship and a - dore.
Now let ev - ery wrong be end - ed, ev - ery sin be cru - ci - fied.
Al - le - lu - ia, al - le - lu - ia to the Tri - une Maj - es - ty!

WORDS: Christopher Wordsworth (1807-1885); rev. vss. 2 & 3 Jubilate Hymns, 1982
MUSIC: Ludwig van Beethoven (1770-1827); adapt. Edward Hodges (1796-1867)

HYMN TO JOY
8.7.8.7.D

290 The Strife Is O'er

Refrain (before verse 1 and after verse 4)
Al - le - lu - ia, al - le - lu - ia, al - le - lu - ia!
1 The strife is o'er, the bat - tle done,
2 The powers of death have done their worst,
3 The three sad days are quick - ly sped,
4 He broke the age - bound chains of hell,
now is the vic - tor's tri - umph won; O let the
and Je - sus has his foes dis - persed: let shouts of
Christ ris - es glo - rious from the dead: all glo - ry
the bars from heaven's high por - tals fell; let hymns of
to Refrain after verse 4
song of praise be sung. Al - le - lu - ia!
ho - ly joy out - burst. Al - le - lu - ia!
to our ris - en Head! Al - le - lu - ia!
praise his tri - umph tell. Al - le - lu - ia!

WORDS: Latin, 17th c.; tr. Francis Pott (1832-1909)
MUSIC: Giovanni Pierluigi da Palestrina (1525-1594); arr. William H. Monk (1823-1889)

VICTORY
8.8.8.Alleluias

Alleluia No. 1

Refrain (Unison)
Al - le - lu - ia, al - le - lu - ia! Give thanks to the ris - en Lord, Al - le -
lu - ia, al - le - lu - ia! Give praise to his name!
Harmony
1 Je - sus is Lord of all the earth.
2 Spread the good news o'er all the earth;
3 We have been cru - ci - fied with Christ.
4 Come, let us praise the liv - ing God,
He is the King of cre - a - tion.
Je - sus has died and has ris - en.
Now we shall live for - ev - er.
joy - ful - ly sing to our Sav - ior.
to Refrain

WORDS and MUSIC: Donald Fishel (1950-)

292 Because You Live, O Christ

1 Be-cause you live, O Christ, the gar-den of the world has come to flow-er,
2 Be-cause you live, O Christ, the spir-it bird of hope is freed for fly-ing,
3 Be-cause you live, O Christ, the rain-bow of your peace will span cre-a-tion,
the dark-ness of the tomb is flood-ed with your res-ur-rec-tion pow-er.
our ca-ges of de-spair no long-er keep us closed and life-de-ny-ing.
the col-ors of your love will draw all hu-man-kind to ad-o-ra-tion.
Refrain
The stone has rolled a-way and death can-not im-pris-on!
O sing this Eas-ter Day, for Je-sus Christ has ris-en,
has ris-en, has ris-en, has ris-en!

WORDS: Shirley Erena Murray (1931-)
MUSIC: J. Oudaen's *David's Psalmen*, 1685; harm. Alice Parker (1925-)

VRUECHTEN
6.11.6.11.Ref.

Christ Is Risen! Shout Hosanna! 293

1 Christ is ris - en! Shout Ho - san - na! Cel - e - brate this day of days!
2 Christ is ris - en! Raise your spir - its from the cav - erns of de - spair.
3 Christ is ris - en! Earth and heav - en nev - er - more shall be the same.
Christ is ris - en! Hush in won - der: all cre - a - tion is a-mazed.
Walk with glad-ness in the morn-ing. See what love can do and dare.
Break the bread of new cre - a - tion where the world is still in pain.
In the des - ert all - sur-round - ing, see, a spread-ing tree has grown.
Drink the wine of res - ur - rec - tion, not a ser - vant, but a friend.
Tell its grim, de - mon - ic cho - rus: "Christ is ris - en! Get you gone!"
Heal-ing leaves of grace a - bound - ing bring a taste of love un - known.
Je - sus is our strong com - pan - ion. Joy and peace shall nev - er end.
God the First and Last is with us. Sing Ho - san - na, ev - ery - one!

WORDS: Brian Wren (1936-)
MUSIC: Polish folk tune; adapt. A. E. Rusbridge (1917-1969)

W̧ ZLOBIE LEZY
8.7.8.7.D.

294 Christ Arose!

1 Low in the grave he lay– Je-sus my Sav-ior, wait-ing the com-ing day– Je-sus my Lord!
2 Vain-ly they watch his bed– Je-sus my Sav-ior, vain-ly they seal the dead– Je-sus my Lord!
3 Death can-not keep his prey– Je-sus my Sav-ior, he tore the bars a-way– Je-sus my Lord!
Refrain
Up from the grave he a-rose, he a-rose, with a might-y tri-umph o'er his foes; he a-rose! he a-rose a vic-tor from the dark do-main, and he lives for-ev-er with his saints to reign. He a-rose! He a-rose! He a-rose! He a-rose! Hal-le-lu-jah! Christ a-rose!

WORDS and MUSIC: Robert Lowry (1826-1899)

CHRIST AROSE
6.5.6.5.Ref.

Jesus Christ Is Risen Today

1 Je - sus Christ is risen to - day, Al - le - lu - ia!
2 Hymns of praise then let us sing, Al - le - lu - ia!
3 But the pains which he en - dured, Al - le - lu - ia!
4 Sing we to our God a - bove, Al - le - lu - ia!
our tri - um - phant ho - ly day, Al - le - lu - ia!
un - to Christ, our heaven - ly King, Al - le - lu - ia!
our sal - va - tion have pro - cured: Al - le - lu - ia!
praise e - ter - nal as his love: Al - le - lu - ia!
who did once, up - on the cross, Al - le - lu - ia!
who en - dured the cross and grave, Al - le - lu - ia!
now a - bove the sky he's King, Al - le - lu - ia!
praise him, all ye heaven - ly host, Al - le - lu - ia!
suf - fer to re - deem our loss, Al - le - lu - ia!
sin - ners to re - deem and save, Al - le - lu - ia!
where the an - gels ev - er sing, Al - le - lu - ia!
Fa - ther, Son, and Ho - ly Ghost, Al - le - lu - ia!

WORDS: Latin hymn, 14th c.; tr. *Lyra Davidica*, 1708, alt.; vs. 4, Charles Wesley (1707-1788)
MUSIC: Robert Williams (1781-1821)

LLANFAIR
7.7.7.7.Alleluias

296 Goodness Is Stronger than Evil

Good-ness is stron-ger than e - vil; love is stron-ger than hate;
light is stron-ger than dark - ness; life is stron-ger than death.
Vic - tory is ours, vic - tory is ours
Oh, vic - tory is ours, vic - tory is
through him who loved us. us.
ours through him who loved us. us.
1
2

WORDS: From *An African Prayer Book*, Selected by Desmond Tutu (1931-)
MUSIC: John L. Bell (1949-)

GOODNESS IS STRONGER
Irregular

His Battle Ended There

Unison
1 His battle ended there, death was o - ver-come.
Je - sus, a - live a - gain, wore the Vic - tor's crown.
Clear - ly sin had failed, good-ness had pre - vailed, Al - le - lu - ia,
al - le - lu - ia; Al - le - lu - ia, al - le - lu - ia.
2 Dread powers of death and sin had him in their hold.
When Je - sus rose a - gain all their plans were foiled.
Je - sus lived a - gain, tri-umphed o - ver sin, Al - le - lu - ia,
3 Dead in the grave he lay, mourned by ev - ery friend.
Those dark and fear - ful days then did reach their end.
God raised him to life, vic - tor in the strife, Al - le - lu - ia,
4 He burst the chains of sin, o - pened death's dark jail.
God filled him with new life, life that could not fail.
Right be - fore their eyes Je - sus did a - rise, Al - le - lu - ia,
5 Lord, by the pains you bore in your dark - est hour,
free us from fear of death, and from all sin's power.
May we with you live, to you our-selves give, Al - le - lu - ia,

WORDS: Tom Colvin (1925-2000); para. African Chewa hymn
MUSIC: Angoni war song; adapt. Tom Colvin (1925-2000)

NCHEU
11.11.10.8.8.

298 The Day of Resurrection!

1 The day of res - ur - rec - tion! Earth, tell it out a - broad;
2 Our hearts be pure from e - vil, that we may see a - right
3 Now let the heavens be joy - ful! Let earth its song be - gin!
the Pass - o - ver of glad - ness, the Pass - o - ver of God.
the Lord in rays e - ter - nal of res - ur - rec - tion light;
The world re - sound in tri - umph, and all that is there - in;
From death to life e - ter - nal, from sin's do - min - ion free,
and, lis - tening to his ac - cents, may hear, so calm and plain,
let all things seen and un - seen their notes of glad - ness blend;
our Christ has brought us o - ver with hymns of vic - to - ry.
his own "all hail" and, hear - ing, may raise the vic - tor strain.
for Christ the Lord has ris - en, our Joy that has no end.

WORDS: John of Damascus, 8th c.; tr. John M. Neale (1818-1866)
MUSIC: Henry T. Smart (1813-1879)

LANCASHIRE
7.6.7.6.D.

That Easter Day with Joy Was Bright 299

1 That Eas - ter day with joy was bright,
2 His ris - en flesh with ra - diance glowed;
3 O Je - sus, strong in gen - tle - ness,
4 Come, ris - en Christ, with us a - bide
the sun shone out with fair - er light,
his wound - ed hands and feet he showed;
come now your - self, our hearts pos - sess,
in this our joy - ful Eas - ter - tide;
when, to their long - ing eyes re - stored,
those scars their sol - emn wit - ness gave
that we may give you all our days
your own re - deemed for - ev - er shield
the glad a - pos - tles saw their Lord.
that Christ was ris - en from the grave.
the trib - ute of our grate - ful praise.
from ev - ery weap - on death can wield.

WORDS: Latin hymn, 5th c.; tr. John M. Neale (1818-1866), alt.
MUSIC: Trier manuscript, 15th c.; adapt. Michael Praetorius (1571-1621); harm. George R. Woodward (1848-1934)

PUER NOBIS
L.M.

300 In the Garden

1 I come to the gar - den a - lone, while the dew is still on the ros - es; and the voice I hear, fall - ing on my ear, the Son of God dis - clos - es.
2 He speaks, and the sound of his voice is so sweet the birds hush their sing - ing, and the mel - o - dy that he gave to me with - in my heart is ring - ing.
3 I'd stay in the gar - den with him though the night a - round me be fall - ing, but he bids me go; through the voice of woe his voice to me is call - ing.
Refrain
And he walks with me, and he talks with me, and he tells me I am his own, and the

WORDS and MUSIC: C. Austin Miles (1868-1946); para. John 20:1-18

GARDEN
8.9.10.7.Ref.

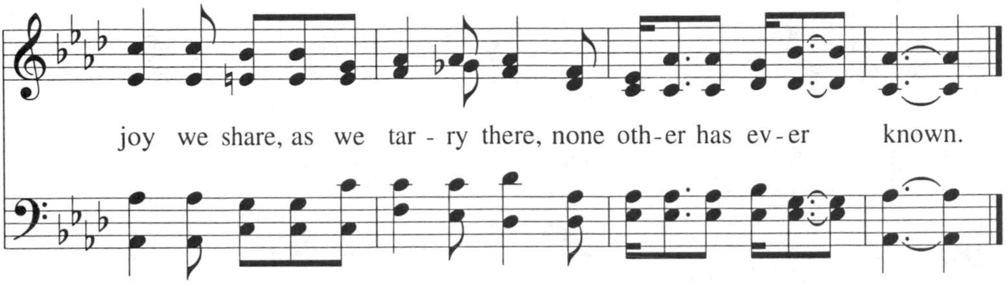
joy we share, as we tar - ry there, none oth-er has ev-er known.

Hallelujah! What a Savior! 301

1 "Man of Sor-rows," what a name for the Son of God, who came
2 Bear - ing shame and scoff - ing rude, in my place con-demned he stood;
3 Guilt - y, vile, and help - less, we; spot - less Lamb of God was he;
4 Lift - ed up was he to die, "It is fin - ished," was his cry;
5 When he comes, our glo - rious King, all his ran-somed home to bring,
ru - ined sin - ners to re - claim! Hal - le - lu - jah! what a Sav - ior!
sealed my par - don with his blood: Hal - le - lu - jah! what a Sav - ior!
full a - tone-ment, can it be? Hal - le - lu - jah! what a Sav - ior!
now in heaven ex - alt - ed high: Hal - le - lu - jah! what a Sav - ior!
then a - new this song we'll sing: Hal - le - lu - jah! what a Sav - ior!

WORDS and MUSIC: Philip P. Bliss (1838-1876)

HALLELUJAH! WHAT A SAVIOR
7.7.7.8.

302 He Lives

1 I serve a ris - en Sav - ior, he's in the world to - day;
2 In all the world a - round me I see his lov - ing care,
3 Re - joice, re - joice, O Chris - tian, lift up your voice and sing
I know that he is liv - ing, what - ev - er some may say;
and though my heart grows wea - ry, I nev - er will de - spair;
e - ter - nal hal - le - lu - jahs to Je - sus Christ the King!
I see his hand of mer - cy, I hear his voice of cheer,
I know that he is lead - ing through all the storm - y blast,
The hope of all who seek him, the help of all who find,
and just the time I need him he's al - ways near.
the day of his ap - pear - ing will come at last.
none oth - er is so lov - ing, so good and kind.

WORDS and MUSIC: Alfred H. Ackley (1887-1960), alt.

ACKLEY
13.13.13.11.Ref.

Refrain
He lives, he lives, Christ Je - sus lives to - day!
he lives, he lives,
He walks with me and talks with me a - long life's nar - row way.
He lives, he lives, sal - va - tion to im - part!
he lives, he lives,
You ask me how I know he lives? He lives with - in my heart.

Jubilate Deo 303

I II III IV V VI
Ju - bi - la - te De - o, ju - bi - la - te De - o, al - le - lu - ia!
In the Lord re - joic - ing! Christ is ris - en from the dead! Al - le - lu - ia!

WORDS: Latin; tr. Taizé Community
MUSIC: Michael Praetorius (1571-1621); arr. Jacques Berthier (1923-1994)

304 Shout for Joy, Loud and Long

1 Shout for joy, loud and long, God be praised with a song! To the Lord we be-long—child-ren of our Mak-er, God the great life giv-er!
2 By God's Word all was made, heaven and earth, light and shade, na-ture's won-ders dis-played, we to rule cre-a-tion from its first foun-da-tion.
3 Yet our pride makes us fall! So Christ came for us all—not the right-eous to call—by his cross and pas-sion, bring-ing us sal-va-tion!
4 Now has Christ tru-ly risen and his Spir-it is given to all those un-der heaven who will walk be-side him, though they once de-nied him!
8vb

WORDS: David Mowbray (1938-)
MUSIC: *Piae Cantiones*, 1582; arr. Gustav T. Holst (1874-1934)

PERSONENT HODIE
6.6.6.6.6.Ref.

Refrain
Shout for joy, joy, joy! Shout for joy, joy, joy!
r.h.
r.h. l.h.
8vb
God is love, God is light, God is ev - er - last - ing!
8vb

He Is Lord

305

C F/C C7 Am/C C7 F C7/F F G9/D Em/G G7 C7
He is Lord, he is Lord! He is ris - en from the dead and he is Lord!
Bb/C C7 F F7 Eb/F F7 Bb Gm7 F/C C7 F
Ev - ery knee shall bow, ev - ery tongue con - fess that Je - sus Christ is Lord!

WORDS and MUSIC: Anonymous; para. Philippians 2:10-11

306 Alleluia! Jesus Is Risen!

Unison
1 Al - le - lu - ia! Je - sus is ris - en! Trum - pets re - sound - ing in glo - ri - ous light! Splen - dor, the Lamb, heav - en for - ev - er! Oh, what a mir - a - cle God has in sight!
2 Walk - ing the way, Christ in the cen - ter tell - ing the sto - ry to o - pen our eyes; break - ing our bread, giv - ing us glo - ry: Je - sus our bless - ing, our con - stant sur - prise.
3 Je - sus the vine, we are the branch - es; life in the Spir - it the fruit of the tree; heav - en to earth, Christ to the peo - ple, gift of the fu - ture now flow - ing to me.
4 Weep - ing, be gone; sor - row, be si - lent: death put a - sun - der, and Eas - ter is bright. Cher - u - bim sing: "O grave, be o - pen!" Clothe us in won - der, a - dorn us in light.
5 Cit - y of God, Eas - ter for - ev - er, gold - en Je - ru - sa - lem, Je - sus the Lamb, riv - er of life, saints and arch - an - gels, sing with cre - a - tion to God the I AM!
Refrain
Je - sus is ris - en and we shall a - rise:

WORDS: Herbert F. Brokering (1926-)
MUSIC: David N. Johnson (1922-1987)

EARTH AND ALL STARS
4.5.10.4.5.10.Ref.

Give God the glo - ry! Al - le - lu - ia!

Good Christians All, Rejoice 307

1 Good Chris-tians all, re - joice and sing! Now is the tri - umph of our King! To all the world glad news we bring:
2 The Lord of life is risen to - day; death's might-y stone is rolled a - way: let ev - ery tongue re - joice and say:
3 We praise in songs of vic - to - ry that love, that life, which can - not die, and sing with hearts up - lift - ed high:
4 Your name we bless, O ris - en Lord, and sing to - day with one ac - cord the life laid down, the life re - stored:
Refrain
"Al - le - lu - ia! Al - le - lu - ia! Al - le - lu - ia!"

WORDS: Cyril A. Alington (1872-1955)
MUSIC: Melchior Vulpius (1560-1615)

GELOBT SEI GOTT
8.8.8.Alleluias

308 This Joyful Eastertide

1 This joy - ful Eas - ter - tide, a - way with sin and sad - ness! Our Lord, the cru - ci - fied, has filled our hearts with glad - ness.
2 My be - ing shall re - joice se - cure with - in God's keep - ing, un - til the trum - pet voice shall wake us from our sleep - ing.
3 Death's wa - ters lost their chill when Je - sus crossed the riv - er. His love shall reach me still; his mer - cy is for - ev - er.
Refrain
Had Christ, who once was slain, not burst his three-day pris - on, our faith would be in

WORDS: George R. Woodward (1848-1934), alt.
MUSIC: J. Oudaen's *David's Psalmen*, 1685

VRUECHTEN
6.7.6.7.Ref.

vain. But now has Christ a - ris - en, a - ris - en, a -
ris - en, but now has Christ a - ris - en!

Christ the Lord Is Risen! 309

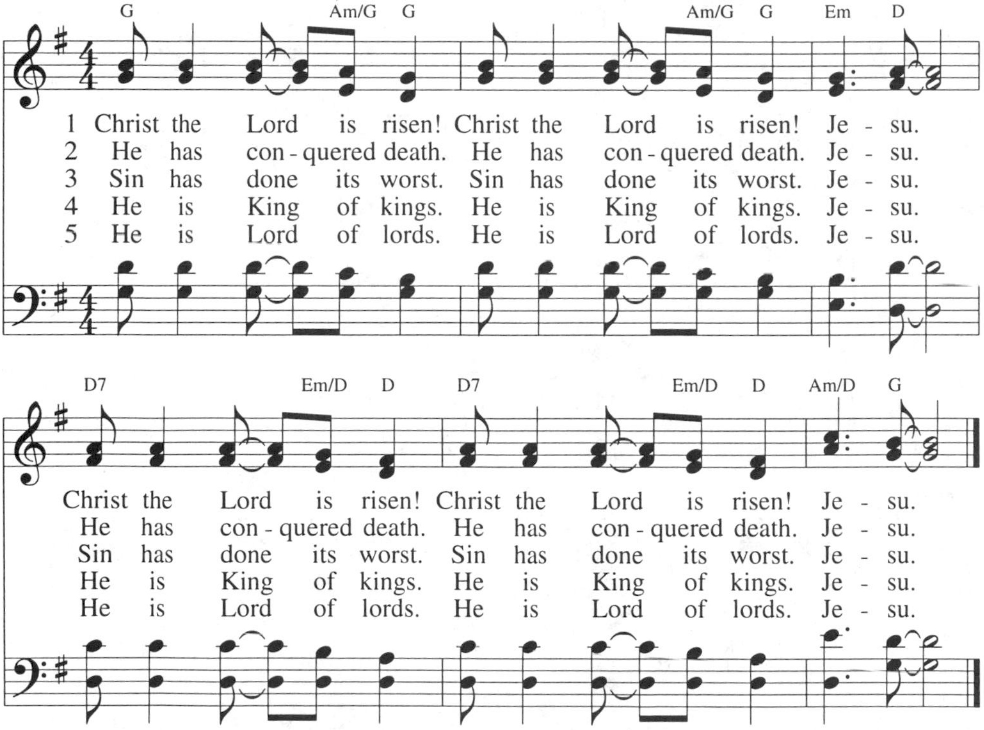
G Am/G G Am/G G Em D
1 Christ the Lord is risen! Christ the Lord is risen! Je - su.
2 He has con - quered death. He has con - quered death. Je - su.
3 Sin has done its worst. Sin has done its worst. Je - su.
4 He is King of kings. He is King of kings. Je - su.
5 He is Lord of lords. He is Lord of lords. Je - su.
D7 Em/D D D7 Em/D D Am/D G
Christ the Lord is risen! Christ the Lord is risen! Je - su.
He has con - quered death. He has con - quered death. Je - su.
Sin has done its worst. Sin has done its worst. Je - su.
He is King of kings. He is King of kings. Je - su.
He is Lord of lords. He is Lord of lords. Je - su.

6 All the world is his.

7 Come and worship him.

8 Christ our Lord is risen!

9 Hallelujah!

WORDS: Tom Colvin (1925-2000)
MUSIC: Ghana folk song; adapt. Tom Colvin (1925-2000); arr. Kevin R. Hackett (1956-)

GARU
Irregular

310 Thine Is the Glory

1 Thine is the glo - ry, ris - en, con-quering Son; end - less is the
2 Lo! Je - sus meets us, ris - en from the tomb; lov - ing - ly he
3 No more we doubt thee, glo - rious Prince of life! Life is nought with-
vic - tory thou o'er death hast won. An - gels in bright rai - ment
greets us, scat - ters fear and gloom. Let his church with glad - ness
out thee: aid us in our strife. Make us more than con-querors,
rolled the stone a - way, kept the fold - ed grave-clothes
hymns of tri - umph sing, for her Lord now liv - eth:
through thy death - less love: bring us safe through Jor - dan
Refrain
where thy bod - y lay.
death hath lost its sting. Thine is the glo - ry, ris - en, con-quering Son;
to thy home a - bove.

WORDS: Edmond L. Budry (1854-1932); tr. R. Birch Hoyle (1875-1939)
MUSIC: George Frideric Handel (1685-1759)

JUDAS MACCABEUS
5.5.6.5.6.5.6.5.Ref.

end - less is the vic - tory thou o'er death hast won.
8

Now the Green Blade Rises 311

Unison
1 Now the green blade ris - es from the bur - ied grain, wheat that in dark earth man - y days has lain; love lives a - gain that with the dead has been;
2 In the grave they laid him, love by ha - tred slain, think - ing that he would nev - er wake a - gain, laid in the earth like grain that sleeps un - seen;
3 Forth he came at Eas - ter, like the ris - en grain, he that for three days in the grave had lain; raised from the dead, my liv - ing Lord is seen;
4 When our hearts are win - tery, griev - ing, or in pain, your touch can call us back to life a - gain, fields of our hearts that dead and bare have been;
love is come a - gain like wheat a - ris - ing green.

WORDS: J.M.C. Crum (1872-1958)
MUSIC: French carol, 15th c.

NOËL NOUVELET
11.10.10.11.

312 Christ Is Alive!

1 Christ is a - live! Let Chris - tians sing. The cross stands
2 Christ is a - live! No long - er bound to dis - tant
3 In ev - ery in - sult, rift, and war, where col - or,
4 Wom - en and men, in age and youth, can feel the
5 Christ is a - live and comes to bring good news to
emp - ty to the sky. Let streets and homes with
years in Pal - es - tine, but sav - ing, heal - ing,
scorn, or wealth di - vide, Christ suf - fers still, yet
Spir - it, hear the call, and find the way, the
this and ev - ery age; till earth and sky and
prais - es ring. Love, drowned in death, shall nev - er die.
here and now, and touch - ing ev - ery place and time.
loves the more, and lives, where e - ven hope has died.
life, the truth, re - vealed in Je - sus, freed for all.
o - cean ring with joy, with jus - tice, love, and praise.
8

WORDS: Brian Wren (1936-)
MUSIC: Thomas Williams' *Psalmodia Evangelica*, 1789

TRURO
L.M.

O Sons and Daughters, Let Us Sing! 313

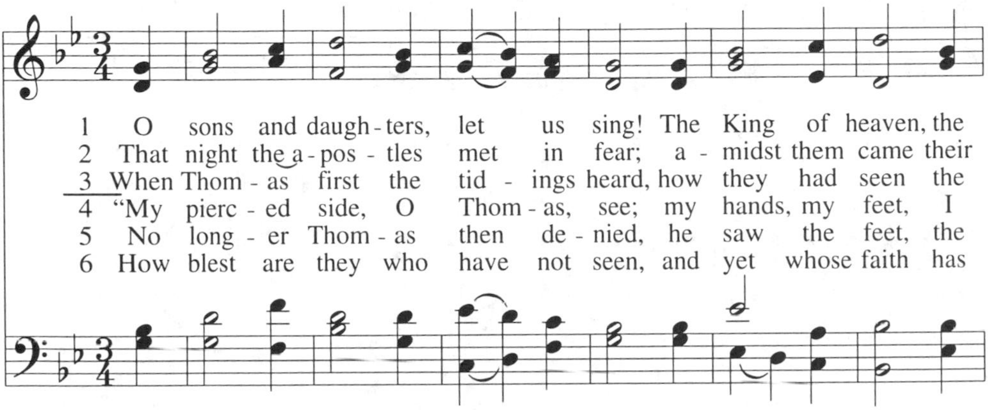
1 O sons and daugh - ters, let us sing! The King of heaven, the
2 That night the a - pos - tles met in fear; a - midst them came their
3 When Thom - as first the tid - ings heard, how they had seen the
4 "My pierc - ed side, O Thom - as, see; my hands, my feet, I
5 No long - er Thom - as then de - nied, he saw the feet, the
6 How blest are they who have not seen, and yet whose faith has

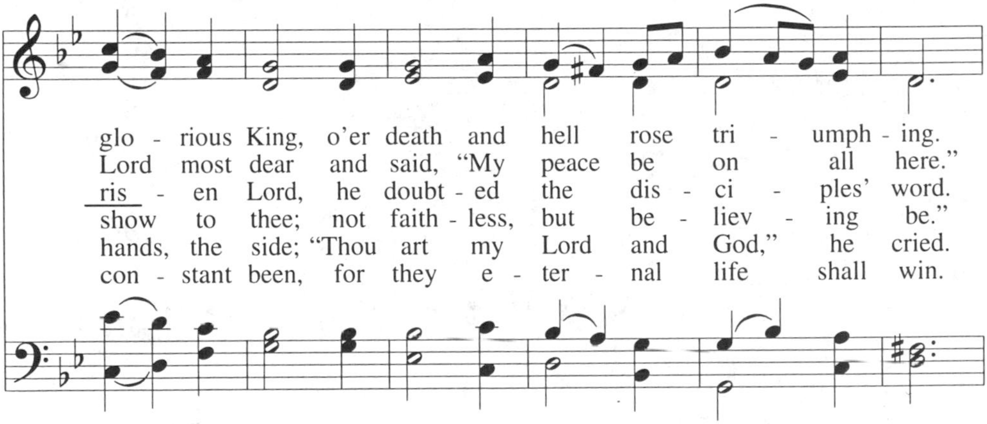
glo - rious King, o'er death and hell rose tri - umph - ing.
Lord most dear and said, "My peace be on all here."
ris - en Lord, he doubt - ed the dis - ci - ples' word.
show to thee; not faith - less, but be - liev - ing be."
hands, the side; "Thou art my Lord and God," he cried.
con - stant been, for they e - ter - nal life shall win.

Al - le - lu - ia! Al - le - lu - ia!

WORDS: Attr. Jean Tisserand (d. 1494); tr. John M. Neale (1818-1866), alt.
MUSIC: French melody, 15th c.; *Airs sur les hymnes sacrez*, 1623

O FILII ET FILIAE
8.8.8.Alleluias

314 Easter Song

Eb Bb Eb Bb Eb Bb Eb Bb Eb Ab Eb
Hear the bells ring-ing, they're sing-ing that we can be born a -
Bb F Bb F Bb Eb Bb Eb Bb
gain. Hear the bells ring-ing, they're
Eb Bb Eb Bb Eb Ab Eb Bb F Bb F Bb
sing - ing, "Christ is ris - en from the dead."
Gm Gm/F Eb maj7 Gm Gm/F
The an - gel up - on the tomb-stone said, "He is ris - en,

WORDS and MUSIC: Anne Herring (1945-)

Ebmaj7
Eb
Cm
Gm/Bb
Abmaj7
Ab
Gm
just as he said. Quick-ly now, go tell his dis - ci-ples that Je - sus
Gm/F
Ebmaj7
Eb
Eb
Bb/D
Cm
Cm/Bb
Ab
Christ is no long - er dead!" Joy to the world, he is ris -
Eb
Ab
Eb
Bb
F
Bb
F
Eb
en, al - le - lu - ia, he's ris - en, al - le - lu - ia, he's ris -
Bb
Eb
Bb
Eb
en, al - le - lu - ia! Al - le - lu - ia!

315 This Is the Feast of Victory

Refrain (Unison)
This is the feast of vic - to - ry for our God.
Al - le - lu - ia! Al - le - lu - ia! Al - le - lu - ia!
1 Wor - thy is Christ, the Lamb who was slain, whose
2 Pow - er, rich - es, wis - dom, and strength, and
3 Sing with all the peo - ple of God, and
4 Bless - ing, hon - or, glo - ry, and might be to
5 For the Lamb who was slain has be -
to Refrain
blood set us free to be peo - ple of God.
hon - or, bless - ing, and glo - ry are his.
join in the hymn of all cre - a - tion.
God and the Lamb for - ev - er. A - men.
gun his reign. Al - le - lu - ia! (to Final Refrain)

WORDS: John W. Arthur (1922-1980); para. Revelation 5:12-13
MUSIC: Richard Hillert (1923-)

FESTIVAL CANTICLE
Irregular

Final Refrain
This is the feast of vic - to - ry for our God.
Al - le - lu - ia! Al - le - lu - ia! Al - le - lu - ia!

Alleluia 316

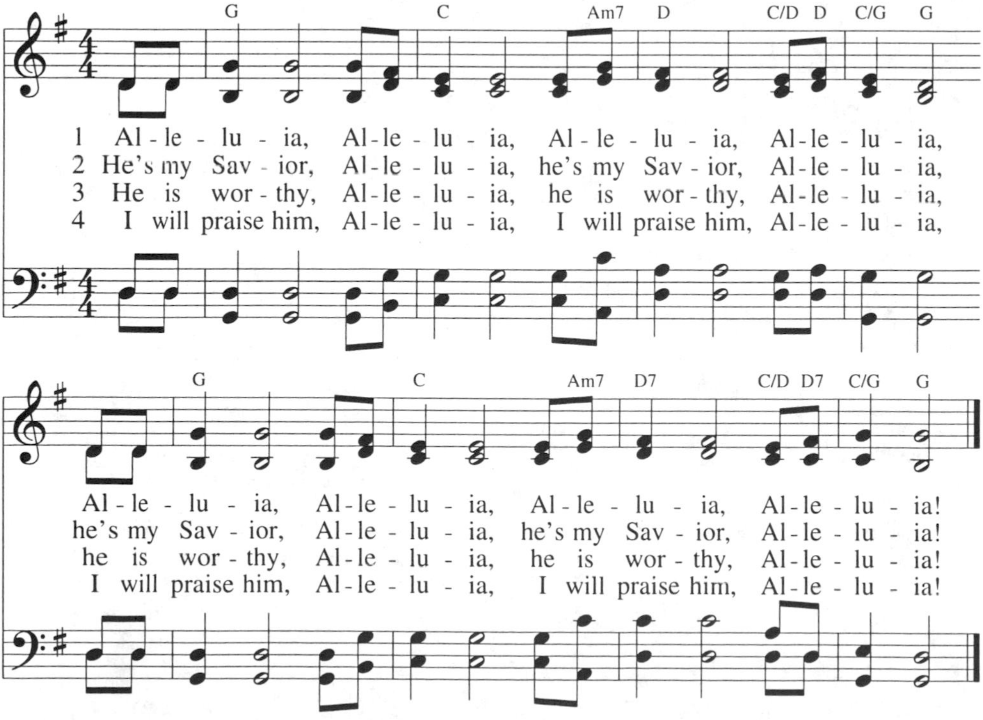
G C Am7 D C/D D C/G G
1 Al - le - lu - ia, Al - le - lu - ia, Al - le - lu - ia, Al - le - lu - ia,
2 He's my Sav - ior, Al - le - lu - ia, he's my Sav - ior, Al - le - lu - ia,
3 He is wor - thy, Al - le - lu - ia, he is wor - thy, Al - le - lu - ia,
4 I will praise him, Al - le - lu - ia, I will praise him, Al - le - lu - ia,
G C Am7 D7 C/D D7 C/G G
Al - le - lu - ia, Al - le - lu - ia, Al - le - lu - ia, Al - le - lu - ia!
he's my Sav - ior, Al - le - lu - ia, he's my Sav - ior, Al - le - lu - ia!
he is wor - thy, Al - le - lu - ia, he is wor - thy, Al - le - lu - ia!
I will praise him, Al - le - lu - ia, I will praise him, Al - le - lu - ia!

WORDS and MUSIC: Jerry Sinclair (1943-1993)

ALLELUIA
L.M.

317 Crown Him with Many Crowns

1 Crown him with man - y crowns, the Lamb up - on his throne.
2 Crown him the Lord of life, who tri-umphed o'er the grave,
3 Crown him the Lord of love; be - hold his hands and side,
4 Crown him the Lord of years, the po - ten - tate of time,

Hark! how the heaven-ly an - them drowns all mu - sic but its own.
and rose vic - to - rious in the strife for those he came to save;
rich wounds, yet vis - i - ble a - bove, in beau - ty glo - ri - fied;
cre - a - tor of the roll - ing spheres, in - ef - fa - bly sub - lime.

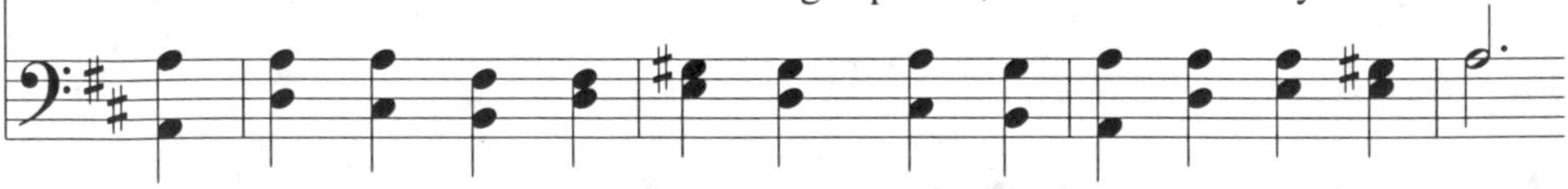

A - wake, my soul, and sing of him who died for thee,
his glo - ries now we sing who died and rose on high,
no an - gels in the sky can ful - ly bear that sight,
All hail, Re - deem - er, hail! for thou hast died for me;

and hail him as thy match-less king through all e - ter - ni - ty.
who died e - ter - nal life to bring, and lives that death may die.
but down-ward bend their burn - ing eyes at mys - ter - ies so bright.
thy praise shall nev - er, nev - er fail through-out e - ter - ni - ty.

8

WORDS: Matthew Bridges (1800-1894) and Godfrey Thring (1823-1903)
MUSIC: George J. Elvey (1816-1893)

DIADEMATA
S.M.D.

Jesus Comes with Clouds Descending 318

1 Je - sus comes with clouds de - scend - ing; see the Lamb for
2 Ev - ery eye shall then be - hold you robed in awe - some
3 Yes, a - men! Let all a - dore you, high on your e -
sin - ners slain! Thou - sand, thou - sand saints at - tend - ing
maj - es - ty; those who jeered and mocked and sold you,
ter - nal throne; crowns and em - pires fall be - fore you,
join to sing the glad re - frain: Al - le - lu - ia!
pierced and nailed you to the tree, shamed and griev - ing,
claim the king - dom for your own. Come, Lord Je - sus,
Al - le - lu - ia! Christ the Lord re - turns to reign!
shamed and griev - ing, shall their true Mes - si - ah see.
come, Lord Je - sus, ev - er - last - ing Christ, come down!

WORDS: Charles Wesley (1707-1788), alt.
MUSIC: Henry T. Smart (1813-1879)

REGENT SQUARE
8.7.8.7.8.7.

319 Shine, Jesus, Shine

Unison
A D/A A E/A
1 Lord, the light of your love is shin - ing,
2 Lord, I come to your awe - some pres - ence,
3 As we gaze on your king - ly bright - ness,
A D/A A E/A D E/D
in the midst of the dark - ness shin - ing; Je - sus, light of the
from the shad - ows in - to your ra - di - ance; by the blood I may
so our fac - es dis - play your like - ness; ev - er chang - ing from
C#m F#m D E/D C#m F#m
world, shine up - on us, set us free by the truth you now bring us,
en - ter your bright - ness, search me, try me, con - sume all my dark - ness,
glo - ry to glo - ry, mir - rored here may our lives tell your sto - ry,
G Esus E G Esus E
shine on me, shine on me.
shine on me, shine on me.
shine on me, shine on me.

WORDS and MUSIC: Graham Kendrick (1950-)

Refrain
A E/A A D Bm A/C♯ Bm/D B7/D♯ E
Shine, Je - sus, shine, fill this land with the Fa-ther's glo - ry;
A E/A A D Bm A/C♯ Bm/D Bm G Esus E
blaze, Spir - it, blaze, set our hearts on fire.
A E/A A D Bm A/C♯ Bm/D B7/D♯ E
Flow, riv - er, flow, flood the na - tions with grace and mer - cy;
A E/A A D Bm A/C♯ Bm/D E7 A D/A
send forth your Word, Lord, and let there be light.
1, 2
E/A D/A
Final ending
E/A D/A A D/A A

320 Alleluia, Sing to Jesus!

1 Al - le - lu - ia, sing to Je - sus! his the scep - ter, his the throne:
2 Al - le - lu - ia! not as or - phans are we left in sor - row now;
3 Al - le - lu - ia! heav-enly High Priest, here on earth our help, our stay;
Al - le - lu - ia! his the tri - umph, his the vic - to - ry a - lone.
Al - le - lu - ia! he is near us; faith be - lieves nor ques-tions how.
Al - le - lu - ia! hear the sin - ful cry to you from day to day.
Hark! the songs of peace-ful Zi - on thun - der like a might-y flood.
Though the cloud from sight re - ceived him when the for - ty days were o'er,
In - ter - ces - sor, Friend of sin - ners, earth's Re - deem - er, hear our plea,
Je - sus, out of ev - ery na - tion, has re - deemed us by his blood.
shall our hearts for - get his prom - ise, "I am with you ev - er - more?"
where the songs of all the sin - less sweep a - cross the crys-tal sea.

WORDS: William C. Dix (1837-1898), alt.
MUSIC: Rowland H. Prichard (1811-1887); arr. Ralph Vaughan Williams (1872-1958)

HYFRYDOL
8.7.8.7.D.

At the Name of Jesus

Unison
1 At the name of Je - sus ev - ery knee shall bow,
2 Hum-bled for a sea - son to re-ceive a name
3 In your hearts en - throne him, there let him sub - due
4 Chris-tians, this Lord Je - sus shall re - turn a - gain
ev - ery tongue con - fess him King of glo - ry now.
from the lips of sin - ners un - to whom he came.
all that is not ho - ly, all that is not true.
with the Fa - ther's glo - ry, when he comes to reign.
'Tis the Fa - ther's plea - sure we should call him Lord,
Faith - ful - ly he bore it, spot - less to the last,
Crown him as your sov - ereign in temp - ta - tion's hour,
For all earth - ly pow - ers soon to him must bow,
who from the be - gin - ning was the might - y Word.
brought it back vic - to - rious when from death he passed.
let his will en - fold you in its might - y power.
so let us con - fess him King of glo - ry now.

WORDS: Caroline Maria Noel (1817-1877); para. Philippians 2:5-11
MUSIC: Ralph Vaughan Williams (1872-1958)

KING'S WESTON
6.5.6.5.D.

322 A Hymn of Glory Let Us Sing!

Unison
1 A hymn of glo - ry let us sing! New hymns through-out the
2 The ho - ly ap - os - tol - ic band up - on the Mount of
3 O Lord, our home-ward path-way bend that our un - wear-ied
4 O ris - en Christ, as - cend - ed Lord, all praise to you let
world shall ring: Al-le - lu - ia! Al-le - lu - ia! Christ, by a road be-
Ol - ives stand, Al-le - lu - ia! Al-le - lu - ia! and with his faith-ful
hearts as - cend, Al-le - lu - ia! Al-le - lu - ia! where, seat - ed on your
earth ac - cord: Al-le - lu - ia! Al-le - lu - ia! You are, while end-less
fore un - trod, as - cends un - to the throne of God. Al-le - lu - ia!
fol-lowers see their Lord as-cend in maj - es - ty. Al-le - lu - ia!
Fa-ther's throne, you reign as King of kings a - lone. Al-le - lu - ia!
a - ges run, with Fa-ther and with Spir - it one. Al-le - lu - ia!
Al-le - lu - ia! Al-le - lu - ia, al-le - lu - ia, al-le - lu - ia!

WORDS: The Venerable Bede, (673-735); tr. *Lutheran Book of Worship*, 1978 LASST UNS ERFREUEN
MUSIC: *Geistliche Kirchengesäng*, Cologne, 1623; harm. Ralph Vaughan Williams (1872-1958) L.M. Alleluias

Hail the Day That Sees Him Rise 323

1 Hail the day that sees him rise, Al - le - lu - ia!
2 There for him high tri - umph waits, Al - le - lu - ia!
3 See! the heaven its Lord re - ceives, Al - le - lu - ia!
4 See! he lifts his hands a - bove! Al - le - lu - ia!
to his throne a - bove the skies; Al - le - lu - ia!
lift your heads, e - ter - nal gates, Al - le - lu - ia!
yet he loves the earth he leaves, Al - le - lu - ia!
See, he shows the prints of love! Al - le - lu - ia!
Christ, the Lamb for sin - ners given, Al - le - lu - ia!
he has con-quered death and sin. Al - le - lu - ia!
though re - turn - ing to his throne, Al - le - lu - ia!
Hark! His gra - cious lips be - stow, Al - le - lu - ia!
en - ters now the high - est heaven. Al - le - lu - ia!
Take the King of glo - ry in! Al - le - lu - ia!
still he calls the world his own. Al - le - lu - ia!
bless - ings on his church be - low. Al - le - lu - ia!

WORDS: Charles Wesley (1707-1788)
MUSIC: Robert Williams (1781-1821); arr. John Roberts (1822-1877)

LLANFAIR
7.7.7.7.Alleluias

324 Christ High-Ascended

Unison
1 Christ high-as - cend - ed, now in glo - ry seat - ed, throned and ex -
2 Christ from the Fa - ther ev - ery power pos - sess - ing, who on his
3 Christ, who in dy - ing won for us sal - va - tion, lives now the
4 Christ in his splen - dor, all do - min - ion gain - ing, Christ with his
5 As at his part - ing, joy shall ban - ish griev - ing, faith in his
alt - ed, vic - to - ry com - plet - ed, death's dread do - min - ion
cho - sen lift - ed hands in bless - ing, sends forth his ser - vants,
first - born of the new cre - a - tion; to win dis - ci - ples
peo - ple ev - er - more re - main - ing, Christ to all ag - es
pres - ence strength - en our be - liev - ing; filled with his Spir - it,
fi - nal - ly de - feat - ed, we are his wit - ness - es.
still in faith con - fess - ing, we are his wit - ness - es.
out of ev - ery na - tion, we are his wit - ness - es.
glo - ri - ous - ly reign - ing, we are his wit - ness - es.
love and power re - ceiv - ing, we are his wit - ness - es.

WORDS: Timothy Dudley-Smith (1926-)
MUSIC: *Paris Antiphoner*, 1681

CHRISTE SANCTORUM
11.11.11.6.

Come, Holy Spirit, Our Souls Inspire 325

1 Come, Holy Spirit, our souls inspire, and lighten with celestial fire; thou the anointing Spirit art, who dost thy sevenfold gifts impart.
2 Thy blessed unction from above is comfort, life, and fire of love; enable with perpetual light the dullness of our mortal sight.
3 Teach us to know the Father, Son, and thee, of both, to be but one; that through the ages all along this may be our endless song:
4 Praise to thy eternal merit, Father, Son, and Holy Spirit. Amen.

WORDS: *Veni Creator Spiritus*, 9th c.; tr. John Cosin (1594-1672), alt.
MUSIC: Plainsong, 4th c.; arr. Healey Willan (1880-1968)

VENI CREATOR SPIRITUS
L.M.

326 Spirit, Spirit of Gentleness

Refrain
D G A D Bm
Spir - it, Spir - it of gen - tle - ness, blow through the wil - der - ness
E A D G A D
call - ing and free; Spir - it, Spir - it of rest - less - ness,
Bm G A7 D G D
stir me from plac - id - ness, wind, wind on the sea.
D G A G D/F♯ A/E
1 You moved on the wa - ters, you called to the deep,
2 You swept through the des - ert, you stung with the sand
3 You sang in a sta - ble, you cried from a hill,
4 You call from to - mor - row, you break an - cient schemes.

WORDS and MUSIC: James K. Manley (1940-)

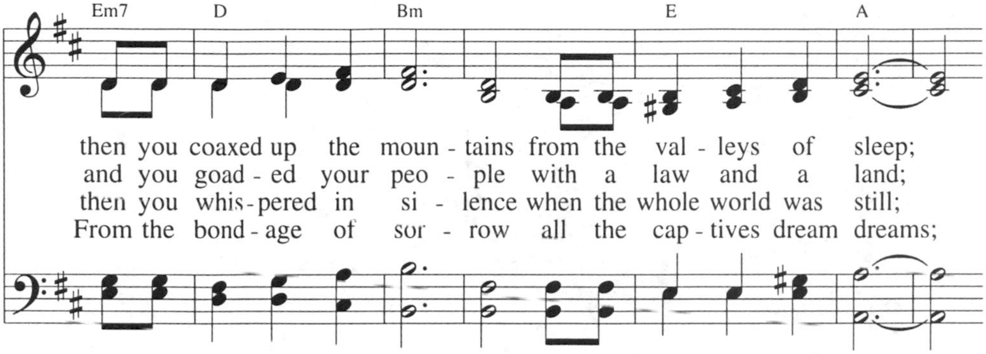
Em7 D Bm E A
then you coaxed up the moun - tains from the val - leys of sleep;
and you goad - ed your peo - ple with a law and a land;
then you whis - pered in si - lence when the whole world was still;
From the bond - age of sor - row all the cap - tives dream dreams;

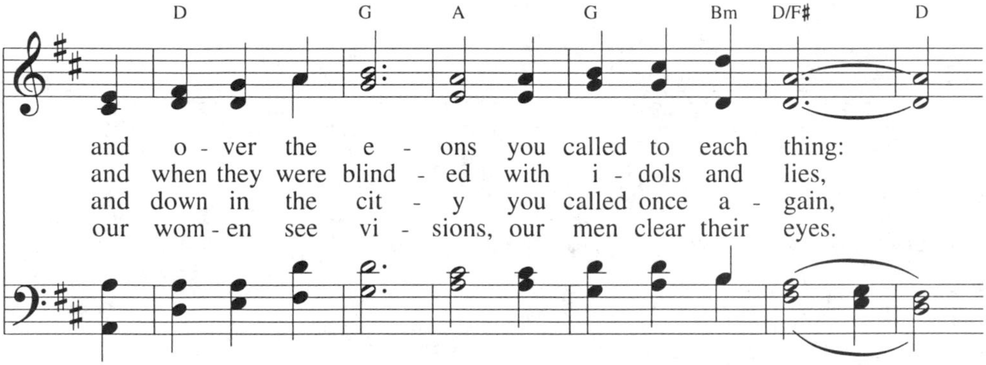
D G A G Bm D/F# D
and o - ver the e - ons you called to each thing:
and when they were blind - ed with i - dols and lies,
and down in the cit - y you called once a - gain,
our wom - en see vi - sions, our men clear their eyes.

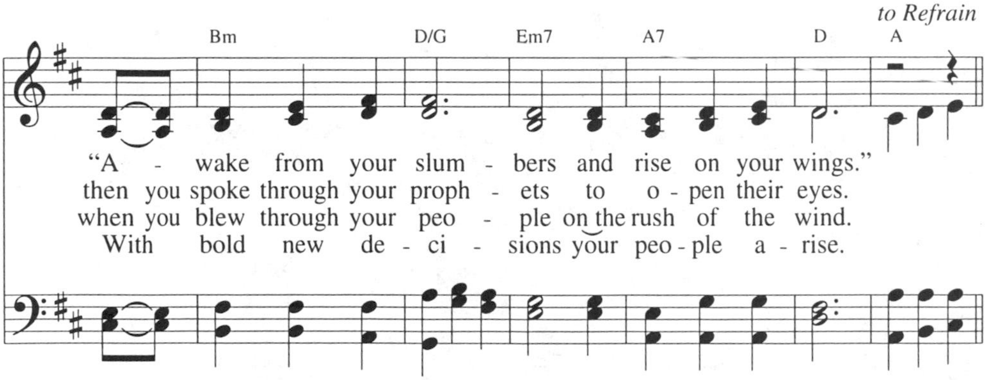
to Refrain
Bm D/G Em7 A7 D A
"A - wake from your slum - bers and rise on your wings."
then you spoke through your proph - ets to o - pen their eyes.
when you blew through your peo - ple on the rush of the wind.
With bold new de - ci - sions your peo - ple a - rise.

327 Like the Murmur of the Dove's Song

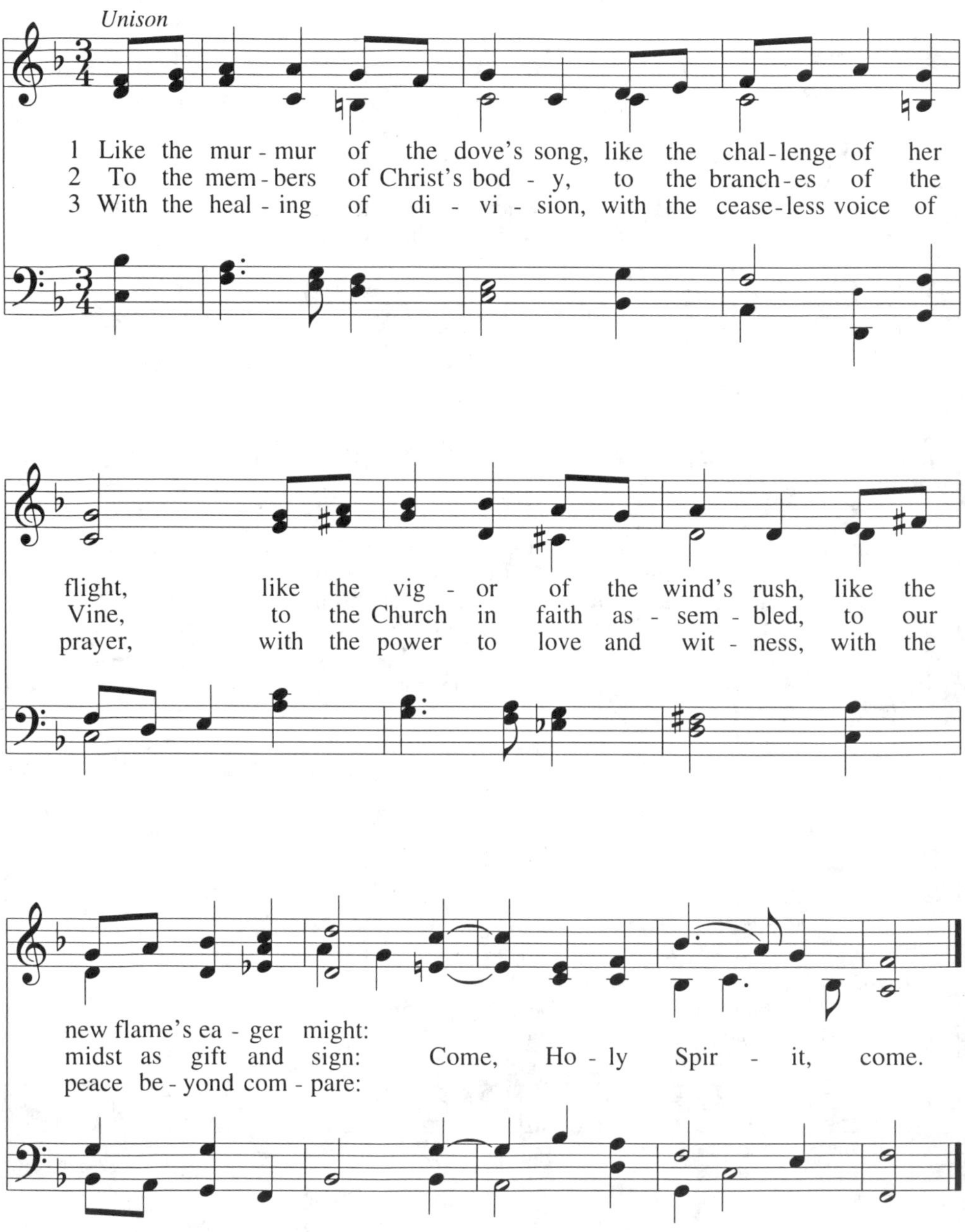
Unison
1 Like the mur - mur of the dove's song, like the chal-lenge of her flight, like the vig - or of the wind's rush, like the new flame's ea - ger might:
2 To the mem-bers of Christ's bod - y, to the branch-es of the Vine, to the Church in faith as - sem - bled, to our midst as gift and sign:
3 With the heal - ing of di - vi - sion, with the cease-less voice of prayer, with the power to love and wit - ness, with the peace be - yond com - pare:
Come, Ho - ly Spir - it, come.

WORDS: Carl P. Daw, Jr. (1944-)
MUSIC: Peter Cutts (1937-)

BRIDEGROOM
8.7.8.7.6.

O Breath of Life

1 O Breath of Life, come sweep - ing through us, re - vive your church with life and power; O Breath of Life, come, cleanse, re - new us, and fit your church to meet this hour.
2 O Wind of God, come bend us, break us, till hum - bly we con - fess our need; then in your ten - der - ness re - make us, re - vive, re - store— for this we plead.
3 O Breath of Love, come breathe with - in us, re - new - ing thought and will and heart; come, Love of Christ, a - fresh to win us, re - vive your church in ev - ery part!

WORDS: Elizabeth Ann P. Head (1850-1936)
MUSIC: Mary J. Hammond (1878-1964)

SPIRITUS VITAE
9.8.9.8.

329 Come, O Spirit, Dwell Among Us

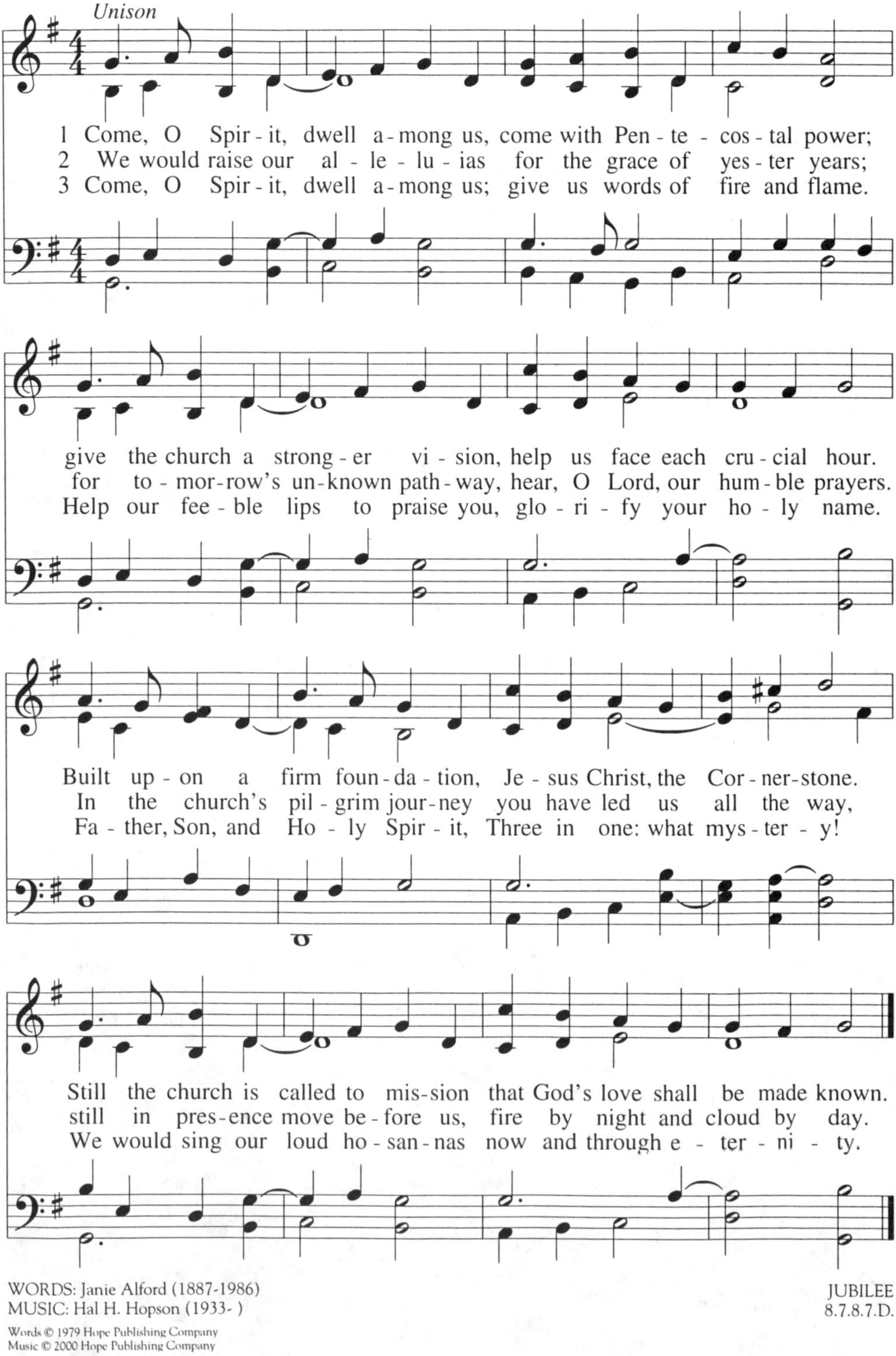
Unison
1 Come, O Spir - it, dwell a - mong us, come with Pen - te - cos - tal power;
2 We would raise our al - le - lu - ias for the grace of yes - ter years;
3 Come, O Spir - it, dwell a - mong us; give us words of fire and flame.
give the church a strong - er vi - sion, help us face each cru - cial hour.
for to - mor-row's un-known path - way, hear, O Lord, our hum - ble prayers.
Help our fee - ble lips to praise you, glo - ri - fy your ho - ly name.
Built up - on a firm foun - da - tion, Je - sus Christ, the Cor - ner-stone.
In the church's pil - grim jour - ney you have led us all the way,
Fa - ther, Son, and Ho - ly Spir - it, Three in one: what mys - ter - y!
Still the church is called to mis-sion that God's love shall be made known.
still in pres-ence move be - fore us, fire by night and cloud by day.
We would sing our loud ho - san - nas now and through e - ter - ni - ty.

WORDS: Janie Alford (1887-1986)
MUSIC: Hal H. Hopson (1933-)

JUBILEE
8.7.8.7.D.

Come Down, O Love Divine 330

1 Come down, O Love di - vine, seek out this soul of mine
2 O let it free - ly burn, till earth - ly pas - sions turn
3 And so the yearn - ing strong with which the soul will long
and vis - it it with your own ar - dor glow - ing:
to dust and ash - es in its heat con - sum - ing:
shall far out - pass the power of hu - man tell - ing:
O Com-fort - er, draw near, with - in my heart ap - pear,
and let your glo - rious light shine ev - er on my sight,
for none can guess God's grace, till love cre - ates a place,
and kin - dle it, your ho - ly flame be - stow - ing.
and clothe me round, the while my path il - lum - ing.
where - in the Ho - ly Spir - it makes a dwell - ing.

WORDS: Bianco da Siena (d. 1434); tr. Richard Frederick Littledale (1833-1890), alt.
MUSIC: Ralph Vaughan Williams (1872-1958)

DOWN AMPNEY
6.6.11.D.

331 Filled with the Spirit's Power

1 Filled with the Spirit's power, with one accord
2 Now with the mind of Christ set us on fire,
3 Widen our love, good Spirit, to embrace
the infant church confessed its risen Lord.
that unity may be our great desire.
the people of all lands and every race.
O Holy Spirit, in the church today
Give joy and peace, give faith to hear your call,
Like wind and fire, with life among us move,
again your power of fellowship display.
and readiness in each to work for all.
till we are known as Christ's and Christians prove.

WORDS: J. R. Peacey (1896-1971)
MUSIC: Cyril V. Taylor (1907-1991)

SHELDONIAN
10.10.10.10.

Let Every Christian Pray 332

1 Let ev - ery Chris - tian pray, this day and ev - ery day, come, Ho - ly Spir - it, come! Was not the church we love com - mis - sioned from a - bove? Come, Ho - ly Spir - it, come!
2 The Spir - it brought to birth the church of Christ on earth to seek and save the lost: God nev - er has with - drawn, since that tre - men - dous dawn, the gifts at Pen - te - cost.
3 On - ly the Spir - it's power can fit us for this hour: Come, Ho - ly Spir - it, come! In - struct, in - spire, u - nite, and help us see your light: Come, Ho - ly Spir - it, come!

WORDS: Fred Pratt Green (1903-2000)
MUSIC: Joseph Barnby (1838-1896)

LAUDES DOMINI
6.6.6.D.

333 Wind Who Makes All Winds That Blow

1 Wind who makes all winds that blow—gusts that bend the sap - lings low,
2 Fire who fuels all fires that burn— suns a - round which plan - ets turn,
3 Ho - ly Spir - it, Wind and Flame, move with - in our mor - tal frame.
gales that heave the sea in waves, stir - rings in the mind's deep caves—
bea - cons mark - ing reefs and shoals, shin - ing truth to guide our souls—
Make our hearts an al - tar pyre, kin - dle them with your own fire.
aim your breath with stead - y power on your church this day, this hour.
come to us as once you came: burst in tongues of sa - cred flame!
Breathe and blow up - on that blaze till our lives, our deeds and ways,
Raise, re - new the life we've lost, Spir - it God of Pen - te - cost.
Light and Pow - er, Might and Strength, fill your church, its breadth and length.
speak that tongue which ev - ery land by your grace shall un - der - stand.

WORDS: Thomas H. Troeger (1945-)
MUSIC: Joseph Parry (1841-1903)

ABERYSTWYTH
7.7.7.7.D.

On Pentecost They Gathered 334

1 On Pen - te - cost they gath - ered quite ear - ly in the day,
2 The peo - ple all a - round them were star - tled and a - mazed
3 God pours the Ho - ly Spir - it on all who would be - lieve,
4 O Spir - it, sent from heav - en on that day long a - go,
a band of Christ's dis - ci - ples, to wor - ship, sing, and pray.
to un - der - stand their lan - guage, as Christ the Lord they praised.
on wom - en, men, and chil - dren who would God's grace re - ceive.
re - kin - dle faith a - mong us in all life's ebb and flow.
A might - y wind came blow - ing, filled all the swirl - ing air,
What u - ni - ver - sal mes - sage, what great good news was here?
That Spir - it knows no lim - it, be - stow - ing life and power.
O give us ears to lis - ten and tongues a - flame with praise,
and tongues of fire a - glow - ing in - spired each per - son there.
That Christ, once dead, is ris - en to van - quish all our fear.
The church, formed and re - form - ing, re - sponds in ev - ery hour.
so peo - ple of all na - tions glad songs of joy shall raise.

WORDS: Jane Parker Huber (1926-)
MUSIC: *Neuvermehrtes Gesangbuch*, 1693; harm. Felix Mendelssohn (1809-1847)

MUNICH
7.6.7.6.D.

335 Christ the Eternal Lord

1 Christ the e - ter - nal Lord whose prom - ise here we claim,
2 Christ the un-chang - ing Word to ev - ery pass - ing age,
3 Christ the re - deem - ing Son who shares our hu - man birth,
4 Christ the un - fad - ing Light of ev - er - last - ing day,
5 Christ the as - cend - ed King ex - alt - ed high a - bove,
whose gifts of grace are free - ly poured on all who name your Name;
whose time - less teach-ings still are heard set forth on Scrip-ture's page;
and by his death sal - va - tion won for ev - ery child of earth;
our morn - ing star in splen - dor bright, the Life, the Truth, the Way;
whose praise un - end - ing a - ges sing, whom yet un - seen we love;
with thank - ful - ness and praise we stand be - fore your throne,
trans - form our thought and mind, en - light - en all who read,
in - spire our hearts, we pray, to tell your love a - broad,
that light of truth you give to serv - ants as to friends,
when mor - tal life is past your voice from heav - en's throne
in - tent to serve you all our days and make your glo - ry known.
with - in your word by faith to find the bread of life in - deed.
that all may hon - or Christ to - day and fol - low him as Lord.
your way to walk, your life to live, till earth's brief jour - ney ends.
shall call your chil - dren home at last to know as we are known.
8

WORDS: Timothy Dudley-Smith (1926-)
MUSIC: George J. Elvey (1816-1893)

DIADEMATA
S.M.D.

Christ Triumphant, Ever Reigning 336

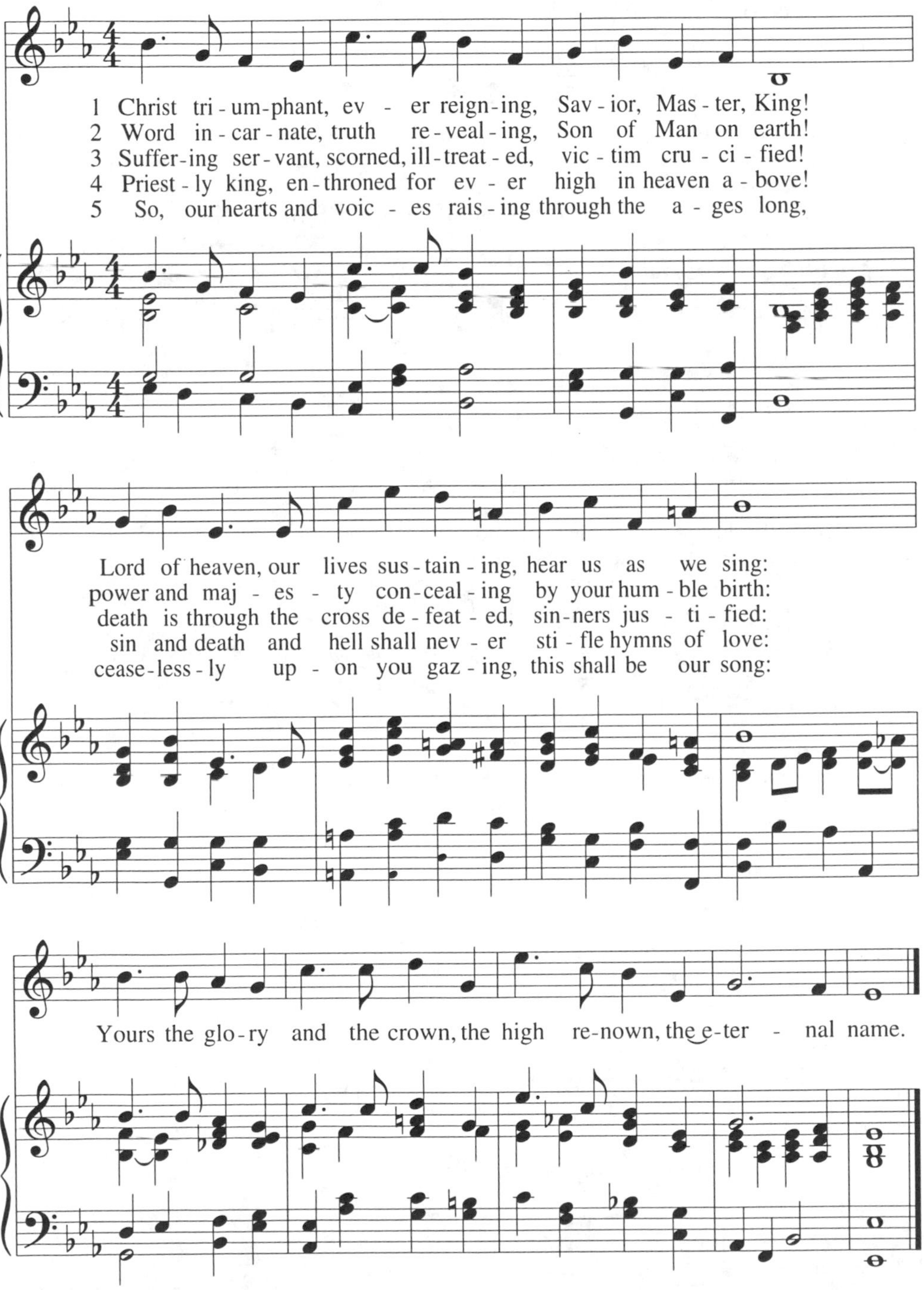
1 Christ tri - um - phant, ev - er reign - ing, Sav - ior, Mas - ter, King!
2 Word in - car - nate, truth re - veal - ing, Son of Man on earth!
3 Suffer - ing ser - vant, scorned, ill - treat - ed, vic - tim cru - ci - fied!
4 Priest - ly king, en - throned for ev - er high in heaven a - bove!
5 So, our hearts and voic - es rais - ing through the a - ges long,
Lord of heaven, our lives sus - tain - ing, hear us as we sing:
power and maj - es - ty con - ceal - ing by your hum - ble birth:
death is through the cross de - feat - ed, sin - ners jus - ti - fied:
sin and death and hell shall nev - er sti - fle hymns of love:
cease - less - ly up - on you gaz - ing, this shall be our song:
Yours the glo - ry and the crown, the high re - nown, the e - ter - nal name.

WORDS: Michael Saward (1932-)
MUSIC: John Barnard (1948-)

GUITING POWER
8.5.8.5.7.9.

337 We Will Glorify

D D/F# G D/F# A/E A D D/F# G D/F# A/E A D
1 We will glo - ri - fy the King of kings, we will glo - ri - fy the Lamb;
2 Lord Je - ho - vah reigns in maj - es - ty, we will bow be - fore his throne;
3 He is Lord of heav - en, Lord of earth, he is Lord of all who live;
4 Hal - le - lu - jah to the King of kings, hal - le - lu - jah to the Lamb;

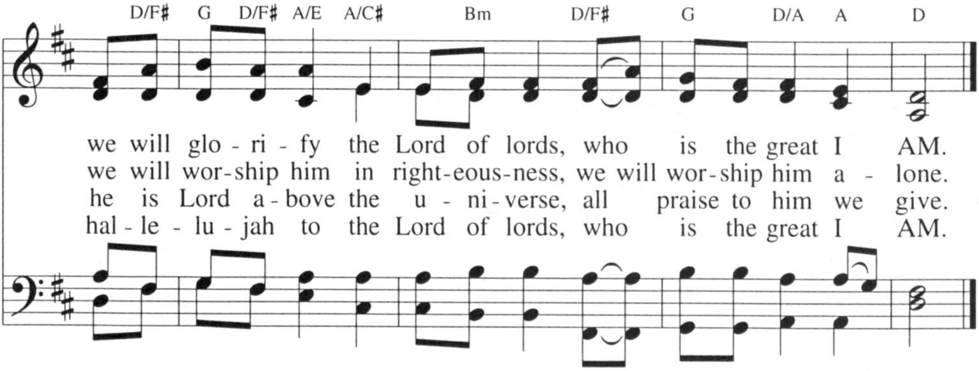
D/F# G D/F# A/E A/C# Bm D/F# G D/A A D
we will glo - ri - fy the Lord of lords, who is the great I AM.
we will wor - ship him in right - eous - ness, we will wor - ship him a - lone.
he is Lord a - bove the u - ni - verse, all praise to him we give.
hal - le - lu - jah to the Lord of lords, who is the great I AM.

WORDS and MUSIC: Twila Paris (1958-)

338 King of Kings

Unison
Em B7 Em
King of kings and Lord of lords, glo - ry, hal - le - lu - jah! King of kings and

WORDS and MUSIC: Sophie Conty (1961-) and Naomi Batya (1961-)

B7
Em
Lord of lords, glo - ry, hal - le - lu - jah! Je - sus, Prince of Peace,

B7
Em
B7
Em
glo-ry, hal-le-lu-jah! Je-sus, Prince of Peace, glo-ry, hal-le-lu-jah!

The Head That Once Was Crowned 339

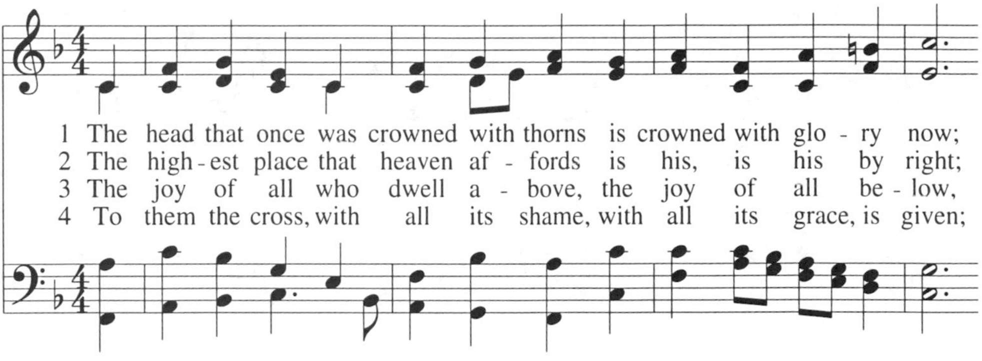
1 The head that once was crowned with thorns is crowned with glo - ry now;
2 The high-est place that heaven af - fords is his, is his by right;
3 The joy of all who dwell a - bove, the joy of all be - low,
4 To them the cross, with all its shame, with all its grace, is given;

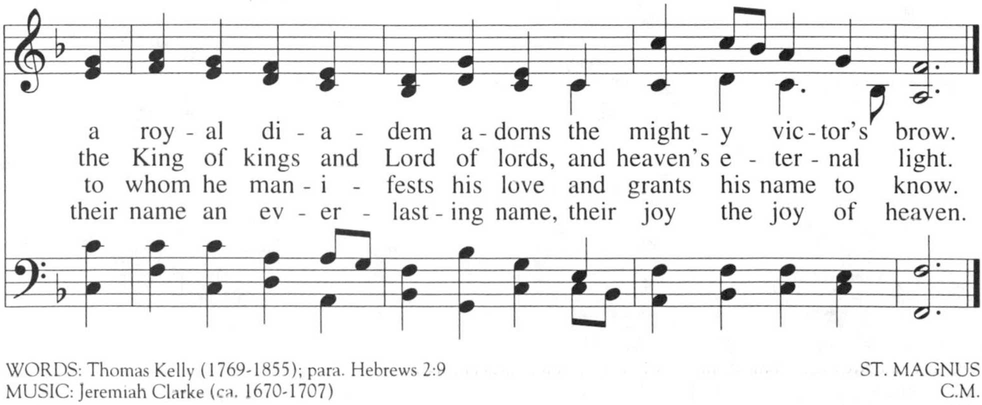
a roy - al di - a - dem a - dorns the might - y vic - tor's brow.
the King of kings and Lord of lords, and heaven's e - ter - nal light.
to whom he man - i - fests his love and grants his name to know.
their name an ev - er - last - ing name, their joy the joy of heaven.

WORDS: Thomas Kelly (1769-1855); para. Hebrews 2:9
MUSIC: Jeremiah Clarke (ca. 1670-1707)

ST. MAGNUS
C.M.

340 Crown Him King of Kings

Ab Cm7 Db Db/Eb Eb7 Ab C7/G Fm Fm/Eb
Crown Him King of kings; Crown Him Lord of lords.
Db Cm7 Ab/C Fm Gb Db/Eb Eb7sus Eb7
Won-der-ful, Coun-sel-or, the Might-y God;
Ab Cm7 Db Bbm7 Eb Eb7 Ab Cm7
Em-man-u-el, God is with us, and
Db Cm7 Ab/C Fm Bbm7 Ab/Bb Eb7 Db/Eb Ab
he shall reign, he shall reign, he shall reign for-ev-er-more.

WORDS and MUSIC: Sharon Damazio (1953-)

Jesus Shall Reign

1 Je - sus shall reign wher - e'er the sun
2 To him shall end - less prayer be made,
3 Peo - ple and realms of ev - ery tongue
4 Let all the peo - ple rise and bring
does its suc - ces - sive jour - neys run;
and end - less prais - es crown his head;
dwell on his love with sweet - est song,
their spe - cial hon - ors to our King;
his king - dom spread from shore to shore,
his name like sweet per - fume shall rise
and in - fant voic - es shall pro - claim
an - gels de - scend with songs a - gain
till moons shall wax and wane no more.
with ev - ery morn - ing sac - ri - fice.
their ear - ly bless - ings on his name.
and earth re - peat the loud A - men.

WORDS: Isaac Watts (1674-1748), alt.; para. Psalm 72
MUSIC: John Hatton (ca. 1710-1793)

DUKE STREET
L.M.

342 Rejoice, the Lord Is King!

1 Re - joice, the Lord is King! Your Lord and King a - dore!
2 Our Sav - ior, Je - sus, reigns, the God of truth and love;
3 His King - dom can - not fail, he rules both earth and heaven;
4 Re - joice in glo - rious hope for Christ the Judge shall come
Re - joice, give thanks, and sing, and tri - umph ev - er - more:
when he had purged our stains, he took his seat a - bove:
the keys of death and hell are to our Je - sus given:
to gath - er all his saints to their e - ter - nal home:
Lift up your heart, lift up your voice!
Re - joice, a - gain I say, re - joice!

WORDS: Charles Wesley (1707-1788); para. Philippians 4:4
MUSIC: John Darwall (1731-1789)

DARWALL'S 148th
6.6.6.6.8.8.

THE CHURCH REDEEMED

343 The Potter's Hand

G
Unison
D/F#
Am
Take me, mold me, use me,
Em
F
C/E
Am
Am/D
C/D D7
fill me; I give my life to the Pot - ter's hand.
G
D/F#
Am
Em
Call me, guide me, lead me, walk be-side me; I
1
F
C/E
Am
Am/D
C/D
D C/D
give my life to the Pot - ter's hand.

WORDS and MUSIC: Darlene Zschech (1965-)

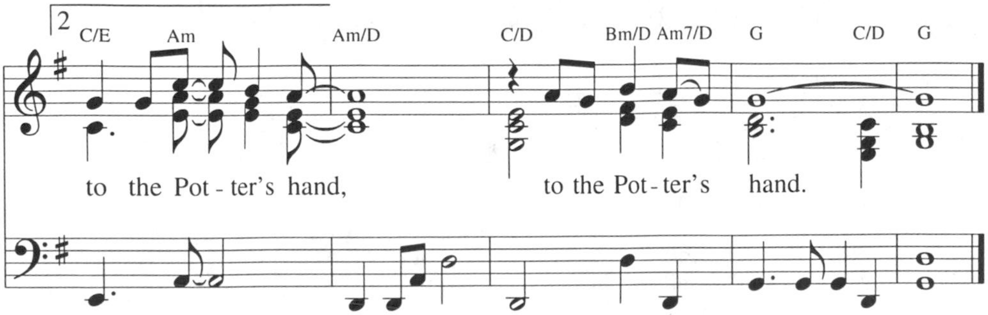
2
C/E Am Am/D C/D Bm/D Am7/D G C/D G
to the Pot - ter's hand, to the Pot - ter's hand.

I Have Decided to Follow Jesus 344

Unison
C C7 F C C/G D9/A G7/B C
1 I have de - cid - ed to fol - low Je - sus, I have de - cid - ed to fol - low Je - sus, I have de - cid - ed to fol - low Je - sus— no turn - ing back, no turn - ing back.
2 The world be - hind me, the cross be - fore me, the world be - hind me, the cross be - fore me, the world be - hind me, the cross be - fore me— no turn - ing back, no turn - ing back.
3 Though none go with me, I still will fol - low, though none go with me, I still will fol - low, though none go with me, I still will fol - low— no turn - ing back, no turn - ing back.
4 Will you de - cide now to fol - low Je - sus? Will you de - cide now to fol - low Je - sus? Will you de - cide now to fol - low Je - sus?— no turn - ing back, no turn - ing back.

WORDS: Anonymous
MUSIC: Indian folk tune

ASSAM
10.10.10.8.

345 Jesus Calls Us o'er the Tumult

1 Je - sus calls us o'er the tu - mult of our life's wild, rest - less sea; day by day his sweet voice sound - eth, say - ing, "Chris - tian, fol - low me."
2 Je - sus calls us from the wor - ship of the vain world's gold - en store, from each i - dol that would keep us, say - ing, "Chris - tian, love me more."
3 In our joys and in our sor - rows, days of toil and hours of ease, still he calls, in cares and pleas - ures, "Chris - tian, love me more than these."
4 Je - sus calls us— by thy mer - cies, Sav - ior, may we hear thy call, give our hearts to thine o - be - dience, serve and love thee best of all.

WORDS: Cecil F. Alexander (1818-1895)
MUSIC: William H. Jude (1851-1922)

GALILEE
8.7.8.7.

O Come to Me, the Master Said 346

1 O come to me, the Mas-ter said, my Fa-ther knows your need;
2 A-bide in me, the Mas-ter said, the true and liv-ing vine;
3 Be-lieve in me, the Mas-ter said, for I have called you friends,
and I shall be, the Mas-ter said, your bread of life in-deed.
my life shall be, the Mas-ter said, poured out for you as wine.
and yours shall be, the Mas-ter said, the life that nev-er ends.
By faith in him we live and grow and share the bro-ken bread,
His bod-y to the cross he gave, his blood he free-ly shed,
And so, with sin and sor-row past, when death it-self is dead,
and all his love and good-ness know, for so the Mas-ter said.
who came in love to seek and save, for so the Mas-ter said.
the Lord shall raise us up at last, for so the Mas-ter said.

WORDS: Timothy Dudley-Smith (1926-)
MUSIC: English melody; arr. Ralph Vaughan Williams (1872-1958)

KINGSFOLD
C.M.D.

347 Lord, You Have Come to the Lakeshore

Tú Has Venido a la Orilla

Unison
D A7 D
1 Lord, you have come to the lake - shore
2 You know so well my pos - ses - sions;
3 You need my hands, full of car - ing,
4 You, who have fished oth - er o - ceans,
1 Tú has ve - ni - do a la o - ri - lla,
2 Tú sa - bes bien lo que ten - go:
3 Tú nec - ce - si - tas mis man - os,
4 Tú, pes - ca - dor de o - tros mar - es,
G A7
look - ing nei - ther for wealth - y nor wise ones;
my boat car - ries no gold and no weap - ons;
through my la - bors to give oth - ers rest,
ev - er longed for by souls who are wait - ing,
no has bus - ca - do ni a sa - bios ni a ri - cos,
en mi bar - ca no hay o - ro - ni es - pa - das,
mi can - san - cio que a o - tros des - can - se,
an - sia e - ter - na de al - mas que es - per - an,
D A7 Dsus D Dsus
you on - ly asked me to fol - low hum - bly.
you will find there my nets and la - bor.
and con - stant love that keeps on lov - ing.
my lov - ing friend, so now you call me.
tan só - lo quie - res que yo te si - ga.
tan só - lo re - des y mi tra - ba - jo.
a - mor que quier - a se - guir a - man - do.
a - mi - go bue - no, que a - si me lla - mas.

WORDS: Cesáreo Gabaraín (1936-1991); para. Matthew 4:18-22
tr. Gertrude C. Suppe (1911-), George Lockwood (1946-),
Raquel Gutiérrez-Achon (1927-), alt.
MUSIC: Cesáreo Gabaraín (1936-1991); arr. Skinner Chávez-Melo (1944-1992)

PESCADOR DE HOMBRES
Irregular.Ref.

Refrain
D7 G D
O Lord, with your eyes you have searched me,
Se - ñor, me has mi - ra - do a los o - jos
A7/C♯ G/B A7 D
and while smil - ing have spo-ken my name;
y son - rien - do has di - cho mi nom - bre;
D7 G F♯m7
now my boat's left on the shore-line be-hind me;
en la a - re - na he de - ja - do mi bar - ca;
B7 Em G/B A7 D
by your side I will seek oth-er seas.
jun - to a ti bus-ca - ré o - tro mar.

348 Softly and Tenderly

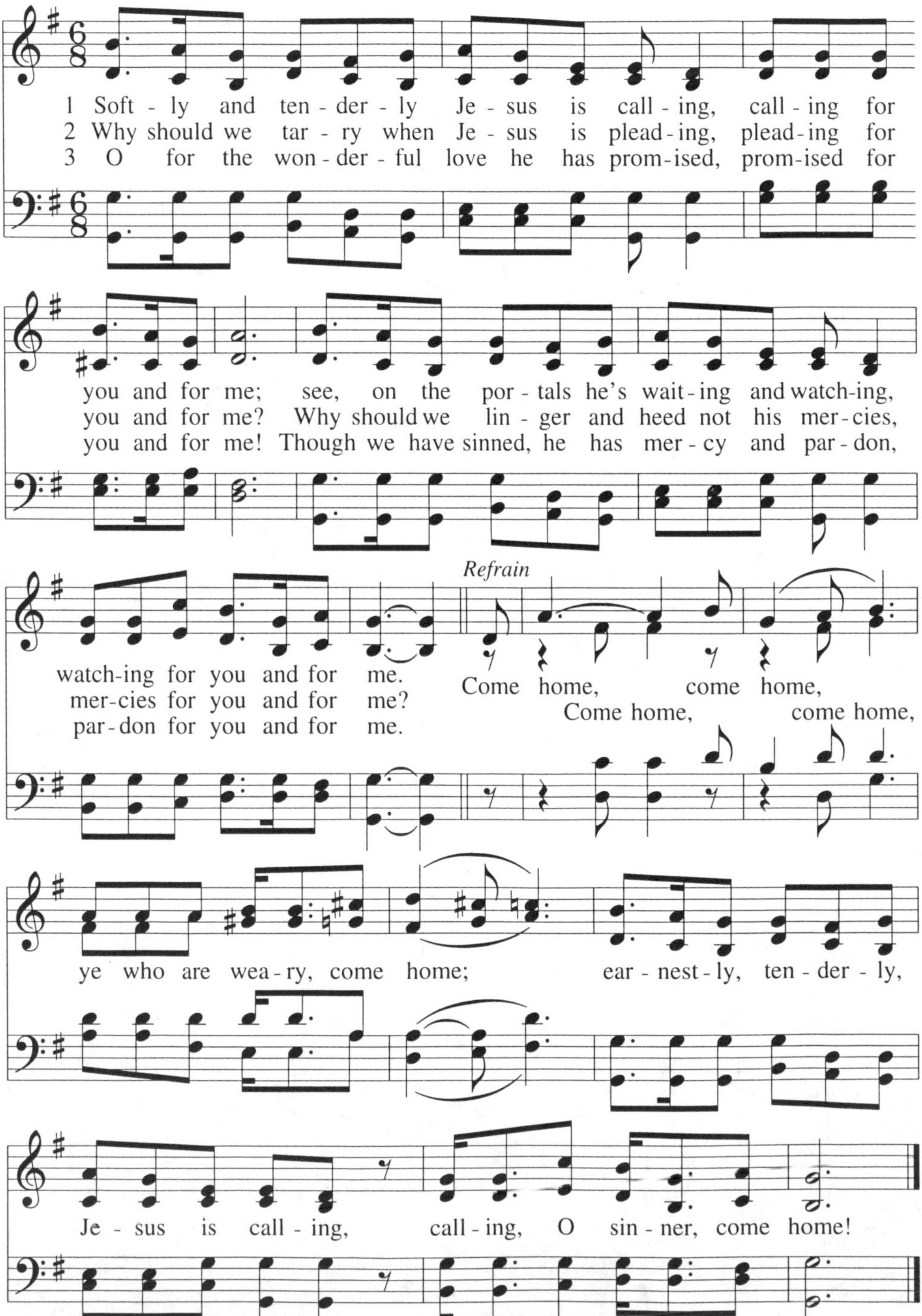
1 Soft - ly and ten - der - ly Je - sus is call - ing, call - ing for
2 Why should we tar - ry when Je - sus is plead - ing, plead - ing for
3 O for the won - der - ful love he has prom - ised, prom - ised for
you and for me; see, on the por - tals he's wait - ing and watch - ing,
you and for me? Why should we lin - ger and heed not his mer - cies,
you and for me! Though we have sinned, he has mer - cy and par - don,
watch - ing for you and for me.
mer - cies for you and for me?
par - don for you and for me.
Refrain
Come home, come home,
Come home, come home,
ye who are wea - ry, come home;
ear - nest - ly, ten - der - ly,
Je - sus is call - ing, call - ing, O sin - ner, come home!

WORDS and MUSIC: Will L. Thompson (1847-1909)

THOMPSON
11.7.11.7.Ref.

Seek Ye First

349

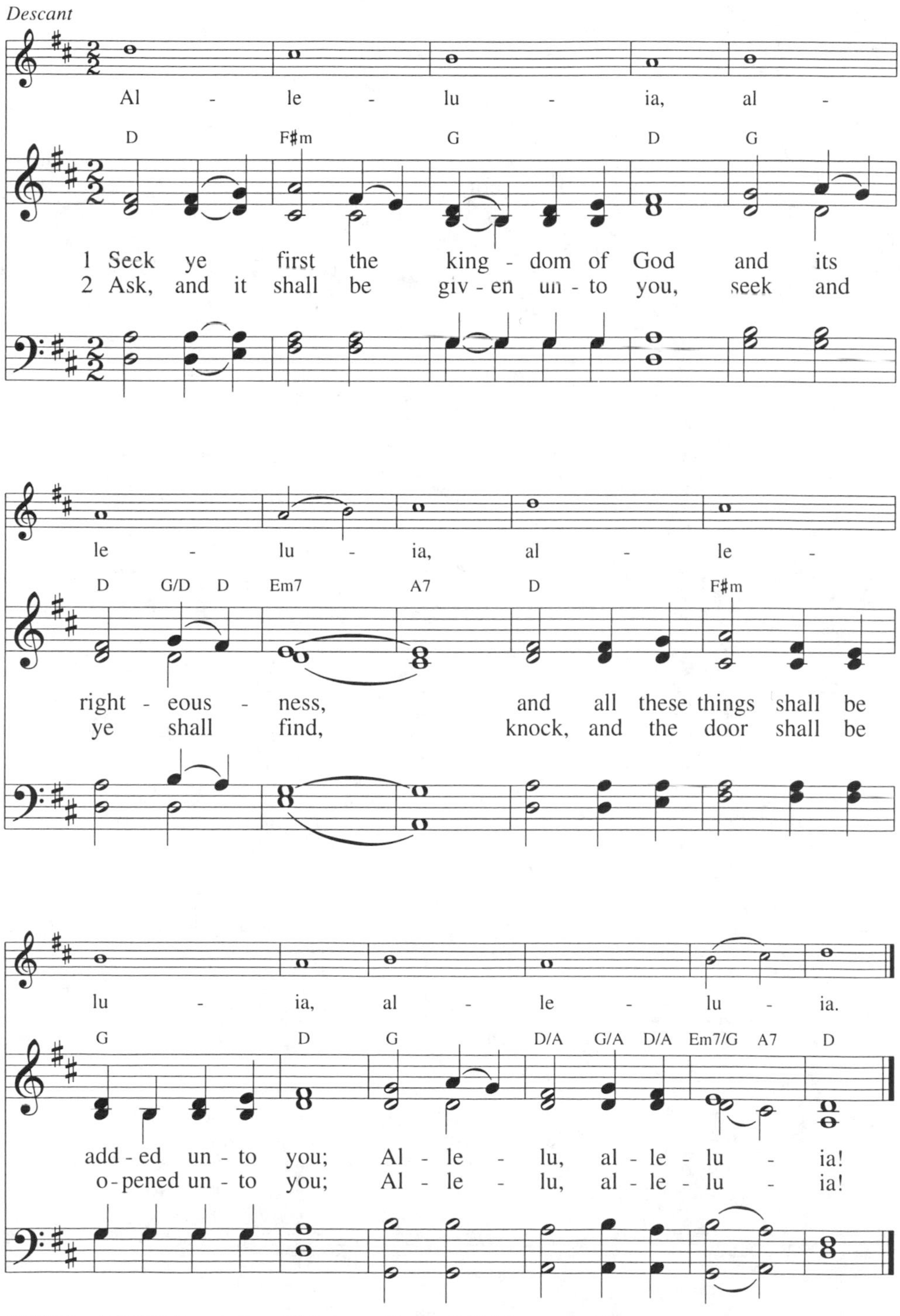
Descant
Al - le - lu - ia, al - le - lu - ia, al - le - lu - ia, al - le - lu - ia.
D F#m G D G
1 Seek ye first the king - dom of God and its
2 Ask, and it shall be giv - en un - to you, seek and
D G/D D Em7 A7 D F#m
right - eous - ness, and all these things shall be
ye shall find, knock, and the door shall be
G D G D/A G/A D/A Em7/G A7 D
add - ed un - to you; Al - le - lu, al - le - lu - ia!
o - pened un - to you; Al - le - lu, al - le - lu - ia!

WORDS and MUSIC: Karen Lafferty (1948-); para. Matthew 6:33, 7:7

350 The Summons

Unison
1 Will you come and fol - low me if I but call your name? Will you go where you don't know and nev - er be the same? Will you let my love be shown, will you let my
2 Will you leave your - self be - hind if I but call your name? Will you care for cruel and kind and nev - er be the same? Will you risk the hos - tile stare should your life at -
3 Will you let the blind - ed see if I but call your name? Will you set the pris - oners free and nev - er be the same? Will you kiss the lep - er clean, and do such as
4 Lord, your sum - mons ech - oes true when you but call my name. Let me turn and fol - low you and nev - er be the same. In your com - pa - ny I'll go where your love and

WORDS: John L. Bell (1949-)
MUSIC: Scottish melody; arr. John L. Bell (1949-)

KELVINGROVE
7.6.7.6.7.7.7.6.

name be known, will you let my life be
tract or scare? Will you let me an - swer
this un - seen, and ad - mit to what I
foot - steps show. Thus I'll move and live and

grown in you and you in me?
prayer in you and you in me?
mean in you and you in me?
grow in you and you in me.

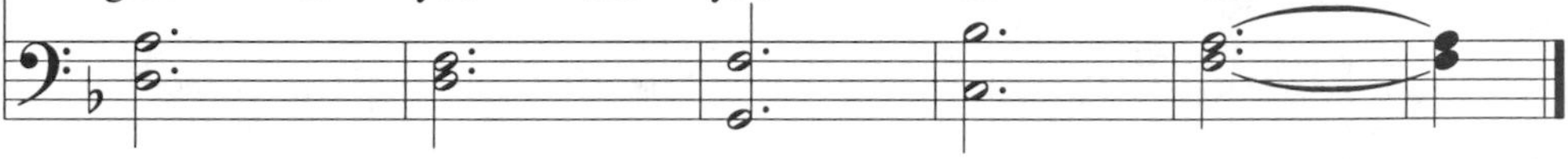

"Take Up Your Cross," the Savior Said 351

1 "Take up your cross," the Sav-ior said, "if you would my dis - ci - ple be; de -
2 Take up your cross, let not its weight fill your weak spir - it with a - larm; his
3 Take up your cross, heed not the shame, nor let your fool-ish pride re - bel; your
4 Take up your cross, and fol - low Christ, nor think till death to lay it down; for

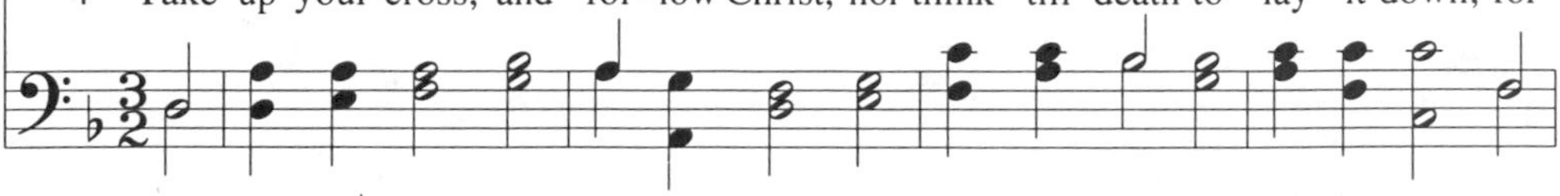

ny your - self, the world for - sake, and hum - bly fol - low af - ter me."
strength shall bear your spir - it up, and nerve your heart, and brace your arm.
Lord for you the cross en - dured, and fought the powers of death and hell.
on - ly they who bear the cross may hope to wear the glo - rious crown.

WORDS: Charles W. Everest (1814-1877), alt.; para. Luke 9:23
MUSIC: *Southern Harmony*, 1835

DISTRESS
L.M.

352 Spirit Song

Unison
Gmaj7 Gmaj7/F# Em7 A7 A7/G
1 O let the Son of God en - fold you with his
2 (O come and) sing this song with glad - ness as your
F#m7 Bm7 Em7
Spir - it and his love. Let him fill your heart and
hearts are filled with joy. Lift your hands in sweet sur -
A7 D Dmaj7 Em7 F#m7 Gmaj7 Gmaj7/F#
sat - is - fy your soul. O let him have the things that
ren - der to his name. O give him all your tears and
Em7 A7 A7/G F#m7 Bm7
hold you, and his Spir - it like a dove will de -
sad - ness; give him all your years of pain, and you'll

WORDS and MUSIC: John Wimber (1934-1997)

Em7
G6/A
G/A
A7
D
C/D
D
scend up - on your life and make you whole.
en - ter in - to life in Je - sus' name.
Refrain
Gmaj7
A7
A9/G
F♯m7
Bm
Je - sus, O Je - sus,
Em7
A7
Dmaj7
C/D
D
come and fill your lambs.
Gmaj7
A7
A9/G
F♯m7
Bm
Je - sus, O Je - sus,
1
2
Em7
G6/A
G/A
D
come and fill your lambs.
2 O come and

353 Grace Greater than Our Sin

1 Mar - vel - ous grace of our lov - ing Lord, grace that ex - ceeds our
2 Dark is the stain that we can - not hide; what can a - vail to
3 Mar - vel - ous, in - fi - nite, match - less grace, free - ly be - stowed on
sin and our guilt, yon - der on Cal - va - ry's mount out - poured,
wash it a - way? Look! there is flow - ing a crim - son tide;
all who be - lieve: you that are long - ing to see his face,
there where the blood of the Lamb was spilt.
whit - er than snow you may be to - day.
will you this mo - ment his grace re - ceive?
Refrain
Grace, grace,
Mar - vel - ous grace,
God's grace,
in - fi - nite grace,
grace that will par - don and cleanse with - in;
grace,
mar - vel - ous
grace, God's grace,
grace, in - fi - nite grace,
grace that is great - er than all our sin.

WORDS: Julia H. Johnston (1849-1919)
MUSIC: Daniel B. Towner (1850-1919)

MOODY
9.9.9.9.Ref.

Just As I Am

1 Just as I am, with - out one plea
2 Just as I am, and wait - ing not
3 Just as I am, though tossed a - bout
4 Just as I am, thou wilt re - ceive,
but that thy blood was shed for me,
to rid my soul of one dark blot,
with man - y a con - flict, man - y a doubt,
wilt wel - come, par - don, cleanse, re - lieve;
and that thou bidd'st me come to thee,
to thee whose blood can cleanse each spot,
fight - ings and fears with - in, with - out,
be - cause thy prom - ise I be - lieve,
O Lamb of God, I come! I come!
O Lamb of God, I come! I come!
O Lamb of God, I come! I come!
O Lamb of God, I come! I come!

WORDS: Charlotte Elliott (1789-1871)
MUSIC: William B. Bradbury (1816-1868)

WOODWORTH
L.M.

355 This Is a Day of New Beginnings

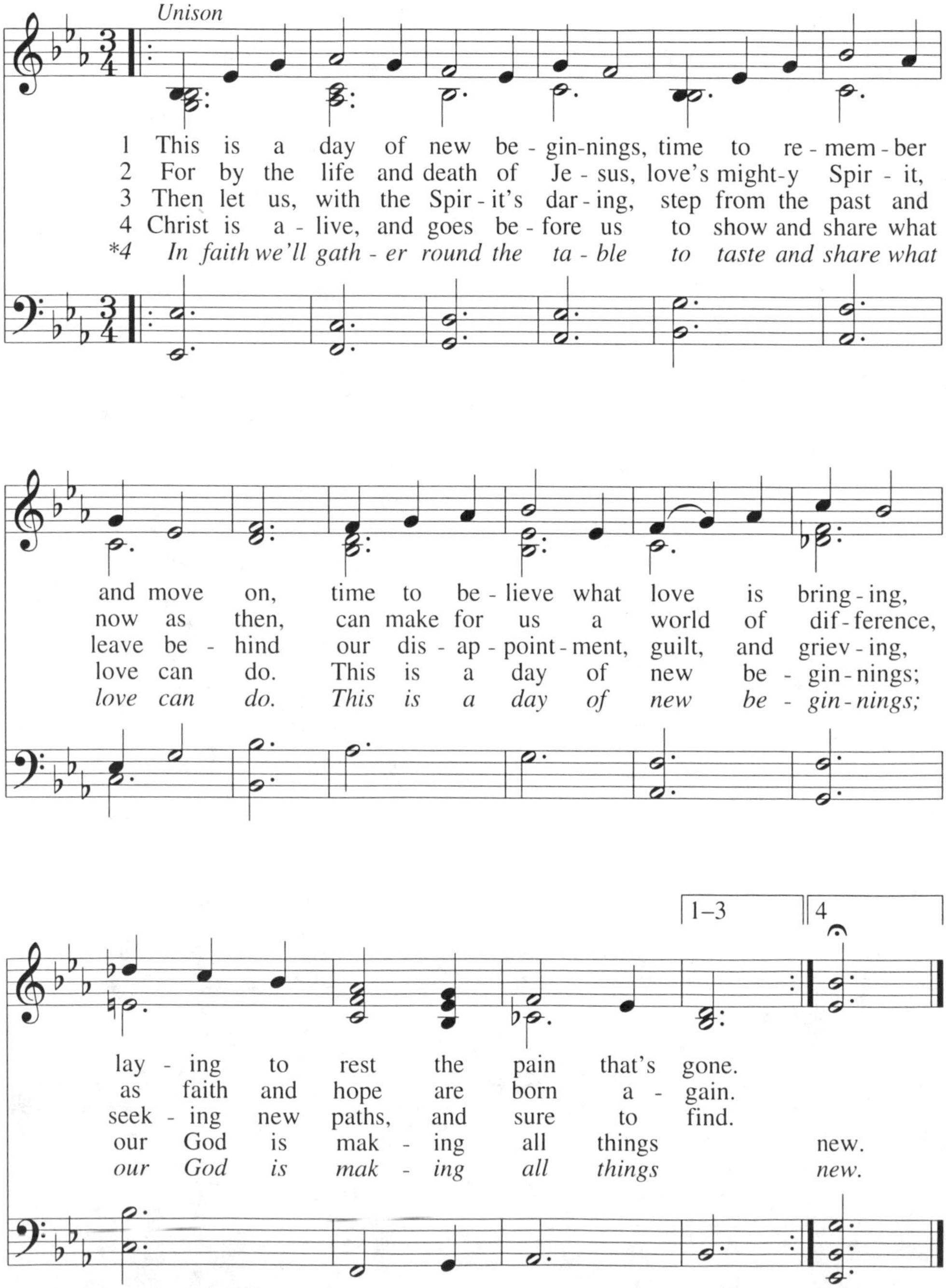
Unison
1 This is a day of new be - gin-nings, time to re - mem - ber
2 For by the life and death of Je - sus, love's might-y Spir - it,
3 Then let us, with the Spir - it's dar - ing, step from the past and
4 Christ is a - live, and goes be - fore us to show and share what
*4 In faith we'll gath - er round the ta - ble to taste and share what
and move on, time to be - lieve what love is bring - ing,
now as then, can make for us a world of dif - ference,
leave be - hind our dis - ap - point - ment, guilt, and griev - ing,
love can do. This is a day of new be - gin - nings;
love can do. This is a day of new be - gin - nings;
1–3
4
lay - ing to rest the pain that's gone.
as faith and hope are born a - gain.
seek - ing new paths, and sure to find.
our God is mak - ing all things new.
our God is mak - ing all things new.

*Alternate text for Holy Communion

WORDS: Brian Wren (1936-)
MUSIC: Carlton R. Young (1926-)

BEGINNINGS
9.8.9.8.

I Will Sing of My Redeemer 356

1 I will sing of my Re - deem-er and his won-drous love to me;
2 I will tell the won-drous sto - ry how, my lost es - tate to save,
3 I will praise my dear Re - deem-er, his tri - umph - ant power I'll tell,
4 I will sing of my Re - deem-er and his heaven-ly love for me;
on the cru - el cross he suf - fered from the curse to set me free.
in his bound - less love and mer - cy he the ran - som free - ly gave.
how the vic - to - ry he giv - eth o - ver sin and death and hell.
he from death to life hath brought me, Son of God, with him to be.
Refrain
Sing, O sing of my Re - deem-er, with his blood he pur-chased me,
on the cross he sealed my par - don, paid the debt, and made me free.

WORDS: Philip P. Bliss (1838-1876)
MUSIC: Rowland H. Prichard (1811-1887)

HYFRYDOL
8.7.8.7.D.

357 Knowing You

Unison
Am F C F G C
1 All I once held dear, built my life up - on, all this
(2 Now my) heart's de - sire is to know you more, to be
(3 Oh, to) know the power of your ris - en life and to
Am F C Am G C
world re - veres and wars to own. All I
found in you, and known as yours. To pos-
know you in your suf - fer - ings. To be -
F G C F/A G C
once thought gain I have count - ed loss, spent and
sess by faith what I could not earn, all sur -
come like you in your death, my Lord, so with
Am F C Am Gsus G
worth - less now com - pared to this.
pass - ing gift of right - eous - ness.
you to live and nev - er die.

WORDS and MUSIC: Graham Kendrick (1950-)

Refrain
F C F G C Am G
Know-ing you, Je - sus, know-ing you, there is no great - er
F C/E F/A
thing. You're my all, you're the best, you're my
C/G F G/F C2/E C/E F2/A
joy, my right-eous-ness, and I love you, Lord.
1, 2
C/G G
2 Now my
3 Oh, to
3
C/G F/G C
I love you, Lord.

358 Love Divine, All Loves Excelling

1 Love di - vine, all loves ex - cel-ling, Joy of heaven to earth come down,
2 Breathe, O breathe thy lov - ing Spir - it in - to ev - ery trou - bled breast;
3 Come, al - might - y to de - liv - er, let us all thy life re - ceive;
4 Fin - ish then thy new cre - a - tion, pure and spot-less let us be;
fix in us thy hum - ble dwell-ing, all thy faith - ful mer - cies crown.
let us all in thee in - her - it, let us find the prom - ised rest.
sud - den - ly re - turn, and nev - er, nev - er - more thy tem - ples leave.
let us see thy great sal - va - tion per - fect - ly re - stored in thee:
Je - sus, thou art all com - pas - sion, pure, un - bound - ed love thou art;
Take a - way the love of sin - ning, Al - pha and O - me - ga be;
Thee we would be al - ways bless-ing, serve thee as thy hosts a - bove,
changed from glo - ry in - to glo - ry, till in heaven we take our place,
vis - it us with thy sal - va - tion, en - ter ev - ery trem - bling heart.
end of faith, as its be - gin - ning, set our hearts at lib - er - ty.
pray and praise thee with - out ceas - ing, glo - ry in thy per - fect love.
till we cast our crowns be - fore thee, lost in won - der, love, and praise.

WORDS: Charles Wesley (1707-1788)
MUSIC: John Zundel (1815-1882)

BEECHER
8.7.8.7.D.

Give Thanks

Unison
F C/E Dm Am
Give thanks with a grate-ful heart, give thanks to the Ho - ly One, give
Bb F/A F Dm Eb Gm/C C7
thanks be-cause he's giv-en Je - sus Christ his Son. Give
Gm/C C7 Am Dm7 Gm7
Son. And now let the weak say "I am strong," let the
C7 Fmaj7 Dm7 Eb
poor say "I am rich," be-cause of what the Lord has done for
Gm/C C7 Gm/C C7 F Bb/F F
us. And us. Give thanks!

WORDS and MUSIC: Henry Smith (1952-)

360 What the Lord Has Done in Me

Unison
Refrain (Parts)
G/A D A7 D D/F# G A
1 Let the weak say, "I am strong." Let the poor say, "I am rich." Let the blind say, "I can see; it's what the Lord has done in me."
2 In-to the riv-er I will wade. There my sins are washed a-way, from the heav-en's mer-cy stream of the Sav-ior's love for me.
3 I will rise from wa-ters deep in-to the sav-ing arms of God. I will sing sal-va-tion songs: Je-sus Christ has set me free!
Bm D A7 Bm D/A
Em9 A7 D Dsus D
Bm A
Ho-san-na, ho-san-na to the Lamb that was slain. Ho-san-na, ho-
Bm Bm/A G D Bm A

WORDS and MUSIC: Reuben Morgan (1975-)

Bm D/A A7 D A/D G/D D
san - na, Je - sus died and rose a - gain (a - gain).

361 Jesus, Your Name

Unison
C Gsus G Fm/C C B♭/C C7
1 Je - sus, your name is pow - er,
2 Je - sus, your name is heal - ing,
3 Je - sus, your name is ho - ly,
F Gsus G C2/E C/E Dm7 G C G/F F
Je - sus, your name is might. Je - sus, your name will
Je - sus, your name gives sight. Je - sus, your name will
Je - sus, your name brings light. Je - sus, your name, a -
C/G Fm6/A♭ Am7 G/A Am7 Dm7 Gsus G7 C
break ev - ery strong - hold, Je - sus, your name is life.
free ev - ery cap - tive, Je - sus, your name is life.
bove ev - ery oth - er, Je - sus, your name is life.

WORDS: Claire Cloninger (1942-)
MUSIC: Morris Chapman (1938-)

362 Wonderful Grace of Jesus

1 Won - der - ful grace of Je - sus, great - er than all my sin;
2 Won - der - ful grace of Je - sus, reach - ing to all the lost,
3 Won - der - ful grace of Je - sus, reach - ing the most de - filed,
how shall my tongue de - scribe it, where shall its praise be - gin?
by it I have been par - doned, saved to the ut - ter - most;
by its trans-form - ing pow - er mak - ing me God's dear child,
Tak - ing a - way my bur - den, set - ting my spir - it free,
chains have been torn a - sun - der, giv - ing me lib - er - ty,
pur - chas - ing peace and heav - en for all e - ter - ni - ty—
for the won - der - ful grace of Je - sus reach - es me.
for the won - der - ful grace of Je - sus reach - es me.
and the won - der - ful grace of Je - sus reach - es me.
Refrain
the match - less grace of Je - sus,
Won - der - ful the match - less grace of Je - sus,

WORDS and MUSIC: Haldor Lillenas (1885-1959)

WONDERFUL GRACE
Irregular

sea, the roll - ing sea;
deep - er than the might - y roll - ing sea;
won - der - ful grace, all suf - fi -
high - er than the moun - tain, spark - ling like a foun - tain, all suf - fi - cient
cient for me, for e - ven me; broad - er than the scope of my trans -
grace for e - ven me; trans -
gres - sions, great - er far than all my sin and shame;
gres - sions, sing it! shame, my sin and shame;
O mag - ni - fy the pre - cious name of Je - sus, praise his name!

363 My Tribute

How can I say thanks for the things you have done for me?
Things so un-de-served, yet you gave to prove your love for me; the
voic-es of a mil-lion an-gels could not ex - press my grat-i - tude.
All that I am, and ev-er hope to be; I owe it all to thee.
Refrain
To God be the glo - ry, to God be the glo - ry,

WORDS and MUSIC: Andraé Crouch (1945-)

to God be the glo - ry for the things he has done.
With his blood he has saved me; with his power he has raised me;
Fine
to God be the glo - ry for the things he has done.
Just let me live my life; let it be pleas-ing, Lord, to thee.
D.S. al Fine
And if I gain an - y praise, let it go to Cal - va - ry. With his

364 Woman in the Night

Unison
1 Wo-man in the night, spent from giv - ing birth,
2 Wo-man at the well, ques - tion the Mes - siah;
3 Wo-man in the house, nur - tured to be meek,
4 Wo-men on the hill, stand when men have fled;
guard our pre - cious light; peace is on the earth.
find your friends and tell: drink your heart's de - sire!
leave your sec - ond place, lis - ten, think, and speak!
Christ needs lov - ing still, though your hope is dead.
Wo-man in the crowd, creep - ing up be - hind,
Wo-man at the feast, let the right - eous stare;
Wo-man on the road, from your sick - ness freed,
Wo-men in the dawn, care and spic - es bring,
touch - ing is al - lowed: seek and you will find!
come and go in peace; love him with your hair!
wit - ness and pro - vide, join - ing word and deed:
ear - li - est to mourn, ear - li - est to sing!
3
3

WORDS: Brian Wren (1936-)
MUSIC: Alfred V. Fedak (1953-)

NEW DISCIPLES
5.5.5.5.D.

Brightly
Come and join the song, wo - men, chil - dren, men.
Je - sus makes us free to live a - gain! gain!
1–3
4

Thank You, Lord 365

G D♯dim7 Em Am A9 D7sus D7 C B7
1 Thank you, Lord, thank you, Lord, thank you,
2 Been so good, been so good, been so
3 Been my friend, been my friend, been my
Em E7/G♯ Am G/B Am/C Em/C♯ G/D D7 C/G G
Lord, I just want to thank you, Lord.
good, I just want to thank you, Lord.
friend, I just want to thank you, Lord.

WORDS and MUSIC: African-American

366 And Can It Be

1 And can it be that I should gain an in - terest
2 He left his Fa - ther's throne a - bove, so free, so
3 Long my im - pris - oned spir - it lay fast bound in
4 No con - dem - na - tion now I dread: Je - sus, and
in the Sav - ior's blood? Died he for me, who caused his
in - fi - nite his grace! Emp - tied him - self of all but
sin and na - ture's night. Thine eye dif - fused a quick - ening
all in him, is mine! A - live in him, my liv - ing
pain? For me, who him to death pur - sued?
love, and bled for A - dam's help - less race!
ray; I woke— the dun - geon flamed with light!
Head, and clothed in righ - teous - ness di - vine,
A - maz - ing love! how can it be that
'Tis mer - cy all, im - mense and free, for,
My chains fell off, my heart was free, I
bold I ap - proach the e - ter - nal throne, and

WORDS: Charles Wesley (1707-1788)
MUSIC: Thomas Campbell (1777-1844)

SAGINA
L.M.D.

thou, my God, shouldst die for me?
O my God, it found out me. A - maz - ing
rose, went forth, and fol - lowed thee. A -
claim the crown, through Christ my own.
love! how can it be that thou, my God, shouldst die for me?
maz-ing love! how can it be that thou, my

Now Let Us Learn of Christ 367

1 Now let us learn of Christ: he speaks, and we shall find he light-ens
(2) love in Christ as he has first loved us; as he en-
(3) grow in Christ and look to things a - bove, and speak the
(4) stand in Christ in ev - ery trial we meet, in all his
1–3
4
our dark mind, so let us learn of Christ. 2 Now let us
dured the cross, so let us love in Christ. 3 Now let us
truth in love; so let us grow in Christ. 4 Now let us
strength com - plete; so let us stand in Christ.

WORDS: Christopher Idle (1938-)
MUSIC: David Peacock (1949-)

PARKSTONE
6.6.6.6.

368 O Happy Day

1 O hap - py day that fixed my choice on thee, my Sav - ior and my God!
2 O hap - py bond, that seals my vows to him who mer - its all my love!
3 'Tis done—the great trans - ac - tion's done; I am my Lord's, and he is mine;
Well may this glow - ing heart re - joice, and tell its rap - tures all a - broad.
Let cheer - ful an - thems fill his house, while to that sa - cred shrine I move.
he drew me, and I fol - lowed on, charmed to con - fess the voice di - vine.
Refrain
Hap - py day, hap - py day, when Je - sus washed my sins a - way!
He taught me how to watch and pray, and live re - joic - ing ev - ery day—
hap - py day, hap - py day, when Je - sus washed my sins a - way!

WORDS: Philip Doddridge (1702 -1751); ref. *Wesleyan Sacred Harp*, 1854
MUSIC: Attr. Edward F. Rimbault (1816-1876)

HAPPY DAY
L.M.Ref.

Christ Is God's Never Changing 'Yes!' 369

Unison
1 Christ is God's nev - er chang - ing 'Yes!' Ev - ery one of God's prom - is - es is con-firmed in the love that died, by the one who was cru - ci - fied.
2 Earth, cor - rupt - ed by sin and shame, scan - dal - ized the Cre - a - tor's name; now the Spir - it of God says 'Yes!' Christ has hon - ored God's ho - li - ness!
3 Je - sus, now, we are called to be 'Yes' our-selves to your vic - to - ry; God a - noints us to serve with you; Yes, the Spir - it will keep us true.
4 Love has con-quered, though Je - sus died; he is ris - en and glo - ri - fied; this is prom - ised, and noth - ing less, all cre - a - tion will an - swer, 'Yes!'
Refrain
'Yes' from God and then, 'Yes' from Christ a - gain! In the Spir - it we say, 'A - men!'

WORDS: Alan Gaunt (1935-)
MUSIC: Jamaican folk tune; adapt. Doreen Potter (1925-1980)

LINSTEAD
L.M.Ref.

370 Healing Grace

D A/C# D Em11 D A/C# D Bm E/G# Asus A
Mer - ci - ful God and Fa - ther, lov - ing us like no oth - er,
G A/G F#m7 Bm7 Em7 Gmaj7 Asus A
hear our prayer, the cry of our hearts, as we come to you; we ac -
F#m7 Bm7 Em9 Em7 G/B A7/C# D
knowl - edge our trans - gres - sions, we con - fess to you our sins,
Bm A G2 G
show us mer - cy and com - pas - sion,

WORDS and MUSIC: John Chisum (1958-) and Gary Sadler (1954-)

D/F# G Em7 A D A/C# D Em11 D A/C# A D
touch our lives with your heal-ing grace a - gain. Re -
A/B Bm A/B Bm7 F#m7 G2 G Asus A Dsus D A/C#
lease us from the past, as we seek your face:
A/B Bm A/B Bm7 F#m7 Em11 Em7
wash us free at last, we re - ceive your love, we re -
D/A A7 G D2/F# D/F#
ceive your heal - ing grace. We re -
Em11 Em7 D/A A7 D
ceive your love, we re - ceive your heal - ing grace.

371 Our Father, We Have Wandered

1 Our Fa - ther, we have wan - dered and hid - den from your face;
2 And now at length dis - cern - ing the e - vil that we do,
3 O Lord of all the liv - ing, both ban - ished and re - stored,
in fool - ish - ness have squan - dered your leg - a - cy of grace.
be - hold us, Lord, re - turn - ing with hope and trust to you.
com - pas - sion - ate, for - giv - ing and ev - er - car - ing Lord,
But now, in ex - ile dwell - ing, we rise with fear and shame,
In haste you come to meet us and home re - joic - ing bring,
grant now that our trans - gress - ing, our faith - less - ness may cease.
as, dis - tant but com - pel - ling, we hear you call our name.
in glad - ness there to greet us with calf and robe and ring.
Stretch out your hand in bless - ing, in par - don, and in peace.

WORDS: Kevin Nichols (1929-)
MUSIC: Hans Leo Hassler (1564-1612); arr. J.S. Bach (1685-1750)

PASSION CHORALE
7.6.7.6.D.

I Then Shall Live 372

1 I then shall live as one who's been for - giv - en;
I'll walk with joy to know my debts are paid. I know my
name is clear be - fore my Fa - ther; I am his child, and
I am not a - fraid. So great - ly par-doned, I'll for - give an -
oth - er; the law of love I glad - ly will o - bey.
2 I then shall live as one who's learned com - pas - sion;
I've been so loved that I'll risk lov - ing, too. I know how
fear builds walls in - stead of bridg - es; I dare to see an -
oth - er's point of view. And when re - la - tion - ships de - mand com -
mit - ment, then I'll be there to care and fol - low through.
3 Your king - dom come a - round and through and in me,
your power and glo - ry, let them shine through me; your hal - lowed
name, oh, may I bear with hon - or, and may your liv - ing
king - dom come in me. The Bread of Life, oh, may I share with
hon - or, and may you feed a hun - gry world through me.

WORDS: Gloria Gaither (1942-)
MUSIC: Jean Sibelius (1865-1957); arr. *Hymnal 1933*

FINLANDIA
11.10.11.10.11.10.

373 Change My Heart, O God

Unison
C Am7 Dm7 G7
Change my heart, O God, make it ev - er true.
C G/B Am7 Dm7
Change my heart, O God,
Dm7/G G7 C Esus E
may I be like you. You are the
3
Am Am7 Dm7 G C
Pot - ter, I am the clay;

WORDS and MUSIC: Eddie Espinosa (1953-)

Esus E Am C/D D7
mold me and make me, this is what I
Gsus G7 C Am7 Dm7
pray. Change my heart, O God,
G7 C G/B Am7
make it ev - er true. Change my heart, O God,
Dm7 Dm7/G G7 C
may I be like you.

374 Refiner's Fire

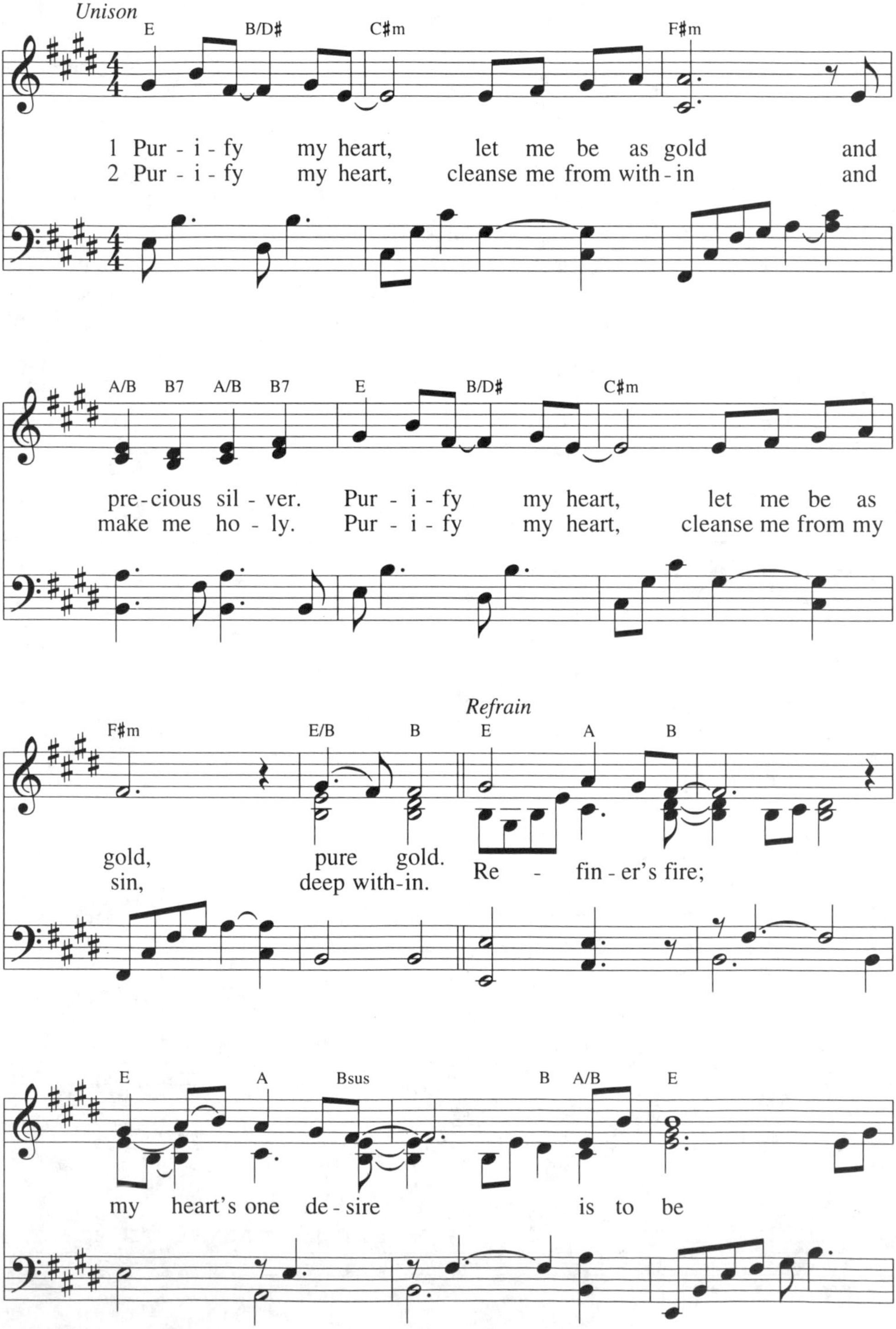
Unison
E B/D# C#m F#m
1 Pur - i - fy my heart, let me be as gold and
2 Pur - i - fy my heart, cleanse me from with - in and
A/B B7 A/B B7 E B/D# C#m
pre - cious sil - ver. Pur - i - fy my heart, let me be as
make me ho - ly. Pur - i - fy my heart, cleanse me from my
F#m E/B B
gold, pure gold.
sin, deep with-in.
Refrain
E A B
Re - fin - er's fire;
E A Bsus B A/B E
my heart's one de - sire is to be

WORDS and MUSIC: Brian Doerksen (20th c.)

B/D♯ B E A E/B Bsus B A/B
ho - ly, set a - part for you, Lord. I choose to
E B/D♯ B E A E/B
be ho - ly, set a - part for you,
B F♯m A/B B Esus E
my Mas - ter, read - y to do your will.

Lord, Have Mercy 375

D Bm F♯m Bm A G G/B
Unison
Lord, have mer - cy, Christ, have
D G Bsus Bm Asus A D
mer - cy, Lord, have mer - cy.

WORDS and MUSIC: John Michael Talbot (20th c.)

376 How Long, O Lord

Dm Dm(♯7) Dm7 Dm6 Gm7
1 How long, O Lord, will you for-get an ans-wer
2 How long, O Lord, will you for-sake and leave me
3 How long, O Lord— but you for-give, with mer-cy
B♭/C C/F F Em7 E♭9 Dm9 Dm9(♯7)
to my prayer? No to-kens of
in this way? When will you come
from a-bove. I find that all
Dm9 G13/D Gm7 B♭/C C7 Fsus2 F
your love I see, your face is turned a-way from me; I
to my re-lief? My heart is o-ver-whelmed with grief, by
your ways are just, I learn to praise you and to trust in

WORDS: Barbara Woollett (1937-); para. Psalm 13
MUSIC: Christopher Norton (1953-)

1, 2
3
Em7 A7 Dm Em7(♭5) A7 Dm G/A A7 Dm
wres - tle with des - pair.
e - vil night and day.
your un - fail - ing love.

Kyrie Eleison

Oré Poriajú Verekó

377

Unison
A D E A
1 Ky-ri - e e - le - i - son, ky-ri - e e - le - i - son, ky-ri-
2 Chri - ste e - le - i - son, Chri - ste e - le - i - son, Chri-
1 O Lord, have mer - cy, O Lord, have mer - cy, O
2 O Christ, have mer - cy, O Christ, have mer - cy, O
1 O - ré po-ria - jú ve-re - kó, *Ñan-de - ya - ra; O
F# Bm E A
e e - le - i - son, ky - ri - e e - le - i - son.
ste e - le - i - son, ky - ri - e e - le - i - son.
Lord, have mer - cy, have mer - cy on us.
Christ, have mer - cy, have mer - cy on us.
ré po-ria - jú ve-re - kó, *Ñan-de - ya - ra.

*A stanza may be added by substituting "Jesu Cristo" for "Ñandeyara."

WORDS: Paraguayan
MUSIC: Guarani Kyrie; harm. Carlton R. Young (1926-)

378 Create in Me a Clean Heart, O God

Bb2 Bb Csus C F Am7
1 Cre - ate in me a clean heart, O
2 Cast me not a - way from your
3 Re - store to me the joy of your sal -
Bb2 Bb D7sus/A D7 G G7/B
God; Cre - ate in me a clean heart, O
pres - ence, cast me not a - way from your
va - tion, re - store to me the joy of your sal -
C2 C Gm6/Bb A A7/C# A7
God; Cre - ate in me a clean heart, O
pres - ence, cast me not a - way from your
va - tion, re - store to me the joy of your sal -

WORDS and MUSIC: John Carter (1930-); para. Psalm 51:10-12

SARADAY
Irregular

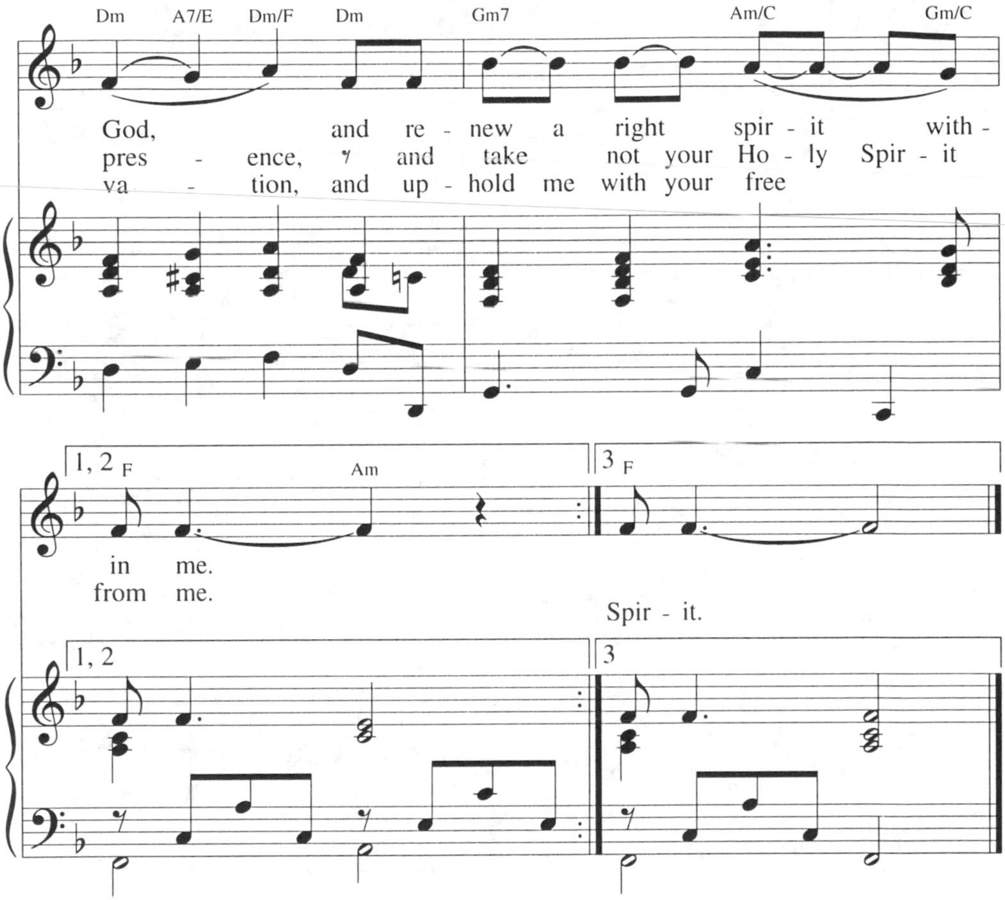
Dm A7/E Dm/F Dm Gm7 Am/C Gm/C
God, and re - new a right spir - it with -
pres - ence, and take not your Ho - ly Spir - it
va - tion, and up - hold me with your free
1, 2 F Am
3 F
in me.
from me.
Spir - it.
1, 2
3

Kyrie

379

1, 3 Ky - ri - e e - lei - son. Ky - ri - e e - lei - son.
2 Chris - te e - lei - son. Chris - te e - lei - son.
1, 3 Lord, have mer - cy. Lord, have mer - cy.
2 Christ, have mer - cy. Christ, have mer - cy.
Ky - ri - e e - le - i - son.
Chris - te e - le - i - son.
Lord, have mer - cy.
Christ, have mer - cy.
8

WORDS: Greek litany
MUSIC: Russian Orthodox

380 Cast Thy Burden upon the Lord

Cast thy burden upon the Lord, and he shall sustain thee; he
never will suffer the righteous to fall: he is at thy
right hand. Thy mercy, Lord, is great and far above the
heavens: let none be made ashamed that wait upon thee.

WORDS: Psalm 55:22, 16:8
MUSIC: Felix Mendelssohn (1809-1847), from *Elijah*

381 Restore in Us, O God

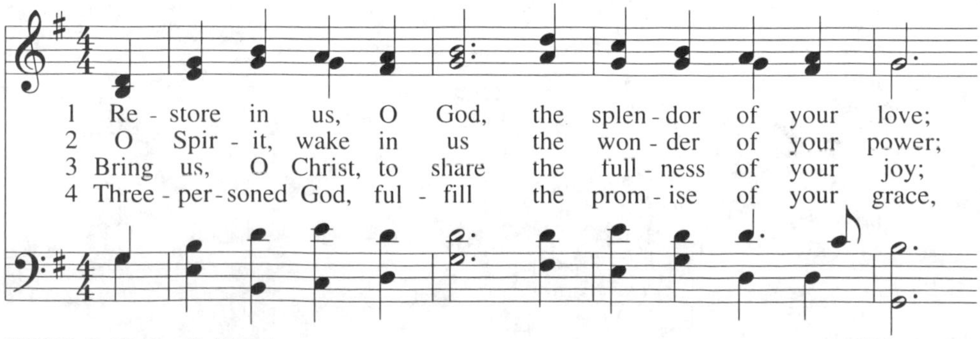
1 Re - store in us, O God, the splen - dor of your love;
2 O Spir - it, wake in us the won - der of your power;
3 Bring us, O Christ, to share the full - ness of your joy;
4 Three - per - soned God, ful - fill the prom - ise of your grace,

WORDS: Carl P. Daw, Jr. (1944-)
MUSIC: *Genevan Psalter*, 1551; adapt. William Crotch (1775-1847)

ST. MICHAEL
S.M.

re - new your im - age in our hearts, and all our sins re - move.
from fruit - less fear un - furl our lives like spring - time bud and flower.
bap - tize us in the ris - en life that death can - not de - stroy.
that we, when all our search - ing ends, may see you face to face.

"Forgive Our Sins as We Forgive" 382

1 "For - give our sins as we for - give," you taught us, Lord, to pray, but you a - lone can grant us grace to live the words we say.
2 How can your par - don reach and bless the un - for - giv - ing heart that broods on wrongs and will not let old bit - ter - ness de - part?
3 In blaz - ing light your cross re - veals the truth we dim - ly knew: what triv - ial debts are owed to us, how great our debt to you.
4 Lord, cleanse the depths with - in our souls and bid re - sent - ment cease. Then, bound to all in bonds of love, our lives will spread your peace.

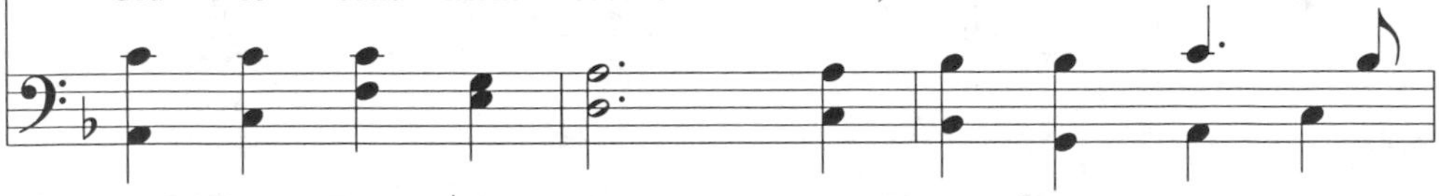

WORDS: Rosamond E. Herklots (1905-1987)
MUSIC: Supplement to the *Kentucky Harmony*, 1820

DETROIT
C.M.

383 If My People's Hearts Are Humbled

Unison
1 If my peo - ple's hearts are hum-bled, if they pray and seek my face,
2 Then my eyes will see their sor - row, then my ears will hear their plea;
if they turn a - way from e - vil, I will not with-hold my grace.
if my peo - ple's hearts are hum-bled, I will set their na - tion free.
I will hear their prayers from heav - en; I will par-don ev - ery sin.
If my peo-ple's hearts are hum-bled, if they pray and seek my face;
If my peo - ple's hearts are hum-bled, I will sure - ly heal their land.
if they turn a - way from e - vil, I will not with-hold my grace.

WORDS: Claire Cloninger (1942-); para. 2 Chronicles 7:14
MUSIC: Leavitt's *The Christian Lyre*, 1830; arr. Jack Schrader (1942-)

PLEADING SAVIOR
8.7.8.7.D.

Rock of Ages

1 Rock of A - ges, cleft for me, let me
2 Not the la - bors of my hands can ful -
3 Noth - ing in my hand I bring, sim - ply
4 While I draw this fleet - ing breath, when my
hide my - self in thee; let the wa - ter and the blood,
fill thy law's de - mands; could my zeal no res - pite know,
to thy cross I cling; na - ked, come to thee for dress,
eyes shall close in death, when I soar to worlds un - known,
from thy wound - ed side which flowed, be of sin the
could my tears for - ev - er flow, all for sin could
help - less, look to thee for grace; foul, I to the
see thee on thy judg - ment throne, Rock of A - ges,
dou - ble cure, save from wrath and make me pure.
not a - tone; thou must save and thou a - lone.
foun - tain fly; wash me, Sav - ior, or I die!
cleft for me, let me hide my - self in thee.

WORDS: Augustus M. Toplady (1740-1778)
MUSIC: Thomas Hastings (1784-1872)

TOPLADY
7.7.7.7.7.7.

385 Search Me, O God

1 Search me, O God, and know my heart to - day; try me, O
2 I praise thee, Lord, for cleans - ing me from sin; ful - fill thy
3 Lord, take my life and make it whol - ly thine; fill my poor
Sav - ior, know my thoughts, I pray. See if there be some wick - ed
Word and make me pure with - in. Fill me with fire where once I
heart with thy great love di - vine. Take all my will, my pas - sion,
way in me; cleanse me from ev - ery sin and set me free.
burned with shame; grant my de - sire to mag - ni - fy thy name.
self, and pride; I now sur - ren - der, Lord—in me a - bide.

WORDS: J. Edwin Orr (1912-1987)
MUSIC: Edward J. Hopkins (1818-1901)

ELLERS
10.10.10.10.

386 Lord Jesus, Think on Me

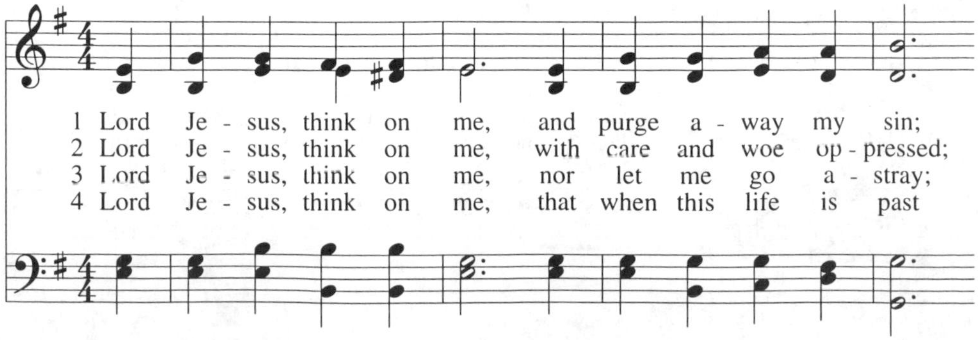
1 Lord Je - sus, think on me, and purge a - way my sin;
2 Lord Je - sus, think on me, with care and woe op - pressed;
3 Lord Je - sus, think on me, nor let me go a - stray;
4 Lord Je - sus, think on me, that when this life is past

WORDS: Synesius of Cyrene (ca. 375-430); tr. Allen W. Chatfield (1808-1896)
MUSIC: William Damon's *Psalms*, 1579

SOUTHWELL
S.M.

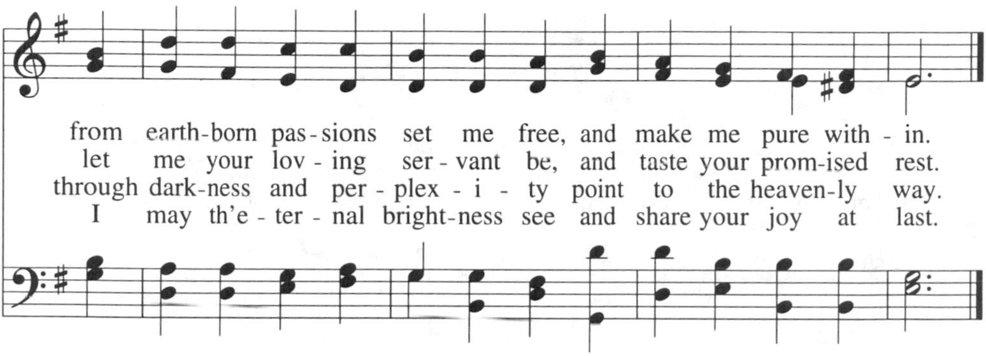
from earth-born pas-sions set me free, and make me pure with - in.
let me your lov - ing ser - vant be, and taste your prom-ised rest.
through dark-ness and per - plex - i - ty point to the heaven-ly way.
I may th'e - ter - nal bright-ness see and share your joy at last.

The Lord Is in His Holy Temple 387

The Lord is in his ho - ly tem - ple, the Lord is in his ho - ly
tem - ple; let all the earth keep si - lence, let all the earth keep
si - lence be - fore him, keep si - lence, keep si - lence be - fore him.

WORDS: Habakkuk 2:20
MUSIC: George F. Root (1820-1895)

QUAM DILECTA
Irregular

388 O God in Whom All Life Begins

1 O God in whom all life be-gins, who births the seed to fruit,
2 U - nite in mu - tual min - is - try our minds and hands and hearts
3 Through tears and laugh-ter, grief and joy, en - large our trust and care;
be - stow your bless-ing on our lives; here let your love find root.
that we may have the grace to seek the power your peace im - parts.
so bind us in com - mu - ni - ty that we may risk and dare.
Bring forth in us the Spir - it's gifts of pa-tience, joy, and peace;
So let our var - ied gifts com-bine to glo - ri - fy your Name
Be with us when we gath - er here to wor-ship, sing, and pray,
de - liv - er us from numb-ing fear, and grant our faith in-crease.
that in all things by word and deed we may your love pro-claim.
then send us forth in power and faith to live the words we say.

WORDS: Carl P. Daw, Jr. (1944-)
MUSIC: English melody; arr. Arthur S. Sullivan (1842-1900)

NOEL
C.M.D.

Put Peace into Each Other's Hands 389

3
4
1 Put peace in - to each oth - er's hands and like a
2 Put peace in - to each oth - er's hands with lov - ing
3 Put peace in - to each oth - er's hands, like bread we
4 As at com - mu - nion, shape your hands in to a
5 Put Christ in - to each oth - er's hands, he is love's
3
treas - ure hold it; pro - tect it like a
ex - pec - ta - tion; be gen - tle in your
break for shar - ing; look peo - ple warm - ly
wait - ing cra - dle; the gift of Christ re -
deep - est meas - ure; in love make peace, give
can - dle flame, with ten - der - ness en - fold it.
words and ways, in touch with God's cre - a - tion.
in the eye: our life is meant for car - ing.
ceive, re - vere, u - nit - ed round the ta - ble.
peace a chance and share it like a treas - ure.

WORDS: Fred Kaan (1929-)
MUSIC: Irish melody

ST. COLUMBA
8.7.8.7.

390 We're Marching to Zion

1 Come, we that love the Lord, and let our joys be known; join in a song with sweet accord, join in a song with sweet accord and thus surround the throne, and thus surround the throne.
2 Let those refuse to sing who never knew our God; but children of the heavenly King, but children of the heavenly King may speak their joys abroad, may speak their joys abroad.
3 The hill of Zion yields a thousand sacred sweets before we reach the heavenly fields, before we reach the heavenly fields, or walk the golden streets, or walk the golden streets.
4 Then let our songs abound, and every tear be dry; we're marching through Emmanuel's ground, we're marching through Emmanuel's ground, to fairer worlds on high, to fairer worlds on high.
Refrain
We're marching to Zion, beautiful, beautiful Zion;

WORDS: Isaac Watts (1674-1748); ref. Robert Lowry (1826-1899)
MUSIC: Robert Lowry (1826-1899)

MARCHING TO ZION
6.6.8.8.6.6.Ref.

we're march-ing up-ward to Zi - on, the beau-ti-ful cit-y of God.

Will You Let Me Be Your Servant 391

Unison
D Em/D D G/D D A/C♯ D
1 Will you let me be your ser - vant,
2 We are pil - grims on a jour - ney,
3 I will hold the Christ - light for you,
4 I will weep when you are weep - ing,
5 When we sing to God and heav - en,
Em/D D G/D D A G D/F♯
let me be as Christ to you? Pray that I might
here to - geth - er on the road; we are here to
in the night - time of your fear; I will hold my
when you laugh I'll laugh with you; I will share your
we shall find such har - mo - ny, born of all we've
Em7 D/A A7 Bm G D/G Em/G G G/A A7 D
have the grace to let you be my ser - vant too.
help each oth - er walk the mile and bear the load.
hand out to you, speak the peace you long to hear.
joy and sor - row till we've seen this jour - ney through.
known to - geth - er of Christ's love and ag - o - ny.

WORDS and MUSIC: Richard Gillard (1953-)

392 Fear Not, Rejoice and Be Glad

Refrain (Unison)

Em
B7
Fear not, re-joice and be glad, the Lord has done a great thing:
Em
Am
Em/B
B7
Em
has poured out his Spir-it on all who live, on those who con-fess his name.
Am
B7
Em
1 The fig tree is bud - ding, the vine bear - ing fruit, the
2 We shall eat in plen - ty and be sat - is - fied, the
3 "My peo - ple will know that I am the Lord; their
4 His chil - dren shall dwell in a bod - y of love, a
Am
E
Am
wheat fields are gold - en with grain. Thrust in the sick - le, the
moun-tains will drip with new wine. "My chil-dren will drink of the
shame I have tak - en a - way. My Spir - it will lead them to -
light to the world they will be. Life shall come forth from the

WORDS: Priscilla Wright (1928-); para. Joel 2:21-29, 3:13-18
MUSIC: Priscilla Wright (1928-); arr. Dale Grotenhuis (1931-)

CLAY
Irregular

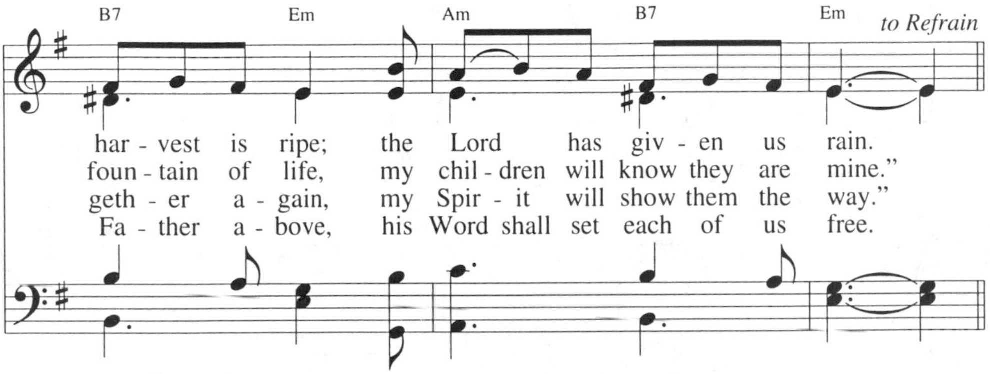
B7 Em Am B7 Em to Refrain
har - vest is ripe; the Lord has giv - en us rain.
foun - tain of life, my chil - dren will know they are mine."
geth - er a - gain, my Spir - it will show them the way."
Fa - ther a - bove, his Word shall set each of us free.

Blest Be the Tie That Binds 393

1 Blest be the tie that binds our hearts in Chris - tian love;
2 Be - fore our Fa - ther's throne we pour our ar - dent prayers;
3 We share our mu - tual woes, each oth - er's bur - dens bear;
4 From sor - row, toil, and pain, and sin we shall be free;

the fel - low - ship of kin - dred minds is like to that a - bove.
our fears, our hopes, our aims are one, our com - forts and our cares.
and oft - en for each oth - er flows the sym - pa - thiz - ing tear.
and per - fect love and friend - ship reign through all e - ter - ni - ty.

WORDS: John Fawcett (1740-1817), alt.
MUSIC: Johann G. Nägeli (1773-1836); arr. Lowell Mason (1792-1872)

DENNIS
S.M.

394 God of All Time

1 God of all time, all sea-sons of our liv - ing, source of our
2 Here in this place, where oth - ers have been build - ing, we come to
3 Spir - it who draws our frag - ile selves to - geth - er, Spir - it who
4 Let us not die from pov - er - ty of car - ing, let us not
spark, pro - tec - tor of our flame, blaz - ing be - fore our birth, be -
claim the leg - a - cy of faith, take in our turn the tell - ing
turns a strang-er to a friend, be at this ta - ble where we
starve, where love is to be shared. Come, break us o - pen to re -
yond our dy - ing, God of all time, we come to sing your name.
of your sto - ry, and, though we trem - ble, speak your hope, your truth.
greet each oth - er, be in the peace we pass from hand to hand.
ceive your heal - ing: your bro - ken bod - y be our wine and bread.

WORDS: Shirley Erena Murray (1931-)
MUSIC: John B. Dykes (1823-1876)

STRENGTH AND STAY
11.10.11.10.

395 The Bond of Love

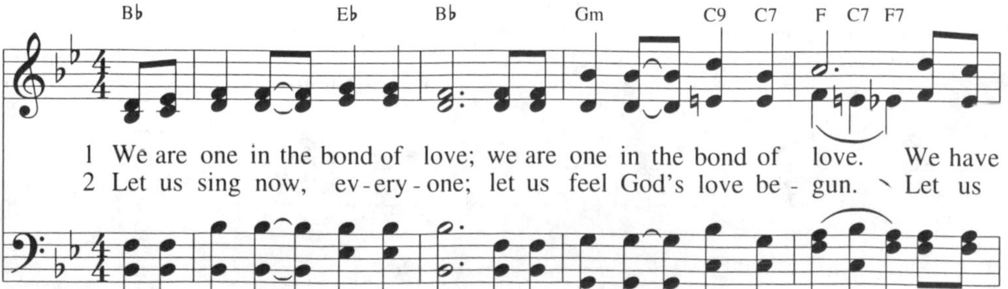
Bb Eb Bb Gm C9 C7 F C7 F7
1 We are one in the bond of love; we are one in the bond of love. We have
2 Let us sing now, ev - ery - one; let us feel God's love be - gun. Let us

WORDS and MUSIC: Otis Skillings (1935-)

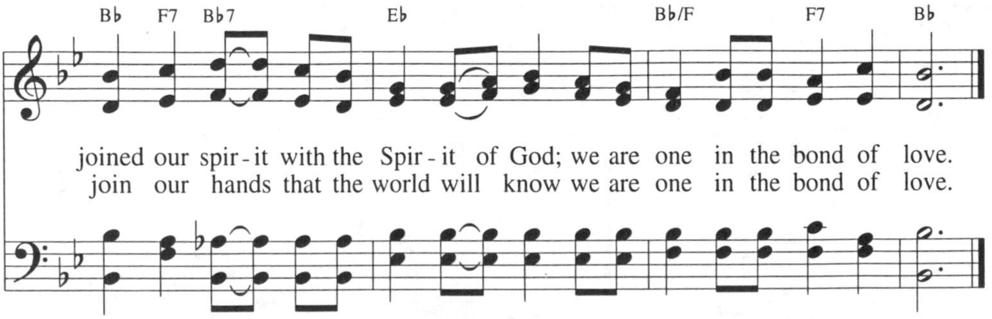
Bb F7 Bb7 Eb Bb/F F7 Bb
joined our spir - it with the Spir - it of God; we are one in the bond of love.
join our hands that the world will know we are one in the bond of love.

Where the Spirit of the Lord Is 396

Eb Ebdim Eb C+ C7 Fm
Where the Spir - it of the Lord is, there is peace. Where the
Bb7 Bbdim7 Bb7 Gm/Bb Bb7 Eb Gm/Bb Bb7 Eb
Spir - it of the Lord is, there is love. There is com - fort in life's
Dbmaj7/Eb Eb7 Abmaj9 Ab Abm6
dark - est hour, there is light and life, there is help and
Eb/Bb Fm/Bb Bb7 Ab/Bb Bb7 Eb Ab/Eb Eb
pow - er in the Spir - it, in the Spir - it of the Lord.

WORDS and MUSIC: Stephen R. Adams (1943-)

397 The Gift of Love

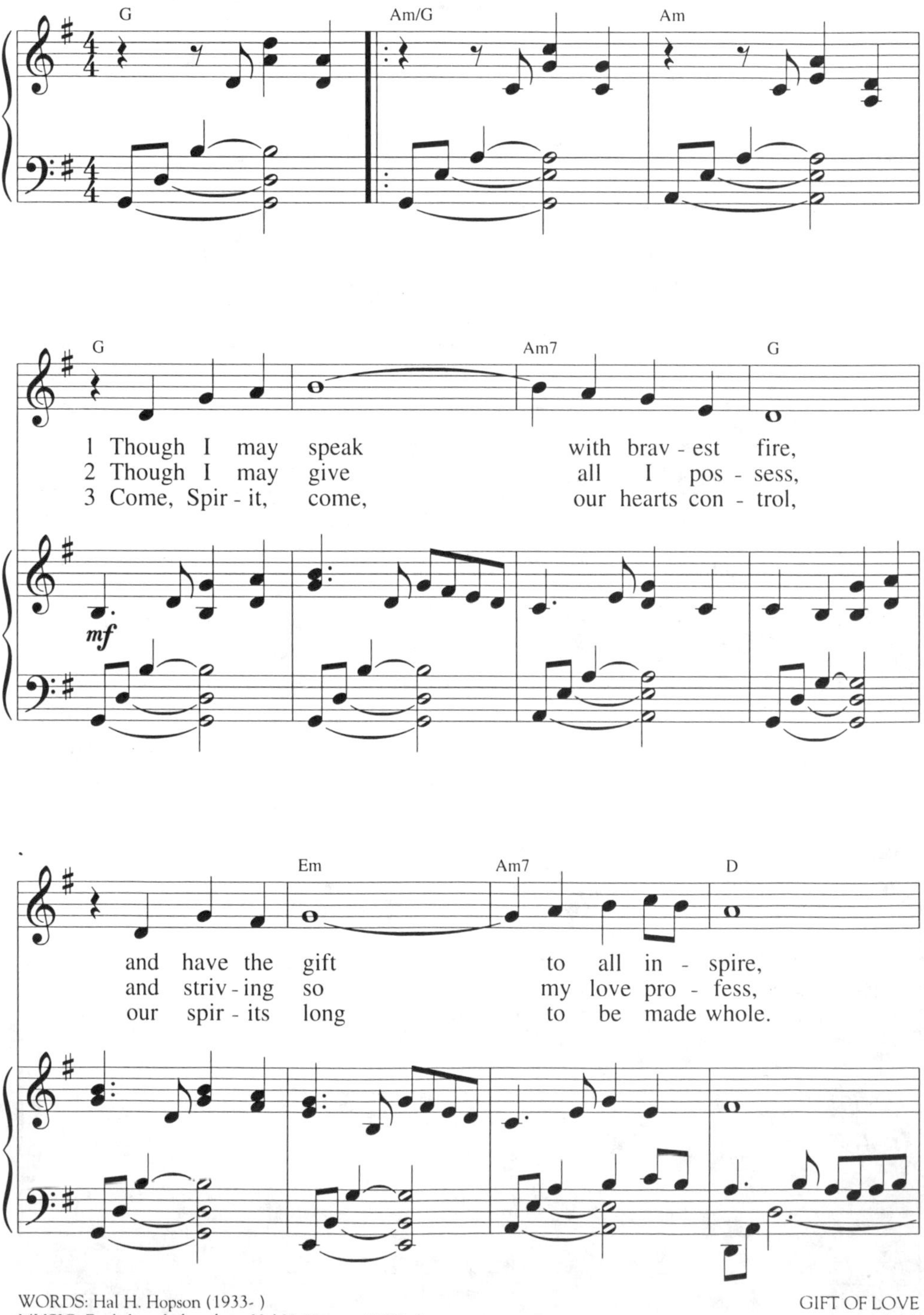
G
Am/G
Am
G
Am7
G
1 Though I may speak with brav - est fire,
2 Though I may give all I pos - sess,
3 Come, Spir - it, come, our hearts con - trol,
mf
Em
Am7
D
and have the gift to all in - spire,
and striv - ing so my love pro - fess,
our spir - its long to be made whole.

WORDS: Hal H. Hopson (1933-)
MUSIC: English melody; adapt. Hal H. Hopson (1933-)

GIFT OF LOVE
L.M.

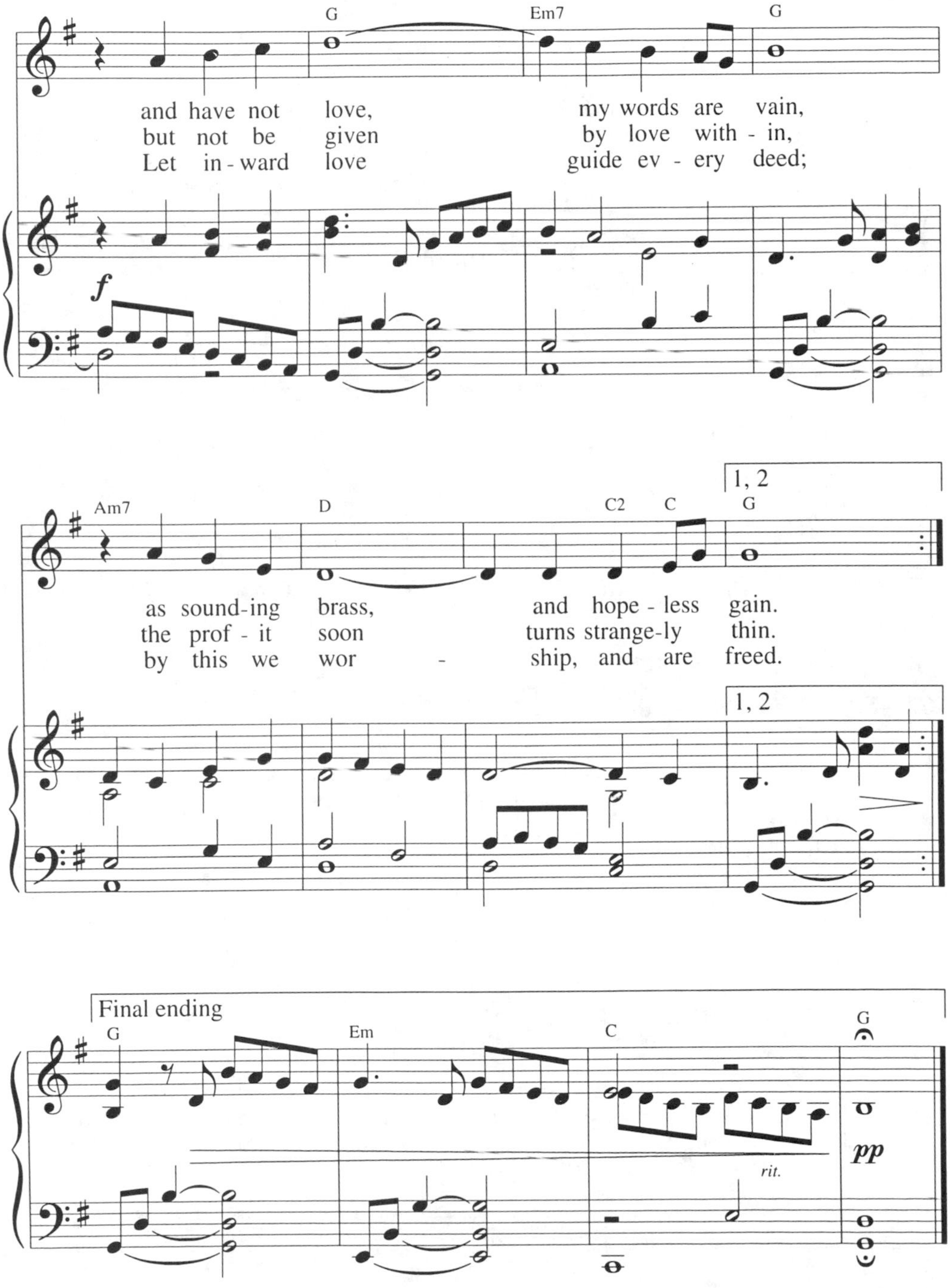
G
Em7
G
and have not love, my words are vain,
but not be given by love with - in,
Let in - ward love guide ev - ery deed;
f
Am7
D
C2
C
1, 2
G
as sound-ing brass, and hope - less gain.
the prof - it soon turns strange-ly thin.
by this we wor - ship, and are freed.
Final ending
Em
rit.
pp

398 O the Deep, Deep Love of Jesus

1 O the deep, deep love of Je - sus, vast, un - mea - sured,
2 O the deep, deep love of Je - sus—spread his praise from
3 O the deep, deep love of Je - sus, love of ev - ery
bound-less, free! Roll - ing as a might - y o - cean in its
shore to shore! How he loves us, ev - er loves us, chang-es
love the best! 'Tis an o - cean vast of bless - ing, 'tis a
full - ness o - ver me! Un - der - neath me, all a - round me,
nev - er, nev - er - more! How he watch - es o'er his loved ones,
ha - ven sweet of rest! O the deep, deep love of Je - sus—
is the cur - rent of thy love— lead - ing on - ward,
died to call them all his own; how for them he's
'tis a heaven of heavens to me; and it lifts me

WORDS: Samuel Trevor Francis (1834-1925)
MUSIC: Thomas J. Williams (1869-1944)

EBENEZER
8.7.8.7.D

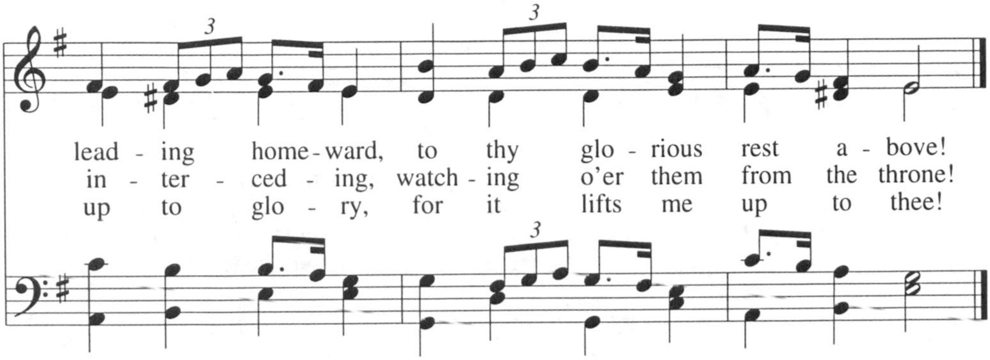
lead - ing home-ward, to thy glo - rious rest a - bove!
in - ter - ced - ing, watch - ing o'er them from the throne!
up to glo - ry, for it lifts me up to thee!

Ubi Caritas et Amor

399

Where True Charity and Love Abide

F C Dm B♭ D G C
U - bi ca - ri - tas et a - mor,
Where true char - i - ty and love a - bide,
F C Dm Gm C F
u - bi ca - ri - tas De - us i - bi est.
God is dwell - ing there; God is dwell - ing there.

WORDS: Latin, 8th c.
MUSIC: Jacques Berthier (1923-1994)

400 Not for Tongues of Heaven's Angels

Unison
1 Not for tongues of heav-en's an - gels, not for wis-dom to dis - cern, not for faith that mas - ters moun - tains, for this bet - ter gift we yearn:
2 Love is hum - ble, love is gen - tle, love is ten - der, true and kind; love is gra - cious, ev - er pa - tient, gen - er - ous of heart and mind:
3 Nev - er jeal - ous, nev - er self - ish, love will not re - joice in wrong; nev - er boast - ful nor re - sent - ful, love be - lieves and suf - fers long:
4 In the day this world is fad - ing faith and hope will play their part; but when Christ is seen in glo - ry love shall reign in ev - ery heart:
may love be ours, O Lord.

WORDS: Timothy Dudley-Smith (1926-); para. 1 Corinthians 13
MUSIC: Peter Cutts (1937-)

BRIDEGROOM
8.7.8.7.6.

Of All the Spirit's Gifts to Me 401

Unison
1 Of all the Spir - it's gifts to me, I
2 The Spir - it shows me love's the root of
3 The Spir - it shows if I pos - sess a
4 Though what's a - head is mys - ter - y, and
5 We go in peace, but made a - ware that,
pray that I may nev - er cease to take and treas - ure
ev - ery gift sent from a - bove, of ev - ery flower, of
love no e - vil can de - stroy, how - ev - er great is
life it - self is ours on lease, each day the Spir - it
in a need - y world like this, our clear - est pur - pose
most these three: love, joy, and peace.
ev - ery fruit, that God is love.
my dis - tress, then this is joy.
says to me, "Go forth in peace!"
is to share love, joy, and peace.

WORDS: Fred Pratt Green (1903-2000)
MUSIC: Austin C. Lovelace (1919-)

THREEFOLD GIFTS
8.8.8.4.

402 He Came Down

G
3
D7
1 He came down that we may have love; he
2 He came down that we may have peace; he
3 He came down that we may have joy; he
4 He came down that we may have life; he

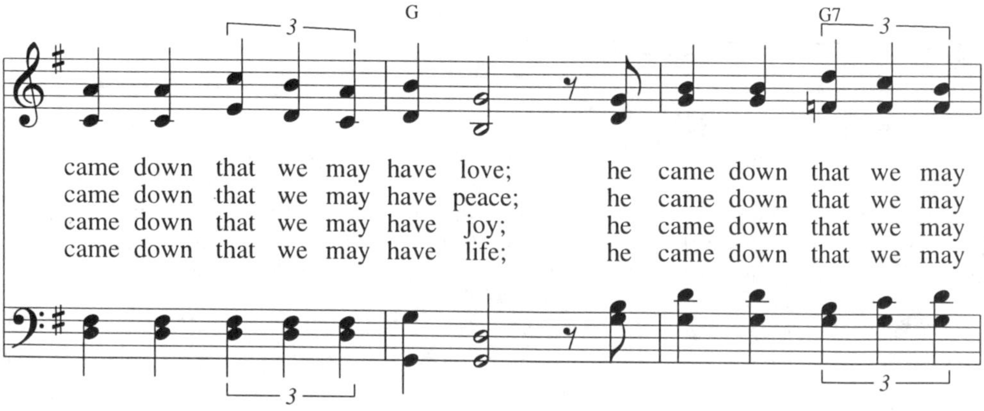
3
G
G7
came down that we may have love; he came down that we may
came down that we may have peace; he came down that we may
came down that we may have joy; he came down that we may
came down that we may have life; he came down that we may

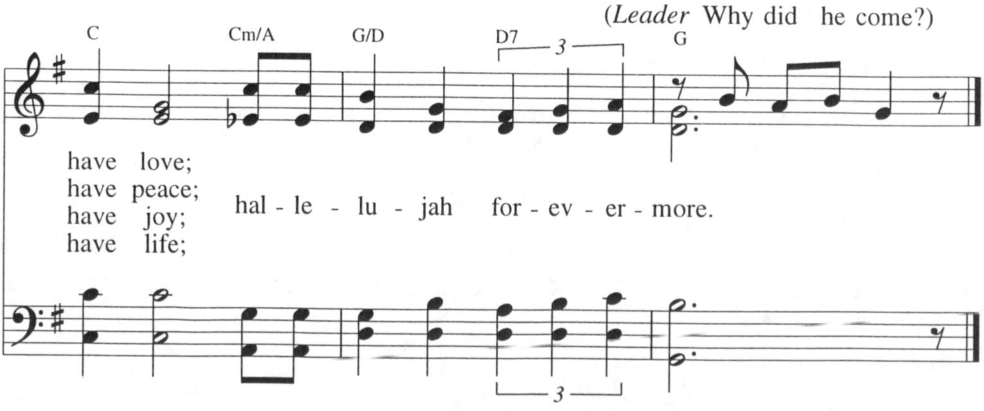
(Leader Why did he come?)
C
Cm/A
G/D
D7
G
have love;
have peace;
have joy;
have life;
hal - le - lu - jah for - ev - er - more.

WORDS and MUSIC: Cameroon; arr. Jane Holstein (1958-)

CAMEROON
Irregular

Come, My Way, My Truth, My Life 403

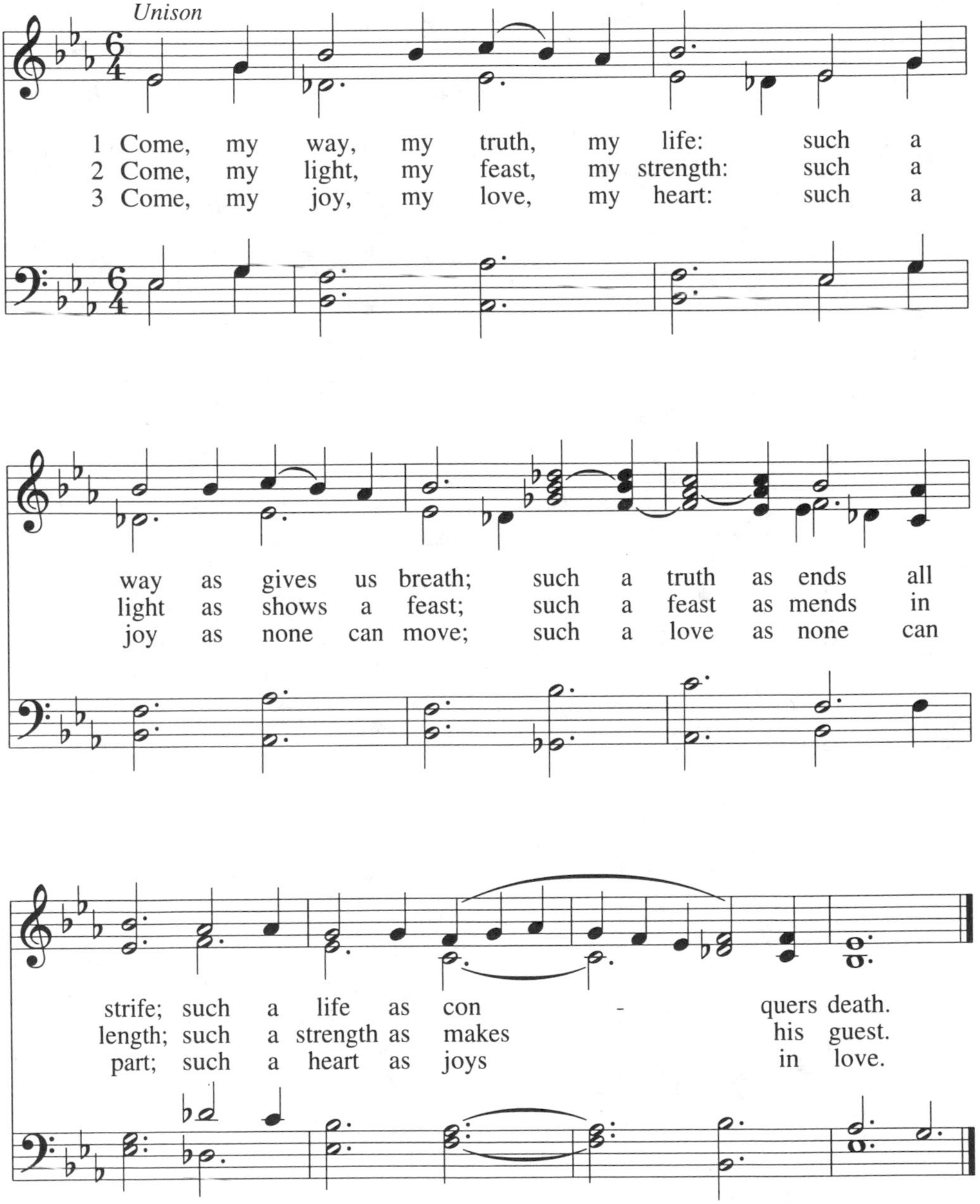
Unison
1 Come, my way, my truth, my life: such a
2 Come, my light, my feast, my strength: such a
3 Come, my joy, my love, my heart: such a
way as gives us breath; such a truth as ends all
light as shows a feast; such a feast as mends in
joy as none can move; such a love as none can
strife; such a life as con - quers death.
length; such a strength as makes his guest.
part; such a heart as joys in love.

WORDS: George Herbert (1593-1633)
MUSIC: Ralph Vaughan Williams (1872-1958)

THE CALL
7.7.7.7.

404 Hope of the World

Unison
1 Hope of the world, O Christ of great com - pas - sion:
2 Hope of the world, God's gift from high - est heav - en,
3 Hope of the world, a - foot on dust - y high - ways,
4 Hope of the world, who by your cross did save us
5 Hope of the world, O Christ, o'er death vic - to - rious,
speak to our fear - ful hearts by con - flict rent;
bring - ing to hun - gry souls the bread of life:
show - ing to wan - dering souls the path of light:
from death and dark de - spair, from sin and guilt:
who by this sign did con - quer grief and pain:
save us, your peo - ple, from con - sum - ing pas - sion,
still let your Spir - it un - to us be giv - en
walk now be - side us, lest the tempt - ing by - ways
we ren - der back the love your mer - cy gave us;
we would be faith - ful to your gos - pel glo - rious;
who by our own false hopes and aims are spent.
to heal earth's wounds and end her bit - ter strife.
lure us a - way from you to end - less night.
take now our lives and use them as you will.
you are our Lord, and you for - ev - er reign!

WORDS: Georgia Harkness (1891-1974), alt.
MUSIC: V. Earle Copes (1921-)

VICAR
11.10.11.10.

My Hope Is Built on Nothing Less 405

1 My hope is built on noth-ing less than Je-sus' blood and right-eous-ness; I dare not trust the sweet-est frame, but whol-ly lean on Je-sus' name.
2 When dark-ness veils his love-ly face, I rest on his un-chang-ing grace; in ev-ery high and storm-y gale, my an-chor holds with-in the veil.
3 His oath, his cov-e-nant, his blood, sup-port me in the whelm-ing flood; when all a-round my soul gives way, he then is all my hope and stay.
4 When he shall come with trum-pet sound, O may I then in him be found: dressed in his right-eous-ness a-lone, fault-less to stand be-fore the throne.
Refrain
On Christ, the sol-id Rock, I stand: all oth-er ground is sink-ing sand; all oth-er ground is sink-ing sand.

WORDS: Edward Mote (1797-1874)
MUSIC: William B. Bradbury (1816-1868)

SOLID ROCK
L.M.Ref.

406 My Faith Has Found a Resting Place

1 My faith has found a rest - ing place, not in de - vice nor creed;
2 E - nough for me that Je - sus saves, this ends my fear and doubt;
3 My heart is lean - ing on the Word, the writ - ten Word of God,
4 My great Phy - si - cian heals the sick, the lost he came to save;
I trust the ev - er - liv - ing One, his wounds for me shall plead.
a sin - ful soul, I come to him, he'll nev - er cast me out.
sal - va - tion by my Sav - ior's name, sal - va - tion through his blood.
for me his pre - cious blood he shed, for me his life he gave.
Refrain
I need no oth - er ar - gu - ment, I need no oth - er plea;
it is e - nough that Je - sus died, and that he died for me.

WORDS: Lidie H. Edmunds, 19th c.
MUSIC: Norwegian melody; arr. William J. Kirkpatrick (1838-1921)

LANDAS
C.M.Ref.

I Know Whom I Have Believed 407

1 I know not why God's won-drous grace to me he has made known,
2 I know not how this sav - ing faith to me he did im - part,
3 I know not how the Spir - it moves, con-vinc-ing me of sin,
4 I know not when my Lord may come, at night or noon-day fair,
nor why, un - wor - thy, Christ in love re - deemed me for his own.
nor how be - liev - ing in his Word wrought peace with-in my heart.
re - veal - ing Je - sus through the Word, cre - at - ing faith in him.
nor if I'll walk the vale with him, or meet him in the air.
Refrain
But "I know whom I have be - liev - ed, and am per-suad-ed that he is
a - ble to keep that which I've com-mit-ted un-to him a-gainst that day."

WORDS: Daniel W. Whittle (1840-1901); para. 2 Timothy 1:12b
MUSIC: James McGranahan (1840-1907)

EL NATHAN
C.M.Ref.

408 I Am Thine, O Lord

1 I am thine, O Lord— I have heard thy voice, and it told thy love to me; but I long to rise in the arms of faith and be clos - er drawn to thee.
2 Con - se - crate me now to thy serv - ice, Lord, by the power of grace di - vine; let my soul look up with a stead - fast hope and my will be lost in thine.
3 O the pure de - light of a sin - gle hour that be - fore thy throne I spend, when I kneel in prayer and with thee, my God, I com-mune as friend with friend.
4 There are depths of love that I can - not know till I cross the nar - row sea; there are heights of joy that I may not reach till I rest in peace with thee.
Refrain
Draw me near - er, near-er, bless-ed Lord, to the cross where thou hast died; draw me near - er, near - er, near - er, bless - ed Lord, to thy pre - cious, bleed - ing side.

WORDS: Fanny J. Crosby (1820-1915)
MUSIC: William H. Doane (1832-1915)

I AM THINE
10.7.10.7.Ref.

God of Our Life

1 God of our life, through all the cir-cling years, we trust in
2 God of the past, our times are in your hand; with us a-
3 God of the com-ing years, thro' paths un-known we fol-low
you; in all the past, through all our hopes and fears, your
bide. Lead us by faith to hope's true Prom-ised Land; be
you; when we are strong, Lord, leave us not a-lone; our
hand we view. With each new day, when morn-ing lifts the
now our guide. With you to bless, the dark-ness shines as
faith re-new. Be now for us in life our dai-ly
veil, we own your mer-cies, Lord, which nev-er fail.
light, and faith's fair vi-sion chang-es in-to sight.
bread, our heart's true home when all our years have sped.

WORDS: Hugh T. Kerr (1872-1950), alt.
MUSIC: Charles H. Purday (1799-1885); arr. John Weaver (1937-)

SANDON
10.4.10.4.10.10.

410 Firm Foundation

Refrain
F Bb F/C Csus F Bb
Je - sus, you're my firm foun - da - tion, I know I can stand
C Dm7 F Bb Asus A
se - cure; Je - sus, you're my firm foun - da - tion,
Bb F C Dm7
I put my hope in your ho - ly Word,
Bb F C Csus F
I put my hope in your ho - ly Word.

WORDS and MUSIC: Nancy Gordon (1955-) and Jamie Harvill (1960-)

Verse Men (Unison)
Women (Unison)
F C/F F F C/F F
1 I have a liv - ing hope,
2 Your Word is faith - ful,
Bb C F Bb/D C/E F
I have a fu - ture;
might - y in pow - er;
Dm7 Fmaj7/C Bb2
God has a plan for me,
God will de - liv - er me,
of
Bb2 F/A All Gm7 C7sus to Refrain
of this I'm sure.
this I'm sure,

411 How Firm a Foundation

1 How firm a foun - da - tion, you saints of the Lord,
2 "Fear not, I am with you, O be not dis - mayed,
3 "When through the deep wa - ters I call you to go,
4 "When through fier - y tri - als your path - way shall lie,
5 "The soul that on Je - sus still leans for re - pose,
is laid for your faith in his ex - cel - lent Word!
for I am your God, and will still give you aid;
the riv - ers of sor - row shall not o - ver - flow;
my grace, all suf - fi - cient, shall be your sup - ply;
I will not, I will not de - sert to its foes;
What more can he say than to you he has said,
I'll strength - en you, help you, and cause you to stand,
for I will be with you in trou - ble to bless,
the flame shall not hurt you, I on - ly de - sign
that soul, though all hell should en - deav - or to shake,
to you who for ref - uge to Je - sus have fled?
up - held by my right - eous, om - nip - o - tent hand.
and sanc - ti - fy to you your deep - est dis - tress.
your dross to con - sume, and your gold to re - fine.
I'll nev - er, no, nev - er, no, nev - er for - sake!"

WORDS: Rippon's *Selection of Hymns*, 1787, alt.; vss. 2-5 para. Isaiah 43:1-5
MUSIC: Funk's *Genuine Church Music*, 1832

FOUNDATION
11.11.11.11.

He Comes to Us As One Unknown 412

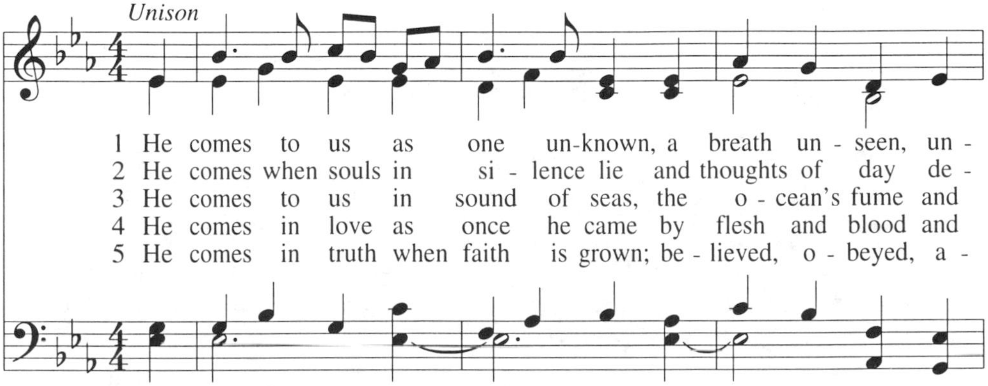
Unison
1 He comes to us as one un-known, a breath un - seen, un -
2 He comes when souls in si - lence lie and thoughts of day de -
3 He comes to us in sound of seas, the o - cean's fume and
4 He comes in love as once he came by flesh and blood and
5 He comes in truth when faith is grown; be - lieved, o - beyed, a -

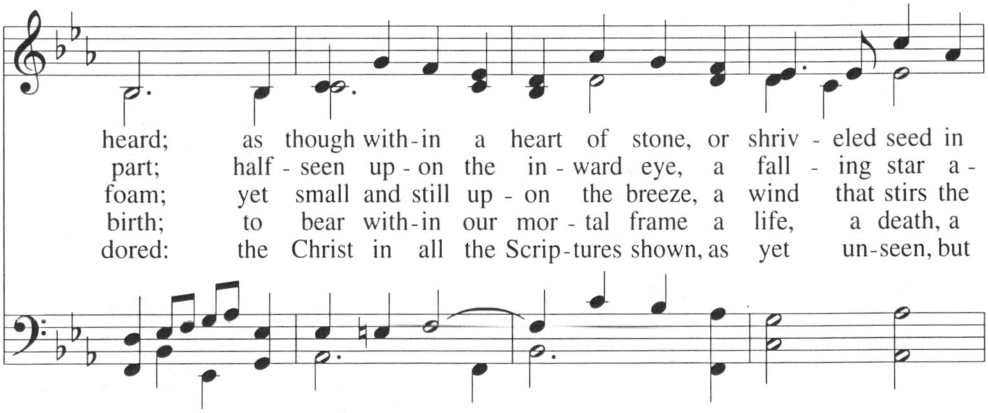
heard; as though with-in a heart of stone, or shriv - eled seed in
part; half - seen up - on the in - ward eye, a fall - ing star a -
foam; yet small and still up - on the breeze, a wind that stirs the
birth; to bear with-in our mor - tal frame a life, a death, a
dored: the Christ in all the Scrip-tures shown, as yet un-seen, but

dark - ness sown, a pulse of be - ing stirred, a pulse of be - ing stirred.
cross the sky of night with-in the heart, of night with-in the heart.
tops of trees, a voice to call us home, a voice to call us home.
sav - ing name, for ev - ery child of earth, for ev - ery child of earth.
not un-known, our Sav - ior and our Lord, our Sav - ior and our Lord.

WORDS: Timothy Dudley-Smith (1926-)
MUSIC: C. Hubert H. Parry (1848-1918)

REPTON
8.6.8.8.6.6.

413 When Our Confidence Is Shaken

1 When our con - fi - dence is shak - en in be - liefs we thought se - cure, when the spir - it in its sick - ness seeks but can - not find a cure, God is ac - tive in the ten - sions of a faith not yet ma - ture, of a faith not yet ma - ture.
2 So - lar sys - tems, void of mean - ing, freeze the spir - it in - to stone; al - ways our re - search - es lead us to the ul - ti - mate un - known. Faith must die, or come full cir - cle to its source in God a - lone, to its source in God a - lone.
3 In the dis - ci - pline of pray - ing, when it's hard - est to be - lieve; in the drudg - er - y of car - ing, when it's not e - nough to grieve; faith, ma - tur - ing, learns ac - cep - tance of the in - sights we re - ceive, of the in - sights we re - ceive.
4 God is love, and thus re - deems us in the Christ we cru - ci - fy; this is God's e - ter - nal an - swer to the world's e - ter - nal why. May we in this faith ma - tur - ing be con - tent to live and die, be con - tent to live and die!

WORDS: Fred Pratt Green (1903-2000)
MUSIC: John Hughes (1873-1932)

CWM RHONDDA
8.7.8.7.8.7.7.

I Know That My Redeemer Lives! 414

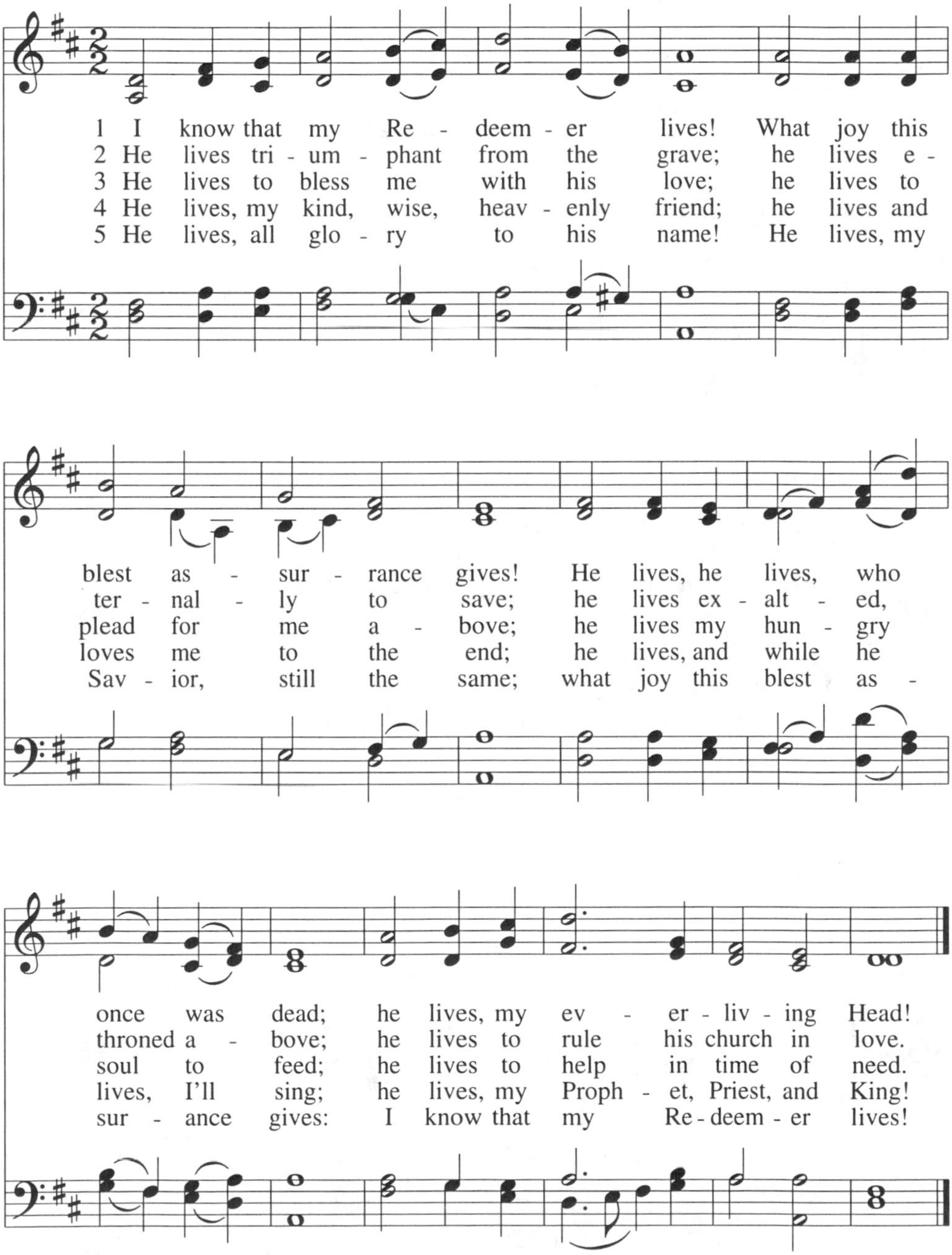
1 I know that my Re - deem - er lives! What joy this blest as - sur - rance gives! He lives, he lives, who once was dead; he lives, my ev - er - liv - ing Head!
2 He lives tri - um - phant from the grave; he lives e - ter - nal - ly to save; he lives ex - alt - ed, throned a - bove; he lives to rule his church in love.
3 He lives to bless me with his love; he lives to plead for me a - bove; he lives my hun - gry soul to feed; he lives to help in time of need.
4 He lives, my kind, wise, heav - enly friend; he lives and loves me to the end; he lives, and while he lives, I'll sing; he lives, my Proph - et, Priest, and King!
5 He lives, all glo - ry to his name! He lives, my Sav - ior, still the same; what joy this blest as - sur - ance gives: I know that my Re - deem - er lives!

WORDS: Samuel Medley (1738-1799), alt.
MUSIC: John Hatton (ca. 1710-1793)

DUKE STREET
L.M.

415 When We Are Living

Pues Si Vivimos

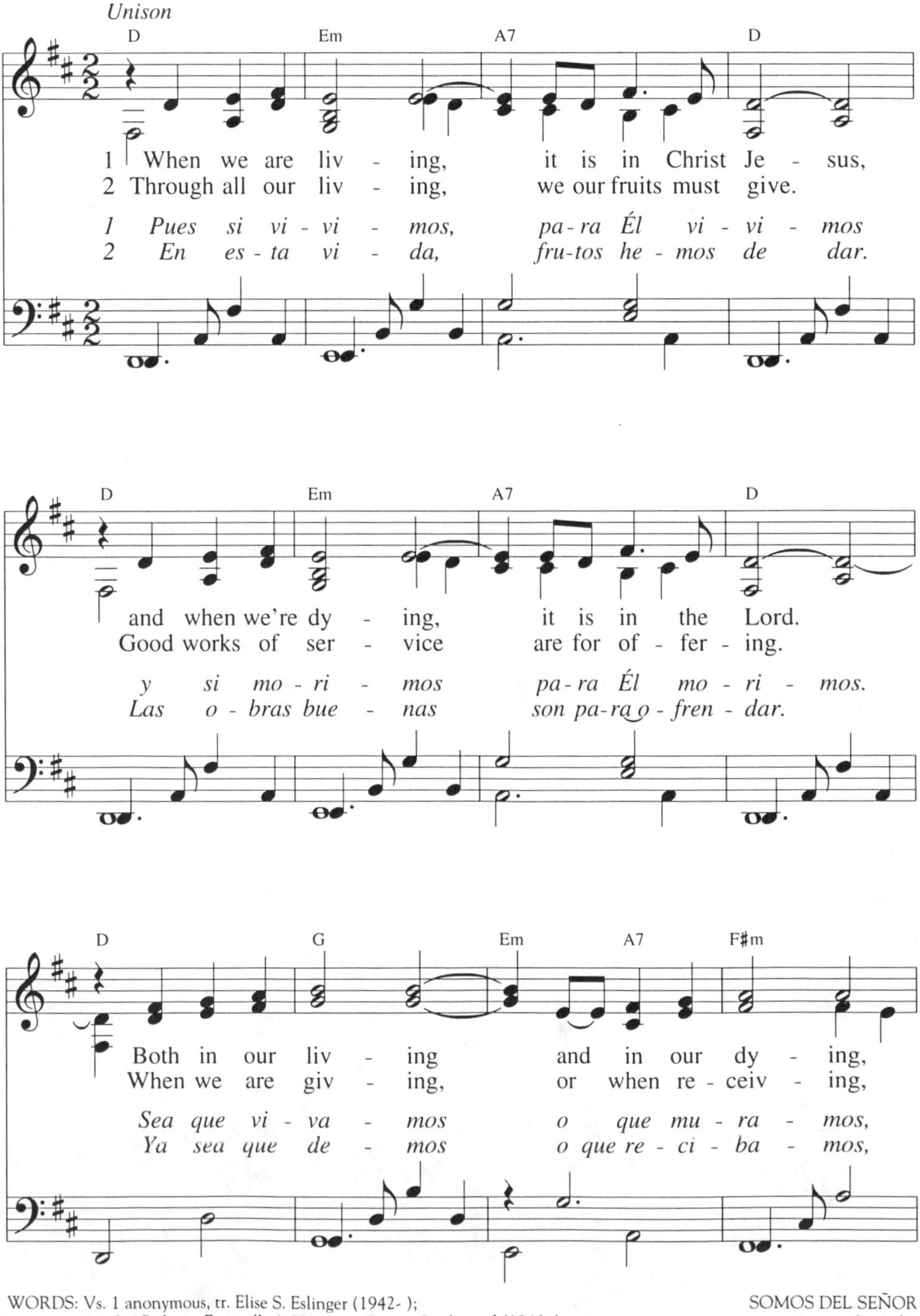
Unison
D Em A7 D
1 When we are liv - ing, it is in Christ Je - sus,
2 Through all our liv - ing, we our fruits must give.
1 Pues si vi - vi - mos, pa - ra Él vi - vi - mos
2 En es - ta vi - da, fru-tos he - mos de dar.
D Em A7 D
and when we're dy - ing, it is in the Lord.
Good works of ser - vice are for of - fer - ing.
y si mo - ri - mos pa - ra Él mo - ri - mos.
Las o - bras bue - nas son pa-ra o - fren - dar.
D G Em A7 F♯m
Both in our liv - ing and in our dy - ing,
When we are giv - ing, or when re - ceiv - ing,
Sea que vi - va - mos o que mu - ra - mos,
Ya sea que de - mos o que re - ci - ba - mos,

WORDS: Vs. 1 anonymous, tr. Elise S. Eslinger (1942-);
vss. 2-4 Roberto Escamilla (1931-), tr. George Lockwood (1946-)
MUSIC: Spanish melody; arr. Hal H. Hopson (1933-)

SOMOS DEL SEÑOR
Irregular

last time
Bm
Em
A7
D
D
we be-long to God, we be-long to God.
so-mos del Se - ñor, so-mos del Se - ñor.

3 'Mid times of sorrow and in times of pain,
when sensing beauty or in love's embrace,
whether we suffer, or sing rejoicing,
we belong to God, we belong to God.

3 En la tristeza y en el dolor,
en la belleza y en el amor,
sea que suframos o que gocemos,
somos del Señor, somos del Señor.

4 Across this wide world, we shall always find
those who are crying with no peace of mind,
but when we help them, or when we feed them,
we belong to God, we belong to God.

4 En este mundo, hemos de encontrar
gente que llora y sin consolar.
Sea que ayudemos o que alimentemos,
somos del Señor, somos del Señor.

God! When Human Bonds Are Broken 416

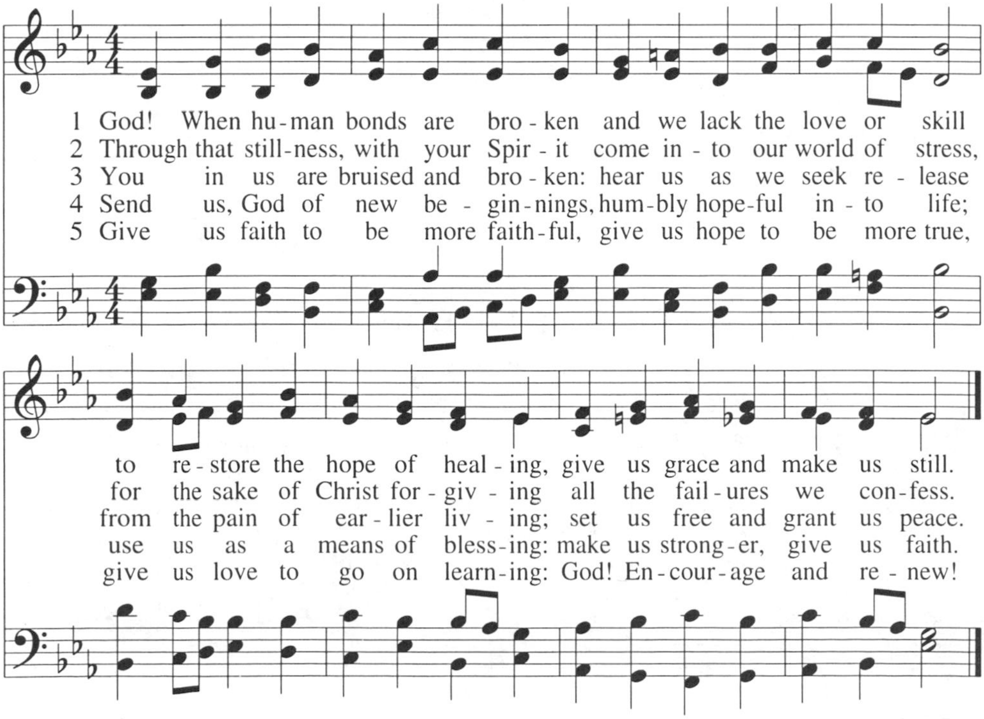
1 God! When hu-man bonds are bro - ken and we lack the love or skill
2 Through that still-ness, with your Spir - it come in - to our world of stress,
3 You in us are bruised and bro - ken: hear us as we seek re - lease
4 Send us, God of new be - gin-nings, hum-bly hope-ful in - to life;
5 Give us faith to be more faith-ful, give us hope to be more true,
to re-store the hope of heal - ing, give us grace and make us still.
for the sake of Christ for - giv - ing all the fail-ures we con-fess.
from the pain of ear - lier liv - ing; set us free and grant us peace.
use us as a means of bless-ing: make us strong-er, give us faith.
give us love to go on learn-ing: God! En-cour-age and re - new!

WORDS: Fred Kaan (1929-)
MUSIC: William H. Monk (1823-1889)

MERTON
8.7.8.7.

417 Not with Naked Eye

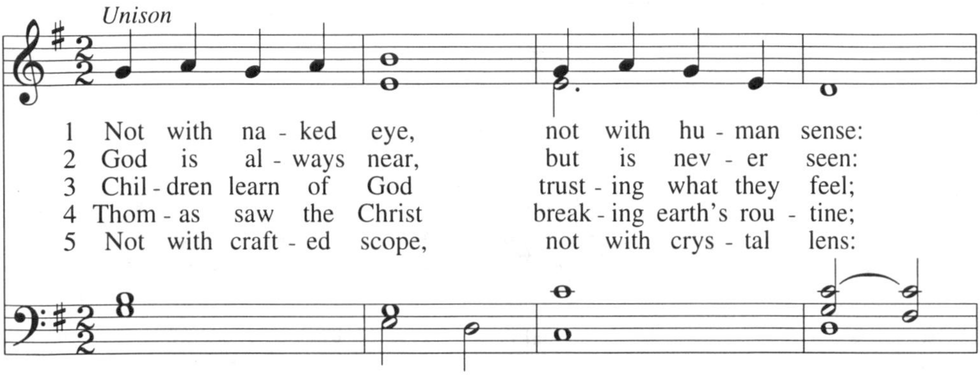
Unison
1 Not with na - ked eye, not with hu - man sense:
2 God is al - ways near, but is nev - er seen:
3 Chil - dren learn of God trust - ing what they feel;
4 Thom - as saw the Christ break - ing earth's rou - tine;
5 Not with craft - ed scope, not with crys - tal lens:

through the eye of faith ob - serve om - ni - po - tence.
Source of heaven and earth and all that lies be - tween.
touch - ing, tast - ing, seek - ing, find - ing what is real.
blessed are those who trust the Ho - ly One un - seen.
vi - sion of the Christ be - gins where see - ing ends.

WORDS and MUSIC: Daniel Charles Damon (1955-)

STITELER
5.5.5.6.

418 Eternal Light, Shine in My Heart

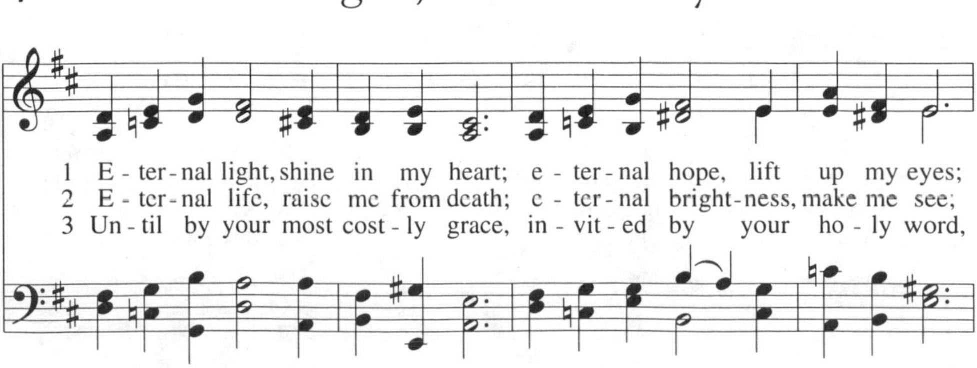
1 E - ter - nal light, shine in my heart; e - ter - nal hope, lift up my eyes;
2 E - ter - nal life, raise me from death; e - ter - nal bright - ness, make me see;
3 Un - til by your most cost - ly grace, in - vit - ed by your ho - ly word,

WORDS: Alcuin, 8th c.; para. Christopher Idle (1938-)
MUSIC: Jane Marshall (1924-)

JACOB
L.M.

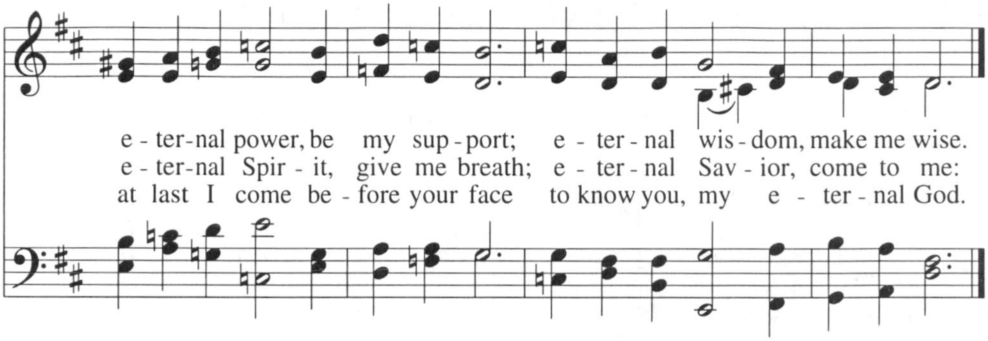
e - ter-nal power, be my sup - port; e - ter - nal wis - dom, make me wise.
e - ter-nal Spir - it, give me breath; e - ter - nal Sav - ior, come to me:
at last I come be - fore your face to know you, my e - ter - nal God.

My Faith Looks Up to Thee 419

1 My faith looks up to thee, thou Lamb of Cal - va - ry,
2 May thy rich grace im - part strength to my faint - ing heart,
3 While life's dark maze I tread, and griefs a - round me spread,
4 When ends life's tran - sient dream, when death's cold, sul - len stream
Sav - ior di - vine! Now hear me while I pray, take all my
my zeal in - spire; as thou hast died for me, O may my
be thou my guide; bid dark-ness turn to day, wipe sor-row's
shall o'er me roll; blest Sav - ior, then, in love, fear and dis -
guilt a - way; O let me from this day be whol - ly thine!
love to thee pure, warm, and change-less be, a liv - ing fire!
tears a - way, nor let me ev - er stray from thee a - side.
trust re-move; O bear me safe a - bove, a ran - somed soul!

WORDS: Ray Palmer (1808-1887)
MUSIC: Lowell Mason (1792-1872)

OLIVET
6.6.4.6.6.6.4.

420 Jesus, the Very Thought of Thee

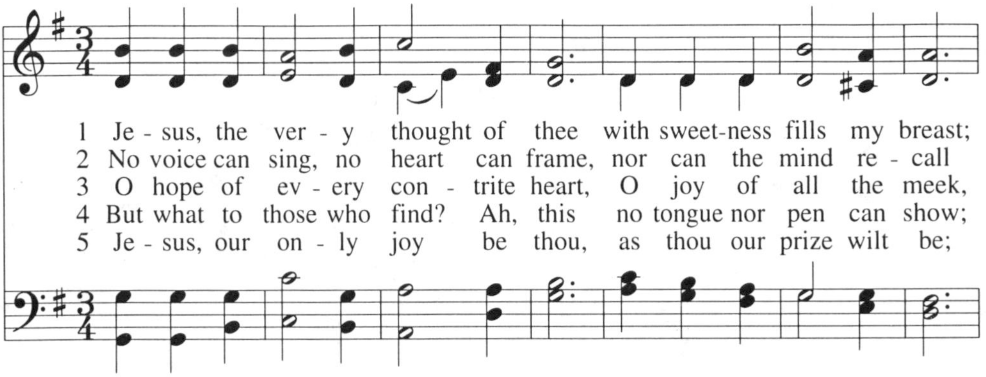
1 Je - sus, the ver - y thought of thee with sweet-ness fills my breast;
2 No voice can sing, no heart can frame, nor can the mind re - call
3 O hope of ev - ery con - trite heart, O joy of all the meek,
4 But what to those who find? Ah, this no tongue nor pen can show;
5 Je - sus, our on - ly joy be thou, as thou our prize wilt be;

but sweet-er far thy face to see, and in thy pres - ence rest.
a sweet-er sound than thy blest name, O Sav - ior of us all!
to those who ask, how kind thou art, how good to those who seek!
the love of Je - sus, what it is none but his loved ones know.
Je - sus, be thou our glo - ry now, and through e - ter - ni - ty.

WORDS: Latin, 12th c.; tr. Edward Caswall (1814-1878)
MUSIC: John B. Dykes (1823-1876)

ST. AGNES
C.M.

421 Nothing Can Trouble

Nada te Turbe

Am
Dm7
G
Em/C
1
F
Noth - ing can trou - ble, noth - ing can fright - en. Those who seek
Na - da te tur - be, na - da te es - pan - te. Quien a Dios

WORDS: St. Teresa of Jesus; Taizé Community, 1986, 1991
MUSIC: Jacques Berthier (1923-1994)

Dm6 E Am
2 F Dm6 E Am
God shall nev - er go want - ing. God a - lone fills us.
tie - ne na - da le fal - ta. So - lo Dios bas - ta.

Amazing Grace! 422

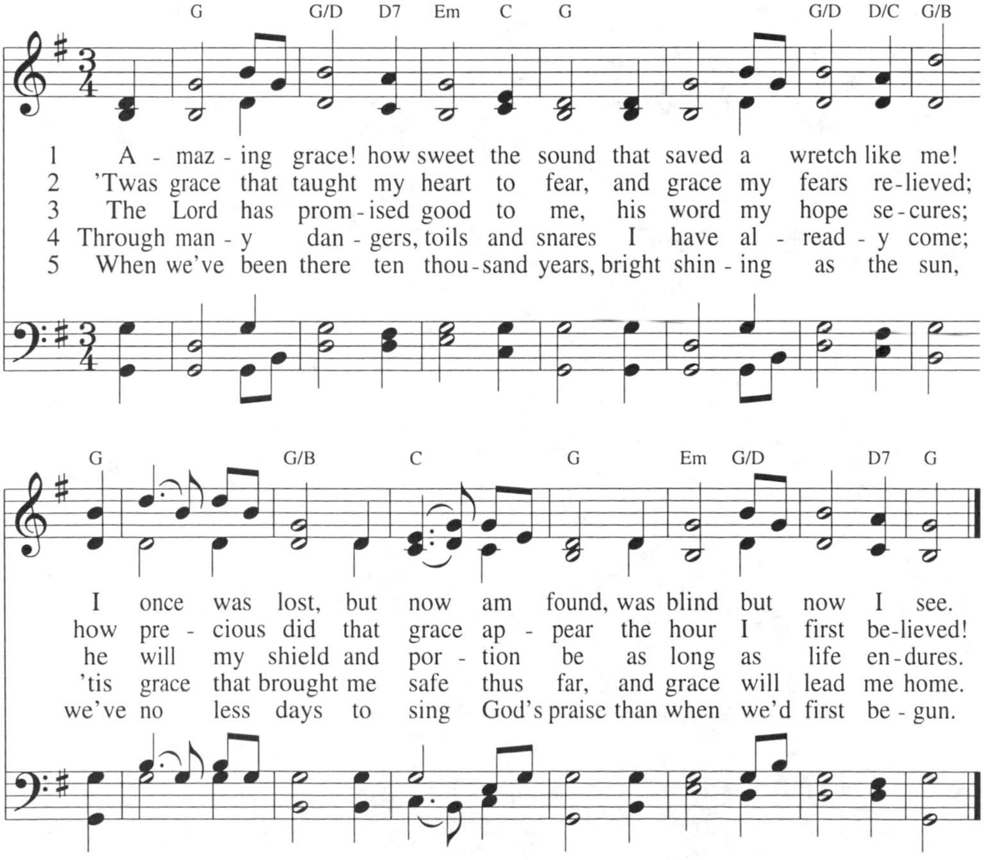
G G/D D7 Em C G G/D D/C G/B
1 A - maz - ing grace! how sweet the sound that saved a wretch like me!
2 'Twas grace that taught my heart to fear, and grace my fears re-lieved;
3 The Lord has prom - ised good to me, his word my hope se - cures;
4 Through man - y dan - gers, toils and snares I have al - read - y come;
5 When we've been there ten thou - sand years, bright shin - ing as the sun,
G G/B C G Em G/D D7 G
I once was lost, but now am found, was blind but now I see.
how pre - cious did that grace ap - pear the hour I first be-lieved!
he will my shield and por - tion be as long as life en-dures.
'tis grace that brought me safe thus far, and grace will lead me home.
we've no less days to sing God's praise than when we'd first be - gun.

WORDS: John Newton (1725-1807), alt.; vs. 5, anonymous
MUSIC: *Virginia Harmony*, 1831; adapt. Edwin O. Excell (1851-1921)

NEW BRITAIN
C.M.

423 Surely It Is God Who Saves Me

1 Sure-ly it is God who saves me; I shall trust and have no fear.
2 Make God's deeds known to the peo-ples; tell out his ex - alt - ed Name.
For the Lord de - fends and shields me and his sav - ing help is near.
Praise the Lord, who has done great things; all his works God's might pro-claim.
So re - joice as you draw wa - ter from sal - va - tion's liv - ing spring;
Zi - on, lift your voice in sing-ing; for with you has come to dwell,
in the day of your de - liv-'rance thank the Lord, his mer-cies sing.
in your ver - y midst, the great and Ho - ly One of Is - ra - el.

WORDS: Carl P. Daw, Jr. (1944-); para. Isaiah 12:1-6
MUSIC: Dutch melody, 18th c.

IN BABILONE
8.7.8.7.D.

How Can I Keep from Singing? 424

F Bb F C
1 My life flows on in end-less song; a-bove earth's lam-en-ta-tion,
2 Through all the tu-mult and the strife, I hear that mu-sic ring-ing.
3 What though my joys and com-forts die? The Lord my Sav-ior liv-eth.
4 The peace of Christ makes fresh my heart, a foun-tain ev-er spring-ing!
F Bb F C7 F
I catch the sweet, though far-off hymn that hails a new cre-a-tion.
It finds an ech-o in my soul. How can I keep from sing-ing?
What though the dark-ness gath-er round? Songs in the night he giv-eth.
All things are mine since I am his! How can I keep from sing-ing?
Refrain
F C Dm C F C F
No storm can shake my in-most calm while to that Rock I'm cling-ing.
F Bb F F/C C7 F
Since Christ is Lord of heav-en and earth, how can I keep from sing-ing?

WORDS and MUSIC: Robert Lowry (1826-1899), alt.

ENDLESS SONG
8.7.8.7.Ref.

425 Christ Beside Me

Unison
C C/E Dm7/F G7 F/C C
1 Christ be - side me, Christ be - fore me,
2 Christ on my right hand, Christ on my left hand,
3 Christ be in all hearts think - ing a - bout me,
4 Christ be - side me, Christ be - fore me,
C Em Am C/E Am/F♯ Gsus G7
Christ be - hind me— King of my heart;
Christ all a - round me— shield in the strife;
Christ be on all tongues tell - ing of me;
Christ be - hind me— King of my heart;
C F Dm7 C/E Am D/F♯
Christ with - in me, Christ be - low me,
Christ in my sleep - ing, Christ in my sit - ting,
Christ be the vi - sion in eyes that see me,
Christ with - in me, Christ be - low me,
Em/G C F G7 C
Christ a - bove me— nev - er to part.
Christ in my ris - ing— light of my life.
in ears that hear me Christ ev - er be.
Christ a - bove me— nev - er to part.

WORDS: James Quinn, S.J. (1919-); adapt. from *St. Patrick's Breastplate*
MUSIC: Gaelic melody; arr. Jack Schrader (1942-)

BUNESSAN
5.5.5.4.D.

Blessed Assurance

1 Bless-ed as - sur - ance, Je - sus is mine! O what a fore - taste of glo - ry di - vine! Heir of sal - va - tion, pur - chase of God, born of his Spir - it, washed in his blood.
2 Per - fect sub - mis - sion, per-fect de - light, vi-sions of rap - ture now burst on my sight; an - gels de - scend - ing, bring from a - bove ech - oes of mer - cy, whis-pers of love.
3 Per - fect sub - mis - sion, all is at rest, I in my Sav - ior am hap - py and blest, watch-ing and wait - ing, look - ing a - bove, filled with his good - ness, lost in his love.
Refrain
This is my sto - ry, this is my song, prais-ing my Sav - ior all the day long; this is my sto - ry, this is my song, prais-ing my Sav - ior all the day long.

WORDS: Fanny J. Crosby (1820-1915)
MUSIC: Phoebe P. Knapp (1839-1908)

ASSURANCE
9.10.9.9.Ref.

427 You Are My All in All

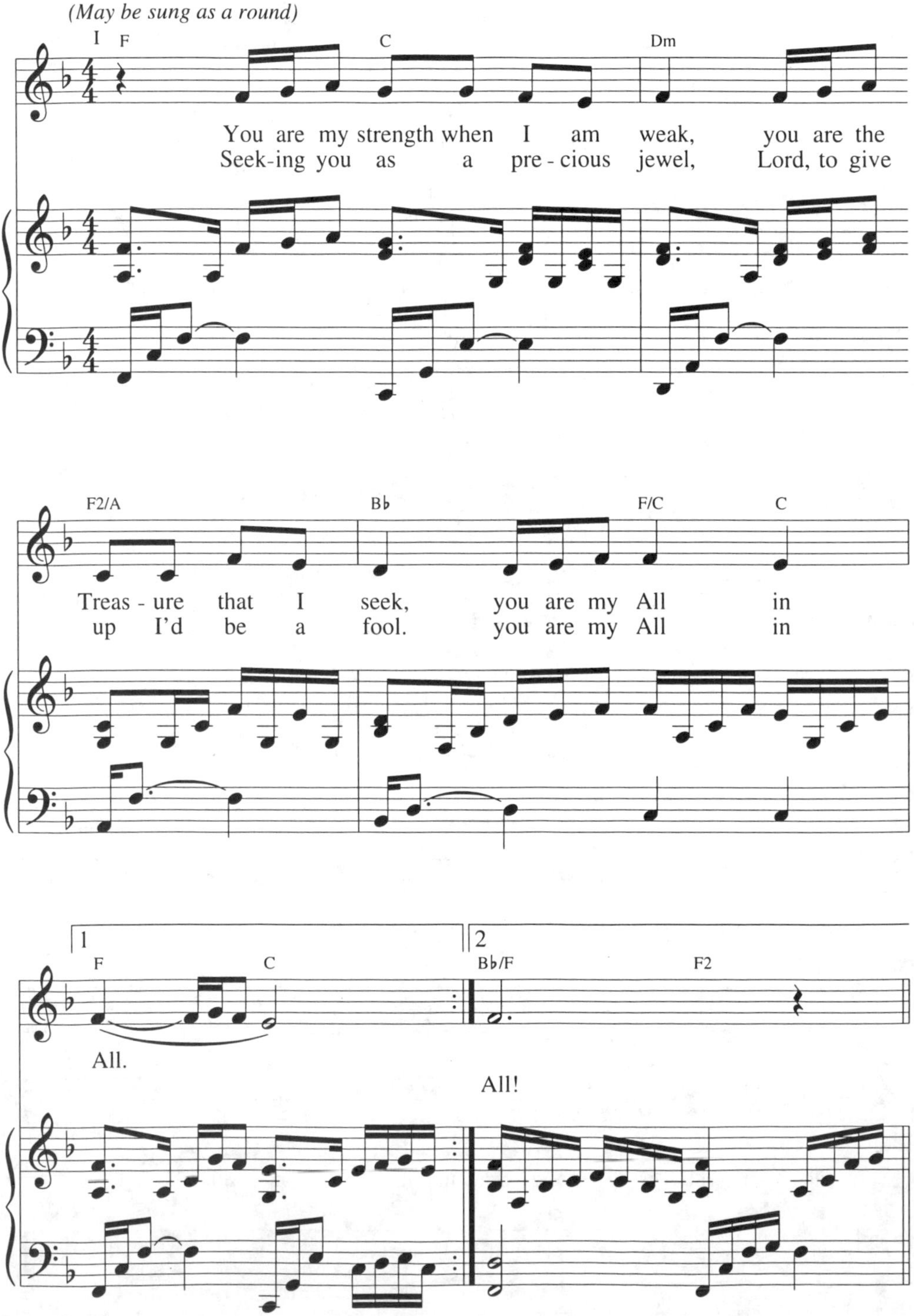
(May be sung as a round)
I
F
C
Dm
You are my strength when I am weak, you are the
Seek-ing you as a pre - cious jewel, Lord, to give
F2/A
B♭
F/C
C
Treas - ure that I seek, you are my All in
up I'd be a fool. you are my All in
1
F
C
All.
2
B♭/F
F2
All!

WORDS and MUSIC: Dennis L. Jernigan (1959-)

II
F
C
Dm7
F2/A
Je - sus, Lamb of God,
B♭
F/C
C
F
C
Wor - thy is your name.
F
C
Dm7
F2/A
Je - sus, Lamb of God,
B♭
F/C
C
B♭/F
F
Wor - thy is your name.
8vb

428 When Peace Like a River

1 When peace like a river attendeth my way, when sorrows like sea billows roll, whatever my lot, thou hast taught me to say, "It is well, it is well with my soul."
2 Though Satan should buffet, though trials should come, let this blest assurance control: that Christ has regarded my helpless estate, and has shed his own blood for my soul.
3 My sin—O, the bliss of this glorious thought, my sin—not in part but the whole, is nailed to the cross and I bear it no more: Praise the Lord, praise the Lord, O my soul!
4 And, Lord, haste the day when my faith shall be sight, the clouds be rolled back as a scroll, the trump shall resound and the Lord shall descend: "Even so"—it is well with my soul.
Refrain
It is well with my soul, it is well, it is well with my soul.
It is well with my soul,

WORDS: Horatio G. Spafford (1828-1888)
MUSIC: Philip P. Bliss (1838-1876)

VILLE DU HAVRE
11.8.11.9.Ref.

If You Will Trust in God to Guide You 429

1 If you will trust in God to guide you, and hope in God through all your ways, God will give strength, what-e'er betide you, and bear you through the evil days. Who trusts in God's unchanging love builds on the rock that will not move.
2 God will embrace your pain and weeping, your helpless anger and distress. If you are in God's care and keeping, in sorrow will God love you less? For Christ, who took for you a cross, will bring you safe through every loss.
3 Sing, pray, and keep God's ways unswerving; so do your own part faithfully, and trust God's word; though undeserving, you'll find God's promise true to be. God never will forsake in need the soul that trusts in God indeed.

WORDS: Georg Neumark (1621-1681);
vss. 1, 3 tr. Catherine Winkworth (1827-1878), alt.; vs. 2 tr. Jaroslav J. Vajda (1919-), alt.
MUSIC: Georg Neumark (1621-1681)

NEUMARK
9.8.9.8.8.8.

430 Be Not Afraid

Verse 1:
G Gsus G Gsus G Gsus
1 You shall cross the bar-ren des-ert, but you shall not die of
G D/F# C Csus2 C C/B Am Am/G
thirst. You shall wan-der far in safe-ty though you do not know the
D/F# G B7 Em Am C F
way. You shall speak your words in for-eign lands and all will un - der -
D G Em A A7 D D7
stand. You shall see the face of God and live.
Refrain
G Gsus G D Am7 D G6 C G/B
Be not a - fraid. I go be-fore you al-ways. Come, fol-low
Bm Em Am D G Gsus G Gsus G C/G G
me, and I will give you rest.

WORDS: Bob Dufford, S.J. (1943-); para. Isaiah 43:2-3, Luke 6:20ff
MUSIC: Bob Dufford, S.J. (1943-); arr. Theophane Hytrek, O.S.F. (20th c.)

Verse 2:
G Gsus G Gsus G Gsus
2 If you pass through rag-ing wa-ters in the sea, you shall not
G D/F# C Csus2 C C/B Am Am/G
drown. If you walk a-mid the burn-ing flames, you shall not be
D/F# G B7 Em Am C F
harmed. If you stand be-fore the power of hell and death is at your
D G Em Am Am/G D D7 to Refrain
side, know that I am with you through it all.
Verse 3:
G Gsus G Gsus G Gsus G D/F#
3 Bless-ed are your poor, for the king-dom shall be theirs.
C Csus2 C C/B Am Am/G D/F#
Blest are you that weep and mourn, for one day you shall laugh.
G B7 Em Am C F
And if wick-ed tongues in-sult and hate you all be-cause of
D G Em Am Am/G D D7 to Refrain
me, bless-ed, bless-ed are you!

431 Jesus, Priceless Treasure

1 Je - sus, price - less treas - ure, source of pur - est pleas - ure, tru - est friend to me: Ah, how long I've pant - ed, and my heart has faint - ed, thirst - ing, Lord, for thee! Thine I am, O spot - less Lamb; I will suf - fer nought to hide thee, nought I ask be - side thee.
2 In thine arms I rest me; foes who would mo - lest me can - not reach me here. Though the earth be shak - ing, ev - ery heart be quak - ing, Je - sus calms my fear. Sin and hell in con - flict fell with their bit - ter storms as - sail me, Je - sus will not fail me.
3 Hence, all fears and sad - ness, for the Lord of glad - ness, Je - sus, en - ters in. Those who love the Fa - ther, though the storms may gath - er, still have peace with - in. Yea, what - e'er I here must bear, still in thee lies pur - est pleas - ure, Je - sus, price - less treas - ure!
8

WORDS: Johann Franck (1618-1677); tr. Catherine Winkworth (1827-1878), alt.
MUSIC: Johann Crüger (1598-1662); harm. J. S. Bach (1685-1750)

JESU, MEINE FREUDE
6.6.5.6.6.5.7.8.6.

As Water to the Thirsty 432

Unison
1 As wa - ter to the thirst - y, as beau - ty to the eyes, as
2 Like calm in place of clam - or, like peace that fol-lows pain, like
3 As sleep that fol-lows fe - ver, as gold in-stead of gray, as
strength that fol-lows weak - ness, as truth in-stead of lies, as
meet - ing af - ter part - ing, like sun - shine af - ter rain, like
free - dom af - ter bond - age, as sun - rise to the day, as
song - time and spring - time and sum - mer-time to be, so
moon - light and star - light and sun - light on the sea, so
home to the trav - eler and all we long to see, so
is my Lord, my liv - ing Lord, so is my Lord to me.

WORDS: Timothy Dudley-Smith (1926-)
MUSIC. T. Brian Coleman (1920-)

OASIS
7.6.7.6.6.6.4.4.6.

433 O Christ the Same

1 O Christ the same, through all our sto - ry's pag - es,
2 O Christ the same, the friend of sin - ners, shar - ing
3 O Christ the same, se - cure with - in whose keep - ing
our loves and hopes, our fail - ures and our fears;
our in - most thoughts, the se - crets none can hide,
our lives and loves, our days and years re - main,
e - ter - nal Lord, the King of all the a - ges,
still as of old up - on your bod - y bear - ing
our work and rest, our wak - ing and our sleep - ing,
un - chang - ing still a - mid the pass - ing years:
the marks of love, in tri - umph glo - ri - fied:
our calm and storm, our plea - sure and our pain:

WORDS: Timothy Dudley-Smith (1926-)
MUSIC: Irish melody; arr. John Barnard (1948-)

LONDONDERRY AIR
11.10.11.10.D.

O liv - ing Word, the source of all cre - a - tion,
O Son of Man, who stooped for us from heav - en,
O Lord of love, for all our joys and sor - rows,
who spread the skies, and set the stars a - blaze,
O Prince of life, in all your sav - ing power,
for all our hopes, when earth shall fade and flee,
O Christ the same, who wrought our whole sal - va - tion,
O Christ the same, to whom our hearts are giv - en,
O Christ the same, be - yond our brief to - mor - rows,
we bring our thanks for all our yes - ter - days.
we bring our thanks for this the pres - ent hour.
we bring our thanks for all that is to be.

434 If Christ Had Not Been Raised from Death

1 If Christ had not been raised from death our faith would be in vain,
2 If Christ still lay with - in the tomb then death would be the end,
3 If Christ had not been tru - ly raised his church would live a lie:
our preach-ing but a waste of breath, our sin and guilt re - main.
and we should face our fi - nal doom with nei - ther guide nor friend.
his name should nev - er - more be praised, his words de - serve to die.
But now the Lord is risen in - deed; he rules in earth and heaven:
But now the Sav - ior is raised up, so when a Chris-tian dies
But now our great Re - deem-er lives; through him we are re - stored:
his Gos - pel meets a world of need— in Christ we are for - given.
we mourn, yet look to God in hope— in Christ the saints a - rise!
his word en - dures, his church re - vives in Christ, our ris - en Lord.

WORDS: Christopher Idle (1938-)
MUSIC: English melody; arr. Ralph Vaughan Williams (1872-1958)

KINGSFOLD
C.M.D.

Like a River Glorious 435

1 Like a riv - er glo - rious is God's per - fect peace, o - ver all vic - to - rious in its bright in - crease: per - fect, yet it flow - eth full - er ev - ery day, per - fect, yet it grow - eth deep - er all the way.
2 Hid - den in the hol - low of his bless - ed hand, nev - er foe can fol - low, nev - er trai - tor stand; not a surge of wor - ry, not a shade of care, not a blast of hur - ry touch the spir - it there.
3 Ev - ery joy or tri - al fall - eth from a - bove, traced up - on our di - al by the Sun of Love; we may trust him ful - ly all for us to do; they who trust him whol - ly find him whol - ly true.
Refrain
Stayed up - on Je - ho - vah, hearts are ful - ly blest, find - ing, as he prom - ised, per - fect peace and rest.

WORDS: Frances R. Havergal (1836-1879)
MUSIC: James Mountain (1844-1933)

WYE VALLEY
6.5.6.5.D.Ref.

436 Grace Alone

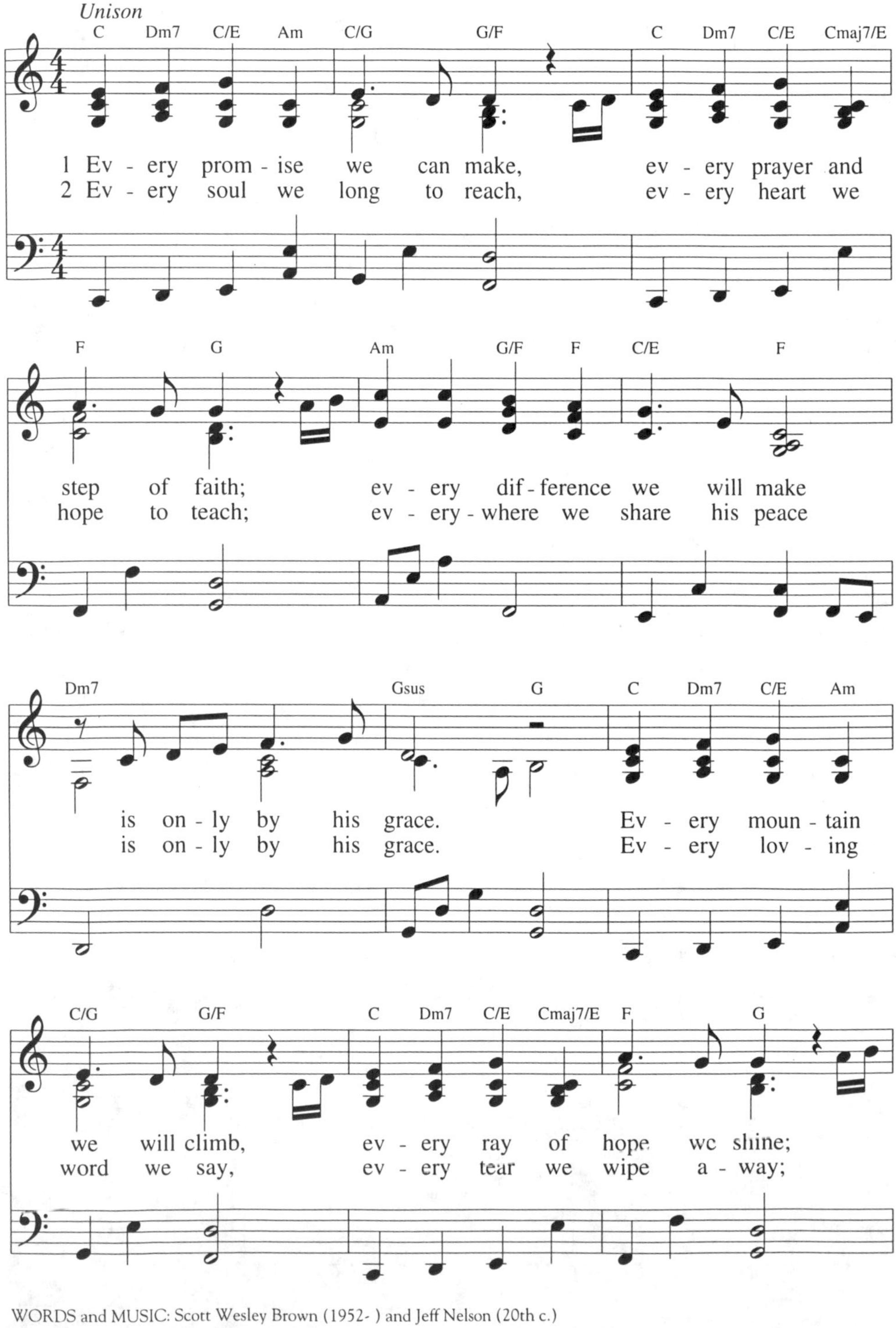
Unison
C Dm7 C/E Am C/G G/F C Dm7 C/E Cmaj7/E
1 Ev - ery prom - ise we can make, ev - ery prayer and
2 Ev - ery soul we long to reach, ev - ery heart we
F G Am G/F F C/E F
step of faith; ev - ery dif - ference we will make
hope to teach; ev - ery - where we share his peace
Dm7 Gsus G C Dm7 C/E Am
is on - ly by his grace. Ev - ery moun - tain
is on - ly by his grace. Ev - ery lov - ing
C/G G/F C Dm7 C/E Cmaj7/E F G
we will climb, ev - ery ray of hope we shine;
word we say, ev - ery tear we wipe a - way;

WORDS and MUSIC: Scott Wesley Brown (1952-) and Jeff Nelson (20th c.)

Am G/F F C/E F Dm7 Gsus G7
ev - ery bless - ing left be - hind is on - ly by his
ev - ery sor - row turned to praise is on - ly by his
Refrain
C C/E F G/B C C/E
grace.
grace.
Grace a - lone which God sup-plies; strength un-
F G/B C C/E F E7/G♯
known he will pro - vide. Christ in us, our cor-ner-
Am C/G Dm7 Gsus Fmaj7/G G7 C
stone, we will go forth in grace a - lone.

437 Jesus Loves Me

1 Je - sus loves me, this I know, for the Bi - ble tells me so!
2 Je - sus loves me, he who died heav-en's gate to o - pen wide;
3 Je - sus loves me! He will stay close be - side me all the way;
Lit - tle ones to him be - long: they are weak, but he is strong.
he will wash a - way my sin, let his lit - tle child come in.
he's pre - pared a home for me, and some day his face I'll see.
Refrain
Yes, Je - sus loves me! Yes, Je - sus loves me!
Yes, Je - sus loves me! The Bi - ble tells me so.

WORDS: Anna B. Warner (1820-1915), alt.
MUSIC: William B. Bradbury (1816-1868)

JESUS LOVES ME
7.7.7.7.Ref.

On Eagle's Wings

Unison
G
D/F#
G
1 You who dwell in the shel-ter of the Lord, who a - bide in his
(2) snare of the fowl - er will nev - er cap-ture you, and fa-mine will
3 You need not fear the ter - ror of the night, nor the ar - row that
D/F#
F
Dm
shad-ow for life, say to the Lord, "My ref - uge, my
bring you no fear, un - der his wings your ref - uge, his
flies by day; though thou - sands fall a - bout you,
F
Gm
Asus
A
Refrain
D
Rock in whom I trust."
faith - ful - ness your shield. And he will raise you up on
near you it shall not come.
Em
A7
D
D7/F#
ea - gle's wings, bear you on the breath of dawn, make you to shine like the
G
A
Bm
F#m
Em7
A
Dsus
D
D.C.
sun and hold you in the palm of his hand. 2 The
Fine

WORDS and MUSIC: Michael Joncas (1951-)

439 Jesus, Lover of My Soul

1 Je - sus, lov - er of my soul, let me to thy bos - om fly,
2 Oth - er ref - uge have I none; hangs my help-less soul on thee;
3 Plen - teous grace with thee is found, grace to cov - er all my sin;
while the near - er wa - ters roll, while the tem-pest still is high;
leave, ah! leave me not a - lone, still sup - port and com - fort me.
let the heal - ing streams a - bound, make and keep me pure with - in.
hide me, O my Sav - ior, hide, till the storm of life is past;
All my trust on thee is stayed, all my help from thee I bring;
Thou of life the foun - tain art, free - ly let me take of thee;
safe in - to the ha - ven guide, O re - ceive my soul at last!
cov - er my de - fense-less head with the shad - ow of thy wing.
spring thou up with - in my heart, rise to all e - ter - ni - ty.

WORDS: Charles Wesley (1707-1788)
MUSIC: Joseph Parry (1841-1903)

ABERYSTWYTH
7.7.7.7.D.

Savior, Like a Shepherd Lead Us 440

1 Sav - ior, like a Shep-herd lead us, much we need thy ten - der care;
2 We are thine, do thou be - friend us, be the guard-ian of our way;
3 Thou hast prom-ised to re - ceive us, poor and sin - ful though we be;
4 Ear - ly let us seek thy fa - vor, ear - ly let us do thy will;
in thy pleas-ant pas-tures feed us, for our use thy folds pre - pare:
keep thy flock, from sin de - fend us, seek us when we go a - stray:
thou hast mer - cy to re - lieve us, grace to cleanse, and power to free:
bless - ed Lord and on - ly Sav - ior, with thy love our bos - oms fill:
Bless-ed Je - sus, bless-ed Je - sus, thou hast bought us, thine we are;
Bless-ed Je - sus, bless-ed Je - sus, hear, O hear us when we pray;
Bless-ed Je - sus, bless-ed Je - sus, ear - ly let us turn to thee;
Bless-ed Je - sus, bless-ed Je - sus, thou hast loved us, love us still;
bless-ed Je - sus, bless-ed Je - sus, thou hast bought us, thine we are.
bless-ed Je - sus, bless-ed Je - sus, hear, O hear us when we pray.
bless-ed Je - sus, bless-ed Je - sus, ear - ly let us turn to thee.
bless-ed Je - sus, bless-ed Je - sus, thou hast loved us, love us still.

WORDS: Attr. Dorothy A. Thrupp (1779-1847); *Hymns for the Young*, 1836
MUSIC: William B. Bradbury (1816-1868)

BRADBURY
8.7.8.7.D.

441 Trust in the Lord

Bb
Bb
(Leader) Trust in the Lord
with
(Congregation) Trust in the Lord
r.h.
l.h.
Gm
Eb
Bb/D
all your heart
and lean not to your own un-der-
with all your heart
Cm7
Eb
Bb/D
Cm7
stand-ing.
In
and lean not to your own un-der-stand-ing.

WORDS and MUSIC: Roland Tabell (1934-); para. Proverbs 3:5-6

Bb/F
Gm
Bb/F
all your ways ac-knowl-edge him
In all your ways ac -
Gm
Eb
F
Eb/Bb
Bb
and he shall di - rect your paths.
knowl-edge him
and
Eb
F
Eb/Bb
Bb
Bb
he shall di - rect your paths.
Trust in the Lord,
ritard.
trust in the Lord!
Trust in the Lord,
trust in the Lord!
ritard.

442 'Tis So Sweet to Trust in Jesus

1 'Tis so sweet to trust in Je - sus, just to take him at his word,
2 O how sweet to trust in Je - sus, just to trust his cleans-ing blood,
3 Yes, 'tis sweet to trust in Je - sus, just from sin and self to cease,
4 I'm so glad I learned to trust you, pre-cious Je - sus, Sav - ior, Friend,
just to rest up - on his prom - ise, just to know, "Thus saith the Lord."
just in sim - ple faith to plunge me 'neath the heal - ing, cleans-ing flood!
just from Je - sus sim - ply tak - ing life and rest, and joy and peace.
and I know that you are with me, will be with me to the end.
Refrain
Je - sus, Je - sus, how I trust him! How I've proved him o'er and o'er!
Je - sus, Je - sus, pre - cious Je - sus! O for grace to trust him more!

WORDS: Louisa M. R. Stead (1850-1917)
MUSIC: William J. Kirkpatrick (1838-1921)

TRUST IN JESUS
8.7.8.7.Ref.

Trust and Obey

1 When we walk with the Lord in the light of his Word, what a
2 Not a bur - den we bear, not a sor - row we share, but our
3 But we nev - er can prove the de - lights of his love un - til
4 Then in fel - low - ship sweet we will sit at his feet, or we'll
glo - ry he sheds on our way! While we do his good will, he a - bides with us
toil he will rich - ly re - pay; not a grief nor a loss, not a frown nor a
all on the al - tar we lay; for the fa - vor he shows and the joy he be -
walk by his side in the way; what he says we will do, where he sends we will
still, and with all who will trust and o - bey.
cross, but is blest if we trust and o - bey.
stows are for them who will trust and o - bey.
go— nev - er fear, on - ly trust and o - bey.
Refrain
Trust and o - bey, for there's
no oth - er way, to be hap - py in Je - sus, but to trust and o - bey.

WORDS: John H. Sammis (1846-1919)
MUSIC: Daniel B. Towner (1850-1919)

TRUST AND OBEY
6.6.9.D.Ref.

444 Rain Down

Refrain (Unison)
F A7 G/B A7 Dm F7 Eb/G F7/A
Rain down, rain down,
Bb F/A Gm7 C7 Gm7/D C7/E
rain down your love on your peo - ple.
F A7 Dm F7 Eb/G F7/A
Rain down, rain down,
3
3
Bb Am7 Gm7 Gm/C Am/C Gm/C Bb/F F
rain down your love, God of life.

WORDS and MUSIC: Jaime Cortez (1963-); arr. John Carter (1930-)

F A7 Dm F7 Eb/G F7/A
1 Faith - ful and true is the word of our God.
2 We who re - vere and find hope in our God
3 God of cre - a - tion, we long for your truth;
Bb F/A G7 C7 Bb/D C7/E
All of God's works are so wor - thy of trust.
live in the kind - ness and joy of God's wing.
you are the wa - ter of life for our thirst.
F A7 Dm F7
God's mer - cy falls on the just and the right;
God will pro - tect us from dark - ness and death;
Grant that your love and your peace touch our hearts,
to Refrain
Bb Gm7 Gm/C Am/C Gm/C F C Bb/D C7/E
full of God's love is the earth.
God will not leave us to starve.
all of our hope lies in you.

445 In the Day of Need

Unison
1 In the day of need may your an - swer be the Lord;
2 May the Lord God give you suc - cess in all your plans;
3 Now I know that God will en - cour - age those he loves;
4 There are some who boast of the weap - ons of the world,
may the God of Ja - cob strength - en you:
may he give you all your heart's de - sire:
he will hear and an - swer from on high;
but the power of God is all our pride;
may he send you help from his high and ho - ly place,
may we sing for joy when we see the bat - tle won,
not a word shall fail of the prom - ise he has made,
those who arm for war shall one day col - lapse and fall,
and sup - port you for the glo - ry of his name.
when the Lord has heard and an - swered ev - ery prayer.
nor the works of his vic - to - ri - ous right hand.
but God's peo - ple stand and in their King pre - vail.

WORDS: Christopher Idle (1938-), alt.; para. Psalm 20
MUSIC: Norman Warren (1934-)

SAMSON
12.9.12.11.

O Love That Will Not Let Me Go 446

1 O Love that will not let me go,
2 O Light that fol - lowest all my way,
3 O Joy that seek - est me through pain,
4 O Cross that lift - est up my head,
I rest my wea - ry soul in thee;
I yield my flick - ering torch to thee;
I can - not close my heart to thee;
I dare not ask to fly from thee;
I give thee back the life I owe, that
my heart re - stores its bor - rowed ray, that
I trace the rain - bow through the rain, and
I lay in dust life's glo - ry dead, and
in thine o - cean depths its flow may rich - er, full - er be.
in thy sun-shine's blaze its day may bright - er, fair - er be.
feel the prom - ise is not vain that morn shall tear - less be.
from the ground there blos - soms red life that shall end - less be.

WORDS: George Matheson (1842-1906)
MUSIC: Albert L. Peace (1844-1912)

ST. MARGARET
8.8.8.8.6.

447 Because He Lives

1 God sent his Son, they called him Je - sus; he came to love, heal, and for - give; he lived and died to buy my par - don, an emp - ty grave is there to prove my Sav - ior lives.
2 How sweet to hold a new-born ba - by, and feel the pride and joy he gives; but great-er still the calm as - sur - ance: this child can face un-cer-tain days be-cause he lives.
3 And then one day I'll cross the riv - er; I'll fight life's fi - nal war with pain; and then as death gives way to vic - tory, I'll see the lights of glo - ry and I'll know he lives.
Refrain
Be-cause he lives I can face to - mor - row; be-cause he lives

WORDS: Gloria Gaither (1942-) and William J. Gaither (1936-)
MUSIC: William J. Gaither (1936-)

RESURRECTION
Irregular

all fear is gone; be-cause I know he holds the fu - ture,
and life is worth the liv - ing just be-cause he lives.

In the Lord I'll Be Ever Thankful 448

In the Lord I'll be ev - er thank - ful, in the Lord I will re -
joice! Look to God, do not be a - fraid. Lift up your
voic - es, the Lord is near; lift up your voic - es, the Lord is near.

WORDS: Taizé Community
MUSIC: Jacques Berthier (1923-1994)

449 Day by Day

Eb
Fm7/Ab
Bb
1 Day by day and with each pass-ing mo - ment, strength I find to
2 Ev - ery day the Lord him - self is near me with a spe - cial
3 Help me then in ev - ery trib - u - la - tion so to trust your
Bb7
Eb
Fm7/Ab
meet my tri - als here; trust-ing in my Fa - ther's wise be - stow-ment,
mer - cy for each hour; all my cares he fain would bear, and cheer me,
prom-is - es, O Lord, that I lose not faith's sweet con - so - la - tion
Bb
Bb7
Eb
I've no cause for wor - ry or for fear. He whose heart is kind be-yond all
he whose name is Coun-sel - or and Power. The pro - tec - tion of his child and
of - fered me with - in your ho - ly Word. Help me, Lord, when toil and trou - ble
Ab
Bb7
Bb7/F
Bb7
Eb
mea - sure gives un - to each day what he deems best—lov - ing - ly, its
trea - sure is a charge that on him-self he laid: "As your days, your
meet - ing, e'er to take, as from a fa-ther's hand, one by one, the

WORDS: Carolina Sandell Berg (1832-1903); tr. Andrew L. Skoog (1856-1934)
MUSIC: Oscar Ahnfelt (1813-1882)

BLOTT EN DAG
10.9.10.9.D.

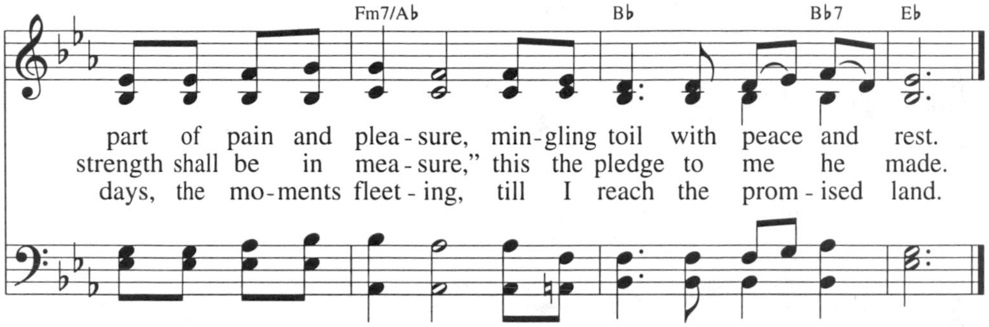
Fm7/A♭ B♭ B♭7 E♭
part of pain and plea - sure, min-gling toil with peace and rest.
strength shall be in mea - sure," this the pledge to me he made.
days, the mo-ments fleet - ing, till I reach the prom - ised land.

Be Still and Know 450

1 Be still and know that I am God,
2 The Lord Al - might - y is our God,
3 In you, O Lord, we put our trust.
be still and know that I am God,
the Lord Al - might - y is our God,
In you, O Lord, we put our trust.
be still and know that I am God.
the Lord Al - might - y is our God.
In you, O Lord, we put our trust.

WORDS and MUSIC: Anonymous; para. Psalm 46:10, 11; 143:8; arr. Jack Schrader (1942-)

451 Be Still, My Soul

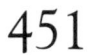

1 Be still, my soul: the Lord is on your side!
2 Be still, my soul: your God will un - der - take
3 Be still, my soul: the hour is has - tening on
Bear pa - tient - ly the cross of grief or pain; leave to your
to guide the fu - ture as he has the past; your hope, your
when we shall be for - ev - er with the Lord, when dis - ap -
God to or - der and pro - vide— in ev - ery change he
con - fi - dence let noth - ing shake— all now mys - te - rious
point - ment, grief, and fear are gone, sor - row for - got, love's
faith - ful will re - main. Be still, my soul: your best, your heaven - ly
shall be bright at last. Be still, my soul: the waves and winds still
pur - est joys re - stored. Be still, my soul: when change and tears are

WORDS: Katherina von Schlegel (18th c.); tr. Jane L. Borthwick (1813-1897), alt.
MUSIC: Jean Sibelius (1865-1957); arr. *Hymnal 1933*

FINLANDIA
10.10.10.10.10.10.

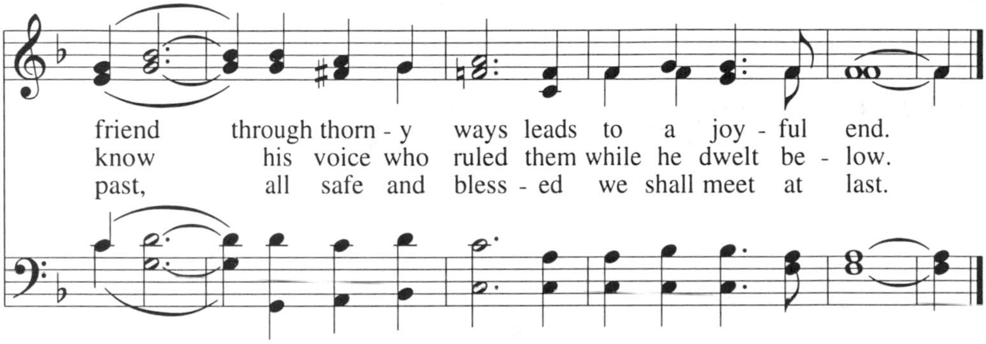
friend through thorn - y ways leads to a joy - ful end.
know his voice who ruled them while he dwelt be - low.
past, all safe and bless - ed we shall meet at last.

Through It All 452

Eb Eb7 Ab Fm7 Bb Cm/Bb
Through it all, through it all, I've learned to trust in
Bb7 Ab/Bb Eb Cm Bb Eb Eb7
Je - sus, I've learned to trust in God; through it all,
Ab Fm7 Bb Cm/Bb Bb7 Ab/Bb Bb7 Eb Ab/Eb Eb
through it all, I've learned to de - pend up - on his Word.

WORDS and MUSIC: Andraé Crouch (1945-)

453 Christ Be My Leader

Unison
1 Christ be my lead - er by night as by day;
2 Christ by my teach - er in age as in youth,
3 Christ be my Sav - ior in calm as in strife;
safe through the dark - ness, for he is the Way.
drift - ing or doubt - ing, for he is the Truth.
death can - not hold me for he is the Life. Nor
Glad - ly I fol - low, my fu - ture his care,
Grant me to trust him; though shift - ing as sand,
dark - ness nor doubt - ing nor sin and its stain can
dark - ness is day - light when Je - sus is there.
doubt can - not daunt me; in Je - sus I stand.
touch my sal - va - tion: with Je - sus I reign.

WORDS: Timothy Dudley-Smith (1926-)
MUSIC: Irish melody; harm. Carlton R. Young (1926-)

SLANE
10.10.10.10.

He Came Singing Love

454

Unison
D D/C# Bm
1 He came sing - ing love and he lived sing - ing love; he
2 He came sing - ing faith and he lived sing - ing faith; he
3 He came sing - ing hope and he lived sing - ing hope; he
4 He came sing - ing peace and he lived sing - ing peace; he
D/F# G D A/C# Bm F#m
died sing - ing love. He a - rose in si - lence.
died sing - ing faith. He a - rose in si - lence.
died sing - ing hope. He a - rose in si - lence.
died sing - ing peace. He a - rose in si - lence.
D G A7 F#m
For the love to go on
For the faith to go on
For the hope to go on
For the peace to go on
we must make it our
Bm G A7 D G D
song; you and I be the sing - ers.

WORDS and MUSIC: Colin Gibson (1933-)

SINGING LOVE
Irregular

455 Take Thou Our Minds, Dear Lord

1 Take thou our minds, dear Lord, we hum - bly pray;
2 Take thou our hearts, O Christ, they are thine own;
3 Take thou our wills, Most High! Hold thou full sway;
4 Take thou our - selves, O Lord, heart, mind, and will;
give us the mind of Christ each pass - ing day;
come thou with - in our souls and claim thy throne;
have in our in - most souls thy per - fect way;
through our sur - ren - dered souls thy plans ful - fill.
teach us to know the truth that sets us free;
help us to shed a - broad thy death - less love;
guard thou each sa - cred hour from self - ish ease;
We yield our - selves to thee— time, tal - ents, all;
grant us in all our thoughts to hon - or thee.
use us to make the earth like heaven a - bove.
guide thou our or - dered lives as thou dost please.
we hear, and hence - forth heed, thy sov - ereign call.

WORDS: William H. Foulkes (1877-1962)
MUSIC: Calvin Weiss Laufer (1874-1938)

HALL
10.10.10.10.

Thy Holy Wings

Unison
1 Thy ho - ly wings, O Sav - ior, spread gent - ly o - ver me
2 Oh, wash me in the wa - ters of No-ah's cleans-ing flood.
and let me rest se - cure - ly through good and ill in thee.
Give me a will - ing spir - it, a heart both clean and good.
Oh, be my strength and por - tion, my rock and hid - ing place,
Oh, take in - to thy keep - ing thy child - ren great and small,
and let my ev - ery mo - ment be lived with - in thy grace.
and while we sweet - ly slum - ber, en - fold us one and all.

WORDS: Carolina Sandell Berg (1832-1903); tr. Gracia Grindal (1943-)
MUSIC: Swedish folk tune; arr. Jane Holstein (1958-)

BRED DINA VIDA VINGAR
7.6.7.6.D.

457 Lord, I Want to Be a Christian

D D G D
1 Lord, I want to be a Chris-tian in my heart, in my heart;
2 Lord, I want to be more lov - ing in my heart, in my heart;
3 Lord, I want to be more ho - ly in my heart, in my heart;
4 Lord, I want to be like Je - sus in my heart, in my heart;
A Bm G D G/D D
Lord, I want to be a Chris-tian in my heart.
Lord, I want to be more lov - ing in my heart.
Lord, I want to be more ho - ly in my heart.
Lord, I want to be like Je - sus in my heart.
G D Bm
In my heart, in my heart, in my heart, in my heart,
D A7 Bm G D
Lord, I want to be a Chris-tian in my heart.
Lord, I want to be more lov - ing in my heart.
Lord, I want to be more ho - ly in my heart.
Lord, I want to be like Je - sus in my heart.

WORDS and MUSIC: African-American spiritual

I WANT TO BE A CHRISTIAN
Irregular

O Jesus, I Have Promised

1 O Je - sus, I have prom - ised to serve you to the end; re -
2 O let me hear you speak - ing in ac - cents clear and still, a -
3 O Je - sus, you have prom - ised to all who fol - low you that
main for - ev - er near me, my Mas - ter and my Friend: I
bove the storms of pas - sion, the mur - murs of self - will. O
where you are in glo - ry, your ser - vant shall be too; and,
shall not fear the bat - tle if you are by my side, nor
speak to re - as - sure me, to has - ten or con - trol; now
Je - sus, I have prom - ised to serve you to the end; O
wan - der from the path - way if you will be my guide.
speak, and make me lis - ten, O guard - ian of my soul.
give me grace to fol - low, my Mas - ter and my Friend.

WORDS: John E. Bode (1816-1874), alt.
MUSIC: Arthur H. Mann (1850-1929)

ANGEL'S STORY
7.6.7.6.D.

459 Come, All Christians, Be Committed

1 Come, all Chris-tians, be com - mit - ted to the ser - vice of the
2 Of your time and tal - ents give now, they are gifts from God a -
3 Come in praise and ad - o - ra - tion, all who on Christ's name be-
Lord; make your lives for him more fit - ted, tune your hearts with one ac -
bove, to be used by Chris-tians free - ly to pro - claim his won-drous
lieve; wor - ship him with con - se - cra - tion, grace and love will you re -
cord. Come in - to his courts with glad - ness, all your sa - cred vows re -
love. Come a - gain to serve the Sav - ior, tithes and of - ferings with you
ceive. For his grace give Christ the glo - ry, for the Spir - it and the
new, turn a - way from sin and sad - ness, be trans-formed with life a - new.
bring; in your work, with Christ find fa - vor, and with joy his prais - es sing.
Word, and re - peat the gos - pel sto - ry un - til all his name have heard.

WORDS: Eva B. Lloyd (1912-), alt.
MUSIC: Attr. B. F. White (1800-1879), *The Sacred Harp*, 1844; arr. James H. Wood (1921-)

BEACH SPRING
8.7.8.7.D.

All for Jesus! 460

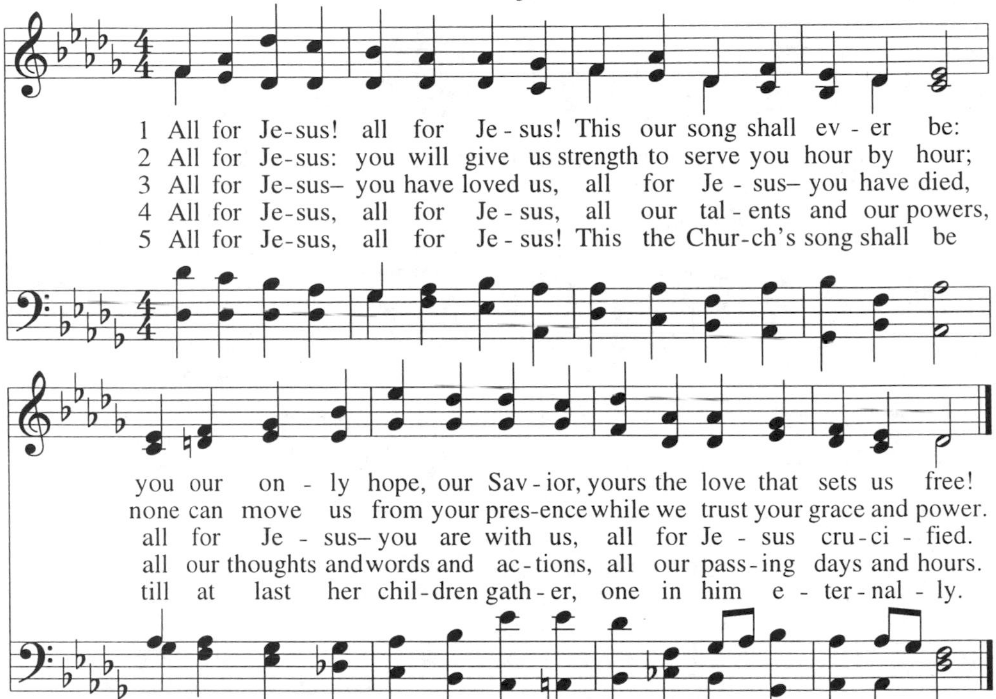
1 All for Je-sus! all for Je - sus! This our song shall ev - er be:
2 All for Je-sus: you will give us strength to serve you hour by hour;
3 All for Je-sus– you have loved us, all for Je - sus– you have died,
4 All for Je-sus, all for Je - sus, all our tal - ents and our powers,
5 All for Je-sus, all for Je - sus! This the Chur-ch's song shall be
you our on - ly hope, our Sav - ior, yours the love that sets us free!
none can move us from your pres-ence while we trust your grace and power.
all for Je - sus– you are with us, all for Je - sus cru - ci - fied.
all our thoughts and words and ac - tions, all our pass - ing days and hours.
till at last her chil - dren gath - er, one in him e - ter - nal - ly.

WORDS: William J. Sparrow-Simpson (1859-1952); rev. Jubilate Hymns, 1982
MUSIC: John Stainer (1840-1901)
ALL FOR JESUS
8.7.8.7.

Breathe on Me, Breath of God 461

1 Breathe on me, breath of God, fill me with life a - new,
2 Breathe on me, breath of God, un - til my heart is pure,
3 Breathe on me, breath of God, so that your will is mine,
4 Breathe on me, breath of God, so shall I nev - er die,
that I may love what - e'er you love, and do what you would do.
un - til with you I will one will, to do and to en - dure.
un - til this earth - ly part of me glows with your fire di - vine.
but live with you the per - fect life of your e - ter - ni - ty.

WORDS: Edwin Hatch (1835-1889), alt.
MUSIC: Robert Jackson (1842-1914)
TRENTHAM
S.M.

462 Renew Your Church

1 Re - new your church, our min - is - tries re - store: both to serve and a - dore. Make us a - gain as salt through-out the land, and as light from a stand. 'Mid som - ber shad - ows of the night, where greed and ha - treds spread their blight, O
2 Teach us your Word, re - veal its truth di - vine, on our path let it shine; tell of your works, your might - y acts of grace, from each page show your face. As you have loved us, sent your Son, and our sal - va - tion now is won, O
3 Teach us to pray, for you are ev - er near, your still voice let us hear. Our souls are rest - less till they rest in you, this the goal we pur - sue. Be - fore your pres - ence keep us still that we may find for us your will, and
4 Teach us to love, with strength of heart and mind, each and all, hu - man-kind; break down old walls of prej - u - dice and hate, leave us not to our fate. As you have loved and given your life to end hos - til - i - ty and strife, O

WORDS: Kenneth L. Cober (1902-), alt.
MUSIC: *The Sacred Harp*, 1844

ALL IS WELL
10.6.10.6.8.8.8.6.

send us forth with power en - dued, help us, Lord, be re - newed.
let our hearts with love be stirred, help us, Lord, know your Word.
seek your guid - ance ev - ery day, teach us, Lord, how to pray.
share your grace from heaven a - bove, teach us, Lord, how to love.

Revive Us Again 463

1 We praise thee, O God, for the Son of thy love, for Je - sus who died and is now gone a - bove.
2 We praise thee, O God, for thy Spir - it of light, who has shown us our Sav - ior and scat - tered our night.
3 All glo - ry and praise to the Lamb that was slain, who has borne all our sins, and has cleansed ev - ery stain.
4 Re - vive us a - gain: fill each heart with thy love; may each soul be re - kin - dled with fire from a - bove.
Refrain
Hal - le - lu - jah! thine the glo - ry; Hal - le - lu - jah, A - men! Hal - le - lu - jah! thine the glo - ry; re - vive us a - gain.

WORDS: William P. Mackay (1839-1885)
MUSIC: John J. Husband (1760-1825)

REVIVE US AGAIN
11.11.Ref.

464 May the Mind of Christ, My Savior

1 May the mind of Christ, my Sav - ior, live in me from day to day,
2 May the Word of God dwell rich - ly in my heart from hour to hour,
3 May the peace of God, my Fa - ther, rule my life in ev - ery-thing,
4 May the love of Je - sus fill me, as the wa - ters fill the sea,
5 May I run the race be - fore me, strong and brave to face the foe,
by his love and power con-trol-ling all I do and say.
so that all may see I tri-umph on - ly through his power.
that I may be calm to com-fort sick and sor - row - ing.
him ex - alt - ing, self a - bas - ing— this is vic - to - ry.
look-ing on - ly un - to Je - sus as I on - ward go.

WORDS: Kate B. Wilkinson (1859-1928)
MUSIC: A. Cyril Barham-Gould (1891-1953)

ST. LEONARDS
8.7.8.5.

465 Lord, Be Glorified

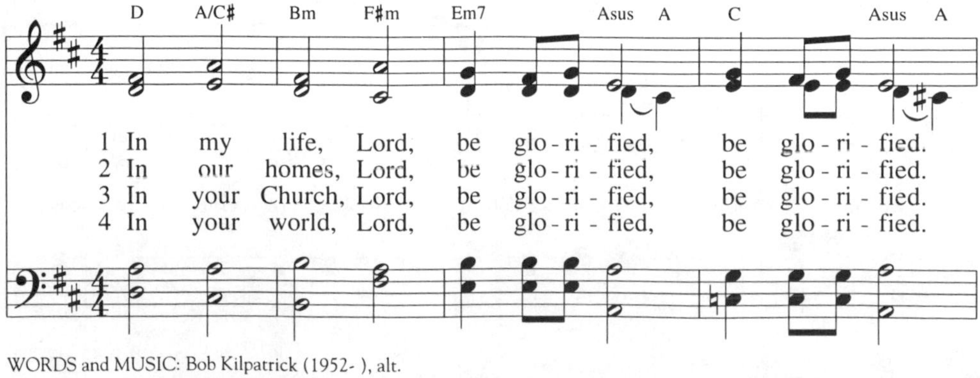
D A/C# Bm F#m Em7 Asus A C Asus A
1 In my life, Lord, be glo - ri - fied, be glo - ri - fied.
2 In our homes, Lord, be glo - ri - fied, be glo - ri - fied.
3 In your Church, Lord, be glo - ri - fied, be glo - ri - fied.
4 In your world, Lord, be glo - ri - fied, be glo - ri - fied.

WORDS and MUSIC: Bob Kilpatrick (1952-), alt.

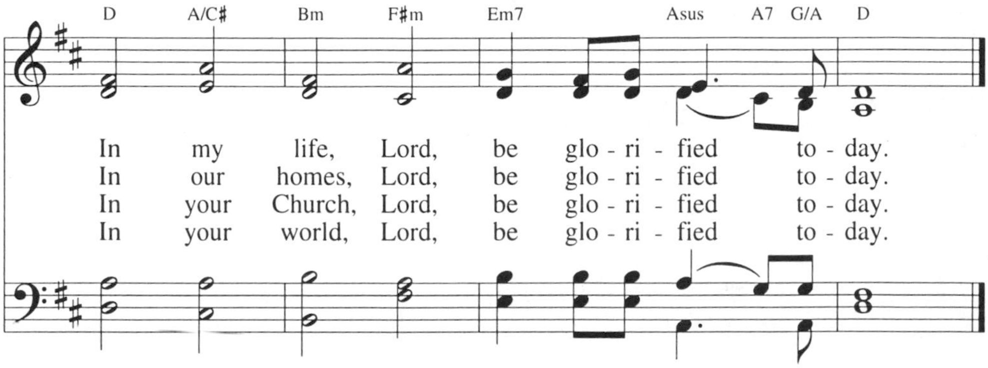
D A/C♯ Bm F♯m Em7 Asus A7 G/A D
In my life, Lord, be glo - ri - fied to - day.
In our homes, Lord, be glo - ri - fied to - day.
In your Church, Lord, be glo - ri - fied to - day.
In your world, Lord, be glo - ri - fied to - day.

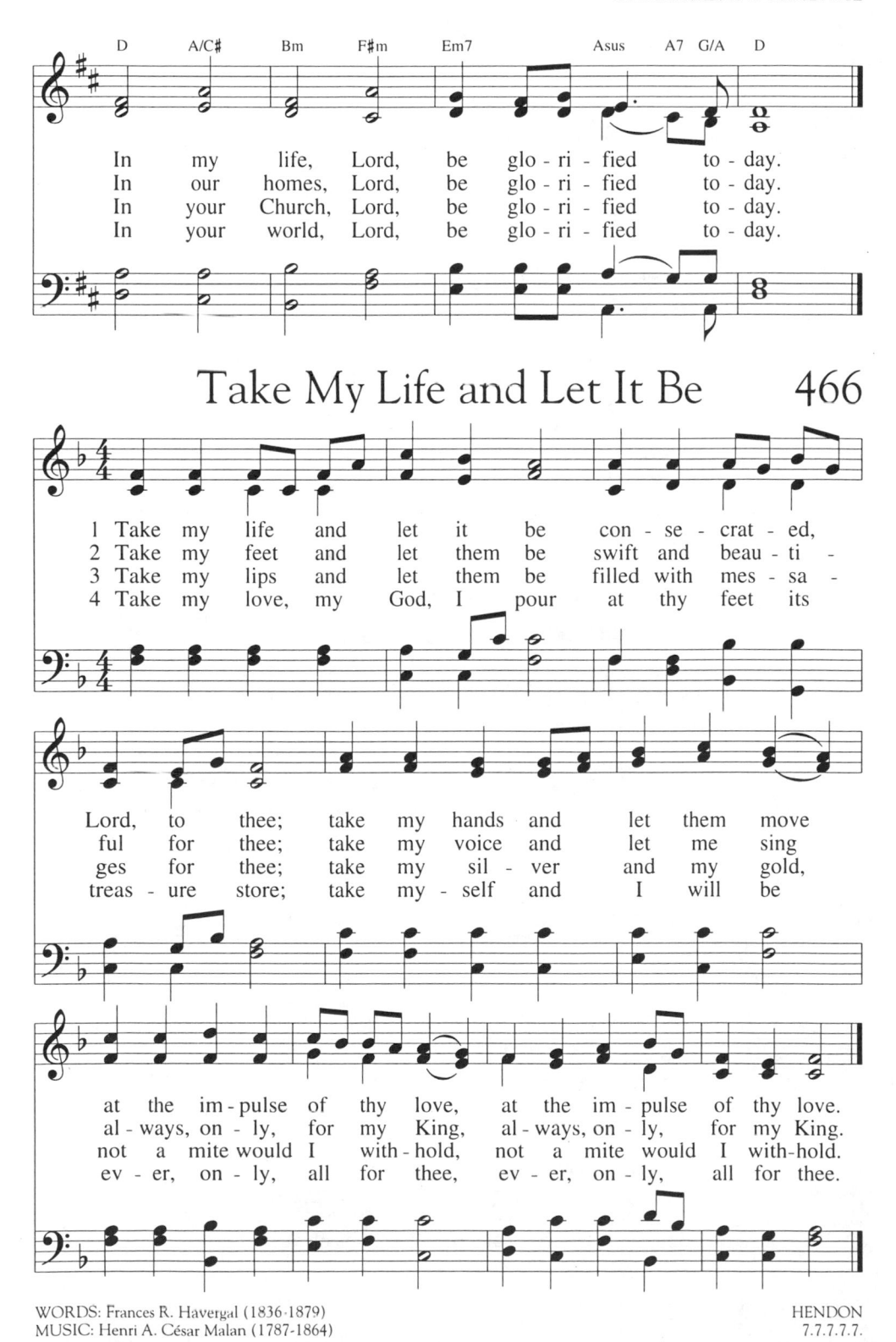

Take My Life and Let It Be 466

1 Take my life and let it be con - se - crat - ed, Lord, to thee; take my hands and let them move at the im - pulse of thy love, at the im - pulse of thy love.
2 Take my feet and let them be swift and beau - ti - ful for thee; take my voice and let me sing al - ways, on - ly, for my King, al - ways, on - ly, for my King.
3 Take my lips and let them be filled with mes - sa - ges for thee; take my sil - ver and my gold, not a mite would I with - hold, not a mite would I with-hold.
4 Take my love, my God, I pour at thy feet its treas - ure store; take my - self and I will be ev - er, on - ly, all for thee, ev - er, on - ly, all for thee.

WORDS: Frances R. Havergal (1836-1879)
MUSIC: Henri A. César Malan (1787-1864)

HENDON
7.7.7.7.7.

467 The Power of Your Love

A E/G# F#m C#m
1 Lord, I come to you; let my heart be changed, re - newed,
2 Lord, un - veil my eyes; let me see you face to face,
F#m D E F#m Bm7 Esus E
flow - ing from the grace that I've found in you.
the knowl-edge of your love as you live in me.
A E/G# F#m C#m
And Lord, I've come to know the weak-ness-es I see in me
Lord, re - new my mind, as your will un - folds in my life,
F#m D Esus E7 A D/A E/A
will be stripped a - way by the power of your love.
in liv-ing ev - ery day by the power of your love.
Refrain
A A7 D E D/A A
Hold me close, let your love sur - round me.
D E E7 A E7sus/B A/C# A7 D
Bring me near, draw me to your side. And as I wait,
E D/A A E/G#
I'll rise up like the ea - gle, and I will soar with
F#m C#m7 D E7 D/A A
you; your Spir - it leads me on in the power of your love.

WORDS and MUSIC: Geoff Bullock (20th c.)

My Jesus, I Love Thee 468

1 My Je - sus, I love thee, I know thou art mine,
2 I love thee be - cause thou hast first lov - ed me,
3 In man - sions of glo - ry and end - less de - light,
for thee all the fol - lies of sin I re - sign;
and pur - chased my par - don on Cal - va - ry's tree;
I'll ev - er a - dore thee in heav - en so bright;
my gra - cious Re - deem - er, my Sav - ior art thou;
I love thee for wear - ing the thorns on thy brow;
I'll sing with the glit - ter - ing crown on my brow;
if ev - er I loved thee, my Je - sus, 'tis now.
if ev - er I loved thee, my Je - sus, 'tis now.
if ev - er I loved thee, my Je - sus, 'tis now.

WORDS: William R. Featherstone (1846-1873)
MUSIC: Adoniram J. Gordon (1836-1895)

GORDON
11.11.11.11.

469 Lord of All Hopefulness

1 Lord of all hope - ful - ness, Lord of all joy,
2 Lord of all ea - ger - ness, Lord of all faith,
3 Lord of all kind - li - ness, Lord of all grace,
4 Lord of all gen - tle - ness, Lord of all calm,
whose trust, ev - er child - like no cares could de - stroy,
whose strong hands were skilled at the plane and the lathe,
your hands swift to wel - come, your arms to em - brace,
whose voice is con - tent - ment, whose pres - ence is balm,
be there at our wak - ing, and give us, we pray, your
be there at our la - bors, and give us, we pray, your
be there at our hom - ing, and give us, we pray, your
be there at our sleep - ing, and give us, we pray, your
bliss in our hearts, Lord, at the break of the day.
strength in our hearts, Lord, at the noon of the day.
love in our hearts, Lord, at the eve of the day.
peace in our hearts, Lord, at the end of the day.

WORDS: Jan Struther (1901-1953)
MUSIC: Irish melody; harm. Jack Schrader (1942-)

SLANE
10.11.11.12.

Dear Lord and Father of Mankind 470

1 Dear Lord and Fa - ther of man - kind, for - give our fool - ish ways! Re - clothe us in our right - ful mind; in pur - er lives thy serv - ice find, in deep - er rev - erence, praise.
2 In sim - ple trust like theirs who heard, be - side the Syr - ian Sea, the gra - cious call - ing of the Lord, let us, like them, with - out a word, rise up and fol - low thee.
3 O sab - bath rest by Gal - i - lee! O calm of hills a - bove, where Je - sus knelt to share with thee the si - lence of e - ter - ni - ty, in - ter - pre - ted by love!
4 Drop thy still dews of qui - et - ness, till all our striv - ings cease; take from our souls the strain and stress, and let our or - dered lives con - fess the beau - ty of thy peace.
5 Breathe through the heats of our de - sire thy cool - ness and thy balm; let sense be dumb, let flesh re - tire; speak through the earth - quake, wind, and fire, O still small voice of calm!

WORDS: John G. Whittier (1807-1892)
MUSIC: Frederick C. Maker (1844-1927)

REST
8.6.8.8.6.

471 As the Deer

Unison
D A/C# Bm Dsus/A D/A
1 As the deer pants for the wa - ter, so my
2 I want you more than gold or sil - ver, on - ly
3 You're my friend and you are my broth - er, e - ven
G A7sus A7 D G/A A7 D A/C#
soul longs af - ter you; you a - lone are my
you can sat - is - fy; you a - lone are the
though you are a king; I love you more than
Bm Dsus/A D/A G Asus A7 D
heart's de - sire and I long to wor - ship you.
real joy-giv - er and the ap - ple of my eye.
an - y oth - er, so much more than an - y - thing!
Refrain
Bm Bm/A G D/F# G Bm/F#
You a - lone are my strength and shield; to you a - lone may my

WORDS and MUSIC: Martin Nystrom (1956-), alt.

Em
F#sus
F#
D
A/C#
spir - it yield. You a - lone are my
Bm
Dsus/A
D/A
G
A7sus
A7
D
heart's de - sire, and I long to wor - ship you.

Turn Your Eyes upon Jesus 472

Turn your eyes up-on Je - sus, look full in his won-der-ful face; and the
things of earth will grow strange-ly dim in the light of his glo-ry and grace.

WORDS and MUSIC: Helen H. Lemmel (1864-1961)

473 What a Friend We Have in Jesus

1 What a friend we have in Je - sus, all our sins and griefs to bear!
2 Have we tri - als and temp - ta - tions? Is there trou - ble an - y - where?
3 Are we weak and heav - y la - den, cum - bered with a load of care?
What a priv - i - lege to car - ry ev - ery - thing to God in prayer!
We should nev - er be dis - cour - aged; take it to the Lord in prayer!
Pre - cious Sav - ior, still our ref - uge— take it to the Lord in prayer!
O what peace we of - ten for - feit, O what need - less pain we bear,
Can we find a friend so faith - ful who will all our sor - rows share?
Do your friends de - spise, for - sake you? Take it to the Lord in prayer!
all be - cause we do not car - ry ev - ery - thing to God in prayer!
Je - sus knows our ev - ery weak - ness; take it to the Lord in prayer!
In his arms he'll take and shield you; you will find a sol - ace there.

WORDS: Joseph M. Scriven (1819-1886)
MUSIC: Charles C. Converse (1832-1918)

CONVERSE
8.7.8.7.D.

I Surrender All

1 All to Je - sus I sur-ren - der, all to him I free - ly give;
2 All to Je - sus I sur-ren - der, hum - bly at his feet I bow,
3 All to Je - sus I sur-ren - der, make me, Sav - ior, whol - ly thine;
4 All to Je - sus I sur-ren - der, Lord, I give my - self to thee;
I will ev - er love and trust him, in his pres-ence dai - ly live.
world - ly pleas-ures all for-sak - en: take me, Je - sus, take me now.
may thy Ho - ly Spir - it fill me, may I know thy power di - vine.
fill me with thy love and pow - er, let thy bless-ing fall on me.
Refrain
I sur-ren-der all,
I sur-ren-der all,
I sur-ren-der all,
I sur-ren-der all,
all to thee, my bless - ed Sav - ior, I sur - ren - der all.

WORDS: Judson W. VanDeVenter (1855-1939)
MUSIC: Winfield S. Weeden (1847-1908)

SURRENDER
8.7.8.7.Ref.

475 Eternal Spirit of the Living Christ

Unison
1 E - ter - nal Spir - it of the liv - ing Christ,
2 Come, pray in me the prayer I need this day;
3 Come with the vi - sion and the strength I need
I know not how to ask or what to say;
help me to see your pur - pose and your will,
to serve my God, and all hu - man - i - ty;
I on - ly know my need, as deep as life,
where I have failed, what I have done a - miss;
ful - fill - ment of my life in love out - poured—
and on - ly you can teach me how to pray.
held in for - giv - ing love, let me be still.
my life in you, O Christ, your love in me.

WORDS: Frank von Christierson (1900-1996)
MUSIC: Alfred Morton Smith (1879-1971)

SURSUM CORDA
10.10.10.10.

I Need Thee Every Hour

G Am/C G/D D G C G
1 I need thee ev - ery hour, most gra - cious Lord;
2 I need thee ev - ery hour, stay thou near by;
3 I need thee ev - ery hour, in joy or pain;
4 I need thee ev - ery hour, teach me thy will,
D G/D D G D/A A7 D
no ten - der voice like thine can peace af - ford.
temp - ta - tions lose their power when thou art nigh.
come quick - ly, and a - bide, or life is vain.
and thy rich prom - is - es in me ful - fill.
Refrain
G C/G G G/D D D7 Em/D D7 G
I need thee, O I need thee; ev - ery hour I need thee!
G/B C G C6 G/D D7 G
O bless me now, my Sav - ior, I come to thee.

WORDS: Annie S. Hawks (1835-1918); ref. Robert Lowry (1826-1899)
MUSIC: Robert Lowry (1826-1899)

NEED
6.4.6.4.Ref.

477 Come and Find the Quiet Center

F Gm F Dm B♭ C B♭ F
1 Come and find the qui - et cen - ter in the crowd - ed life we lead,
2 Si - lence is a friend who claims us, cools the heat and slows the pace,
3 In the Spir - it let us trav - el, o - pen to each oth - er's pain,
F Gm F Dm B♭ C7 B♭ F
find the room for hope to en - ter, find the frame where we are freed:
God it is who speaks and names us, knows our be - ing, touch - es base,
let our loves and fears un - rav - el, cel - e - brate the space we gain:
F C Dm F B♭
clear the cha - os and the clut - ter, clear our eyes, that we can see
mak - ing space with - in our think - ing, lift - ing shades to show the sun,
there's a place for deep - est dream - ing, there's a time for heart to care,
C Dm B♭ F Gm Am B♭ F
all the things that real - ly mat - ter, be at peace, and sim - ply be.
rais - ing cour - age when we're shrink - ing, find - ing scope for faith be - gun.
in the Spir - it's live - ly schem - ing there is al - ways room to spare!

WORDS: Shirley Erena Murray (1931-)
MUSIC: Attr. B. F. White (1800-1879), *The Sacred Harp*, 1844; arr. Ronald A. Nelson (1927-)

BEACH SPRING
8.7.8.7.D.

Sweet Hour of Prayer

1 Sweet hour of prayer, sweet hour of prayer, that calls me from a world of care,
2 Sweet hour of prayer, sweet hour of prayer, the joys I feel, the bliss I share
3 Sweet hour of prayer, sweet hour of prayer, your wings shall my pe - ti - tion bear
and bids me at my Fa-ther's throne make all my wants and wish-es known.
of those whose anx-ious spir - its burn with strong de - sires for your re - turn!
to him whose truth and faith - ful - ness en - gage the wait - ing soul to bless.
In sea - sons of dis - tress and grief my soul has oft - en found re - lief,
With such I has - ten to the place where God my Sav - ior shows his face,
And since he bids me seek his face, be - lieve his Word, and trust his grace,
and oft es-caped the tempt-er's snare by your re - turn, sweet hour of prayer.
and glad - ly take my sta - tion there, and wait for you, sweet hour of prayer.
I'll cast on him my ev - ery care, and wait for you, sweet hour of prayer.

WORDS: William W. Walford (1772-1850), alt.
MUSIC: William B. Bradbury (1816-1868)

SWEET HOUR
L.M.D.

479 Near the Cross

F Bb/F F C7 Dm Bb F F/C C
1 Je - sus, keep me near the cross; there a pre - cious foun - tain,
2 Near the cross, a trem - bling soul, love and mer - cy found me;
3 Near the cross! O Lamb of God, bring its scenes be - fore me;
4 Near the cross I'll watch and wait, hop - ing, trust - ing ev - er,
F Bb/F F C7 Dm Bb F/C C C7 F
free to all, a heal - ing stream, flows from Cal - vary's moun - tain.
there the bright and morn - ing star sheds its beams a - round me.
help me walk from day to day with its shad - ow o'er me.
till I reach the gold - en strand just be - yond the riv - er.
Refrain
F Bb F Bb/F F F/C C
In the cross, in the cross, be my glo - ry ev - er,
F Gm/F F A7/E Dm Bb F/C C C7 F
till my rap - tured soul shall find rest be - yond the riv - er.

WORDS: Fanny J. Crosby (1820-1915)
MUSIC: William H. Doane (1832-1915)

NEAR THE CROSS
7.6.7.6.Ref.

Open My Eyes, That I May See 480

1 O-pen my eyes, that I may see glimps-es of truth you have for me;
2 O-pen my ears, that I may hear voic-es of truth you send so clear;
3 O-pen my mouth, and let me bear glad-ly the warm truth ev-ery-where;
place in my hands the won-der-ful key that shall un-lock and set me free.
and while the mes-sage sounds in my ear, ev-ery-thing false will dis-ap-pear.
o-pen my heart, and let me pre-pare love with your chil-dren thus to share.
Si-lent-ly now, on bend-ed knee, read-y I wait your will to see;
o-pen my eyes, il-lu-mine me, Spir-it di-vine!
o-pen my ears, il-lu-mine me, Spir-it di-vine!
o-pen my heart, il-lu-mine me, Spir-it di-vine!

WORDS and MUSIC: Clara H. Scott (1841-1897), alt.

OPEN MY EYES
8.8.9.8.8.8.8.4.

481 Every Time I Feel the Spirit

Refrain
Ev-ery time I feel the Spir-it mov-ing in my heart I will pray.
Yes, ev-ery time I feel the Spir-it mov-ing in my heart I will pray.
1 Up - on the moun - tain, when my Lord spoke, out of God's
2 Jor - dan riv - er, chil - ly and cold, it chills the
mouth came fire and smoke. Looked all a - round me,
bod - y but not the soul. There is but one train

WORDS and MUSIC: African-American spiritual, alt.; arr. Melva W. Costen (1933-)

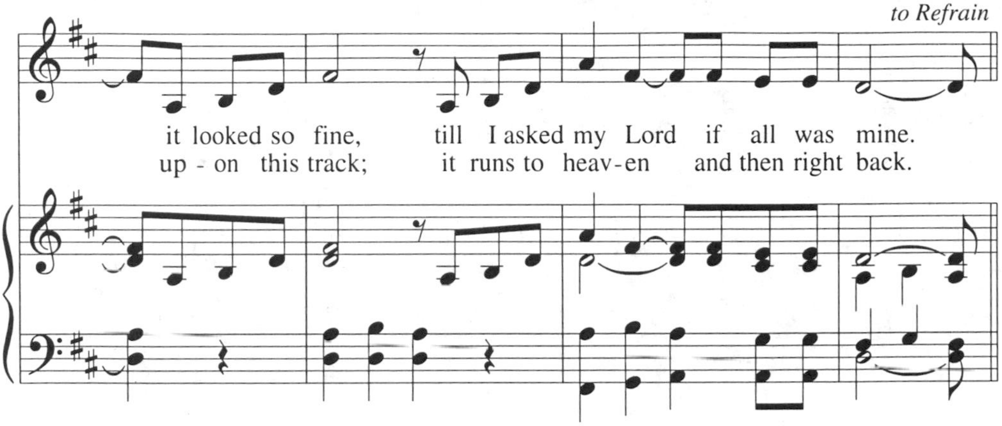
to Refrain
it looked so fine, till I asked my Lord if all was mine.
up - on this track; it runs to heav-en and then right back.

Sanctuary 482

F♯m/A Em/A D A
Lord, pre - pare me to be a sanc - tu - ar - y,
G Em7 D A F♯m/A Em/A D
pure and ho - ly, tried and true; with thanks - giv - ing,
A G F♯m/A G/A D
I'll be a liv - ing sanc - tu - ar - y for you.

WORDS and MUSIC: John Thompson (1950-) and Randy Scruggs (20th c.)

483 Take Time to Be Holy

1 Take time to be ho - ly, speak oft with your Lord;
2 Take time to be ho - ly, the world rush - es on;
3 Take time to be ho - ly, let him be your guide,
a - bide in him al - ways, and feed on his Word.
spend much time in se - cret with Je - sus a - lone.
and run not be - fore him, what - ev - er be - tide.
Make friends of God's chil - dren; help those who are weak;
By look - ing to Je - sus, like him you shall be;
In joy or in sor - row, still fol - low your Lord,
for - get - ting in noth - ing his bless - ing to seek.
your friends in your con - duct his like - ness will see.
and look - ing to Je - sus, still trust in his Word.

WORDS: William D. Longstaff (1822-1894), alt.
MUSIC: George C. Stebbins (1846-1945)

HOLINESS
6.5.6.5.D.

O Lord, Hear My Prayer 484

Em C6 D G C Am6 B
1 O Lord, hear my prayer, O Lord, hear my prayer: when I call an - swer me.
2 The Lord is my song, the Lord is my praise: all my hope comes from God.
Em C6 D G6 Am B Em
O Lord, hear my prayer, O Lord, hear my prayer, come and lis - ten to me.
The Lord is my song, the Lord is my praise: God, the well-spring of life.

WORDS: Taizé Community, 1982; para. Psalm 102
MUSIC: Jacques Berthier (1923-1994)

Into My Heart 485

F C C7 F
In - to my heart, in - to my heart, come in - to my heart, Lord Je - sus;
Bb F/A C7sus/G C7/G C7 F Bb F/A C7/G C7 F/A C C7 F
come in to-day, come in to stay, come in - to my heart, Lord Je - sus.

WORDS and MUSIC: Harry D. Clarke (1888-1957)

INTO MY HEART
L.M.

486 Have Thine Own Way, Lord!

1 Have thine own way, Lord! Have thine own way! Thou art the
2 Have thine own way, Lord! Have thine own way! Search me and
3 Have thine own way, Lord! Have thine own way! Wound-ed and
4 Have thine own way, Lord! Have thine own way! Hold o'er my
Pot - ter, I am the clay. Mold me and make me aft - er thy
try me, Mas-ter, to - day! Whit-er than snow, Lord, wash me just
wea - ry, help me, I pray! Pow - er—all pow - er— sure - ly is
be - ing ab - so - lute sway! Fill with thy Spir - it till all shall
will, while I am wait - ing yield - ed and still.
now, as in thy pres - ence hum - bly I bow.
thine! Touch me and heal me, Sav - ior di - vine!
see Christ on - ly, al - ways, liv - ing in me!

WORDS: Adelaide A. Pollard (1862-1934)
MUSIC: George C. Stebbins (1846-1945)

ADELAIDE
5.4.5.4.D.

487 Kum Ba Yah

D
G
D
1 *Kum ba yah, my Lord, kum ba yah! Kum ba yah, my Lord, kum ba
2 Some-one's cry-ing, Lord, kum ba yah! Some-one's cry-ing, Lord, kum ba
3 Some-one's sing-ing, Lord, kum ba yah! Some-one's sing-ing, Lord, kum ba
4 Some-one's pray-ing, Lord, kum ba yah! Some-one's pray-ing, Lord, kum ba

*Come by here

WORDS and MUSIC: African-American spiritual

KUM BA YAH
8.8.8.5.

A7 D G D G D A7 D
yah! Kum ba yah, my Lord, kum ba yah! O Lord, kum ba yah!
yah! Some-one's cry-ing, Lord, kum ba yah! O Lord, kum ba yah!
yah! Some-one's sing-ing, Lord, kum ba yah! O Lord, kum ba yah!
yah! Some-one's pray-ing, Lord, kum ba yah! O Lord, kum ba yah!

I Lift My Eyes to the Quiet Hills 488

Unison
1 I lift my eyes to the qui-et hills in the
2 I lift my eyes to the qui-et hills, to a
3 I lift my eyes to the qui-et hills with a
4 I lift my eyes to the qui-et hills and my

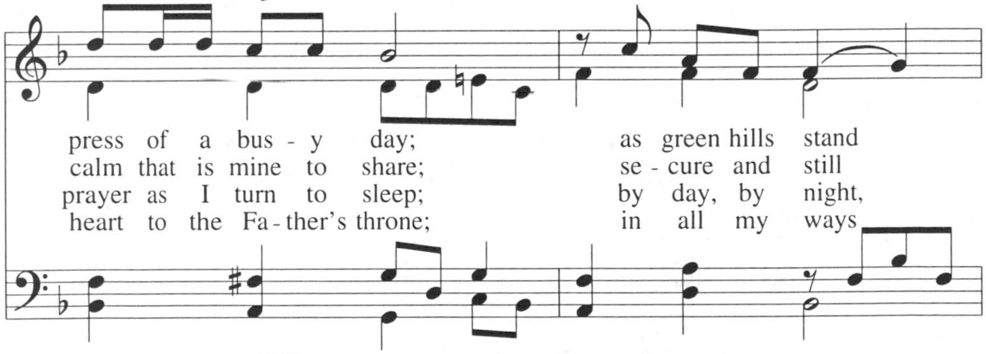
press of a bus-y day; as green hills stand
calm that is mine to share; se-cure and still
prayer as I turn to sleep; by day, by night,
heart to the Fa-ther's throne; in all my ways

in a dust-y land so God is my strength and stay.
in the Fa-ther's will and kept by the Fa-ther's care.
thro' the dark and light my Shep-herd will guard his sheep.
to the end of days the Lord will pre-serve his own.

WORDS: Timothy Dudley-Smith (1926-)
MUSIC: Michael Baughen (1930-) and Elisabeth Crocker (1950-)

DAVOS
4.5.8.4.5.7.

489 Lord, Listen to Your Children Praying

Eb
Eb7
Db/Ab
Ab
Eb
Lord, listen to your children praying,
Lord, send your
F7
Bb7
Eb
Eb7
Spirit in this place;
Lord, listen to your children
Db/Ab
Ab
Adim7
Eb/Bb
Bb7
Ab/Eb
Eb
praying, send us love, send us power, send us grace.

WORDS and MUSIC: Ken Medema (1943-)

CHILDREN PRAYING
Irregular

490 Hear Our Prayer, O Lord

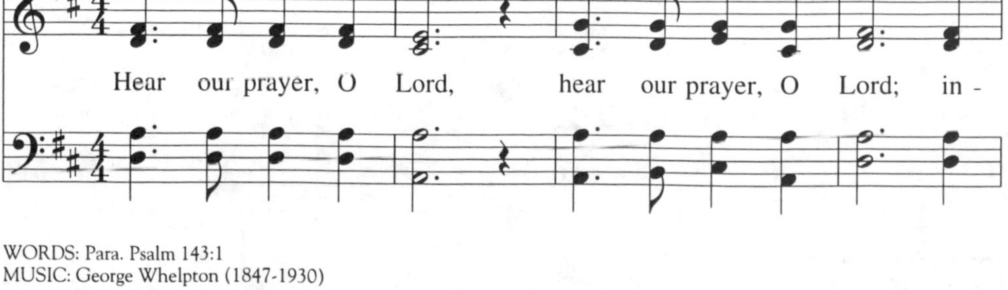
Hear our prayer, O Lord,
hear our prayer, O Lord; in -

WORDS: Para. Psalm 143:1
MUSIC: George Whelpton (1847-1930)

cline thine ear to us, and grant us thy peace. A - men.

Open Our Eyes 491

D A7/E D/F# G2 G Em7 A7 G/D D
1 O - pen our eyes, Lord, we want to see Je - sus,
2 O - pen our ears, Lord, and help us to lis - ten,
Bm Bm7/A Gmaj7
1
Em A7sus A7 G/D
to reach out and touch him, and say that we love
o - pen our eyes,
D
him.
2
Em A7 Em/D D
Lord, we want to see Je - sus.

WORDS and MUSIC: Bob Cull (1949-); arr. David Allen (1941-)

492 Spirit of the Living God

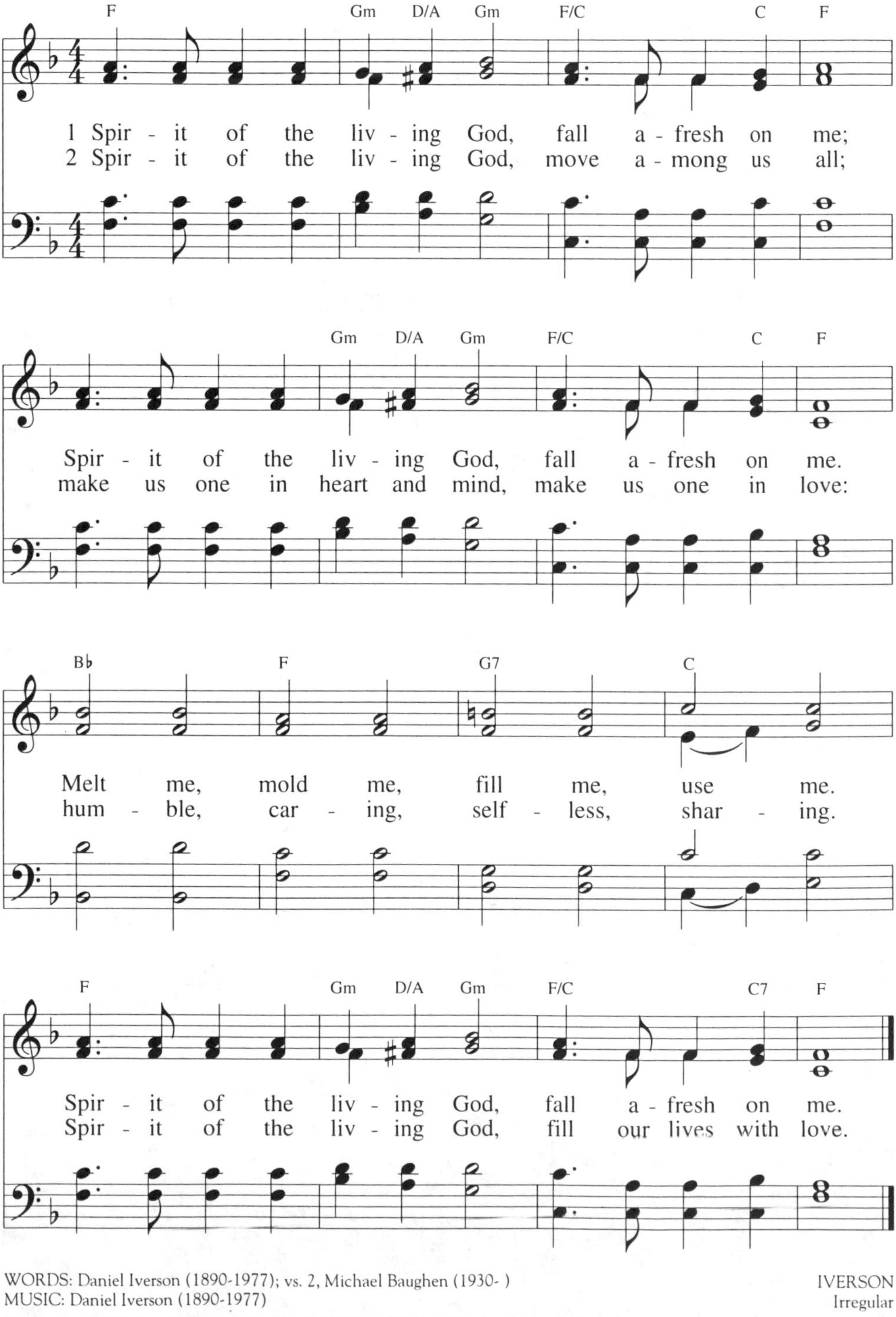
F Gm D/A Gm F/C C F
1 Spir - it of the liv - ing God, fall a - fresh on me;
2 Spir - it of the liv - ing God, move a - mong us all;
Gm D/A Gm F/C C F
Spir - it of the liv - ing God, fall a - fresh on me.
make us one in heart and mind, make us one in love:
B♭ F G7 C
Melt me, mold me, fill me, use me.
hum - ble, car - ing, self - less, shar - ing.
F Gm D/A Gm F/C C7 F
Spir - it of the liv - ing God, fall a - fresh on me.
Spir - it of the liv - ing God, fill our lives with love.

WORDS: Daniel Iverson (1890-1977); vs. 2, Michael Baughen (1930-)
MUSIC: Daniel Iverson (1890-1977)

IVERSON
Irregular

Cares Chorus

493

Unison
C
G/B
Am
Cmaj7/G
I cast all my cares up-on you, I
F
3
C/E
Dm
Gsus
G
lay all of my bur - dens down at your feet. And
C
G/B
C/B♭
F/A
Fm/A♭
an - y-time that I don't know what to do. I will
C2/G
C/G
G7sus
G7
F/C
C
cast all my cares up-on you.

WORDS and MUSIC: Kelly Willard (1956-)

494 Step by Step

G
D/F#
C/E
D7
G
O God, you are my God, and I will ev-er praise you. O
G
D/F#
C/E
D7
G
God, you are my God, and I will ev-er praise you. I will
Em
C/E
D
C
Am
C/D
seek you in the morn-ing, and I will learn to walk in your ways; and
G
D/F#
Am7
D7
C/D
G
step by step you'll lead me, and I will fol-low you all of my days.

WORDS and MUSIC: Beaker (20th c.)

Stand by Me

Eb
Ab
Eb
1 When the storms of life are rag - ing, stand by me; when the
2 In the midst of trib - u - la - tion, stand by me; in the
3 In the midst of faults and fail - ures, stand by me; in the
4 When I'm grow - ing old and fee - ble, stand by me; when I'm
Bb7sus
Bb7
storms of life are rag - ing, stand by me. When the
midst of trib - u - la - tion, stand by me. When the
midst of faults and fail - ures, stand by me. When I've
grow - ing old and fee - ble, stand by me. When my
Eb
Eb/Bb
Bdim7
Cm
world is toss - ing me like a ship up - on the sea,
hosts of sin as - sail, and my strength be - gins to fail,
done the best I can, and my friends mis - un - der - stand,
life be-comes a bur - den, and I'm near - ing chil - ly Jor-dan,
Eb/Bb
Ab/Bb
Eb
thou who rul - est wind and wa - ter, stand by me.
thou who nev - er lost a bat - tle, stand by me.
thou who know - est all a - bout me, stand my me.
O thou Lil - y of the Val - ley, stand by me.

WORDS and MUSIC: Charles A. Tindley (1851-1933); arr. Daniel L. Ridout (1899-1982), alt.

STAND BY ME
11.11.7.7.11.

496 Leaning on the Everlasting Arms

1 What a fel-low-ship, what a joy di-vine, lean-ing on the ev-er-last-ing arms; what a bless-ed-ness, what a peace is mine, lean-ing on the ev-er-last-ing arms.
2 O how sweet to walk in this pil-grim way, lean-ing on the ev-er-last-ing arms; O how bright the path grows from day to day, lean-ing on the ev-er-last-ing arms.
3 What have I to dread, what have I to fear, lean-ing on the ev-er-last-ing arms? I have bless-ed peace with my Lord so near, lean-ing on the ev-er-last-ing arms.
Refrain
Lean - ing, lean - ing, safe and se-cure from all a-larms; lean - ing, lean - ing, lean-ing on the ev-er-last-ing arms.
Lean-ing on Je - sus, lean-ing on Je - sus, lean-ing on Je - sus, lean-ing on Je - sus,

WORDS: Elisha A. Hoffman (1839-1929)
MUSIC: Anthony J. Showalter (1858-1924)

SHOWALTER
10.9.10.9.Ref.

Find Us Faithful

O may all who come be - hind us find us faith - ful;
may the fire of our de - vo - tion light their way.
May the foot - prints that we leave lead them to be - lieve,
and the lives we live in - spire them to o - bey.
O may all who come be - hind us find us faith - ful.

WORDS and MUSIC: Jon Mohr (1955-), alt.

498 Lead Me, Guide Me

Refrain
Eb F7 Bb F7 Bb Eb7
Lead me, guide me, a - long the way,
Ab Gm/Bb Fm/Bb Eb Bb7 Eb
for if you lead me, I can - not stray.
Eb Db7 C7
Lord, let me walk each day with you,
Fm C7 Fm Eb/Bb F9 Bb7 Eb Ab/Eb Eb
lead me my whole life through.

WORDS: Doris Akers (1922-1995), alt.
MUSIC: Doris Akers (1922-1995); arr. Richard Smallwood (1948-)

LEAD ME
Irregular

Eb Eb/Db C7 Fm Fm7 Bb7
1 I am weak and I need your strength and power to en-
2 Help me walk in the paths of right - eous - ness; be my
3 I am lost if you take your hand from me, I am
Fm Fm/Bb Gm/Bb Fm/Bb Eb/Bb Bb7 Eb
dure with grace my weak - est hour. Help me
aid when Sa - tan and sin op - press. I am
blind with - out your light to see. Lord, for-
Eb7 Fm/Ab C7/G Fm
through the dark - ness your face to see.
trust - ing you what - e'er may be.
ev - er may I your ser - vant be.
to Refrain
Eb/Bb F9 Bb7 Ab/Bb Bb7 Eb Ab/Eb Eb
Lead me, O Lord, lead me.

499 He Leadeth Me

1 He lead - eth me, O bless - ed thought! O words with heaven - ly
2 Lord, I would clasp thy hand in mine, nor ev - er mur - mur
3 And when my task on earth is done, when by thy grace the
com - fort fraught! What - e'er I do, where - e'er I be, still
nor re - pine; con - tent, what - e'er my lot may be, since
vic - tory's won, e'en death's cold wave I will not flee, since
'tis God's hand that lead - eth me.
'tis my God who lead - eth me.
God through Jor - dan lead - eth me.
Refrain
He lead - eth me, he lead - eth me, by his own hand he lead - eth me; his faith - ful fol - lower I would be, for by his hand he lead - eth me.

WORDS: Joseph H. Gilmore (1834-1918)
MUSIC: William B. Bradbury (1816-1868)

HE LEADETH ME
L.M.Ref.

Precious Lord, Take My Hand 500

1 Pre - cious Lord, take my hand, lead me on, let me stand,
2 When my way grows drear, pre-cious Lord, lin - ger near,
3 When the dark - ness ap - pears and the night draws near,
I am tired, I am weak, I am worn;
when my life is al - most gone;
and the day is past and gone,
through the storm, through the night, lead me on to the light:
hear my cry, hear my call, hold my hand lest I fall:
at the riv - er I stand, guide my feet, hold my hand:
take my hand, pre - cious Lord, lead me home.
take my hand, pre - cious Lord, lead me home.
take my hand, pre - cious Lord, lead me home.

WORDS and MUSIC: Thomas A. Dorsey (1899-1993)

PRECIOUS LORD
6.6.9.6.6.9.

501 Guide Me, O Thou Great Jehovah

1 Guide me, O thou great Je - ho - vah, pil - grim through this bar - ren land;
2 O - pen now the crys - tal foun-tain, whence the heal - ing stream doth flow;
3 When I tread the verge of Jor - dan, bid my anx - ious fears sub - side;
I am weak, but thou art might - y— hold me with thy power - ful hand:
let the fire and cloud-y pil - lar lead me all my jour - ney through:
bear me through the swell - ing cur - rent, land me safe on Ca - naan's side:
Bread of heav - en, Bread of heav - en, feed me till I want no
Strong De - liv - erer, strong De - liv - erer, be thou still my strength and
Songs of prais - es, songs of prais - es I will ev - er give to
more, (want no more,) feed me till I want no more.
shield, (strength and shield,) be thou still my strength and shield.
thee, (give to thee,) I will ev - er give to thee.

WORDS: William Williams (1717-1791); tr. Peter Williams (1722-1796) and others
MUSIC: John Hughes (1873-1932)

CWM RHONDDA
8.7.8.7.8.7.7.

Be Thou My Vision

502

1 Be thou my Vi - sion, O Lord of my heart;
2 Be thou my Wis - dom, and thou my true Word,
3 High King of heav - en, my vic - to - ry won,
naught be all else to me, save that thou art—
I ev - er with thee and thou with me, Lord;
may I reach heav - en's joys, O bright heaven's Sun!
thou my best thought, by day or by night,
thou and thou on - ly, first in my heart,
Heart of my own heart, what - ev - er be - fall,
wak - ing or sleep - ing, thy pres - ence my light.
high King of heav - en, my Treas - ure thou art.
still be my Vi - sion, O Rul - er of all.

WORDS: Irish hymn, 8th c.; tr. Mary E. Byrne (1880-1931); versed Eleanor H. Hull (1860-1935)
MUSIC: Irish melody; arr. Jack Schrader (1942-)

SLANE
10.10.10.10.

503 O God, Your Constant Care and Love

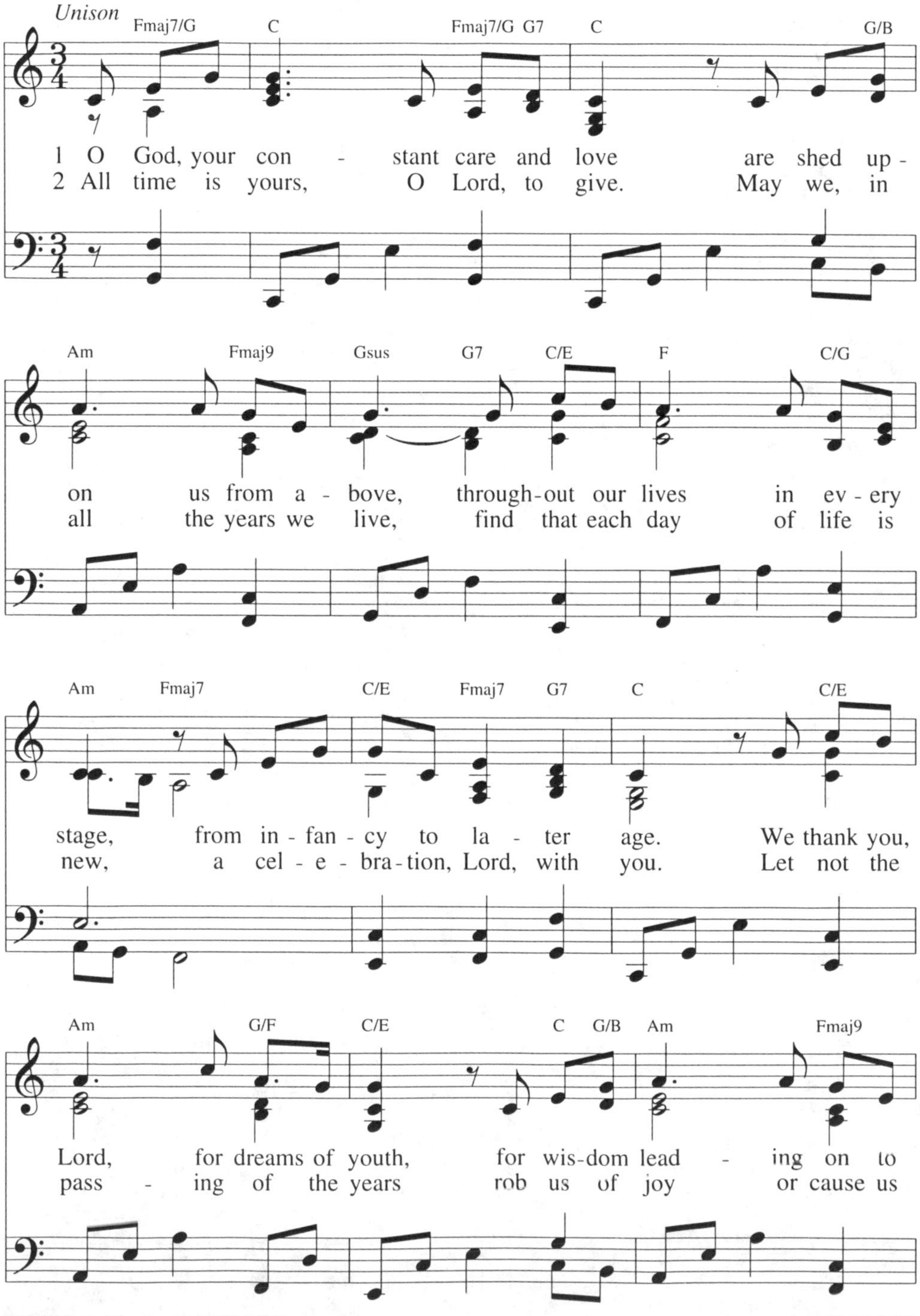
Unison
Fmaj7/G C Fmaj7/G G7 C G/B
1 O God, your con - stant care and love are shed up -
2 All time is yours, O Lord, to give. May we, in
Am Fmaj9 Gsus G7 C/E F C/G
on us from a - bove, through-out our lives in ev - ery
all the years we live, find that each day of life is
Am Fmaj7 C/E Fmaj7 G7 C C/E
stage, from in - fan - cy to la - ter age. We thank you,
new, a cel - e - bra - tion, Lord, with you. Let not the
Am G/F C/E C G/B Am Fmaj9
Lord, for dreams of youth, for wis-dom lead - ing on to
pass - ing of the years rob us of joy or cause us

WORDS: H. Glen Lanier (1925-1978)
MUSIC: Twila Paris (1958-)

LAMB OF GOD
8.8.8.8.D.

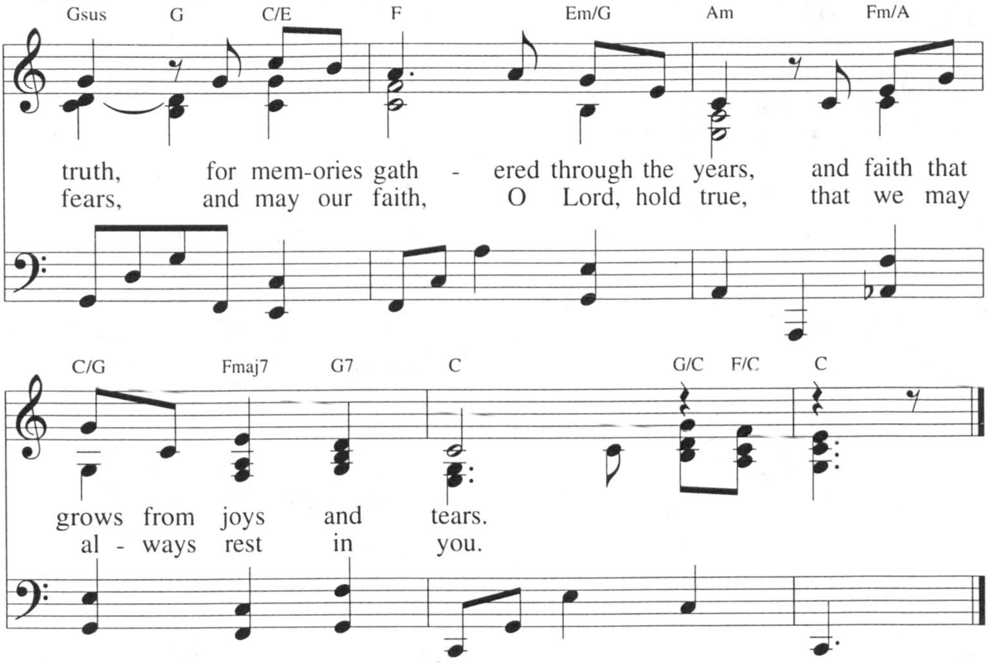
Gsus G C/E F Em/G Am Fm/A
truth, for mem-ories gath - ered through the years, and faith that
fears, and may our faith, O Lord, hold true, that we may
C/G Fmaj7 G7 C G/C F/C C
grows from joys and tears.
al - ways rest in you.

Just a Closer Walk with Thee 504

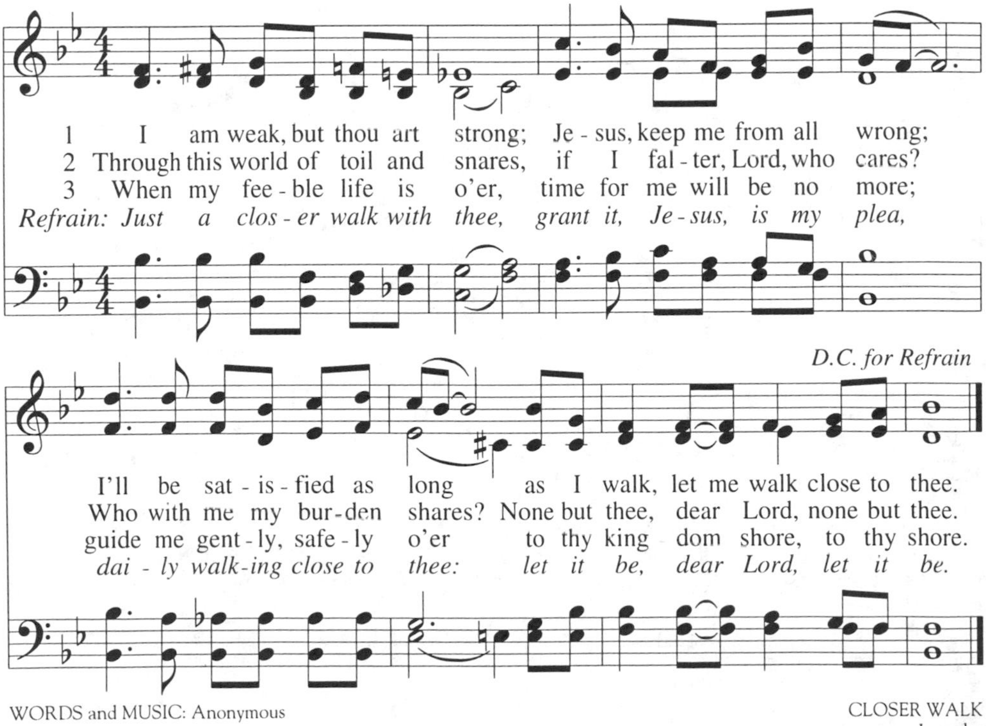
1 I am weak, but thou art strong; Je - sus, keep me from all wrong;
2 Through this world of toil and snares, if I fal - ter, Lord, who cares?
3 When my fee - ble life is o'er, time for me will be no more;
Refrain: Just a clos - er walk with thee, grant it, Je - sus, is my plea,
D.C. for Refrain
I'll be sat - is - fied as long as I walk, let me walk close to thee.
Who with me my bur - den shares? None but thee, dear Lord, none but thee.
guide me gent - ly, safe - ly o'er to thy king - dom shore, to thy shore.
dai - ly walk-ing close to thee: let it be, dear Lord, let it be.

WORDS and MUSIC: Anonymous

CLOSER WALK
Irregular

505 All the Way My Savior Leads Me

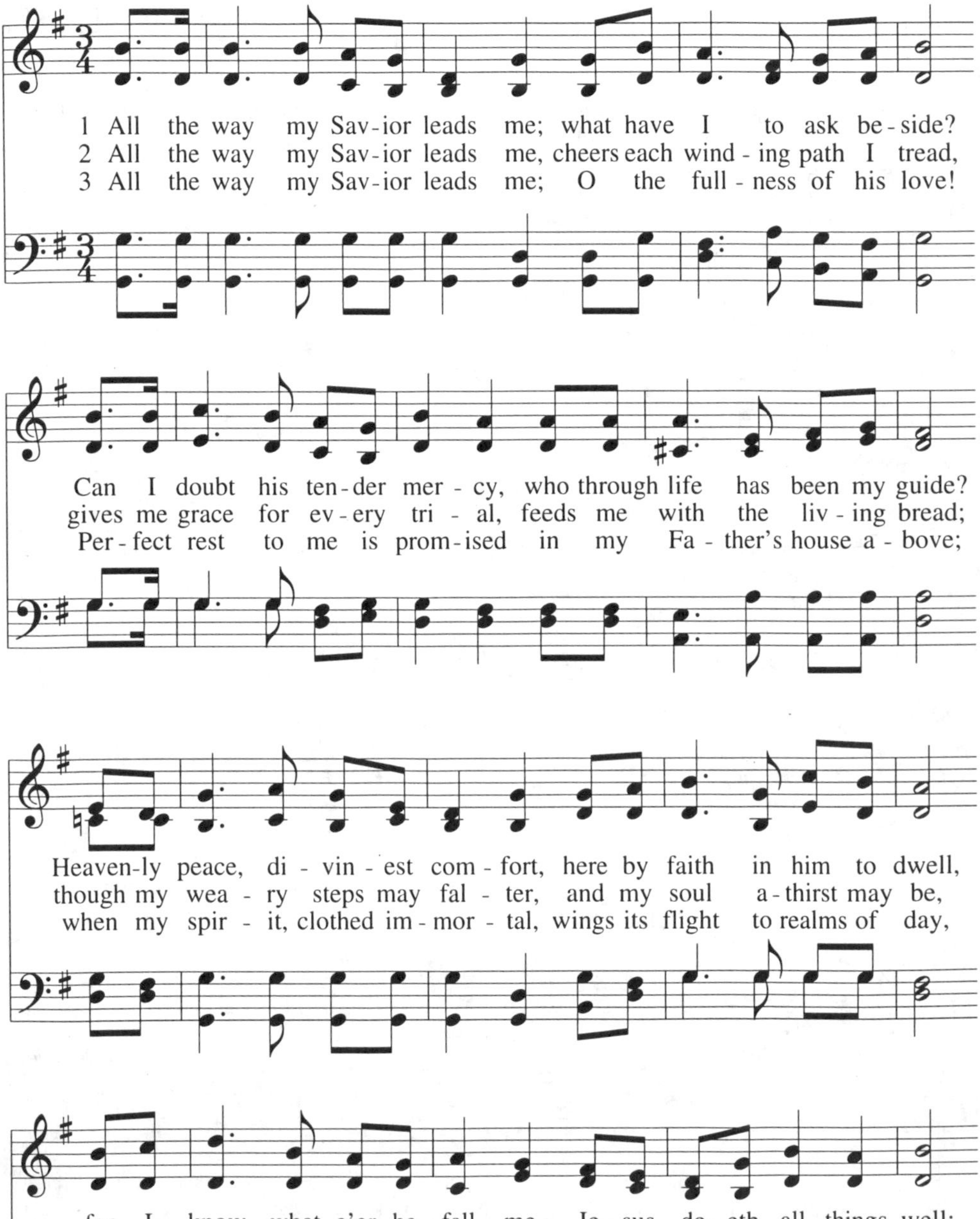
1 All the way my Sav-ior leads me; what have I to ask be-side?
2 All the way my Sav-ior leads me, cheers each wind-ing path I tread,
3 All the way my Sav-ior leads me; O the full-ness of his love!
Can I doubt his ten-der mer-cy, who through life has been my guide?
gives me grace for ev-ery tri-al, feeds me with the liv-ing bread;
Per-fect rest to me is prom-ised in my Fa-ther's house a-bove;
Heaven-ly peace, di-vin-est com-fort, here by faith in him to dwell,
though my wea-ry steps may fal-ter, and my soul a-thirst may be,
when my spir-it, clothed im-mor-tal, wings its flight to realms of day,
for I know, what-e'er be-fall me, Je-sus do-eth all things well;
gush-ing from the rock be-fore me, lo! a spring of joy I see;
this my song through end-less a-ges, Je-sus led me all the way;

WORDS: Fanny J. Crosby (1820-1915)
MUSIC: Robert Lowry (1826-1899)

ALL THE WAY
8.7.8.7.D.

for I know, what-e'er be-fall me, Je-sus do-eth all things well.
gush-ing from the rock be-fore me, lo! a spring of joy I see.
this my song through end-less a-ges, Je-sus led me all the way.

I Want Jesus to Walk with Me 506

Unison
Dm A7/E Dm A7 Dm Am Dm N.C.
1 I want Je-sus to walk with me; I want
2 In my tri-als, Lord, walk with me; in my
3 When I'm in trou-ble, Lord, walk with me; when I'm in
F C7/G F/A F A7/E Dm A7/C♯ A7 Dm C9/E C7
Je-sus to walk with me; all a-long my pil-grim
tri-als, Lord, walk with me; when my heart is al-most
trou-ble, Lord, walk with me; when my head is bowed in
Dm Dm7/C B♭ C7 Dm B♭ Gm7 A7 Dm Gm6 Dm
jour-ney, Lord, I want Je-sus to walk with me.
break-ing, Lord, I want Je-sus to walk with me.
sor-row, Lord, I want Je-sus to walk with me.

WORDS and MUSIC: African-American spiritual

WALK WITH ME
Irregular

507 A Mighty Fortress Is Our God

1 A might-y for-tress is our God, a bul-wark nev-er fail-ing;
2 Did we in our own strength con-fide, our striv-ing would be los-ing,
3 And though this world, with dev-ils filled, should threat-en to un-do us,
4 That word a-bove all earth-ly powers, no thanks to them, a-bid-eth;
our help-er he, a-mid the flood of mor-tal ills pre-vail-ing.
were not the right man on our side, the man of God's own choos-ing.
we will not fear, for God hath willed his truth to tri-umph through us.
the Spir-it and the gifts are ours thro' him who with us sid-eth.
For still our an-cient foe doth seek to work us woe; his craft and power are
Dost ask who that may be? Christ Je-sus, it is he; Lord Sab-a-oth his
The Prince of Dark-ness grim, we trem-ble not for him; his rage we can en-
Let goods and kin-dred go, this mor-tal life al-so; the bod-y they may
great, and, armed with cru-el hate, on earth is not his e-qual.
name, from age to age the same, and he must win the bat-tlc.
dure, for lo, his doom is sure; onc lit-tle word shall fell him.
kill: God's truth a-bid-eth still; his king-dom is for-ev-er.

WORDS: Martin Luther (1483-1546); tr. Frederick H. Hedge (1805-1890)
MUSIC: Martin Luther (1483-1546)

EIN' FESTE BURG
8.7.8.7.6.6.6.6.7.

Lead On, O King Eternal

1 Lead on, O King E - ter - nal, the day of march has come;
2 Lead on, O King E - ter - nal, till sin's fierce war shall cease,
3 Lead on, O King E - ter - nal, we fol - low, not with fears;
hence-forth in fields of con - quest your tents shall be our home.
and ho - li - ness shall whis - per the sweet A - men of peace;
for glad-ness breaks like morn - ing wher - e'er your face ap - pears;
Through days of prep - a - ra - tion your grace has made us strong,
for not with swords loud clash - ing, nor roll of stir - ring drums,
your cross is lift - ed o'er us; we jour - ney in its light;
and now, O King E - ter - nal, we lift our bat - tle song.
with deeds of love and mer - cy the heaven - ly king - dom comes.
the crown a - waits the con - quest: lead on, O God of might.

WORDS: Ernest W. Shurtleff (1862-1917)
MUSIC: Henry T. Smart (1813-1879)

LANCASHIRE
7.6.7.6.D.

509 Onward, Christian Soldiers

1 On - ward, Chris - tian sol - diers, march - ing as to war,
2 Like a might - y ar - my moves the Church of God;
3 Crowns and thrones may per - ish, king - doms rise and wane,
4 On - ward, then, you peo - ple, join our hap - py throng,
with the cross of Je - sus go - ing on be - fore:
Chris - tians, we are tread - ing where the saints have trod;
but the Church of Je - sus con - stant will re - main;
blend with ours your voic - es in the tri - umph song;
Christ, the roy - al Mas - ter, leads a - gainst the foe;
we are not di - vid - ed, all one bod - y we,
gates of hell can nev - er 'gainst that Church pre - vail;
glo - ry, laud, and hon - or un - to Christ the King:
for - ward in - to bat - tle, see his ban - ners go.
one in hope and doc - trine, one in char - i - ty.
we have Christ's own prom - ise, and that can - not fail.
this thro' count - less a - ges with the an - gels sing.

WORDS: Sabine Baring-Gould (1834-1924), alt.
MUSIC: Arthur S. Sullivan (1842-1900)

ST. GERTRUDE
6.5.6.5.D.Ref.

Refrain
On - ward, Chris-tian sol - diers, march-ing as to war,

with the cross of Je - sus go - ing on be - fore.

Am I a Soldier of the Cross 510

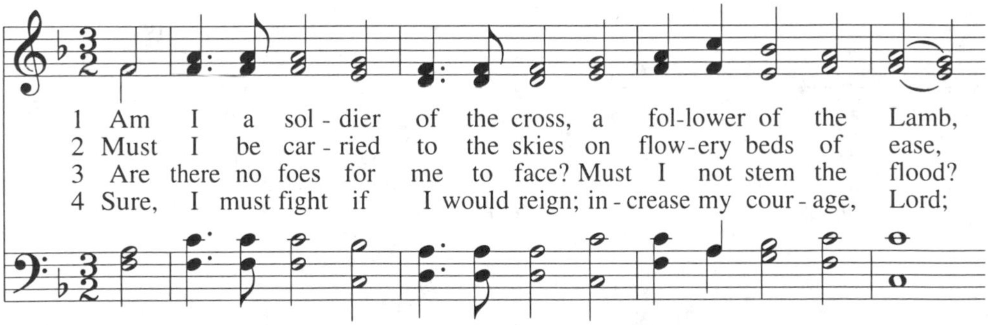
1 Am I a sol - dier of the cross, a fol-lower of the Lamb,
2 Must I be car - ried to the skies on flow-ery beds of ease,
3 Are there no foes for me to face? Must I not stem the flood?
4 Sure, I must fight if I would reign; in - crease my cour - age, Lord;

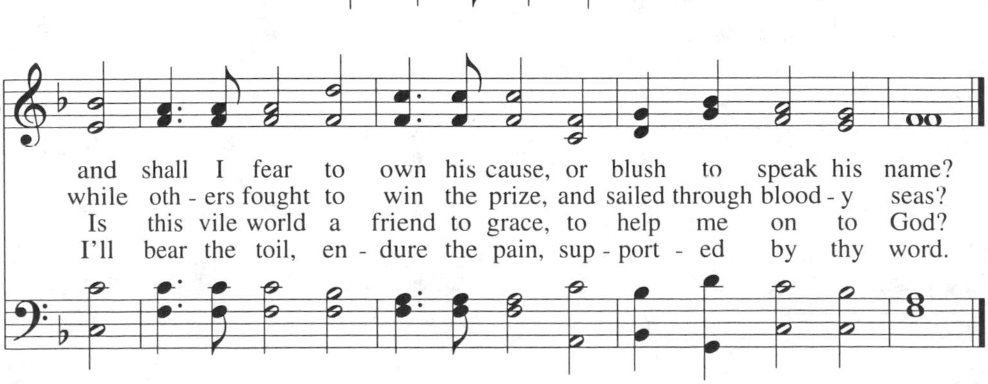
and shall I fear to own his cause, or blush to speak his name?
while oth - ers fought to win the prize, and sailed through blood - y seas?
Is this vile world a friend to grace, to help me on to God?
I'll bear the toil, en - dure the pain, sup - port - ed by thy word.

WORDS: Isaac Watts (1674-1748)
MUSIC: Thomas A. Arne (1710-1778)

ARLINGTON
C.M.

511 The Battle Belongs to the Lord

Unison
Em
D/E
D
N.C.
C
G
Refrain
1 In heav-en-ly ar - mor we'll en - ter the land, the bat-tle be-longs to the Lord. No weap-on that's fash - ioned a-gainst us will stand, the bat-tle be-longs to the Lord.
2 When the pow-er of dark-ness comes in like a flood, the bat-tle be-longs to the Lord. He's raised up a stan - dard, the power of his blood, the bat-tle be-longs to the Lord.
3 When your en - e - my press - es in hard, do not fear, the bat-tle be-longs to the Lord. Take cour-age, my friend, your re-demp-tion is near, the bat-tle be-longs to the Lord.
And we sing glo - ry, hon - or, pow-er and strength to the Lord. We sing

WORDS and MUSIC: Jamie Owens-Collins (1955-)

G D C D G Cmaj7 D Em
glo - ry, hon - or, pow - er and strength to the Lord!

We Shall Overcome 512

1 We shall o - ver - come, we shall o - ver - come, we shall
o - ver - come some - day!
Refrain
Oh, deep in my heart
I do be - lieve we shall o - ver - come some - day!

2 The Lord will see us through.
3 We'll walk hand in hand.
4 We are not afraid (today).
5 The truth shall make us free.
6 We shall live in peace.

WORDS and MUSIC: African-American spiritual, arr. William Farley Smith (1941-)

MARTIN
Irregular

513 Stand Up, Stand Up for Jesus

1 Stand up, stand up for Je - sus, you sol - diers of the cross, lift high his roy - al ban - ner, it must not suf - fer loss; from vic - tory un - to vic - tory his ar - my shall he lead, till ev - ery foe is van - quished and Christ is Lord in - deed.
2 Stand up, stand up for Je - sus, the trum - pet call o - bey; forth to the might - y con - flict in this his glo - rious day. You that are brave, now serve him a - gainst un - num - bered foes; let cour - age rise with dan - ger, and strength to strength op - pose.
3 Stand up, stand up for Je - sus, stand in his strength a - lone; the arm of flesh will fail you—you dare not trust your own; put on the gos - pel ar - mor, each piece put on with prayer; where du - ty calls, or dan - ger, be nev - er want - ing there.
4 Stand up, stand up for Je - sus, the strife will not be long; this day the noise of bat - tle, the next, the vic - tor's song: to those who con - quer e - vil a crown of life shall be; they with the King of glo - ry shall reign e - ter - nal - ly.

WORDS: George Duffield (1818-1888)
MUSIC: George J. Webb (1803-1887)

WEBB
7.6.7.6.D.

Be Strong in the Lord

1 Be strong in the Lord, and be of good cour-age; your might-y De-fend-er is al-ways the same. Mount up with wings, as the ea-gle as-cend-ing; vic-tory is sure when you call on his name.
2 So put on the ar-mor the Lord has pro-vid-ed, and place your de-fense in his un-fail-ing care. Trust him for he will be with you in bat-tle, light-ing your path to a-void ev-ery snare.
3 Be strong in the Lord, and be of good cour-age; your might-y Com-mand-er will van-quish the foe. Fear not the bat-tle for the vic-tory is al-ways his; he will pro-tect you where-ev-er you go.
Refrain
Be strong, be strong, be strong in the Lord, and be of good cour-age for he is your guide. Be strong, be strong, be strong in the Lord, and re-joice for the vic-tory is yours.

WORDS: Linda Lee Johnson (1947-)
MUSIC: Tom Fettke (1941-)

STRENGTH
11.11.11.10.

515 Hymn of Promise

Unison
1 In the bulb there is a flow - er; in the seed, an ap - ple
2 There's a song in ev - ery si - lence, seek-ing word and mel - o -
3 In our end is our be - gin - ning; in our time, in - fin - i -
tree; in co - coons, a hid - den prom - ise: but - ter - flies will soon be
dy; there's a dawn in ev - ery dark - ness bring-ing hope to you and
ty; in our doubt there is be - liev - ing; in our life, e - ter - ni-
free! In the cold and snow of win - ter there's a spring that waits to
me. From the past will come the fu - ture; what it holds, a mys-ter-
ty; in our death, a res - ur - rec - tion; at the last, a vic - to-
be, un-re-vealed un-til its sea-son, some-thing God a-lone can see.
y, un-re-vealed un-til its sea-son, some-thing God a-lone can see.
ry, un-re-vealed un-til its sea-son, some-thing God a-lone can see.

WORDS and MUSIC: Natalie Sleeth (1930-1992)

PROMISE
8.7.8.7.D.

Grief of Ending, Wordless Sorrow 516

Unison
1 Grief of end - ing, word - less sor - row, pain of part - ing, dry or weep - ing, on our lips and in our bod - ies, lov - ing God, to you we of - fer.
2 Times re - mem - bered, joy dis - cov - ered, love and friend - ship, voice and ges - ture, pre - cious, love - ly, one and on - ly, giv - ing God, we tell and treas - ure.
3 Word of prom - ise, lift our sing - ing, blend - ing griev - ing with be - liev - ing. In your hands is all com - plet - ed, last - ing God, our hope and meas - ure.
4 Christ a - mong us, Spir - it - breath - ing, safe com - pan - ion, in your keep - ing, death is birth to res - ur - rec - tion, liv - ing God, our joy for - ev - er.

WORDS: Brian Wren (1936-)
MUSIC: Peter Cutts (1937-)

MOUNT AUBURN
L.M.

517 Christ the Victorious

1 Christ the Vic - to - ri - ous, give to your ser - vants
2 On - ly Im - mor - tal One, Might - y Cre - a - tor!
3 God - spo - ken proph - e - cy, word at cre - a - tion:
4 Christ the Vic - to - ri - ous, give to your ser - vants
rest with your saints in the re - gions of light.
We are your crea - tures and chil - dren of earth.
"You came from dust and to dust shall re - turn."
rest with your saints in the re - gions of light.
Grief and pain end - ed, and sigh - ing no long - er,
From earth you formed us, both glo - rious and mor - tal,
Yet at the grave shall we raise up our glad song,
Grief and pain end - ed, and sigh - ing no long - er,
there may they find ev - er - last - ing life.
and to the earth shall we all re - turn.
"Al - le - lu - ia, al - le - lu - ia!"
there may they find ev - er - last - ing life.

WORDS: Carl. P. Daw, Jr. (1944-)
MUSIC: Alexis Lvov (1799-1870)

RUSSIAN HYMN
11.10.11.9.

Give Thanks for Life

Unison
1 Give thanks for life, the meas - ure of our days,
2 Give thanks for those who made their life a light
3 And for our own, our liv - ing and our dead,
4 Give thanks for hope, that, like the wheat, the grain
mor - tal, we pass through beau - ty that de - cays, yet
caught from the Christ - flame, burst - ing through the night, who
thanks for the love by which our life is fed, a
ly - ing in dark - ness does its life re - tain, in
sing to God our hope, our love, our praise:
touched the truth, who burned for what is right:
love not changed by time or death or dread:
res - ur - rec - tion to grow green a - gain:
Al - le - lu - ia! Al - le - lu - ia!

WORDS: Shirley Erena Murray (1931-)
MUSIC: Ralph Vaughan Williams (1872-1958)

SINE NOMINE
10.10.10.Alleluias

519 On Jordan's Stormy Banks I Stand

1 On Jor-dan's storm-y banks I stand, and cast a wish-ful eye
2 O'er all those wide ex-tend-ed plains shines one e-ter-nal day;
3 When shall I reach that hap-py place and be for-ev-er blest?
4 Filled with de-light, my rap-tured soul would here no long-er stay;
to Ca-naan's fair and hap-py land, where my pos-ses-sions lie.
there God the Son for-ev-er reigns and scat-ters night a-way.
When shall I see my Fa-ther's face and in his bos-om rest?
though Jor-dan's waves a-round me roll, fear-less I'd launch a-way.
Refrain
I am bound for the prom-ised land, I am bound for the prom-ised
land; O who will come and go with me? I am bound for the prom-ised land.

WORDS: Samuel Stennett (1727-1795)
MUSIC: American melody; arr. Rigdon M. McIntosh (1836-1899) and Donald P. Hustad (1918-)

PROMISED LAND
C.M.Ref.

Swing Low, Sweet Chariot 520

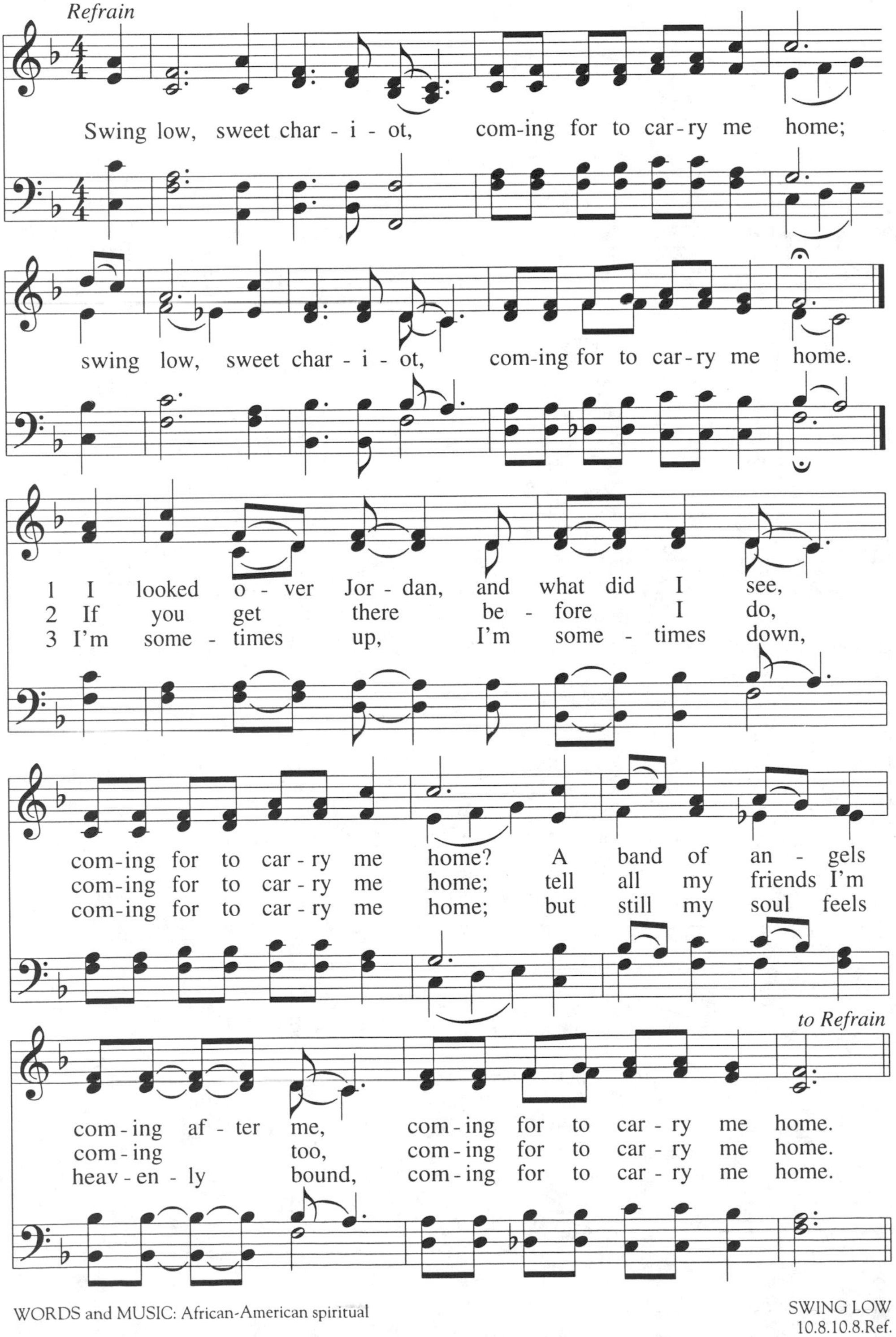
Refrain
Swing low, sweet char - i - ot, com-ing for to car-ry me home;
swing low, sweet char - i - ot, com-ing for to car-ry me home.
1 I looked o - ver Jor - dan, and what did I see,
2 If you get there be - fore I do,
3 I'm some - times up, I'm some - times down,
com-ing for to car - ry me home? A band of an - gels
com-ing for to car - ry me home; tell all my friends I'm
com-ing for to car - ry me home; but still my soul feels
to Refrain
com - ing af - ter me, com - ing for to car - ry me home.
com - ing too, com - ing for to car - ry me home.
heav - en - ly bound, com - ing for to car - ry me home.

WORDS and MUSIC: African-American spiritual

SWING LOW
10.8.10.8.Ref.

521 Abide with Me

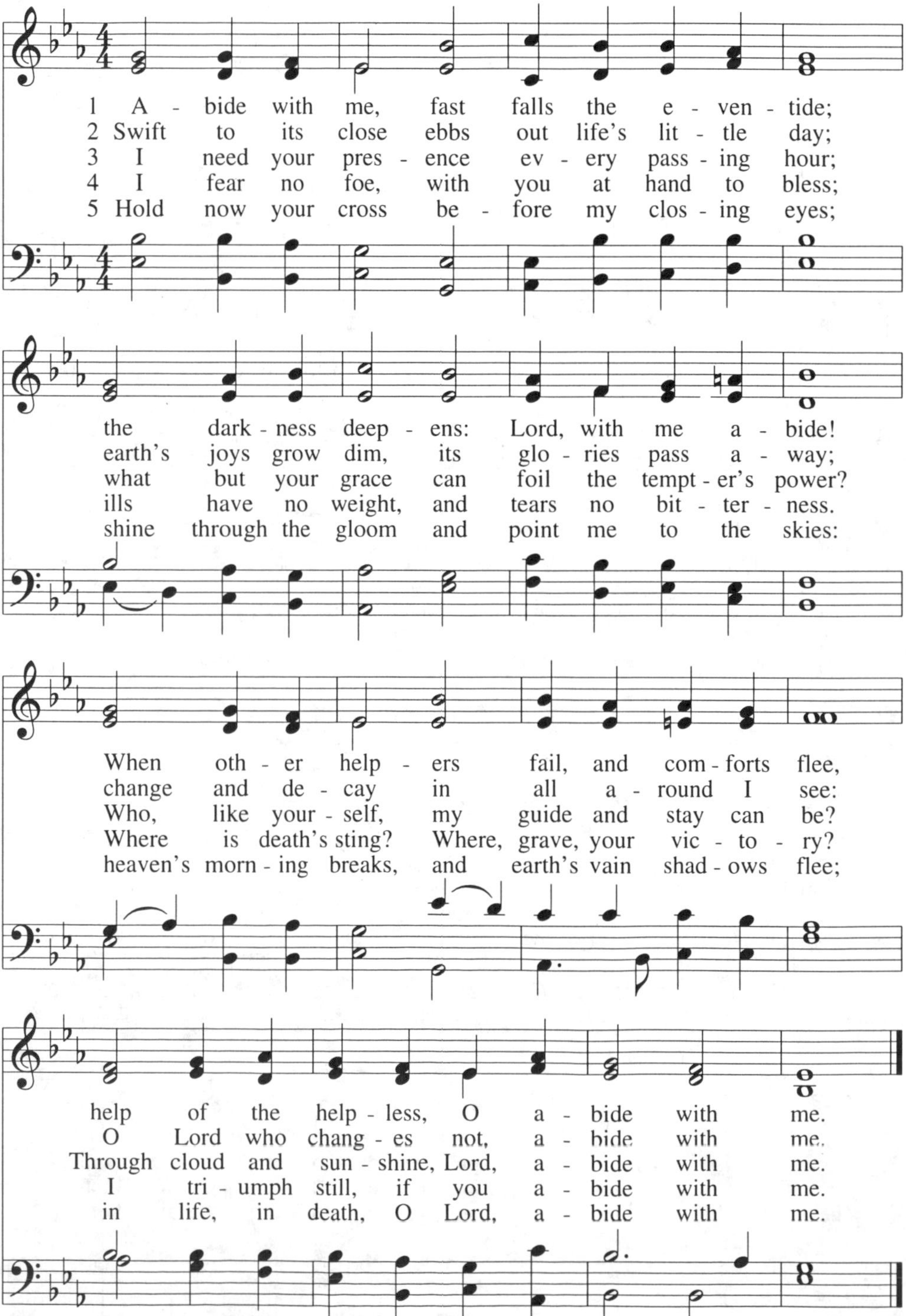
1 A - bide with me, fast falls the e - ven - tide;
the dark - ness deep - ens: Lord, with me a - bide!
When oth - er help - ers fail, and com - forts flee,
help of the help - less, O a - bide with me.
2 Swift to its close ebbs out life's lit - tle day;
earth's joys grow dim, its glo - ries pass a - way;
change and de - cay in all a - round I see:
O Lord who chang - es not, a - bide with me.
3 I need your pres - ence ev - ery pass - ing hour;
what but your grace can foil the tempt - er's power?
Who, like your - self, my guide and stay can be?
Through cloud and sun - shine, Lord, a - bide with me.
4 I fear no foe, with you at hand to bless;
ills have no weight, and tears no bit - ter - ness.
Where is death's sting? Where, grave, your vic - to - ry?
I tri - umph still, if you a - bide with me.
5 Hold now your cross be - fore my clos - ing eyes;
shine through the gloom and point me to the skies:
heaven's morn - ing breaks, and earth's vain shad - ows flee;
in life, in death, O Lord, a - bide with me.

WORDS: Henry F. Lyte (1793-1847), alt.
MUSIC: William H. Monk (1823-1889)

EVENTIDE
10.10.10.10.

Shall We Gather at the River 522

1 Shall we gath-er at the riv - er, where bright an - gel feet have trod, with its crys - tal tide for - ev - er flow-ing by the throne of God?
2 Ere we reach the shin-ing riv - er, lay we ev - ery bur - den down; grace our spir - its will de - liv - er, and pro - vide a robe and crown.
3 Soon we'll reach the shin-ing riv - er, soon our pil - grim-age will cease; soon our hap - py hearts will quiv - er with the mel - o - dy of peace.
Refrain
Yes, we'll gath - er at the riv - er, the beau - ti - ful, the beau - ti - ful riv - er;
gath-er with the saints at the riv - er that flows by the throne of God.

WORDS and MUSIC: Robert Lowry (1826-1899)

HANSON PLACE
8.7.8.7.Ref.

523 Soon and Very Soon

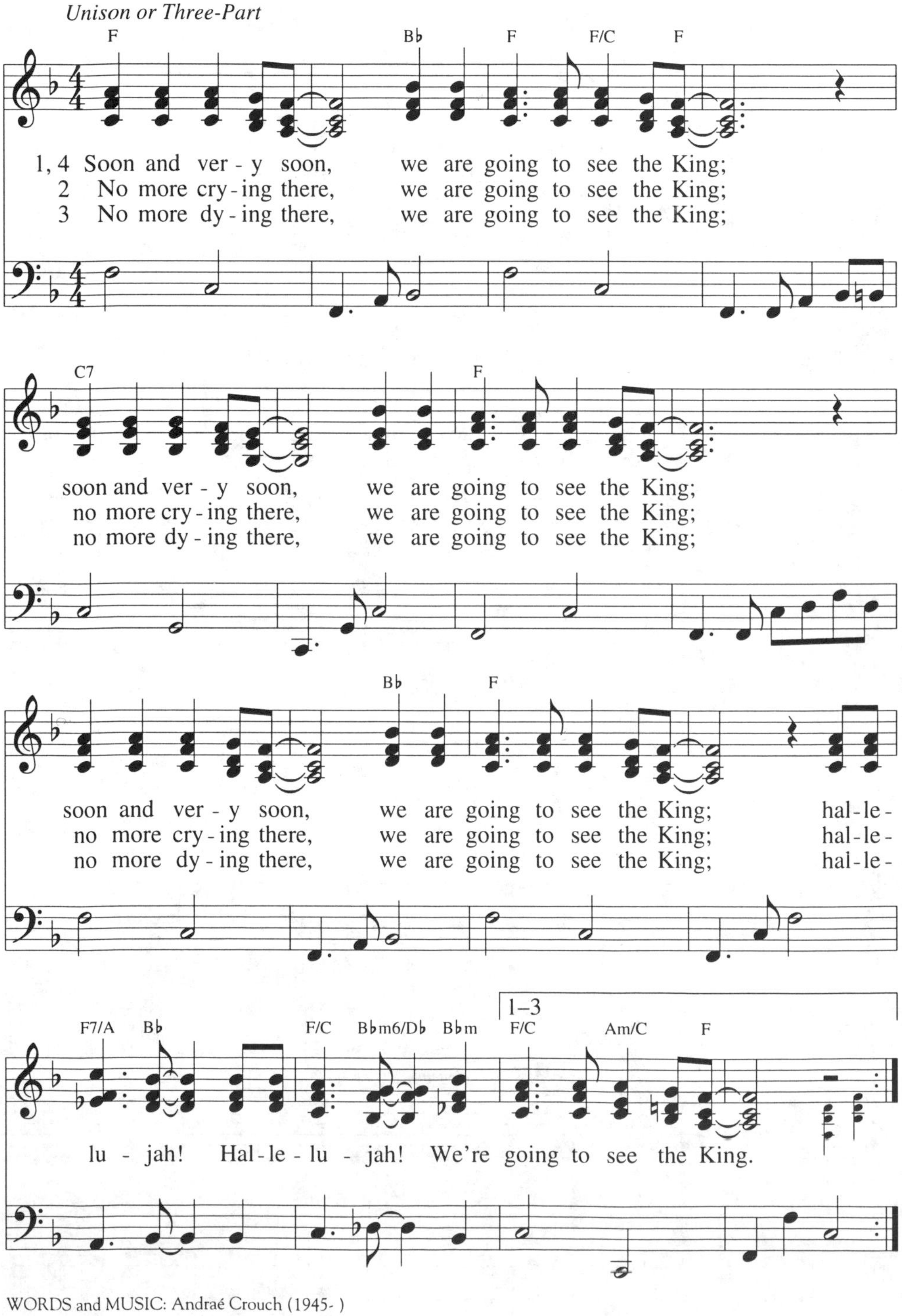
Unison or Three-Part
F Bb F F/C F
1, 4 Soon and ver - y soon, we are going to see the King;
2 No more cry - ing there, we are going to see the King;
3 No more dy - ing there, we are going to see the King;
C7 F
soon and ver - y soon, we are going to see the King;
no more cry - ing there, we are going to see the King;
no more dy - ing there, we are going to see the King;
Bb F
soon and ver - y soon, we are going to see the King; hal - le -
no more cry - ing there, we are going to see the King; hal - le -
no more dy - ing there, we are going to see the King; hal - le -
1–3
F7/A Bb F/C Bbm6/Db Bbm F/C Am/C F
lu - jah! Hal - le - lu - jah! We're going to see the King.

WORDS and MUSIC: Andraé Crouch (1945-)

4
F/C Am/C F G7 C7 F G7 C7 F
going to see the King! Hal - le - lu - jah! Hal - le - lu - jah!

Lord of the Living

524

Unison
1 Lord of the liv - ing, in your name as - sem - bled, we join to
2 Help us to trea - sure all that will re - mind us of the en -
3 May we, when - ev - er tempt - ed to de - jec - tion, strong - ly re -
4 God, you can lift us from the grave of sor - row in - to the
thank you for the life re - mem - bered. Hold us, en - fold us,
rich - ment in the days be - hind us. Your love has set us
cap - ture thoughts of res - ur - rec - tion. You gave us Je - sus
pres - ence of your own to - mor - row; give to your peo - ple
to your chil - dren giv - ing hope in be - liev - ing.
in the gen - er - a - tions, God of cre - a - tion.
to de - feat our sad - ness with Eas - ter glad - ness.
for the day's af - flic - tion your ben - e - dic - tion.

WORDS: Fred Kaan (1929-)
MUSIC: *Paris Antiphoner*, 1681; arr. Erik Routley (1917-1982)

CHRISTE SANCTORUM
10.11.11.6.

525 When We All Get to Heaven

1 Sing the won-drous love of Je - sus, sing his mer - cy and his grace;
2 While we walk the pil - grim path-way clouds will o - ver - spread the sky,
3 Let us then be true and faith-ful, trust - ing, serv - ing ev - ery day;
4 On-ward to the prize be - fore us! Soon his beau - ty we'll be - hold;
in the man - sions bright and bless - ed he'll pre - pare for us a place.
but when trav - eling days are o - ver, not a sha - dow, not a sigh.
just one glimpse of him in glo - ry will the toils of life re - pay.
soon the pearl - y gates will o - pen, we shall tread the streets of gold.
Refrain
When we all get to heav - en, what a day of re -
When we all what a
joic - ing that will be! When we all see
day of re - joic - ing that will be! When we all

WORDS: Eliza E. Hewitt (1851-1920)
MUSIC: Emily D. Wilson (1865-1942)

HEAVEN
8.7.8.7.Ref.

Je - sus we'll sing and shout the vic - to - ry.
shout, and shout the vic - to - ry.

How Blest Are They 526

1 How blest are they who trust in Christ when we and those we love must part: we yield them up, for go they must, but do not lose them from our heart.
2 In rip - ened age, their har - vest reaped, or gone from us in youth or prime, in Christ they have e - ter - nal life, re - leased from all the bonds of time.
3 In Christ, who tast - ed death for us, we rise a - bove our nat - ural grief, and wit - ness to a strick - en world the strength and splen - dor of be - lief.

WORDS: Fred Pratt Green (1903-2000)
MUSIC: Robert A. Schumann (1810-1856)

CANONBURY
L.M.

527 Steal Away

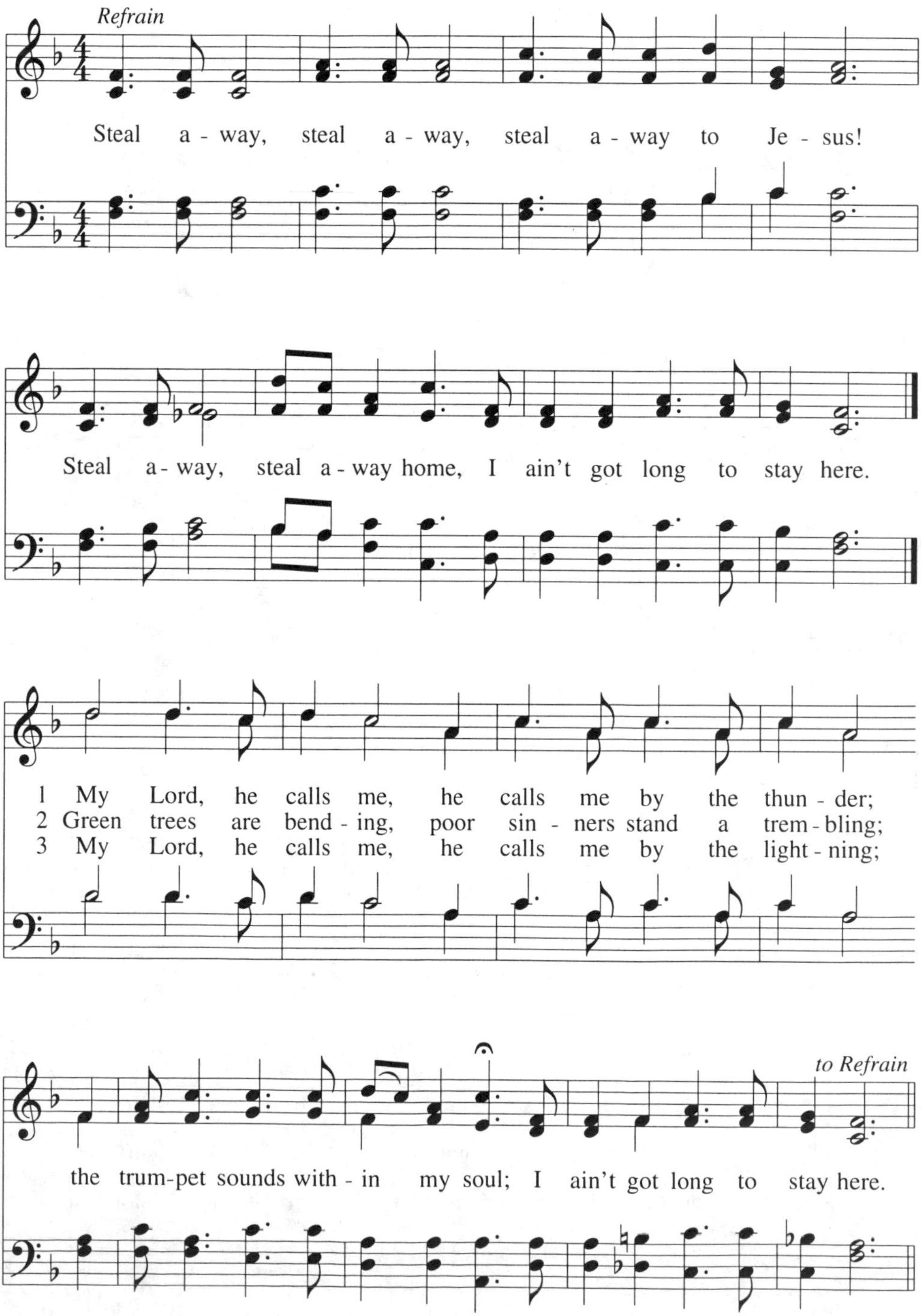
Refrain
Steal a - way, steal a - way, steal a - way to Je - sus!
Steal a - way, steal a - way home, I ain't got long to stay here.
1 My Lord, he calls me, he calls me by the thun - der;
2 Green trees are bend - ing, poor sin - ners stand a trem - bling;
3 My Lord, he calls me, he calls me by the light - ning;
the trum-pet sounds with - in my soul; I ain't got long to stay here.
to Refrain

WORDS and MUSIC: African-American spiritual

STEAL AWAY
Irregular

Here from All Nations

1 Here from all na - tions, all tongues, and all peo - ples,
2 These have come out of the hard - est op - pres - sion;
3 Gone is their thirst and no more shall they hun - ger;
4 He will go with them to clear liv - ing wa - ter
5 Bless - ing and glo - ry and wis - dom and pow - er
count - less the crowd, but their voic - es are one;
now they may stand in the pres - ence of God,
God is their shel - ter, his pow - er at their side:
flow - ing from springs which his mer - cy sup - plies;
be to the Sav - ior a - gain and a - gain;
vast is the sight and ma - jes - tic their sing - ing:
serv - ing their Lord day and night in his tem - ple,
sun shall not pain them, no burn - ing will tor - ture;
gone is their grief and their tri - als are o - ver,
might and thanks - giv - ing and hon - or for - ev - er
"God has the vic - tory; he reigns from the throne."
ran - somed and cleansed by the Lamb's pre - cious blood.
Je - sus the Lamb is their shep - herd and guide.
God wipes a - way ev - ery tear from their eyes.
be to our God: Hal - le - lu - jah! A - men.

WORDS: Christopher Idle (1938-)
MUSIC: *Paris Antiphoner*, 1681

O QUANTA QUALIA
11.10.11.10.

529 For All the Saints

Unison, verses 1, 2, 5 and 6.

1 For all the saints who from their la - bors rest, who thee by faith be - fore the world con - fessed, thy name, O Je - sus, be for - ev - er blest.
2 Thou wast their rock, their for - tress and their might; thou, Lord, their cap - tain in the well-fought fight; thou in the dark - ness drear, their one true light.
5 But lo! there breaks a yet more glo - rious day: the saints tri - um - phant rise in bright ar - ray; the King of glo - ry pass - es on his way.
6 From earth's wide bounds and o - cean's far - thest coast, through gates of pearl streams in the count - less host, sing - ing to Fa - ther, Son, and Ho - ly Ghost:
Al - le - lu - ia! Al - le - lu - ia!

WORDS: William W. How (1823-1897)
MUSIC: Ralph Vaughan Williams (1872-1958)

SINE NOMINE
10.10.10.Alleluias

Harmony, verses 3 and 4.

3 O blest com - mun - ion, fel - low - ship di - vine!
4 And when the strife is fierce, the war - fare long,
We fee - bly strug - gle; they in glo - ry shine.
steals on the ear the dis - tant tri - umph song,
Yet all are one in thee, for all are thine.
and hearts are brave a - gain and arms are strong.
to verses 5 and 6
Al - le - lu - ia!
Al - le - lu - ia! Al - le - lu - ia!

530 Faith of Our Fathers

1 Faith of our fa - thers, liv - ing still in spite of dun - geon,
2 Faith of our moth - ers, we will love both friend and foe in
3 Faith of the mar - tyrs who, though bound, were still in heart and
fire, and sword. O how our hearts beat high with joy
all our strife, and preach it, too, as love knows how,
con - science true. How blest would be their chil - dren's fate,
when-e'er we hear that glo - rious Word! Faith of our fa - thers,
by kind - ly words and vir - tuous life! Faith of our moth - ers,
if they, like them, should live for you! Faith of the mar - tyrs,
ho - ly faith, we will be true to you till death.

WORDS: Frederick W. Faber (1814-1863), alt.
MUSIC: Henri F. Hemy (1818-1888); arr. James G. Walton (1821-1905)

ST. CATHERINE
8.8.8.8.8.8.

Rejoice in God's Saints

1 Re - joice in God's saints, to - day and all days;
2 Some march with e - vents to turn them God's way;
3 Re - joice in those saints, un - praised and un - known,
4 Re - joice in God's saints, to - day and all days;
a world with - out saints for - gets how to praise.
some need to with - draw, the bet - ter to pray;
who bear some - one's cross or shoul - der their own;
a world with - out saints for - gets how to praise.
Their faith in ac - quir - ing the hab - it of prayer,
some car - ry the gos - pel through fire and through flood:
they shame our com - plain - ing, our com - forts, our cares:
In lov - ing, in liv - ing, they prove it is true:
their depth of a - dor - ing, Lord, help us to share.
our world is their par - ish; their pur - pose is God.
what pa - tience in car - ing, what cour - age, is theirs!
the way of self - giv - ing, Lord, leads us to you.

WORDS: Fred Pratt Green (1903-2000)
MUSIC: William Croft (1678-1727)

HANOVER
10.10.11.11.

532 Isaiah the Prophet Has Written of Old

Unison
1 I - sa - iah the proph - et has writ - ten of old how
2 Yet na - tions still prey on the meek of the world, and
God's new cre - a - tion shall come. In - stead of the thorn tree, the
con - flict turns par - ent from child. Your peo - ple de - spoil all the
fir tree shall grow; the wolf shall lie down with the lamb.
sweet-ness of earth, the brier and the thorn tree grow wild.
The moun - tains and hills shall burst forth in - to song, the
God, bring to fru - i - tion your will for the earth, that
peo - ples be led forth in peace, for the earth shall be filled with the
no one shall hurt or de - stroy, that wis - dom and jus - tice shall

WORDS: Joy F. Patterson (1931-)
MUSIC: *Southern Harmony* 1835; harm. Austin C. Lovelace (1919-)

SAMANTHRA
11.8.11.8.D.

knowl-edge of God as the wa - ters cov - er the sea.
reign in the land and your peo - ple shall go forth in joy.

Joy in the Morning 533

Unison
1 There'll be joy in the morn-ing on that day, there'll be joy in the morn-ing on that day, for the day-light will dawn when the dark - ness is gone, there'll be joy in the morn-ing on that day.
2 There'll be peace and con-tent-ment ev - er - more, there'll be peace and con-tent-ment ev - er - more, ev - ery heart, ev - ery voice on that day will re - joice, there'll be peace and con-tent-ment ev - er - more.
3 There'll be love and for-give-ness ev - ery - where, there'll be love and for-give-ness ev - ery-where, and the way of the Lord will that day be re - stored, there'll be love and for-give-ness ev - ery-where.

WORDS and MUSIC: Natalie Sleeth (1930-1992); arr. Roland Tabell (1934-)

JOY IN THE MORNING
Irregular

534 When the King Shall Come Again

1 When the King shall come a - gain all his power re - veal - ing;
2 In the des - ert trees take root, fresh from God's cre - a - tion;
3 Strength-en fee - ble hands and knees; faint - ing hearts, be cheer - ful!
4 There God's high - way shall be seen where no roar - ing li - on,
splen - dor shall an - nounce his reign, life and joy and heal - ing:
plants and flowers and sweet - est fruit join the cel - e - bra - tion.
God who comes for such as these, seeks and saves the fear - ful.
noth - ing e - vil or un - clean walks the road to Zi - on:
earth no long - er in de - cay, hope no more frus - trat - ed;
Riv - ers spring up from the earth, bar - ren lands a - dorn - ing:
Deaf ears hear the si - lent tongues sing a - way their weep - ing;
ran-somed peo - ple, home-ward bound, all your prais - es voic - ing,
this is God's re - demp-tion - day long - ing - ly a - wait - ed.
val - leys, this is your new birth; moun-tains, greet the morn - ing!
blind eyes see the life - less ones walk - ing, run - ning, leap - ing.
see your Lord with glo - ry crowned, share in his re - joic - ing!
8

WORDS: Christopher Idle (1938-)
MUSIC: *Piae Cantiones*, 1582

TEMPUS ADEST FLORIDUM
7.6.7.6.D.

Face to Face

535

1 Face to face with Christ my Sav - ior, face to face– what will it be
2 On - ly faint - ly now I see him, with the dark-ening veil be-tween;
3 What re-joic - ing in his pres-ence when are ban-ished grief and pain,
4 Face to face! O bliss-ful mo-ment! Face to face– to see and know;
when with rap-ture I be - hold him, Je-sus Christ who died for me?
but a bless-ed day is com - ing when his glo - ry shall be seen.
when the crook-ed ways are straight-ened and the dark things shall be plain.
face to face with my Re-deem - er, Je-sus Christ who loves me so.
Refrain
Face to face I shall be-hold him, far be-yond the star-ry sky;
face to face in all his glo - ry, I shall see him by and by!

WORDS: Carrie E. Breck (1855-1934)
MUSIC: Grant C. Tullar (1869-1950)

FACE TO FACE
8.7.8.7.Ref.

536 Through the Darkness of the Ages

1 Through the dark - ness of the a - ges, through the sor - rows
2 Boun - ty of two thou - sand har - vests, beau - ty of two
3 Count - less flowers have bloomed and with - ered, count - less noons are
4 Mas - ter, we shall sing your prais - es, man of sor - rows,
of the days, strength of wea - ry gen - er - a - tions,
thou - sand springs; He who framed the times and sea - sons
sealed in night, shat - tered thrones and fal - len em - pires,
God of power, for the mea - sured march of sea - sons
lift - ing hearts in hope and praise, light in dark - ness, joy in
has vouch - safed us great - er things. Word of God who spoke cre-
realms and rich - es lost from sight. Christ, your king - dom still in-
shall at last bring in the hour when, as light - ning leaps the
sor - row, pres - ence to al - lay all fears, Je - sus,
a - tion speaks for - give - ness, speaks to save, gath - ers
creas - es as the cen - tu - ries un - fold. Grain that
heav - ens, you re - turn to lead us home. You have

WORDS: Hilary Jolly (1945-)
MUSIC: Cyril V. Taylor (1907-1991)

ABBOT'S LEIGH
8.7.8.7.D.

NEW CREATION

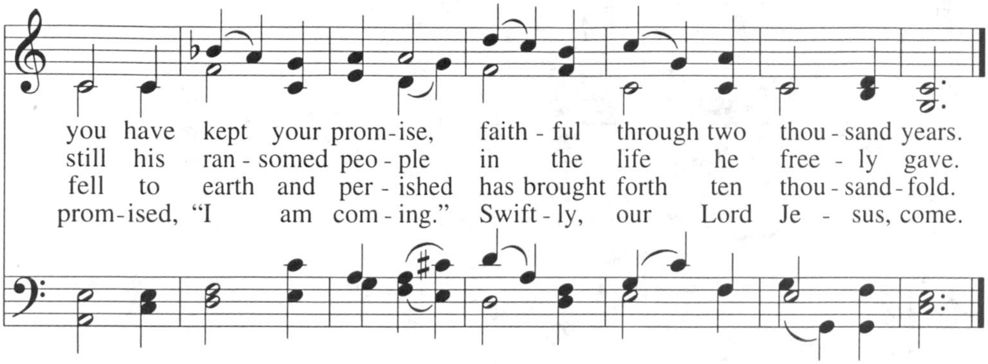
you have kept your prom-ise, faith-ful through two thou-sand years.
still his ran-somed peo-ple in the life he free-ly gave.
fell to earth and per-ished has brought forth ten thou-sand-fold.
prom-ised, "I am com-ing." Swift-ly, our Lord Je-sus, come.

537 My Lord! What a Morning

Refrain
My Lord! what a morn-ing; my Lord! what a morn-ing;
O, my Lord! what a morn-ing, when the stars be-gin to fall.
1 You'll hear the trum-pet sound
2 You'll hear the sin-ner cry to wake the na-tions un-der-ground,
3 You'll hear the Chris-tian shout
to Refrain
look-ing to my God's right hand when the stars be-gin to fall.

WORDS and MUSIC: African-American spiritual; arr. Donald P. Hustad (1918-)

BURLEIGH
Irregular

538 Deep River

Deep riv - er, my home is o - ver Jor - dan.
Deep riv - er, Lord, I want to cross o - ver in - to camp-ground.
Oh, don't you want to go to that gos - pel feast, that
prom - ised land where all is peace? Oh,
deep riv - er, Lord, I want to cross o - ver in - to camp-ground.

WORDS and MUSIC: African-American spiritual

DEEP RIVER
Irregular

O Day of Peace

Unison
1 O day of peace that dim - ly shines through all our
2 Then shall the wolf dwell with the lamb, nor shall the
hopes and prayers and dreams, guide us to jus - tice, truth, and
fierce de - vour the small; as beasts and cat - tle calm - ly
love, de - liv - ered from our self - ish schemes. May swords of
graze, a lit - tle child shall lead them all. Then en - e -
hate fall from our hands, our hearts from en - vy find re-lease, till by God's
mies shall learn to love, all crea-tures find their true ac-cord; the hope of
grace our war-ring world shall see Christ's prom-ised reign of peace.
peace shall be ful - filled, for all the earth shall know the Lord.

WORDS: Carl P. Daw, Jr. (1944-)
MUSIC: C. Hubert H. Parry (1848-1918)

JERUSALEM
L.M.D.

540 Two Thousand Years Since Bethlehem

1 Two thou-sand years since Beth-le-hem first wel-comed Je-sus' birth:
2 Two thou-sand years since Gal-i-lee where Je-sus preached and healed;
3 Two thou-sand years since Cal-va-ry, the hill where Je-sus died;
4 Two thou-sand years since Pen-te-cost: the Ho-ly Spir-it came
5 Two thou-sand years of Chris-tian faith have changed our his-to-ry,

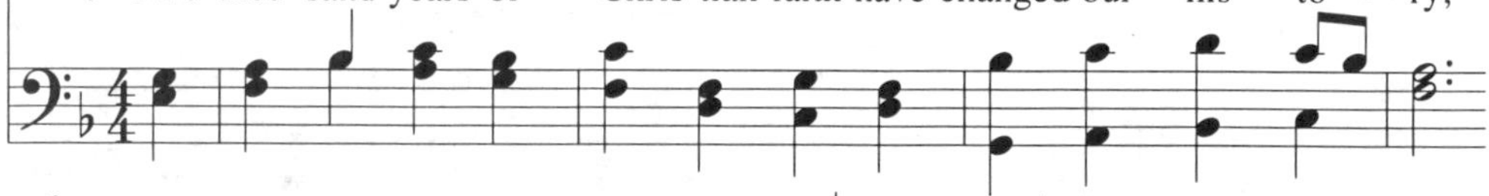

the start-ling truth be-gan to dawn that God had come to earth.
in words of truth and works of power God's king-dom was re-vealed.
the Lamb of God, the sin-less one, for me was cru-ci-fied.
in sound of might-y, rush-ing wind and tongues of liv-ing flame;
for Je-sus is the Lord of time and of e-ter-ni-ty.

And as he grew and lived and taught a dif-ferent way un-furled:
As young and old and rich and poor re-spond-ed to his call,
But soon he rose up from the grave to reign in vic-to-ry;
a gift to all who will be-lieve and live the Je-sus way;
For all who seek a bet-ter way, than fail-ure, sin and pain,

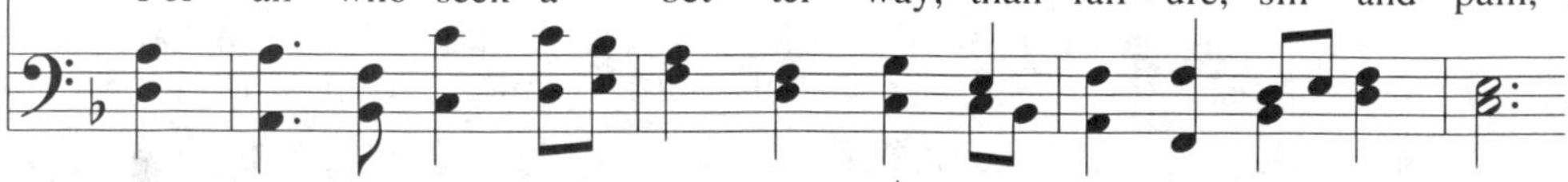

a way of joy and love and peace, a new start for the world!
they found what we may find to-day: a new start for us all!
good news I scarce-ly can be-lieve: a new start won for me!
the power of God we may re-ceive, a new start from to-day!
still Je-sus Christ makes all things new: a chance to start a-gain!

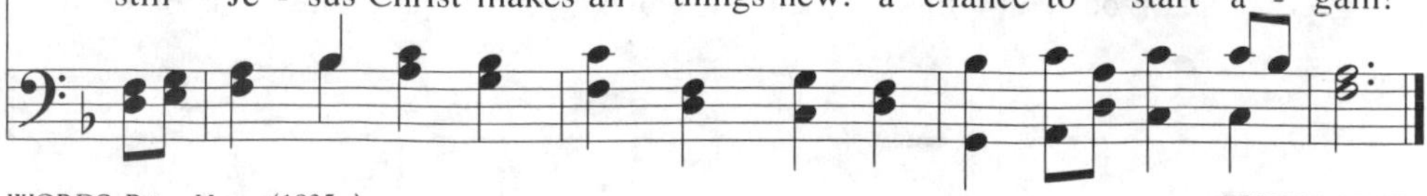

WORDS: Brian Hoare (1935-)
MUSIC: English melody; harm. Ralph Vaughan Williams (1872-1958)

FOREST GREEN
8.6.8.6.D.

THE CHURCH IN THE WORLD

541 Church of God, Elect and Glorious

1 Church of God, e - lect and glo - rious, ho - ly na - tion, cho - sen race;
2 God has called you out of dark - ness in - to his most mar - velous light;
3 Once you were an al - ien peo - ple, stran - gers to God's heart of love;
4 Church of God, e - lect and ho - ly, be the peo - ple he in - tends;
called as God's own spe - cial peo - ple, roy - al priests and heirs of grace:
brought his truth to life with - in you, turned your blind - ness in - to sight.
but he brought you home in mer - cy, cit - i - zens of heaven a - bove.
strong in faith and swift to an - swer each com - mand your Mas - ter sends:
know the pur - pose of your call - ing, show to all his might - y deeds;
Let your light so shine a - round you that God's name is glo - ri - fied;
Let his love flow out to oth - ers, let them feel a Fa - ther's care;
roy - al priests, ful - fill your call - ing through your sac - ri - fice and prayer;
tell of love which knows no lim - its, grace that meets all hu - man needs.
and all find fresh hope and pur - pose in Christ Je - sus cru - ci - fied.
that they too may know his wel - come and his count - less bless ings share.
give your lives in joy - ful serv - ice—sing his praise, his love de - clare.

WORDS: James E. Seddon (1915-1983), para. 1 Peter 2:9-12
MUSIC: John Wyeth's *Repository of Sacred Music*, 1813

NETTLETON
8.7.8.7.D.

They Did Not Build in Vain 542

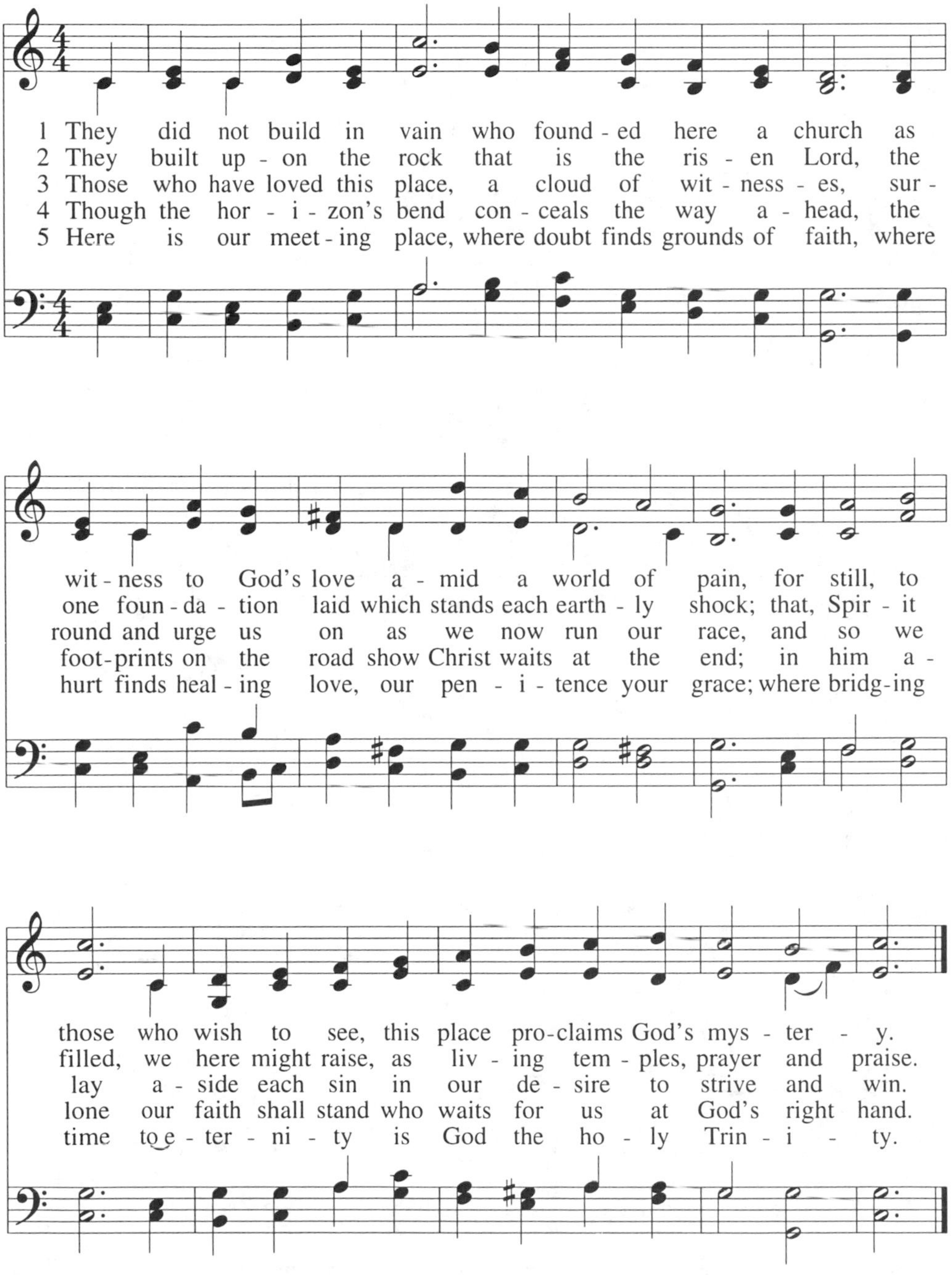
1 They did not build in vain who found - ed here a church as
2 They built up - on the rock that is the ris - en Lord, the
3 Those who have loved this place, a cloud of wit - ness - es, sur -
4 Though the hor - i - zon's bend con - ceals the way a - head, the
5 Here is our meet - ing place, where doubt finds grounds of faith, where
wit - ness to God's love a - mid a world of pain, for still, to
one foun - da - tion laid which stands each earth - ly shock; that, Spir - it
round and urge us on as we now run our race, and so we
foot-prints on the road show Christ waits at the end; in him a -
hurt finds heal - ing love, our pen - i - tence your grace; where bridg-ing
those who wish to see, this place pro-claims God's mys - ter - y.
filled, we here might raise, as liv - ing tem - ples, prayer and praise.
lay a - side each sin in our de - sire to strive and win.
lone our faith shall stand who waits for us at God's right hand.
time to e - ter - ni - ty is God the ho - ly Trin - i - ty.

WORDS: Alan Luff (1928-)
MUSIC: John Darwall (1731-1789)

DARWALL'S 148th
6.6.6.6.8.8.

543 Come Build a Church

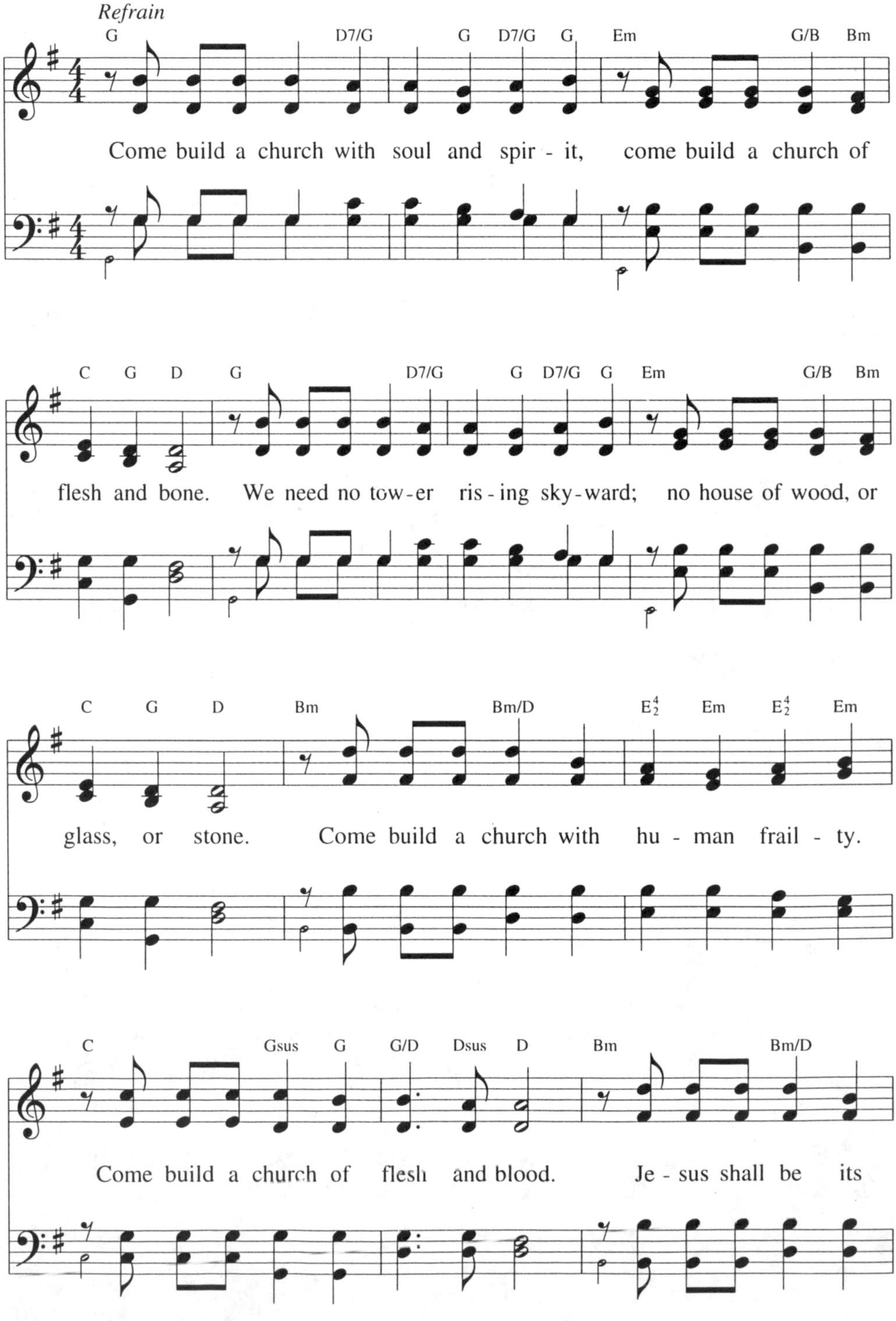
Refrain
G D7/G G D7/G G Em G/B Bm
Come build a church with soul and spir - it, come build a church of
C G D G D7/G G D7/G G Em G/B Bm
flesh and bone. We need no tow-er ris-ing sky-ward; no house of wood, or
C G D Bm Bm/D E4 2 Em E4 2 Em
glass, or stone. Come build a church with hu - man frail - ty.
C Gsus G G/D Dsus D Bm Bm/D
Come build a church of flesh and blood. Je - sus shall be its

WORDS and MUSIC: Ken Medema (1943-)

E4/2 Em E4/2 Em Am G/B C Csus2 C C6 G C/G G
sure foun-da-tion. It shall be built by the hand of God.
D G/D D G/D G/B C G
1 Let us see the tongues of fi - re. Let us hear the
2 Let us know the love un-ceas-ing, which a-lone can
3 Guide our feet in peace-ful path-ways. Teach us peace of
G/D D G/D D G/D
great wind roar. Let us know the awe and won-der,
loose the bounds, reach-ing out a-cross the cha-sms,
heart and mind; peace with God and all God's chil-dren;
G/B C G G/D D Am B B/D#
that we've on-ly glimpsed be-fore. Let us feel the
bring-ing walls of ha-tred down. Let us taste the
till we leave our wars be-hind. Sure-ly joy will
Em E4/2 Em Am B B/D# Em E4/2 Em Bm C# C#/E#
strength of pas-sion, which can make us laugh and weep. Let us know this
sweet com-mun-ion, where the cir-cle nev-er ends. Hold us in the
come and find us like a breeze that cools the night; like the rain up-
to Refrain
F#m F#4/2 F#m Bm G/B C Em A Am Am/C C/D
great a-wake-ning. For so long we've been a-sleep.
sweet con-nec-tion, turn-ing strang-ers in-to friends.
on the des-ert; like a can-dle's gen-tle light.

544 The Church's One Foundation

1 The Church's one foun - da - tion is Je - sus Christ her Lord;
2 E - lect from ev - ery na - tion, yet one o'er all the earth,
3 Though with a scorn - ful won - der we see her sore op - pressed,
4 'Mid toil and trib - u - la - tion, and tu - mult of her war,
5 Yet she on earth hath un - ion with God, the Three in One,
she is his new cre - a - tion, by wa - ter and the word:
her char - ter of sal - va - tion: one Lord, one faith, one birth;
by schisms rent a - sun - der, by her - e - sies dis - tressed:
she waits the con - sum - ma - tion of peace for - ev - er - more,
and mys - tic sweet com - mun - ion with those whose rest is won:
from heaven he came and sought her to be his ho - ly bride;
one ho - ly name she bless - es, par - takes one ho - ly food,
yet saints their watch are keep - ing, their cry goes up, "How long?"
till with the vi - sion glo - rious her long - ing eyes are blest,
O hap - py ones and ho - ly! Lord, give us grace that we,
with his own blood he bought her, and for her life he died.
and to one hope she press - es with ev - ery grace en - dued.
and soon the night of weep - ing shall be the morn of song.
and the great Church vic - to - rious shall be the Church at rest.
like them, the meek and low - ly, on high may dwell with thee.

WORDS: Samuel J. Stone (1839-1900)
MUSIC: Samuel S. Wesley (1810-1876)

AURELIA
7.6.7.6.D.

How Lovely, Lord, How Lovely 545

Unison
1 How love - ly, Lord, how love - ly is your a - bid - ing place;
2 In your blest courts to wor - ship, O God, a sin - gle day
3 A sun and shield for - ev - er are you, O Lord Most High;
my soul is long - ing, faint - ing, to feast up - on your grace.
is bet - ter than a thou - sand if I from you should stray.
you show - er us with bless - ings; no good will you de - ny.
The spar - row finds a shel - ter, a place to build her nest;
I'd rath - er keep the en - trance and claim you as my Lord
The saints, your grace re - ceiv - ing, from strength to strength shall go,
and so your tem - ple calls us with - in its walls to rest.
than rev - el in the rich - es the ways of sin af - ford.
and from their life shall riv - ers of bless - ing o - ver - flow.

WORDS: Arlo D. Duba (1929-); para. Psalm 84
MUSIC: Hal H. Hopson (1933-)

MERLE'S TUNE
7.6.7.6.D.

546 Built on the Rock

1 Built on the Rock the Church does stand, e - ven when stee - ples are
2 Not in a tem - ple made with hands God the Al - might - y is
3 We are God's house of liv - ing stones built for his own hab - i-
4 Through all the pass - ing years, O Lord, grant that, when church bells are
fall - ing; Christ builds his church in ev - ery land; bells still are
dwell - ing; high in the heavens his tem - ple stands, all earth - ly
ta - tion; he fills our hearts, his hum - ble thrones, grant-ing us
ring - ing, man - y may come to hear God's word where he this
chim-ing and call - ing, call-ing the young and old to rest, call-ing the
tem-ples ex - cel - ling. Yet he who dwells in heaven a - bove choos-es to
life and sal - va - tion. Were two or three to seek God's face, he in their
prom-ise is bring - ing: "I know my own, my own know me; you, not the
souls of those dis - tressed, long-ing for life ev - er - last - ing.
live with us in love, mak-ing our bod - ies his tem - ple.
midst would show his grace, bless-ings up - on them be - stow - ing.
world, my face shall see; my peace I leave with you. A - men."

WORDS: Nikolai F. S. Grundtvig (1783-1872); tr. Carl Doving (1867-1937)
MUSIC: Ludvig M. Lindeman (1812-1887)

KIRKEN DEN ER ET
8.8.8.8.8.8.8.

We Are God's People 547

Unison
1 We are God's peo - ple, the cho - sen of the Lord,
2 We are God's loved ones, the Bride of Christ our Lord,
3 We are the Bod - y of which the Lord is Head,
4 We are a tem - ple, the Spir - it's dwell - ing place,
born of his Spir - it, es - tab - lished by his Word; our
for we have known it, the love of God out - poured; now
called to o - bey him, now ris - en from the dead; he
formed in great weak - ness, a cup to hold God's grace; we
cor - ner - stone is Christ a - lone, and strong in him we stand: O
let us learn how to re - turn the gift of love once given: O
wills us be a fam - i - ly, di - verse yet tru - ly one: O
die a - lone, for on its own each em - ber los - es fire: yet
let us live trans - par - ent - ly, and walk heart to heart and hand in hand.
let us share each joy and care, and live with a zeal that pleas - es Heaven.
let us give our gifts to God, and so shall his work on earth be done.
joined in one the flame burns on to give warmth and light, and to in - spire.

WORDS: Bryan Jeffery Leech (1931-)
MUSIC: Johannes Brahms (1833-1897); arr. Fred Bock (1939-1998)

SYMPHONY
11.11.14.8.9.

548 Come, Great God of All the Ages

1 Come, great God of all the a - ges, make your earth - ly
2 Come, Christ Je - sus, flesh and spir - it, sure foun - da - tion,
3 Come, great Spir - it, in and with us, tune our ears to
4 Come, O come, in cel - e - bra - tion, house-hold of the
mis - sion known; speak through ev - ery deed and per - son,
cor - ner - stone, help us form the church e - ter - nal,
hear your call; through the mov - ing of your pres - ence,
one true God, in com - mit - ment and re - joic - ing
let your way and will be shown. Guide the church to
may your vi - sion be our own. Send a mes - sage
let re - deem - ing love re - call min - is - try in
let us go where Christ has trod; as we act in
true com - mit - ment, give di - rec - tion now, we ask;
to each fol - lower, lead all peo - ple to your way;
ded - i - ca - tion, love em - bod - ied in our deeds;
faith and rev - erence, let us, Lord, the fu - ture see,

WORDS: Mary Jackson Cathey (1926-)
MUSIC: Cyril V. Taylor (1907-1991)

ABBOT'S LEIGH
8.7.8.7.D.

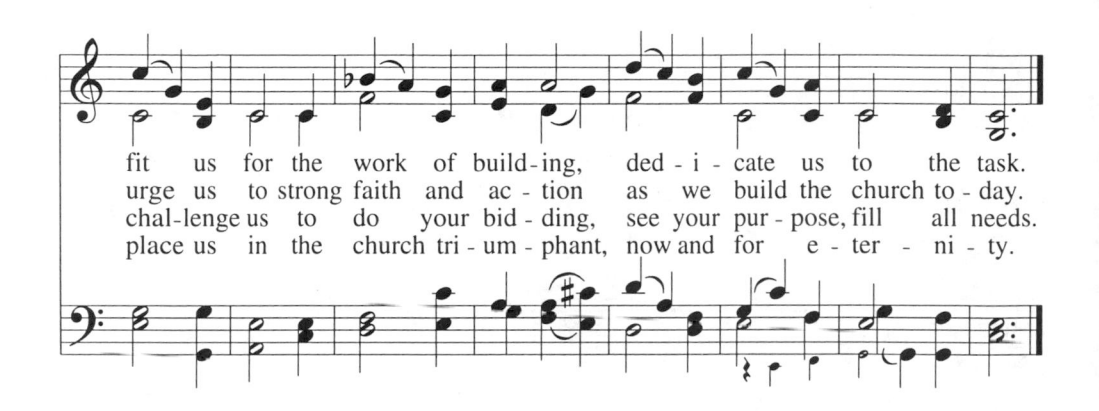

fit us for the work of build-ing, ded - i - cate us to the task.
urge us to strong faith and ac - tion as we build the church to - day.
chal-lenge us to do your bid - ding, see your pur - pose, fill all needs.
place us in the church tri - um - phant, now and for e - ter - ni - ty.

I Love Your Kingdom, Lord 549

1 I love your king - dom, Lord, the house of your a - bode,
2 I love your Church, O God— her walls be - fore you stand,
3 For her my tears shall fall, for her my prayers as - cend,
4 Be - yond my high - est joy I prize her heaven-ly ways,
5 Sure as your truth shall last, to Zi - on shall be given

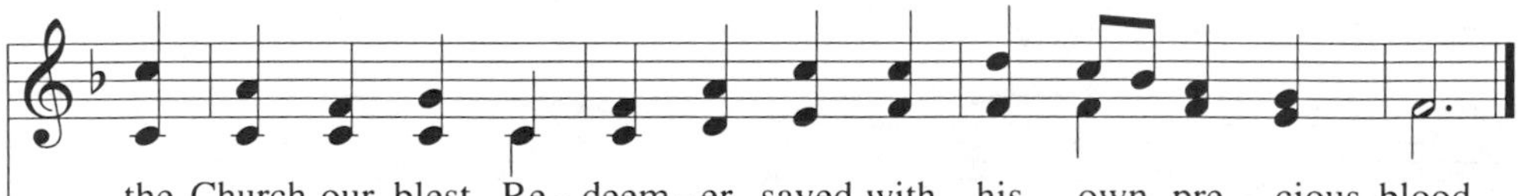

the Church our blest Re - deem - er saved with his own pre - cious blood.
dear as the ap - ple of your eye, and grav - en on your hand.
to her my cares and toils be given till toils and cares shall end.
her sweet com-mun - ion, sol - emn vows, her hymns of love and praise.
the bright-est glo - ries earth can yield, and bright - er bliss of heaven.

WORDS: Timothy Dwight (1752-1817), alt.; para. Psalm 26:8
MUSIC: Aaron Williams' *New Universal Psalmodist*, 1770

ST. THOMAS
S.M.

550 We Are the Church

Refrain (Unison)
I am the church! You are the church! We are the church to - geth - er! All who fol - low Je - sus, all a - round the world! Yes, we're the church to - geth - er!
1 The church is not a build-ing, the church is not a stee - ple, the church is not a rest - ing place, the church is a peo - ple.
2 We're man - y kinds of peo - ple, with man - y kinds of fac - es, all col - ors and all a - ges, too, from all times and plac - es.
3 Some-times the church is march-ing, some-times it's brave - ly burn - ing, some - times it's rid - ing, some-times hid - ing, al - ways it's learn - ing.
4 And when the peo - ple gath - er, there's sing - ing and there's pray - ing, there's laugh-ing and there's cry - ing some-times, all of it say - ing:
5 At Pen - te - cost some peo - ple re - ceived the Ho - ly Spir - it and told the Good News through the world to all who would hear it.
to Refrain

WORDS and MUSIC: Richard K. Avery (1934-) and Donald S. Marsh (1923-)

PORT JERVIS
7.7.8.7.Ref.

As a Fire Is Meant for Burning

Unison
1 As a fire is meant for burn - ing with a bright and warm-ing flame,
2 We are learn - ers; we are teach - ers; we are pil - grims on the way.
3 As a green bud in the spring-time is a sign of life re-newed,
so the church is meant for mis - sion, giv - ing glo - ry to God's name.
We are seek - ers; we are giv - ers; we are ves - sels made of clay.
so may we be signs of one - ness 'mid earth's peo - ples, man - y - hued.
Not to preach our creeds or cus - toms, but to build a bridge of care,
By our gen - tle, lov - ing ac - tions, we would show that Christ is light.
As a rain - bow lights the heav - ens when a storm is past and gone,
we join hands a - cross the na - tions, find - ing neigh-bors ev - ery - where.
In a hum - ble, lis-tening spir - it, we would live to God's de - light.
may our lives re - flect the ra - diance of God's new and glo-rious dawn.

WORDS: Ruth Duck (1947-)
MUSIC: Attr. B. F. White (1800-1879), *The Sacred Harp*, 1844; arr. Jack Schrader (1942-)

BEACH SPRING
8.7.8.7.D.

552 We All Are One in Mission

1 We all are one in mis - sion, we all are one in call,
2 We all are called for serv - ice to wit - ness in God's name.
3 We all be - hold one vi - sion, a stark re - al - i - ty:
4 Now let us be u - nit - ed and let our song be heard.
our var - ied gifts u - nit - ed by Christ, the Lord of all.
Our min - is - tries are dif - ferent, our pur - pose is the same:
the au - thor of sal - va - tion was nailed up - on a tree.
Now let us be a ves - sel for God's re - deem - ing Word.
A sin - gle, great com - mis - sion com - pels us from a - bove
to touch the lives of oth - ers by God's sur - pris - ing grace,
Yet res - ur - rect - ed Jus - tice gives rise that we may share
We all are one in mis - sion, we all are one in call,
to plan and work to - geth - er that all may know Christ's love.
so ev - 'ry folk and na - tion may feel God's warm em - brace.
free re - con - cil - i - a - tion and hope a - mid de - spair.
our var - ied gifts u - nit - ed by Christ, the Lord of all.

WORDS: Rusty Edwards (1955-)
MUSIC: Samuel S. Wesley (1810-1876)

AURELIA
7.6.7.6.D.

Go to the World!

Unison
1 Go to the world! Go in - to all the earth.
2 Go to the world! Go in - to ev - ery place.
3 Go to the world! Go strug - gle, bless, and pray;
4 Go to the world! Go as the ones I send,
Go preach the cross where Christ re - news life's worth,
Go live the word of God's re - deem - ing grace.
the nights of tears give way to joy - ous day.
for I am with you till the age shall end,
bap - tiz - ing as the sign of our re - birth.
Go seek God's pres - ence in each time and space.
As ser - vant church, you fol - low Christ's own way.
when all the hosts of glo - ry cry, "A - men."
1–3
4
1–3 Al - le - lu - ia!
4 Al - le - lu - ia!

WORDS: Sylvia G. Dunstan (1955-1993)
MUSIC: Charles V. Stanford (1852-1924)

ENGELBERG
10.10.10.Alleluias

554 We Have Heard the Joyful Sound

1 We have heard the joy - ful sound: Je - sus saves! Je - sus saves!
2 Send it on the roll - ing tide: Je - sus saves! Je - sus saves!
3 Sing a - bove the bat - tle strife: Je - sus saves! Je - sus saves!
4 Give the winds a might - y voice: Je - sus saves! Je - sus saves!
Spread the ti - dings all a - round: Je - sus saves! Je - sus saves!
Tell to sin - ners far and wide: Je - sus saves! Je - sus saves!
By his death and end - less life: Je - sus saves! Je - sus saves!
Let the na - tions now re - joice: Je - sus saves! Je - sus saves!
Bear the news to ev - ery land, climb the steeps and cross the waves;
Sing, you is - lands of the sea! Ech - o back, you o - cean caves!
Sing it soft - ly through the gloom, when the heart for mer - cy craves;
Shout sal - va - tion full and free, high - est hills and deep - est caves;
on - ward! 'tis our Lord's com - mand: Je - sus saves! Je - sus saves!
Earth shall keep her ju - bi - lee: Je - sus saves! Je - sus saves!
sing in tri - umph o'er the tomb: Je - sus saves! Je - sus saves!
this our song of vic - to - ry: Je - sus saves! Je - sus saves!

WORDS: Priscilla J. Owens (1829-1907)
MUSIC: William J. Kirkpatrick (1838-1921)

JESUS SAVES
7.6.7.6.7.7.7.6.

When the Church of Jesus

Unison
1 When the Church of Je - sus shuts its out - er door,
2 If our hearts are lift - ed where de - vo - tion soars
3 Lest the gifts we of - fer, mon - ey, tal - ents, time,
lest the roar of traf - fic drown the voice of prayer:
high a - bove this hun - gry, suf-fering world of ours:
serve to salve our con - science, to our se - cret shame:
may our prayers, Lord, make us ten times more a - ware
lest our hymns should drug us to for - get its needs,
Lord, re - prove, in - spire us by the way you give;
that the world we ban - ish is our Chris - tian care.
forge our Chris-tian wor - ship in - to Chris - tian deeds.
teach us, dy - ing Sav - ior, how true Chris - tians live.

WORDS: Fred Pratt Green (1903-2000)
MUSIC: Ralph Vaughan Williams (1872-1958)

KING'S WESTON
6.5.6.5.D.

556 Go Forth in His Name

Unison
Verse
D G/D A/D D
1 We are his chil - dren, the fruit of his suf - fering,
2 Count - less the souls that are stum - bling in dark - ness,
3 Lis - ten, the wind of the Spir - it is blow - ing, the
Bm Em/B C Asus A
saved and re - deemed by his blood;
why do we sleep in the light?
end of the age is so near;
D G/D A/C♯ A/B Bm
called to be ho - ly, a light to the na - tions,
Je - sus com - mands us to go make dis - ci - ples,
powers in the earth and the heav - ens are shak - ing.
C C/B C/A C/G Asus A
clothed with his power, filled with his love.
this is our cause, this is the fight.
Je - sus, our Lord soon shall ap - pear.

WORDS and MUSIC: Graham Kendrick (1950-)

Refrain (parts)
Bm A/B Bm A Bm Bm/A Gmaj7 A/G
Go forth in his name, pro - claim - ing
Gmaj7 A Bm Em7 A
"Je - sus reigns." Now is the time for the
F#m7 Bm7 G D G D Em7 G/A
church to a - rise and pro - claim him, "Je - sus, Sav - ior, Re - deem - er and
1
D G/D A/D A/C#
to Refrain
Lord."
2
D G/D A/D G/D
to Verse
Lord."
Last time
Asus A D G/D Dmaj7 G/A D G/D D
Lord." Je - sus is Lord, Je - sus is Lord.

557 Pass It On

D Em7 F♯m G G/B F♯m/A A
1 It on - ly takes a spark to get a fire go - ing,
2 What a won-drous time is spring when all the trees are bud - ding,
3 I wish for you, my friend, this hap - pi - ness that I've found—
D Em7 F♯m G G/B F♯m/A A
and soon all those a - round can warm up in its glow - ing;
the birds be - gin to sing, the flow - ers start their bloom - ing;
on God you can de - pend, it mat - ters not where you're bound;
D/F♯ G A/G D/F♯ Em7 F♯m Bm
that's how it is with God's love, once you've ex - per - i - enced it:
that's how it is with God's love, once you've ex - per - i - enced it:
I'll shout it from the moun-tain top, I want my world to know:
Bm Em D/F♯ G A A7 D
you spread God's love to ev - ery - one, you want to pass it on.
you want to sing, it's fresh like spring, you want to pass it on.
the Lord of love has come to me, I want to pass it on.

WORDS and MUSIC: Kurt Kaiser (1934-)

The World Is Full of Stories 558

Unison
1 The world is full of sto - ries, of sto - ries that have passed
2 The world is full of sto - ries, new sto - ries peo - ple tell,
3 The world is full of sto - ries that cap - ture and en - thral;
4 It tells us of the an - guish God's love was bound to bear,
to us a - long the a - ges; great sto - ries that still last,
and young and old come un - der the sto - ry - tell - er's spell
but joy - ful faith dis - cov - ers that one tran-scends them all:
to con - quer death and e - vil and fath - om our des - pair.
to tell of hu - man feel - ings drawn deep from heart and mind,
which stirs i - mag - i - na - tion and o - pens wide our eyes
God's love as told in Je - sus, who shared our life on earth,
As we re - peat the sto - ry, hope comes to life and thrives,
more true than fact: their mean - ing the sur - est we can find.
to du - ty and con - vic - tion, to won - der and sur - prise.
and hu - man re - cre - a - tion be - gin - ning at his birth.
to make the love of Je - sus the sto - ry of our lives.

WORDS: Alan Gaunt (1935-)
MUSIC: Hal H. Hopson (1933-)

MERLE'S TUNE
7.6.7.6.D.

559 Here I Am, Lord

Unison
G Am/G D7/G C/G
1 I, the Lord of sea and sky, I have heard my
2 I, the Lord of snow and rain, I have borne my
3 I, the Lord of wind and flame, I will tend the
G D G Em Am7 C
peo - ple cry. All who dwell in dark and sin
peo - ple's pain. I have wept for love of them,
poor and lame. I will set a feast for them,
Am D7/G D/F# D/C G Am/G D7/G
my hand will save. I who made the stars of night,
they turn a - way. I will break their hearts of stone,
my hand will save. Fin-est bread I will pro-vide
C/G G D G Em
I will make their dark - ness bright. Who will bear my
give them hearts for love a - lone. I will speak my
till their hearts be sat - is - fied. I will give my

WORDS: Daniel L. Schutte (1947-); para. Isaiah 6:8
MUSIC: Daniel L. Schutte (1947-); arr. Michael Pope (20th c.), Daniel L. Schutte (1947-), John Weissrock (20th c.)

Refrain
Am7 C Am G/B C6 slowing D D7/F#
light to them? Whom shall I send?
Word to them. Whom shall I send? Here I
life to them. Whom shall I send?
a tempo
G Gsus G D7/A C/E D7 G
am, Lord. Is it I, Lord? I have
C/G Am G/B C6 D D7/F#
heard you call - ing in the night. I will
G Gsus G C/G G C/E D7 G
go, Lord, if you lead me. I will
Am7 C/D D G C/G G
hold your peo - ple in my heart.

560 I Love to Tell the Story

1 I love to tell the sto - ry of un - seen things a - bove, of
2 I love to tell the sto - ry, 'tis pleas - ant to re - peat what
3 I love to tell the sto - ry, for those who know it best seem
Je - sus and his glo - ry, of Je - sus and his love. I love to tell the
seems, each time I tell it, more won - der - ful - ly sweet. I love to tell the
hun - ger - ing and thirst - ing to hear it like the rest. And when in scenes of
sto - ry be - cause I know 'tis true; it sat - is - fies my long - ings as
sto - ry, for some have nev - er heard the mes - sage of sal - va - tion from
glo - ry I sing the new, new song, 'twill be the old, old sto - ry that
noth - ing else can do.
God's own Ho - ly Word.
I have loved so long.
Refrain
I love to tell the sto - ry, 'twill be my theme in

WORDS: A. Catherine Hankey (1834-1911)
MUSIC: William G. Fischer (1835-1912)

HANKEY
7.6.7.6.D.Ref.

glo - ry, to tell the old, old sto - ry of Je - sus and his love.

Christ for the World! We Sing 561

1 Christ for the world! we sing; the world to Christ we bring
2 Christ for the world! we sing; the world to Christ we bring
3 Christ for the world! we sing; the world to Christ we bring
4 Christ for the world! we sing; the world to Christ we bring
with lov - ing zeal— the poor and them that mourn, the faint and
with fer - vent prayer— the way - ward and the lost, by rest - less
with one ac - cord— with us the work to share, with us re -
with joy ful song— the new - born souls whose days, re - claimed from
o - ver - borne, sin - sick and sor - row - worn, for Christ to heal.
pas - sions tossed, re - deemed at count - less cost from dark de - spair.
proach to dare, with us the cross to bear, for Christ our Lord.
er - ror's ways, in - spired with hope and praise, to Christ be - long.

WORDS: Samuel Wolcott (1813-1886)
MUSIC: Felice de Giardini (1716-1796); arr. Russell Schulz-Widmar (1944-)

ITALIAN HYMN
6.6.4.6.6.6.4.

562 We've a Story to Tell to the Nations

1 We've a sto - ry to tell to the na - tions, that shall turn their hearts to the right, a sto - ry of truth and mer - cy, a sto - ry of peace and light, a sto - ry of peace and light.
2 We've a song to be sung to the na - tions, that shall lift their hearts to the Lord, a song that shall con - quer e - vil and shat - ter the spear and sword, and shat - ter the spear and sword.
3 We've a mes - sage to give to the na - tions, that the Lord who reigns high a - bove has sent us his Son to save us, and show us that God is love, and show us that God is love.
4 We've a Sav - ior to show to the na - tions, who the path of sor - row has trod, that all of the world's great peo - ples might come to the truth of God, might come to the truth of God.
Refrain
For the dark-ness shall turn to dawn-ing, and the dawn-ing to noon-day bright;

WORDS and MUSIC: H. Ernest Nichol (1862-1928)

MESSAGE
10.8.8.7.7.Ref.

and Christ's great king-dom shall come on earth, the king-dom of love and light.

Song for the Nations 563

1 May we be a shin - ing light to the na - tions, a shin - ing
2 May we bring a word of hope to the na - tions, a word of
3 May we be a heal - ing balm to the na - tions, a heal - ing
4 May we sing a song of joy to the na - tions, a song of
5 May your king - dom come to the na - tions, your will be
light to the peo-ples of the earth, till the whole world sees the
life to the peo-ples of the earth, till the whole world knows there's sal-
balm to the peo-ples of the earth, till the whole world knows the
praise to the peo-ples of the earth, till the whole world rings with the
done in the peo-ples of the earth, till the whole world knows that
glo - ry of your name. May your pure light shine through us.
va - tion thro' your name. May your mer - cy flow through us.
pow - er of your name. May your heal - ing flow through us.
prais - es of your name. May your song be sung through us.
Je - sus Christ is Lord. May your king-dom come on earth.

WORDS and MUSIC: Chris Christensen (1957-); arr. Tom Fettke (1941-)

564 God Is Working His Purpose Out

I
II
1 God is work - ing his pur - pose out, as
2 From the east to ut - most west, where
3 March we forth in the strength of God, with the
4 All we can do is noth - ing worth un -
year suc - ceeds to year: God is work-ing his
hu - man feet have trod, by the mouth of man - y
ban-ner of Christ un - furled, that the light of the glo - rious
less God bless-es the deed. Vain - ly we hope for the
pur - pose out, the time is draw - ing near.
mes - sen - gers goes forth the voice of God,
Gos - pel of truth may shine through-out the world.
har - vest - tide till God gives life to the seed. Yet

WORDS: Arthur C. Ainger (1841-1919)
MUSIC: Martin Shaw (1875-1958)

PURPOSE
Irregular

1–3
4
Near - er and near - er draws the time, the time that shall sure - ly be, when the earth shall be filled with the glo - ry of God as the wa - ters cov - er the sea.
"Give ear to me, you con - ti - nents, you isles, give ear to me, that the earth may be filled with the glo - ry of God as the wa - ters cov - er the sea."
Fight we the fight with sor - row and sin to set the cap - tives free, that the earth may be filled with the glo - ry of God as the wa - ters cov - er the sea.
near - er and near - er draws the time, the time that shall sure - ly be, when the earth shall be filled with the glo - ry of God as the wa - ters cov - er the sea.

565 O Christians, Haste

1 O Chris-tians, haste, your mis-sion high ful-fill-ing,
2 Pro-claim to ev-ery peo-ple, tongue, and na-tion,
3 Give of your sons to bear the mes-sage glo-rious;
to tell the world that God is one who cares,
that God, in whom we live and move, is love.
give of your daugh-ters, speed them on their way.
that God who made all na-tions is not will-ing
Tell how God stooped to save a lost cre-a-tion,
Pour out your soul for them in prayer vic-to-rious,
one life should per-ish, lost in deep de-spair.
and died on earth that we might live a-bove.
till God shall bring a new and joy-ful day.

WORDS: Mary A. Thomson (1834-1923), alt.
MUSIC: James Walch (1837-1901)

TIDINGS
11.10.11.10.Ref.

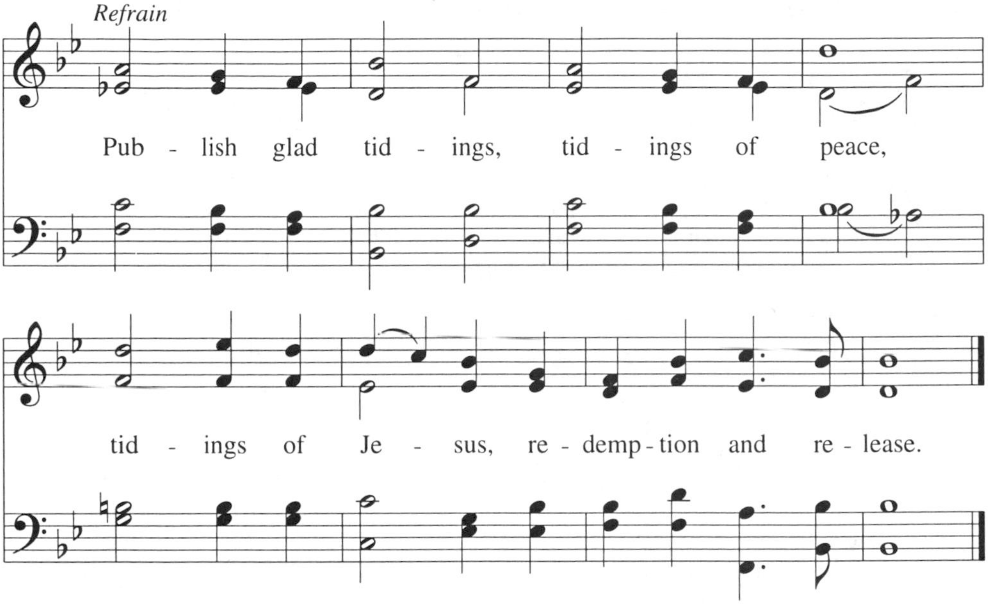
Refrain
Pub - lish glad tid - ings, tid - ings of peace,
tid - ings of Je - sus, re - demp - tion and re - lease.

Your Servant Comes This Hour 566

1 Your ser - vant comes this hour in true hu - mil - i - ty, be - liev - ing in your call, O God, and answ - ering, "Lord, send me."
2 Your ser - vant kneels in prayer, a - wait - ing from a - bove the touch which sets their life a - part for min - i - stries of love.
3 Your ser - vant stands this day im - plant - ed in the word; pre - pared to share the ho - ly truth, pro - claim it lamp and sword.
4 Your ser - vant leaves this place with con - fi - dence se - cure, and by the Ho - ly Spir - it bears the fruit which shall en - dure.

WORDS: Constance Cherry (1953-)
MUSIC: William H. Walter (1825-1893)

FESTAL SONG
S.M.

567 With Welcome Heart We Greet You, Lord

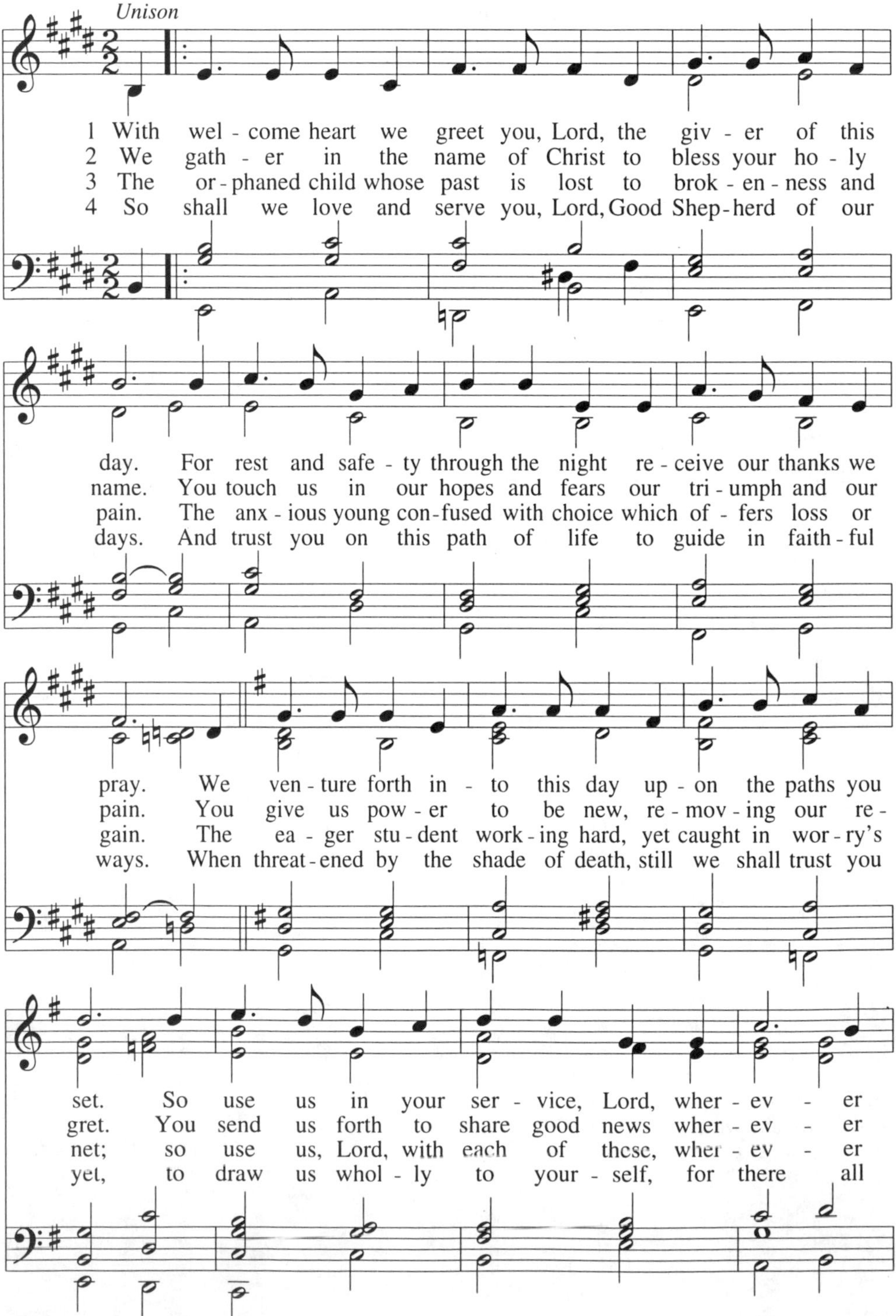
Unison
1 With wel - come heart we greet you, Lord, the giv - er of this
2 We gath - er in the name of Christ to bless your ho - ly
3 The or - phaned child whose past is lost to brok - en - ness and
4 So shall we love and serve you, Lord, Good Shep - herd of our
day. For rest and safe - ty through the night re - ceive our thanks we
name. You touch us in our hopes and fears our tri - umph and our
pain. The anx - ious young con - fused with choice which of - fers loss or
days. And trust you on this path of life to guide in faith - ful
pray. We ven - ture forth in - to this day up - on the paths you
pain. You give us pow - er to be new, re - mov - ing our re -
gain. The ea - ger stu - dent work - ing hard, yet caught in wor - ry's
ways. When threat - ened by the shade of death, still we shall trust you
set. So use us in your ser - vice, Lord, wher - ev - er
gret. You send us forth to share good news wher - ev - er
net; so use us, Lord, with each of these, wher - ev - er
yet, to draw us whol - ly to your - self, for there all

WORDS: Fred R. Anderson (1941-)
MUSIC: John Weaver (1937-)

GALLANT
8.6.8.6.D.

1–3
4
need is met. (2) We
need is met. (3) The
need is met. (4) So
need is met.

People Need the Lord 568

Unison
C
Dm
C/E
1 Peo-ple need the Lord, peo-ple need the
2 Peo-ple need the Lord, peo-ple need the
F
G
G/F
C/E
Lord; at the end of bro - ken dreams,
Lord; when will we re - al - ize
1
Dm
G
2
Dm
G7
F/G
C
he's the o - pen door. peo-ple need the Lord.

WORDS and MUSIC: Greg Nelson (1948-) and Phill McHugh (1951-); arr. David Allen (1941-)

Use tune of #285 in The Worshiping Church

569 God of Grace and God of Glory

1 God of grace and God of glo - ry, on your peo - ple
2 Lo! the hosts of e - vil round us scorn your Christ, as -
3 Heal your chil - dren's war - ring mad - ness, bend our pride to
4 Save us from weak res - ig - na - tion to the e - vils
pour your power; crown your an - cient Church's sto - ry, bring its
sail his ways! Fears and doubts too long have bound us— free our
your con - trol; shame our wan - ton, self - ish glad - ness, rich in
we de - plore; let the gift of your sal - va - tion be our
bud to glo - rious flower. Grant us wis - dom, grant us cour - age
hearts to work and praise. Grant us wis - dom, grant us cour - age
things and poor in soul. Grant us wis - dom, grant us cour - age
glo - ry ev - er - more. Grant us wis - dom, grant us cour - age,
for the fac - ing of this hour, for the fac - ing of this hour.
for the liv - ing of these days, for the liv - ing of these days.
lest we miss your king-dom's goal, lest we miss your king - dom's goal.
serv - ing you whom we a - dore, serv - ing you whom we a - dore.

WORDS: Harry E. Fosdick (1878-1969), alt.
MUSIC: John Hughes (1873-1932)

CWM RHONDDA
8.7.8.7.8.7.7.

As Saints of Old Their First-fruits Brought 570

1 As saints of old their first-fruits brought of vine-yard, flock, and field
2 A world in need now sum-mons us to la - bor, love, and give,
3 With grat - i - tude and hum-ble trust we bring our best to you,
to God, the giv - er of all good, the source of boun-teous yield;
to make our life an of - fer - ing to God, that all may live.
not just to serve your cause, but share your love with neigh-bors too.
so we to - day our first-fruits bring: the wealth of this good land,
The church of Christ is call - ing us to make the dream come true:
O God, who gave your - self to us in Je - sus Christ your Son,
of farm and mar - ket, shop and home, of mind and heart and hand.
a world re-deemed, by Christ-like love, all life in Christ made new.
help us to give our - selves each day un - til life's work is done.

WORDS: Frank von Christierson (1900-1996), alt.
MUSIC: English melody; harm. Ralph Vaughan Williams (1872-1958)

FOREST GREEN
8.6.8.6.D.

571 Christ, You Call Us All to Service

1 Christ, you call us all to serv-ice, call us all who fol - low you;
2 Teach us how to work to - geth - er, broth-ers, sis - ters, side by side,
3 Let us be a ser - vant peo-ple, re - con-cil - ing, end - ing strife,
plant in us a deep com-mit-ment all your work and will to do.
e - qual part-ners in the strug-gle, in the cause of truth al - lied.
seek - ing ways more just of shar-ing and of or - dering hu - man life.
Fire a pas-sion for your jus-tice, in us kin - dle love of peace;
To each one some gift is giv - en, man or wo-man, young or old;
Fill us with a glow-ing vi - sion of this world as it should be;
help us heal the bro - ken-heart-ed, to the cap - tive bring re - lease.
help us use each skill and tal - ent your great pur - pose to un - fold.
send us forth to change that vi - sion in - to blest re - al - i - ty.

WORDS: Joy F. Patterson (1931-)
MUSIC: Dutch melody, 18th c.; arr. Julius Röntgen (1855-1933)

IN BABILONE
8.7.8.7.D.

God, Whose Giving Knows No Ending 572

1 God, whose giv-ing knows no end-ing, from your rich and end-less store:
2 Skills and time are ours for press-ing toward the goals of Christ, your Son:
3 Trea-sure, too, you have en-trust-ed, gain through powers your grace con-ferred;
na-ture's won-der, Je-sus' wis-dom, cost-ly cross, grave's shat-tered door,
all at peace in health and free-dom, rac-es joined, the Church made one.
ours to use for home and kin-dred, and to spread the Gos-pel Word.
gift-ed by you, we turn to you, of-fer-ing up our-selves in praise;
Now di-rect our dai-ly la-bor, lest we strive for self a-lone;
O-pen wide our hands in shar-ing, as we heed Christ's age-less call,
thank-ful song shall rise for-ev-er, gra-cious do-nor of our days.
born with tal-ents, make us ser-vants fit to an-swer at your throne.
heal-ing, teach-ing, and re-claim-ing, serv-ing you by lov-ing all.

WORDS: Robert L. Edwards (1915-), alt.
MUSIC: C. Hubert H. Parry (1848-1918)

RUSTINGTON
8.7.8.7.D.

573 How Clear Is Our Vocation, Lord

Unison
1 How clear is our vo - ca - tion, Lord, when
2 But if, for - get - ful, we should find your
3 We mar - vel how your saints be - come in
4 In what you give us, Lord, to do, to -
once we heed your call: to live ac - cord - ing
yoke is hard to bear; if world - ly pres - sures
hin - dranc - es more sure; whose joy - ful vir - tues
geth - er or a - lone, in old rou - tines and
to your word, and dai - ly learn, re - freshed, re - stored, that
fray the mind, and love it - self can - not un - wind its
put to shame the cas - ual way we wear your name, and
ven - tures new may we not cease to look to you, the
you are Lord of all, and will not let us fall.
tan - gled skein of care: our in - ward life re - pair.
by our faults ob - scure your power to cleanse and cure.
cross you hung up - on— all you en - deav - ored done.

WORDS: Fred Pratt Green (1903-2000)
MUSIC: C. Hubert H. Parry (1848-1918)

REPTON
8.6.8.8.6.6.

I'm Gonna Live So God Can Use Me 574

F Bb/F F Gm/F F
1 I'm gon-na live so God can use me
(I'm gon-na live so) (God can
F7 Bb Eb/Bb Bb F Bb/F
an - y time and an - y - where.
use me) (an - y time) (an - y -
F N.C. F Bb/F F A7
I'm gon-na live so God can use me
where.) (I'm gon-na live so)
Dm Bb6 F/C Dm7 G7 C7 F Bb/F F
an - y time and an - y - where.
(an - y time) (an - y - where.)

2 I'm gonna work... 3 I'm gonna pray... 4 I'm gonna sing...

WORDS and MUSIC: African-American spiritual

I'M GONNA LIVE
Irregular

575 Lord, Whose Love Through Humble Service

1 Lord, whose love through hum-ble ser - vice bore the weight of hu-man need,
2 Still your chil - dren wan-der home-less; still the hun - gry cry for bread;
3 As we wor - ship, grant us vi - sion, till your love's re - veal-ing light
4 Called by wor - ship to your ser - vice, forth in your dear name we go,
who up - on the cross, for - sak - en, of - fered mer - cy's per - fect deed;
still the cap - tives long for free - dom; still in grief we mourn our dead.
in its height and depth and great-ness, dawns up - on our quick-ened sight,
to the child, the youth, the a - ged, love in liv - ing deeds to show;
we, your ser - vants, bring the wor-ship not of voice a - lone, but heart,
As, O Lord, your deep com - pas - sion healed the sick and freed the soul,
mak-ing known the needs and bur - dens your com-pas-sion bids us bear,
hope and health, good will and com-fort, coun - sel, aid, and peace we give,
con - se - crat - ing to your pur - pose ev - ery gift that you im - part.
use the love your Spir - it kin - dles still to save and make us whole.
stir-ring us to tire-less striv - ing, your a - bun-dant life to share.
that your ser vants, Lord, in free - dom may your mer - cy know and live.

WORDS: Albert F. Bayly (1901-1984) BEACH SPRING
MUSIC: Attr. B. F. White (1800-1879); *The Sacred Harp*, 1844; harm. Ronald A. Nelson (1927-) 8.7.8.7.D.

Make Me a Servant

576

Unison
G
Em
D7sus/A
D7sus
D7
D7sus/A
Make me a ser - vant, hum - ble and meek, Lord, let me
C/D
D7
C/G
G
Am/G
G
B7
Em
Em7/D
lift up those who are weak; and may the prayer of my
Em/C#
Cm6
G/B
D7sus/A
G/B
heart al-ways be: make me a ser-vant, make me a
Am7/C
G/D
D7sus
D7
C/G
G
ser - vant, make me a ser - vant to - day.

WORDS and MUSIC: Kelly Willard (1956-)

577 Sing a New Church

1 Sum-moned by the God who made us rich in our di - ver - si - ty,
2 Ra - diant ris - en from the wa - ter; robed in ho - li - ness and light,
3 Trust the good-ness of cre - a - tion; trust the Spir - it strong with - in.
4 Bring the hopes of ev - ery na - tion; bring the art of ev - ery race.
5 Draw to - geth - er at one ta - ble all the hu - man fam - i - ly;
gath-ered in the name of Je - sus, rich - er still in u - ni - ty:
male and fe - male in God's im - age, male and fe - male, God's de - light:
Dare to dream the vi - sion prom-ised sprung from seed of what has been.
Weave a song of peace and jus - tice; let it sound through time and space.
shape a cir - cle ev - er wid - er and a peo - ple ev - er free.
Refrain
Let us bring the gifts that dif - fer and, in splen-did, var - ied ways,
sing a new church in - to be - ing, one in faith and love and praise.

WORDS: Delores Dufner, O.S.B. (20th c.)
MUSIC: John Wyeth's *Repository of Sacred Music*, 1813

NETTLETON
8.7.8.7.D.

So Send I You

1 So send I you— by grace made strong to tri - umph o'er hosts of
2 So send I you— to take to souls in bond - age the Word of
3 So send I you— my strength to know in weak-ness, my joy in
4 So send I you— to bear my cross with pa - tience, and then one
hell, o'er dark-ness, death, and sin, my name to bear and in that name to
truth that sets the cap - tive free, to break the bonds of sin, to loose death's
grief, my per - fect peace in pain, to prove my power, my grace, my prom-ised
day with joy to lay it down, to hear my voice, "Well done, my faith - ful
1–3
4
con - quer— so send I you, my vic - to - ry to win.
fet - ters— so send I you, to bring the lost to me.
pres - ence— so send I you, e - ter - nal fruit to gain.
ser - vant—come, share my throne, my king-dom, and my crown!"
"As the Fa - ther has sent me, so send I you."

WORDS: Margaret Clarkson (1915-)
MUSIC: John W. Peterson (1921-)

TORONTO
11.10.11.10.Coda

579 This Is a Time to Remember

Unison
1 This is a time to re - mem-ber the great-ness of the Lord;
he has so faith-ful-ly led us as prom-ised in his Word;
he has so boun-ti-fully giv - en his grace like fresh-ening rain;
he has so lov - ing-ly par-doned and made us whole a - gain.
2 This is a time to re - mem-ber the glo - ries that have been;
this is a time to press on-ward to vis - tas yet un - seen;
Christ is a-live in his peo-ple, he meets us face to face;
grant-ing the power of his Spir - it to serve him in this place.
3 This is a time to re - mem-ber the Church is his, not ours;
this is a time to sur - ren - der our-selves, our wealth, our powers;
this is a time to be ser-vants— to give our-selves a - way,
build-ing the Church of the fu - ture un - til the com - ing day.

WORDS and MUSIC: Bryan Jeffery Leech (1931-); arr. Roland Tabell (1934-)

DUDLEY
14.14.14.14.

We Are Called to Be God's People 580

1 We are called to be God's peo - ple, show-ing by our lives his grace,
2 We are called to be God's ser - vants, work-ing in his world to - day;
3 We are called to be God's proph-ets, speak-ing for the truth and right,
one in heart and one in spir - it, sign of hope for all the race.
tak - ing his own task up - on us, all his sa - cred words o - bey.
stand-ing firm for god - ly jus - tice, bring-ing e - vil things to light.
Let us show how he has changed us, and re - made us as his own,
Let us rise, then, to his sum - mons, ded-i - cate to him our all,
Let us seek the cour-age need - ed, our high call-ing to ful - fill,
let us share our life to - geth - er as we shall a - round his throne.
that we may be faith - ful ser - vants, quick to an - swer now his call.
that the world may know the bless-ing of the do - ing of God's will.

WORDS: Thomas A. Jackson (1931-), alt.
MUSIC: Franz Joseph Haydn (1732-1809)

AUSTRIAN HYMN
8.7.8.7.D.

581 Called as Partners in Christ's Service

1 Called as part-ners in Christ's ser-vice, called to min-is-tries of grace,
2 Christ's ex-am-ple, Christ's in-spir-ing, Christ's clear call to work and worth,
3 Thus new pat-terns for Christ's mis-sion, in a small or glob-al sense,
4 So God grant us for to-mor-row ways to or-der hu-man life
we re-spond with deep com-mit-ment fresh new lines of faith to trace.
let us fol-low, nev-er fal-tering, rec-on-cil-ing folk on earth.
help us bear each oth-er's bur-dens, break-ing down each wall or fence.
that sur-round each per-son's sor-row with a calm that con-quers strife.
May we learn the art of shar-ing, side by side and friend with friend,
Men and wom-en, rich-er, poor-er, all God's peo-ple, young and old,
Words of com-fort, words of vi-sion, words of chal-lenge, said with care,
Make us part-ners in our liv-ing, our com-pas-sion to in-crease,
e-qual part-ners in our car-ing to ful-fill God's cho-sen end.
blend-ing hu-man skills to-geth-er gra-cious gifts from God un-fold.
bring new power and strength for ac-tion, make us col-leagues, free and fair.
mes-sen-gers of faith, thus giv-ing hope and con-fi-dence and peace.

WORDS: Jane Parker Huber (1926-)
MUSIC: John Zundel (1815-1882)

BEECHER
8.7.8.7.D.

O Jesus Christ, May Grateful Hymns Be Rising 582

1 O Je - sus Christ, may grate - ful hymns be ris - ing,
2 Grant us new cour - age, sac - ri - fi - cial, hum - ble,
3 Show us your Spir - it, brood - ing o'er each cit - y,
in ev - ery cit - y for your love and care;
strong in your strength to ven - ture and to dare;
as you once wept a - bove Je - ru - sa - lem,
in - spire our wor - ship, grant the glad sur - pris - ing
to lift the fall - en, guide the feet that stum - ble,
seek - ing to gath - er all in love and pit - y,
that your blest Spir - it rous - es ev - ery - where.
seek out the lone - ly and God's mer - cy share.
and heal - ing those who touch your gar - ment's hem.

WORDS: Bradford Gray Webster (1898-1991)
MUSIC: Alfred Scott-Gatty (1847-1918)

WELWYN
11.10.11.10.

583 You Call Us, Lord

1 You call us, Lord, to be a peo - ple set a - part,
2 You call us, Lord, to care for self and neigh - bor too,
3 You call us, Lord, to be good stew - ards of the earth;
4 You call us, Lord, to serve: to die that we may live,
to feel with thought - ful mind and think with ten - der heart.
to take the risk, and dare to show what love can do.
to tend it as a place of bless - ed - ness and worth.
to know we best re - ceive when joy - ful - ly we give.
Refrain
Thus cho - sen, now, O Lord, we ask for faith in your
un - fail - ing grace to make us e - qual to the task.

WORDS: Jane Marshall (1924-)
MUSIC: John David Edwards (1806-1885)

RHOSYMEDRE
6.6.6.6.8.8.8.

Come, Celebrate the Call of God 584

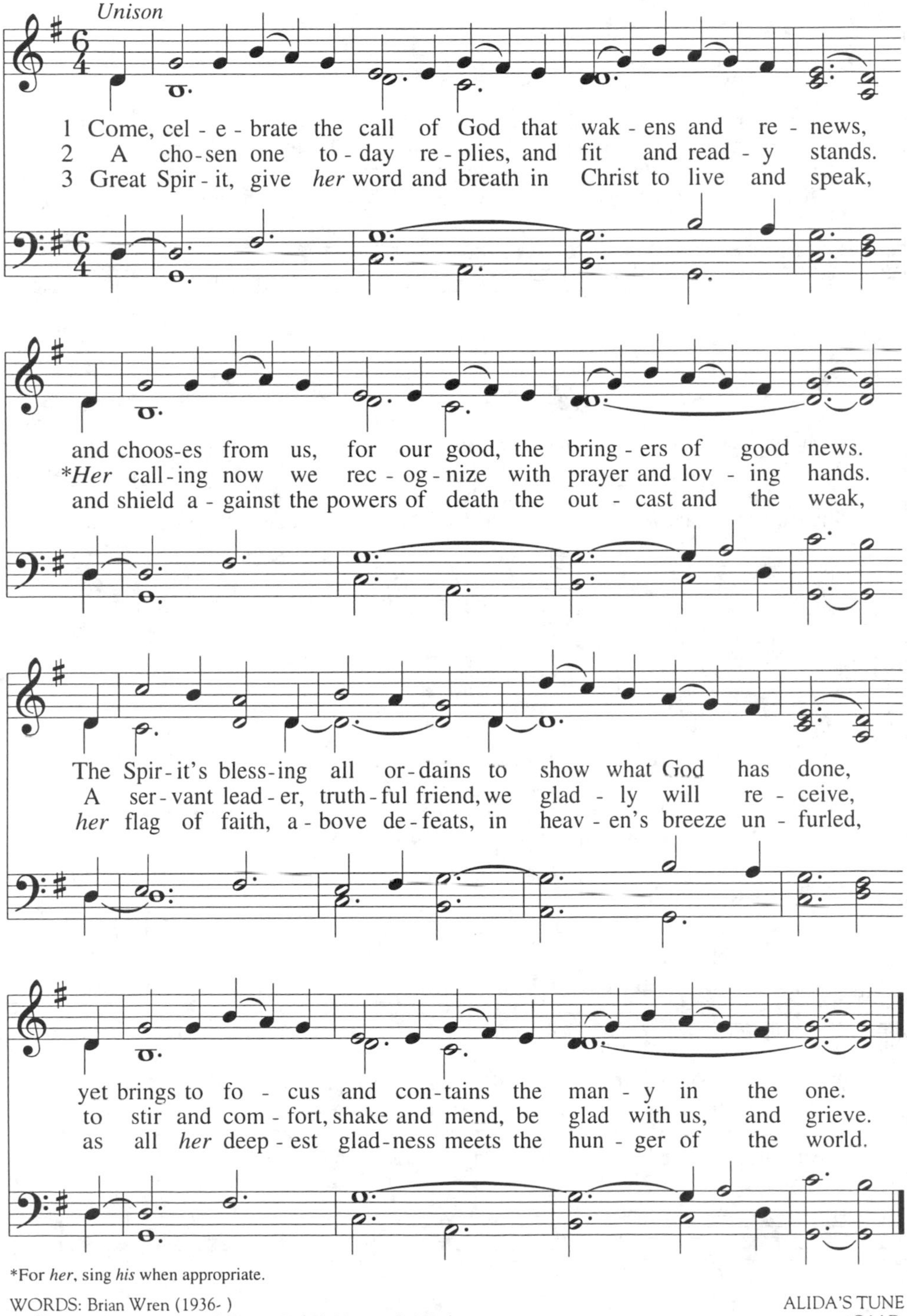
Unison
1 Come, cel - e - brate the call of God that wak - ens and re - news,
2 A cho - sen one to - day re - plies, and fit and read - y stands.
3 Great Spir - it, give her word and breath in Christ to live and speak,
and choos - es from us, for our good, the bring - ers of good news.
*Her call - ing now we rec - og - nize with prayer and lov - ing hands.
and shield a - gainst the powers of death the out - cast and the weak,
The Spir - it's bless - ing all or - dains to show what God has done,
A ser - vant lead - er, truth - ful friend, we glad - ly will re - ceive,
her flag of faith, a - bove de - feats, in heav - en's breeze un - furled,
yet brings to fo - cus and con - tains the man - y in the one.
to stir and com - fort, shake and mend, be glad with us, and grieve.
as all her deep - est glad - ness meets the hun - ger of the world.

*For *her*, sing *his* when appropriate.

WORDS: Brian Wren (1936-)
MUSIC: Early American melody; arr. Hal H. Hopson (1933-)

ALIDA'S TUNE
C.M.D.

585 A Prophet-Woman Broke a Jar

1 A proph-et-wom-an broke a jar, by Love's di-vine ap-point-ing.
2 A faith-ful wom-an left a tomb by Love's di-vine com-mis-sion.
3 Though wom-an-wis-dom, wom-an-truth, for cen-tu-ries were hid-den,
4 The Spir-it knows, the Spir-it calls, by Love's di-vine or-dain-ing,
With rare per-fume she filled the room, pre-sid-ing and a-noint-ing.
She saw, she heard, she preached the Word, a-ris-ing from sub-mis-sion.
un-sung, un-writ-ten, and un-heard, de-rid-ed and for-bid-den,
the friends we need to serve and lead, their powers and gifts un-chain-ing.
A proph-et-wom-an broke a jar, the sneers of scorn de-fy-ing.
A faith-ful wom-an left a tomb, with res-ur-rec-tion gos-pel.
the Spir-it's breath, the Spir-it's fire, on free and slave de-scend-ing,
The Spir-it knows, the Spir-it calls, from wom-en, men and chil-dren,
With rare per-fume she filled the room, pre-par-ing Christ for dy-ing.
She saw, she heard, she preached the Word, a-pos-tle to a-pos-tles.
can tum-ble our di-vid-ing walls, our shame and sad-ness mend-ing.
the friends we need, to serve and lead. Re-joice, and make them wel-come!

WORDS: Brian Wren (1936-)
MUSIC: Walter K. Stanton (1891-1978)

MEGERRAN
8.7.8.7.D.

Our Cities Cry to You, O God 586

Unison
1 Our cit - ies cry to you, O God, from out their pain and strife;
2 Yet still you walk our streets, O Christ! We know your pres - ence here
3 Your peo - ple are your hands and feet to serve your world to - day,
4 O heal - ing Sav - ior, Prince of Peace, sal - va - tion's source and sum,
you made us for your - self a - lone, but we choose al - ien life.
where hum - ble Chris-tians love and serve in god - ly grace and fear.
our lives the book our cit - ies read to help them find your way.
for you our bro - ken cit - ies cry: O come, Lord Je - sus, come!
Our goals are plea - sure, gold, and power; in - jus - tice stalks our earth;
O Word made flesh, be seen in us! May all we say and do
O pour your sov - ereign Spir - it out on heart and will and brain:
With truth your roy - al di - a - dem, with right-eous-ness your rod,
in vain we seek for rest, for joy, for sense of hu - man worth.
af - firm you God In - car - nate still and turn sad hearts to you!
in - spire your church with love and power to ease our cit - ies' pain!
O come, Lord Je - sus, bring to earth the cit - y of our God!

WORDS: Margaret Clarkson (1915-) SALVATION
MUSIC: *Kentucky Harmony*, 1816; harm. *Songs for Liturgy and More Hymns and Spiritual Songs*, 1971 C.M.D.

587 Make Me a Channel of Your Peace

Prayer of St. Francis

D G/D G/A D
1 Make me a chan-nel of your peace. Where there is ha-tred
2 Make me a chan-nel of your peace. Where there's de-spair in
3 Make me a chan-nel of your peace. It is in par-don-
Bm C Asus A7 Em
let me bring your love. (love.) Where there is in-ju-
life let me bring hope. (hope.) Where there is dark-ness,
ing that we are par-doned, (par-doned,) in giv-ing of our-
Em7 G/A A Em
ry, your par-don, Lord, and where there's doubt, true
on-ly light, and where there's sad-ness,
selves that we re-ceive, and in dy-ing that we're
1, 2
A A7 D D7 to Refrain
faith in you. O
ev-er joy. O
3
A A7 D
born to e-ter-nal life.

WORDS and MUSIC: Sebastian Temple (1928-1998); arr. Jane Holstein (1958-)

PRAYER OF ST. FRANCIS
Irregular

Dedicated to Mrs. Frances Tracy

Refrain
G
Em7
F♯m
Bm7
Em7
Mas-ter, grant that I may nev - er seek so much to be con-
A7
D
D7
G
Em7
soled as to con - sole, to be un - der - stood, as to un - der-
F♯m
Bm7
E
E7
A
Em
A
stand, to be loved, as to love with all my soul.

A Charge to Keep I Have 588

1 A charge to keep I have, a God to glo - ri - fy, a
2 To serve the pres - ent age, my call-ing to ful - fill, O
3 Arm me with watch - ful care as in thy sight to live, and
4 Help me to watch and pray, and still on thee re - ly, O
nev - er - dy - ing soul to save, and fit it for the sky.
may it all my powers en - gage to do my Mas - ter's will!
now thy serv - ant, Lord, pre - pare a strict ac - count to give!
let me not my trust be - tray, but press to realms on high.

WORDS: Charles Wesley (1707-1788)
MUSIC: Lowell Mason (1792-1872)

BOYLSTON
S.M.

589 O Master, Let Me Walk with Thee

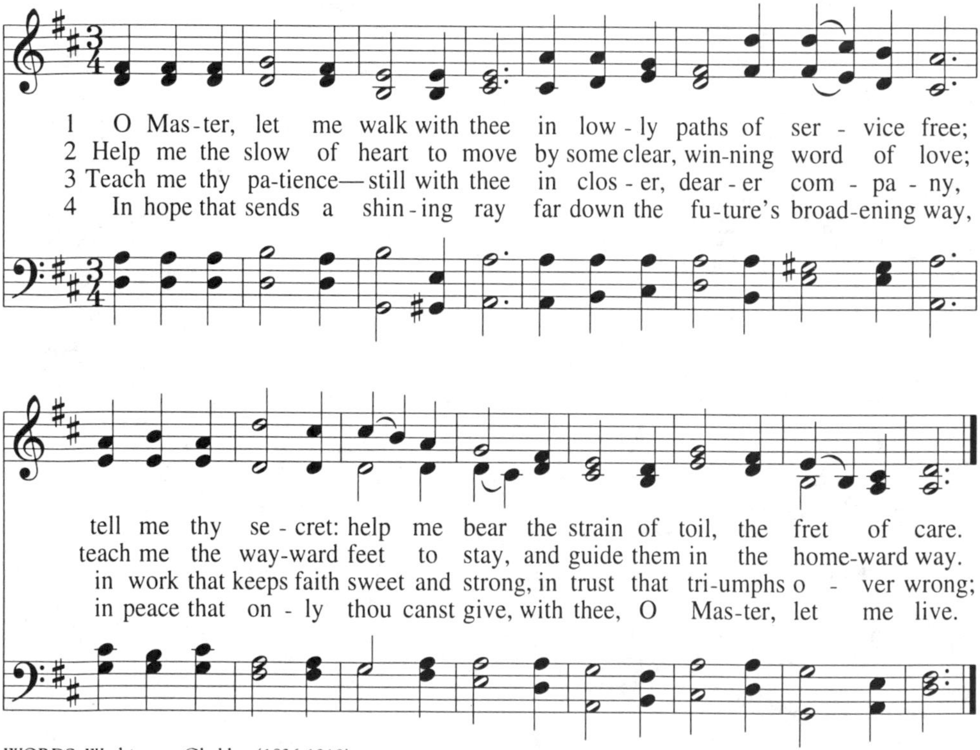
1 O Mas-ter, let me walk with thee in low - ly paths of ser - vice free;
2 Help me the slow of heart to move by some clear, win-ning word of love;
3 Teach me thy pa-tience—still with thee in clos - er, dear - er com - pa - ny,
4 In hope that sends a shin - ing ray far down the fu-ture's broad-ening way,
tell me thy se - cret: help me bear the strain of toil, the fret of care.
teach me the way-ward feet to stay, and guide them in the home-ward way.
in work that keeps faith sweet and strong, in trust that tri-umphs o - ver wrong;
in peace that on - ly thou canst give, with thee, O Mas-ter, let me live.

WORDS: Washington Gladden (1836-1918)
MUSIC: H. Percy Smith (1825-1898)

MARYTON
L.M.

590 Rise Up, O Saints of God!

1 Rise up, O saints of God! From vain am - bi - tions turn; Christ
2 Speak out, O saints of God! De - spair en - gulfs earth's frame; as
3 Rise up, O saints of God! His king-dom's task em - brace; re -
4 Give heed, O saints of God! Cre - a - tion cries in pain; stretch
5 Com - mit your hearts to seek the paths which Christ has trod; and

WORDS: Norman O. Forness (1936-)
MUSIC: William H. Walter (1825-1893)

FESTAL SONG
S.M.

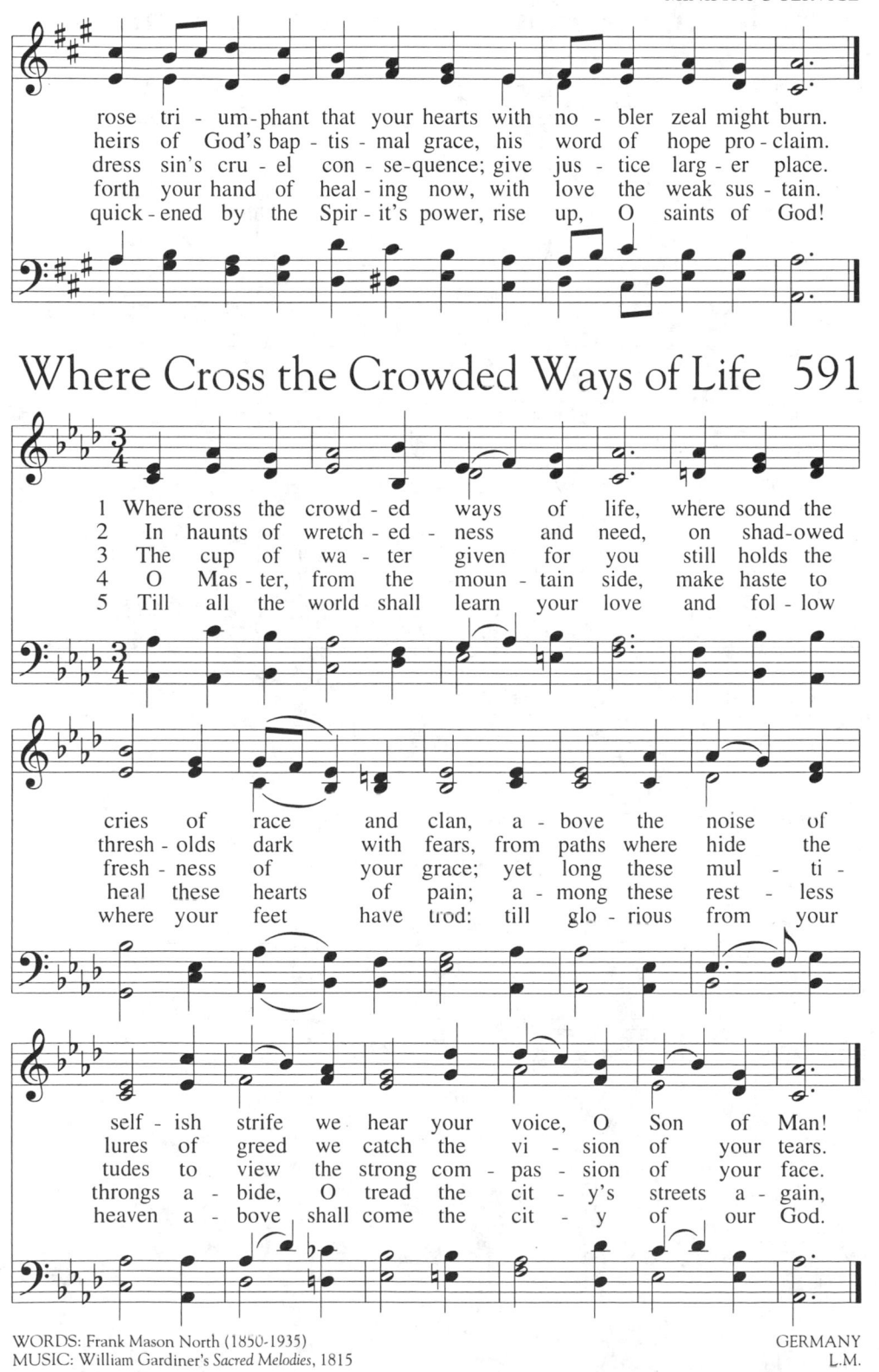

rose tri - um-phant that your hearts with no - bler zeal might burn.
heirs of God's bap - tis - mal grace, his word of hope pro - claim.
dress sin's cru - el con - se-quence; give jus - tice larg - er place.
forth your hand of heal - ing now, with love the weak sus - tain.
quick - ened by the Spir - it's power, rise up, O saints of God!

Where Cross the Crowded Ways of Life 591

1 Where cross the crowd - ed ways of life, where sound the
2 In haunts of wretch - ed - ness and need, on shad-owed
3 The cup of wa - ter given for you still holds the
4 O Mas - ter, from the moun - tain side, make haste to
5 Till all the world shall learn your love and fol - low

cries of race and clan, a - bove the noise of
thresh - olds dark with fears, from paths where hide the
fresh - ness of your grace; yet long these mul - ti -
heal these hearts of pain; a - mong these rest - less
where your feet have trod: till glo - rious from your

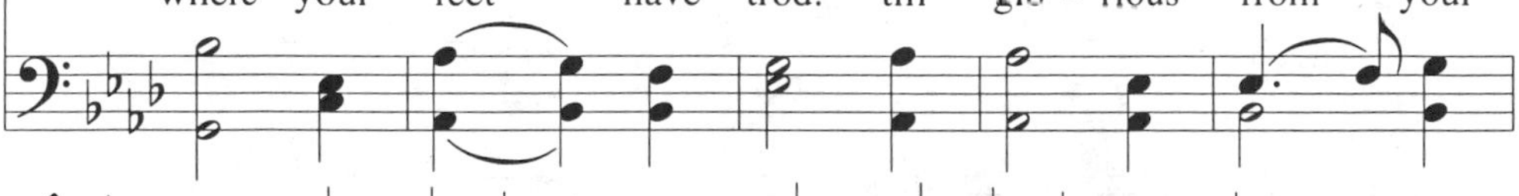

self - ish strife we hear your voice, O Son of Man!
lures of greed we catch the vi - sion of your tears.
tudes to view the strong com - pas - sion of your face.
throngs a - bide, O tread the cit - y's streets a - gain,
heaven a - bove shall come the cit - y of our God.

WORDS: Frank Mason North (1850-1935)
MUSIC: William Gardiner's *Sacred Melodies*, 1815

GERMANY
L.M.

592 Lord, You Give the Great Commission

1 Lord, you give the great com-mis-sion: "Heal the sick and
2 Lord, you call us to your ser-vice: "In my name bap-
3 Lord, you make the com - mon ho-ly: "This my bod - y,
4 Lord, you show us love's true meas-ure: "Fa - ther, what they
5 Lord, you bless with words as - sur-ing: "I am with you
preach the word." Lest the church ne - glect its mis-sion
tize and teach." That the world may trust your prom-ise,
this my blood." Let us all, for earth's true glo-ry,
do, for - give." Yet we hoard as pri - vate treas-ure
to the end." Faith and hope and love re - stor-ing,
and the gos - pel go un-heard, help us wit - ness
life a - bun - dant meant for each, give us all new
dai - ly lift life heav - en-ward, ask - ing that the
all that you so free - ly give. May your care and
may we serve as you in-tend, and, a - mid the
to your pur-pose with re - newed in-teg - ri - ty:
fer - vor, draw us clos - er in com-mu - ni - ty:
world a - round us share your chil-dren's lib - er - ty:
mer - cy lead us to a just so - ci - e - ty:
cares that claim us, hold in mind e - ter - ni - ty:

WORDS: Jeffery Rowthorn (1934-)
MUSIC: Cyril V. Taylor (1907-1991)

ABBOT'S LEIGH
8.7.8.7.D.

With the Spir-it's gifts em-power us for the work of min-is-try.

Lord, Speak to Me 593

1 Lord, speak to me, that I may speak in
2 O lead me, Lord, that I may lead the
3 O teach me, Lord, that I may teach the
4 O fill me with your full - ness, Lord, un -

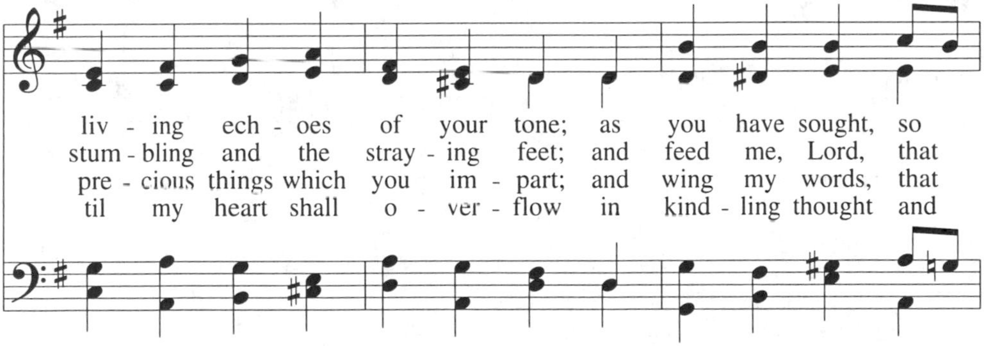
liv - ing ech - oes of your tone; as you have sought, so
stum - bling and the stray - ing feet; and feed me, Lord, that
pre - cious things which you im - part; and wing my words, that
til my heart shall o - ver - flow in kind - ling thought and

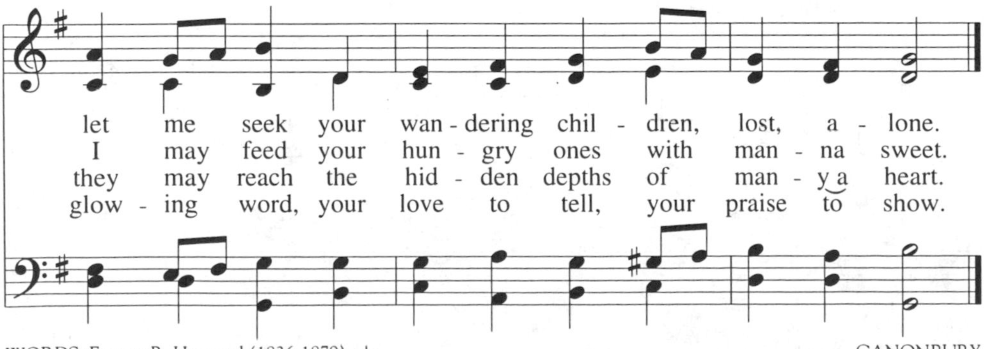
let me seek your wan - dering chil - dren, lost, a - lone.
I may feed your hun - gry ones with man - na sweet.
they may reach the hid - den depths of man - y a heart.
glow - ing word, your love to tell, your praise to show.

WORDS: Frances R. Havergal (1836-1879), alt.
MUSIC: Robert A. Schumann (1810-1856)

CANONBURY
L.M.

594 We Are Your People

1 We are your peo - ple, Spir - it of grace,
2 Joined in com - mu - ni - ty, treas - ured and fed,
3 Rich in di - ver - si - ty, help us to live
4 Glad of tra - di - tion, help us to see
5 Spir - it, u - nite us, make us, by grace,
you dare to make us to all our neigh - bors, Christ's liv - ing
may we dis - cov - er gifts in each oth - er, will - ing to
clos - er than neigh - bors, o - pen to strang - ers, a - ble to
in all life's chang - ing, where you are lead - ing, where our best
will - ing and read - y, Christ's liv - ing bod - y, lov - ing the
1–4
5
voice, hands and face.
lead and be led.
clash and for - give.
ef - forts should be.
whole hu - man race.

WORDS: Brian Wren (1936-)
MUSIC: John W. Wilson (1905-1992)

WHITFIELD
Irregular

They'll Know We Are Christians 595

Unison
1 We are one in the Spir - it; we are one in the Lord.
2 We will walk with each oth - er; we will walk hand in hand.
3 We will work with each oth - er; we will work side by side.
4 All praise to the Fa - ther, from whom all things come.
We are one in the Spir - it; we are one in the Lord.
We will walk with each oth - er; we will walk hand in hand.
We will work with each oth - er; we will work side by side.
And all praise to Christ Je - sus, his on - ly Son.
And we pray that all u - ni - ty may one day be re - stored.
And to - geth - er we'll spread the news that God is in our land.
And we'll guard each one's dig - ni - ty and save each one's pride.
And all praise to the Spir - it, who makes us one.
Refrain
And they'll know we are Chris-tians by our love, by our love.
Yes, they'll know we are Chris-tians by our love.

WORDS and MUSIC: Peter Scholtes (1938-); para. John 13:35

596 Help Us Accept Each Other

Unison
1 Help us ac - cept each oth - er as Christ ac - cept - ed us;
2 Teach us, O Lord, your les - sons, as in our dai - ly life
3 Let your ac - cept - ance change us, so that we may be moved
4 Lord, for to - day's en - coun - ters with all who are in need,
teach us as sis - ter, broth - er, each per - son to em - brace.
we strug - gle to be hu - man and search for hope and faith.
in liv - ing sit - u - a - tions to do the truth in love;
who hun - ger for ac - cep - tance, for right - eous - ness and bread,
Be pres - ent, Lord, a - mong us and bring us to be - lieve
Teach us to care for peo - ple, for all, not just for some,
to prac - tice your ac - cept - ance un - til we know by heart
we need new eyes for see - ing, new hands for hold - ing on:
we are our - selves ac - cept - ed, and meant to love and live.
to love them as we find them, or as they may be - come.
the ta - ble of for - give - ness, and laugh - ter's heal - ing art.
re - new us with your Spir - it; Lord, free us, make us one!

WORDS: Fred Kaan (1929-)
MUSIC: John Ness Beck (1930-1986)

BECK
7.6.7.6.D.

Here, O Lord, Your Servants Gather 597

Unison
1 Here, O Lord, your ser-vants gath-er, hand we link with hand;
2 Man-y are the tongues we speak, scat-tered are the lands,
3 Na-ture's se-crets o-pen wide, chang-es nev-er cease.
4 Grant, O God, an age re-newed, filled with death-less love;
look-ing toward our Sav-ior's cross, joined in love we stand.
yet our hearts are one in God, one in love's de-mands.
Where, O, where can wea-ry souls find the source of peace?
help us as we work and pray, send us from a-bove
As we seek the realm of God, we u-nite to pray:
E'en in dark-ness hope ap-pears, call-ing age and youth:
Un-to all those sore dis-tressed, torn by end-less strife:
truth and cour-age, faith and power, need-ed in our strife:
Je-sus, Sav-ior, guide our steps, for you are the Way.
Je-sus, teach-er, dwell with us, for you are the Truth.
Je-sus, heal-er, bring your balm, for you are the Life.
Je-sus, Mas-ter, be our Way, be our Truth, our Life.

WORDS: Tokuo Yamaguchi (20th c.); tr. Everett M. Stowe (20th c.)
MUSIC: Isao Koizumi (1907-1992)

TOKYO
7.5.7.5.D.

598 Glorious Things of Thee Are Spoken

1 Glo - rious things of thee are spo - ken, Zi - on, cit - y of our God;
2 See, the streams of liv - ing wa - ters, spring-ing from e - ter - nal love,
3 Round each hab - i - ta - tion hov-ering, see the cloud and fire ap - pear,
4 Sav - ior, since of Zi - on's cit - y I through grace a mem - ber am,
he whose Word can - not be bro - ken formed you for his own a - bode.
well sup - ply your sons and daugh-ters and all fear of want re - move.
for a glo - ry and a cov - ering, show - ing that the Lord is near!
let the world de - ride or pit - y, I will glo - ry in your name.
On the Rock of A - ges found - ed, what can shake your sure re - pose?
Who can faint while such a riv - er ev - er will their thirst as - suage?
Thus de - riv - ing from their ban - ner light by night and shade by day,
Fad - ing are the world's best plea - sures, all its bloat - ed pomp and show;
With sal - va - tion's walls sur - round - ed, you may smile at all your foes.
Grace, which like the Lord, the giv - er, nev - er fails from age to age.
safe they feed up - on the man - na which God gives them on their way.
sol - id joys and last - ing trea - sures none but Zi - on's chil - dren know.

WORDS: John Newton (1725-1807), alt.
MUSIC: Franz Joseph Haydn (1732-1809)

AUSTRIAN HYMN
8.7.8.7.D.

Shadow and Substance

Unison
1 Shad - ow and sub - stance, won - der and mys - ter - y,
2 We are your im - age, formed in com - mu - ni - ty;
3 Nam - ing the name - less Spir - it of u - ni - ty,
spell - bind - ing spin - ner of at - oms and earth;
sis - ters and broth - ers of Ad - am and Eve.
scan - ning the heav - ens for signs of your care;
soul of the cos - mos, per - son and en - er - gy,
You gave us col - or, cus - tom and his - to - ry;
God of the a - ges, give us hu - mil - i - ty;
source of our be - ing: we sing of your worth.
teach us to hon - or what oth - ers re - ceive.
guide us to mys - ti - cal un - ion in prayer.

WORDS and MUSIC: Daniel Charles Damon (1955-)

TWILIGHT
5.6.10.D.

600 In Christ There Is No East or West

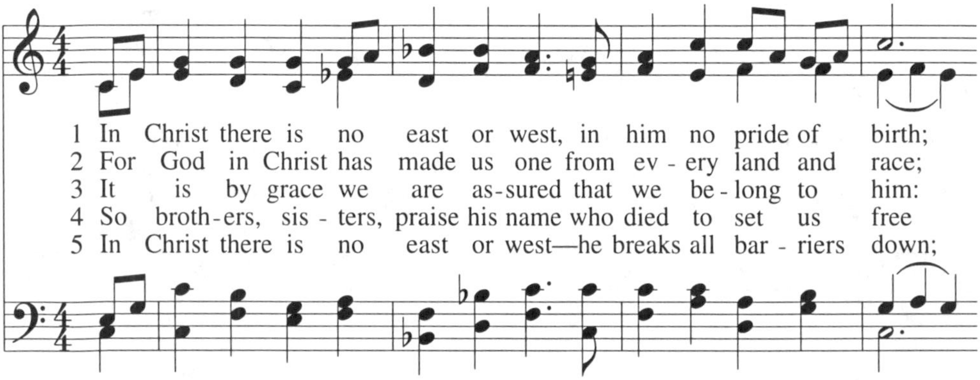
1 In Christ there is no east or west, in him no pride of birth;
2 For God in Christ has made us one from ev - ery land and race;
3 It is by grace we are as-sured that we be - long to him:
4 So broth-ers, sis - ters, praise his name who died to set us free
5 In Christ there is no east or west—he breaks all bar - riers down;

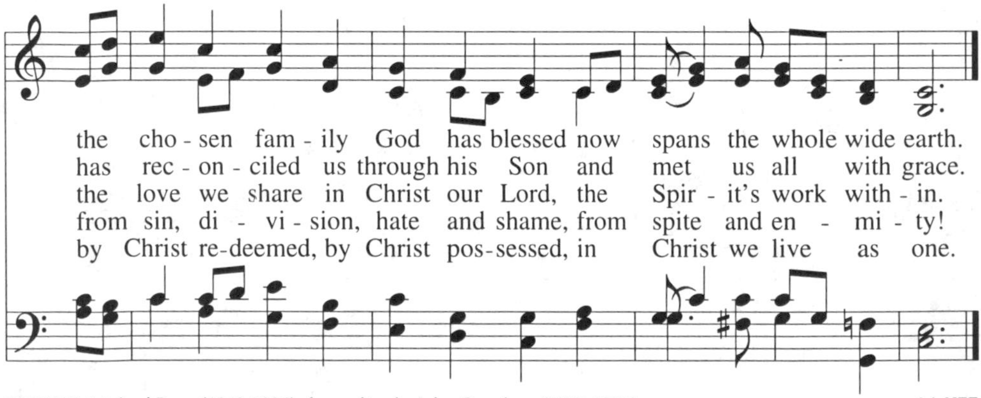
the cho - sen fam - ily God has blessed now spans the whole wide earth.
has rec - on - ciled us through his Son and met us all with grace.
the love we share in Christ our Lord, the Spir - it's work with - in.
from sin, di - vi - sion, hate and shame, from spite and en - mi - ty!
by Christ re-deemed, by Christ pos-sessed, in Christ we live as one.

WORDS: Michael Perry (1942-1996); from a line by John Oxenham (1852-1941) — McKEE
MUSIC: African-American melody; arr. Harry T. Burleigh (1866-1949) — C.M.

601 Dear Christ, Uplifted from the Earth

1 Dear Christ, uplifted from the earth,
your arms stretched out above
through every culture, every birth,
to draw an answering love.

2 Still east and west your love extends
and always, near and far,
you call and claim us as your friends
and love us as we are.

3 Where age and gender, class and race,
divide us to our shame,
you see a person and a face,
a neighbor with a name.

4 May we, accepted as we are,
yet called in grace to grow,
reach out to others, near and far,
your healing love to show.

Brian Wren (1936-)

Suggested tune:
McKEE, no. 600

Who Is My Mother, Who Is My Brother? 602

Unison
1 Who is my moth - er, who is my broth - er?
2 Dif - ferent - ly a - bled, dif - ferent - ly la - beled
3 Love will re - late us— col - or or sta - tus
4 Bound by one vis - ion, met for one mis - sion
All those who gath - er round Je - sus Christ:
wid - en the cir - cle round Je - sus Christ,
can't seg - re - gate us, round Je - sus Christ:
we claim each oth - er, round Je - sus Christ:
Spir - it - blown peo - ple born from the gos - pel
crutch - es and stig - mas, cul - tures' en - ig - mas
fam - i - ly fail - ings, hu - man de - rail - ings—
here is my moth - er, here is my broth - er,
sit at the ta - ble, round Je - sus Christ.
all come to - geth - er round Je - sus Christ.
all are ac - cept - ed, round Je - sus Christ.
kin - dred in Spir - it, through Je - sus Christ.

WORDS: Shirley Erena Murray (1931-)
MUSIC: Jack Schrader (1942-)

KINDRED
5.5.9.5.5.9.

603 In Christ There Is No East or West

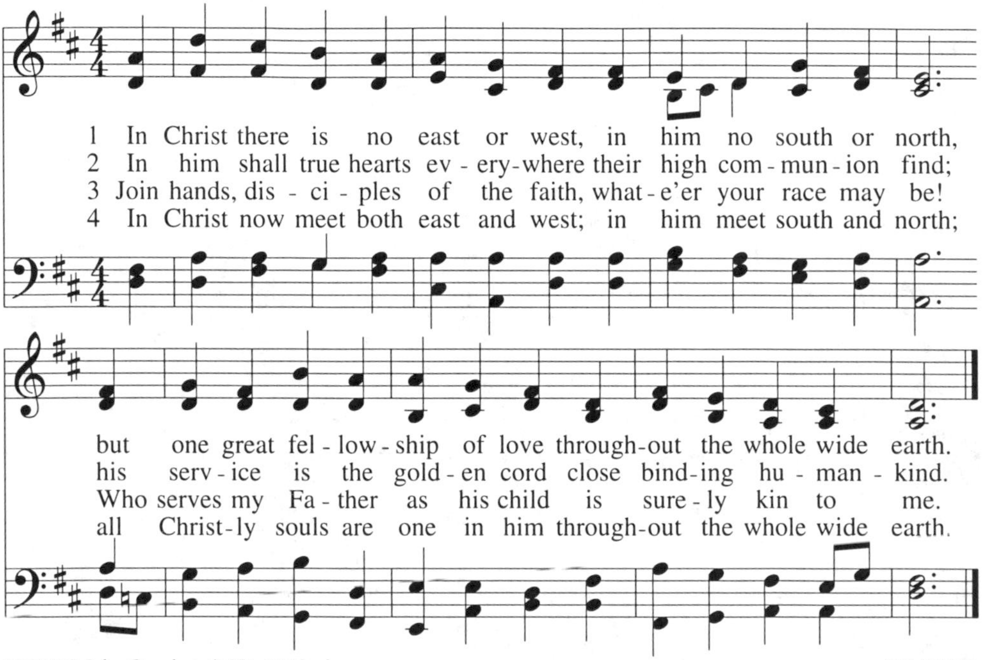
1 In Christ there is no east or west, in him no south or north,
2 In him shall true hearts ev - ery-where their high com - mun - ion find;
3 Join hands, dis - ci - ples of the faith, what - e'er your race may be!
4 In Christ now meet both east and west; in him meet south and north;
but one great fel - low - ship of love through-out the whole wide earth.
his serv - ice is the gold - en cord close bind-ing hu - man - kind.
Who serves my Fa - ther as his child is sure - ly kin to me.
all Christ - ly souls are one in him through-out the whole wide earth.

WORDS: John Oxenham (1852-1941), alt.
MUSIC: Alexander R. Reinagle (1799-1877)

ST. PETER
C.M.

604 Great God, as We Are Gathering

Unison
1 Great God, as we are gath - er - ing, you watch your peo - ple come;
2 Great God, with - in this gath - er - ing, quell en - mi - ty and fear,
3 Great God of man - y gath - er - ings, you make your peo - ple one;
4 Great God, as from this gath - er - ing we go our sep-arate ways,
as yet, we're walk - ing out of step, help us to walk as one.
bring hon - es - ty and o - pen-ness, make un - der - stand-ing clear.
from dif - ferent back-grounds, ways and lives, our jour-neys have be - gun.
we're joined by you, we go as one, to trav - el all our days.

WORDS: Andrew Pratt (1948-)
MUSIC: *Kentucky Harmony*, 1813

MORNING SONG
C.M.

The Family Prayer Song

605

Unison
Ab2
Db/Ab
Ab
Come and fill our homes with your pres - ence; you a - lone are
Eb/G
Eb
Db/F
Eb
Ab
Db
wor - thy of our rev - erence. As for me and my house,
Eb
Ab
Db/F
Eb
Ab
Db
we will serve the Lord. As for me and my house,
Eb
Ab
Db/F
Eb
Ab
Db
we will serve the Lord. As for me and my house,
Eb
Edim7
Fm
F7
Bbm
Eb
Db/Eb
Db/Ab
Ab
we will serve the Lord; we will serve the Lord.

WORDS and MUSIC: Morris Chapman (1938-)

606 As Your Family, Lord, Meet Us Here

1 As your fam - ily, Lord, meet us here, as your fam - ily, Lord, meet us
2 At your ta - ble, Lord, we are fed, at your ta - ble, Lord, we are
3 Fill our spir - its, Lord, with your love, fill our spir - its, Lord, with your
4 Make us faith - ful, Lord, to your will, make us faith - ful, Lord, to your
5 As your fam - ily, Lord, meet us here, as your fam - ily, Lord, meet us

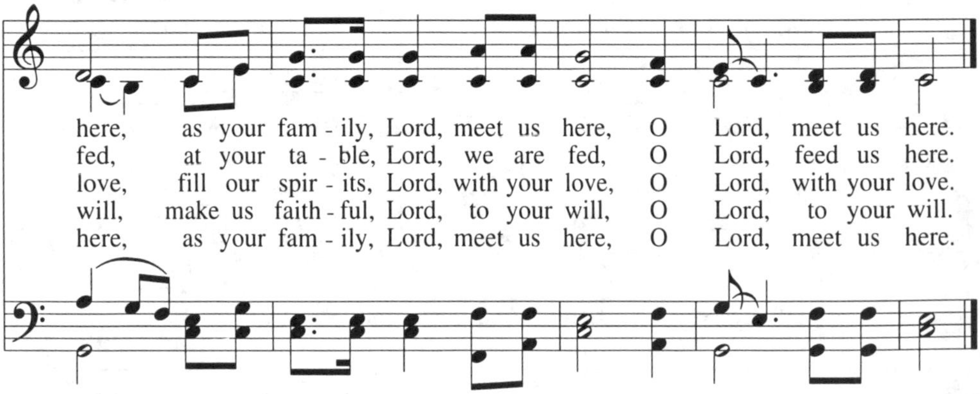
here, as your fam - ily, Lord, meet us here, O Lord, meet us here.
fed, at your ta - ble, Lord, we are fed, O Lord, feed us here.
love, fill our spir - its, Lord, with your love, O Lord, with your love.
will, make us faith - ful, Lord, to your will, O Lord, to your will.
here, as your fam - ily, Lord, meet us here, O Lord, meet us here.

WORDS: Anonymous
MUSIC: African-American spiritual

KUM BA YAH
8.8.8.5.

607 Happy the Home When God Is There

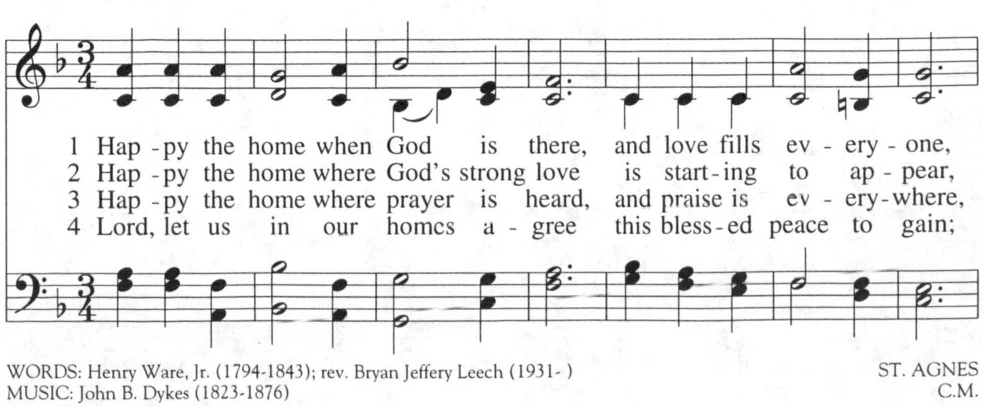
1 Hap - py the home when God is there, and love fills ev - ery - one,
2 Hap - py the home where God's strong love is start - ing to ap - pear,
3 Hap - py the home where prayer is heard, and praise is ev - ery - where,
4 Lord, let us in our homes a - gree this bless - ed peace to gain;

WORDS: Henry Ware, Jr. (1794-1843); rev. Bryan Jeffery Leech (1931-)
MUSIC: John B. Dykes (1823-1876)

ST. AGNES
C.M.

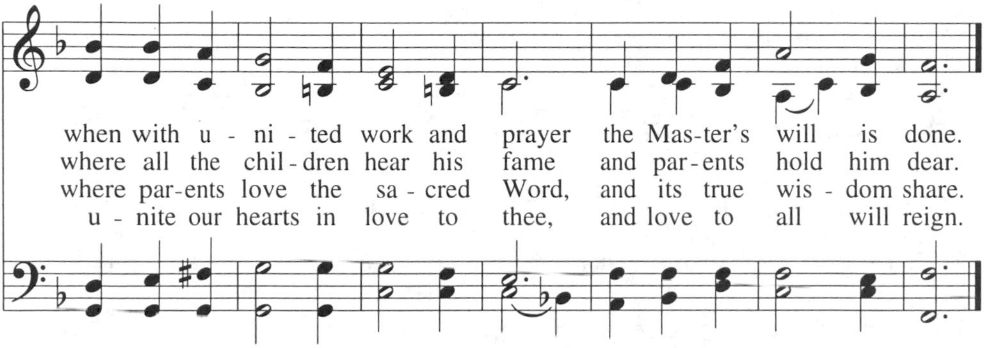
when with u - ni - ted work and prayer the Mas-ter's will is done.
where all the chil - dren hear his fame and par - ents hold him dear.
where par-ents love the sa - cred Word, and its true wis - dom share.
u - nite our hearts in love to thee, and love to all will reign.

Lord of Our Growing Years 608

1 Lord of our grow - ing years, with us from in - fan - cy,
2 Lord of our strong-est years, stretch - ing our youth - ful powers,
3 Lord of our mid - dle years, giv - er of stead-fast - ness,
4 Lord of our old - er years, steep though the road may be,
5 Lord of our clos - ing years, al - ways your prom - ise stands;
laugh - ter and quick - dried tears, fresh-ness and en - er - gy:
lov - ers and pi - o - neers when all the world seems ours:
cour - age that per - se - veres when there is small suc - cess:
rid us of fool - ish fears, bring us se - ren - i - ty:
hold us when death ap - pears, safe - ly with - in your hands:
Refrain
Your grace sur-rounds us all our days—for all your gifts we bring our praise.

WORDS: David Mowbray (1938-)
MUSIC: James V. Lee (1892-1959)

EASTVIEW
6.6.6.6.Ref.

609 Come to a Wedding

Unison
1 Come to a wed - ding, come to a bless - ing,
come on a day when hap - pi - ness sings!
Come rain or sun, come win - ter or sum - mer,
cel - e - brate love and all that it brings.
2 Thanks for the love that holds us to - geth - er—
par - ent and child, and lov - er and friend:
thanks to the God whose love is our cen - ter,
source of com - pas - sion, know-ing no end.
3 Love is the gift, and love is the giv - er,
love is the gold that makes the day shine,
love for - gets self to care for the oth - er,
love chang-es life from wa - ter to wine.
4 Come to this wed - ding, ask - ing a bless - ing
for all the years that liv - ing will prove:
health of the bod - y, health of the spir - it—
now to you both we of - fer our love.

WORDS: Shirley Erena Murray (1931-)
MUSIC: Gaelic melody; arr. Jack Schrader (1942-)

BUNESSAN
5.5.5.4.D.

O Perfect Love

1 O per - fect Love, all hu - man thought tran - scend - ing,
2 O per - fect Life, be now their full as - sur - ance
3 Grant them the joy which bright - ens earth - ly sor - row;
low - ly we kneel in prayer be - fore your throne,
of ten - der char - i - ty and stead - fast faith,
grant them the peace which calms all earth - ly strife,
that theirs may be the love which knows no end - ing,
of pa - tient hope and qui - et, brave en - dur - ance,
and to life's day the glo - rious un - known mor - row
whom you for - ev - er - more u - nite in one.
with child - like trust that fears no pain or death.
that dawns up - on e - ter - nal love and life.

WORDS: Dorothy F. Gurney (1858-1932), alt.
MUSIC: Joseph Barnby (1838-1896)

O PERFECT LOVE
11.10.11.10.

611 As Man and Woman We Were Made

Unison
1 As man and wom - an we were made that love be found and
2 Now Je - sus lived and gave his love to make our life and
3 And Je - sus died to live a - gain, so praise the love that,
4 Then spread the ta - ble, clear the hall, and cel - e - brate till
life be - gun, so praise the Lord who made us two, and
lov - ing new; so cel - e - brate with him to - day and
come what may, can bring the dawn and clear the skies, and
day is done; let peace go deep be - tween us all and
praise the Lord when two are one: praise for the love that
drink the joy he of - fers you, that makes the sim - ple
waits to wipe all tears a - way; and let us hope for
joy be shared by ev - ery - one; laugh and make mer - ry
comes to life through child or par - ent, hus - band, wife.
mo - ment shine and chang - es wa - ter in - to wine.
what shall be, be - liev - ing where we can - not see.
with your friends, and praise the love that nev - er ends.

WORDS: Brian Wren (1936-)
MUSIC: English carol; arr. Ralph Vaughan Williams (1872-1958)

SUSSEX CAROL
8.8.8.8.8.8.

When Love Is Found

1 When love is found and hope comes home, sing and be glad that two are one. When love explodes and fills the sky, praise God and share our Maker's joy.
2 When love has flowered in trust and care, build both each day, that love may dare to reach beyond home's warmth and light, to serve and strive for truth and right.
3 When love is tried as loved ones change, hold still to hope though all seems strange, till ease returns, and love grows wise through listening ears and opened eyes.
4 When love is torn and trust betrayed, pray strength to love till torments fade, till lovers keep no score of wrong, but hear through pain love's Easter song.
5 Praise God for love, praise God for life, in age or youth, in calm or strife. Lift up your hearts, let love be fed through death and life in broken bread.

WORDS: Brian Wren (1936-)
MUSIC: English melody; adapt. Hal H. Hopson (1933-)

GIFT OF LOVE
L.M.

613 Your Love, O God, Has Called Us

1 Your love, O God, has called us here, for all love finds its source in you,
2 O gra-cious God, you con - se - crate all that is love - ly, good, and true.
3 O God of love, in - spire our life, re-veal your will in all we do.
the per - fect love that casts out fear, the love that Christ makes ev - er new.
Bless those who in your pres-ence wait and ev - ery day their love re - new.
Join ev - ery hus-band, ev - ery wife in mu-tual love and love for you.

WORDS: Russell Schulz-Widmar (1944-)
MUSIC: Henry W. Baker (1821-1877)

QUEBEC
8.8.8.8.

614 Let There Be Peace on Earth

Let there be peace on earth, and let it be - gin with me;
let there be peace on earth, the peace that was meant to be.

WORDS: Sy Miller (1908-1971) and Jill Jackson (1913-1995), alt.
MUSIC: Sy Miller (1908-1971) and Jill Jackson (1913-1995); harm. Charles H. Webb (1933-)

With God our cre - a - tor, chil - dren all are we.
Let us walk with each oth - er in per - fect har - mo - ny.
Let peace be - gin with me; let this be the mo - ment now.
With ev - ery step I take, let this be my sol - emn vow:
to take each mo - ment and live each mo - ment in peace e - ter - nal - ly.
Let there be peace on earth, and let it be - gin with me.

615 Community of Christ

1 Com - mu - ni - ty of Christ, who make the cross your own,
2 Com - mu - ni - ty of Christ, look past the church - 's door
3 Com - mu - ni - ty of Christ, through whom the word must sound—
4 When men - ace melts a - way, so shall God's will be done,
live out your creed and risk your life for God a - lone:
and see the ref - u - gee, the hun - gry, and the poor.
cry out for jus - tice and for peace the whole world round:
the cli - mate of the world be peace and Christ its sun;
the God who wears your face, to whom all worlds be - long,
Take hands with the op - pressed, the job - less in your street,
dis - arm the powers that war and all that can de - stroy,
our cur - ren - cy be love and kind - li - ness our law,
whose chil - dren are of ev - ery race and ev - ery song.
take towel and wa - ter, that you wash your neigh - bor's feet.
turn bombs to bread, and tears of an - guish in - to joy.
our food and faith be shared as one for ev - er - more.

WORDS: Shirley Erena Murray (1931-)
MUSIC: Hebrew melody; arr. Meyer Lyon (1751-1797)

LEONI
6.6.8.4.D.

We Meet You, O Christ

Unison
1 We meet you, O Christ, in man - y a guise;
2 In mil - lions a - live, a - way and a - broad,
3 We hear you, O Man,* in ag - o - ny cry;
4 You choose to be made at one with the earth;
your im - age we see in sim - ple and wise.
in - volved in our life, you live down the road.
for free - dom you march, in ri - ots you die.
the dark of the grave pre - pares for your birth.
You live in a pal - ace, ex - ist in a shack.
Im - pris - oned in sys - tems, you long to be free.
Your face in the pa - pers we read and we see.
Your death is your ris - ing, cre - a - tive your word:
We see you, the gar - dener, a tree on your back.
We wit - ness you, Je - sus, still bear - ing your tree.
The tree must be plant - ed by hu - man de - cree.
the tree springs to life and our hope is re - stored!

*or Christ

WORDS: Fred Kaan (1929-)
MUSIC: Carl F. Schalk (1929-)

STANLEY BEACH
10.10.11.11.

617 A Place at the Table

1 For ev - ery - one born, a place at the ta - ble, for
2 For wo - man and man, a place at the ta - ble, re -
3 For young and for old, a place at the ta - ble, a
4 For just and un - just, a place at the ta - ble, a -
5 For ev - ery - one born, a place at the ta - ble, to
ev - ery - one born, clean wa - ter and bread, a
vis - ing the roles, de - cid - ing the share, with
voice to be heard, a part in the song, the
bus - er, a - bused, with need to for - give, in
live with - out fear, and sim - ply to be, to
shel - ter, a space, a safe place for grow - ing, for
wis - dom and grace, di - vid - ing the pow - er, for
hands of a child in hands that are wrink - led, for
an - ger, in hurt, a mind - set of mer - cy, for
work, to speak out, to wit - ness and wor - ship, for

WORDS: Shirley Erena Murray (1931-)
MUSIC: Jane Marshall (1924-)

TABLESONG
11.10.11.10.Ref.

Refrain
ev - ery - one born, a star o - ver - head,
wo - man and man, a sys - tem that's fair,
young and for old, the right to be - long, and God will de - light when
just and un - just, a new way to live,
ev - ery - one born, the right to be free,
we are cre - a - tors of jus - tice and joy, com - pas - sion and peace: yes,
God will de - light when we are cre - a - tors of jus - tice, jus - tice and joy!

618 Go Down, Moses

Unison
Parts
1 When Is - rael was in E-gypt's land, Let my peo-ple go;
2 The Lord told Mo - ses what to do, Let my peo-ple go;
3 They jour-neyed on at his com-mand, Let my peo-ple go;
4 Oh, let us all from bond-age flee, Let my peo-ple go;
Unison
Parts
op-pressed so hard they could not stand, Let my peo-ple go.
to lead the He-brew chil-dren through, Let my peo-ple go.
and came at length to Ca-naan's land, Let my peo-ple go.
and let us all in Christ be free, Let my peo-ple go.
Refrain
Go down, Mo - ses, way down in E-gypt's land;
(go down)
tell old Phar - aoh: Let my peo - ple go!

WORDS and MUSIC: African-American spiritual

GO DOWN, MOSES
Irregular

Because He Died and Is Risen 619

Unison
Dm A Dm
1 Be-cause he died and is ris-en, be-cause he
(2) stroys walls be-tween us, his peace de-
(3) give you," said Je-sus, "my peace I
(4) yond un-der-stand-ing, the peace be-
D7 Gm A/E
died and is ris-en, be-cause he died
stroys walls be-tween us, his peace de-stroys
give you," said Je-sus, "my peace I give
yond un-der-stand-ing, the peace be-yond
A/C# Dm B♭7 F Gm7
and is ris-en, we now have peace with God through
walls be-tween us, for on-ly he can rec-on-
you," said Je-sus, "don't let your heart be trou-bled;
un-der-stand-ing will guard the hearts and minds of
1–3 A Gm/B♭ A N.C.
Je-sus Christ our Lord. 2 His peace de-
cile us both to God. 3 "My peace I
do not be a-fraid." 4 The peace be-
4 A7 Dm
those who pray.

WORDS: Michael Baughen (1930-)
MUSIC: Israeli melody; arr. Michael Baughen (1930-)

ISRAELI
8.8.8.12.

620 O Lord, You Gave Your Servant John

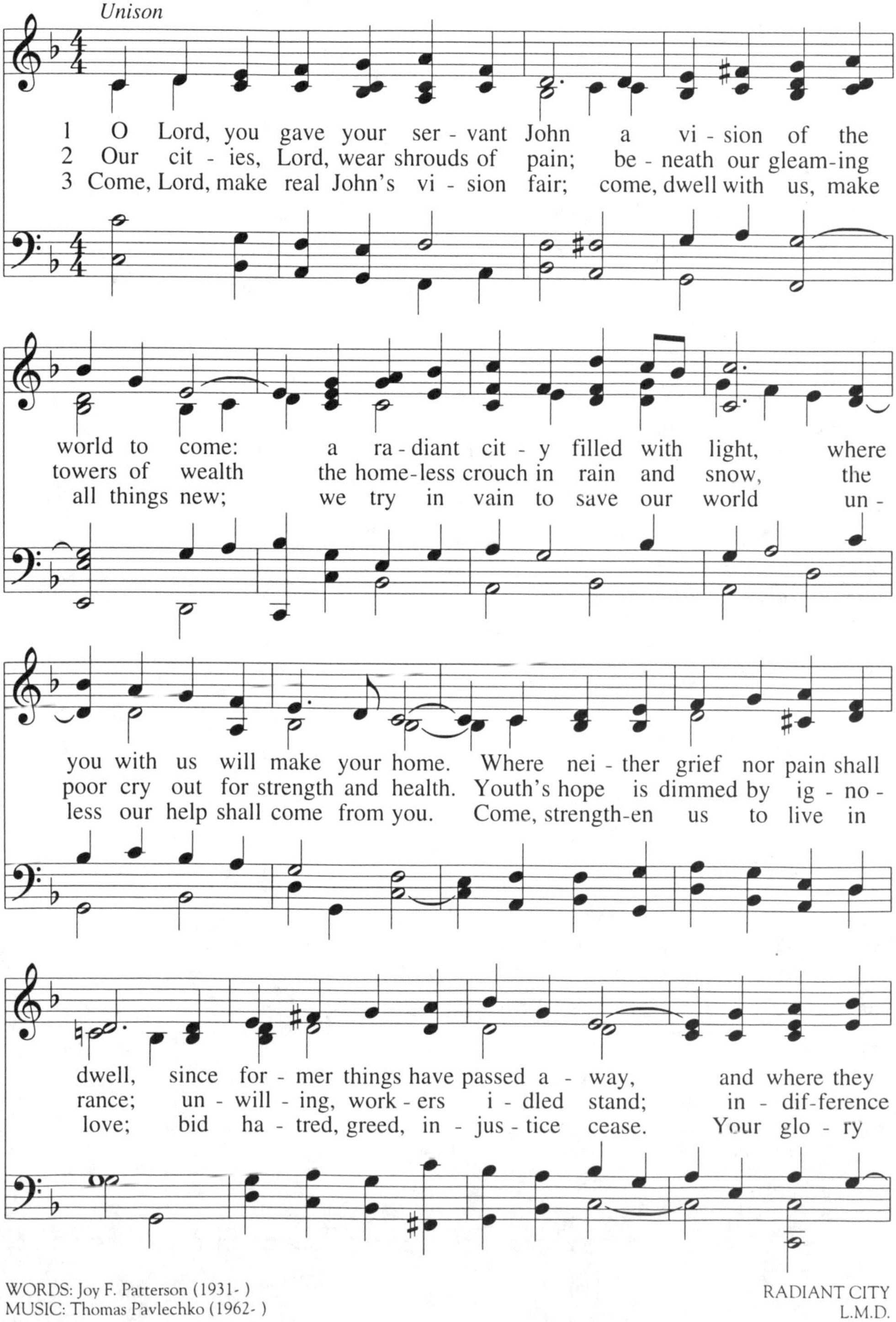
Unison
1 O Lord, you gave your ser - vant John a vi - sion of the world to come: a ra - diant cit - y filled with light, where you with us will make your home. Where nei - ther grief nor pain shall dwell, since for - mer things have passed a - way, and where they
2 Our cit - ies, Lord, wear shrouds of pain; be - neath our gleam-ing towers of wealth the home-less crouch in rain and snow, the poor cry out for strength and health. Youth's hope is dimmed by ig - no - rance; un - will - ing, work - ers i - dled stand; in - dif-ference
3 Come, Lord, make real John's vi - sion fair; come, dwell with us, make all things new; we try in vain to save our world un - less our help shall come from you. Come, strength-en us to live in love; bid ha - tred, greed, in - jus - tice cease. Your glo - ry

WORDS: Joy F. Patterson (1931-)
MUSIC: Thomas Pavlechko (1962-)

RADIANT CITY
L.M.D.

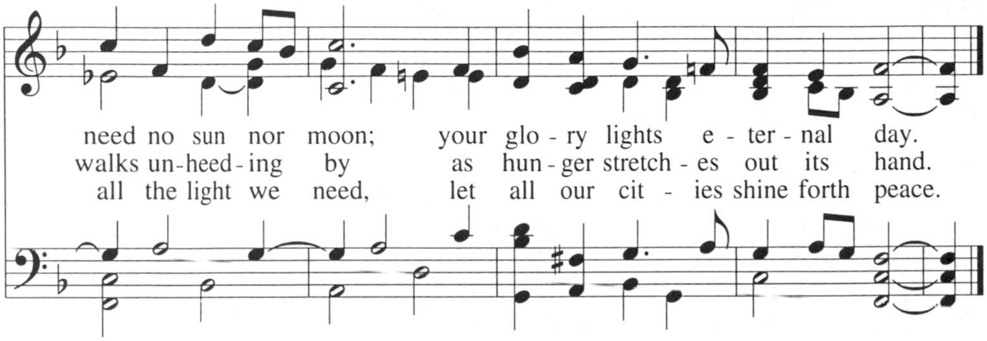
need no sun nor moon; your glo - ry lights e - ter - nal day.
walks un-heed - ing by as hun - ger stretch - es out its hand.
all the light we need, let all our cit - ies shine forth peace.

For the Healing of the Nations 621

1 For the heal - ing of the na - tions, Lord, we pray with one ac - cord,
2 Lead your peo - ple in - to free-dom, from de - spair your world re - lease,
3 All that kills a - bun - dant liv - ing, let it from the earth be banned:
4 You, Cre - a - tor - God, have writ - ten your great name on hu - man-kind;
for a just and e - qual shar ing of the things that earth af - fords.
that, re-deemed from war and ha - tred, all may come and go in peace.
pride of sta - tus, race, or school-ing, dog - mas that ob - scure your plan.
for our grow - ing in your like-ness, bring the life of Christ to mind;
To a life of love in ac - tion help us rise and pledge our word.
Show us how, through care and good-ness, fear will die and hope in - crease.
In our com - mon quest for jus - tice may we hal - low life's brief span.
that by our re - sponse and serv - ice earth its des - ti - ny may find.

WORDS: Fred Kaan (1929-)
MUSIC: Henry T. Smart (1813-1879)

REGENT SQUARE
8.7.8.7.8.7.

622 When Will People Cease Their Fighting?

1 When will peo - ple cease their fight - ing? When will ar - mies
2 Floods and earth-quakes, drought and fam - ine plague the world with
3 As we strive for peace with vig - or, hop - ing to be
wage no war, na - tions con - quer not their neigh - bor,
awe - some ill, but far great - er is war's hor - ror
shown the way, we are strength-ened in the knowl - edge
weap - ons i - dle, used no more? When will guns and bombs be
caused by hu - man, stub - born will. Blest are those who, work - ing,
of a fu - ture, per - fect day; for we know that deep - er,
si - lent? When will cap - tives be set free? All cre -
pray - ing, pur - pose in their hearts to be in - stru -
rich - er peace is ours when Christ shall reign: then will

WORDS: Constance Cherry (1953-)
MUSIC: C. Hubert H. Parry (1848-1918)

RUSTINGTON
8.7.8.7.D.

a - tion groans in long - ing for the world's true lib - er - ty.
ments of peace, com - mit - ted to the na - tions' har - mo - ny.
all our swords be plow-shares and God's chil - dren free from pain.

The Church of Christ in Every Age 623

1 The church of Christ in ev - ery age, be - set by change but Spir - it - led, must claim and test its her - i - tage and keep on ris - ing from the dead.
2 A - cross the world, a - cross the street, the vic - tims of in - jus - tice cry for shel - ter and for bread to eat, and nev - er live un - til they die.
3 Then let the ser - vant church a - rise, a car - ing church that longs to be a part - ner in Christ's sac - ri - fice, and clothed in Christ's hu - man - i - ty.
4 For Christ a - lone, whose blood was shed, can cure the fe - ver in our blood, and teach us how to share our bread and feed the starv - ing mul - ti - tude.
5 We have no mis - sion but to serve in full o - be - dience to our Lord: to care for all, with - out re - serve, and spread Christ's lib - er - at - ing word.

WORDS: Fred Pratt Green (1903-2000)
MUSIC: William Knapp (1698-1768)

WAREHAM
L.M.

624 When the Poor Ones

Cuando el Pobre

Unison
Dm A7 B♭
1 When the poor ones who have noth-ing share with strang-ers,
2 When at last all those who suf - fer find their com - fort,
1 Cuan-do el po - bre na - da tie - ne y aun re - par - te,
2 Cuan - do su - fre un hom-bre y lo - gra su con - sue - lo,
D7 Gm C7 F
when the thirst-y wa-ter give un - to us all,
when they hope though e - ven hope seems hope-less-ness,
cuan-do el hom - bre pa - sa sed y a - gua nos da,
cuan-do es-pe - ra y no se can - sa de es-pe - rar,
F E7 A7 Dm
when the wound-ed in their weak-ness strength-en oth - ers,
when we love though hate at times seems all a-round us,
cuan-do el dé - bil a su her-ma - no for - ta - le - ce,
cuan-do a-ma - mos, aun-que el o - dio nos ro - de - e,
Refrain B♭ A7 Dm
then we know that God still goes that road with us,
va Dios mis - mo en nues-tro mis - mo ca - mi - nar,

WORDS: J. A. Olivar (20th c.) and Miguel Manzano (20th c.); tr. George Lockwood (1946-), alt.
MUSIC: J. A. Olivar (20th c.) and Miguel Manzano (20th c.); arr. Alvin Schutmaat (1921-1988)

EL CAMINO
12.11.12.Ref.

D7 Gm Dm A7 Dm Gm Dm
then we know that God still goes that road with us.
va Dios mis - mo en nues-tro mis - mo ca - mi - nar.

3 When our joy fills up
our cup to overflowing,
when our lips can speak
no words other than true,
when we know that love
for simple things is better,
Refrain

4 When our homes are filled
with goodness in abundance,
when we learn how to make
peace instead of war,
when each stranger that we meet
is called a neighbor,
Refrain

3 Cuando crece la alegría y
nos inunda,
cuando dicen nuestros
labios la verdad,
cuando amamos
el sentir de los sencillos,
Estribillo

4 Cuando abunda el bien
y llena los hogares,
cuando un hombre donde hay
guerra pone paz,
cuando "hermano"
e llamamos al extraño,
Estribillo

All Who Love and Serve Your City 625

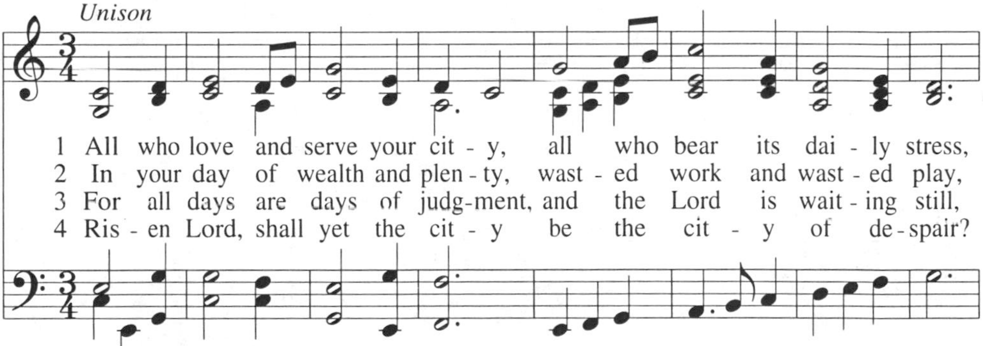
Unison
1 All who love and serve your cit - y, all who bear its dai - ly stress,
2 In your day of wealth and plen - ty, wast - ed work and wast - ed play,
3 For all days are days of judg-ment, and the Lord is wait - ing still,
4 Ris - en Lord, shall yet the cit - y be the cit - y of de - spair?

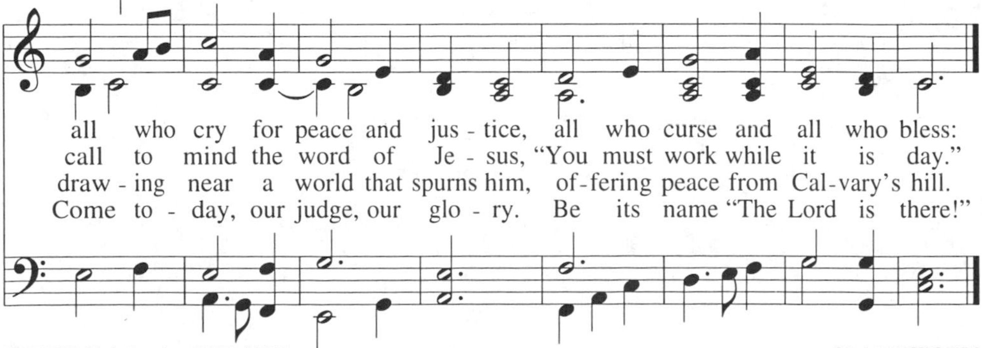
all who cry for peace and jus - tice, all who curse and all who bless:
call to mind the word of Je - sus, "You must work while it is day."
draw - ing near a world that spurns him, of - fering peace from Cal - vary's hill.
Come to - day, our judge, our glo - ry. Be its name "The Lord is there!"

WORDS: Erik Routley (1917-1982)
MUSIC: *The United States Sacred Harmony*, 1799; harm. Carlton R. Young (1926-)

CHARLESTOWN
8.7.8.7.

626 O God of Every Nation

1 O God of ev - ery na - tion, of ev - ery race and land,
2 From search for wealth and pow - er and scorn of truth and right,
3 Keep bright in us the vi - sion of days when war shall cease,
re - deem your whole cre - a - tion with your al - might - y hand;
from trust in bombs that show - er de - struc - tion through the night,
when ha - tred and di - vi - sion give way to love and peace,
where hate and fear di - vide us, and bit - ter threats are hurled,
from pride of race and sta - tion and blind-ness to your way,
till dawns the morn - ing glo - rious when truth and jus - tice reign,
in love and mer - cy guide us, and heal our strife - torn world.
de - liv - er ev - ery na - tion, e - ter - nal God, we pray.
and Christ shall rule vic - to - rious o'er all the world's do - main.

WORDS: William W. Reid, Jr. (1923-)
MUSIC: Welsh melody; harm. David Evans (1874-1948)

LLANGLOFFAN
7.6.7.6.D.

Now It Is Evening

Unison
G D/F# C/G G
1 Now it is eve - ning: lights of the cit - y
2 Now it is eve - ning: lit - tle ones sleep - ing
3 Now it is eve - ning: food on the ta - ble
4 Now it is eve - ning: here in our meet - ing
Am7 G/B C Dsus D
bid us re - mem - ber Christ is our light.
bid us re - mem - ber Christ is our peace.
bids us re - mem - ber Christ is our life.
may we re - mem - ber Christ is our friend.
Bm Em Am Dsus D
Man - y are lone - ly, who will be neigh - bor?
Some are ne - glect - ed, who will be neigh - bor?
Man - y are hun - gry, who will be neigh - bor?
Some may be strang - ers, who will be neigh - bor?
Am7 G/B C D G
Where there is car - ing, Christ is our light.
Where there is car - ing, Christ is our peace.
Where there is shar - ing, Christ is our life.
Where there's a wel - come, Christ is our friend.

WORDS: Fred Pratt Green (1903-2000)
MUSIC: David Haas (1957-)

EVENING HYMN
5.5.5.4.D.

628 We Cannot Measure How You Heal

F F/A Gm7 C Am7 Dm7 Gm7 C7
1 We can - not meas - ure how you heal or
2 The pain that will not go a - way, the
3 So some have come who need your help and
F F/A B♭ F/A Gm7 C C7
an - swer ev - ery suf - ferer's prayer, yet
guilt that clings from things long past, the
some have come to make a - mends, as
F F/A Gm7 C Am7 Dm7 Gm7 C7
we be - lieve your grace re - sponds where
fear of what the fu - ture holds, are
hands which shaped and saved the world are
F F/A B♭ F/A Gm7 F
faith and doubt u - nite to care. Your
pres - ent as if meant to last. But
pres - ent in the touch of friends. Lord,

WORDS: John L. Bell (1949-)
MUSIC: Scottish melody; arr. John L. Bell (1949-)

YE BANKS AND BRAES
8.8.8.8.D.

Am7 Dm7 Dm Gm7 C7 B♭/C
hands, though blood - ied on the cross, sur -
pres - ent too is love which tends the
let your Spir - it meet us here to
F Am7 B♭ Gm7 C7sus C7
vive to hold and heal and warn, to
hurt we nev - er hoped to find, the
mend the bod - y, mind, and soul, to
F Cm/E♭ D7 Gm C7
car - ry all through death to life and
pri - vate ag - o - nies in - side, the
dis - en - tan - gle peace from pain, and
F Dm B♭ F/A Gm7 F
cra - dle chil - dren yet un - born.
mem - o - ries that haunt the mind.
make your bro - ken peo - ple whole.

629 Strong, Gentle Children

Unison
G C/G G C/G
1 Strong, gen - tle chil - dren, God made you beau - ti - ful,
2 Strong, hurt - ing chil - dren, an - gry and ter - ri - fied,
3 Strong, know - ing chil - dren, ut - ter your cry a - loud,
Bm Em7 Am7 D
gave you the wis - dom and pow - er you need;
o - pen the se - crets your life has con - cealed;
hon - or the wis - dom God gave you at birth;
G C/G G C/G
speak in the still - ness all you are long - ing for;
though you are wound - ed, know you are not to blame;
speak to your el - ders till they have heard your voice;
Bm7 Em7 Am7 D7 G
live out your call - ing to love and to lead.
cry out your sto - ry till truth is re - vealed.
sing out your vi - sion of heal - ing on earth.

WORDS and MUSIC: Daniel Charles Damon (1955-)

TWILIGHT
5.6.10.D

Healer of Our Every Ill 630

Refrain (Unison)
D Em7/D D G/D A7/D D Bm A Bm/A G A
Heal-er of our ev-ery ill, light of each to-mor-row,
F#m Em/B Bm Em7 F#7 G D/F# Em D A/C# A7 D
give us peace be-yond our fear, and hope be-yond our sor-row.
Bm F#m/A G
1 You who know our fears and sad-ness, grace us with your
2 In the pain and joy be-hold-ing, how your grace is
3 Give us strength to love each oth-er, ev-ery sis-ter,
4 You who know each thought and feel-ing, teach us all your
to Refrain
F Em D/F# G Bm A/C# A7
peace and glad-ness. Spir-it of all com-fort, fill our hearts.
still un-fold-ing. Give us all your vi-sion, God of love.
ev-ery broth-er. Spir-it of all kind-ness, be our guide.
way of heal-ing. Spir-it of com-pas-sion, fill each heart.

WORDS and MUSIC: Marty Haugen (1950-)

631 There Is a Balm in Gilead

Refrain (Unison)
There is a balm in Gil-e-ad to make the wound-ed whole,
there is a balm in Gil-e-ad to heal the sin-sick soul.
1 Some-times I feel dis-cour-aged, and think my work's in vain,
2 If you can-not preach like Pe-ter, if you can-not pray like Paul,
3 Don't ev-er feel dis-cour-aged, for Je-sus is your friend;
to Refrain
but then the Ho-ly Spir-it re-vives my soul a-gain.
you can tell the love of Je-sus, and say, "He died for all."
and if you lack for knowl-edge he'll ne'er re-fuse to lend.

WORDS and MUSIC: African-American spiritual

BALM IN GILEAD
Irregular

When Aimless Violence Takes Those We Love 632

1 When aim - less vi - o - lence takes those we love,
2 When pass - ing years rob sight and strength and mind
3 Our faith may flick - er low, and hope grow dim,
4 Be - cause your Son knew a - go - ny and loss,
5 Through long, grief - dark - ened days help us, dear Lord,
when ran - dom death strikes child - hood's prom - ise down,
yet fail to still a strong - ly beat - ing heart,
yet you, O God, are with us in our pain;
felt des - o - la - tion, grief, and scorn and shame,
to trust your grace for cour - age to en - dure,
when wrench - ing loss be - comes our dai - ly bread,
and grief be - comes the fab - ric of our days,
you grieve with us and for us day by day,
we know you will be with us, come what may,
to rest our souls in your sup - port - ing love,
we know, O God, you leave us not a - lone.
dear Lord, you do not stand from us a - part.
and with us, shar - ing sor - row, will re - main.
your lov - ing pres - ence near, al - ways the same.
and find our hope with - in your mer - cy sure.

WORDS: Joy F. Patterson (1931-)
MUSIC: Thomas Pavlechko (1962-)

GREENBELT
10.10.10.10.

633 Healer of My Soul

Unison
D F♯m G A D
1, 3 Heal - er of my soul,
2 Keep - er of my soul, on
F♯m G A Bm F♯m
keep me at eve - ning. Keep me at morn-ing,
rough course far - ing. Help and safe-guard my
G A Em D/F♯ Gmaj7 Asus A Asus G/D D
1, 3
keep me at noon, heal - er of my soul.
means this night, keep - er of my
2
G/D Dsus D Bm Asus A Bm A G G2
soul. I am tired, a - stray and stum-bling,

WORDS and MUSIC: John Michael Talbot (20th c.)

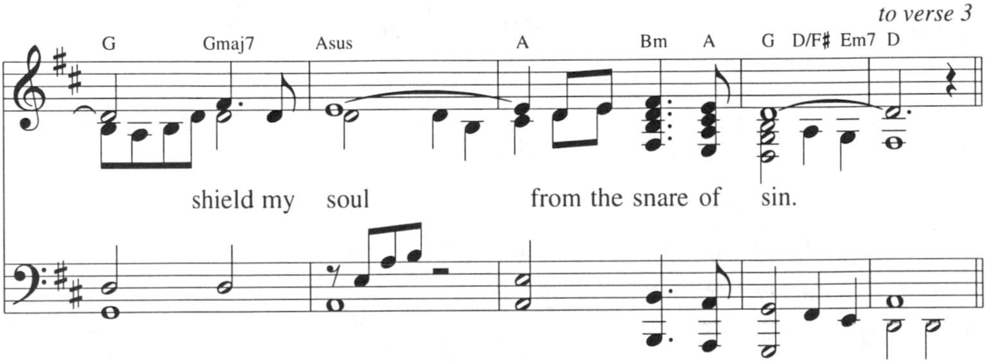
to verse 3
G Gmaj7 Asus A Bm A G D/F# Em7 D
shield my soul from the snare of sin.

Jesus' Hands Were Kind Hands 634

Unison
1 Je - sus' hands were kind hands, do - ing good to all, heal - ing pain and
2 Take my hands, Lord Je - sus, let them work for you; make them strong and
sick - ness, bless - ing chil - dren small, wash - ing tired feet and
gen - tle, kind in all I do; let me watch you, Je - sus,
sav-ing those who fall; Je-sus' hands were kind hands, do-ing good to all.
till I'm gen - tle too, till my hands are kind hands, quick to work for you.

WORDS: Margaret Cropper (1886-1980)
MUSIC: French melody

AU CLAIR DE LA LUNE
11.11.11.11.

635 And Jesus Said

1 And Je - sus said: don't be a - fraid. I've
2 And Je - sus said: don't be a - fraid. I
3 And Je - sus said: don't be a - fraid. I
come to turn your fear to hope, I've come to take you through the
know your emp - ti - ness and grief, I hear your words of un - be -
am the Way, I am the Light, I am the Truth that holds you
deep, to be your friend un - til the end, and give your
lief, but if you will, I'll heal your soul and give your
tight, and in God's home you have a room, a place of

WORDS: Shirley Erena Murray (1931-)
MUSIC: Donald P. Hustad (1918-)

DAISY HILL
8.8.8.4.4.8.

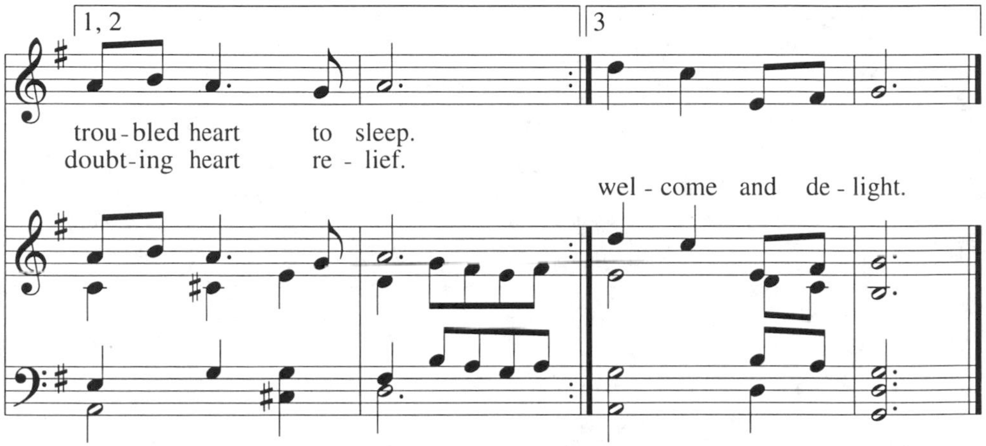
1, 2
3
trou-bled heart to sleep.
doubt-ing heart re - lief.
wel - come and de - light.

Heal Me, Hands of Jesus 636

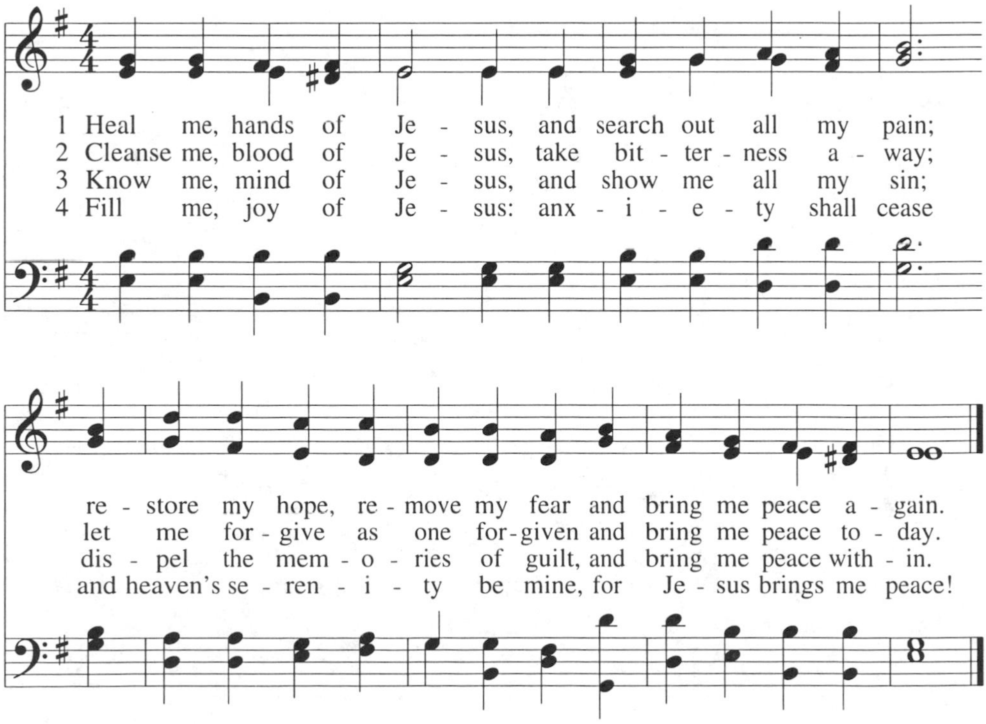
1 Heal me, hands of Je - sus, and search out all my pain;
2 Cleanse me, blood of Je - sus, take bit - ter - ness a - way;
3 Know me, mind of Je - sus, and show me all my sin;
4 Fill me, joy of Je - sus: anx - i - e - ty shall cease
re - store my hope, re - move my fear and bring me peace a - gain.
let me for - give as one for-given and bring me peace to - day.
dis - pel the mem - o - ries of guilt, and bring me peace with - in.
and heaven's se - ren - i - ty be mine, for Je - sus brings me peace!
8

WORDS: Michael Perry (1942-1996)
MUSIC: Herbert S. Irons (1834-1905), alt.

SOUTHWELL
S.M.

637 His Strength Is Perfect

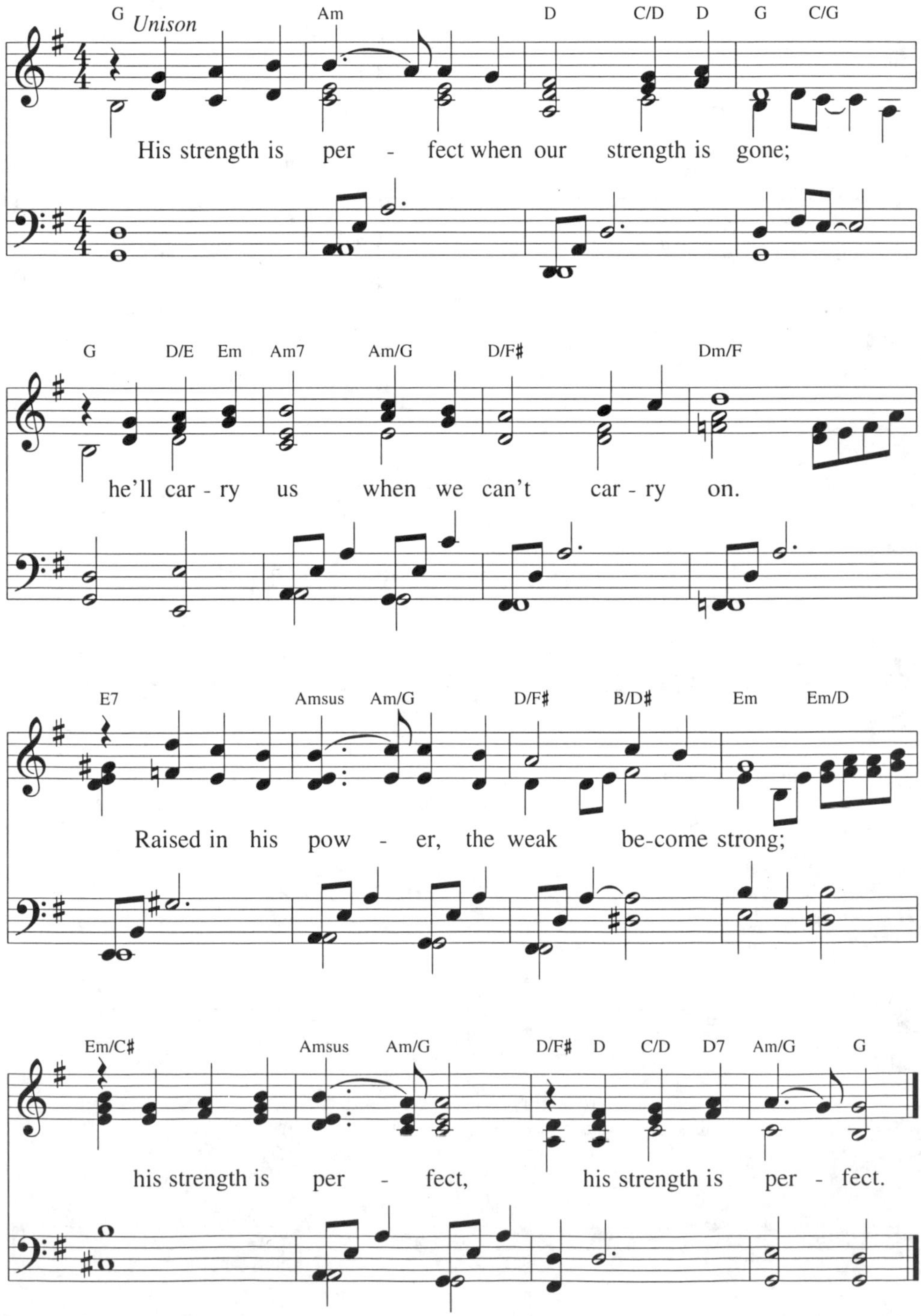
G Unison
Am
D
C/D
D
G
C/G
His strength is per - fect when our strength is gone;
G
D/E
Em
Am7
Am/G
D/F#
Dm/F
he'll car - ry us when we can't car - ry on.
E7
Amsus
Am/G
D/F#
B/D#
Em
Em/D
Raised in his pow - er, the weak be-come strong;
Em/C#
Amsus
Am/G
D/F#
D
C/D
D7
Am/G
G
his strength is per - fect, his strength is per - fect.

WORDS and MUSIC: Steven Curtis Chapman (1962-) and Jerry Salley (20th c.)

O Christ, the Healer, We Have Come 638

1 O Christ, the heal - er, we have come to
2 From ev - ery ail - ment flesh en - dures our
3 In con - flicts that de - stroy our health we
4 Grant that we all, made one in faith, in
pray for health, to plead for friends. How can we fail to
bod - ies clam - or to be freed; yet in our hearts we
rec - og - nize the world's dis - ease; our com - mon life de -
your com - mu - ni - ty may find the whole - ness that, en -
be re - stored when reached by love that nev - er ends?
would con - fess that whole - ness is our deep - est need.
clares our ills. Is there no cure, O Christ, for these?
rich - ing us, shall reach the whole of hu - man - kind.

WORDS: Fred Pratt Green (1903-2000)
MUSIC: Robert A. Schumann (1810-1856)

CANONBURY
L.M.

639 He Is Able

Unison
He is a - ble, more than a - ble to ac-
comp-lish what con-cerns me to-day. He is a - ble, more than a -
- ble to han-dle an - y-thing that comes my way.
He is a - ble, more than a - ble to do much more than
I could ev - er dream. He is a - ble, more than a -

WORDS and MUSIC: Rory Noland (20th c.) and Greg Ferguson (20th c.)

- ble to make me what he wants me to be.

From Miles Around 640

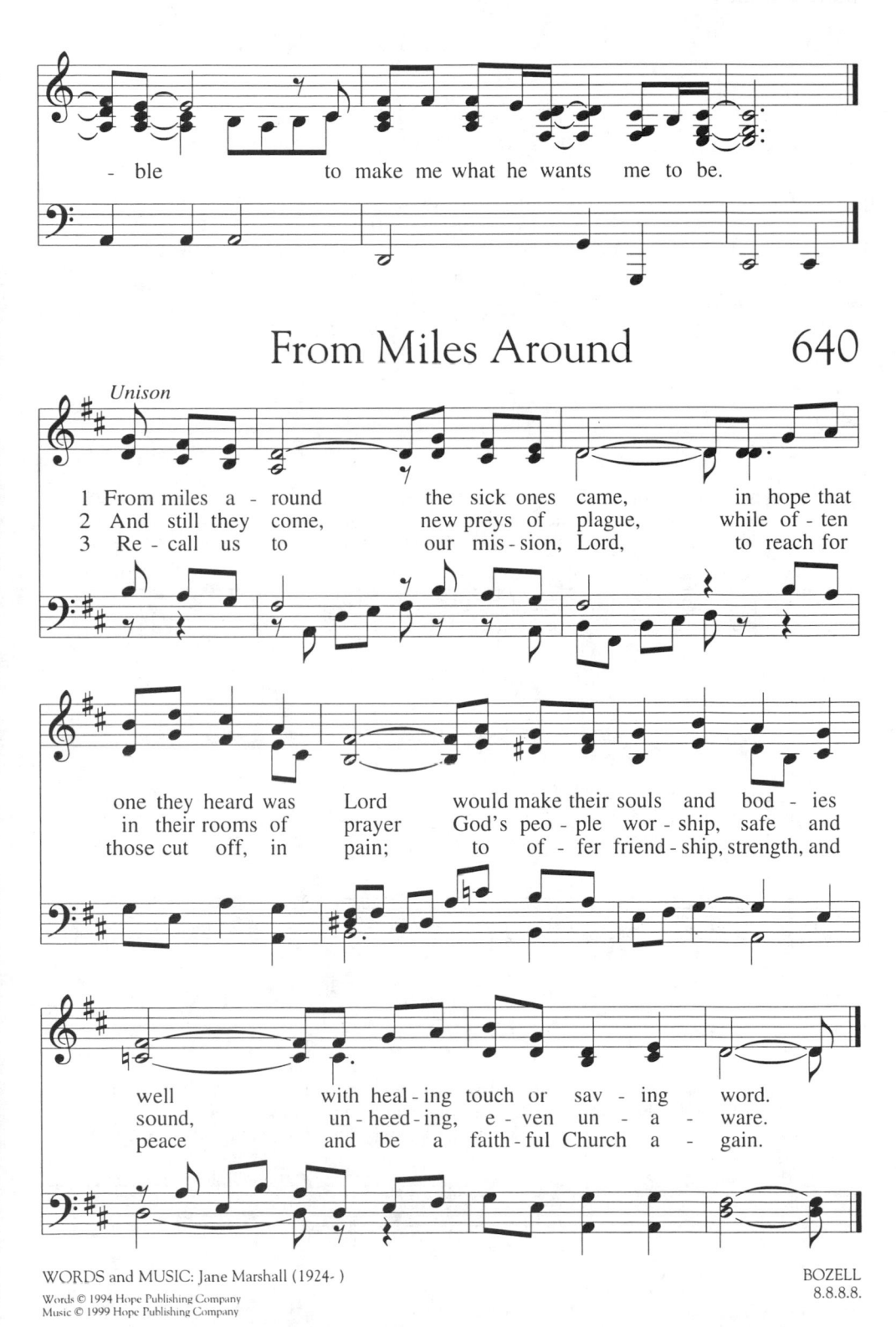

Unison
1 From miles a - round the sick ones came, in hope that
2 And still they come, new preys of plague, while of - ten
3 Re - call us to our mis - sion, Lord, to reach for

one they heard was Lord would make their souls and bod - ies
in their rooms of prayer God's peo - ple wor - ship, safe and
those cut off, in pain; to of - fer friend - ship, strength, and

well with heal - ing touch or sav - ing word.
sound, un - heed - ing, e - ven un - a - ware.
peace and be a faith - ful Church a - gain.

WORDS and MUSIC: Jane Marshall (1924-)

BOZELL
8.8.8.8.

641 For the Music of Creation

1 For the mu-sic of cre-a-tion, for the song your Spir-it sings,
2 Psalms and sym-pho-nies ex-alt you, drum and trum-pet, string and reed,
3 All the voic-es of the a-ges in tran-scen-dent cho-rus meet,
for your sound's di-vine ex-pres-sion, burst of joy in liv-ing things:
sim-ple mel-o-dies ac-claim you, tunes that rise from deep-est need,
wor-ship lift-ing up the sens-es, hands that praise, and danc-ing feet;
God, our God, the world's com-pos-er, hear us, ech-oes of your voice;
hymns of long-ing and be-long-ing, car-ols from a cheer-ful throat,
o-ver dis-cord and di-vi-sion mu-sic speaks your joy and peace,
mu-sic is your art, your glo-ry, let the hu-man heart re-joice!
lilt of lul-la-by and love song catch-ing heav-en in a note.
har-mo-ny of earth and heav-en, song of God that can-not cease!

WORDS: Shirley Erena Murray (1931-)
MUSIC: C. Hubert H. Parry (1848-1918)

RUSTINGTON
8.7.8.7.D.

Earth and All Stars

1 Earth and all stars, loud rush-ing plan - ets
2 Trum - pet and pipes, loud clash-ing cym - bals
3 Steel and ma-chines, loud pound-ing ham - mers sing to the
4 Class-rooms and labs, loud boil - ing test tubes
5 Knowl-edge and truth, loud sound-ing wis - dom
Hail, wind, and rain, loud blow-ing
Harp, lute and lyre, loud hum-ming
Lord a new song! Lime-stone and beams, loud build-ing
Ath - lete and band, loud cheer-ing
Daugh-ter and son, loud pray-ing
snow - storm
cel - los
work - ers sing to the Lord a new song! God has done
peo - ple
mem - bers
Refrain
mar - vel-ous things. We will sing prais-es with a new song!

WORDS: Herbert F. Brokering (1926-), alt.
MUSIC: David N. Johnson (1922-1987)

EARTH AND ALL STARS
4.5.7.4.5.7.Ref.

643 Colorful Creator

Unison
1 Col - or - ful Cre - a - tor, God of mys - ter - y,
2 Har - mo - ny of a - ges, God of lis - tening ear,
3 Au - thor of our jour - ney, God of near and far,
4 God of truth and beau - ty, Po - et of the Word,
thank you for the art - ist teach - ing us to see
thank you for com - pos - ers tun - ing us to hear
praise for tale and dra - ma tell - ing who we are,
may we be cre - a - tors by the Spir - it stirred,
glimps - es of the mean - ing of the com - mon - place,
ech - oes of the Gos - pel in the songs we sing,
strip - ping to the es - sence strug - gles of our day,
o - pen to your pres - ence in our joy and strife,
vi - sions of the ho - ly in each hu - man face.
sounds of love and long - ing from the deep - est spring.
times of change and con - flict when we choose our way.
ves - sels of the ho - ly cours - ing through our life.
1–3
4

WORDS: Ruth Duck (1947-)
MUSIC: Carlton R. Young (1926-)

HOUGHTON
11.11.11.11.

God, Who Stretched the Spangled Heavens 644

Unison
1 God, who stretched the span - gled heav - ens, in - fi - nite in time and place,
2 Proud-ly rise our mod - ern cit - ies, state - ly build-ings row on row;
3 We have con-quered worlds un - dreamed of since the child-hood of our race;
4 As each far ho - ri - zon beck - ons, may it chal-lenge us a - new,
flung the suns in burn - ing ra - diance through the si - lent fields of space,
yet their win-dows, blank, un - feel - ing, stare on can-yoned streets be - low,
known the ec - sta - sy of wing-ing through un - chart - ed realms of space;
chil - dren of cre - a - tive pur - pose, serv - ing oth - ers, honor-ing you.
we, your chil - dren, in your like-ness, share in - ven - tive powers with you.
where the lone - ly drift un - no - ticed in the cit - y's ebb and flow,
probed the se - crets of the at - om, yield-ing un - im - ag - ined power,
May our dreams prove rich with prom - ise, each en - deav - or well be - gun.
Great Cre - a - tor, still cre - at - ing, show us what we yet may do.
lost to pur-pose and to mean-ing, scarce-ly car - ing where they go.
fac - ing us with life's de - struc - tion or our most tri - um-phant hour.
Great Cre - a - tor, give us guid - ance till our goals and yours are one.

WORDS: Catherine Cameron (1927-)
MUSIC: *Columbian Harmony*, 1825

HOLY MANNA
8.7.8.7.D.

645 When the Morning Stars Together

1 When the morn-ing stars to - geth - er their Cre - a - tor's glo - ry sang,
2 When in syn - a - gogue and tem - ple voic - es raised the psalm-ists' songs,
3 Voice and in - stru - ment in un - ion through the a - ges spoke your praise.
4 Lord, we bring our gift of mu - sic; touch our lips and fire our hearts,
and the an - gel host all shout - ed till with joy the heav - ens rang,
of - fer - ing the ad - o - ra - tion that a - lone to you be - longs;
Plain-song, tune - ful hymns, and an - thems told your faith - ful, gra - cious ways.
teach our minds and train our sens - es, fit us for this sa - cred art.
then your wis - dom and your great-ness their ex - ult - ant mu - sic told,
when the sing - ers and the cym - bals with the trum - pet made ac - cord,
Choir and or - ches - tra and or - gan, each a sa - cred of - fering brought,
Then with skill and con - se - cra - tion we would serve you, Lord, and give
all the beau - ty and the splen - dor that your might - y works un - fold.
glo - ry filled the house of wor - ship, and all knew your pres - ence, Lord.
while, in - spired by your own Spir - it, po - et and com - pos - er wrought.
all our powers to glo - ri - fy you, and in serv - ing ful - ly live.

WORDS: Albert F. Bayly (1901-1984)
MUSIC: *Tochter Sion*, 1741

WEISSE FLAGGEN
8.7.8.7.D.

THE CHURCH IN WORSHIP

646 As We Gather

Unison
D
F#m7
G
Gmaj7/A
A7
As we gath - er may your Spir - it work with - in us,
A7sus
as we gath - er may we glo - ri - fy your Name.
A
A/C#
Bm7
Know - ing well that as our hearts be - gin to wor - ship,
Em7
G/A
D/A
we'll be blessed be - cause we came,
we'll be blessed be - cause we came.

WORDS and MUSIC: Mike Fay (20th c.) and Tommy Coomes (1946-)

We Have Come to Join in Worship 647

1 We have come to join in wor - ship and a - dore the Lord our God.
2 See them gath - er all a - round you, those he bought at such a cost;
3 Let us love our God su - preme-ly; let us love each oth - er, too.
Let us come in prayer, ex - pect - ing God to speak his might - y Word.
see the wea - ry, see the hurt - ing, see the lone - ly, see the lost.
Let us care for all his peo - ple till our God makes all things new.
All is vain un - less the Spir - it of the Ho - ly One comes down.
Be his hand, and touch the need - y; be his gos - pel, let it sound!
Christ will call us home to heav - en; at his ban-quet we'll sit down;
Chris - tians, pray, and ho - ly man - na will be show-ered all a - round.
Be his bod - y, and sweet man - na will be show-ered all a - round.
Christ him - self will rise and serve us liv - ing man - na all a - round.

WORDS: Ken Bible (1950-) and George Atkins (18th c.)
MUSIC: *Columbian Harmony*, 1825; attr. William Moore (19th c.)

HOLY MANNA
8.7.8.7.D.

648 You're Worthy of My Praise

G
(Echo)
F2
F
1 I will wor - ship with
2 I will bow down, to
Unison
1 I will wor - ship with all of my heart.
2 I will bow down to hail you as King.
F2
F
C
all of my heart. I will praise you
hail you as King. I will serve you
I will praise you with
I will serve you, give you
C/G
G
Am7
G/B
Am/C
D7
with all my strength.
and give you ev - ery - thing.
all of my strength.
ev - ery - thing.
G
F2
F
I will seek you in
I will lift up my
I will seek you in all of my days.
I will lift up my eyes to your throne.

WORDS and MUSIC: David Ruis (20th c.)

F2
F
C
all of my days.
eyes to your throne.
I will fol - low
I will trust you,
I will fol - low
I will trust you,
in
I will
C/G
G
Am7
G/B
Am/C
D7
all your ways.
trust in you a - lone.
all of your ways.
trust you a - lone.
Refrain
G
D/F#
Bm/D
D
C
I will give you all my wor - ship,
I will give you
Am
Em/A
Am/D
D7
G
D/F#
Bm/D
D
all my praise.
You a - lone I long to wor - ship,
C
Am
Em/B
Am/C
D7
G
Am/G
G
you a - lone are wor - thy of my praise.

649 Gather Us In

Unison
D A/C# C G Gm/Bb Dm
1 Here in this place, the new light is stream-ing, shad-ows of doubt are
2 We are the young, our lives are a mys - tery; we are the old, who
3 Here we re - ceive new life in the wa - ters; here we re - ceive the
4 Not just in build - ings, small and con - fin - ing, not in some heav - en,
C G D A/C# C G
van - ished a - way. See in this space our fears and our dream-ings,
yearn for your face. We have been sung through-out all of his - tory,
bread of new birth; here you shall call your sons and your daugh-ters,
light years a - way, here in this place the new light is shin - ing;
Gm/Bb Dm C Am7 D
brought here to you in the light of this day.
called to be light to the whole hu - man race.
call us a - new to be salt for the earth.
now is God pres - ent, and now is the day.
A C/G D/F# G A C/G
Gath - er us in, the lost and for - sak - en; gath - er us in; our
Gath - er us in, the rich and the haugh - ty; gath - er us in, the
Give us to drink the wine of com - pas - sion; give us to eat the
Gath - er us in and hold us for - ev - er; gath - er us in and

WORDS and MUSIC: Marty Haugen (1950-)

GATHER US IN
Irregular

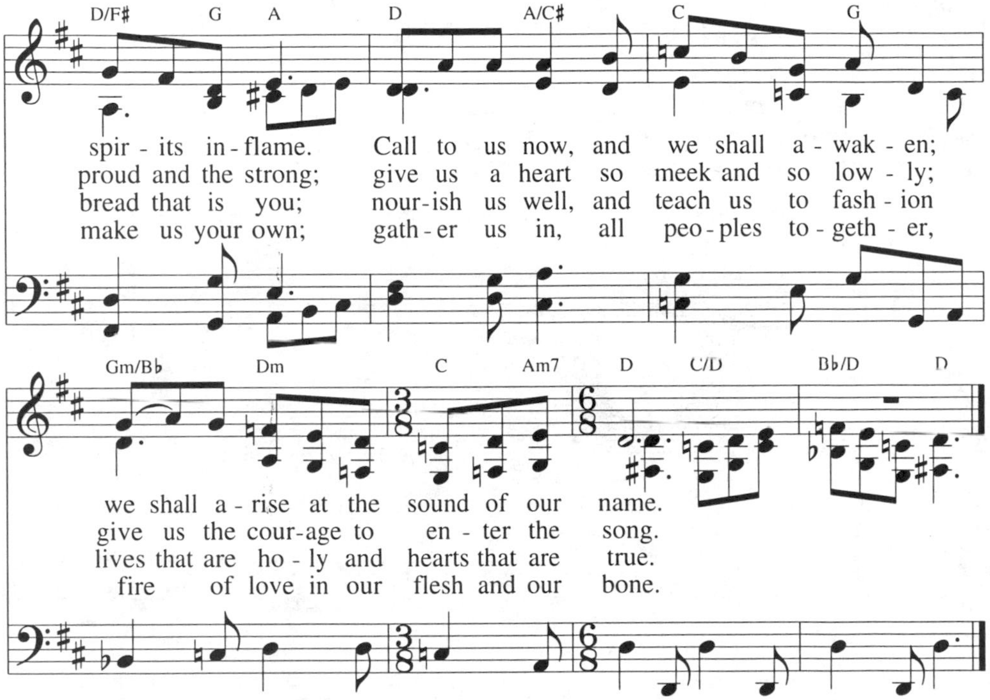
D/F# G A D A/C# C G
spir - its in - flame. Call to us now, and we shall a - wak - en;
proud and the strong; give us a heart so meek and so low - ly;
bread that is you; nour - ish us well, and teach us to fash - ion
make us your own; gath - er us in, all peo - ples to - geth - er,
Gm/Bb Dm C Am7 D C/D Bb/D D
we shall a - rise at the sound of our name.
give us the cour - age to en - ter the song.
lives that are ho - ly and hearts that are true.
fire of love in our flesh and our bone.

650 Rejoice in the Lord Always

I
II
Re - joice in the Lord al - ways, a - gain I say, re - joice! Re -
III
joice in the Lord al - ways, a - gain I say, re - joice! Re - joice! Re - joice! A -
IV
gain I say, re - joice! Re - joice! Re - joice! A - gain I say, re - joice!

WORDS: Philippians 4:4
MUSIC: Anonymous

651 We Bring the Sacrifice of Praise

D A7 D
We bring the sac - ri - fice of praise in - to the
G Em7 D/A A7 D A7
house of the Lord; we bring the sac - ri - fice of
D G A7 D D7 G Em7
praise in - to the house of the Lord. And we of - fer up to
F♯m7 Bm7 Em A7 D A//E D/F♯ D7
you the sac - ri - fic - es of thanks - giv - ing; and we
G Em7 F♯m7 Bm7 Em A7 D G/D D
of - fer up to you the sac - ri - fic - es of joy.

WORDS and MUSIC: Kirk Dearman (1952-)

This Is the Day

Unison
This is the day, this is the day that the Lord has made, that the
Lord has made; we will re-joice, we will re-joice and be
glad in it, and be glad in it. This is the day that the
Lord has made; we will re-joice and be glad in it.
This is the day, this is the day that the Lord has made.

WORDS and MUSIC: Les Garrett (1944-), para. Psalm 118:24

653 I Will Call upon the Lord

(Echo, 2nd time only)
C F/C C Dm7/C C F/C
I will call up-on the Lord
Unison
I will call up-on the Lord who is wor-thy to be
Cmaj7 F/C C F/C Cmaj7 F/C
who is wor-thy to be praised; so shall I be
praised; so shall I be saved from my en - e - mies.
C F/C C/G F/G 1 C F/G
saved from my en - e - mies. I will call up-on the
I will call up-on the Lord.

WORDS and MUSIC: Michael O'Shields (1948-); para. Psalm 18

2
C F/G C F C/E
Lord. The Lord liv-eth and bless-ed be the Rock, and let the God
F C/E C G
of my sal - va - tion be ex - alt - ed. The
C F C/E
Lord liv - eth and bless - ed be the Rock, and let the God
1
F C/E C G7 F/C C
of my sal - va - tion be ex - alt - ed. The
2
G7 C F/C C
alt - ed.

654 Holy Ground

Unison
We are stand - ing on ho - ly ground,
and I know that there are an - gels all a -
round. Let us praise
Je - sus now; We are
stand - ing in his pres-ence on ho - ly ground.
8vb

WORDS and MUSIC: Geron Davis (1960-)

Come Away from Rush and Hurry 655

Unison
1 Come a - way from rush and hur - ry to the still - ness of God's peace;
2 In the pas - tures of God's good - ness we lie down to rest our soul.
3 Come, then, chil - dren, with your bur - dens— life's con - fu - sions, fears and pain.
from our vain am - bi - tion's wor - ry, come to Christ to find re - lease.
From the wa - ters of God's mer - cy we drink deep - ly, are made whole.
Leave them at the cross of Je - sus; take in - stead his king - dom's reign.
Come a - way from noise and clam - or, life's de - mands and fren - zied pace;
At the ta - ble of God's pres - ence all the saints are rich - ly fed.
Bring your thirsts, for he will quench them— he a - lone will sat - is - fy.
come to join the peo - ple gath - ered here to seek and find God's face.
With the oil of God's a - noint - ing in - to ser - vice we are led.
All our long - ings find at - tain - ment when to self we glad - ly die.

WORDS: Marva J. Dawn (1948-) BEACH SPRING
MUSIC: Attr. B. F. White (1800-1879), *The Sacred Harp*, 1844; arr. Jack Schrader (1942-) 8.7.8.7.D.

656 Open the Eyes of My Heart

Refrain
E2
Bsus/D♯
O-pen the eyes of my heart, Lord, o-pen the eyes of my heart,
A2/C♯
A
1
E2
Esus
I want to see you, I want to see you;
2
E2
B
C♯m
see you. To see you high and lift - ed up,
A
Bsus
B
shin-ing in the light of your glo - ry; pour out your power and love
C♯m
F♯m7
Bsus
to Refrain
as we sing, "Ho - ly, ho - ly, ho - ly."
Coda
E2
Bsus/D♯
Ho - ly, ho - ly, ho - ly, ho - ly, ho - ly, ho-
A2/C♯
A
- ly; ho - ly, ho - ly, ho - ly, I want to
1 Repeat as desired
E2
Esus
2
E2
E
see you. see you.

WORDS and MUSIC: Paul Baloche (1962-)

He Has Made Me Glad

I will en - ter his gates with thanks - giv - ing in my heart; I will
en - ter his courts with praise. I will say, "This is the day that the
Lord has made!" I will re - joice for he has made me glad.
1
He has made me glad, he has made me glad, I will re - joice for
he has made me glad.
2
will re - joice for he has made me glad.

WORDS and MUSIC: Leona Von Brethorst (1923-)

658 Awesome God

Em
Bm7
Em
Bm7
Em
Bm7
Em
Em/D
Unison
Our
C
G
D
God is an awe-some God, he reigns from
Em
D/E
Em
C
G
heav-en a - bove with wis - dom, power and love— Our
Repeat Ending
Song Ending
Am
Em/B
B7
Em
Em/D
Em
God is an awe-some God! Our God!

WORDS and MUSIC: Rich Mullins (20th c.)

Jesus, We Are Here

Jesu Tawa Pano

1 Je - sus, we are here; Je - sus, we are here; Je - sus, we are here; we are here for you.
1 Je - su ta - wa pa - no; Je - su ta - wa pa - no; Je - su ta - wa pa - no; ta - wa pa - no mu zi - ta ren - yu.
2 Sav - ior, we are here; Sav - ior, we are here; Sav - ior, we are here; we are here for you.
3 Spir - it, we are here; Spir - it, we are here; Spir - it, we are here; we are here for you.
(Leader) wel - come Je - sus.
Mam - bo Je - su.
wel - come Sav - ior.
wel - come Spir - it.

WORDS and MUSIC: Patrick Matsikenyiri (1937-)

660 I Sing Praises

N.C.
Dmaj7
E/D
1 I sing prais-es to your name, O Lord, prais-es to your
(2) name, O Lord, glo - ry to your
C♯m7
F♯m
Bm7
D/E E D/E E
name, O Lord, for your name is great and great-ly to be
name, O Lord,
Amaj7
A/C♯
Dmaj7
E/D
praised;
I sing prais-es to your name, O Lord, prais-es to your
I give glo - ry to your name, O Lord, glo - ry to your
C♯m7
F♯m
Bm7
name, O Lord, for your name is great and
name, O Lord,

WORDS and MUSIC: Terry MacAlmon (1955-)

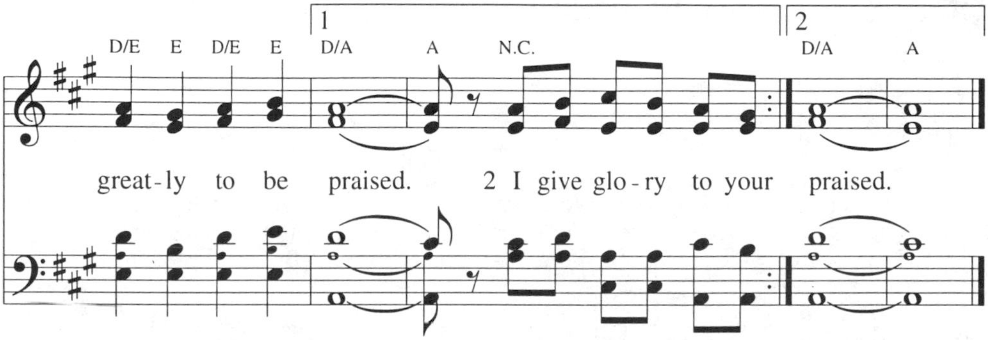
1
2
D/E E D/E E D/A A N.C. D/A A
great-ly to be praised. 2 I give glo-ry to your praised.

All People That on Earth Do Dwell 661

1 All people that on earth do dwell, sing to the Lord with cheerful voice; him serve with joy, his praise forth tell, come ye before him and rejoice.
2 Know that the Lord is God indeed; without our aid he did us make; we are his folk, he doth us feed, and for his sheep he doth us take.
3 O enter then his gates with praise, approach with joy his courts unto; praise, laud and bless his name always, for it is seemly so to do.
4 For why? The Lord our God is good, his mercy is forever sure; his truth at all times firmly stood, and shall from age to age endure.

WORDS: William Kethe (ca. 1530-1594); para. Psalm 100
MUSIC: Louis Bourgeois (ca. 1510-1561); *Genevan Psalter*, 1551

OLD 100th
L.M.

662 Thanks to God Whose Word Was Spoken

Unison
1 Thanks to God whose Word was spo - ken in the deed that made the earth: his the voice that called a na - tion, his the fires that tried its worth. God has spo - ken, God has spo - ken, praise God for his o - pen Word.
2 Thanks to God whose Word in - car - nate heights and depths of life did share; deeds and words and death and ris - ing, grace in hu - man form de - clare.
3 Thanks to God whose Word is an - swered by the Spir - it's voice with - in; here we drink of joy un - mea - sured, life re - deemed from death and sin. God is speak - ing,

WORDS: R. T. Brooks (1918-1985); alt.
MUSIC: Peter Cutts (1937-)

WYLDE GREEN
8.7.8.7.4.7.

God's Holy Ways Are Just and True 663

1 God's ho - ly ways are just and true, his prom - i - ses are ev - er
2 Bring back to mind his grace and love, our needs pro-vid - ed from a -
3 Tell once a - gain his deeds of old, the sto - ry of our might-y
new: O praise him, al - le - lu - ia! Let ev - ery heart with prais - es
bove: O praise him, al - le - lu - ia! He kept his word and Je - sus
God: O praise him, al - le - lu - ia! For all his glo-rious works and
sing and make this house with voic - es ring: O praise him, O
came to make a peo - ple for his name: O praise him, O
ways we shall re-joice through end-less days: O praise him, O
praise him! Al-le - lu - ia, al-le - lu - ia, al - le - lu - ia!
praise him! Al-le - lu - ia, al-le - lu - ia, al - le - lu - ia!
praise him! Al-le - lu - ia, al-le - lu - ia, al - le - lu - ia!

WORDS: Barbara Woollett (1937-); para. Psalm 111
MUSIC: *Geistliche Kirchengesäng*, Cologne, 1623; arr. Ralph Vaughan Williams (1872-1958)

LASST UNS ERFREUEN
L.M.Alleluias

664 Thy Word

Refrain (Unison)
F C/E F
Thy Word is a lamp un-to my feet and a
Bb/D C/E F
light un - to my path.
C Gm Dm Am Bb C7
1 When I feel a-fraid, think I've lost my way, still you're there right be-
2 I will not for-get your love for me, and yet my heart for - ev - er is
Bb/F F C Gm Dm Am
side me. And noth-ing will I fear as long as you are near.
wan - der-ing. Je - sus, be my guide and hold me to your side; and

WORDS: Amy Grant (1960-); para. Psalm 119:105
MUSIC: Michael W. Smith (1957-)

to Refrain
Bb C D Csus C C7
Please be near me to the end.
I will love you to the end.

Break Now the Bread of Life 665

1 Break now the bread of life, dear Lord, to me, as once you broke the loaves be - side the sea. Be - yond the sa - cred page I seek you, Lord; my spir - it longs for you, O liv - ing Word.
2 Bless your own Word of truth, dear Lord, to me, as when you blessed the bread by Gal - i - lee. Then shall all bond - age cease, all fet - ters fall; and I shall find my peace, my All in all!
3 You are the bread of life, dear Lord, to me; your ho - ly Word the truth that res - cues me. Give me to eat and live with you a - bove; teach me to love your truth, for you are love.
4 O send your Spir - it now, dear Lord, to me, that he may touch my eyes and make me see. Show me the truth made plain with - in your Word, for in your book re - vealed I see the Lord.

WORDS: Mary A. Lathbury (1841-1913); vs. 3-4, Alexander Groves (1842-1909), alt.
MUSIC: William F. Sherwin (1826-1888), alt.

BREAD OF LIFE
6.4.6.4.D.

666 Blest Are They

Gsus G D/F# C
1 Blest are they, the poor in spir - it, theirs is the
2 Blest are they, the low - ly ones, they shall in -
3 Blest are they who show mer - cy, mer - cy
4 Blest are they who seek peace. They are the
5 Blest are you who suf - fer hate, all be -
Dsus Gsus G Gsus G
king - dom of God. Blest are they,
her - it the earth. Blest are they who
shall be theirs. Blest are they, the
child - ren of God. Blest are they who
cause of me. Re - joice be glad,
D/F# C Dsus D C/G G
full of sor - row, they shall be con - soled.
hun - ger and thirst, they shall have their fill.
pure of heart, they shall see God.
suf - fer in faith, the glo - ry of God is theirs.
yours is the king - dom; shine for all to see.

WORDS and MUSIC: David Haas (1957-)

Refrain
C
D
G
D/F♯
Em
G/D
Re - joice and be glad!
C
G/B
Am7
A/C♯
D
C
Bless - ed are you, ho - ly are you! Re - joice
D
Em
Em/D
C
D
and be glad! Yours is the king - dom of
To verses
Final
Gsus
C/G
G
C/G
C/D
G
God!

667 God Has Spoken by the Prophets

1 God has spo - ken by the proph-ets, spo - ken the un - chang - ing Word,
2 God has spo - ken by Christ Je - sus, Christ, the ev - er - last - ing Son,
3 God is speak-ing by the Spir - it, speak-ing to our hearts a - gain;
each from age to age pro-claim - ing God, the one, the right - eous Lord!
bright-ness of the Fa - ther's glo - ry, with the Fa - ther ev - er one;
in the age - long Word de - clar - ing God's own mes-sage, now as then.
'Mid the world's de - spair and tur - moil one firm an - chor hold - ing fast:
spo - ken by the Word in - car - nate, God of God, ere time was born;
Through the rise and fall of na - tions one sure faith yet stand - ing fast:
God e - ter - nal reigns for - ev - er, God the first and God the last.
Light of light, to earth de - scend - ing, Christ, as God in hu - man form.
God a - bides, the Word un - chang - ing, God the first and God the last.

WORDS: George W. Briggs (1875-1959)
MUSIC: Ludwig van Beethoven (1770-1827)

HYMN TO JOY
8.7.8.7.D.

Wonderful Words of Life 668

1 Sing them o - ver a - gain to me, won-der - ful words of life;
2 Christ, the bless-ed One, gives to all won-der - ful words of life;
3 Sweet - ly ech - o the gos - pel call, won-der - ful words of life;
let me more of their beau - ty see, won-der - ful words of life.
sin - ner, list to the lov - ing call, won-der - ful words of life.
of - fer par-don and peace to all, won-der - ful words of life.
Words of life and beau - ty, teach me faith and du - ty:
All so free - ly giv - en, woo - ing us to heav - en:
Je - sus, on - ly Sav - ior, sanc - ti - fy for - ev - er:
Refrain
Beau-ti - ful words, won-der-ful words, won-der-ful words of life.
life.

WORDS and MUSIC: Philip P. Bliss (1838-1876)

WORDS OF LIFE
8.6.8.6.6.6.Ref.

669 Jesus, Come, for We Invite You

1 Je - sus, come, for we in - vite you, guest and mas - ter,
2 Je - sus, come! trans - form our pleas-ures, guide us in - to
3 Je - sus, come in new cre - a - tion, heaven brought near by
4 Je - sus, come! sur - prise our dull - ness; make us will - ing
friend and Lord; now, as once at Ca - na's wed - ding,
paths un - known; bring your gifts, com - mand your ser - vants,
power di - vine; give your un - ex - pect - ed glo - ry,
to re - ceive more than we can yet im - ag - ine,
speak, and let us hear your word: lead us through our
let us trust in you a - lone: though your hand may
chang ing wa - ter in - to wine: rouse the faith of
all the best you have to give: let us find your
need or doubt-ing, hope be born and joy re - stored.
work in se - cret, all shall see what you have done.
your dis - ci - ples— come, our first and great - est Sign!
hid - den rich - es, taste your love, be - lieve, and live!

WORDS: Christopher Idle (1938-)
MUSIC: Sicilian melody, 18th c.

SICILIAN MARINERS
8.7.8.7.8.7.

O Word of God Incarnate 670

1 O Word of God in - car - nate, O Wis - dom from on high,
2 The Church, from her dear Mas - ter, re - ceived the gift di - vine,
3 O make your Church, dear Sav - ior, a lamp of pur - est gold,
O Truth un - changed, un - chang - ing, O Light of our dark sky:
and still that light is lift - ed on all the earth to shine.
to bear be - fore the na - tions your true light as of old;
we praise you for the ra - diance that from the hal - lowed page,
It is the chart and com - pass that, all life's voy - age through,
teach us, your wan-dering pil - grims, by this our path to trace,
a lan - tern to our foot - steps, shines on from age to age.
'mid mists and rocks and quick - sands, still guides, O Christ, to you.
till, clouds and dark - ness end - ed, we see you face to face!

WORDS: William W. How (1823-1897)
MUSIC: *Neuvermehrtes Gesangbuch*, 1693; adapt. Felix Mendelssohn (1809-1847)

MUNICH
7.6.7.6.D.

671 Lord, We Hear Your Word

1 Lord, we hear your Word with glad - ness: you have spo - ken—
2 May we hear with un - der - stand - ing, by your Spir - it
3 You have spo - ken— yours the ful - ness, ours the wealth of
we re - joice: words of love and life and free - dom—
taught and led; may the springs of all our be - ing
this your Word: debt - ors, then, as liv - ing let - ters
help us make their truth our choice! Now in ho - ly cel - e -
by your Liv - ing Word be fed; may our hearts ac - cept with
we must make your Gos - pel heard! By your Spir - it's power trans-
bra - tion for your Word we wor - ship you; spo - ken,
meek - ness all the grace your light makes known; may o -
form us; shed your sav - ing Light a - broad till our

WORDS: Margaret Clarkson (1915-)
MUSIC: William P. Rowlands (1860-1937)

BLAENWERN
8.7.8.7.D.

writ - ten, known in Je - sus, ours to - day to prove a - new.
be - dience mark our foot - steps till we make each word our own!
lives by love in ac - tion show our world the truth of God!

This Is the Threefold Truth 672

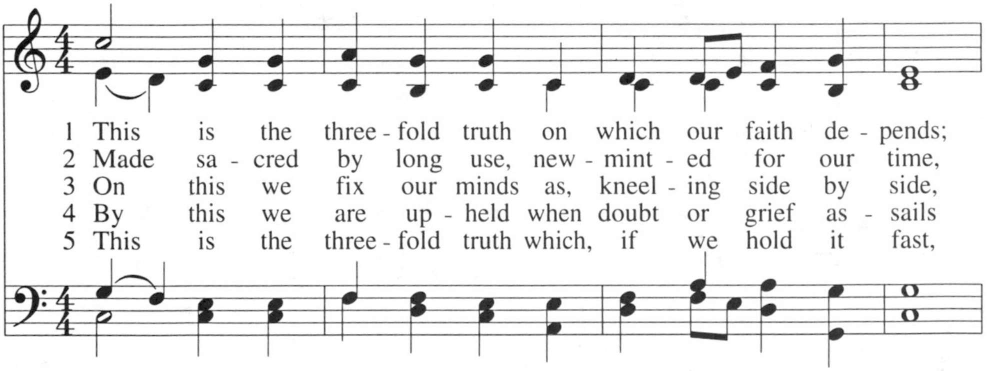
1 This is the three - fold truth on which our faith de - pends;
2 Made sa - cred by long use, new - mint - ed for our time,
3 On this we fix our minds as, kneel - ing side by side,
4 By this we are up - held when doubt or grief as - sails
5 This is the three - fold truth which, if we hold it fast,

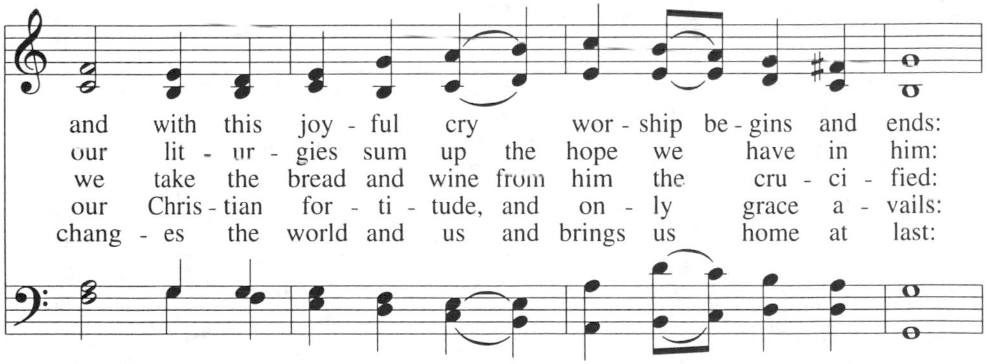
and with this joy - ful cry wor - ship be - gins and ends:
our lit - ur - gies sum up the hope we have in him:
we take the bread and wine from him the cru - ci - fied:
our Chris - tian for - ti - tude, and on - ly grace a - vails:
chang - es the world and us and brings us home at last:

Christ has died! Christ is ris - en! Christ will come a - gain!

WORDS: Fred Pratt Green (1903-2000)
MUSIC: Jack Schrader (1942-)

ACCLAMATIONS
12.12.12.

673 We Believe in God Almighty

Unison
1 We be-lieve in God Al-might-y, mak-er of the earth
2 We be-lieve in Christ the Sav-ior, Son of God and Son
3 We be-lieve in God the Spir-it, pres-ent in our lives
and sky; all we see and all that's hid-den is his work un-
of Man; born of Ma-ry, preach-ing, heal-ing, cru-ci-fied, yet
to-day; speak-ing through the proph-ets' writ-ings, guid-ing trav-elers
ceas-ing-ly: God our Fa-ther's lov-ing kind-ness,
risen a-gain: he as-cend-ed to the Fa-ther,
on their way: to our hearts he brings for-give-ness,
with us till the day we die— ev-er-more and ev-er-more.
there in glo-ry long to reign— ev-er-more and ev-er-more.
and the hope of end-less joy— ev-er-more and ev-er-more.

WORDS: David Mowbray (1938-)
MUSIC: Plainsong, 13th c; harm. C. Winfred Douglas (1867-1944)

DIVINUM MYSTERIUM
8.7.8.7.8.7.7.

What a Mighty God

Unison (or 3 parts)

G C/G G Am/G G C G C/D
1 What a might - y God we serve, what a
(2 Let us) sing and praise the Lord, let us
(3 Let us) shout and praise his name, let us
(4 What a) might - y God we serve, what a
G Am/G G A7 D (Am D7) C/D G Dm7 G G7 C
might - y God we serve; what a might - y God we serve,
sing and praise the Lord; let us sing and praise the Lord,
shout and praise his name; let us shout and praise his name,
might - y God we serve; what a might - y God we serve,
Am G/D Am/D G/D D7 G
1–3
(Am G)
what a might - y God we serve!
let us sing and praise the Lord!
let us shout and praise his name!
what a might - y God we serve!
C/D
2 Let us
3 Let us
4 What a
4
G (Am G) Am/G G
serve!

WORDS and MUSIC: African folk song; adapt. Jack Schrader (1942-)

675 I Believe in Jesus

Unison
E A E/B B
1 I be-lieve in Je - sus,
2 I be-lieve in you, Lord,
E A B
I be-lieve he is the Son of God.
I be-lieve you are the Son of God.
E A E/B B
I be-lieve he died and rose a-gain.
I be-lieve you died and rose a-gain.
E A B
I be-lieve he paid for us all.
I be-lieve you paid for us all.

WORDS and MUSIC: Marc Nelson (20th c.)

Descant I be-lieve that he's (you're) here
A B/D# E E/G#
And I be-lieve that he's here now,
And I be-lieve that you're here now,
A B E E/G#
stand-ing in our midst.
with the pow - er to
A B/D# E E/G#
Here with the pow - er to heal now,
heal,
A B 1 E A/C# A/B 2 E
and the grace to for - give.
give.

676 Come, Be Baptized

C G/B F/A C/G G C G/B
1 Come as a child, come to the wa - ters; to the fam - ily of God,
2 Come as a child, come, sons and daugh-ters, draw from the well
F/A C/G G Am Em/G F G/F
come, sons and daugh-ters. Come to the riv - er, the Lord, the life -
life - giv - ing wa - ters. Drink of the riv - er, the Lord, the life -
C2 Dm/F Em Dm/F Dm7 G
giv - er; wash in the love that is sent from a - bove.
giv - er; feel how it pours out the life that is yours.
Refrain
C Em7 F C F
Come, be bap - tized in the name of the Fa - ther; come, be

WORDS and MUSIC: Gary Alan Smith (1947-); arr. Jack Schrader (1942-)

COME, BE BAPTIZED
Irregular.Ref.

C D7/A G Am Em/G
bap-tized in the name of the Son; come, be bap-tized in the
F6 C/G Dm7 Am/E Dm/F F G C
name of the Spir-it; come, be bap-tized in love.

Child of Blessing, Child of Promise 677

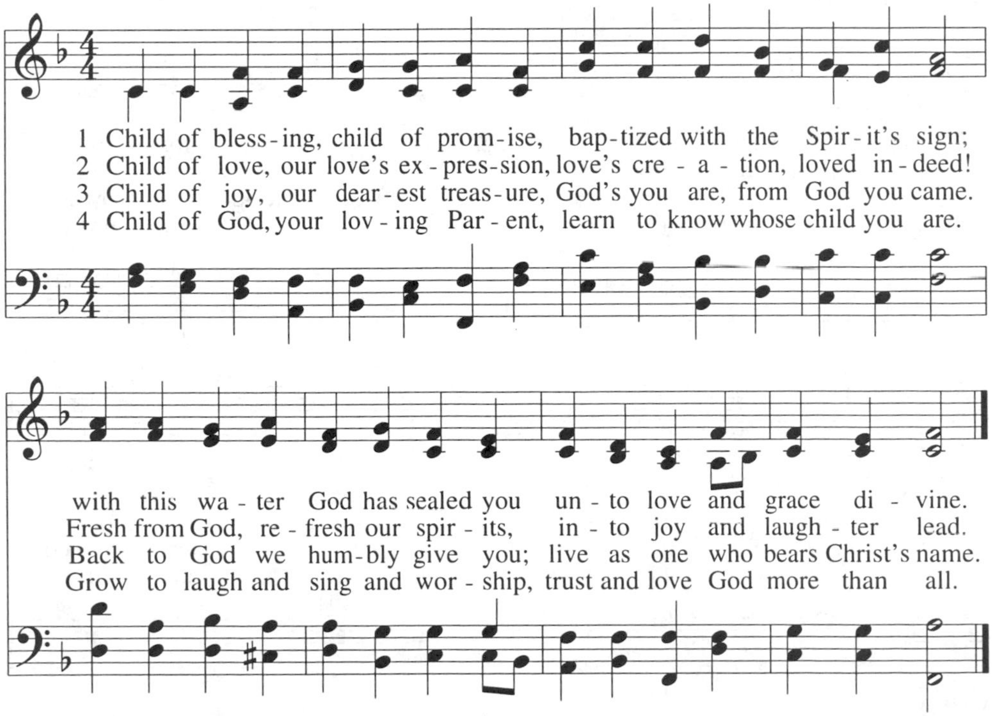
1 Child of bless-ing, child of prom-ise, bap-tized with the Spir-it's sign;
2 Child of love, our love's ex-pres-sion, love's cre-a-tion, loved in-deed!
3 Child of joy, our dear-est treas-ure, God's you are, from God you came.
4 Child of God, your lov-ing Par-ent, learn to know whose child you are.
with this wa-ter God has sealed you un-to love and grace di-vine.
Fresh from God, re-fresh our spir-its, in-to joy and laugh-ter lead.
Back to God we hum-bly give you; live as one who bears Christ's name.
Grow to laugh and sing and wor-ship, trust and love God more than all.

WORDS: Ronald S. Cole-Turner (1948-)
MUSIC: Attr. Christian F. Witt (1660-1716); adapt. Henry J. Gauntlett (1805-1876)

STUTTGART
8.7.8.7.

678 In Water We Grow

Unison
1 In wa - ter we grow, se - cure in the womb,
2 In wa - ter we wash: the dirt of each day,
3 In wa - ter we dive, and can - not draw breath,
4 In wa - ter we dwell, for by its deep flow
and speech - less - ly know love's safe - ty and room.
its trou - ble and rush are car - ried a - way.
then sur - face a - live, re - bound - ing from death.
through blood - stream and cell, we live, think, and grow.
Bap - tiz - ing and bless - ing, we pub - lish for good
In Christ re - cre - at - ed by love's cleans - ing art,
Our old self goes un - der, in Christ dead and drowned.
Praise God, love out - flow - ing, whose well of new birth
the free - ing, ca - ress - ing safe - keep - ing of God.
self - will and self - ha - tred dis - solve and de - part.
We rise, washed in won - der, by love clad and crowned.
bap - tiz - es our know - ing, and wa - ters the earth.

WORDS: Brian Wren (1936-)
MUSIC: Carl F. Schalk (1929-)

STANLEY BEACH
10.10.11.11.

Baptized in Water

Unison
1 Bap - tized in wa - ter, sealed by the Spir - it,
2 Bap - tized in wa - ter, sealed by the Spir - it,
3 Bap - tized in wa - ter, sealed by the Spir - it,
cleansed by the blood of Christ, our King;
dead in the tomb with Christ, our King;
marked with the sign of Christ, our King;
heirs of sal - va - tion, trust - ing his prom - ise,
one with his ris - ing, freed and for - giv - en,
born of one Fa - ther, we are his chil - dren,
faith - ful - ly now God's prais - es we sing.
thank - ful - ly now God's prais - es we sing.
joy - ful - ly now God's prais - es we sing.

WORDS: Michael Saward (1932-)
MUSIC: Gaelic melody; harm. David Evans (1874-1948)

BUNESSAN
5.5.5.4.D.

680 Borning Cry

Unison
G Gmaj7 Am/G G Am/G Gmaj7 Am/G
1 I was there to hear your born - ing cry, I'll be
2 When you heard the won - der of the Word I was
3 In the mid - dle a - ges of your life, not too
G Gmaj7 Am/G G Am6/G
there when you are old. I re - joiced the day you
there to cheer you on. You were raised to praise the
old, no long - er young, I'll be there to guide you
G Am/G G C/E Am7 D7sus D7 G (Fine)
were bap - tized to see your life un - fold.
liv - ing Lord to whom you now be - long.
through the night, com - plete what I've be - gun.
C G/B Am G
I was there when you were but a child with a
If you find some - one to share your time, and you
When the eve - ning gent - ly clos - es in and you

WORDS and MUSIC: John C. Ylvisaker (1937-)

WATERLIFE
Irregular

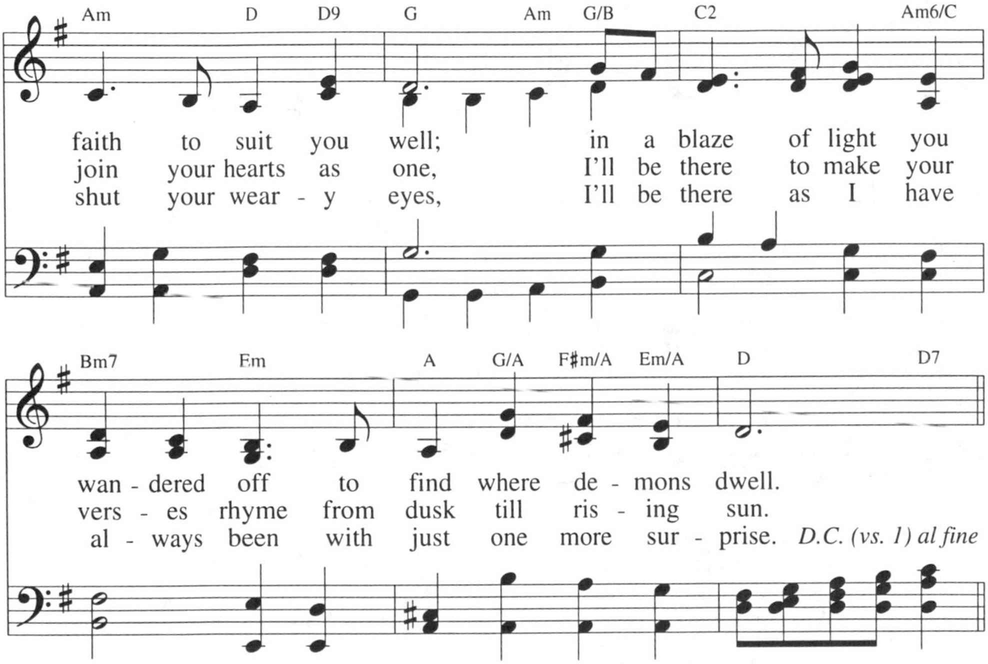
Am D D9 G Am G/B C2 Am6/C
faith to suit you well; in a blaze of light you
join your hearts as one, I'll be there to make your
shut your wear - y eyes, I'll be there as I have
Bm7 Em A G/A F♯m/A Em/A D D7
wan - dered off to find where de - mons dwell.
vers - es rhyme from dusk till ris - ing sun.
al - ways been with just one more sur - prise.
D.C. (vs. 1) al fine

Lord, We Bring to You Our Children 681

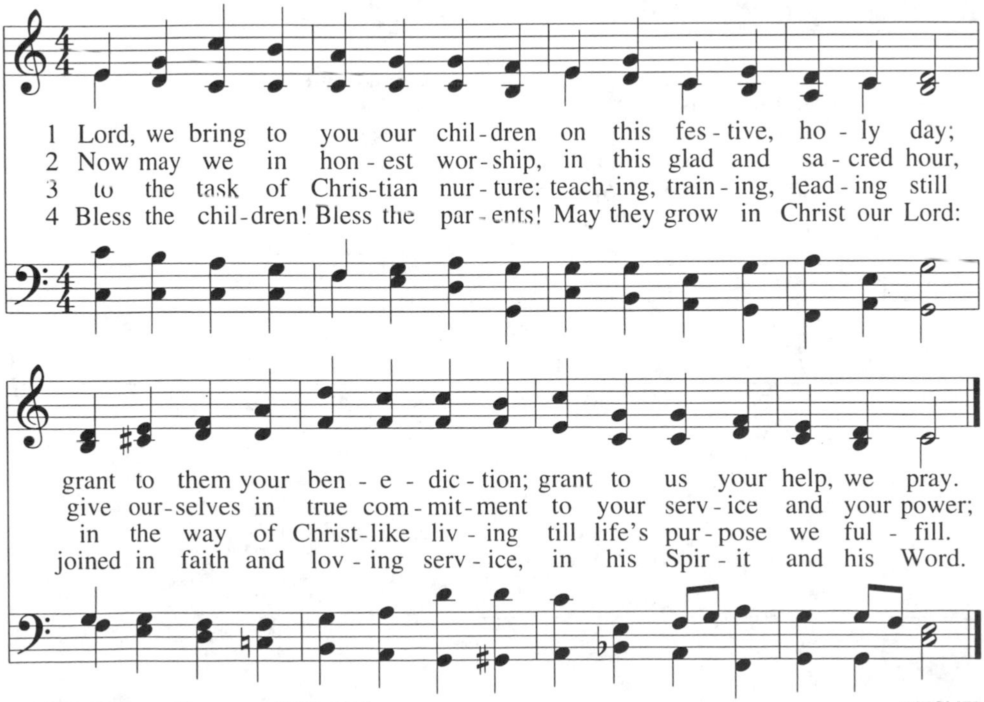
1 Lord, we bring to you our chil-dren on this fes-tive, ho - ly day;
2 Now may we in hon-est wor-ship, in this glad and sa-cred hour,
3 to the task of Chris-tian nur-ture: teach-ing, train-ing, lead-ing still
4 Bless the chil-dren! Bless the par-ents! May they grow in Christ our Lord:
grant to them your ben - e - dic - tion; grant to us your help, we pray.
give our-selves in true com-mit-ment to your serv-ice and your power;
in the way of Christ-like liv - ing till life's pur-pose we ful - fill.
joined in faith and lov - ing serv - ice, in his Spir - it and his Word.

WORDS: Frank von Christierson (1900-1996)
MUSIC: John Stainer (1840-1901)

WYCLIFF
8.7.8.7.

682 The Fruit of Love

1 The fruit of love, this gift of life,
2 This ten - der child is known by you,
3 A ba - by's fu - ture waits with hope
4 With hum - ble joy we rec - og - nize
5 We praise you, Fa - ther, God a - lone.
we place, O God, with - in your care.
in - clined to truth and e - vil too.
en - vel - oped with the Spir - it's grace.
a task that on - ly has be - gun.
We praise you, Je - sus, Son of love.
To know your grace and guid - ing hand
Would you pro - tect this one we love
To - mor - row's prom - ise can be glimpsed
A sa - cred charge lies in our arms
And to the Spir - it, Ho - ly One,
in years to come is now our prayer.
from sin and harm its whole life through?
with - in this in - fant's ti - ny face.
to cra - dle faith and pass it on.
we sing our praise. A - men. A - men.

WORDS: Gregory E. Asimakoupoulos (1952-)
MUSIC: English melody; adapt. Hal H. Hopson (1933-)

GIFT OF LOVE
L.M.

Little One, Born to Bring 683

Unison
1 Lit - tle one, born to bring us such love,
2 Hold us, dear God, as this child is held
3 Can - cel our an - ger, tem - per our tears,
4 Ho - ly and ten - der Spir - it of God,
lit - tle one, wrapped a - round by our prayer,
close to your heart, to com - fort our pain;
ban - ish the blame we keep to our cost,
you do not leave us strug - gling a - lone;
giv - en and tak - en, light - ing our life,
we too are chil - dren, chil - dren of time,
tell us the words we long to be - lieve:
sleep - ing or wak - ing, bless us with peace,
now we re - turn you in - to God's care.
need - ing to turn and trust you a - gain.
nev - er a child of yours will be lost.
take him/her, en - fold him/her: s/he is your own.

WORDS: Shirley Erena Murray (1931-)
MUSIC: Joy F. Patterson (1931-)

KORU
9.9.9.9.

684 For the Life That You Have Given

For the life that you have giv - en, for the love in Christ made known,
with these fruits of time and la - bor, with these gifts that are your own:
here we of - fer, Lord, our prais-es; heart and mind and strength we bring;
give us grace to love and serve you, liv - ing what we pray and sing.

WORDS: Carl P. Daw, Jr., (1944-)
MUSIC: Leavitt's *The Christian Lyre*, 1830

PLEADING SAVIOR
8.7.8.7.D.

What Gift Can We Bring 685

Unison
1 What gift can we bring, what pres - ent, what to - ken?
2 Give thanks for the Past, for those who had vi - sion,
3 Give thanks for To - mor - row, full of sur - pris - es,
4 This gift we now bring, this pres - ent, this to - ken,
What words can con - vey it— the joy of this day?
who plant - ed and wa - tered so dreams could come true.
for know - ing what - ev - er To - mor - row may bring,
these words can con - vey it— the joy of this day!
When grate - ful we come, re - mem - bering, re - joic - ing,
Give thanks for the Now, for stud - y, for wor - ship,
God gives us his word that al - ways, for - ev - er,
When grate - ful we come, re - mem - bering, re - joic - ing,
what song can we of - fer in hon - or and praise?
for mis - sion that bids us turn prayer in - to deed.
we rest in his keep - ing and live in his love.
this song we now of - fer in hon - or and praise!

WORDS and MUSIC: Jane Marshall (1924-)

ANNIVERSARY SONG
11.11.11.11.

686 What Does the Lord Require

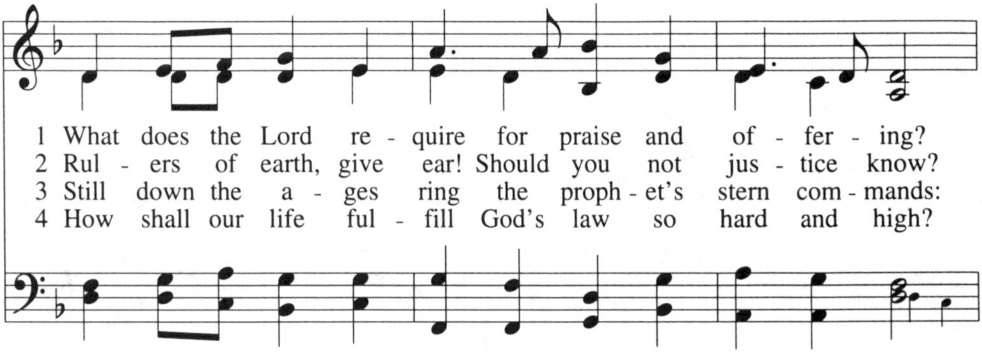
1 What does the Lord re - quire for praise and of - fer - ing?
2 Rul - ers of earth, give ear! Should you not jus - tice know?
3 Still down the a - ges ring the proph - et's stern com - mands:
4 How shall our life ful - fill God's law so hard and high?

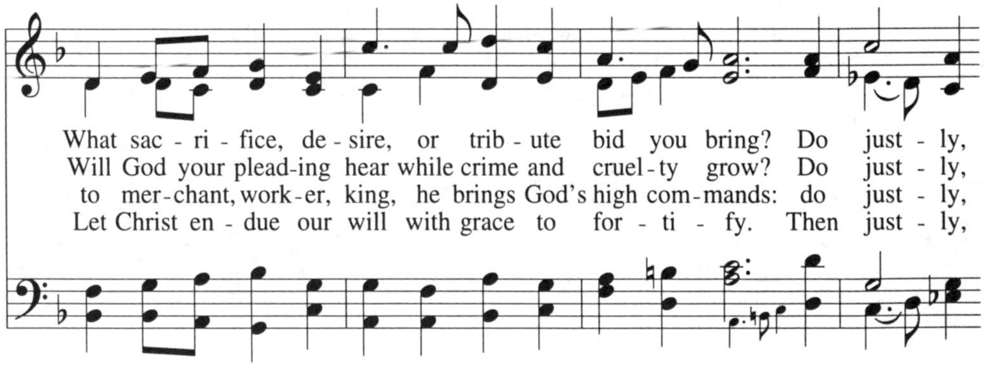
What sac - ri - fice, de - sire, or trib - ute bid you bring? Do just - ly,
Will God your plead-ing hear while crime and cruel - ty grow? Do just - ly,
to mer-chant, work-er, king, he brings God's high com-mands: do just - ly,
Let Christ en - due our will with grace to for - ti - fy. Then just - ly,

1–3
4
love mer - cy, walk hum - bly with your God.
love mer - cy, walk hum - bly with your God.
love mer - cy, walk hum - bly with your God.
in mer - cy, we'll hum - bly walk with God.

WORDS: Albert F. Bayly (1901-1984), alt; para. Micah 6:6-8
MUSIC: Erik Routley (1917-1982)

SHARPTHORNE
6.6.6.6.3.3.6.

All Things Are Yours! 687

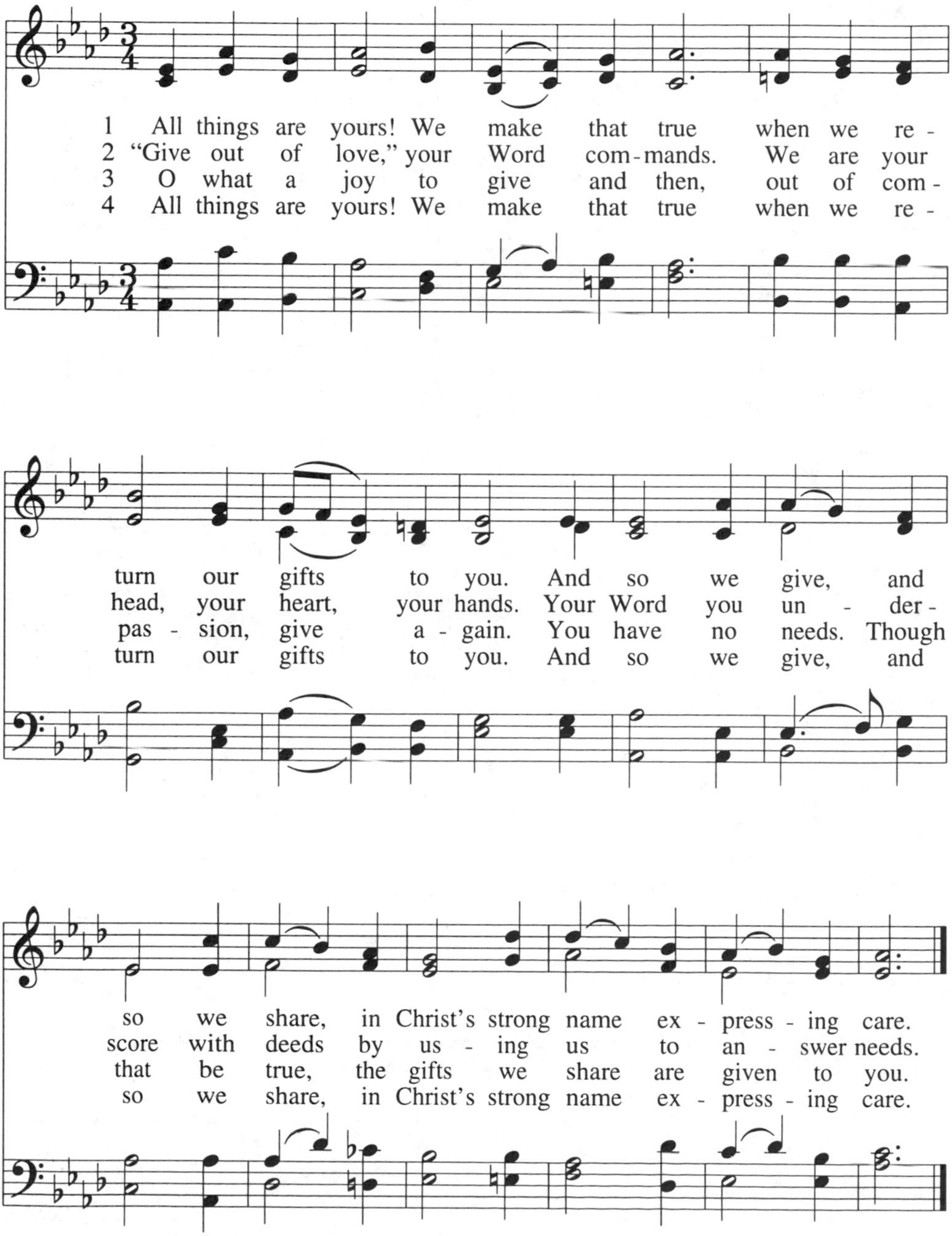
1 All things are yours! We make that true when we re -
2 "Give out of love," your Word com-mands. We are your
3 O what a joy to give and then, out of com -
4 All things are yours! We make that true when we re -
turn our gifts to you. And so we give, and
head, your heart, your hands. Your Word you un - der -
pas - sion, give a - gain. You have no needs. Though
turn our gifts to you. And so we give, and
so we share, in Christ's strong name ex - press - ing care.
score with deeds by us - ing us to an - swer needs.
that be true, the gifts we share are given to you.
so we share, in Christ's strong name ex - press - ing care.

WORDS: Bryan Jeffery Leech (1931-)
MUSIC: William Gardiner's *Sacred Melodies*, 1815

GERMANY
L.M.

688 We Give Thee but Thine Own

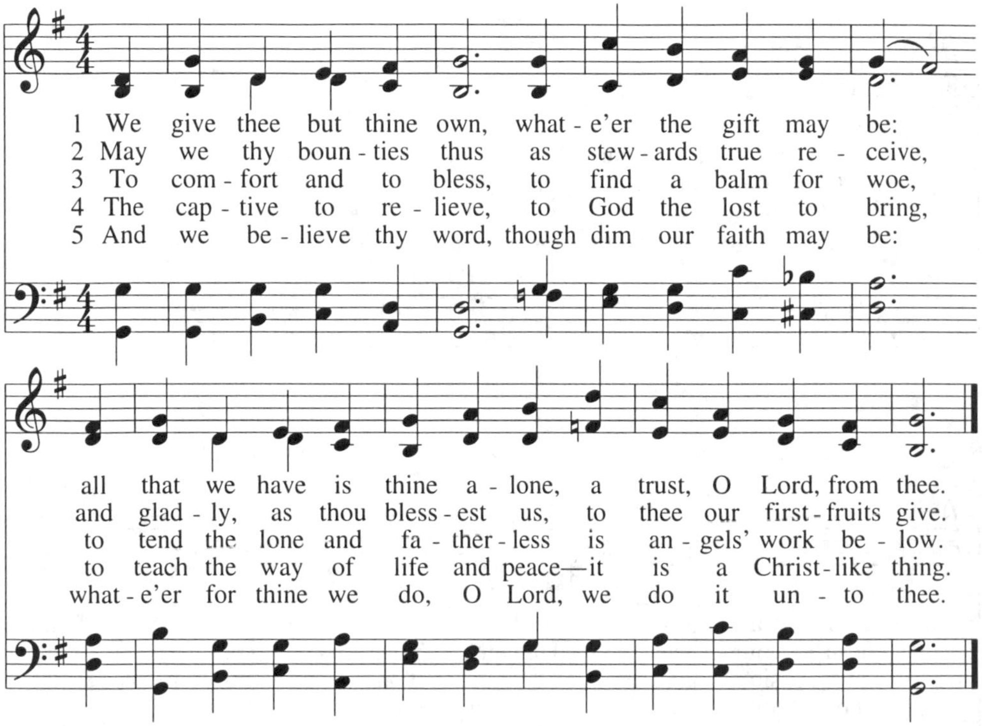
1 We give thee but thine own, what-e'er the gift may be:
2 May we thy boun-ties thus as stew-ards true re-ceive,
3 To com-fort and to bless, to find a balm for woe,
4 The cap-tive to re-lieve, to God the lost to bring,
5 And we be-lieve thy word, though dim our faith may be:
all that we have is thine a-lone, a trust, O Lord, from thee.
and glad-ly, as thou bless-est us, to thee our first-fruits give.
to tend the lone and fa-ther-less is an-gels' work be-low.
to teach the way of life and peace—it is a Christ-like thing.
what-e'er for thine we do, O Lord, we do it un-to thee.

WORDS: William W. How (1823-1897)
MUSIC: Mason and Webb's *Cantica Laudis*, 1850

SCHUMANN
S.M.

689 One Bread, One Body

Refrain (Unison)
N.C. G C/G G C/G G D Em Bsus B
One bread, one bod-y, one Lord of all,
Em D G Em A7 D7
one cup of bless-ing which we bless. And

WORDS: John B. Foley (1939-)
MUSIC: John B. Foley (1939-); arr. Gary Alan Smith (1947-), alt.

G C/G G C/G G D Em Bsus B
we, though man-y through-out the earth,
Em D G Em A7 D7 G C G
we are one bod - y in this one Lord.
Em D Em D
1 Gen - tile or Jew, ser - vant or free,
2 Man - y the gifts, man - y the works,
3 Grain for the fields, scat-tered and grown,
Em F Am D D7 to Refrain
wom-an or man, no more.
one in the Lord of all. One
gath-ered to one, for all.

690 We Remember You

Unison
G/B C D7 Gsus
1 We re-mem-ber you, we re-mem-ber you;
2 Pre-cious, ris-en Lamb, Je-sus who was slain,
G Em G/D A/C#
by your sac-ri-fice of love all glo-ry now is due.
now en-throned in glo-ry, for-ev-er you will reign.
D G/B C D/C G/B D/F#
At this ta-ble here mer-cy hov-ers near.
Glad-ly we em-brace both these signs of grace.
Em7 G/D C Am D7 C/G G
Thanks is of-fered up; in this bread and cup we re-mem-ber you.

WORDS and MUSIC: Walt Harrah (1948-)

EUCHARIST
Irregular

With the Body That Was Broken 691

Unison
1 With the bod - y that was bro - ken, to the bod - y
2 In the cross of Christ con - fid - ing, by the cross we
3 Fed by break-ing and out - pour - ing, joined in break-ing -
who pro - claim, by the blood that is life's to - ken,
bear as sign, through the Spir - it's gifts and guid - ing,
forth of praise, given the peace of God's re - stor - ing,
for the life found in his name: so the Word-made-flesh has
with these gifts of bread and wine: so the church in faith a -
sent in peace to live al - ways: so we show forth our a -
spo - ken, and his pres - ence here we claim.
bid - ing keeps the feast Christ made di - vine.
dor - ing as God's ser - vants all our days.

WORDS: Carl P. Daw, Jr. (1944-)
MUSIC: French melody, 17th c.; harm. Ralph Vaughan Williams (1872-1958)

PICARDY
8.7.8.7.8.7.

692 Eat This Bread and Never Hunger

Refrain (Unison)
Eat this bread and nev-er hun-ger, drink this cup and nev-er thirst;
Christ in-vites us to the ta-ble where the last be-come the first.
1 Ask - ing for a cup of wa - ter,
2 Walk - ing down a des - ert high - way,
3 Weep - ing for his friend at grave - side,
Je - sus touched for - bid - den ground; and the wom - an,
Je - sus healed a man born blind; soon the man be -
Je - sus felt the pain of death; yet he knew God's
to Refrain
with a ques - tion, told the world what she had found.
came a wit - ness to the truth we seek and find.
power to wak - en: liv - ing wa - ter, liv - ing breath.

WORDS and MUSIC: Daniel Charles Damon (1955-)

MODESTO
8.7.8.7.Ref.

Bread of the World

Bread of the world, in mer - cy bro - ken, Wine of the
soul, in mer - cy shed, by whom the words of life were spo - ken,
and in whose death our sins are dead: look on the heart by sor-row
bro - ken, look on the tears by sin - ners shed; and be your
feast to us the to - ken that by your grace our souls are fed.

WORDS: Reginald Heber (1783-1826)
MUSIC: Louis Bourgeois (ca. 1510-1561); *Genevan Psalter*, 1551

RENDEZ À DIEU
9.8.9.8.D.

694 Come, Let Us Eat

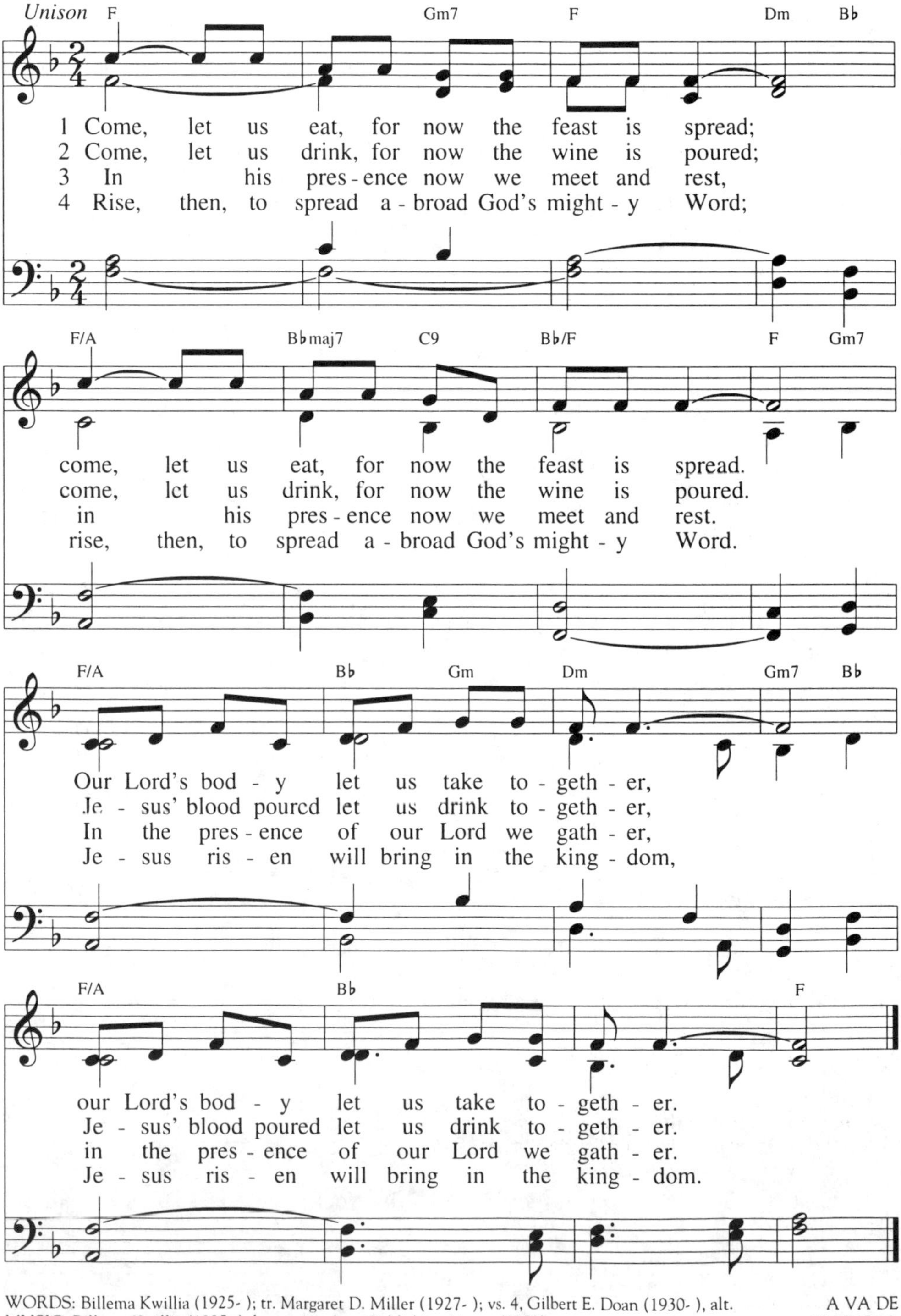
Unison
F Gm7 F Dm B♭
1 Come, let us eat, for now the feast is spread;
2 Come, let us drink, for now the wine is poured;
3 In his pres - ence now we meet and rest,
4 Rise, then, to spread a - broad God's might - y Word;
F/A B♭maj7 C9 B♭/F F Gm7
come, let us eat, for now the feast is spread.
come, let us drink, for now the wine is poured.
in his pres - ence now we meet and rest.
rise, then, to spread a - broad God's might - y Word.
F/A B♭ Gm Dm Gm7 B♭
Our Lord's bod - y let us take to - geth - er,
Je - sus' blood poured let us drink to - geth - er,
In the pres - ence of our Lord we gath - er,
Je - sus ris - en will bring in the king - dom,
F/A B♭ F
our Lord's bod - y let us take to - geth - er.
Je - sus' blood poured let us drink to - geth - er.
in the pres - ence of our Lord we gath - er.
Je - sus ris - en will bring in the king - dom.

WORDS: Billema Kwillia (1925-); tr. Margaret D. Miller (1927-); vs. 4, Gilbert E. Doan (1930-), alt.
MUSIC: Billema Kwillia (1925-); harm. Augsburg Publishing House (1972)

A VA DE
10.10.10.10.

As We Gather at Your Table

Unison
1 As we gath - er at your ta - ble, as we lis - ten to your word,
2 Turn our wor-ship in - to wit - ness in the sac - ra - ment of life;
3 Gra-cious Spir - it, help us sum - mon oth - er guests to share that feast
help us know, O God, your pres - ence; let our hearts and minds be stirred.
send us forth to love and serve you, bring-ing peace where there is strife.
where tri - um-phant Love will wel - come those who had been last and least.
Nour-ish us with sa - cred sto - ry till we claim it as our own;
Give us, Christ, your great com-pas - sion to for - give as you for-gave;
There no more will en - vy bind us nor will pride our peace de - stroy,
teach us through this ho - ly ban - quet how to make Love's vic - tory known.
may we still be - hold your im - age in the world you died to save.
as we join with saints and an - gels to re - peat the sound-ing joy.

WORDS: Carl P. Daw, Jr. (1944-)
MUSIC: Attr. B. F. White (1800-1879), *The Sacred Harp*, 1844; arr. Jack Schrader (1942-)

BEACH SPRING
8.7.8.7.D.

696 Come, Share the Lord

1 We gath-er here in Je-sus' name, his love is burn-ing in our hearts like liv-ing flame; for through his lov-ing Son the Fa-ther makes us one: come, take the bread, come, drink the wine, come, share the Lord.
2 He joins us here, he breaks the bread, the Lord who pours the cup is ris-en from the dead; the one we love the most is now our gra-cious host: come, take the bread, come, drink the wine, come, share the Lord.
3 We'll gath-er soon where an-gels sing; we'll see the glo-ry of our Lord and com-ing King; now we an-tic-i-pate the feast for which we wait: come, take the bread, come, drink the wine, come, share the Lord.
Fine
(1) No one is a stran-ger here, ev-ery-one be-longs;
(2) We are now a fam-i-ly of which the Lord is head;
8

WORDS and MUSIC: Bryan Jeffery Leech (1931-)

DIVERNON
Irregular

to verses 2 and 3
find - ing our for - give-ness here, we in turn for-give all wrongs.
though un - seen he meets us here in the break - ing of the bread.

Eat This Bread 697

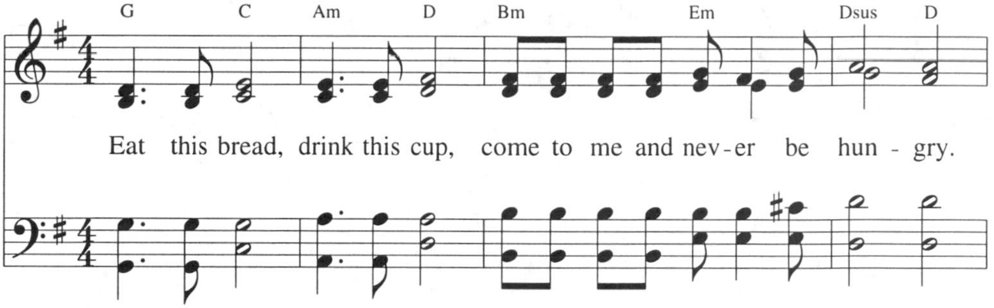
G C Am D Bm Em Dsus D
Eat this bread, drink this cup, come to me and nev-er be hun - gry.

G D Em Bm C Dsus D G
Eat this bread, drink this cup, trust in me and you will not thirst.

WORDS: Robert Batastini (1942-) and the Taizé Community
MUSIC: Jacques Berthier (1923-1994)

698 Let Us Talents and Tongues Employ

1 Let us tal - ents and tongues em - ploy, reach - ing out with a
2 Christ is a - ble to make us one, at the ta - ble he
3 Je - sus calls us in, sends us out bear - ing fruit in a
shout of joy: bread is bro - ken, the wine is poured,
set the tone, teach - ing peo - ple to live to bless,
world of doubt, gives us love to tell, bread to share:
Refrain
Christ is spo - ken and seen and heard.
love in word and in deed ex - press. Je - sus lives a - gain,
God (Im - man - u - el) ev - ery - where!

WORDS: Fred Kaan (1929-)
MUSIC: Jamaican folk tune; adapt. Doreen Potter (1925-1980)

LINSTEAD
L.M.Ref.

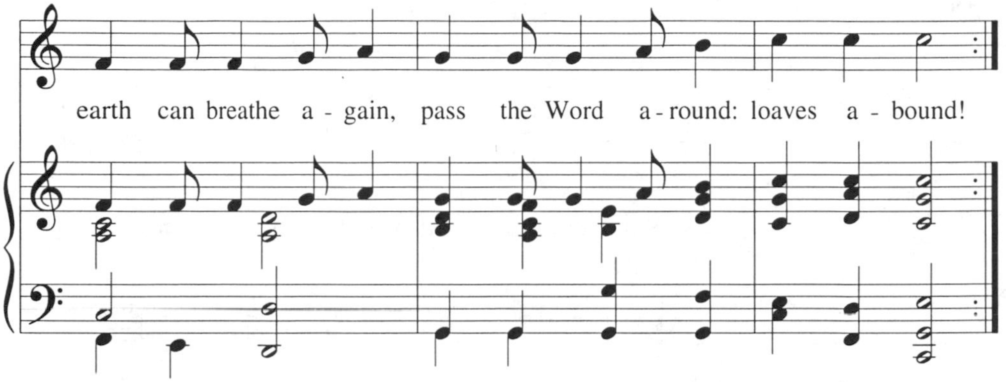
earth can breathe a - gain, pass the Word a - round: loaves a - bound!

Let Us Break Bread Together 699

Unison
Eb Cm Ab Fm/Bb Bb7 Eb Ab/Eb Eb Eb/G
1 Let us break bread to - geth-er on our knees; let us break
2 Let us drink wine to - geth-er on our knees; let us drink
3 Let us praise God to - geth-er on our knees; let us praise
Bb7/F Cm7 F F7 Bb Bbsus Bb
Refrain
N.C. Eb Gm C7 C7/E
bread to - geth-er on our knees.
wine to - geth-er on our knees.
God to - geth-er on our knees.
When I fall on my knees, with my
Fm Fm/Eb Bb7/D Ab/C Bb7 Eb Cm Fm7 Fm/Bb Bb7 Eb Ab Eb
face to the ris-ing sun, O Lord, have mer-cy on me.

WORDS and MUSIC: African-American spiritual; arr. Carlton R. Young (1926-)

LET US BREAK BREAD
10.10.Ref.

700 Now the Silence

Unison
Now the si - lence Now the peace Now the emp - ty hands up -
lift - ed Now the kneel - ing Now the plea Now the Fa - ther's
arms in wel - come Now the hear - ing Now the power
Now the ves - sel brimmed for pour - ing

WORDS: Jaroslav J. Vajda (1919-)
MUSIC: Carl F. Schalk (1929-)

NOW
Irregular

Now the bod - y Now the blood Now the joy - ful
cel - e - bra - tion Now the wed - ding Now the songs
Now the heart for - giv - en leap - ing Now the Spir - it's
vis - i - ta - tion Now the Son's e - piph - a - ny
Now the Fa - ther's bless - ing Now Now Now

701 There's a Quiet Understanding

1 There's a qui - et un - der-stand - ing when we're gath - ered
2 And we know when we're to - geth - er, shar - ing love and
in the Spir - it; it's a prom-ise that he gives us, when we
un - der-stand - ing, that our broth-ers and our sis - ters feel the
gath - er in his name. There's a love we feel in Je - sus,
one-ness that he brings. Thank you, thank you, thank you, Je - sus,
there's a man - na that he feeds us; it's a prom-ise that he gives us,
for the way you love and feed us, for the man - y ways you lead us,
1
2
(Repeat, ad lib.)
when we gath - er in his name.
thank you, thank you, Lord.

WORDS and MUSIC: Tedd Smith (1927-)

QUIET UNDERSTANDING
Irregular

We Come as Guests Invited 702

1 We come as guests in - vit - ed when Je - sus bids us dine,
2 We eat and drink, re - ceiv - ing from Christ the grace we need,
3 One bread is ours for shar - ing, one sin - gle fruit - ful vine,
his friends on earth u - nit - ed to share the bread and wine;
and in our hearts be - liev - ing on him by faith we feed;
our fel - low - ship de - clar - ing re - newed in bread and wine:
the bread of life is bro - ken, the wine is free - ly poured
with won - der and thanks - giv - ing for love that knows no end,
re newed, sus-tained, and giv - en by to - ken, sign, and word,
for us, in sol - emn to - ken of Christ our dy - ing Lord.
we find in Je - sus liv - ing our ev - er - pres - ent friend.
the pledge and seal of heav - en, the love of Christ our Lord.

WORDS: Timothy Dudley-Smith (1926-)
MUSIC: Johann Steurlein (1546-1613)

WIE LIEBLICH IST DER MAIEN
7.6.7.6.D.

703 I Am the Bread of Life

A F♯m A/C♯ C♯m
1 I am the bread of life; you who
2 The bread that I will give is my
3 Un - less you eat of the
4 I am the res - ur - rec - tion,
5 Yes, Lord, we be - lieve that
D Esus E
come to me shall not hun - ger; you who be -
flesh for the life of the world; and if you
flesh of the Son of Man and
I am the life. If you be -
you are the Christ, the
A/C♯ C♯m7 D E/D A/C♯ C♯m/E
lieve in me shall not thirst. No one can come to
eat of this bread, you shall live for -
drink of his blood, and drink of his
lieve in me, ev - en though you
Son of God who has

WORDS and MUSIC: Suzanne Toolan (1927-); arr. Betty Pulkingham (1928-)

F♯m F♯m/E Dmaj7 Bm/D E
me un - less the Fa - ther beck - ons.
ev - er, you shall live for - ev - er.
blood you shall not have life with - in you.
die, you shall live for - ev - er.
come in - to the world.
Refrain
A/C♯ E/B A D E
And I will raise you up, and I will raise you up,
A D Esus E7 A
and I will raise you up on the last day.

704 We Meet as Friends at Table

Unison
1 We meet as friends at ta - ble, to lis - ten, and be heard, u -
2 With food and drink for shar - ing the ta - ble soon is spread. The
3 We share our lives and long - ings, and when the meal is done we
4 Ful - filled, and glad to fol - low wher - ev - er Christ may lead, we
nit - ed by the Spir - it, at - ten - tive to the Word. Through
free - dom meal of Je - sus is crowned with wine and bread, and
pray as friends at ta - ble, and prom - ise to be one. To
jour - ney from the ta - ble to love a world in need with
prayer and con - ver - sa - tion we tune our var - ied views to
all, with - out ex - cep - tion, may eat, and speak, and stay, for
Christ, and to each oth - er, we cheer - ful - ly be - long: a -
pa - tience, truth and kind - ness, that jus - tice may in - crease and
Christ, whose love has made us the bear - ers of good news.
this is Christ's own ta - ble where none are turned a - way.
part, our hope is fruit - less; to - geth - er, we are strong.
all may sit at ta - ble in free - dom, joy, and peace.

WORDS: Brian Wren (1936-)
MUSIC: Hal H. Hopson (1933-)

MEAL OF LOVE
7.6.7.6.D.

You Satisfy the Hungry Heart 705

Refrain (Unison)
You sat-is-fy the hun-gry heart with gift of fin-est wheat;
come give to us, O sav-ing Lord, the bread of life to eat.
1 As when the shep herd calls his sheep, they know and heed his voice;
2 With joy-ful lips we sing to you our praise and grat-i-tude,
3 Is not the cup we bless and share the blood of Christ out-poured?
4 The mys-tery of your pres-ence, Lord, no mor-tal tongue can tell:
5 You give your-self to us, O Lord; then self-less let us be,
to Refrain
so when you call your fam-ily, Lord, we fol-low and re-joice.
that you should count us wor-thy, Lord, to share this heaven-ly food.
Do not one cup, one loaf, de-clare our one-ness in the Lord?
whom all the world can-not con-tain comes in our hearts to dwell.
to serve each oth-er in your name in truth and char-i-ty.

WORDS: Omer Westendorf (1916-1998)
MUSIC: Robert E. Kreutz (1922-1996)

FINEST WHEAT
C.M.Ref.

706 I Come with Joy

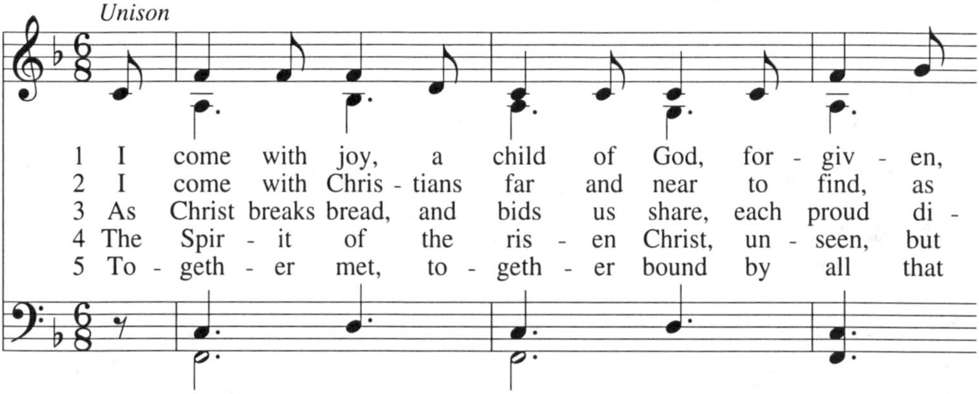
Unison
1 I come with joy, a child of God, for - giv - en,
2 I come with Chris - tians far and near to find, as
3 As Christ breaks bread, and bids us share, each proud di -
4 The Spir - it of the ris - en Christ, un - seen, but
5 To - geth - er met, to - geth - er bound by all that

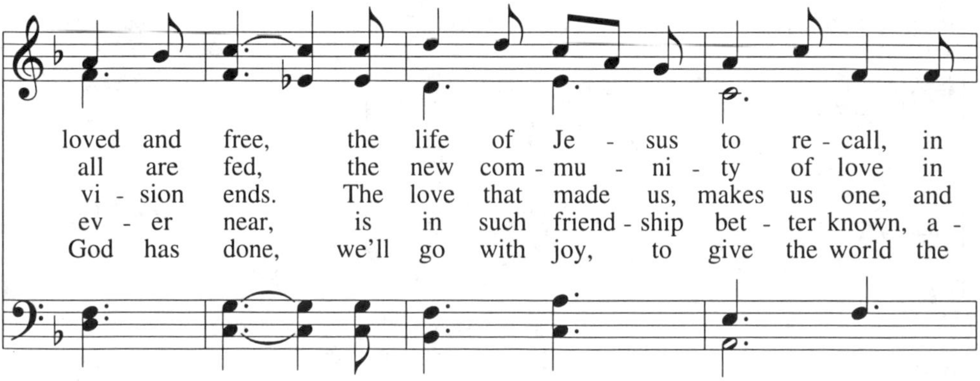
loved and free, the life of Je - sus to re - call, in
all are fed, the new com - mu - ni - ty of love in
vi - sion ends. The love that made us, makes us one, and
ev - er near, is in such friend - ship bet - ter known, a -
God has done, we'll go with joy, to give the world the

love laid down for me, in love laid down for me.
Christ's com - mun - ion bread, in Christ's com - mun - ion bread.
stran - gers now are friends, and stran - gers now are friends.
live a - mong us here, a - live a - mong us here.
love that makes us one, the love that makes us one.

WORDS: Brian Wren (1936-)
MUSIC: American melody; arr. Austin C. Lovelace (1919-)

DOVE OF PEACE
8.6.8.6.6.

We Thank You, God, for Feeding Us 707

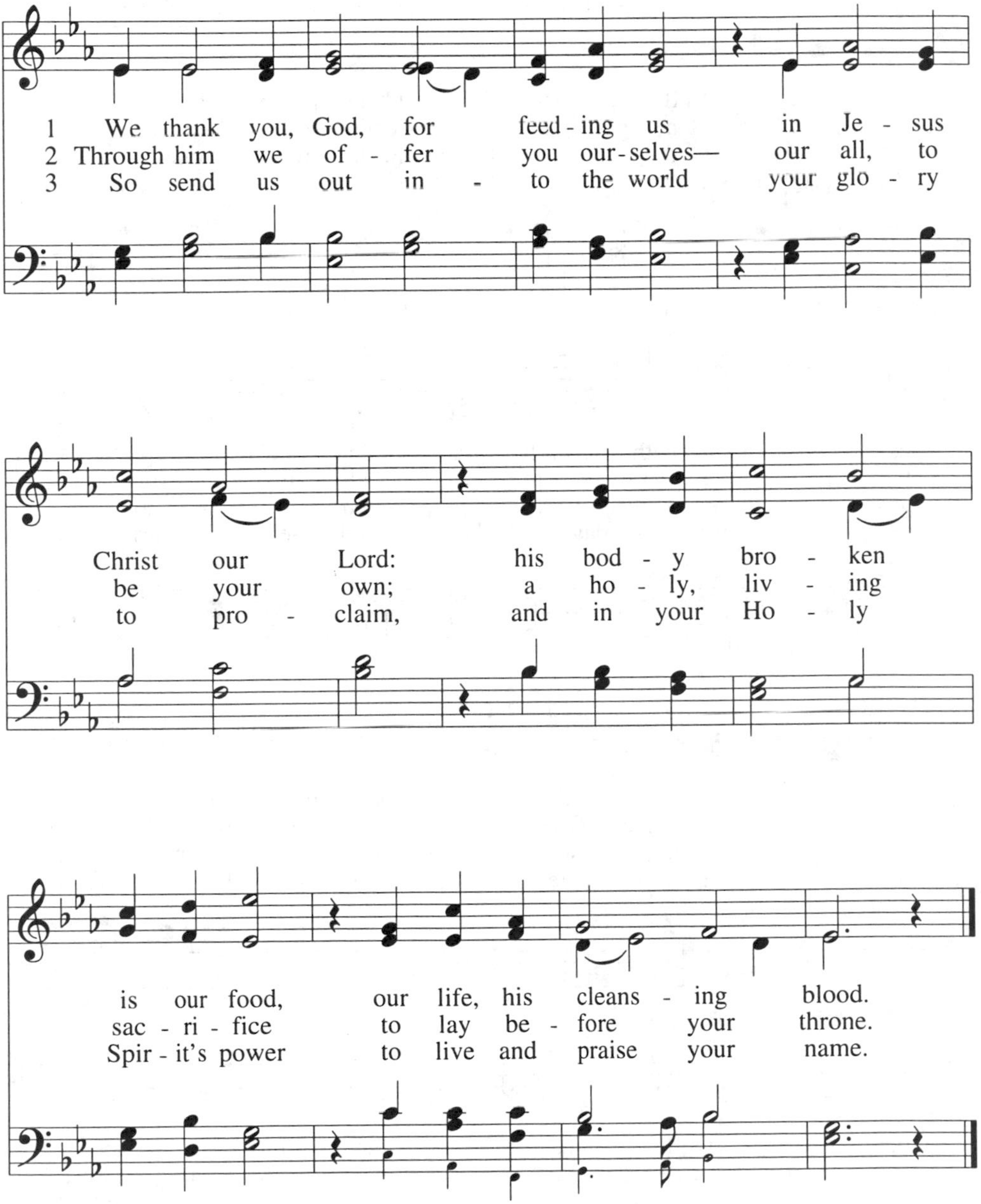
1 We thank you, God, for feed-ing us in Je-sus Christ our Lord: his bod-y bro-ken is our food, our life, his cleans-ing blood.
2 Through him we of-fer you our-selves— our all, to be your own; a ho-ly, liv-ing sac-ri-fice to lay be-fore your throne.
3 So send us out in-to the world your glo-ry to pro-claim, and in your Ho-ly Spir-it's power to live and praise your name.

WORDS: Michael Perry (1942-1996)
MUSIC: Erik Routley (1917-1982)

EVANSTON NEW
C.M.

708 Go Forth for God

1 Go forth for God, go to the world in peace; be of good
2 Go forth for God, go to the world in love; strength - en the
3 Go forth for God, go to the world in strength; hold fast the
4 Go forth for God, go to the world in joy, to serve God's
cour - age, armed with heaven - ly grace, in God's good Spir - it
faint, give cour - age to the weak; help the af - flict - ed;
good, be ur - gent for the right; ren - der to no one
peo - ple ev - ery day and hour, and serv - ing Christ, our
dai - ly to in - crease, till in the king - dom we see face to
rich - ly from a - bove God's love sup - plies the grace and power we
e - vil; Christ at length shall o - ver - come all dark-ness with his
ev - ery gift em - ploy, re - joic - ing in the Ho - ly Spir - it's
face. Go forth for God, go to the world in peace.
seek. Go forth for God, go to the world in love.
light. Go forth for God, go to the world in strength.
power. Go forth for God, go to the world in joy.

WORDS: J. R. Peacey (1896-1971)
MUSIC: *Genevan Psalter*, 1551; harm. C. Winfred Douglas (1867-1944), alt.

GENEVA 124
10.10.10.10.10.

Hallelujah! We Sing Your Praises 709

Refrain
Am G C G
Hal - le - lu - jah! We sing your prais - es, all our
D G Am G G7 Am G Am/C
hearts are filled with glad - ness. Hal - le - lu - jah! We sing your
G/D Em D G/D Am/D G
prais - es, all our hearts are filled with glad - ness.
Am G C G D G Am G
1 Christ the Lord to us said: I am wine, I am bread,
2 Now he sends us all out, strong in faith, free of doubt,
to Refrain (after repeat)
G7 Am G Am/C G/D Em D G/D Am/D G
I am wine, I am bread, give to all who thirst and hun - ger.
strong in faith, free of doubt. Tell to all the joy - ful Gos - pel.

WORDS and MUSIC: South African

HALELUYA! PELO TSO RONA
Irregular

710 The Trees of the Field

Unison
Em B7 Em B7 Em D7/F#
You shall go out with joy and be led forth with peace; the
G C/G G D/F# D B/D# N.C. Em B7 Em
moun-tains and the hills will break forth be - fore you; there'll be shouts of joy,
B7 Em B/F# F#m Em/G B7 Em
and all the trees of the field will clap, will clap their hands.
D7 N.C. G C/G G D
And all the trees of the field will clap their hands, the
D7 G D7 G C/G G
trees of the field will clap their hands, the trees of the field will

* = clap hands.

WORDS: Steffi Geiser Rubin (1950-); para. Isaiah 55:12
MUSIC: Stuart Dauermann (1944-)

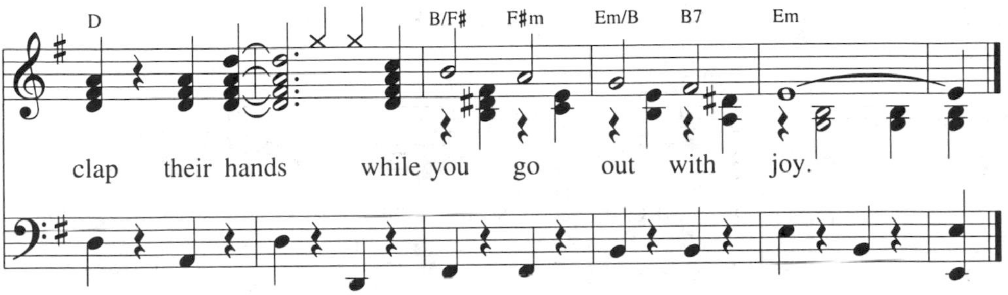
D
B/F#
F#m
Em/B
B7
Em
clap their hands while you go out with joy.

Savior, Again to Your Dear Name 711

1 Sav - ior, a - gain to your dear name we raise with one ac - cord our part - ing hymn of praise; we give you thanks be - fore our wor - ship cease, and now de - part - ing, wait your word of peace.
2 Grant us your peace up - on our home-ward way; with you be - gan, with you shall end the day; guard now the lips from sin, the hearts from shame, that in this house have called up - on your name.
3 Grant us your peace, Lord, through the com - ing night; turn all our dark - ness to your per - fect light; then, while we sleep, our hope and strength re - new, for dark and light are both a - like to you.
4 Grant us your peace through-out our earth - ly life: com - fort in sor - row, cour - age in the strife; then, when your voice shall make our con - flict cease, call us, O Lord, to your e - ter - nal peace.

WORDS: John Ellerton (1826-1893)
MUSIC: Edward J. Hopkins (1818-1901)

ELLERS
10.10.10.10.

712 Sent Forth by God's Blessing

Unison
1 Sent forth by God's bless-ing our true faith con - fess-ing, the
2 With praise and thanks-giv - ing to God ev - er liv - ing, the
peo - ple of God from this dwell - ing take leave. The
tasks of our ev - ery - day life we will face. Our
ser - vice is end - ed, O now be ex - tend - ed the
faith ev - er shar - ing, in love ev - er car - ing, em -
fruits of our wor - ship in all who be - lieve. The
brac - ing God's chil - dren of each tribe and race. With

WORDS: Omer Westendorf (1916-1998)
MUSIC: Welsh folk tune; harm. Leland Sateren (1913-)

ASH GROVE
6.6.11.6.6.11.D.

seed of the teach - ing, re - cep - tive souls reach - ing, shall
your grace you feed us, with your light now lead us: u -
blos - som in ac - tion for God and for all. God's
nite us as one in this life that we share. Then
grace did in - vite us, and love shall u - nite us to
may all the liv - ing with praise and thanks - giv - ing give
work for God's king - dom and an - swer the call.
hon - or to Christ and that name which we bear.

713 Send Me, Jesus

Leader
1 Send me, Lord.
All
1 Send me, Je - sus, send me, Je - sus, send me,
(2) Je - sus, lead me, Je - sus, lead me,
(3) Je - sus, fill me, Je - sus, fill me,
1, 2
3
2 Lead me, Lord.
3 Fill me, Lord.
Je - sus, send me, Lord.
Je - sus, lead me, Lord.
Je - sus, fill me,
2 Lead me,
3 Fill me,
Lord.

WORDS: South African
MUSIC: Thuma Mina

THUMA MINA
4.4.4.3.

714 Shalom, My Friends

Shalom Chaverim

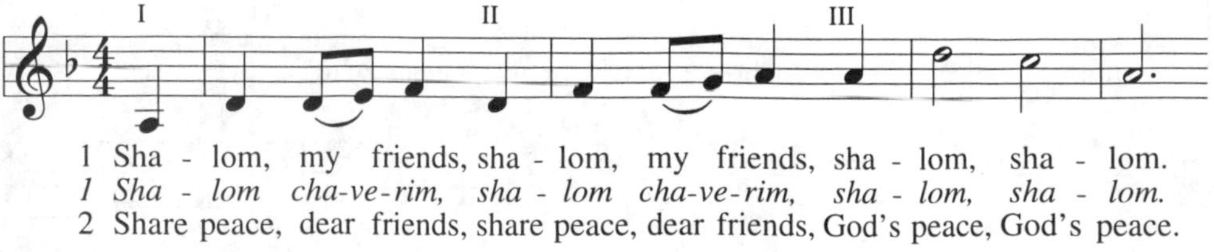
I
II
III
1 Sha - lom, my friends, sha - lom, my friends, sha - lom, sha - lom.
1 Sha - lom cha-ve-rim, sha - lom cha-ve-rim, sha - lom, sha - lom.
2 Share peace, dear friends, share peace, dear friends, God's peace, God's peace.

WORDS: Israeli round; English tr. Donald P. Hustad (1918-)
MUSIC: Hebrew melody

Sha - lom, my friends, sha - lom, my friends, sha - lom, sha - lom.
Sha - lom cha-ve-rim, sha - lom cha-ve-rim, sha - lom, sha - lom.
Share peace, dear friends, share peace, dear friends, God's peace, God's peace.

Now Let Us from This Table Rise 715

I
II
1 Now let us from this ta - ble rise, re - newed in bod - y, mind, and soul; with Christ we die and rise a - gain, his self - less love has made us whole.
2 With minds a - lert, up - held by grace, to spread the Word in speech and deed, we fol - low in the steps of Christ, at one with all in hope and need.
3 To fill each hu - man house with love, it is the sac - ra - ment of care; the work that Christ be - gan to do we hum - bly pledge our - selves to share.
4 Then give us grace, Com - pan - ion God, to choose a - gain the pil - grim way; and help us to ac - cept with joy the chal - lenge of to - mor - row's day.

WORDS: Fred Kaan (1929-)
MUSIC: Thomas Tallis (ca. 1505-1585)

TALLIS' CANON
L.M.

716 God Be with You

1 God be with you till we meet a-gain, by his coun-sels guide, up-hold you,
2 God be with you till we meet a-gain, 'neath his wings pro-tect-ing hide you,
3 God be with you till we meet a-gain; if life's per-ils should con-found you,
with his sheep se-cure-ly fold you; God be with you till we meet a-gain.
dai-ly man-na still pro-vide you; God be with you till we meet a-gain.
God will put his arms a-round you; God be with you till we meet a-gain.

WORDS: Jeremiah E. Rankin (1828-1904)
MUSIC: William G. Tomer (1833-1896)

GOD BE WITH YOU
9.8.9.8.

717 Go Now in Peace

1 Go now in peace; though friends must part, your
2 Go now in hope, and hope-ful stay, though
3 Go now in faith, through time and chance, un-
pres-ence lives in ev-ery heart. Your gifts to us no
shad-owed val-leys hide your way; through good and e-vil,
til we join the wed-ding dance as part-ners of the

WORDS: Brian Wren (1936-)
MUSIC: Thomas Tallis (ca. 1505-1585)

TALLIS' CANON
L.M.

words can tell: go now in peace, in Christ go well.
joy and pain, with God, in Spir - it, you re - main.
Three - in - One, where all is end - ed and be - gun.

Forth in Your Name 718

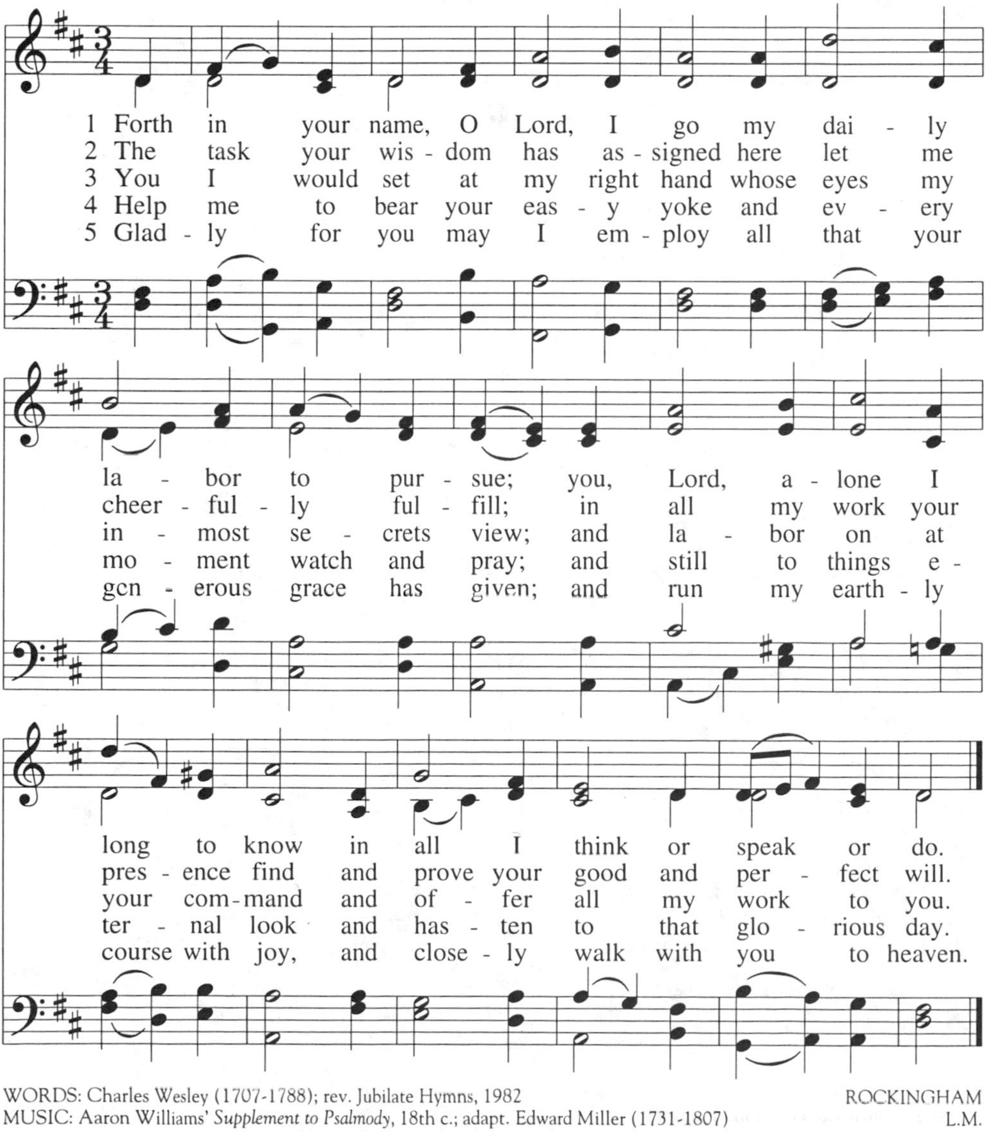
1 Forth in your name, O Lord, I go my dai - ly
2 The task your wis - dom has as - signed here let me
3 You I would set at my right hand whose eyes my
4 Help me to bear your eas - y yoke and ev - ery
5 Glad - ly for you may I em - ploy all that your
la - bor to pur - sue; you, Lord, a - lone I
cheer - ful - ly ful - fill; in all my work your
in - most se - crets view; and la - bor on at
mo - ment watch and pray; and still to things e -
gen - erous grace has given; and run my earth - ly
long to know in all I think or speak or do.
pres - ence find and prove your good and per - fect will.
your com - mand and of - fer all my work to you.
ter - nal look and has - ten to that glo - rious day.
course with joy, and close - ly walk with you to heaven.

WORDS: Charles Wesley (1707-1788); rev. Jubilate Hymns, 1982 ROCKINGHAM
MUSIC: Aaron Williams' *Supplement to Psalmody*, 18th c.; adapt. Edward Miller (1731-1807) L.M.

719 Go, My Children, with My Blessing

1 Go, my chil-dren, with my bless-ing, nev-er a-lone.
2 Go, my chil-dren, sins for-giv-en, at peace and pure.
3 Go, my chil-dren, fed and nour-ished, clos-er to me;
4 I, the Lord, will bless and keep you and give you peace;
Wak-ing, sleep-ing, I am with you; you are my own.
Here you learned how much I love you, what I can cure.
grow in love and love by serv-ing, joy-ful and free.
I, the Lord, will smile up-on you and give you peace:
In my love's bap-tis-mal riv-er I have made you mine for
Here you heard my dear Son's sto-ry; here you touched him, saw his
Here my Spir-it's pow-er filled you; here his ten-der com-fort
I, the Lord, will be your Fa-ther, Sav-ior, Com-fort-er, and
ev-er. Go, my chil-dren, with my bless-ing— you are my own.
glo-ry. Go, my chil-dren, sins for-giv-en, at peace and pure.
stilled you. Go, my chil-dren, fed and nour-ished, joy-ful and free.
Broth-er. Go, my chil-dren, I will keep you and give you peace.

WORDS: Jaroslav J. Vajda (1919-)
MUSIC: Welsh melody

AR HYD Y NOS
8.4.8.4.8.8.8.4.

With Grateful Heart I Thank You, Lord 720

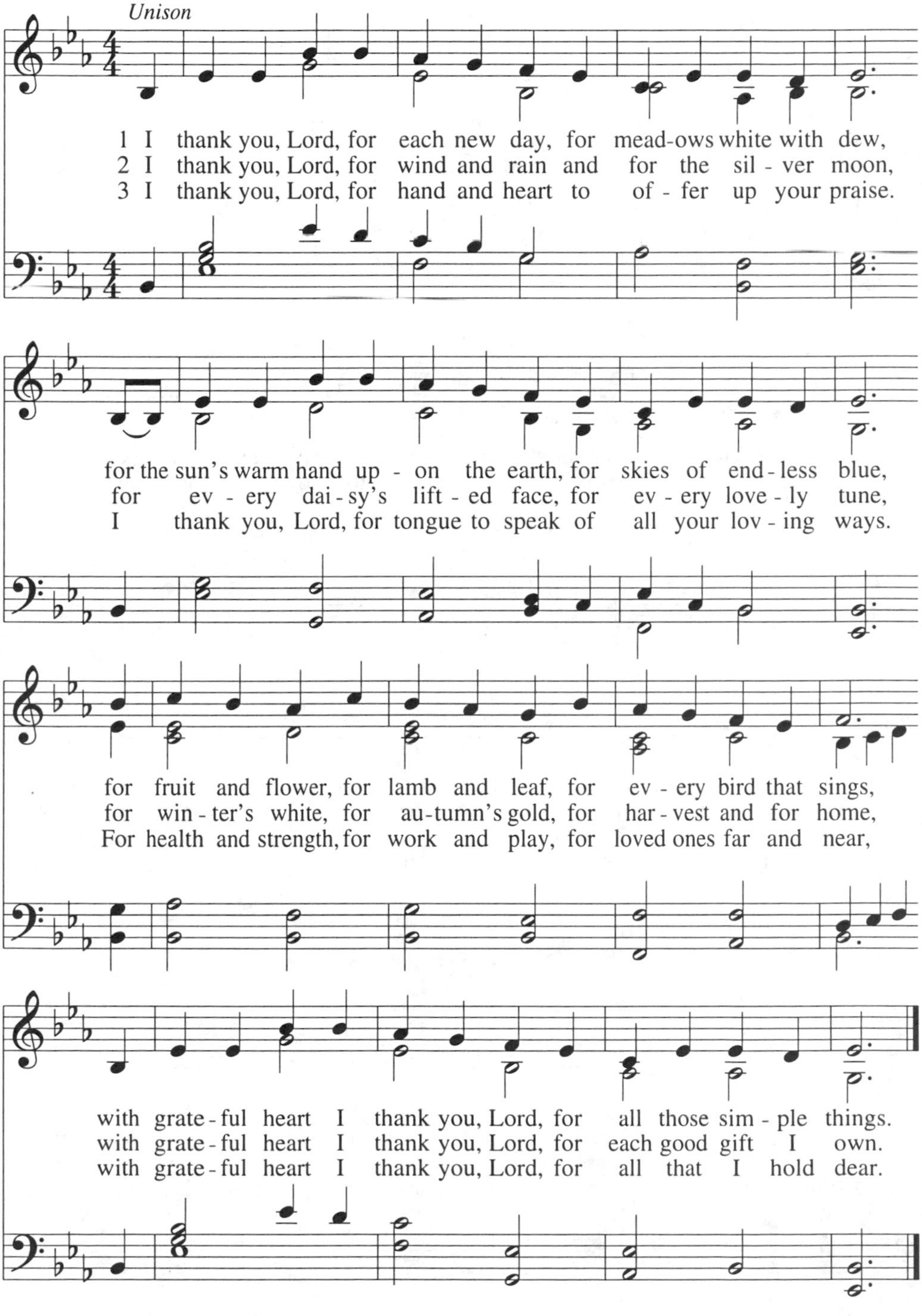
Unison
1 I thank you, Lord, for each new day, for mead-ows white with dew,
2 I thank you, Lord, for wind and rain and for the sil - ver moon,
3 I thank you, Lord, for hand and heart to of - fer up your praise.
for the sun's warm hand up - on the earth, for skies of end - less blue,
for ev - ery dai - sy's lift - ed face, for ev - ery love - ly tune,
I thank you, Lord, for tongue to speak of all your lov - ing ways.
for fruit and flower, for lamb and leaf, for ev - ery bird that sings,
for win - ter's white, for au - tumn's gold, for har - vest and for home,
For health and strength, for work and play, for loved ones far and near,
with grate - ful heart I thank you, Lord, for all those sim - ple things.
with grate - ful heart I thank you, Lord, for each good gift I own.
with grate - ful heart I thank you, Lord, for all that I hold dear.

WORDS and MUSIC: Mary Kay Beall (1943-)

GRATUS
C.M.D.

721 Come, Ye Thankful People, Come

1 Come, ye thank-ful peo - ple, come; raise the song of har - vest home.
2 All the world is God's own field, fruit un - to his praise to yield,
3 For the Lord our God shall come and shall take his har - vest home,
4 E - ven so, Lord, quick - ly come to your fi - nal har - vest home,
All is safe - ly gath - ered in ere the win - ter storms be - gin.
wheat and tares to - geth - er sown, un - to joy or sor - rows grown.
from his field shall in that day all of - fens - es purge a - way,
gath - er all your peo - ple in, free from sor - row, free from sin,
God, our ma - ker, does pro - vide for our wants to be sup - plied;
First the blade, and then the ear, then the full corn shall ap - pear,
give his an - gels charge at last in the fire the tares to cast,
there, for - ev - er pu - ri - fied, in your pres - ence to a - bide.
come to God's own tem - ple, come, raise the song of har - vest home.
Lord of har - vest, grant that we whole - some grain and pure may be.
but the fruit - ful ears to store in his gar - ner ev - er - more.
Come, with all your an - gels, come, raise the glo - rious har - vest home.

WORDS: Henry Alford (1810-1871), alt.
MUSIC: George J. Elvey (1816-1893)

ST. GEORGE'S, WINDSOR
7.7.7.7.D.

Praise and Thanksgiving

Unison
C C/E Dm7/F G7 F/C C
1 Praise and thanks - giv - ing, God, we would of - fer
2 God bless the la - bor we bring to serve you;
3 You are pro - vid - ing food for your chil - dren,
4 Then will your bless - ing reach ev - ery peo - ple,
C Em Am C/E Am/F# Gsus G7
for all things liv - ing, you have made good:
that with our neigh - bor we may be fed.
your wis - dom guid - ing teach - es us share
all lands con - fess - ing your gra - cious hand.
C F Dm7 C/E Am D/F#
har - vest of sown fields, fruits of the or - chard,
Sow - ing or till - ing, we would work with you;
one with an - oth - er so that, re - joic - ing,
Where you are reign - ing no one will hun - ger,
Em/G C F G7 C
hay from the mown fields, blos - som and wood.
har - vest - ing, mill - ing for dai - ly bread.
oth - ers may know you and praise your care.
your love sus - tain - ing, fruit - ful the land.

WORDS: Albert F. Bayly (1901-1984), alt.
MUSIC: Gaelic melody; arr. Jack Schrader (1942-)

BUNESSAN
5.5.5.4.D.

723 For the Fruit of All Creation

1 For the fruit of all cre - a - tion, thanks be to God.
2 In the just re - ward of la - bor, God's will is done.
3 For the har - vests of the Spir - it, thanks be to God.
For his gifts to ev - ery na - tion, thanks be to God.
In the help we give our neigh - bor, God's will is done.
For the good we all in - her - it, thanks be to God.
For the plow - ing, sow - ing, reap ing, si - lent growth while we are
In our world-wide task of car - ing for the hun - gry and de -
For the won - ders that as - tound us, for the truths that still con -
sleep - ing, fu - ture needs in earth's safe - keep - ing, thanks be to God.
spair - ing, in the har - vests we are shar - ing, God's will is done.
found us, most of all, that love has found us, thanks be to God.

WORDS: Fred Pratt Green (1903-2000), alt.
MUSIC: Welsh melody; harm. Luther O. Emerson (1820-1915)

AR HYD Y NOS
8.4.8.4.8.8.8.4.

Sing to the Lord of Harvest 724

Unison
1 Sing to the Lord of har - vest, sing songs of love and praise;
2 God makes the clouds rain good - ness, the des - erts bloom and spring,
3 Bring to this sa - cred al - tar the gifts his good-ness gave,
with joy - ful hearts and voic - es your al - le - lu - ias raise.
the hills leap up in glad - ness, the val - leys laugh and sing.
the gold - en sheaves of har - vest, the souls Christ died to save.
By him the roll - ing sea - sons in fruit - ful or - der move;
God fills them with his full - ness, all things with large in - crease;
Your hearts lay down be - fore him when at his feet you fall,
sing to the Lord of har - vest a joy - ous song of love.
he crowns the year with bless - ing, with plen - ty and with peace.
and with your lives a - dore him who gave his life for all.

WORDS: John Samuel Bewley Monsell (1811-1875)
MUSIC: Johann Steurlein (1546-1613)

WIE LIEBLICH IST DER MAIEN
7.6.7.6.D.

725 Thanks to God for My Redeemer

1 Thanks to God for my Re-deem - er, thanks for all thou dost pro-vide!
2 Thanks for prayers that thou hast an-swered, thanks for what thou dost de - ny!
3 Thanks for ros - es by the way - side, thanks for thorns their stems con-tain!
Thanks for times now but a mem - ory, thanks for Je - sus by my side!
Thanks for storms that I have weath - ered, thanks for all thou dost sup - ply!
Thanks for home and thanks for fire - side, thanks for hope, that sweet re - frain!
Thanks for pleas - ant, balm - y spring-time, thanks for dark and drear - y fall!
Thanks for pain and thanks for plea - sure, thanks for com - fort in de - spair!
Thanks for joy and thanks for sor - row, thanks for heaven-ly peace with thee!
Thanks for tears by now for - got - ten, thanks for peace with - in my soul!
Thanks for grace that none can meas - ure, thanks for love be-yond com-pare!
Thanks for hope in the to - mor - row, thanks through all e - ter - ni - ty!

WORDS: August Ludvig Storm (1862-1914); tr. Carl E. Backstrom (1901-1984)
MUSIC: John A. Hultman (1861-1942)

TACK O GUD
8.7.8.7.D.

We Praise You, O God

1 We praise you, O God, our Re - deem - er, Cre - a - tor;
2 We wor - ship you, God of our fa - thers and moth - ers;
3 With voic - es u - nit - ed our prais - es we of - fer,
in grate - ful de - vo - tion our trib - ute we bring;
through life's storm and tem - pest our guide you have been;
our songs of thanks - giv - ing to you we now raise;
we lay it be - fore you; we kneel and a - dore you;
when per - ils o'er - take us, you nev - er for - sake us,
your strong arm will guide us, our God is be - side us,
we bless your ho - ly name: glad prais - es we sing.
and with your help, O Lord, our bat - tles we win.
to you, our great Re - deem - er, for - ev - er be praise!

WORDS: Julia C. Cory (1882-1963), alt.
MUSIC: *Nederlandtsch Gedenckclanck*, 1626; arr. Edward Kremser (1838-1914)

KREMSER
12.11.12.11.

727 America, the Beautiful

1 O beau - ti - ful for spa-cious skies, for am - ber waves of grain,
2 O beau - ti - ful for pil - grim feet, whose stern, im - pas-sioned stress
3 O beau - ti - ful for he - roes proved in lib - er - at - ing strife,
4 O beau - ti - ful for pa - triot dream that sees be-yond the years
for pur - ple moun-tain maj - es - ties a - bove the fruit - ed plain!
a thor-ough-fare for free-dom beat a - cross the wil - der - ness!
who more than self their coun - try loved, and mer - cy more than life!
thine al - a - bas - ter cit - ies gleam, un-dimmed by hu - man tears!
A - mer - i - ca! A - mer - i - ca! God shed his grace on thee,
A - mer - i - ca! A - mer - i - ca! God mend thine ev - ery flaw,
A - mer - i - ca! A - mer - i - ca! May God thy gold re - fine,
A - mer - i - ca! A - mer - i - ca! God shed his grace on thee,
and crown thy good with broth - er - hood from sea to shin - ing sea!
con - firm thy soul in self - con - trol, thy lib - er - ty in law!
till all suc-cess be no - ble-ness, and ev - ery gain di - vine!
and crown thy good with broth - er - hood from sea to shin - ing sea!

WORDS: Katharine L. Bates (1859-1929)
MUSIC: Samuel A. Ward (1848-1903)

MATERNA
C.M.D.

God of the Ages, Whose Almighty Hand 728

Trumpets before each stanza
1 God of the a - ges, whose al - might - y hand leads forth in beau - ty all the star - ry band of shin - ing worlds in splen - dor through the skies, our grate - ful songs be - fore your throne a - rise.
2 Your love di - vine has led us in the past, in this free land by you our lot is cast; be now our rul - er, guard - ian, guide, and stay, your Word our law, your paths our cho - sen way.
3 From war's a - larms, from dead - ly pes - ti - lence, be your strong arm our ev - er sure de - fense; your true re - li - gion in our hearts in - crease, your boun - teous good - ness nour - ish us in peace.
4 Re - fresh your peo - ple on their toil - some way, lead us from night to nev - er - end - ing day; fill all our lives with heaven-born love and grace, and songs of praise we'll lift be - fore your face!

WORDS: Daniel C. Roberts (1841-1907), alt.
MUSIC: George W. Warren (1828-1902)

NATIONAL HYMN
10.10.10.10.

729 Lift Every Voice and Sing

1 Lift ev - ery voice and sing till earth and heav - en ring,
2 Ston - y the road we trod, bit - ter the chast - ening rod,
3 God of our wea - ry years, God of our si - lent tears,
ring with the har - mon - ies of lib - er - ty;
felt in the days when hope un - born had died;
thou who hast brought us thus far on the way;
let our re joic - ing rise, high as the lis - tening skies,
yet with a stead - y beat, have not our wea - ry feet
thou who hast, by thy might, led us in - to the light,
let it re - sound loud as the roll - ing sea.
come to the place for which our peo - ple sighed?
keep us for - ev - er in the path, we pray.

WORDS: James Weldon Johnson (1871-1938), alt.
MUSIC: J. Rosamond Johnson (1873-1954)

LIFT EVERY VOICE
Irregular

Sing a song full of the faith that the dark past has taught us,
We have come o - ver a way that with tears has been wa - tered,
Lest our feet stray from the plac - es, our God, where we met thee,
sing a song full of the hope that the pres - ent has brought
we have come, tread - ing our path through the blood of the slaugh -
lest, our hearts drunk with the wine of the world, we for - get
us; fac - ing the ris - ing sun of our new day be -
tered, out from the gloom - y past, till now we stand at
thee; shad-owed be - neath thy hand, may we for - ev - er
gun, let us march on till vic - to - ry is won.
last where the white gleam of our bright star is cast.
stand, true to our God, true to our na - tive land.

730 Mine Eyes Have Seen the Glory

1 Mine eyes have seen the glo - ry of the com - ing of the Lord;
2 I have seen him in the watch-fires of a hun - dred cir - cling camps,
3 He has sound - ed forth the trum - pet that shall nev - er call re - treat;
4 In the beau - ty of the lil - ies Christ was born a - cross the sea,
he is tramp - ling out the vin - tage where the grapes of wrath are stored;
they have build - ed him an al - tar in the eve - ning dews and damps;
he is sift - ing out the hearts of all be - fore his judg - ment seat.
with a glo - ry in his bos - om that trans - fig - ures you and me;
he hath loosed the fate - ful light - ning of his ter - ri - ble swift sword;
I can read his right - eous sen - tence by the dim and flar - ing lamps;
O be swift, my soul, to an - swer him; be ju - bi - lant, my feet!
as he died to make us ho - ly, let us die to make all free,
his truth is march - ing on.
his day is march - ing on.
Our God is march - ing on.
while God is march - ing on.
Refrain
Glo - ry, glo - ry, hal - le - lu - jah! Glo - ry, glo - ry, hal - le -

WORDS: Julia Ward Howe (1819-1910)
MUSIC: American melody, 19th c.

BATTLE HYMN
15.15.15.6.Ref.

lu - jah! Glo - ry, glo - ry, hal - le - lu - jah! His truth is march-ing on.

My Country, 'Tis of Thee 731

1 My coun - try, 'tis of thee, sweet land of lib - er - ty,
2 My na - tive coun - try, thee, land of the no - ble free,
3 Let mu - sic swell the breeze, and ring from all the trees
4 Our fa - thers' God, to thee, Au - thor of lib - er - ty,
of thee I sing: land where my fa - thers died, land of the
thy name I love; I love thy rocks and rills, thy woods and
sweet free-dom's song: let mor - tal tongues a - wake, let all that
to thee we sing: long may our land be bright with free-dom's
pil - grims' pride, from ev - ery moun - tain - side let free - dom ring!
tem - pled hills; my heart with rap - ture thrills like that a - bove.
breathe par - take; let rocks their si - lence break, the sound pro - long.
ho - ly light; pro - tect us by thy might, great God, our King!

WORDS: Samuel F. Smith (1808-1895)
MUSIC: *Thesaurus Musicus*, 1744

AMERICA
6.6.4.6.6.6.4.

732 Glory to God, Glory in the Highest

Leader
Dm Gm B♭ Dm
Glo-ry to God, glo-ry to God, glo-ry in the high - est!
All
Dm Gm B♭ Dm
Glo-ry to God, glo-ry to God, glo-ry in the high - est!
Leader
Dm C Dm Dm C Dm
To God be glo-ry for-ev - er!
All
To God be glo-ry for-ev - er!
Leader
C Dm C Dm
Leader
C Dm C Dm
Al-le-lu-ia! A-men!
Al-le-lu-ia! A-men!
Group 1
Group 1, 2
Al-le-lu-ia! A-men! Al-le-lu-ia! A-men! Al-le-lu-ia! A-men!
Leader
C Dm C Dm C Dm C Dm
Al-le-lu-ia! A-men!
Group 1, 2, 3
Al-le-lu-ia! A-men! Al-le-lu-ia! A-men! Al-le-lu-ia! A-men! Al-le-lu-ia! A - men!

WORDS: Traditional
MUSIC: Peruvian melody

Glory Be to the Father

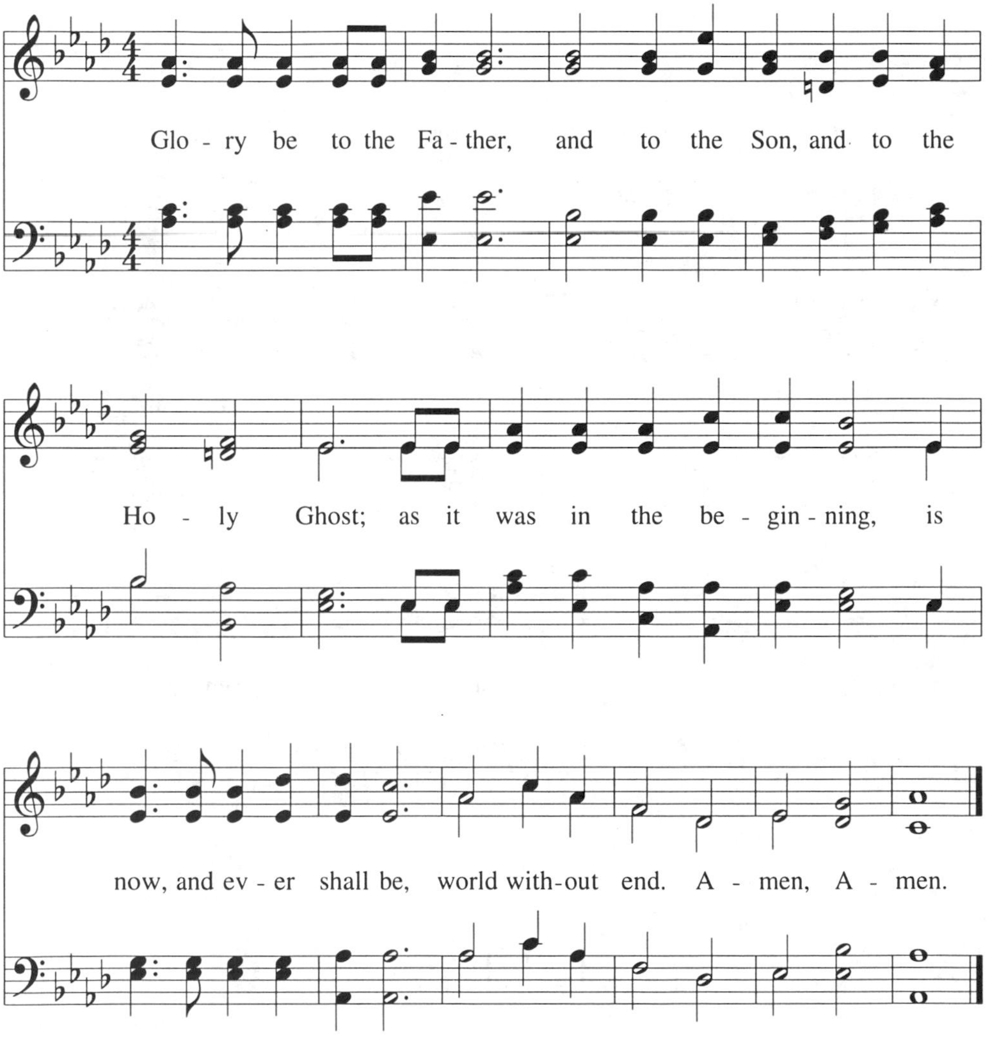
Glo - ry be to the Fa - ther, and to the Son, and to the
Ho - ly Ghost; as it was in the be - gin - ning, is
now, and ev - er shall be, world with-out end. A - men, A - men.

WORDS: *Gloria Patri*, 2nd c.
MUSIC: Christoph Meineke (1782-1850)

MEINEKE
Irregular

734 Glory Be to the Father

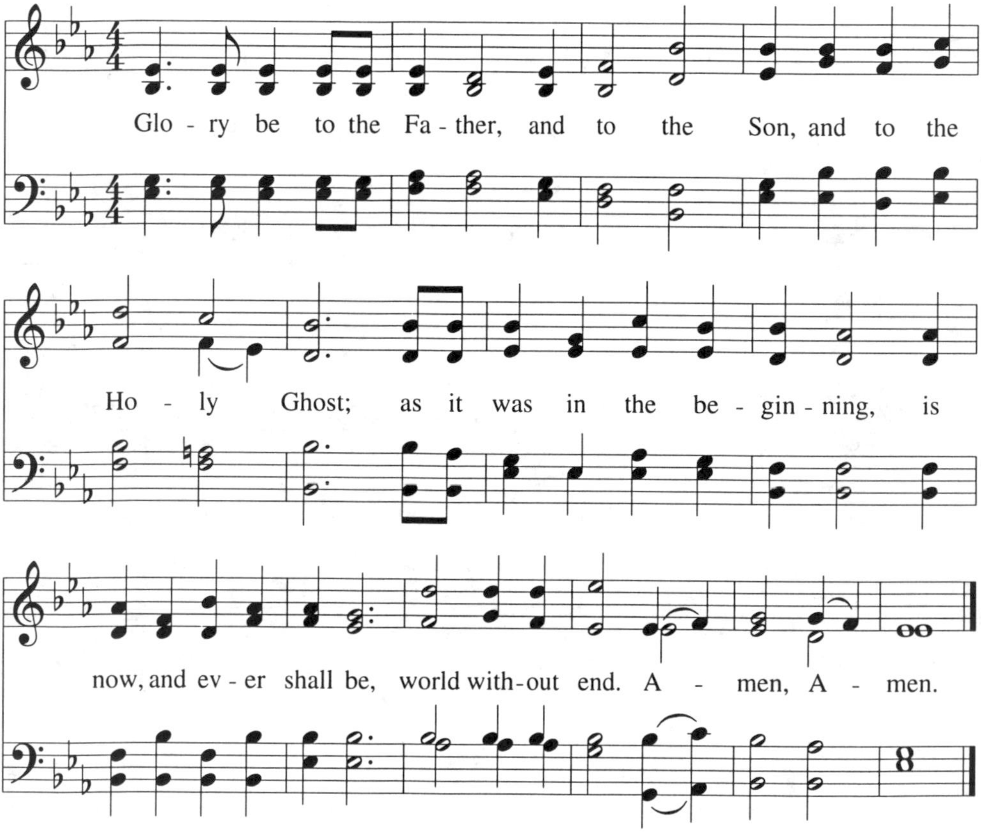
Glo - ry be to the Fa - ther, and to the Son, and to the
Ho - ly Ghost; as it was in the be - gin - ning, is
now, and ev - er shall be, world with-out end. A - men, A - men.
8

WORDS: *Gloria Patri*, 2nd c.
MUSIC: Henry W. Greatorex (1813-1858)

GREATOREX
Irregular

735 Hallelujah
Heleluyan

I
II
III
Hal - le - lu - jah, hal - le - lu - jah; hal - le, hal - le - lu - jah;
He - le - lu - yan, he - le - lu - yan; he - le, he - le - lu - yan;
hal - le - lu - jah, hal - le - lu - jah; hal - le, hal - le - lu - jah.
he - le - lu - yan, he - le - lu - yan; he - le, he - le - lu - yan.

WORDS and MUSIC: Muscogee (Creek) Indian; transcription by Charles H. Webb (1933-)

Celtic Alleluia 736

Al - le - lu - ia, al - le - lu - ia.
Al - le - lu - ia, al - le - lu - ia.

WORDS: Christopher Walker (1947-)
MUSIC: Fintan O'Carroll (d. 1977) and Christopher Walker (1947-)

Holy, Holy, Holy 737

Santo, Santo, Santo

D F#m/A A7 A7/B Bm G A7/G G G/D D
Ho - ly, ho - ly, ho - ly, my heart, my heart a - dores you. My
San - to, san - to, san - to, mi co - ra - zon te a - do - ra. Mi
G A7/G D A/C# Bm Bm/A Em7 A7 G/A D
heart is glad to say the words: you are Ho - ly, Lord!
co - ra - zon te sa - be de-cir: san - to e - res Señ - or.

WORDS and MUSIC: Latin American, 20th c.; arr. Allen Pote (1945-)

738 Holy, Holy, Holy Lord

F Gm/F F Bb/F F C
Ho - ly, ho - ly, ho - ly Lord, God of power and
F C/E Dm F7/C Bb F C/E
might, heaven and earth are filled with your glo - ry: Ho -
Dm Gm C7 Fsus F Dm Am/C Bb F/A
san - na in the high - est. Bless - ed is he who comes
Gm7 F/A Bb C7 F F7/C
in the name of the Lord; ho - san - na in the
Bb F C/E Dm Gm C7 Bb/F F
high - est. Ho - san - na in the high - est.

WORDS: *Sanctus*
MUSIC: American melody; arr. Jack Schrader (1942-)

LAND OF REST
C.M.

739 "Holy, Holy, Holy"

"Santo, Santo, Santo"

Unison
Em
D
"Ho - ly, ho - ly, ho - ly," an - gel hosts are sing - ing. "Ho - ly, ho - ly,
"San - to, san - to, san - to," can-tan se - ra - fi - nes. "San - to, san - to,
Am
Em
ho - ly is the Lord our God. Ho - ly, ho - ly, ho - ly is
san - to, Dios es el Se - ñor. San - to, san - to, san - to es
E7
Am
B7
Em
B7
God, the Lord of might. Your glo - ry fills the heav-ens, your glo - ry fills the
fuer - te nue-stro Dios. Tu glo - ria lle-na los cie - los, la tie - rra lle-na es-
Em7
Am
Em
B7
Em
earth." Ho - san - na in the high - est, ho - san - na is our song.
tá." Ho - san-na en las al - tu - ras, ho - san - na la can - ción.

WORDS: Spanish; tr. Bert Polman (1945-); para. Isaiah 6:3
MUSIC: Spanish melody; harm. AnnaMae Meyer Bush (1947-)

MERENGUE
Irregular

740 The Lord's Prayer

Unison
Our Fa - ther, who art in heav - en,
hal-low-ed be thy name. Thy king-dom
come, thy will be done on earth as it is in
heav - en. Give us this day our dai - ly bread, and for-

WORDS: Matthew 6:9-13
MUSIC: Albert Hay Malotte (1895-1964); arr. Donald P. Hustad (1918-)

give us our debts, as we for-give our debt-ors.
And lead us not in-to temp-ta-tion but de-liv-er us from
e-vil: for thine is the king-dom, and the pow-er,
and the glo-ry, for-ev-er,
A-men. A-men.

741 Amen, Sing Praises to the Lord!

Amen, Siakudumisa!

Refrain
Leader O sing ye!
Ma - si - thi!
A - men, sing prais - es to the Lord!
A - men, si - a - ku - du - mi - sa!
Sing prais - es to the Lord!
Si - a - ku - du - mi - sa!
O sing ye!
Ma - si - thi!
A-men, sing prais-es to the Lord!
A-men, si - a - ku-du-mi - sa!
A-men, re-joice.
A-men, ba-wo.
Sing prais-es to the Lord!
Si - a - ku-du-mi - sa!
A-men, re-
A-men, ba-
1
O sing ye!
Ma-si - thi!
A-men, re-joice.
A-men, ba-wo.
A-men, sing prais-es to the Lord!
A-men, si - a - ku-du-mi - sa!
joice,
wo,
re-joice, re-joice.
ba-wo, ba-wo.
Sing prais-es to the Lord!
Si - a - ku-du-mi - sa!

WORDS and MUSIC: S. C. Molefe (20th c.);
verses by Hal H. Hopson (1933-); para. Psalm 100

AMEN SIAKUDUMISA
Irregular

2
Verses (Optional choir or solo)
Lord! 1 Come with sounds of thank - ful praise;
sa! 2 Come and bless God's ho - ly name;
Lord! 1 Come with sounds of thank - ful
sa! 2 Come and bless God's ho - ly
come with joy - ful sing - ing. Let ev - ery heart and voice be raised,
we are God's own peo - ple. God's love is ev - er - more the same,
praise; with joy - ful sing - ing. Ev - ery voice be
name; we are God's peo - ple. Come and sing a
to Refrain
sing a joy - ful song. Sing, re - joice. Sing, re - joice.
sing a joy - ful song. Sing, re - joice. Sing, re - joice.
raised, sing a song.
song, sing a song.

742 Amen

p
A - men,
p
Ch.
p legato sempre
Sw.
cresc.
Ped.
mp
mf
a - men, a - men, a -
a - men, a - men, a - men, a - men,
mp
mf
a - men, a - men,
cresc.
a - men, a - men, a -
Sw.
mp
cresc.
mf

MUSIC: John Rutter (1945-), adapt. by the composer from the anthem *The Lord Bless You and Keep You*

mp
rall.
molto rall.
p dim.
pp
men, a - men, a - men, a - men.
a - men, a - men, a - men.
a - men, a - men, a - men.
men, a - men, a - men.
dim.
mp
dim.
p dim.
pp

743 Amen

A-men, a - men.

MUSIC: Dresden

Amen 744

A-men, a-men, a - men.

MUSIC: Danish

745 Amen

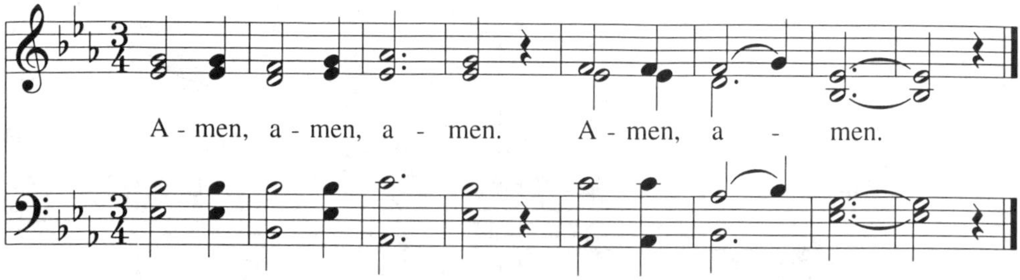
A - men, a - men, a - men. A - men, a - men.

MUSIC: Franz Schubert (1797-1828)

746 Amen

A - men, a - men, a - men, a - men, a - men.

WORDS and MUSIC: African-American spiritual; arr. Nelsie T. Johnson (1912-)

747 Go with Us, Lord

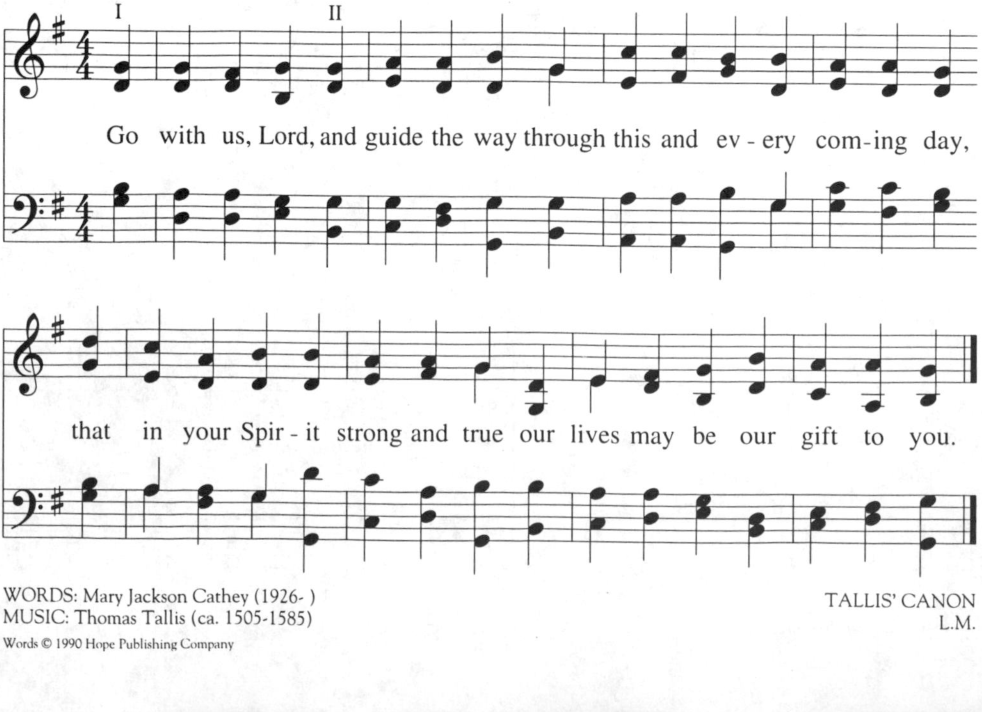
I
II
Go with us, Lord, and guide the way through this and ev - ery com-ing day,
that in your Spir - it strong and true our lives may be our gift to you.

WORDS: Mary Jackson Cathey (1926-)
MUSIC: Thomas Tallis (ca. 1505-1585)

TALLIS' CANON
L.M.

Lord, Dismiss Us with Your Blessing 748

1 Lord, dis - miss us with your bless-ing; fill our hearts with
2 Thanks we give and ad - o - ra - tion for your gos - pel's
joy and peace; let us each, your love pos - sess - ing,
joy - ful sound; may the fruits of your sal - va - tion
tri - umph in re - deem - ing grace; O di - rect us
in our hearts and lives a - bound; ev - er faith - ful,
and pro - tect us trav - eling through this wil - der - ness.
ev - er faith - ful to your truth may we be found.

WORDS: Attr. John Fawcett (1740-1817)
MUSIC: Sicilian melody, 18th c.

SICILIAN MARINERS
8.7.8.7.8.7.

749 The Lord Bless You and Keep You

The Lord bless you and keep you. The Lord lift his coun - te - nance up-
on you, and give you peace,
on you, and give you peace, and give you
The Lord make his face to shine up -
and give you peace. The Lord make his face to shine up -
peace.
on you and be gra - cious un - to you, be gra - cious;
on you and be gra - cious, and be gra - cious;

WORDS: Numbers 6:24–26
MUSIC: Peter C. Lutkin (1858-1931)

1 (optional ending)
the Lord be gra-cious, gra-cious un - to you. A - men.
2 you.
A -
mp
cresc.
you. A - men, A -
you. A - men, A - men, A -
p
p
you. A - men, A - men, A -
men, A - men, A -
f
dim.
- men, A - men, A - men,
men, A - men, A -
f
dim.
men, A - men, A -
men, A - men, A - men.
rit.
pp
A - men, A - men.
- men, A - men, A - men.
rit.
pp
men, A - men, A - men.

INDEXES

Index of Copyright Owners and Administrators

Listed here are the names and addresses of the copyright owners and administrators whose works appear in this hymnal. All copyrighted material is included here with the permission of the owners and no further use of these copyrights may be made without obtaining permission directly from the appropriate owner. Abbreviated notices appear below those works under copyright throughout the book. Complete copyright notices are listed below following the alphabetical listing of Copyright Owners and Administrators.

Material in the public domain is neither noted on its respective page nor listed in this index. Every effort has been made to determine and locate the owners of all the materials that appear in this book. The publisher regrets any errors or omissions and upon written notice will make necessary corrections in subsequent printings.

Abingdon Press (See The Copyright Company)
Akers, Doris (See Hal Leonard Corporation)
Archdiocese of Philadelphia, 222 N. 17th Avenue, Philadelphia, PA 19103 – (215) 587-3696
Augsburg Fortress Publishers, P.O. Box 1209, Minneapolis, MN 55440-1209 – (612) 330-3300
Augsburg Publishing House (See Augsburg Fortress)
BMG Music Publishing, 1400 18th Avenue South, Nashville, TN 37212 – (615) 858-1300
BMG Songs (See EMI Christian Music Publishing)
Birdwing Music (See EMI Christian Music Publishing)
Board of Publication, Lutheran Church in America (See Augsburg Fortress Publishers)
Bob Kilpatrick Music (See Lorenz Publishing Company)
Brentwood-Benson Music Publishing, 741 Cool Springs Blvd., Franklin, TN 37067 – (615) 261-3342
Brethren Press, 1451 Dundee Avenue, Elgin, IL 60120 (847) 742-5100
Brier Patch Music, 4324 Canal SW, Grandville, MI 49418 (616) 534-6571
Bud John Songs, Inc. (See EMI Christian Music Publishing)
Broadman Press (See Genevox Music Group)
C.A. Music (See Music Services)
CRC Publications, 2850 Kalamazoo Avenue, SE, Grand Rapids, MI 49560 – (616) 224-0785
Cartford, Gerhard, 2279 Commonwealth Avenue, St. Paul, MN 55108
Careers-BMG Music Publishing, Inc. (See BMG Music Publishing)
Celebration (See The Copyright Company)
Centro de Pastoral Liturgica (See OCP Publications)
Chavez-Melo, Juan Francisco, Arenal 48-10, 01050 Mexico D.F. , Mexico
Cole-Turner, Ronald, 4737 Gwynne Road, Memphis, TN 38117
Coomesietunes (See The Copyright Company)
CopyCare USA (See. The Copyright Company)
Copyright Company, The, 40 Music Square East, Nashville, TN 37203 – (615) 244-5588
Costen, Melva W., P.O. Box 42497, Atlanta, GA 30311 (404) 696-5900
Cortez, Jaime (See OCP Publications)
Crouch Music (See EMI Christian Music Publishing)
David Higham Associates, Ltd., 5-8 Lower Street, Golden Square, London W1R 4HA , England 020-7437-7888
Dawn, Marva J., Christians Equipped for Ministry, 304 Fredricksburg Way, Vancouver, WA 98664-2147
Dayspring Music, Inc., P.O. Box 128469, Nashville, TN 37212-8469 – (615) 321-5000
Derry Music Company, 1299 Fourth Street, Suite 409, San Rafael, CA 94901-3030 - (415) 451-6130
Doubleday, 1540 Broadway, New York, NY 10036 (212) 782-8957
Dufford, Robert J. (See New Dawn Music)
Dufner, Delores (See OCP Publications)
E.C. Schirmer Music Company, 138 Ipswich Street, Boston, MA 02215 – (617) 236-1935
E.H. Freeman (Address unknown)
EMI Christian Music Publishing, P.O. Box 5085, Brentwood, TN 37024 – (615) 371-4400
Ears to Hear Music (See EMI Christian Music Publishing)
F.E.L. Publications (See Lorenz Publishing Company)
Fairhill Music, Inc., P.O. Box 4467, Oceanside, CA 92052 (760) 806-3672
Farquharson, Walter, Box 58, Saltcoats, Sask. S0A 3R0 Canada
Foley, S. J., John B. (See New Dawn Music)
Forness, Norman O., 38 E. Stevens Street, Gettysburg, PA 17325 – (717) 334-6893
Fred Bock Music Company, P.O. Box 570567, Tarzana, CA 91357 – (818) 996-6181
Frederick Harris Music, 529 Speers Road, Oakville, Ontario L6K 2G4 , Canada – (905) 501-1595
Full Armor Music. (See The Kruger Organisation, Inc.)
G. Schirmer, Inc., 257 Park Avenue, S., New York, NY 10010 – (212) 254-2100
GIA Publications, Inc., 7404 S. Mason Avenue, Chicago, IL 60638 – (708) 496-3800
Gabriel Music, P.O. Box 840999, Houston, TX 77282-0999
Gabaraín, Cesareo (See OCP Publications)
Gaither, William J. (See Gaither Copyright Management)
Gaither Copyright Management, P.O. Box 737, Alexandria, IN 46001 – (765) 724-8233
Gaither Music Company (See Gaither Copyright Management)
General Board of Global Ministries, GBG Musik, 475 Riverside Drive, Room 350, New York, NY 10115
Genevox Music Group, 127 Ninth Avenue North, Nashville, TN 37234 – (615) 251-2000
Greg Nelson Music (See EMI Christian Music Publishing)
Grindal, Gracia (See Selah Publishing Co.)
H.W. Gray Company, The (See Warner Bros. Publications)
Hal Leonard Corporation, P.O. Box 13819, Milwaukee, WI 53213 – (414) 774-3630
Hark! Productions, Inc., 4624 Allendale Drive, St. Paul, MN 55127 – (651) 653-9540
Harold Ober Associates, 425 Madison Avenue, New York, NY 10017 – (212) 759-8600
HarperCollins Religious (See The Copyright Company)
Hillert, Richard, 1620 Clay Court, Melrose Park, IL 60160

Hillsong Publishing (See Integrity Music, Inc.)
Hinshaw Music, Inc., P.O. Box 470, Chapel Hill, NC 27514-0470 – (919) 933-1691
Historic Church of the Ascension, Atlantic City, NJ, 30 S. Kentucky Avenue, Atlantic City, NJ 08401-7028 (609) 344-0615
Hope Publishing Company, 380 S. Main Place, Carol Stream, IL 60188 – (630) 665-3200 (800) 323-1049
House of Mercy Music (See The Copyright Company)
Huber, Jane Parker (See Westminster/John Knox Press)
Hymn Society, The (See Hope Publishing Company)
Hymnal Project, The (See Brethren Press)
Integrated Copyright Group, P.O. Box 24149, Nashville, TN 37202 – (615) 329-3999
Integrity's Hosanna! Music, Inc. (See Integrity Music, Inc.)
Integrity Music, Inc., 1000 Cody Road, Mobile, AL 36695-3425 – (334) 633-9000
International Commission on English in the Liturgy, 1522 K Street, NW, Suite 1000, Washington, DC 20005-1202 – (202) 347-0800
JASRAC, 6-12, 3-Chome Uehara, Shibuyaku, Tokyo 151-0064, Japan – (03) 3481-2121
J. Curwen & Sons, Ltd. (See G. Schirmer, Inc.)
Jabusch, Willard, Calvert House, 5735 S. University Avenue, Chicago, IL 60637
Jan-Lee Music, P.O. Box 4, West Charleston, VT 05872
John T. Benson Publishing Co. (See Brentwood-Benson Music Publishing)
Jonathan Mark Music (See Gaither Copyright Management)
Jubilate Hymns (See Hope Publishing Company)
Kaanapali Music (See Integrated Copyright Group)
Ken Medema Music, 4324 Canal SW, Grandville, MI 49418– (616) 534-6571
Kid Brothers of St. Frank Publishing (See BMG Songs)
Kingsway's ThankYou Music (See EMI Christian Music Publishing)
Kruger Organisation, Inc., The, 4501 Connecticut Avenue, NW, Suite 711, Washington, DC 20008
Koizumi, Isao (See JASRAC)
Lanny Wolfe Music (See Gaither Copyright Management)
Latter Rain Music (See EMI Christian Music Publishing)
Lee, Geonyong, Korean Institute of Arts, 700 Seocho-Dong, Schocho-ky, Seoul, Korea
Lehsem Music (See Integrated Copyright Group)
Les Presses de Taizé (See GIA Publications, Inc.)
Lillenas Publishing Company (See The Copyright Company)
Lorenz Publishing Company, The Lorenz Corporation, P.O. Box 802, Dayton, OH 45401-0802
Lumko Institute, P.O. Box 5058, Delmenville 1403, South Africa – (011) 827-8924
Lutheran Book of Worship (See Augsburg Fortress Publishers)
Lutheran World Federation, Box 2100, CH 1211 Geneva 2, Switzerland – (022) 791-61-11
Make Way Music (See Music Services)
Malcolm Music (See Shawnee Press)
Manley, James K., 690 Persian Drive, #67, Sunnyvale, CA 94089 – (408) 747-0667
Manna Music, Inc., P.O. Box 218, Pacific City, OR 97135 – (503) 965-6112
Manzano, Miguel (See OCP Publications)
Maranatha! Music (See The Copyright Company)
Maranatha Praise, Inc. (See The Copyright Company)
Marshall, Madeleine Forell (See Augsburg Fortress Publishers)
Marty, Micah, 175 E Delaware Place, Apt. # 8401, Chicago, IL 60611
McKinney Music (See Genevox Music Group)
Meadowgreen Music Company (See EMI Christian Music Publishing)
Mercy/Vineyard Publishing (See Music Services)
Morgan, Reuben (See Integrity Music, Inc.)
Mountain Spring Music (See EMI Christian Music Publishing)
Multisongs (See BMG Music Publishing)
Music & Media International (See Integrated Copyright Group)
Music Services, 209 Chapelwood Drive, Franklin, TN 37064 – (615) 794-9015
New Dawn Music, 5536 NE Hassalo, Portland, OR 97213-3638 – (503) 281-1191
New Song Creations, 175 Heggie Lane, Erin, TN 37061
Novello & Company (See G. Schirmer, Inc.)
OCP Publications, 5536 NE Hassalo, Portland, OR 97213-3638 – (503) 281-1191
O'Carroll, Fintan (See OCP Publications)
Olivar, J. A. (See OCP Publications)
Oxford University Press, 198 Madison Avenue, New York, NY 10016-4314 – (212) 726-6000
Pamela Kay Music (See EMI Christian Music Publishing)
Pavane Publishing, 26565 Mazur Drive, Rancho Palos Verdes, CA 90275 – (310) 375-8688
People of Destiny International (See The Copyright Company)
Pilgrim Press, 700 Prospect Avenue, Fourth Floor, Cleveland, OH 44115-1100 – (216) 736-3755
Pilot Point Music (See The Copyright Company)
Quinn, S.J, James (See Selah Publishing Co., Inc.)
Renewal Servicing, P.O. Box 17, Shepperton, Middlesex TW17 8NU, England
Presbyterian Board of Education (See Westminster John Knox Press)
Resource Publications, Inc., 160 E. Virginia Street, Suite 290, San Jose, CA 95112-5876
Richards, John (See Renewal Servicing)
River Oaks Music Company (See EMI Christian Music Publishing)
Robb, John D., c/o Rodey, Dickason, Sloan, Akin & Robb, 20 First Plaza, Suite 700, Albuquerque, NM 87103
Rocksmith Music (See Trust Music Management)
Rufus Music (See Gaither Copyright Management)
Rusbridge, Rosalind, Bristol Churches Housing Association, 7 York Court, Wilder Street, Bristol, BS2 8QH, England
San Pablo Internacional (See OCP Publications)
Sanchez, Pete Jr. (See Gabriel Music Inc.)
Sandi's Songs Music (See Gaither Copyright Management)
Schutte, Daniel L. (See New Dawn Music)
Scripture in Song (See Integrity Music, Inc.)
Seerveld, Calvin, Institute for Christian Studies, 229 College Street, Toronto, Ontario M5T 1R4 Canada
Selah Publishing Co., Inc., Box 3037, Kingston, NY 12401-0902 – www.selahpub.com – (845) 338-2816
Shade Tree Publishing (See The Copyright Company)
Shawnee Press, 257 Park Avenue, S., New York, NY 10010 (212) 254-2100
Shepherd's Fold Music (See EMI Christian Music Publishing)

Shepherd's Heart Music, Inc. (See Dayspring Music, Inc.)
Singspiration Music (See Brentwood-Benson Music Publishing)
Songchannel Music Company (See EMI Christian Music Publishing)
Sosa, Pablo (See OCP Publications)
Sound III, Inc. (See Warner Bros. Publications)
Sparrow Song (See EMI Christian Music Publishing)
St. Francis Music Company (See Derry Music Company)
St. Frank Publishing (See BMG Music Publishing)
Stainer & Bell Ltd. (See Hope Publishing Company)
Starke, Stephen, c/o St. John Lutheran Church, 1664 Amelith Road, Bay City, MI 48706 – (517) 686-0176
Stassen, Linda (See New Song Creations)
StraightWay Music (See EMI Christian Music Publishing)
Tabell, Roland, 2653 Gardi Street, Duarte, CA 91010
Troeger, Thomas (See Oxford University Press)
Trust Music Management, P.O. Box 22274, Carmel, CA 93922-0274 – (831) 626-1030
Trustees for Methodist Church Purposes (UK) (See Hope Publishing Company)
Tutu, Desmond (See Doubleday)
Unichappell Music, Inc. (See Hal Leonard Corporation)
United Methodist Publishing House, The (See The Copyright Company)
United Reformed Church, The, 86 Tavistock Place, London WC1H 9RT, England
Universal-MCA Music Publishing (See Warner, Bros. Publications)
Universal-PolyGram Int'l Publishing (See Warner, Bros. Publications)
Utterbach Music Inc. (See Warner Bros. Publications)
Utryck (See Walton Music Corp.)
Vajda, Jaroslav, 3534 Brookstone So. Drive, St. Louis, MO 63129-2900 – (314) 892-9473
Van Ness Press (See Genevox Music Group)
WGRG The Iona Community (See GIA Publications, Inc.)
Walker, Christopher (See OCP Publication)
Walton Music, 170 NE 33rd Street, Ft. Lauderdale, FL 33307 – (973) 743-6444
Warner Bros. Publications, 15800 NW 48th Avenue, Miami, FL 33014 – (305) 620-1500
Waterloo Music Ltd., 3 Regina Street, N., Waterloo, Ontario N2J 4A5 , Canada – (519) 886-4990
Westminster/John Knox Press, 100 Witherspoon Street, Louisville, KY 40202-1396 – (502) 569-5060
Whole Armor Music (See The Kruger Organisation, Inc.)
Wilbur, Richard, c/o Harcourt, Inc., 6277 Sea Harbor Drive, 6th Floor, Orlando, FL 32887-6777 (407) 345-3274
Willing Heart Music (See The Copyright Company)
Word Music, Inc., P.O. Box 128469, Nashville, TN 37212-8469 – (615) 321-5000
Word of God Music, The (See The Copyright Company)
World Library Publications, 3825 N. Willow Road, Schiller Park, IL 60176- (800) 621-5197
Yardley, H. Francis, c/o Jean Yardley, 8 Riverview Circle, Unit 22, Cochrane, Alta. T0L 1W4 Canada
Ylvisaker, John C., Box 321, Waverly, IA 50677 www.ylvisaker.com or www.borningcry.com (319) 352-4396; Fax (319) 352-0765
ZionSong Music, P.O. Box 574044, Orlando, FL 32857 (407) 851-7377
Zschech, Darlene (See Integrity Music, Inc.)

1 Words © 1979 Hope Publishing Company. All rights reserved. Music © 1942, Ren. 1970 Hope Publishing Company. All rights reserved.

3 Words © 1982 Jubilate Hymns (Admin. Hope Publishing Company). All rights reserved.

4 Words & Music © 1973 Bud John Songs, Inc. (ASCAP) (Admin. EMI Christian Music Publishing)

5 Words & Music © 1998 Hope Publishing Company. All rights reserved.

7 Words © 1972 Hope Publishing Company. All rights reserved.

8 Words © 1974 Hope Publishing Company. All rights reserved.

9 Words © 1984 Hope Publishing Company. All rights reserved.

10 Words & Music © 1972, 1974 Daniel L. Schutte. Administered by New Dawn Music, 5536 NE Hassalo, Portland, OR 97213. All rights reserved. Used with permission.

12 Words & Music © 1977 Scripture In Song (a div. of Integrity Music, Inc.) All rights reserved. International copyright secured. Used by permission. c/o Integrity Music, Inc., 1000 Cody Road, Mobile, AL 36695

13 Words © 1973 Hope Publishing Company. All rights reserved. Music © 1973 Jubilate Hymns (Admin. Hope Publishing Company). All rights reserved.

15 Words English Tran. © Gerhard Cartford. Used by permission. Music Arr. © 2001 Hope Publishing Company. All rights reserved.

18 Words & Music © 1989 Universal-PolyGram International Publishing, Inc. and Utterbach Music Inc. All rights for Utterbach Music Inc. Controlled and Administered by Universal-PolyGram International Publishing, Inc. All rights reserved. Used by permission.

19 Words & Music © 1984 Scripture In Song (a div. of Integrity Music, Inc.) All rights reserved. International copyright secured. Used by permission. c/o Integrity Music, Inc., 1000 Cody road, Mobile, AL 36695.

20 Words © 1982 Jubilate Hymns (Admin. Hope Publishing Company). All rights reserved.

22 Words © 1939, 1966 by E.C. Schirmer Music Company. Used by permission.

24 Words from *A Singing Faith*, © 1978 Jane Parker Huber. Used by permission of Westminster John Knox Press.

25 Words © 1989 Hope Publishing Company. All rights reserved.

26 Music Arr. © 2001 Hope Publishing Company. All rights reserved.

27 Words © 1987 Hope Publishing Company. All rights reserved. Music Harm. © 1964 Abingdon Press (Administered by The Copyright Company, Nashville, TN) All rights reserved. International copyright secured. Used by permission.

28 Words © 1971 Walter Farquharson. Used by permission.

29 Words © 1983 Jaroslav J. Vajda. Used by permission. Music © 1983 GIA Publications, Inc. All rights reserved.

32 Words © 1979 The Hymn Society (Admin. Hope Publishing Company). All rights reserved.

33 Words & Music © 1976 Resource Publications, Inc. Words Tr. & Music Arr. © 1989 The United Methodist Publishing House (Administered by The Copyright Company, Nashville, TN). All rights reserved. International copyright secured. Used by permission.

35 Words © 1957 Harold Ober Associates. Used by permission. Music © 1927 Oxford University Press. Used by permission.

36 Words © 1975, 1983 Hope Publishing Company. All rights reserved. Music © 1990 Hope Publishing Company. All rights reserved.

37 Words © 1973 The Hymn Society (Admin. Hope Publishing Company). All rights reserved.

38 Words & Music © 1992 Hope Publishing Company. All rights reserved.

39 Words © 1995 Stephen P. Starke. Used by permission. Music © 1975 Hope Publishing Company. All rights reserved.

41 Words © 1962, Ren. 1990 Hope Publishing Company. All rights reserved.

42 Words & Music © 1981 Meadowgreen Music Company (ASCAP) (Admin. EMI Christian Music Publishing)

43 Words & Music © 1981 Rocksmith Music c/o Trust Music Management, Inc., P.O. Box 22274, Carmel, California 93922-0274

44 Words & Music © 1972 Bud John Songs, Inc. (ASCAP) (Admin. EMI Christian Music Publishing)

45 Words & Music © 1989 Integrity's Hosanna! Music (ASCAP). All rights reserved. International copyright secured. Used by permission. c/o Integrity Music, Inc., 1000 Cody Road, Mobile, AL 36695.

47 Words & Music © 1977 Pete Sanchez, Jr. (ASCAP). Administered by Gabriel Music Inc., P.O. Box 840999, Houston, TX 77284-0999 USA

49 Music © 1970 The Hymn Society (Admin. Hope Publishing Company). All rights reserved.

50 Words & Music © 1982 Meadowgreen Music (ASCAP) (Admin. EMI Christian Music Publishing)

51 Words & Music © 1953 S.K. Hine. Assigned to Manna Music, Inc., 35255 Brooten Road, Pacific City, OR 97135. Renewed 1981. All rights reserved. Used by permission.

52 Words & Music © 1984 Integrity's Hosanna! Music (ASCAP). All rights reserved. International copyright secured. Used by permission. c/o Integrity Music, Inc., 1000 Cody Road., Mobile, AL 36695.

53 Words & Music © 1988 People of Destiny International (Administered by CopyCare USA c/o The Copyright Company, Nashville, TN). All rights reserved. International copyright secured. Used by permission.

54 Words & Music © 1986 BMG Songs, Inc. (ASCAP) and Pamela Kay Music (ASCAP) (Admin. EMI Christian Music Publishing)

55 Words © 1975, 1995 Hope Publishing Company. All rights reserved. Music © 1977 Hope Publishing Company. All rights reserved.

57 Words & Music © 1987 Integrity's Hosanna! Music (ASCAP). All rights reserved. International copyright secured. Used by permission. c/o Integrity Music, Inc., 1000 Cody Road, Mobile, AL 36695.

58 Words & Music © 1986 Hope Publishing Company. All rights reserved.

62 Words & Music © 1989 Maranatha Praise, Inc. (Administered by The Copyright Company, Nashville, TN). All rights reserved. International copyright secured. Used by permission.

64 Words © 1982 Jubilate Hymns (Admin. Hope Publishing Company). All rights reserved.

69 Words & Music © 1983 Integrity's Hosanna! Music (ASCAP). All rights reserved. International copyright secured. Used by permission. c/o Integrity Music, Inc., 1000 Cody Road, Mobile, AL 36695.

70 Words © 1969 Hope Publishing Company. All rights reserved. Music © 1982 Jubilate Hymns (Admin. Hope Publishing Company). All rights reserved.

72 Words & Music © 1923, Ren. 1951 Hope Publishing Company. All rights reserved.

73 Words © 1990 Hope Publishing Company. All rights reserved. Music © 1932 Oxford University Press. Used by permission.

75 Words © 1974 Hope Publishing Company. All rights reserved.

76 Words & Music © 1994 Hope Publishing Company. All rights reserved.

78 Words © 1982 Hope Publishing Company. All rights reserved.

79 Music Harm. © 1964 Abingdon Press (Administered by The Copyright Company, Nashville, TN) All rights reserved. International copyright secured. Used by permission.

80 Music Arr. © 1986 Word Music, Inc. (ASCAP), 65 Music Square West, Nashville, TN 37203. All rights reserved. Made in the U.S.A. International copyright secured. Used by permission.

83 Words © Board of Publication, Lutheran Church in America; administered by Augsburg Fortress. Used by permission.

85 Words & Music © 1978 House of Mercy Music (Administered by Maranatha! Music c/o The Copyright Company, Nashville, TN). All rights reserved. International copyright secured. Used by permission.

87 Music Arr. © 1927 Oxford University Press. Used by permission.

88 Words & Music © 1989 Maranatha Praise, Inc. (Administered by The Copyright Company, Nashville, TN). All rights reserved. International copyright secured. Used by permission.

89 Words & Music © 1974 Augsburg Publishing House; administered by Augsburg Fortress. Used by permission.

92 Words & Music © 1974 Dayspring Music, Inc. (BMI), 65 Music Square West, Nashville, TN 37203. All rights reserved. Made in the U.S.A. International copyright secured. Used by permission.

93 Words © 1987 Hope Publishing Company. All rights reserved.

94 Words & Music © 1993 Darlene Zschech/Hillsong Publishing (Admin. in U.S. and Canada by Integrity's Hosanna! Music) (ASCAP). All rights reserved. International copyright secured. Used by permission. c/o Integrity Music, Inc., 1000 Cody Road., Mobile, AL 36695.

97 Words & Music © 1986 Kingsway's ThankYou Music (Admin. EMI Christian Music Publishing)

98 Words & Music © 1984 Lehsem Music, LLC (ASCAP)/ Singspiration Music (ASCAP) (Both admin. Music & Media International, Inc./Kaanapali Music) and BMG Songs, Inc. (ASCAP). All rights reserved. Used by permission.

99 Words © 1991 GIA Publications, Inc. All rights reserved.

101 Words © 1984 Hope Publishing Company. All rights reserved.
Music © 1982 Jubilate Hymns (Admin. Hope Publishing Company). All rights reserved.

102 Words & Music © 1959. Renewed 1987 by Manna Music, Inc., 35255 Brooten Road, Pacific City, OR 97135. All rights reserved. Used by permission.

103 Words & Music © 1983 ZionSong Music, P.O. Box 574044, Orlando, FL 32857. All rights reserved. International copyright secured. Used by permission.

104 Words © 1999 Hope Publishing Company. All rights reserved.

105 Words & Music © 1998 Kingsway's ThankYou Music (Admin. EMI Christian Music Publishing)

107 Words © 1989 Hope Publishing Company. All rights reserved.

108 Words & Music © 1970 William J. Gaither (Admin. Gaither Copyright Management)

110 Words © 1957, 1984, Ren. 1985 Hope Publishing Company. All rights reserved.

115 Words & Music © 1976 Latter Rain Music (ASCAP) (Admin. EMI Christian Music Publishing)

116 Words & Music © 1973 Singspiration Music (ASCAP) (Admin. by Brentwood-Benson Music Publishing, Inc.) All rights reserved. Used by permission.

117 Words & Music © 1982 Birdwing Music (ASCAP)/BMG Songs (ASCAP)/Ears to Hear Music (ASCAP) (Admin. EMI Christian Music Publishing)

118 Words & Music © 1963 Stainer & Bell Ltd. (Admin. Hope Publishing Company). All rights reserved.

120 Words vs. 5 & Music © 1974 Linda Stassen, New Song Creations, 175 Heggie Lane, Erin, TN 37061, USA. All rights reserved. International copyright secured. Used by permission only.

121 Words © 1969 Hope Publishing Company. All rights reserved.

122 Words & Music © 1985 StraightWay Music (ASCAP)/Mountain Spring Music (ASCAP) (Admin. EMI Christian Music Publishing)

125 Words & Music © 1986 River Oaks Music Company (BMI) (Admin. EMI Christian Music Publishing)/Gaither Music Company/Sandi's Songs Music (Admin. Gaither Copyright Mgmt.) All rights reserved. Used by permission.

126 Words & Music © 1963, 1975 by Fred Bock Music Company

127 Words & Music © 1982 Mercy/Vineyard Publishing (ASCAP) (Admin. Music Services)

128 Words © 1978 John Richards/Renewal Servicing. Used by permission.

129 Words & Music © 1986 Kingsway's ThankYou Music (Admin. EMI Christian Music Publishing)

130 Words © 1969, 1997 Hope Publishing Company. All rights reserved.
Music © 1969 Hope Publishing Company. All rights reserved.

131 Words & Music © 1977 Lanny Wolfe Music. All rights controlled by Gaither Copyright Management. Used by permission.

133 Words © 1979, 1995 Hope Publishing Company. All rights reserved.
Music © 1979 Hope Publishing Company. All rights reserved.

134 Words & Music © 1962. Renewed 1990 by Manna Music, Inc., 35255 Brooten Road, Pacific City, OR 97135. All rights reserved. Used by permission.

135 Words © 1987 The Hymn Society (Admin. Hope Publishing Company). All rights reserved.

137 Words © 1988 Van Ness Press (Admin. Genevox Music Group) Used by permission.
Music © 1988 McKinney Music (Admin. Genevox Music Group) Used by permission.

139 Words © 1983, 1995 Hope Publishing Company. All rights reserved.
Music © 1983 Hope Publishing Company. All rights reserved.

140 Words © 1982 H. Francis Yardley. Used by permission.
Music Harm. © 1927 Oxford University Press. Used by permission.

141 Words © 1981 The Hymn Society (Admin. Hope Publishing Company). All rights reserved.

142 Words © 1966 Hope Publishing Company. All rights reserved.

143 Words & Music © 1972 Maranatha! Music (Administered by The Copyright Company, Nashville, TN). All rights reserved. International copyright secured. Used by permission.

145 Words & Music © 1996 Hark! Productions. Used by permission.

146 Words & Music © 1976 Maranatha! Music (Administered by The Copyright Company, Nashville, TN). All rights reserved. International copyright secured. Used by permission.

147 Words © 1989 Hope Publishing Company. All rights reserved. Music Harm. © 1998 Hope Publishing Company. All rights reserved.

149 Words © 1989 Hope Publishing Company. All rights reserved.

150 Words © 1982 Jubilate Hymns (Admin. Hope Publishing Company). All rights reserved.
Music Arr. © 1995 Augsburg Fortress. Used by permission.

152 Words © 1982 Hope Publishing Company. All rights reserved.

157 Words & Music © 1988 Geonyong Lee. Used by permission.

158 Words © 1973 Jubilate Hymns (Admin. Hope Publishing Company). All rights reserved.
Music © 1983 Hope Publishing Company. All rights reserved.

159 Words © 1966, 1985 Willard F. Jabusch. Used by permission. Israeli Folk Song, Arr. by John Ferguson. From *The Hymnal of the United Church of Christ* (The Pilgrim Press, 1974). © 1974 The Pilgrim Press. Used by permission.

160 Words & Music © 1983 GIA Publications, Inc. All rights reserved.

161 Words © 1960 David Higham Assoc. Ltd. Used by permission.
Music © 1928 Oxford University Press. Used by permission.

162 Words & Music © 1993 Hope Publishing Company. All rights reserved.

163 Words & Music © 1993 Centro de Pastoral Liturgica. Administered by OCP Publications, 5536 NE Hassalo, Portland, OR 97213. All rights reserved. Used with permission.
Words Tr. © 1995 Madeleine Forell Marshall, administered by Augsburg Fortress.

165 Words © 1989 Hope Publishing Company. All rights reserved.
Music © 1998 Hope Publishing Company. All rights reserved.

166 Words & Music © 1984 Les Presses de Taizé (France) Used by permission of GIA Publications, Inc., exclusive agent. All rights reserved.

167 Words © 1971 Hope Publishing Company. All rights reserved.
Music Arr. © 1924 (Renewed) J. Curwen & Sons, Ltd. International copyright secured. All rights reserved. Reprinted by permission of G. Schirmer, Inc.

168 Words © 1984 Calvin Seerveld, Institute for Christian Studies, Toronto

169 Music © 1955, Ren.1983 E.H. Freeman

170 Words © 1987 Hope Publishing Company. All rights reserved.
Music © 1991 The Hymnal Project. Used by permission of Brethren Press, 1451 Dundee Avenue, Elgin, IL 60120.

171 Words & Music © 1984 Hope Publishing Company. All rights reserved.

172 Words from *A Singing Faith,* © 1986 Jane Parker Huber. Used by permission of Westminster John Knox Press.

173 Words & Music © 1979 Les Presses de Taizé (France). Used by permission of GIA Publications, Inc., exclusive agent. All rights reserved.

174 Music © 1984 Les Presses de Taizé (France). Used by permission of GIA Publications, Inc., exclusive agent. All rights reserved.

175 Words © 1999 Hope Publishing Company. All rights reserved.

177 Words & Music © 1974 Scripture In Song (a div. of Integrity Music, Inc.) All rights reserved. International copyright secured. Used by permission. c/o Integrity Music, Inc., 1000 Cody Road, Mobile, AL 36695.

178 Words & Music © 1976 C.A. Music (div. of C.A. Records, Inc.) (Admin. Music Services). All rights reserved. (ASCAP)

187 Music Arr. © 1989 Hope Publishing Company. All rights reserved.

192 Words & Music © 1991 Word Music, Inc. (ASCAP), 65 Music Square West, Nashville, TN 37203 and Rufus Music (Admin. Gaither Copyright Management). All rights reserved. Made in the U.S.A. International copyright secured. Used by permission.

194 Words & Music © 1964 Stainer & Bell Ltd. (Admin. Hope Publishing Company). All rights reserved.

195 Music © 1989, Pablo Sosa. Published by OCP Publications, 5536 NE Hassalo, Portland, OR 97213. All rights reserved. Used with permission.

197 Words © 1986 Jubilate Hymns (Admin. Hope Publishing Company). All rights reserved.
Music © 1992 Hope Publishing Company. All rights reserved.

199 Words & Music © 1987 GIA Publications, Inc. All rights reserved.

201 Music Arr. © 1990 Hope Publishing Company. All rights reserved.

202 Words vs. 2 © 1989 Hope Publishing Company. All rights reserved.

204 Words © 1968 Hope Publishing Company. All rights reserved.
Music Arr. © 1924 (Renewed) J. Curwen & Sons, Ltd. International copyright secured. All rights reserved. Reprinted by permission of G. Schirmer, Inc.

206 Words "A Christmas Hymn" from *Advice to a Prophet and Other Poems,* © 1961 and renewed 1989 by Richard Wilbur, reprinted by permission of Harcourt, Inc.
Music © 1984 GIA Publications, Inc. All rights reserved.

207 Words Tr. & Music Arr. © 1954 John D. Robb

208 Words © 1993 Hope Publishing Company. All rights reserved.

209 Music Arr. © 1997 Hope Publishing Company. All rights reserved.

210 Music © 1962, Ren. 1990 The H.W. Gray Company (Admin. Warner Bros. Publications U.S. Inc.) All rights reserved. Used by permission.

211 Words & Music © 1969 Hope Publishing Company. All rights reserved.

212 Words & Music © 1979 Les Presses de Taizé (France). Used by permission of GIA Publications, Inc., exclusive agent. All rights reserved.

213 English Text of *'Twas in the Moon of Wintertime* by J.E. Middleton. Used by permission of The Frederick Harris Music Co., Limited, Mississauga, Ontario, Canada. All rights reserved.

214 Words & Music Arr. © 1963, 1980 Utryck (Admin. Walton Music)

215 Words & Music © 1976 Hope Publishing Company. All rights reserved.

216 Words & Music © 1978, 1981 Les Presses de Taizé (France) Used by permission of GIA Publications, Inc., exclusive agent. All rights reserved.

217 Words & Music © 2000 Hope Publishing Company. All rights reserved.

219 Music Arr. by Jeffrey Radford. From *The New Century Hymnal* (The Pilgrim Press, Cleveland, 136). © 1992 The Pilgrim Press. Used by permission.

221 Music © Rosalind Rusbridge

223 Words & Music © 1994 Hope Publishing Company. All rights reserved.

224 Music Arr. © 1986 Word Music, Inc. (ASCAP), 65 Music Square West, Nashville, TN 37203. All rights reserved. Made in the U.S.A. International copyright secured. Used by permission.

225 Words & Music © 1934 (Renewed) by G. Schirmer, Inc. (ASCAP). International copyright secured. All rights reserved. Reprinted by permission of G. Schirmer, Inc.

226 Words & Music © 1976 by Malcolm Music (BMI), a division of Shawnee Press, Inc. and Derry Music Company, successor to St. Francis Music Company. International copyright secured. All rights reserved. Reprinted by permission.

227 Words © 1965 Jubilate Hymns (Admin. Hope Publishing Company). All rights reserved.
Music © 1965, 1986 Jubilate Hymns (Admin. Hope Publishing Company). All rights reserved.

230 Words © 1978 *Lutheran Book of Worship*. Reprinted by permission of Augsburg Fortress.

231 Words © 1992 GIA Publications, Inc. All rights reserved.

234 Words © 1982 Jubilate Hymns (Admin. Hope Publishing Company). All rights reserved.

237 Words © 1985 Oxford University Press. Used by permission.

238 Words & Music © 1963, 1980 Utryck (Admin. Walton Music Corp.)

239 Words © 1984 Hope Publishing Company. All rights reserved.
Music Arr. © 2001 Hope Publishing Company. All rights reserved.

240 Words & Music © 1979, 1988 Les Presses de Taizé (France). Used by permission of GIA Publications, Inc., exclusive agent. All rights reserved.

241 Words © 1980 Hope Publishing Company. All rights reserved.

243 Words Rev. © 1982 Jubilate Hymns (Admin. Hope Publishing Company). All rights reserved.

245 Words © 1988 Hope Publishing Company. All rights reserved.
Music Arr. © 2001 Hope Publishing Company. All rights reserved.

246 Words © 1977, 1995 Hope Publishing Company. All rights reserved.
Music © 1985 Hope Publishing Company. All rights reserved.

247 Words © 1990 Hope Publishing Company. All rights reserved.

248 Words & Music © 1970 Celebration (Administered by The Copyright Company, Nashville, TN). All rights reserved. International copyright secured. Used by permission.

250 Words © 1993 Hope Publishing Company. All rights reserved.

251 Words & Music © 1996 Meadowgreen Music Company (ASCAP) (Admin. EMI Christian Music Publishing) /Maranatha Praise, Inc. (Administered by The Copyright Company, Nashville, TN). All rights reserved. International copyright secured. Used by permission.

254 Words vss. 2-4 © 1996 Hope Publishing Company. All rights reserved.

259 Words & Music © 1989 Make Way Music (Admin. by Music Services in the Western Hemisphere). All rights reserved. (ASCAP)

266 Words & Music © 1985 Mercy/Vineyard Publishing (ASCAP) (Admin. Music Services)

269 Music Arr. © 1993 Jubilate Hymns (Admin. Hope Publishing Company). All rights reserved.

270 Words & Music © 1975 Word Music, Inc. (ASCAP), 65 Music Square West, Nashville, TN 37203. All rights reserved. Made in the U.S.A. International copyright secured. Used by permission.

271 Words & Music © 1974 Birdwing Music (ASCAP)/BMG Songs (ASCAP) (Admin. EMI Christian Music Publishing)

273 Words © 1969, 1997 Hope Publishing Company. All rights reserved.
Music © 1969, 1989 Hope Publishing Company. All rights reserved.

274 Words © 1988 Hope Publishing Company. All rights reserved.

275 Words © 1974 Hope Publishing Company. All rights reserved.
Music Harm. © 1990 Hope Publishing Company. All rights reserved.

276 Words & Music © 1992 Hope Publishing Company. All rights reserved.

278 Words © 1973 Hope Publishing Company. All rights reserved.

279 Words © 1968 Hope Publishing Company. All rights reserved.
Music © 1969, 1982 Jubilate Hymns (Admin. Hope Publishing Company). All rights reserved.

281 Words & Music © 1985 StraightWay Music (ASCAP)/Mountain Spring Music (ASCAP) (Admin. EMI Christian Music Publishing)

282 Words & Music © 1998 WGRG The Iona Community (Scotland). Used by permission of GIA Publications, Inc., exclusive agent. All rights reserved.

285 Words & Music © 1981 Les Presses de Taizé (France). Used by permission of GIA Publications, Inc., exclusive agent. All rights reserved.

286 Words & Music © 1984 Les Presses de Taizé (France). Used by permission of GIA Publications, Inc., exclusive agent. All rights reserved.

287 Words & Music © 1974 Hope Publishing Company. All rights reserved.

289 Words vss. 2 & 3 © 1982 Jubilate Hymns (Admin. Hope Publishing Company). All rights reserved.

291 Words & Music © 1973 The Word of God Music (Administered by The Copyright Company, Nashville, TN). All rights reserved. International copyright secured. Used by permission.

292 Words © 1987 Hope Publishing Company. All rights reserved.
Music Harm. © 1969 Hope Publishing Company. All rights reserved.

293 Words © 1986 Hope Publishing Company. All rights reserved.
Music © Rosalind Rusbridge

296 Words from *An African Prayer Book* selected by Desmond Tutu, © 1995 by Desmond Tutu. Used by permission of Doubleday, a division of Random House, Inc. Music © 1997 WGRG The Iona Community (Scotland). Used by permission of GIA Publications, Inc., exclusive agent. All rights reserved.

297 Words & Music © 1976 Hope Publishing Company. All rights reserved.

302 Words & Music © 1933, renewed 1962 Word Music, Inc. (ASCAP), 65 Music Square West, Nashville, TN 37203. All rights reserved. Made in the U.S.A. International copyright secured. Used by permission.

303 Words & Music © 1978, 1990 Les Presses de Taizé (France) Used by permission of GIA Publications, Inc., exclusive agent. All rights reserved.

304 Words © 1982 Jubilate Hymns (Admin. Hope Publishing Company). All rights reserved. Music Arr. © 1924 (Renewed) J. Curwen & Sons, Ltd. International copyright secured. All rights reserved. Reprinted by permission of G. Schirmer, Inc.

306 Text is reprinted by permission from *With One Voice*, © 1995 Augsburg Fortress. Music © 1969 *Contemporary Worship 1: Hymns*, administered by Augsburg Fortress. Used by permission.

307 Words © 1958, Ren. 1986 Hope Publishing Company. All rights reserved.

309 Words & Music © 1969 Hope Publishing Company. All rights reserved.

311 Words © 1928 Oxford University Press. Used by permission.

312 Words © 1975, 1995 Hope Publishing Company. All rights reserved.

314 Words & Music © 1974 Latter Rain Music (ASCAP) (Admin. EMI Christian Music Publishing)

315 Words © 1978 *Lutheran Book of Worship*. Reprinted by permission of Augsburg Fortress. Music © 1975, 1988 Richard Hillert. Used by permission.

316 Words & Music © 1972. Renewed 2000 by Manna Music, Inc., 35255 Brooten Road, Pacific City, OR 97135. All rights reserved. Used by permission.

319 Words & Music © 1987 Make Way Music (Admin. by Music Services in the Western Hemisphere). All rights reserved. ASCAP

321 Music © 1925 Oxford University Press

322 Words © 1978 *Lutheran Book of Worship*. Reprinted by permission of Augsburg Fortress.

324 Words © 1984 Hope Publishing Company. All rights reserved.

325 Music Arr. © 1995 Waterloo Music Co. Used by permission.

326 Words & Music © 1978 James K. Manley. Used by permission.

327 Words © 1982 Hope Publishing Company. All rights reserved. Music © 1969 Hope Publishing Company. All rights reserved.

329 Words © 1979 Hope Publishing Company. All rights reserved. Music © 2000 Hope Publishing Company. All rights reserved.

331 Words © 1978 Hope Publishing Company. All rights reserved. Music © 1985 Hope Publishing Company. All rights reserved.

332 Words © 1971 Hope Publishing Company. All rights reserved.

333 Words © 1983 Thomas H. Troeger (Admin. Oxford University Press). Used by permission.

334 Words from *A Singing Faith*, © 1981 Jane Parker Huber. Used by permission of Westminster John Knox Press.

335 Words © 1999 Hope Publishing Company. All rights reserved.

336 Words © 1966 Jubilate Hymns (Admin. Hope Publishing Company). All rights reserved. Music © 1982 Jubilate Hymns (Admin. Hope Publishing Company). All rights reserved.

337 Words & Music © 1982 Singspiration Music (ASCAP) (Admin. by Brentwood-Benson Music Publishing, Inc.) All rights reserved. Used by permission.

338 Words & Music © 1980 Maranatha Praise, Inc. (Administered by The Copyright Company, Nashville, TN) All rights reserved. International copyright secured. Used by permission.

340 Words & Music © 1991 Integrity's Hosanna! Music (ASCAP). All rights reserved. International copyright secured. Used by permission. c/o Integrity Music, Inc., 1000 Cody Road, Mobile, AL 36695.

343 Words & Music © 1997 Darlene Zschech/Hillsong Publishing (Admin. in U.S. and Canada by Integrity's Hosanna! Music) (ASCAP). All rights reserved. International copyright secured. Used by permission. c/o Integrity Music, Inc., 1000 Cody Road., Mobile, AL 36695.

346 Words © 1988 Hope Publishing Company. All rights reserved.

347 Words & Music © 1979, 1987, 1989 Cesareo Gabaraín. Published by OCP Publications, 5536 NE Hassalo, Portland, OR 97213. All rights reserved. Used with permission. Words Tr. © 1989 The United Methodist Publishing House (Administered by The Copyright Company, Nashville, TN) All rights reserved. International copyright secured. Used by permission.

349 Words & Music © 1972 Maranatha! Music (Administered by The Copyright Company, Nashville, TN). All rights reserved. International copyright secured. Used by permission.

350 Words & Music © 1987 WGRG The Iona Community (Scotland). Used by permission of GIA Publications, Inc., exclusive agent. All rights reserved.

352 Words & Music © 1979 Mercy/Vineyard Publishing (ASCAP) (Admin. Music Services). Used by permission.

355 Words © 1983, 1987 Hope Publishing Company. All rights reserved. Music © 1987 Hope Publishing Company. All rights reserved.

357 Words & Music © 1994 Make Way Music (Admin. by Music Services in the Western Hemisphere). All rights reserved. (ASCAP)

359 Words & Music © 1978 Integrity's Hosanna! Music (ASCAP). All rights reserved. International copyright secured. Used by permission. c/o Integrity Music, Inc., 1000 Cody Road, Mobile, AL 36695.

360 Words & Music © 1998 Reuben Morgan/Hillsong Publishing (Admin. in U.S. and Canada by Integrity's Hosanna! Music) (ASCAP). All rights reserved. International copyright secured. Used by permission. c/o Integrity Music, Inc., 1000 Cody Road, Mobile, AL 36695.

361 Words & Music © 1990 Maranatha Praise, Inc. (Administered by The Copyright Company, Nashville, TN) and Word Music, Inc. (ASCAP), 65 Music Square West, Nashville, TN 37203. All rights reserved. Made in the U.S.A. International copyright secured. Used by permission.

363 Words & Music © 1971 Bud John Songs, Inc. (ASCAP) (Admin. by EMI Christian Music Publishing)

364 Words © 1983, 1995 Hope Publishing Company. All rights reserved.
Music © 1990 Selah Publishing Co., Inc. All rights reserved. Used by permission.

367 Words © 1980 Jubilate Hymns (Admin. Hope Publishing Company). All rights reserved.
Music © 1982 Jubilate Hymns (Admin. Hope Publishing Company). All rights reserved.

369 Words © 1997 Stainer & Bell Ltd. (Admin. Hope Publishing Company). All rights reserved.
Music © 1975 Hope Publishing Company. All rights reserved.

370 Words & Music © 1994 Integrity's Hosanna! Music (ASCAP) & Integrity's Praise! Music (BMI) All rights reserved. International copyright secured. Used by permission. c/o Integrity Music, Inc., 1000 Cody Road, Mobile, AL 36695.

371 Words from the *Resource Collection of Hymns and Service Music for the Liturgy,* © 1981, International Committee on English in the Liturgy, Inc. All rights reserved.

372 Words © 1981 Gaither Music Company. All rights controlled by Gaither Copyright Management. Used by permission.
Music Arr. © 1933, Ren. 1961 Presbyterian Board of Education. Used by permission of Westminster John Knox Press.

373 Words & Music © 1982 Mercy/Vineyard Publishing (ASCAP) (Admin. Music Services). Used by permission.

374 Words & Music © 1990 Mercy/Vineyard Publishing (ASCAP) (Admin. Music Services). Used by permission.

375 Words & Music © 1988 Birdwing Music (ASCAP) (Admin. EMI Christian Music Publishing)

376 Words © 1990 Jubilate Hymns (Admin. Hope Publishing Company). All rights reserved.
Music © 1993 HarperCollins Religious (Administered by The Copyright Company, Nashville, TN). All rights reserved. International copyright secured. Used by permission.

377 Music Harm. © 1996 General Board of Global Ministries, GBG Musik, 475 Riverside Dr., New York, NY 10115. All rights reserved.

378 Words & Music © 1997 Hope Publishing Company. All rights reserved.

381 Words © 1989 Hope Publishing Company. All rights reserved.

382 Words © 1969 Oxford University Press. Used by permission.

383 Words © 1986 Word Music, Inc. (ASCAP), 65 Music Square West, Nashville, TN 37203. All rights reserved. Made in the U.S.A. International copyright secured. Used by permission.
Music Arr. © 2001 Hope Publishing Company. All rights reserved.

388 Words © 1990 Hope Publishing Company. All rights reserved.

389 Words © 1989 Hope Publishing Company. All rights reserved.

391 Words & Music © 1977 Scripture In Song (a div. of Integrity Music, Inc.) All rights reserved. International copyright secured. Used by permission. c/o Integrity Music, Inc., 1000 Cody Road, Mobile, AL 36695.

392 Words & Music © 1971 Celebration (Administered by The Copyright Company, Nashville, TN). All rights reserved. International copyright secured. Used by permission.

394 Words © 1992 Hope Publishing Company. All rights reserved.

395 Words & Music © 1971 Lillenas Publishing Company (Administered by The Copyright Company, Nashville, TN). All rights reserved. International copyright secured. Used by permission.

396 Words & Music © 1973 Pilot Point Music (Administered by The Copyright Company, Nashville, TN). All rights reserved. International copyright secured. Used by permission.

397 Words & Music © 1972 Hope Publishing Company. All rights reserved.

399 Music © 1979 Les Presses de Taizé (France). Used by permission of GIA Publications, Inc., exclusive agent. All rights reserved.

400 Words © 1985 Hope Publishing Company. All rights reserved.
Music © 1969 Hope Publishing Company. All rights reserved.

401 Words © 1979 Hope Publishing Company. All rights reserved.
Music © 1987 Hope Publishing Company. All rights reserved.

402 Music Arr. © 2001 Hope Publishing Company. All rights reserved.

404 Words © 1954, Ren. 1982 The Hymn Society (Admin. Hope Publishing Company). All rights reserved.
Music © 1963 Abingdon Press (Administered by The Copyright Company, Nashville, TN). All rights reserved. International copyright secured. Used by permission.

409 Words © 1958 *Service Book and Hymnal,* administered by Augsburg Fortress.
Music Arr. © 1990 Hope Publishing Company. All rights reserved.

410 Words & Music © 1994 Integrity's Hosanna! Music (ASCAP) & Integrity's Praise! Music (BMI). All rights reserved. International copyright secured. Used by permission. c/o Integrity Music, Inc., 1000 Cody Road, Mobile, AL 36695.

412 Words © 1973 Hope Publishing Company. All rights reserved.

413 Words © 1971 Hope Publishing Company. All rights reserved.

415 Words Tr. © 1989 The United Methodist Publishing House (Administered by The Copyright Company, Nashville, TN). All rights reserved. International copyright secured. Used by permission.
Music Arr. © 1998 Hope Publishing Company. All rights reserved.

416 Words © 1989 Hope Publishing Company. All rights reserved.

417 Words & Music © 1994 Hope Publishing Company. All rights reserved.

418 Words © 1982 Jubilate Hymns (Admin. Hope Publishing Company). All rights reserved.
Music © 1984 GIA Publications, Inc. All rights reserved.

421 Words & Music © 1986, 1991 Les Presses de Taizé (France). Used by permission of GIA Publications, Inc., exclusive agent. All rights reserved.

423 Words © 1982, 1990 Hope Publishing Company. All rights reserved.

425 Words © 1969 James Quinn, S.J. (Selah Publishing Co., Inc., North American administrator). All rights reserved. Used by permission.
Music Arr. © 1989 Hope Publishing Company. All rights reserved.

427 Words & Music © 1990 Shepherd's Heart Music, Inc. (admin. by Dayspring Music, Inc.) (BMI), 65 Music Square West, Nashville, TN 37203. All rights reserved. Made in the U.S.A. International copy right secured. Used by permission.

429 Words vs. 2 © 1978 *Lutheran Book of Worship*, administered by Augsburg Fortress.

430 Words & Music © 1975, 1978 Robert J. Dufford, S.J. and New Dawn Music, 5536 NE Hassalo, Portland, OR 97213. All rights reserved. Used with permission.

432 Words © 1979 Hope Publishing Company. All rights reserved.
Music © 1979 Stainer & Bell Ltd. and The Trustees for Methodist Church Purposes (UK) (Admin. Hope Publishing Company). All rights reserved.

433 Words © 1984 Hope Publishing Company. All rights reserved.
Music Arr. © 1982 Jubilate Hymns (Admin. Hope Publishing Company). All rights reserved.

434 Words © 1985 Jubilate Hymns (Admin. Hope Publishing Company). All rights reserved.

436 Words & Music © 1998 Maranatha! Music (Administered by The Copyright Company, Nashville, TN). All rights reserved. International copyright secured. Used by permission.

438 Words & Music by Michael Joncas © 1979 New Dawn Music, 5536 NE Hassalo, Portland, OR 97213. All rights reserved. Used with permission.

441 Words & Music © 1981 Roland Tabell, 2653 Gardi St., Duarte, CA 91010-1331

444 Words & Music © 1992 Jaime Cortez. Published by OCP Publications, 5536 NE Hassalo, Portland, OR 97213. All rights reserved. Used with permission.

445 Words & Music © 1973 Jubilate Hymns (Admin. Hope Publishing Company). All rights reserved.

447 Words & Music © 1971 William J. Gaither, Inc. All rights controlled by Gaither Copyright Management. Used by permission.

448 Words & Music © 1986, 1991 Les Presses de Taizé (France). Used by permission of GIA Publications, Inc., exclusive agent. All rights reserved.

450 Music Arr. © 1989 Hope Publishing Company. All rights reserved.

451 Music Arr. © 1933, Ren. 1961 Presbyterian Board of Education. Used by permission of Westminster John Knox Press.

452 Words & Music © 1971. Renewed 1999 by Manna Music, Inc., 35255 Brooten Road, Pacific City, OR 97135. All rights reserved. Used by permission.

453 Words © 1964 Hope Publishing Company. All rights reserved.
Music Harm. © 1964 Abingdon Press (Administered by The Copyright Company, Nashville, TN). All rights reserved. International copyright secured. Used by permission.

454 Words & Music © 1994 Hope Publishing Company. All rights reserved.

456 English Words © 1983 Gracia Grindal. Admin. Selah Publishing Co., Inc. All rights reserved. Used by permission.
Music Arr. © 2001 Hope Publishing Company. All rights reserved.

459 Words © 1966 Broadman Press (Admin. Genevox Music Group). Used by permission.
Music Arr. © 1958, Ren. 1986 Broadman Press (Admin. Genevox Music Group). Used by permission.

460 Words © 1978 Novello & Company Ltd., London. International copyright secured. All rights reserved. Reprinted by permission.

465 Words & Music © 1978 Bob Kilpatrick Ministries. Assigned 1998 Lorenz Publishing Company, a division of The Lorenz Corporation. All rights reserved. Used by permission.

467 Words & Music © 1992 Word Music, Inc (ASCAP), 65 Music Square West, Nashville, TN 37203/Maranatha! Music (admin. by Word Music, Inc.) (ASCAP), 65 Music Square West, Nashville, TN 37203. All rights reserved. Made in the U.S.A. International copyright secured. Used by permission.

469 Words © 1931 Oxford University Press. Used by permission.
Music Harm. © 1989 Hope Publishing Company. All rights reserved.

471 Words & Music © 1984 Maranatha Praise, Inc. (Administered by The Copyright Company, Nashville, TN). All rights reserved. International copyright secured. Used by permission.

475 Words © 1974 The Hymn Society (Admin. Hope Publishing Company). All rights reserved.
Music © 1941 Historic Church of the Ascension, Atlantic City, NJ. Used by permission.

477 Words © 1992 Hope Publishing Company. All rights reserved.
Music Arr. © 1978 *Lutheran Book of Worship*; administered by Augsburg Fortress. Used by permission.

481 Music Arr. © 1990 Melva W. Costen. Used by permission.

482 Words & Music © 1982 Whole Armor Music and Full Armor Music. Administered by The Kruger Organisation, Inc. International copyright secured. All rights reserved. Used by permission.

484 Words & Music © 1982 Les Presses de Taizé (France). Used by permission of GIA Publications, Inc., exclusive agent. All rights reserved.

485 Words & Music © 1924, Ren. 1952 Hope Publishing Company. All rights reserved.

488 Words © 1973 Hope Publishing Company. All rights reserved. Music © 1973 Jubilate Hymns (Admin. Hope Publishing Company). All rights reserved.

489 Words & Music © 1973 Hope Publishing Company. All rights reserved.

491 Words & Music © 1976 Maranatha! Music (Administered by The Copyright Company, Nashville, TN). All rights reserved. International copyright secured. Used by permission.

492 Words & Music © 1935, Ren. 1963 Birdwing Music (ASCAP) (Admin. EMI Christian Music Publishing) Words vs. 2 © 1982 Jubilate Hymns (Admin. Hope Publishing Company)

493 Words & Music © 1978 Maranatha Praise, Inc. (Administered by The Copyright Company, Nashville, TN). All rights reserved. International copyright secured. Used by permission.

494 Words & Music © 1991 BMG Songs, Inc. and Kid Brothers of St. Frank Publishing (ASCAP). All rights on behalf of Kid Brothers of St. Frank Publishing administered by BMG Songs, Inc. (ASCAP)

495 Music Arr. © 1965 Abingdon Press (Administered by The Copyright Company, Nashville, TN). All rights reserved. International copyright secured. Used by permission.

497 Words & Music © 1987 Jonathan Mark Music (Admin. Gaither Copyright Management) and Birdwing Music (ASCAP) (Admin. EMI Christian Music Publishing) All rights reserved. Used by permission.

498 Words & Music © 1953 by Doris Akers. Copyright Renewed. All rights administered by Unichappell Music, Inc. International copyright secured. All rights reserved.

500 Words & Music © 1938 by Unichappell Music, Inc. Copyright Renewed. International copyright secured. All rights reserved.

502 Music Arr. © 1989 Hope Publishing Company. All rights reserved.

503 Words © 1976 The Hymn Society (Admin. Hope Publishing Company). All rights reserved. Music © 1985 StraightWay Music/Mountain Spring Music (Admin. EMI Christian Music Publishing)

511 Words & Music © 1984 Fairhill Music (ASCAP)

512 Music Arr. © 1989 The United Methodist Publishing House (Administered by The Copyright Company, Nashville, TN). All rights reserved. International copyright secured. Used by permission.

514 Words & Music © 1979 Hope Publishing Company. All rights reserved.

515 Words & Music © 1986 Hope Publishing Company. All rights reserved.

516 Words © 1993 Hope Publishing Company. All rights reserved. Music © 1992 Hope Publishing Company. All rights reserved.

517 Words © 1982 Hope Publishing Company. All rights reserved.

518 Words © 1987 Hope Publishing Company. All rights reserved.

519 Music Arr. © 1990 Hope Publishing Company. All rights reserved.

523 Words & Music © 1976 Bud John Songs, Inc. (ASCAP)/Crouch Music (ASCAP) (Admin. EMI Christian Music Publishing)

524 Words © 1968 Hope Publishing Company. All rights reserved. Music Arr. © 1976 Hinshaw Music, Inc. Used with permission.

526 Words © 1972 The Hymn Society (Admin. Hope Publishing Company). All rights reserved.

528 Words © 1973 Jubilate Hymns (Admin. Hope Publishing Company). All rights reserved.

531 Words © 1973 Hope Publishing Company. All rights reserved.

532 Words © 1982 The Hymn Society (Admin. Hope Publishing Company). All rights reserved. Music Harm. © 1986 GIA Publications, Inc. All rights reserved.

533 Words & Music © 1977 Hope Publishing Company. All rights reserved.

534 Words © 1982 Jubilate Hymns (Admin. Hope Publishing Company). All rights reserved.

536 Words © 1999 Jubilate Hymns (Admin. Hope Publishing Company). All rights reserved. Music © 1942, Ren. 1970 Hope Publishing Company. All rights reserved.

537 Music Arr. © 1990 Hope Publishing Company. All rights reserved.

539 Words © 1982 Hope Publishing Company. All rights reserved.

540 Words © 1999 Jubilate Hymns (Admin. Hope Publishing Company). All rights reserved.

541 Words © 1982 Jubilate Hymns (Admin. Hope Publishing Company). All rights reserved.

542 Words © 1990 Hope Publishing Company. All rights reserved.

543 Words & Music © 1993 Ken Medema Music/Brier Patch Music

545 Words © 1986 Hope Publishing Company. All rights reserved. Music © 1983 Hope Publishing Company. All rights reserved.

546 Words © 1958 *Service Book and Hymnal*, administered by Augsburg Fortress.

547 Words & Music Arr. © 1976 by Fred Bock Music Company

548 Words © 1990 Hope Publishing Company. All rights reserved. Music © 1942, Ren.1970 Hope Publishing Company. All rights reserved.

550 Words & Music © 1972 Hope Publishing Company. All rights reserved.

551 Words © 1992 GIA Publications, Inc. All rights reserved. Music Arr. © 1992 Hope Publishing Company. All rights reserved.

552 Words © 1986 Hope Publishing Company. All rights reserved.

553 Words © 1991 GIA Publications, Inc. All rights reserved.

555 Words © 1969 Hope Publishing Company. All rights reserved. Music © 1925 Oxford University Press. Used by permission.

556 Words & Music © 1990 Make Way Music (Admin. by Music Services in the Western Hemisphere). All rights reserved. (ASCAP)

557 Words & Music © 1969 Bud John Songs, Inc. (ASCAP) (Admin. EMI Christian Music Publishing)

558 Words © 1991 Stainer & Bell Ltd. (Admin. Hope Publishing Company). All rights reserved. Music © 1983 Hope Publishing Company. All rights reserved.

559 Words & Music © 1981 Daniel L. Schutte and New Dawn Music, 5536 NE Hassalo, Portland, OR 97213. All rights reserved. Used with permission.

561 Music Arr. © 2001 Hope Publishing Company. All rights reserved.

563 Words & Music © 1986 Integrity's Hosanna! Music (ASCAP). All rights reserved. International copyright secured. Used by permission. c/o Integrity Music, Inc., 1000 Cody Road, Mobile, AL 36695.

564 Music © 1931 Oxford University Press. Used by permission.

566 Words © 1999 Hope Publishing Company. All rights reserved.

567 Words & Music © 1999 Hope Publishing Company. All rights reserved.

568 Words & Music © 1983 River Oaks Music Company (BMI)/Shepherd's Fold Music (BMI) (Admin. EMI Christian Music Publishing)

570 Words © 1961, Ren. 1989 The Hymn Society (Admin. Hope Publishing Company). All rights reserved.

571 Words © 1994 Hope Publishing Company. All rights reserved.

572 Words © 1961, Ren. 1989 The Hymn Society (Admin. Hope Publishing Company). All rights reserved.

573 Words © 1982 Hope Publishing Company. All rights reserved.

575 Words © 1961 Oxford University Press. Used by permission. Music Harm. © 1978 *Lutheran Book of Worship*, administered by Augsburg Fortress.

576 Words & Music © 1982 Willing Heart Music (Administered by Maranatha! Music c/o The Copyright Company, Nashville, TN)/Maranatha! Music (Administered by The Copyright Company, Nashville, TN). All rights reserved. International copyright secured. Used by permission.

577 Words © 1993 Delores Dufner. Published by OCP Publications, 5536 NE Hassalo, Portland, OR 97213. All rights reserved. Used with permission

578 Words & Music © 1964 Singspiration Music (ASCAP) (Admin. by Brentwood-Benson Music Publishing, Inc.) All rights reserved. Used by permission.

579 Words & Music © 1982 Pavane Publishing. Used by permission.

580 Words © 1975 Broadman Press (Admin. Genevox Music Group). Used by permission.

581 Words from *A Singing Faith,* © 1981 Jane Parker Huber. Used by permission of Westminster John Knox Press.

582 Words © 1954, Ren. 1982 The Hymn Society (Admin. Hope Publishing Company). All rights reserved.

583 Words © 1992 Hope Publishing Company. All rights reserved.

584 Words & Music Arr. © 1993 Hope Publishing Company. All rights reserved.

585 Words © 1993 Hope Publishing Company. All rights reserved. Music © 1951 Oxford University Press. Used by permission.

586 Words © 1987 Hope Publishing Company. All rights reserved.

587 Dedicated to Mrs. Frances Tracy. Words & Music © 1967 OCP Publications, 5536 NE Hassalo, Portland, OR 97213. All rights reserved. Used with permission.

590 Words © 1978 Norman O. Forness. Used by permission.

592 Words © 1978 Hope Publishing Company. All rights reserved. Music © 1942, Ren. 1970 Hope Publishing Company. All rights reserved.

594 Words © 1975, 1995 Hope Publishing Company. All rights reserved. Music © 1980 Hope Publishing Company. All rights reserved.

595 Words & Music © 1966, 1967 F.E.L. Publications. Assigned 1991 Lorenz Publishing Company, a division of The Lorenz Corporation. All rights reserved. Used by permission.

596 Words © 1975 Hope Publishing Company. All rights reserved. Music © 1977 Hope Publishing Company. All rights reserved.

597 Words Tr. © 1958 The United Methodist Publishing House (Administered by The Copyright Company, Nashville, TN). All rights reserved. International copyright secured. Used by permission. Music © 1958 by Isao Koizumi. Used by permission of JASRAC. License No. 0011624-001.

599 Words & Music © 1994 Hope Publishing Company. All rights reserved.

600 Words © 1982 Jubilate Hymns (Admin. Hope Publishing Company). All rights reserved.

601 Words © 1973, 1995 Hope Publishing Company. All rights reserved.

602 Words & Music © 1992 Hope Publishing Company. All rights reserved.

604 Words © 1996 Stainer & Bell Ltd. (Admin. Hope Publishing Company). All rights reserved.

605 Words & Music © 1994 Maranatha Praise, Inc. (Administered by The Copyright Company, Nashville, TN). All rights reserved. International copyright secured. Used by permission.

607 Words Rev. © 1976 by Fred Bock Music Company

608 Words © 1982 Jubilate Hymns (Admin. Hope Publishing Company). All rights reserved. Music © 1959 The United Reformed Church. Used by permission.

609 Words © 1992 Hope Publishing Company. All rights reserved. Music Arr. © 1989 Hope Publishing Company. All rights reserved.

611 Words © 1983 Hope Publishing Company. All rights reserved.

612 Words © 1983 Hope Publishing Company. All rights reserved. Music © 1972 Hope Publishing Company. All rights reserved.

613 Words © 1982 Hope Publishing Company. All rights reserved.

614 Words & Music © 1955, Ren. 1983 Jan-Lee Music. Used by permission.

615 Words © 1992 Hope Publishing Company. All rights reserved.

616 Words © 1968 Hope Publishing Company. All rights reserved. Music © 1989 The United Methodist Publishing House (Administered by The Copyright Company, Nashville, TN). All rights reserved. International copyright secured. Used by permission.

617 Words © 1998 Hope Publishing Company. All rights reserved. Music © 1999 Hope Publishing Company. All rights reserved.

619 Words & Music Arr. © 1984 Jubilate Hymns (Admin. Hope Publishing Company). All rights reserved.

620 Words © 1989 Hope Publishing Company. All rights reserved. Music © 1994 Hope Publishing Company. All rights reserved.

621 Words © 1968 Hope Publishing Company. All rights reserved.

622 Words © 1990 Hope Publishing Company. All rights reserved.

623 Words © 1971 Hope Publishing Company. All rights reserved.

624 Words & Music © 1971 J.A. Olivar, Miguel Manzano, and San Pablo Internacional-SSP. All rights reserved. Sole U.S. Agent: OCP Publications, 5536 NE Hassalo, Portland, OR 97213. Used with permission. Words Tr. © 1980 The United Methodist Publishing House (Administered by The Copyright Company, Nashville, TN). All rights reserved. International copyright secured. Used by permission.

625 Words © 1969 by Stainer & Bell Ltd. (Admin. Hope Publishing Company). All rights reserved. Music Harm. © 1965 Abingdon Press (Administered by The Copyright Company, Nashville, TN). All rights reserved. International copyright secured. Used by permission.

626 Words © 1958, Ren. 1986 The Hymn Society (Admin. Hope Publishing Company). All rights reserved. Music Harm. © 1927 Oxford University Press. Used by permission.

627 Words © 1974 Hope Publishing Company. All rights reserved. Music © 1985 GIA Publications, Inc. All rights reserved.

628 Words & Music © 1989 WGRG The Iona Community (Scotland). Used by permission of GIA Publications, Inc., exclusive agent. All rights reserved.

629 Words & Music © 1993 Hope Publishing Company. All rights reserved.

630 Words & Music © 1987 GIA Publications, Inc. All rights reserved.

632 Words © 1994 Hope Publishing Company. All rights reserved. Music © 1996 Hope Publishing Company. All rights reserved.

633 Words & Music © 1983 Birdwing Music (ASCAP)/BMG Songs (ASCAP) (Admin. EMI Christian Music Publishing)

634 Words © 1979 Stainer & Bell Ltd. (Admin. Hope Publishing Company). All rights reserved.

635 Words © 1999 Hope Publishing Company. All rights reserved. Music © 2001 Hope Publishing Company. All rights reserved.

636 Words © 1982 Jubilate Hymns (Admin. Hope Publishing Company). All rights reserved.

637 Words & Music © 1988 Sparrow Song (BMI)/Greg Nelson Music (BMI) (Admin. EMI Christian Music Publishing) and Careers-BMG Music Publishing, Inc. (BMI)/Multisongs (a div. of Careers-BMG Music Publishing, Inc.)(SESAC)

638 Words © 1969 Hope Publishing Company. All rights reserved.

639 Words & Music © 1989 Maranatha Praise, Inc. (Administered by The Copyright Company, Nashville, TN). All rights reserved. International copyright secured. Used by permission.

640 Words © 1994 Hope Publishing Company. All rights reserved. Music © 1999 Hope Publishing Company. All rights reserved.

641 Words © 1992 Hope Publishing Company. All rights reserved.

642 Words & Music © 1968 Augsburg Publishing House, administered by Augsburg Fortress.

643 Words & Music © 1993 Hope Publishing Company. All rights reserved.

644 Words © 1967 Hope Publishing Company. All rights reserved.

645 Words © 1969 Oxford University Press. Used by permission.

646 Words & Music © 1981 Coomesietunes/Maranatha! Music (Administered by The Copyright Company, Nashville, TN). All rights reserved. International copyright secured. Used by permission.

647 Words & Music © 1997 Integrity's Hosanna! Music (ASCAP), c/o Integrity Music, Inc., 1000 Cody Road, Mobile, AL 36695 and Word Music, Inc. (ASCAP), 65 Music Square West, Nashville, TN 37203. All rights reserved. Made in the U.S.A. International copyright secured. Used by permission.

648 Words & Music © 1991 Shade Tree Publishing (Administered by Maranatha! Music, c/o The Copyright Company, Nashville, TN) and Maranatha Praise, Inc. (Administered by The Copyright Company, Nashville, TN). All rights reserved. International copyright secured. Used by permission.

649 Words & Music © 1982 GIA Publications, Inc. All rights reserved.

651 Words & Music © 1984 John T. Benson Publishing Co. (ASCAP) (Admin. by Brentwood-Benson Music Publishing, Inc.) All rights reserved. Used by permission.

652 Music © 1967 Scripture In Song (a div. of Integrity Music, Inc.) All rights reserved. International copyright secured. Used by permission. c/o Integrity Music, Inc., 1000 Cody Road, Mobile, AL 36695.

653 Words & Music © 1994 Universal-MCA Music Publishing, a division of Universal Studios, Inc. and Sound III, Inc. All rights for Sound III, Inc. Controlled and Administered by Universal-MCA Music Publishing, a division of Universal Studios, Inc. All rights reserved. Used by permission.

654 Words & Music © 1983 Meadowgreen Music Company (ASCAP)/Songchannel Music Company (ASCAP) (Admin. EMI Christian Music Publishing)

655 Words © 1999 Marva J. Dawn. From *A "Royal" Waste of Time: The Splendor of Worshiping God and Being Church for the World*, W.B. Eerdmans. Music Arr. © 1992 Hope Publishing Company. All rights reserved.

656 Words & Music © 1997 Integrity's Hosanna! Music (ASCAP). All rights reserved. International copyright secured. Used by permission. c/o Integrity Music, Inc., 1000 Cody Road, Mobile, AL 36695.

657 Words & Music © 1976 Maranatha Praise, Inc. (Administered by The Copyright Company, Nashville, TN). All rights reserved. International copyright secured. Used by permission.

658 Words & Music © 1988 BMG Songs, Inc. (ASCAP)

659 Words & Music © 1990, 1996 General Board of Global Ministries, GBG Musik, 475 Riverside Dr., New York, NY 10115. All rights reserved.

660 Words & Music © 1989 Integrity's Hosanna! Music (ASCAP). All rights reserved. International copyright secured. Used by permission. c/o Integrity Music, Inc., 1000 Cody Road, Mobile, AL 36695.

662 Words © 1954, Ren. 1982 Hope Publishing Company. All rights reserved.
Music © 1966 Hope Publishing Company. All rights reserved.

663 Words © 1990 Jubilate Hymns, Ltd. (Admin. Hope Publishing Company). All rights reserved.

664 Words & Music © 1984 Meadowgreen Music Company (ASCAP) (Admin EMI Christian Music Publishing) /Word Music, Inc. (ASCAP), 65 Music Square West, Nashville, TN 37203. All rights reserved. Made in the U.S.A. International copyright secured. Used by permission.

666 Words & Music © 1985 GIA Publications, Inc. All rights reserved.

667 Words © 1953, Ren. 1981 The Hymn Society (Admin. Hope Publishing Company). All rights reserved.

669 Words © 1982 Jubilate Hymns (Admin. Hope Publishing Company). All rights reserved.

671 Words © 1987 Hope Publishing Company. All rights reserved.

672 Words & Music © 1980 Hope Publishing Company. All rights reserved.

673 Words © 1982 Jubilate Hymns (Admin. Hope Publishing Company). All rights reserved.

674 Words & Music © 1995 Hope Publishing Company. All rights reserved.

675 Words & Music © 1987 Mercy/Vineyard Publishing (ASCAP) (Admin. Music Services). Used by permission.

676 Words & Music © 1982 Hope Publishing Company. All rights reserved.

677 Words © 1981 Ronald S. Cole-Turner.

678 Words © 1993 Hope Publishing Company. All rights reserved.
Music © 1989 The United Methodist Publishing House (Administered by The Copyright Company, Nashville, TN) All rights reserved. International copyright secured. Used by permission.

679 Words © 1982 Jubilate Hymns (Admin. Hope Publishing Company). All rights reserved.
Music Harm. © 1927 Oxford University Press. Used by permission.

680 Words & Music © 1985 John C. Ylvisaker, Box 321, Waverly, IA 50677.

681 Words © 1976 The Hymn Society (Admin. Hope Publishing Company). All rights reserved.

682 Words © 1996 Hope Publishing Company. All rights reserved.
Music © 1972 Hope Publishing Company. All rights reserved.

683 Words © 1999 Hope Publishing Company. All rights reserved.
Music © 1996 Hope Publishing Company. All rights reserved.

684 Words © 1990 Hope Publishing Company. All rights reserved.

685 Words & Music © 1982 Hope Publishing Company. All rights reserved.

686 Words © 1949 Oxford University Press. Used by permission.
Music © 1969 Hope Publishing Company. All rights reserved.

687 Words © 1989 Hope Publishing Company. All rights reserved.

689 Words & Music © 1978 John B. Foley, S.J. and New Dawn Music, 5536 NE Hassalo, Portland, OR 97213. All rights reserved. Used with permission.

690 Words & Music © 2000 Hope Publishing Company. All rights reserved.

691 Words © 1989 Hope Publishing Company. All rights reserved.

692 Words & Music © 1993 Hope Publishing Company. All rights reserved.

694 Words vss. 1-3 & Music © Lutheran World Federation
Words vs. 4 & Music Harm. © 1972 *Contemporary Worship 4: Hymns for Baptism and Holy Communion*, administered by Augsburg Fortress

695 Words © 1989 Hope Publishing Company. All rights reserved.
Music Arr. © 1992 Hope Publishing Company. All rights reserved.

696 Words & Music © 1984 by Fred Bock Music Company

697 Words & Music © 1984 Les Presses de Taizé (France) Used by permission of GIA Publications, Inc., exclusive agent. All rights reserved.

698 Words & Music © 1975 Hope Publishing Company. All rights reserved.

699 Music Arr. © 1965 Abingdon Press (Administered by The Copyright Company, Nashville, TN). All rights reserved. International copyright secured. Used by permission.

700 Words & Music © 1969 Hope Publishing Company. All rights reserved.

701 Words & Music © 1973 Hope Publishing Company. All rights reserved.

702 Words © 1984 Hope Publishing Company. All rights reserved.

703 Words & Music © 1966, 1970, 1986, 1993 GIA Publications, Inc. All rights reserved.

704 Words & Music © 1996 Hope Publishing Company. All rights reserved.

705 Words & Music © Copyright permission obtained, Archdiocese of Philadelphia, 1977. All rights reserved.

706 Words © 1971,1995 Hope Publishing Company. All rights reserved.
Music Arr. © 1977 Hope Publishing Company. All rights reserved.

707 Words © 1992 Jubilate Hymns (Admin. Hope Publishing Company). All rights reserved.
Music © 1990 Hope Publishing Company. All rights reserved.

708 Words © 1984 Hope Publishing Company. All rights reserved.

709 Words & Music © 1984 Utryck (Admin. Walton Music Corp.)

710 Words & Music © 1975 Lillenas Publishing Company (Administered by The Copyright Company, Nashville, TN). All rights reserved. International copyright secured. Used by permission.

712 Words © 1964 World Library Publications, 3825 N. Willow Rd., Schiller Park, IL 60176. All rights reserved. Used by permission.
Music Harm. © 1972 *Contemporary Worship 4: Hymns for Baptist and Holy Communion*, administered by Augsburg Fortress.

713 Words & Music © 1984 Utryck (Admin. Walton Music Corp.)

714 Words Tr. © 1990 Hope Publishing Company. All rights reserved.

715 Words © 1968 Hope Publishing Company. All rights reserved.

717 Words © 1993 Hope Publishing Company. All rights reserved.

718 Words Rev. © 1982 Jubilate Hymns (Admin. Hope Publishing Company). All rights reserved.

719 Words © 1983 Jaroslav J. Vajda. Used by permission.

720 Words & Music © 1991 Hope Publishing Company. All rights reserved.

722 Words © 1988 Oxford University Press. Used by permission.
Music Arr. © 1989 Hope Publishing Company. All rights reserved.

723 Words © 1970 Hope Publishing Company. All rights reserved.

735 Music Transcription © 1989 The United Methodist Publishing House (Administered by The Copyright Company, Nashville, TN) All rights reserved. International copyright secured. Used by permission.

736 Words & Music © 1985 Fintan O'Carroll and Christopher Walker. Published by OCP Publications, 5536 NE Hassalo, Portland, OR 97213. All rights reserved. Used with permission.

737 Music Arr. © 1998 Hope Publishing Company. All rights reserved.

738 Music Arr. © 1995 Hope Publishing Company. All rights reserved.

739 Words & Music Harm. © 1987 CRC Publications, Grand Rapids, MI 49560. 1-800-333-8300. All rights reserved. Used by permission.

740 Words & Music © 1935 G. Schirmer, Inc. (ASCAP). International copyright secured. All rights reserved. Reprinted by Permission of G. Schirmer, Inc.

741 Words & Music © 1991 Lumko Institute, P.O. Box 5058, Delmenville, 1403, South Africa

742 Music © 1981 Oxford University Press (Admin. Hinshaw Music, Inc.) Printed with permission.

747 Words © 1990 Hope Publishing Company. All rights reserved.

Photographs

Copyright © Micah Marty.
From *Our Hope for Years to Come.*
Reprinted by permission.

Scriptural Index

Genesis
1:1 28, 30, 32, 45, 139, 141, 145, 147, 304, 388, 524, 599, 643, 673, 726, 733, 734
1:1-23 559
1:1-25 33
1:1-31 17, 26, 79, 662
1:2 128
1:2-3 74, 142
1:3 319
1:3-26 536
1:5 652
1:6 9
1:7 141
1:11 388
1:14 394, 515
1:14-17 31
1:14-19 141, 644
1:16 248, 728
1:21-31 31
1:26 38, 55
1:26-27 28, 577
1:26-28 48
1:26-30 36
1:27 24, 55, 599, 621, 644
1:28 21
1:31 577, 722
2:2 39
2:7 48, 388, 418, 517
2:15 28, 36
2:16 31
2:19-20 37
2:24 611, 612
3:8 300
3:15 202
3:17-19 179, 638
3:19 517
8:22 72, 724
9:12-16 29
9:12-17 446, 551
11:9 191
12:1 326
12:1-3 170, 584, 593
12:2-3 204, 416, 722
15:1 156
18:18 168
22:8 116
26:24 411, 448
28:12 426
28:15 506
28:16 133

Exodus
2:23 559
3:6 16, 257, 337
3:7 559
3:10-13 618
3:20 15
5:1-2 618
10:2 607
13:21 22, 501, 748
13:21-22 598
15:1 15, 122, 298, 674, 729
15:1-2 58
15:2 52, 484
15:6 101, 422
15:11 101, 658
15:13 499, 508
15:18 226
15:20-21 58
15:21 122
15:22-27 430
15:26 450
16:7 35
16:15 716
16:16 598
16:31 409, 505, 647, 701
17:1-7 430
17:5-7 505
19:18 481
20:3 345
23:16 570
23:19 570, 688
33:11 408, 601
33:12-14 747
33:12-15 476
33:14 1
33:19 63
33:20 48
33:22 384, 439
34:6 61, 370, 371, 749
34:6-7 503
35:4-29 459, 722
39:3 71

Leviticus
11:45 374
19:2 374
20:8 374
22:9 374
25:11 554
26:4 394

Numbers
6:22-27 719
6:25 438
11:23 726
14:18 371, 503
14:21 146
18:20 502
21:8-9 287
24:17 223

Deuteronomy
1:6-8 538
1:31 82
2:7 22, 506
4:31 63
4:34 658
5:1-21 326
6:4 139
6:4-5 684
6:4-9 497, 682
6:5 11, 132, 198
6:6-9 417, 524, 607
7:7 170
7:19 726
8:2 579
8:16 409, 647, 701
10:17 45, 658, 674
10:18 688
10:21 15, 52
11:14 394
14:29 79
16:20 539
24:19-21 723
26:19 662
27:19 539
28:12 394
28:58 658
31:6 2, 75, 417, 514, 569
31:7 569
31:7-8 430
31:23 569
32:3 56, 112
32:10 549
32:11 438
32:48-52 519
33:25 449
33:27 418, 496, 716

Joshua
1:2 538
1:5 75, 417
1:5-7 430
1:5-9 411
1:7 569
1:18 569
3:13 499
4:1-3 501
4:5-7 524
4:6-7 607
9:2 500
10:25 569
23:5 519
23:14 667
24:15 344, 605, 607

Judges
5:20 22

Ruth
1:16-18 497

1 Samuel
1:17 714
1:21-28 681
2:2 136, 737
3:1-21 559, 584
3:9 593
7:3 230
7:12 68, 422
15:22 235, 443, 686
15:29 72
17:47 511, 726

2 Samuel
9:7 617
22:2 115
22:3 94
22:4 114
22:31 64, 94

1 Kings
8:20 667
8:27 189
13:11-13 412
19:11-13 326, 470
19:12 432, 462

2 Kings
2:11-12 520

1 Chronicles
16:8 359, 448
16:25 103, 126
16:29 733, 734
22:13 569
28:20 569
29:11 43
29:13 14
29:14 458
29:28 526

2 Chronicles
6:15 728
7:14 370, 383
20:6 738
20:15 511, 514, 726
29:30 337
32:7 569

Ezra
9:13 262

Nehemiah
1:5 658
9:5-7 11
9:17 749
9:19 22
9:31 63
9:32 45, 674

Esther
4:14 569

Job
1:21 83, 428, 683, 741
10:8-9 492
10:16 658
12:10 80
13:15 444
14:1 521
14:14 409
19:25 10, 77, 117, 189, 302, 318, 414, 434, 653
22:26 71
23:10 374
25:2 53
26:7 37
28:21 48
33:26 381
36:5 45
37:14 15
37:22 658
38:1-7 35, 728
38:1-21 32
38:1-33 26
38:7 21, 22, 59, 180, 235, 645, 641, 642
38:12 154
38:18-38 31
38:31-33 724
38:33 248
42:1-3 65

Psalms
1:1-6 494
1:3 48, 428, 488, 515, 724
1:4 67
2:6 390
2:12 94
3:1 590
3:3 2, 422, 425, 438, 545, 633
4:1 445
4:5 651
4:6 438
4:8 432, 469
5:2 2
5:3 35, 111, 136, 300
5:11 25, 54, 94, 304

Psalms, contd.
7:10 2, 422, 438, 633
7:17 363, 448
8:1 31, 42, 97, 101, 642, 728
8:1-2 6
8:1-9 28, 63, 79, 599, 720
8:2 267, 341, 417, 585, 629
8:3 21, 24, 33, 40, 51, 644
8:5 339
8:5-8 38
8:9 97, 101
9:1 3, 15
9:2 657
9:7 56, 142
9:9 74, 423
10:12 644
10:17 471
10:18 2
11:7 539
12:6 444
13:1-5 376
13:6 15, 25, 729
16:1 94
16:2 150
16:8 380
16:9 88
16:11 131, 135, 525, 535, 706
17:6 489, 490
17:8 84, 90, 435, 439, 549
18:1 85, 471
18:2 2, 102, 115, 384, 423, 424, 501, 507, 653
18:35 500
19:1 3, 21, 39, 51, 59, 63, 644, 728, 738, 739
19:1-4 6, 33, 599, 642
19:4 424
19:5 230
19:6 22
19:14 77, 85, 115, 384, 653, 726
20:1-9 445
20:2 84
20:5 43
20:7 429, 450
21:6 535, 657
21:7 376
22:1 206
22:1-5 376
22:3 136, 138, 151
22:4 728
22:6 473
22:28 45
23 73, 86, 343, 593, 655, 661, 701, 717
23:1 1
23:1-2 488, 573
23:1-9 152
23:2 9, 440, 477, 499
23:2-3 428
23:3 170, 498, 505
23:4 506
23:5 627
23:6 71, 608, 680
24:1 9, 28, 36, 37, 176, 309
24:7 176, 267, 271, 342, 513
24:7-10 3, 159, 323, 657
24:8 45, 511
24:9 176, 271
25:4 593
25:6 63
25:7 386
25:9 453
26:8 549
27:1 76, 423, 496, 685
27:4 123, 357, 545
27:5 90, 435
27:11 499, 508
27:14 166, 514
28:2 352
28:7 2, 359, 363, 422, 471, 501, 633
28:9 73, 86
28:14 9
29:2 18, 66, 96, 143, 148, 363
29:11 539, 614, 728
30:1 43
30:4 15, 56, 138, 142
30:5 432, 446, 515, 544, 553, 725
30:11 436, 524
30:12 359, 363
31:2 94, 476
31:3 115, 440, 593
31:15 409, 503
31:16 376
31:20 94
32:7 90, 435, 439, 456
32:8 505
32:11 304, 657
33:1 15, 56, 113, 142
33:3 67
33:4 72
33:5-6 31
33:6 662
33:9 662
33:12 727, 731
33:20 84, 422
33:21 2
34:1-466
34:2 4, 41, 261
34:3 11, 43, 88, 145, 146, 385
34:4 56, 115, 142
34:8 94
34:14 389, 539, 614
34:18 683
34:19 452
34:22 429
35:9 706
35:18 359, 363
35:27 304
35:28 96
36:7 84, 94
36:9 256
37:4 71, 421
37:7 412, 477
37:11 539
37:24 80, 438, 499, 500, 728
37:25 421, 452, 608, 680
38:11 473
40:1 166, 490
40:3 8, 13, 142, 426, 560, 642
40:4 526
40:5 572
40:8 374, 457, 486, 588
40:16 88, 122, 657
40:17 115, 501
42:1 471
42:1-2 431
42:1-4 545
42:2 444
42:3 632
42:4 549
42:5 75, 410, 451
42:8 111
42:11 71, 428
43:3 730
44:3 726
44:4 342
44:8 114
45:1 420
45:2 123
45:4 268, 658
45:15 212
45:17 138
46 507
46:1 56, 84, 94, 471, 637
46:2 431
46:4 68, 435, 522
46:7 445
46:7-9 728
46:10 1, 122, 129, 186, 232, 387, 412, 450, 451, 477, 483, 637
46:11 450
47:1 14, 94
47:2 51, 658
47:6 15, 25, 56, 88, 142, 674
47:9 122
48:1 51, 653, 660
48:14 14, 501
49:14 518
50:1 45, 111
50:10 21
51:1 379
51:1-9 370
51:7 353, 386, 486
51:7-12 456
51:8 212
51:10 104, 170, 386, 461, 467, 631
51:10-12 328, 378, 381
51:11 134, 492
51:12 385
51:16 686
51:16-17 235
51:17 420
52:8 376
53:6 159
55 429
55:1 487
55:17 107
55:22 380, 493
56:3 441
56:4 423, 441
56:11 423, 441
56:13 76, 500
57:1 379, 699
57:5 122, 738, 739
57:7 15
57:9-11 12
57:10 48
57:11 122, 738, 739
59:1 445
59:16 14, 15, 35
60:12 315
61:2 115, 384
61:2-3 529
61:4 94
62:1 446
62:5 428, 446, 484
62:8 94
63:1 432, 440, 494, 648, 665
63:3 145, 146
63:4 14, 352, 700
63:6 579
63:7 15
63:8 80, 438, 683, 728
65:5 658
65:6 31
65:11 724
65:13 8, 13, 304
66:1 94
66:1-2 96
66:2 15, 56, 142
66:3 51, 658
66:4 49
66:5 444, 658
66:6 113
66:7 45
66:8 138
66:10 374
67 554, 748
67:1 422, 438
67:2 168
67:3 626
67:4 212, 657
67:6 724
67:7 81
68:3 113
68:4 18, 741
68:5 2, 423, 688
68:8 499
68:19 68
68:35 51, 658
69:29 445
69:30 145, 741
69:33 476
70:4 88, 657
70:5 115, 501
71 518
71:1-18 632
71:1-24 94, 113
71:2 490
71:3 115
71:5 469
71:5-9 503
71:6-9 608, 680
71:9 495
71:16 45
71:17-21 608, 680
71:18 495
72:11 341
72:12 476
72:15 111
73:24 716
73:25 431
73:26 456
74:21 741
75:1 359, 448
76:12 730
77:9 63
77:11 579
77:12 45
77:15 45

77:19 65
78:1 490
78:36-37 371
78:38 63
79:13 8
80:1 73, 86, 440
80:5 632
81:10 421
81:16 705
82:3 688
84:1-3 545
84:2 457, 476
84:3 2, 29
84:7 545
84:10 535
84:10-12 545
84:11 438
84:12 120
85:6 328, 462, 463
85:7 376
86:1 476
86:11 11
86:12 145, 146
86:15 61
87:3 598
88:2 490
89 60
89:1 14, 15
89:5 15, 136
89:7 658
89:8 45
89:13 728
89:14 503, 539
89:26 115
90:1-5 84
90:1-17 632
90:5-10 48
90:7-15 638
90:10 571
90:12 518
90:14-15 536
90:17 197, 466
91:1 446
91:1-16 438
91:2 94, 115, 450
91:3 514, 728
91:4 439, 716
91:7 207, 380, 633
91:9 94
91:11 721
91:14 445
92:1-2 503
92:4 88
92:8 122
92:15 115, 384, 424, 653
93:1 101
93:4 45, 113
94:19 428
94:22 115
95:1 14, 15, 54, 87, 93, 94, 95, 115, 197
95:1-8 9
95:2 41, 140, 448, 720, 722
95:4-5 63, 80
95:6 31, 114, 182, 337, 648, 699, 700, 724
96:1 8, 10, 13, 15, 49, 142, 642
96:2 35, 741
96:2-3 554
96:4 50, 660
96:6 101
96:8 66
96:10 56
96:12 8
97:1 56, 142
97:2 539
97:9 47, 122
97:10 142
98:1 10, 13, 15, 142, 315, 560, 642, 726
98:1-9 8
98:3 170
98:4-6 7
98:4-9 179
98:8 641, 710
98:8-9 21, 724
99:3 51, 136, 658
99:4 45, 539, 663
99:5 43, 151, 737
99:9 43, 151, 737
100 5, 147, 661
100:1 22, 143
100:2 112, 119, 289
100:3 517
100:4 359, 448, 459, 657, 720
101:1 15
102:27 409, 490
103 4, 82, 142
103:1-3 60
103:1-6 71
103:2 41, 572
103:3 579, 638
103:4 77
103:5 67, 352, 471
103:11 57
103:12 428, 601
103:13 83
103:14 473
103:17 41
103:19 21, 342
103:22 59
104 2, 23
104:1 43, 101
104:2 48, 644
104:19 394
105:4 370
105:5 579
106:3 539
106:48 71
107:1 363, 365, 720
107:2 133
107:6 115
107:9 170, 352, 421, 444, 471
107:16 290
107:22 651
107:23-30 74
107:25 31
107:29 431
107:32 43
107:43 4
108:1 15
108:5 146
110:3 101
110:4 72
111 663
111:3 101
111:5 421
111:7 72
111:9 658
113:2 741
113:3 111
115:9 2
115:16 37
116:7 428
116:12 284, 685
116:13 484
116:16 14
116:17 40, 140, 484, 651, 722, 726
117:1 138
118:14 11, 71
118:19-24 657
118:24 113, 392, 652
118:27 438
118:28 43, 363, 365
119:11 668
119:27 15
119:28 620
119:41 376
119:57 456
119:76 94
119:89 27, 667
119:105 330, 444, 462, 514, 566, 664, 668, 670
119:114 2, 422, 456, 633
119:120 53
119:130 670
119:172 96
121 488
121:1 418
121:2 84
121:3 633
121:4 56
121:7 633
122:1 368
122:6 614
124:1 77
125:2 488
126:3 4
126:5 432
126:6 724
127:1 564
127:2 711
130:5 166, 444
130:12 381
132:9 304
133:1 134, 331, 701, 712
134 39
136 63
136:1 363, 365, 720
137:1-9 430
137:3 7, 113
137:5-6 549
138:2 699
139:1 385
139:1-4 718
139:1-16 682
139:7-8 425
139:7-10 31
139:9-10 499
139:12 111, 190, 248, 409, 453, 711
139:13-14 388
139:13-16 678
139:23 49, 385, 485, 486, 569
139:23-24 347, 636
139:24 499, 500, 508
140:7 115, 501
140:12 476
141:1-2 107
143:8 64, 136, 307, 450
143:9 90, 435, 476
143:10 486, 588
143:12 376
144:2 2, 115, 423, 501, 633
145:1 43
145:2 111
145:3 50
145:4 45
145:5 101
145:6 658
145:9 2
145:10 136, 138
145:12 45
145:13 41, 72
145:17 64
145:21 23
146:2 111, 426
146:6 72, 79
146:10 56, 142
147:1 15, 54, 88
147:4 642
147:5 45
147:14 352, 705
148 6, 17, 33
148:3 40
148:7-12 13, 710
148:9 40, 724
149:1 13, 15, 67, 142, 642
149:2 390
149:4 383
149:10 59
150 5, 6, 7, 13, 46, 147, 645
150:1-6 8, 10
150:2 95
150:3-5 641, 642
150:6 22, 34, 44, 71, 79, 94, 142

Proverbs
3:5 496
3:5-6 429, 441, 493, 513, 590, 610
3:14 580
3:26 429
4:18 22, 91, 496, 562
4:23 484
13:19 428
14:26 94
15:1 389
15:27 36
15:29 490
16:18 170
16:24 668
17:3 374
18:10 18, 94
18:24 417, 627, 635
19:21 65
21:15 539
22:6 497, 607, 681
22:19 429, 441
23:11 423
25:25 432
27:1 401
29:7 539
29:23 170
29:25 450
30:5 94, 438
31:25-31 585
31:28 497
31:30 518

Ecclesiastes
3:1 78, 394, 503

Ecclesiastes, contd.
3:1-8 248, 515, 608, 680
3:4 118
3:8 614
3:11 16, 40, 409
3:20 330
5:7 53
12:1 579

Song of Solomon
2:1 123, 190, 242
2:4 22
4:16 642

Isaiah
1:17 539, 615
1:18 208, 256, 353, 354, 486
1:21 625
1:26 625
2:4 28, 29, 37, 157, 160, 539, 562, 615, 622, 626
2:10 101
2:19 101
2:21 101
6:1-3 58, 739
6:1-4 59
6:1-8 2, 131, 232, 374, 387, 559, 654, 656
6:1-9 584
6:1-10 6, 17
6:2 48
6:3 4, 136, 138, 139, 145, 151, 737
6:5-7 11
6:8 443, 574, 580, 659, 713
6:8-9 566
6:9 177
7:14 92, 154, 160, 163, 168, 172, 178, 180, 182, 211, 237, 340
9:2 154, 155, 160, 208, 222, 233, 235, 296, 319, 559, 562, 649, 670
9:6 42, 45, 69, 102, 105, 137, 145, 153, 157, 185, 197, 338, 340, 449, 586, 674
9:7 341, 626
11:1 154, 158, 190
11:1-10 243
11:2 325
11:6 677
11:6-9 539
11:9 191, 312, 532, 564
11:10 158
12:2-6 423, 442
12:5 363
14:27 564
21:11 164
25:4 84, 439
25:8 290
25:11 170
26:3 20, 433, 435
26:4 441
26:9 665
29:16 343
29:19 420
29:23 53
30:15 419, 701
30:18 166, 539
30:21 154
30:28 730
32:2 255, 534
32:15 534, 724
33:20-21 598
35:1 724
35:1-2 190
35:1-10 534
35:2 535
35:10 101, 390, 517
36:16 532
37:17 490
39:10 67
40:1 155
40:1-4 152
40:1-5 161
40:3 152, 155, 156, 174, 179
40:3-4 535
40:5-6 155
40:8 662
40:9 50, 85, 448
40:10 45, 683
40:11 73, 80, 82, 83, 86, 95, 440
40:12 435
40:12-14 26
40:13 467, 613
40:18 60
40:26 26, 45
40:31 16, 231, 419, 438, 514, 613
41:10 683
41:13 498
41:17-20 430
42:3 77
42:6 79
42:7 656
42:8 114
42:9 55, 355, 503
42:16 155
43:1 251, 371
43:1-2 405, 428, 531
43:1-3 73, 86, 429, 719
43:1-5 411
43:1-7 430, 632
43:2 74, 380, 452, 506, 726
44:6 726
44:23 13, 710, 724
45:6 69
45:9 343
45:21 69
45:22 472
46:4 82, 83, 683
46:10 65
47:8 69
48:10 374
48:13 728
48:17 726
48:18 435
49:5 135
49:7 72
49:13 8
49:15 81
49:16 80, 435, 549
50:10 2
51:11 113, 390
51:17 164
52:7 21, 56, 187, 218, 222, 307, 466, 557, 564, 565, 730, 731
52:8 152
52:10 174
53:2 190
53:3 301
53:3-4 259, 262, 284, 536, 632
53:3-6 104
53:4 95, 109, 258, 263, 277, 473, 562
53:4-5 93, 97, 336
53:4-6 632
53:5 61, 263, 290, 624, 638
53:5-6 371, 586
53:6 159, 539
53:7 268, 280
53:10 243
53:11 1
54:11 625
54:14 625
54:17 511
55:1 444, 479, 655
55:1-2 430
55:3 490
55:5 256
55:6 494
55:8 64, 417, 610
55:10 388
55:11 444
55:12 14, 163, 188, 641, 706, 708, 710, 724
55:12-13 25, 532
56:1 539
57:12 328
58:8 202
59:1 500
59:16 111
59:19 511
60:1 89, 91, 164, 231
60:3 189
60:16 45
61:1 307
61:1-2 89, 93, 158, 160, 199, 231, 534, 571, 615
61:1-3 156, 360, 436
61:1-8 654
61:3 113
61:8 539
61:10 366, 522
63:1 45
63:1-4 730
63:9 82
63:16 726
64:8 343, 373, 486, 551
65:24 27
65:25 532, 539, 622
66:5 145, 146, 337, 465
66:12 435
66:13 135

Jeremiah
3:12 63
8:22 631
9:7 374
9:24 539
10:6 45
10:12 27
18:1-4 328, 486
18:5-6 551
18:6 343, 373
23:5 13
27:5 726
29:11 72, 78, 83, 410, 422, 447, 564, 663, 682
29:13 202, 383
30:7 69
30:10 539
31:3 446
31:10 73, 86
31:12 721
31:13 10, 436, 524
31:33 461
31:33-34 559
31:34 539
32:19 65
32:39 604
46:27 539
50:5 390

Lamentations
2:3 136
3:22 61, 409
3:22-23 35, 60, 62, 72, 663
3:22-24 64, 503
3:23 2, 75, 78, 111, 685
3:41 14, 700

Ezekiel
18:31 467
34:24 444
34:26 579
36:26 461, 467
43:2 161
48:35 625

Daniel
2:21 234
3:26 112
4:3 667
4:9 32
4:34 667
7:9 16, 48, 148
9:4 51
9:9 63
9:18 490
12:3 529

Hosea
6:1 371
10:12 444

Joel
2:21-29 392
2:28 334, 502
2:28-29 6, 503, 571, 581, 629
2:28-32 326, 548, 585
2:31 243
3:10 29, 504, 622
3:13-18 392

Amos
4:12 161
6:3-7 625

Micah
4:3 157, 539, 562
5:2 170, 180, 185, 242
6:6-8 686
6:8 24, 539, 571, 617

Nahum
1:7 94, 429

Habakkuk
2:3 409
2:14 564
2:20 232, 387
3:2 51, 53

Zephaniah
2:11 658
3:17 45

Haggai
2:6 556
2:7 153, 154, 471

Zechariah
4:6 475, 647
6:13 97
8:19 389
9:9 152
12:10 318
13:1 256
13:9 374

Malachi
3:2-3 330
3:3 374
3:6 72, 398, 451, 521
3:10 570
4:2 91, 185, 208, 235, 248, 293

Matthew
1:1 230
1:18 229
1:18-23 181
1:21 153, 177, 227, 447
1:21-23 211
1:23 92, 121, 154, 160, 163, 168, 172, 178, 180, 182, 185, 189, 199, 340, 649
1:24 237
2:1 209
2:1-10 243
2:1-12 165, 167, 184, 187, 189, 193, 196, 210, 215, 225, 227, 229, 233, 234, 235, 236, 238, 247, 540
2:2 223
2:5 180
2:6 1, 153, 242
2:9 224
2:9-10 209
2:16 207
3:1-10 175
3:1-12 239
3:3 152, 155, 161, 174, 179
3:11 140, 518
3:13-15 247
3:13-17 128, 239, 241
3:16 32, 132, 134, 140, 149, 352
3:17 101
4:1 128
4:1-11 252
4:1-17 244
4:10 230
4:11 654
4:16 208
4:18-22 449, 470
4:19 345, 346, 347, 350, 430, 573
4:20 344
4:21 118
4:23 159
4:23-24 638
4:23-25 742
4:24 93
5:1 591
5:3 58
5:3-10 170, 430
5:3-12 666
5:4 231, 404
5:5 113, 183, 544
5:6 457, 560
5:7 377
5:8 113, 298
5:9 587
5:12 382
5:13 649
5:13-14 462
5:14 392, 518, 559, 563, 587, 627
5:14-16 556, 670
5:15 544
5:16 110, 135, 156, 530, 541, 551, 575, 580
5:18 27, 667
5:22 400
5:26-27 29
5:43-44 187, 587
5:45 444, 724
6:6 483
6:8 346, 429
6:9 28, 125, 135, 607
6:9-10 46
6:9-13 332, 740
6:10 168, 217, 372, 532, 555, 562, 563, 723
6:11 409, 627, 722
6:12 587, 695
6:13 626
6:24 121
6:25-34 21, 472
6:28-29 730
6:30 30
6:33 132, 349, 483, 590, 740
6:34 524
7:6-7 302
7:7 132, 349, 420, 590, 740
7:7-12 421
7:14 236, 302, 496
7:24 424, 429, 542, 653
7:24-26 405
7:26 453
8:8 638
8:12 537
8:13 638
8:16 93
8:17 638
8:18 26, 495
8:19 344, 458
8:19-22 345
8:22 347, 350, 430, 573
8:23-27 26, 74, 192, 495, 725
8:28-33 93
8:34 655
9:2-8 638
9:9 344
9:18-26 491
9:20-22 364
9:21-22 638
9:32-33 93
9:33 93
9:35 638
9:36 586
9:37 724
9:41 591
10:1 578
10:8 474, 479, 557, 572, 592
10:9-14 578
10:22 510
10:32 529
10:34 99
10:38 252, 253, 691
10:39 587
11:5 58, 160, 192
11:10 702
11:15 334, 480, 491, 671
11:19 61, 149, 279, 320, 473, 627
11:28 153, 190, 346, 348, 386, 430, 469, 473, 493, 655, 702
11:28-30 9
11:29 80, 367, 573, 718
12:15 638
12:15-16 540, 640
12:18 101, 123
12:20 77
12:21 442
12:22 93, 638
12:46-50 602
12:48 606
12:50 486
13:17 167
13:36-43 721
13:43 438, 529
13:44 431
13:45 427
13:55 237
14:13-21 698
14:14 638
14:16 623
14:22-23 74
14:22-32 495
14:22-33 56, 192, 242, 725
14:27 569
14:29 345
14:36 638
15:14 79
15:28 638
15:29-31 160
15:29-38 665
15:30 638
16:13-16 703
16:18 509, 542, 544, 546, 579, 598
16:24 252, 253, 344, 350, 474, 510, 531, 615, 655
16:24-25 351
16:27 321
17:1-5 245
17:1-8 247, 654, 656
17:1-13 246
17:2 99, 107
17:8 425, 502
17:18 93, 638
17:21-35 596
18:2-6 629
18:3 417, 437
18:5 437
18:20 1, 124, 125, 524, 546, 567, 586, 606, 627, 646, 701
18:21 596
18:21-35 372
18:30 567
18:32 259
18:35 382
19:2 638
19:13-15 93
19:14 95, 203, 205, 267, 417, 469, 585, 629, 634, 677, 681, 682, 719
19:19 273, 723
19:21 460, 474
19:27 344, 350
19:30 165, 359
20:16 165, 359, 695
20:23 253
20:26 576
21:1-9 152, 158, 159, 176, 266, 271
21:4-9 206
21:6 181
21:8-9 265, 267, 268
21:9 95, 230, 250, 269, 591, 738, 739
21:11 242
21:14 638
21:16 267, 341, 585
21:33 491
22:2-14 696
22:4 702
22:8-10 695
22:13 181
22:32 371, 712
22:37 11, 132, 198, 460, 684
22:37-39 210, 462
22:39 187, 27
22:42 230
23:12 170, 304, 383, 586
23:23 555
23:37 582, 649
24:4-8 622
24:14 562
24:29-31 243
24:35 108, 667
24:42 407
25:1 230
25:1-13 164
25:5 230
25:14-30 572
25:21 576
25:21-23 578, 497
25:31-40 199, 578, 616, 624, 647
25:31-46 555, 596, 623
25:34-36 627
25:35 723
25:40 133, 199, 458, 575
26:6-16 585
26:13 459
26:15 121
26:17-29 274
26:24 167
26:26 389

Matthew, contd.
26:26-28 139, 275, 691, 698, 700
26:26-29 592, 690
26:26-38 707
26:27-29 697
26:28 346
26:30 7, 322, 711
26:33 344
26:36 272
26:36-46 249, 286, 742
26:37 301
26:39 277, 486
26:39-41 461, 588
26:40 272
26:41 718
26:52 445, 539
26:56 521
26:58 344, 345
26:63 280
26:64 45
26:69-75 504
26:70-75 262
27:4 97
27:21-23 262
27:27-31 284
27:27-41 278
27:28 279
27:29 279, 281, 339
27:31-45 279
27:33-44 260, 263, 540, 742
27:35 283
27:39-43 262
27:41 97, 281
27:45 258, 267
27:46 206
27:54 261, 479, 675
27:54-56 255
27:55-56 364
27:57-65 253
27:60 311
28:1 364
28:1-8 297, 303, 310, 311, 314, 447, 540
28:1-10 290, 313
28:2 288, 294, 312
28:6 289, 295
28:8 516
28:8-10 585
28:9 298
28:10 283, 334
28:18-19 553
28:18-20 578, 707, 709
28:19 89, 218, 556, 676
28:19-20 592, 678
28:20 75, 104, 203, 205, 320, 417, 425, 430, 442, 449, 521

Mark
1:3 155
1:1-8 156
1:3-5 175
1:3-8 239, 244
1:8 140
1:9-11 128, 132, 239, 241
1:9-13 247
1:10 149
1:11 101
1:12 128
1:12-13 252
1:13 654
1:15 673
1:16-20 449, 470
1:19 118
1:29-39 249
1:32-34 93, 640
1:34 638
1:35 478
1:45 640
2:3-12 638
2:28 507
3:7-12 540, 640
3:10 638
3:31-35 602
4:16 671
4:26-29 721
4:28 311
4:31-35 26
4:35-41 495
4:36-41 192, 725
4:37 242
4:37-41 431
5:8 93
5:23 628, 638
5:25-29 582
5:25-34 364, 491
5:28 638
5:45-52 495
6:3 237
6:7-13 578
6:13 638
6:30-43 698
6:31 374
6:34 568
6:35-44 665
6:37 623
6:45-51 56, 74, 192, 242, 725
6:56 638
7:26-29 93
7:32-37 192
8:24 665
8:27-29 703
8:34 252, 253, 474, 531, 615, 691
8:34-35 351
8:38 510
9:2 99
9:2-3 107
9:2-13 245, 246, 247, 654, 656
9:7 101
9:24 91, 354, 413, 516, 628, 635, 664
9:29 561
9:35 692
9:50 389
10:13-16 93
10:14 95, 203, 205, 267, 437, 469, 585, 629, 634, 677, 719
10:14-16 681, 682, 683
10:15 162
10:16 83, 95, 203, 205, 267, 437, 469, 473, 585, 634, 681, 719
10:21 531
10:28 474
10:31 165, 359
10:38-39 253
10:45 1, 123, 198, 244, 273, 531, 584
10:46 79, 192, 665
10:52 638
11:1-10 152, 158, 159, 176, 266, 271
11:7-10 206
11:8-10 265, 268
11:9 95, 250, 269, 738, 739
12:29 684
12:29-31 273
12:30 11, 132, 198
12:31-33 187
13:5-8 622
13:26 535
13:26-27 243
13:31 108
13:37 426, 479
14:3-9 585
14:13-21 665
14:15 275, 276
14:22 389
14:22-23 690, 697
14:22-24 139, 691, 698, 700, 707
14:22-25 274, 592
14:24 346
14:26 7, 322, 711
14:32-42 249, 286, 742
14:36 277
14:38 588
14:43 244
14:61 280
14:62 3
14:66-72 504
15:15-18 578
15:16-20 278
15:17 279, 284, 339
15:20 262, 279, 284
15:21-47 283
15:22-32 237, 260, 263, 540, 742
15:22-33 279
15:37 244
15:38-39 261
15:39 675
15:39-41 255
15:40-41 364
15:42 253
15:46 311
16:1 364
16:1-8 290, 297, 298, 303, 310, 311, 314, 447, 540
16:2 589
16:6 288, 294, 334
16:6-7 313
16:8 253, 516
16:9-10 585
16:14-20 322
16:15 89, 459, 561, 592
16:15-18 553, 707, 709
16:16 554
16:19 312, 320, 323, 673
16:20-480

Luke
1:17 156
1:26-38 167, 169, 171, 172, 584
1:29-34 211
1:31 177, 220, 447
1:32-33 194
1:33 341
1:34 168
1:35-45 128
1:38 504, 576, 579, 715
1:44 212
1:46 173, 385, 646
1:46-55 41, 170, 172
1:49 136, 151
1:68-79 158
1:78 154
1:79 389, 402
2:1-12 181, 222
2:1-16 227
2:1-20 186, 193, 200, 213, 364, 540
2:6 194
2:6-7 220
2:6-20 184, 188, 189
2:7 199
2:7-12 225
2:7-20 221
2:8-14 161, 202, 210, 228, 229
2:8-15 191, 209
2:8-16 182, 187
2:8-20 196, 198, 217, 218, 225
2:10 179
2:10-14 185
2:11 183, 211, 216
2:12-16 742
2:13 197
2:13-14 165, 224, 238
2:14 119, 195, 212, 214, 215, 219, 223, 240, 389, 402, 732
2:16 141, 199, 203, 205, 207, 214, 249
2:21 211
2:21-40 681, 682
2:25-35 192
2:28 141, 237
2:30 730
2:32 153
2:35 184, 207
2:39-40 141
2:40 540
2:41-48 742
2:41-50 249
2:51 242
2:52 183
2:76-79 156
3:2-10 175
3:2-17 239, 244
3:4 155
3:16 140, 518
3:21-22 128, 132, 239, 241, 247
3:22 101, 149
4:1 128
4:1-3 252
4:1-13 244
4:4 335
4:14-19 159
4:18 58, 79, 96, 107, 156, 571
4:18-19 89, 93, 141, 158, 160, 192, 199, 231, 360, 534, 561, 575, 578, 615, 647
4:33-35 93
4:40 159, 638
5:1-3 742
5:15 638
5:16 531
5:18-26 638

Luke, contd.
5:26 **277**
6:1-12 **449, 470**
6:17-19 **540, 640**
6:18 **638**
6:19 **638**
6:27 **596**
6:32-35 **187**
6:38 **583**
7:16 **53**
7:22 **192**
7:34 **90**
7:43 **259**
7:50 **711**
8:5-8 **722**
8:19-21 **602**
8:22-25 **26, 74, 192, 451, 495, 725**
8:23 **203, 205, 242**
8:24 **90, 431, 439**
8:28 **29-93**
8:35 **449, 470**
8:43-48 **364, 582**
8:47-50 **638**
9:1-5 **578**
9:2 **592**
9:10-17 **698**
9:11 **638**
9:12-17 **665**
9:13 **623**
9:18-20 **703**
9:23 **252, 253, 350, 430, 474, 510, 531, 573, 615, 655, 691**
9:23-24 **351**
9:28-36 **245, 247, 654, 656**
9:35 **101**
9:42 **93, 638**
9:51 **247**
9:57-62 **458**
9:61 **350**
10:2 **724**
10:7 **723**
10:21 **417, 629**
10:27 **11, 132, 187, 273, 601**
10:27-29 **594**
10:29 **601**
10:29-36 **624**
10:29-37 **273**
10:33-37 **273**
10:36-37 **627**
10:38-42 **486**
11:1 **462, 531**
11:2 **28, 46, 135, 217, 372, 532, 563**
11:2-4 **332**
11:2-13 **740**
11:3 **409, 449, 627, 722**
11:4 **382, 587, 695**
11:8-9 **302**
11:8-10 **267**
11:9 **202, 349, 420**
11:9-10 **132**
11:11-13 **135, 489**
11:12 **478**
12:1 **591**
12:15 **36**
12:31 **132, 590, 740**
13:14 **638**
13:30 **165, 359, 692, 695**
13:34 **582**
14:4 **638**
14:11 **304, 383**
14:13 **58**
14:15-24 **559**
14:16-24 **696**
14:21 **647**
14:21-24 **695**
14:27 **252, 253, 351**
15:1-7 **68**
15:4-6 **440**
15:11-24 **371**
15:11-32 **29, 348**
15:20 **700**
15:23-24 **611**
17:10 **363**
17:11-19 **365**
17:15 **638**
17:21 **508**
17:33 **372**
18:9-14 **235**
18:13 **375, 377, 379**
18:14 **383**
18:15-16 **681**
18:15-17 **93**
18:16 **95, 267, 437, 469, 585, 629, 634, 682, 683, 719**
18:16-17 **677**
18:17 **162**
18:22 **474**
18:28 **537**
18:30 **517**
18:42 **638**
18:43 **741**
19:9 **368**
19:10 **68, 234, 332, 346, 406, 554**
19:12-27 **572**
19:29-38 **152, 158, 159, 176, 266, 271**
19:35-40 **206**
19:36-38 **265, 268**
19:41-44 **582**
21:2-4 **466**
21:10-19 **622**
21:25-28 **243**
21:27 **730**
21:28 **511**
21:33 **108**
21:36 **81, 588**
22:1-6 **585**
22:7-13 **274**
22:12 **275, 276**
22:15 **55**
22:17 **696**
22:17-20 **139, 691, 698, 700, 707**
22:19 **389, 627, 690**
22:19-22 **592**
22:19-23 **697**
22:20 **346**
22:27 **276**
22:31 **252**
22:32 **624**
22:40 **478**
22:40-46 **249, 742**
22:41-44 **277**
22:42 **486**
22:43 **654**
22:51 **638**
22:55-62 **504**
22:69 **99**
23:3 **471**
23:3-43 **263**
23:26-43 **284**
23:26-44 **279**
23:26-56 **283**
23:33 **242, 540**
23:33-43 **237, 260, 742**
23:34 **97, 592**
23:40-43 **66, 575**
23:42 **256, 285, 386**
23:46 **80**
23:47 **741**
23:47-49 **261, 479**
23:49 **255, 364**
23:53 **253, 311**
24:1 **313, 364**
24:1-10 **290, 297, 303, 310, 311, 314, 447, 540**
24:1-12 **298**
24:5 **524**
24:6 **288, 294, 313**
24:12 **253**
24:13-16 **675**
24:13-35 **443**
24:15 **404, 506**
24:23 **312**
24:29 **521**
24:31 **480, 656**
24:32 **425, 506, 590, 696**
24:36 **1**
24:36-49 **306**
24:36-53 **322**
24:45-49 **553**
24:49 **556**
24:49-53 **320**
24:50 **324**
24:50-51 **323**

John
1:1 **26, 145, 167, 181, 237, 321, 599, 733, 734**
1:1-2 **30, 45, 229, 258, 263, 279, 291, 309, 662**
1:1-3 **101, 104, 110, 139, 147, 211, 243, 304, 388, 673, 726**
1:1-4 **346**
1:1-5 **97**
1:3 **126**
1:4 **26, 101, 175, 319, 418, 627**
1:4-5 **107**
1:4-9 **121**
1:5 **93, 190**
1:6-18 **182**
1:8-9 **175**
1:9 **48, 61, 76, 91, 93, 101, 107, 144, 156, 186, 231, 233, 250, 446, 529, 627**
1:9-12 **180**
1:11-14 **262**
1:13-14 **168**
1:14 **26, 88, 89, 91, 97, 104, 107, 148, 149, 167, 172, 177, 179, 181, 183, 184, 185, 189, 199, 226, 228, 232, 237, 247, 267, 336, 412, 439, 548, 586, 615, 662, 665, 667, 670**
1:19-28 **239**
1:28 **156**
1:29 **96, 116, 117, 242, 281, 282, 301, 323, 353, 419, 427, 540**
1:29-34 **256**
1:29-39 **510**
1:31-34 **241**
1:32 **128, 132, 247**
1:36 **419**
2 **443**
2:1-11 **247, 669**
2:9 **609, 611**
2:9-10 **243**
2:25 **109, 385, 630**
3:1-8 **314**
3:3 **185**
3:5 **547, 678**
3:8 **333, 426**
3:13-17 **463**
3:14 **301, 601**
3:14-15 **287**
3:16 **26, 40, 63, 66, 88, 89, 101, 117, 180, 181, 200, 204, 211, 221, 225, 226, 259, 261, 348, 359, 447, 517, 562**
3:16-17 **124, 198, 402**
3:17 **63**
4:1-14 **692**
4:1-26 **364**
4:5-7 **524**
4:6 **589**
4:7-14 **655**
4:8 **565**
4:8-14 **93**
4:10 **444, 591**
4:13 **432, 505, 528**
4:13-14 **676**
4:14 **439**
4:16 **565**
4:24 **143**
4:25-27 **691**
4:35 **724**
4:39 **568**
4:39-42 **692**
5:10 **638**
5:12-13 **317**
5:13 **638**
5:16-17 **262**
5:23 **123**
5:24 **356**
5:39 **665**
6:1-13 **665**
6:5-13 **698**
6:15-21 **56, 74, 192, 242, 725**
6:31 **701**
6:33 **501**
6:33-48 **414**
6:35 **335, 346, 404, 528, 649, 703, 705**
6:35-38 **693**
6:35-40 **692, 697**
6:37 **61, 79, 354, 406**
6:38 **486**
6:41 **649, 705, 709**
6:41-51 **703**
6:44 **84, 368**
6:47-51 **715**
6:48-335, 559, 709
6:49 **701**
6:51 **232, 505, 559, 702, 709**
6:53-59 **709**
6:54 **702**
6:63 **134, 328**
6:66 **521**
6:68 **26, 668**
7:23 **638**

John, contd.
7:37 **444, 473**
7:38 **424**
8:12 **27, 59, 121, 123, 144, 180, 231, 319, 344, 403, 453, 551, 565, 627, 635**
8:28 **601**
8:31 **443**
8:32 **24, 440, 455, 512, 665, 730**
8:32-36 **156, 222, 480**
8:33-36 **109**
8:36 **55, 124, 364, 440, 460, 530**
8:58 **181**
9:1-12 **692**
9:3-5 **93**
9:4 **625**
9:4-5 **556**
9:5 **76, 156, 175, 231, 319, 519, 551, 627**
9:25 **79, 192, 422, 665**
9:39-41 **93**
10:3 **300, 440**
10:4-18 **705**
10:7-9 **568**
10:9 **554**
10:10 **110, 442, 453, 575**
10:11 **1**
10:11-15 **706**
10:11-16 **488**
10:14 **1, 73, 86, 102, 352, 440, 546, 567**
10:14-16 **99**
10:16 **1**
10:27 **300, 345, 350**
10:28 **488**
10:29 **683**
10:30 **667**
10:35 **598**
11:2-44 **96**
11:25-26 **311, 703**
11:26 **461**
11:28 **348**
11:33-34 **692**
11:35 **559**
11:44 **543**
12:1-8 **585**
12:3 **253**
12:12-15 **152, 158, 159, 176, 265, 266, 267, 268, 271**
12:13 **18, 19, 95, 206, 250, 269, 738, 739**
12:21 **491, 656**
12:24 **311, 446, 515, 518, 583, 587, 715**
12:26 **350, 430, 458, 499, 590**
12:27 **225**
12:28 **146**
12:32 **264, 275, 287, 301, 305**
12:32-34 **601**
12:34 **301**
12:46 **121, 319, 551**
13:1 **55, 81, 275, 348, 398, 437, 440**
13:1-15 **634**
13:1-17 **273, 391**
13:2-17 **55**
13:3-5 **97**
13:4-5 **275**
13:6-11 **678**
13:13 **15**
13:14 **276**
13:15 **555, 593**
13:20 **601**
13:34 **187, 397, 402, 595, 600, 603**
13:35 **210, 395**
13:37 **143**
14:1 **86, 421, 442**
14:1-3 **168, 437**
14:1-4 **468, 505**
14:1-6 **635**
14:2 **386, 525**
14:2-3 **310**
14:3 **51, 148, 183, 260, 458**
14:6 **66, 105, 110, 154, 175, 194, 312, 335, 354, 453, 568, 597**
14:9 **121**
14:12-14 **104**
14:13 **125**
14:15 **135**
14:15-16 **176**
14:15-21 **130, 149, 332, 475, 630**
14:16 **73, 127, 128**
14:16-17 **330**
14:18 **320**
14:19 **346, 447**
14:23-669
14:25 **141**
14:25-27 **130, 149, 241, 396, 525, 630**
14:26 **127, 325**
14:27 **121, 275, 389, 402, 421, 464, 546, 589, 610, 619, 627, 635, 691, 714, 711, 749**
15:1 **306**
15:1-4 **346**
15:3 **230**
15:5 **327, 698**
15:7 **483**
15:8 **578**
15:10 **443**
15:11 **275**
15:11-12 **273, 397**
15:12 **187, 202, 372, 468, 596**
15:13 **270, 398, 612, 706**
15:13-15 **473**
15:14 **443, 601**
15:15 **346**
15:17 **402**
15:18-19 **374**
16:5-16 **244**
16:5-20 **104**
16:8 **133, 407**
16:12 **325**
16:13 **154, 325, 327**
16:13-14 **673**
16:20-22 **516**
16:22 **402**
16:24 **125, 402**
16:33 **81, 121, 389, 589, 591, 627**
17:6-26 **254**
17:9 **244**
17:13 **386**
17:14 **374**
17:20-21 **604**
17:20-23 **621**
17:21 **276**
17:22 **547**
17:22-23 **551**
17:23 **331**
18:16-18 **504**
18:25-27 **504**
18:28 **272**
18:36 **508**
18:37 **242**
19:1-5 **284**
19:2 **339**
19:16-42 **283**
19:17-18 **585**
19:17-24 **237, 260, 263, 540, 742**
19:25 **261, 479**
19:30 **272, 288, 301**
19:34 **256, 280**
19:36-38 **267**
19:37 **262, 318**
19:42 **311**
20:1 **364**
20:1-8 **290, 297, 311, 447**
20:1-9 **253, 314**
20:1-18 **298**
20:2 **312**
20:10-18 **300**
20:17 **635**
20:18 **288, 294**
20:19 **310**
20:19-23 **516, 675**
20:19-29 **313**
20:21 **275, 578**
20:22 **128, 328, 333, 358, 418, 461**
20:24-29 **58, 299, 417**
20:24-31 **413**
20:25-28 **317**
20:26 **675**
20:27 **323**
20:28 **102**
20:29 **320**
21:15 **345**
21:15-17 **623**
21:15-19 **468, 593**
21:19 **350, 430, 499, 573**
21:19-21 **334**
21:24-31 **354**
21:27 **276**
21:27-28 **302**

Acts
1:1 **715**
1:1-3 **312**
1:1-11 **32**
1:8 **24, 128, 133, 140, 148, 327, 333, 474, 553, 565, 571, 584, 671, 707, 713**
1:8-10 **324**
1:9 **88**
1:9-11 **342, 656**
1:10-11 **168, 523**
1:11 **232, 301, 321, 536, 672, 721**
1:12-14 **597**
1:14 **478, 561**
2:1-3 **128, 134, 327**
2:1-4 **132, 244, 326, 328, 331, 332, 392, 492, 540, 550, 559, 713**
2:1-13 **334, 528**
2:2 **145, 333, 556**
2:2-3 **329, 543**
2:3 **150, 325, 330, 463**
2:4 **140**
2:5-12 **597**
2:11 **15, 96**
2:14-41 **558, 631**
2:16-21 **629**
2:17 **502, 503**
2:17-18 **6, 329, 334, 548, 571, 581, 585, 617**
2:17-21 **326**
2:18 **492**
2:19 **15**
2:20 **243**
2:21 **108, 125, 406, 554, 653**
2:24 **288, 294**
2:28 **127**
2:34 **3**
2:36 **305**
2:38 **127, 676**
2:38-39 **334**
2:39 **417, 585, 677**
2:41 **679, 715**
2:42 **699**
2:42-47 **37, 133, 4 74, 478, 492, 552, 580, 604, 687, 701, 704**
2:43 **53**
3:1 **478**
3:6 **675**
3:15 **310**
4:12 **108, 109, 125, 406, 486**
4:13 **569**
4:21 **66**
4:25-28 **27**
4:29 **569**
4:31-35 **474**
4:32-35 **37, 492, 552, 604, 687**
4:33 **307, 327**
5:1-11 **604**
5:32 **324**
5:42 **307**
6:2 **575**
6:4 **478**
7:1-53 **558**
7:34 **559**
7:48 **546**
7:55 **3, 168**
8:4 **560**
8:36 **679**
8:38 **678**
9:1-18 **584**
10:36 **307**
10:38 **107**
11:15 **492**
11:16 **140**
12:7 **96**
12:17 **366**
13:47 **392, 518, 563, 670**
14:7 **307, 724**
14:21 **307**
15:9 **374, 461**
15:11 **353, 362, 422**
15:14 **27**
15:36-41 **604**
16:23-32 **366**
16:25 **113, 478, 631**

Acts, contd.
16:31 675
17:18 307
17:22-31 56
17:24 546, 550
17:24-28 139
17:25 48
17:28 1, 36, 46, 77, 110, 565
20:22 328
20:24 718
20:28 229, 356, 544
20:32 716
20:35 583
20:36-38 516
20:38 393
22:11 107
22:16 678
24:10-21 558
26:2-23 558

Romans
1:1 576
1:16 133, 380, 560
1:19 48
1:20 418
1:26 48
2:10 389
3:23 568
3:24 3, 353, 436
4:22 69
5:1 3, 447, 543, 619
5:1-8 573
5:2-21 353
5:5 155, 325, 330
5:6 284, 406
5:6-8 366
5:8 142, 406
5:15 436, 439
5:17 101, 436
5:17-21 362
5:20 436
6:4 140, 356, 678, 679, 715
6:14 17, 96, 436
6:18 55, 440
6:23 26, 356, 568
8:1 366
8:2 55, 222, 385
8:9-11 134
8:14 671
8:15-17 372, 649, 719
8:16 27, 148, 556, 600, 603, 662
8:16-17 426, 683
8:18 528
8:19 25
8:19-20 534
8:22 179, 187, 590, 626
8:26 284, 475, 487
8:26-27 416
8:28 725
8:28-39 226, 408
8:29 505
8:30-39 452
8:31 725
8:31-39 61, 348
8:32 51
8:34 168
8:36-39 422, 510
8:37 310
8:37-38 57
8:37-39 53, 62, 244, 308, 411, 414, 446, 575, 610
8:38-39 83, 453, 460
9:21 343
9:33 380
10:1-568
10:9 15, 101, 102, 305, 354, 712
10:9-10 128, 331, 485, 675
10:11 380
10:12 64
10:13 125, 653
10:15 307
10:17 407
11:6 353
11:29 573
11:32-36 226
11:33-36 53, 64, 65, 147, 149, 235, 398, 408, 658, 688
11:35-36 687
11:36 363
12:1 64, 258, 261, 263, 333, 404, 460, 466, 572, 684
12:1-2 132, 143, 252, 374, 385, 443, 455, 459, 467, 474, 555, 575, 579, 580, 707
12:2 718
12:3-8 594, 691
12:5 395
12:7 576
12:8 688
12:10 596
12:12 208
12:15 391, 531, 591
12:16 614
12:18 389, 614
12:21 708
13:8 615
13:9 273
13:9-10 601
13:11 564
13:11-12 164
13:14 405
14:4 513
14:8 415
14:9 305
14:10 730
14:11 321
14:12 572
14:19 389
15:1 708
15:5 331
15:7 596, 601
15:12 243
15:13 404
15:16 130
16:27 363

1 Corinthians
1:9 435
1:18 258
1:22 142
1:22-25 260
1:24 97
1:27 437, 504
2:2 460, 178
2:3 637
2:7 643
2:9 37, 64, 164, 226, 417, 420, 433, 644, 669
2:14 133, 136, 325, 334, 417
2:16 331, 455
2:28 3
3:5 576
3:6 685
3:9 689, 721, 723
3:11 405, 410, 411
3:16 482, 543, 546, 547
4:2 24, 525
4:7 459
4:12 580
5:2 400
5:7-8 298
6:11 370, 679
6:19 330, 482, 543, 546
6:20 440, 466, 505, 687
7:15 389, 539
7:31 521
9:7 509
9:19-22 576
9:24 464
9:24-27 718
10:1-4 678
10:1-13 29
10:4 255, 384
10:12 304
10:13 476, 513
10:14-17 394, 702
10:16 75, 389, 690, 694, 705, 707, 709
10:16-17 689
10:17 139
10:24 400
10:31 718
11:17-26 672, 702
11:17-34 704
11:23 696
11:23-24 389
11:23-25 274, 691, 697, 700
11:23-26 139, 394, 592, 694, 698, 707
11:24-25 1, 627, 690, 693
11:25 75
11:26-28 699
11:28 606, 706
11:33-34 389
12:1-7 687
12:1-13 552
12:1-26 331
12:1-30 594
12:1-31 691
12:3 15, 119, 128
12:4-6 577, 689
12:4-7 388
12:7 571
12:7-10 628
12:7-11 492, 585
12:7-12 581
12:8-11 325
12:12-13 130, 157, 544, 595, 600, 603, 604, 687, 689
12:13 140, 676
12:14-16 586
12:24 388
12:24-26 388
12:27 327, 547, 581
12:31 401
13:1-13 399, 400, 612
13:4 144
13:4-7 609
13:8 142
13:12 32, 66, 82, 117, 183, 277, 334, 335, 353, 381, 397, 418, 467, 472, 525, 535, 539, 579, 610, 649, 670, 708
13:13 454, 518
14:1 400
14:26 7, 645
14:26-28 388
14:33-35 585
15 189
15:1-11 290, 298
15:2 288
15:2-4 672
15:3 289, 291, 406
15:4-5 673
15:9 94, 100, 106
15:12-19 434
15:12-20 308, 414
15:22 252, 311
15:25 539
15:26 404
15:50-54 428
15:50-58 308
15:51 515
15:51-52 537
15:52 10, 29, 243, 405, 527
15:53-55 521
15:54 17, 226, 296, 297, 324, 523
15:54-55 292, 453, 310, 317
15:55 208, 288, 313, 381, 499, 524
15:56 291
15:57 289, 356, 499
15:58 503, 513
16:13 510, 513
16:22 527, 586
16:23 362

2 Corinthians
1:3 2
1:3-7 388, 683
1:4 477
1:20 369, 429, 442
1:22 135
2:14 363
3:2 558, 586, 671
3:17 55, 133, 396, 492
3:18 24, 319, 358, 535
4:1-6 427
4:4 507, 564
4:5-7 552
4:6 230, 656
4:7 437, 551
4:7-12 132, 251, 351, 360, 547, 578, 637
4:8-12 64
4:16 449
4:18 560
5:2 505
5:5 426
5:6-8 384
5:10 110, 588, 730
5:14 68, 257
5:15 43
5:17 89, 192, 358
5:17-20 24
5:18 157
5:18-20 185

2 Corinthians, contd.
5:19-21 600, 603
5:21 150, 277, 284, 301
6:1 353
6:2 354, 700
6:13 124
6:16 482, 543, 546
7:10 383
8:1-5 624
8:9 227, 244, 353, 359, 362
9:7 684
9:8 422
9:15 40, 226, 363
10:1 97, 389
10:3 509
11:25-26 275
12:1-10 132
12:7-10 638
12:9 251, 362, 411, 451, 578, 637
12:9-10 90, 351
12:10 165, 427, 504
13:11 389
13:14 362, 748

Galatians
1:5 363
2:11-14 604
2:20 255, 262, 291, 302, 486, 544
3:13 356
3:16 170
3:26-20 462
3:26-29 604, 626, 706
3:27 366
3:28 93, 124, 393, 581, 585, 600, 603, 689
3:28-30 601
4:4 186, 394
4:4-5 544
5:1 55, 124, 513
5:7 464
5:11 264
5:13 576
5:13-14 273
5:14 601
5:22 134, 289, 326, 397, 401, 469, 610, 714
5:22-23 165, 400, 402, 533, 723
5:22-24 388
5:22-26 331
5:23 389
5:25 132
5:25-26 544
6:2 372, 393, 575, 581
6:9 78
6:10 596
6:14 242, 251, 255, 258, 260, 261, 264, 287, 384, 446, 479, 509
6:15 89
6:18 362

Ephesians
1:6 479
1:7 66, 353, 354, 362, 363, 727
1:9 366
1:12-13 442
1:13 135, 142, 578, 679
1:14 426
1:15-23 631
1:18 656
1:19 45, 564
1:20 3, 99
1:22 366
1:23 421
2:1 348
2:4 63, 270, 277
2:5 311
2:5-9 353
2:6 363
2:8 55, 406, 436
2:8-9 82, 106, 284, 384, 422, 569
2:10 24
2:12 568
2:13 256
2:13-18 121
2:14 157, 276, 627
2:14-15 124, 402, 619, 626, 689
2:14-16 93, 600, 603
2:14-17 695
2:14-18 99, 462, 585, 604
2:14-19 601
2:14-22 581
2:19 547, 706
2:20 329, 436, 548
3:17 321, 397
3:18 244, 575
3:18-19 61
3:19 464, 593
3:20 610, 639
3:20-21 78
3:21 363, 465
4:1 588
4:1-3 24
4:2 273, 330, 372, 389
4:3 331
4:4 588
4:4-6 509
4:5 140, 678
4:7-8 26
4:7-13 592, 594, 691
4:7-16 581
4:8 322, 324, 335, 669
4:11 580
4:13 331, 681
4:15 367, 596
4:16 388
4:18 136
4:28 37
4:30 68, 135, 146
4:32 372, 382, 393, 695
5:2 460
5:8 27, 248, 443, 518
5:14 230, 438, 543
5:18-19 334
5:19 7, 25, 49, 54, 87, 113, 119, 501, 577, 582, 641, 674
5:19-20 388, 645
5:21 596, 610
5:22 613
5:31 612
6:3 613
6:4 557, 607, 682
6:7 576
6:10 45, 504
6:10-11 514
6:10-17 508
6:10-18 584
6:10-19 511
6:11-17 513
6:12 578
6:13 500
6:14 366
6:17 148
6:18 481

Philippians
1:6 65, 358, 608, 639, 680, 715
1:19-26 527
1:21 70, 526
2:1-6 576
2:1-7 580
2:1-10 367, 584
2:1-11 228, 257, 433
2:2 1
2:3 400
2:5 331, 464
2:5-8 97, 366
2:5-11 321
2:6-8 99, 168
2:6-11 141
2:7 1
2:7-8 142, 185
2:8 565
2:9 123, 125, 177
2:9-10 43, 45
2:9-11 16, 108, 114, 117, 137, 305, 318, 361, 724
2:10 9, 76, 100, 102, 106, 109, 115, 138, 150, 181, 187, 188, 337, 404, 648
2:10-11 563
2:11 15, 101, 119, 128, 291, 513
2:13 133, 243
2:15 230
2:19 337
3:1 650
3:5-14 472
3:7 502
3:7-8 261
3:7-10 357
3:9 69
3:10 255, 302, 457, 718
3:12-14 70, 464
3:13-14 355
3:14 24, 525, 579
3:18 507
4:2-3 604
4:4 113, 302, 342, 650, 652
4:4-7 113, 482
4:5 389
4:6 473
4:7 447, 464, 539, 619
4:8-9 613
4:11 499
4:13 90, 582, 637, 639
4:19 385, 421, 436, 572, 663, 721

Colossians
1:11 738
1:12 529
1:14 66, 142
1:15 89, 97, 121, 147, 185, 199, 208, 226, 324, 417, 667
1:16 126
1:17 27, 110
1:18 547
1:20 626
1:23 576
1:26 65
1:27 75, 104, 366, 404, 425, 486, 518
2:2 712
2:9 199
2:12 140, 356, 678, 679
2:13 695
2:14 428
2:15 290
3:1 99, 168, 312, 679
3:1-2 289
3:5 36
3:11 462, 585
3:12 389, 400
3:13 23, 382, 596, 695
3:14 330, 331, 358, 395
3:15 148, 153, 389, 402, 627
3:15-16 464
3:16 7, 25, 49, 54, 87, 113, 119, 577, 641, 674
3:16-17 388
3:17 645
3:21 682
4:2 478
4:12 367

1 Thessalonians
2:7 135
3:13 620
4:8 121
4:13 434, 526, 711
4:13-18 672
4:14 301
4:16 29, 51, 189, 405, 428, 537, 721
4:16-18 243, 318
4:17 66, 324, 342, 407, 451
5:13 389, 539, 714
5:14 576, 708
5:16 208, 327
5:17 478, 483
5:18 359, 363, 720, 725
5:19 518
5:21-22 708

2 Thessalonians
1:9 43, 97, 101
1:10 531
1:10-12 646
1:11 588
1:12 465
2:9 507
2:13 130
2:15 513
2:17 620
3:16 402

1 Timothy
1:1 404
1:14 362
1:15 66, 198

1 Timothy, contd.
1:17 48, 63, 102, 317, 417, 508, 517, 732
2:2 389, 477
2:3-4 562
2:8 14, 700
2:11-15 585
3:3 389
3:15 548
4:10 442
4:12 497
4:12-13 629
6:11 389
6:12 288, 508, 510, 529
6:14 302
6:15 43, 92, 309, 317, 338
6:17 421
6:18 37

2 Timothy
1:3-7 497
1:6 708
1:6-7 629
1:7 381
1:9 573
1:10 208, 302
1:11-12 406
1:12 68, 407, 510
2:1-2 551, 557
2:1-7 497
2:2 593, 688
2:3 367, 508, 509, 510
2:5 223, 522
2:8 40
2:12 339, 453, 513
2:19 410, 411
2:21 459, 574, 593
2:22 485
2:24 576, 579
3:3 513
4:2 589, 708
4:7 248, 288, 464
4:8 260, 302, 342, 468, 508, 513, 522
4:18 363

Titus
2:1-8 113
2:10 441
2:11 353
2:12 474
2:13 302, 404, 426
2:13-14 356
2:14 374, 663
3:5 63, 384
3:7 3, 362

Hebrews
1:1 667
1:2 24, 126, 150, 181
1:3 3, 17, 32, 97, 101, 144, 322, 324
1:3-7 182
1:6 185
1:13 27
2:3 358
2:7-9 317
2:9 182, 310, 342, 526
2:9-10 339
2:11 121, 211
2:13 441
2:14 289
2:14-17 555
2:18 639
3:2 462
3:3 99, 124, 126, 569
3:6 569
3:8 9
4:9 505, 529
4:9-11 153
4:10 503
4:12 70, 566, 668
4:13 572
4:14-16 62, 239, 241, 414, 478, 632
4:15 132, 183, 227, 244, 312, 336
4:15-16 97, 252
4:16 393
5:8 97
6:6 262
6:13 16
6:19 405, 518, 667
7:2 539
7:21 72
7:24-26 414
7:25 168, 244, 320, 398, 554
8:1 97, 101, 324
9:22 256, 489
9:23-28 168
9:27-28 625
9:28 248, 295, 426, 544
10:1 319
10:10 295
10:14 374
10:23 518
10:25 524, 646
11 531, 663
11:1 417, 628
11:1-40 497, 558
11:3 150
11:6 590
11:9 522
11:11 536
11:13 501, 529
11:16 519
11:32-40 573
11:34 578, 637
11:35-38 530
11:36-37 510
11:39 564
12:1 578
12:1-2 70, 464, 525
12:1-3 248, 344, 497, 542
12:2 260, 295, 339, 351, 367, 419, 483, 656
12:3 253
12:6 81
12:12 534, 56, 582, 590, 708
12:14 389, 483, 714
13:2 594, 627, 706
13:5 75, 90, 104, 411, 417, 726
13:8 14, 433, 685
13:15 111, 572, 651
13:16 37
13:20 1, 73, 86, 352, 402, 435, 440, 464, 488, 539, 714
13:21 43, 363

James
1:2 128, 385, 435, 528
1:3 374
1:5 569, 572, 631
1:12 468
1:13-15 740
1:16-18 48
1:17 13, 16, 40, 46, 72, 82, 84, 398, 405, 433, 458, 572, 649, 667, 670, 684
1:22 530
1:22-25 388, 553
1:27 555, 728
2:8 273
2:18 712
2:23 408, 601
3:17 234
4:6 41, 170
4:8 461
4:10 55
4:13 628
4:14 518
5:1-2 170
5:1-6 620
5:8 513
5:11 377
5:13 7, 25, 54, 111, 113, 473, 478, 501

1 Peter
1:2 130
1:3 314
1:5 633
1:6 78, 435, 528
1:7 374, 385, 541, 727
1:8 200, 335, 420, 662
1:9-10-144
1:10 191
1:10-12 167, 201, 649, 729
1:16 483, 556
1:19 71, 353, 549
1:21 667
1:25 27, 662, 667
2:2 457
2:4-5 482
2:4-7 262
2:5 546, 550
2:6 436
2:9 11, 27, 88, 100, 106, 453
2:9-10 71, 319, 541, 547, 562, 580, 670
2:10-11 234
2:14 547
2:21 499
2:21-23 280
2:23 367
2:24 463, 678
3:1-7 613
3:3 518
3:4 389
3:7 686
3:8 614
3:11 389, 539
3:15 148, 321, 389, 558, 589
3:21 678
4:8 400
4:10-11 691
4:11 363, 637
4:12 411, 473
5:1-4 440
5:1-7 149
5:1-11 584
5:2 36, 593
5:4 102, 468
5:5 400
5:5-6 586, 590
5:6 41, 45, 155, 383, 566
5:7 23, 380, 493
5:8 507
5:8-9 481

2 Peter
1:1 573
1:4 41, 442
1:6 43
1:10 588
1:16 97, 101
1:17 469
1:19 91, 105, 223, 230, 664
1:21 673
3:9 82, 243, 565, 625, 667
3:11 374
3:13 145, 293, 620
3:18 363, 681

1 John
1:1 671
1:1-4 557
1:5 27, 248, 304, 453
1:7 96, 248, 256, 356, 374, 443
1:9 28, 348, 370, 374, 385, 416, 419, 463, 675
2:17 108
2:20 325
3:1 83, 101, 257, 258, 259, 263, 270, 277, 362, 372, 398, 677, 683
3:2 66
3:3 518
3:16 259
3:16-20 630
3:17 555
3:18 388, 530, 671, 715
3:18-21 480
3:18-24 596
4:7 187, 402
4:7-11 210
4:7-12 595, 596, 647
4:8 58, 399, 401, 565
4:11 557
4:11-12 273
4:12 610
4:16 58, 59, 157, 304, 413, 612
4:16-18 613
4:17 730
4:18 150
4:19 109, 143, 270, 367, 372, 468
4:19-21 647
5:4 512
5:6 384
5:14-15 487

2 John
12 402

3 John
2 609

Jude
14 95, 318
24 83, 142, 402, 500, 535, 639
24-25 463
25 43, 97, 101, 119, 265, 465

Revelation
1:1-11 3
1:5 14, 96, 256, 354, 368
1:6 43
1:7 183, 189, 232, 243, 318, 472
1:8 19, 181, 246, 358, 667, 733, 734
1:9 620
1:16 107, 656
1:17 293, 525
1:18 288, 302, 312, 324, 342, 371, 480, 712
2:1 124
2:10 260, 351, 522, 530
2:17 647
2:28 230, 235
3:7 154
3:10 476
3:11 260
3:21 517, 673
4:1-11 3, 51, 164, 232
4:4-10 318
4:6 67, 522
4:6-11 17, 48, 59, 138
4:7-11 34, 44
4:8 151, 737
4:8-10 111, 136
4:8-11 16, 305
4:9 363
4:10 358
4:11 43, 50, 99, 116, 126, 137, 316, 322, 648
5:1-14 117
5:2 119, 126, 360
5:3 136
5:5 243
5:6 103
5:6-14 257, 337, 509
5:6-16 232
5:9 52, 67, 100, 106, 142, 192, 256, 287, 320, 528, 544, 560, 600, 603, 604, 642, 690
5:9-10 204
5:9-14 7, 17, 34, 44, 48, 14, 138, 164, 182
5:10 294
5:11-13 103, 123
5:11-14 3, 60, 315
5:12 50, 116, 119, 281, 427, 463
5:12-13 43
5:12-14 98
5:13 112, 137, 181, 244
5:13-14 51
5:14 553
6:11 138, 522
6:12 243
6:12-17 537
6:14 428
7:7 535
7:9 529
7:9-10 334, 565
7:9-12 155
7:9-17 6, 17, 34, 44, 49, 96, 114, 138, 164, 182, 509, 528, 626
7:11 112, 181, 724
7:11-17 3, 60, 232
7:12 511, 553
7:14 256
7:17 67, 390, 393, 451, 523, 721
8:34 155
11:9 712
11:15 19, 92, 138, 179, 226, 318, 341, 539
11:17 19
12:11 256, 354
14:1 152, 287
14:3 7
14:4 344, 499
14:6 712
14:13 529
14:14 70, 100, 106
14:15 392
14:34 731
15:3 41, 116, 663
16:7 663
17:14 64, 77, 92, 100, 106, 137, 232, 234, 309, 317, 337, 338, 339, 340
17:16 184
19:1 112, 119, 208, 316, 735, 736
19:1-6 301
19:1-7 58
19:1-8 232, 302
19:1-10 313
19:2 663
19:3-4 71, 208, 316, 735, 736
19:4 87, 553
19:6 56, 208, 316, 735, 736
19:6-7 320
19:6-12 317
19:7 88, 363, 392, 650, 696
19:9 696
19:11 50, 509
19:13 256
19:15 730
19:16 58, 77, 92, 100, 106, 137, 184, 232, 234, 309, 317, 337, 338, 339, 340
20:6 92, 318
20:11 142
21:1 145, 293
21:1-4 620
21:2 591
21:3 26
21:3-4 523
21:4 67, 390, 393, 451, 525, 528, 535, 721
21:5 55
21:6 358, 444, 667
21:9 544
21:21 67
21:22 337
21:23 107, 116, 236, 243, 248, 620
21:27 519
22:1 519, 522
22:2 621
22:3 179
22:4 287
22:4-5 16
22:5 92, 236, 294, 519
22:6 246
22:11 525
22:12 175
22:13 246, 293, 358, 667
22:16 92, 105, 123, 223, 230, 235, 335, 479
22:17 444, 489, 668, 692, 702
22:20 153, 168, 318, 523, 536, 586, 621, 721
22:21 362

Index of Hymn Tunes

A LA RU 207
A PURPLE ROBE 279
A VA DE 694
ABBOT'S LEIGH 1, 536, 548, 592
ABERYSTWYTH 333, 439
ABINGDON 55
ACCLAMATIONS 672
ACKLEY 302
ADELAIDE 486
ADESTE FIDELES 114, 182
ALIDA'S TUNE 584
ALL FOR JESUS 460
ALL IS WELL 462
ALL THE WAY 505
ALLELUIA 316
AMEN SIAKUDUMISA 741
AMERICA 731
AMSTEIN 36
AMSTERDAM 46
ANDUJAR 206
ANGEL'S STORY 458
ANNIVERSARY SONG 685
ANNUNCIATION 171
ANTIOCH 179
AR HYD Y NOS 719, 723
ARLINGTON 510
ASH GROVE 22, 712
ASSAM 344
ASSURANCE 426
AU CLAIR DE LA LUNE 634
AURELIA 544, 552
AUSTRIAN HYMN 17, 580, 598
AWAY IN A MANGER 203
AZMON 96

BALM IN GILEAD 631
BARBARA ALLEN 150
BATTLE HYMN 730
BEACH SPRING 459, 477, 551, 575, 655, 695
BECK 596
BEECHER 358, 581
BEGINNINGS 355
BEREDEN VÄG FÖR HERRAN 152
BESANÇON 161
BLAENWERN 671
BLANTYRE 211
BLOTT EN DAG 449
BOYLSTON 588
BOZELL 640
BRADBURY 440
BREAD OF LIFE 665
BRED DINA VIDA VINGAR 456
BRIDEGROOM 327, 400
BROTHER JAMES' AIR 73

BUNESSAN 35, 78, 425, 609, 679, 722
BURLEIGH 537

CALYPSO CAROL 227
CAMEROON 402
CANONBURY 32, 526, 593, 638
CANTAD AL SEÑOR 15
CANTIQUE DE NOEL 187
CAROL 191
CHARLESTOWN 625
CHEREPONI 273
CHILDREN PRAYING 489
CHRIST AROSE 294
CHRISTE SANCTORUM 121, 140, 324, 524
CHRISTMAS 228
CLAY 392
CLEANSING FOUNTAIN 256
CLOSER WALK 504
COME, BE BAPTIZED 676
CONRAD 49
CONVERSE 473
CORONATION 106
CRADLE SONG 205
CRANHAM 196
CRIMOND 86
CRUCIFER 287
CRUSADER'S HYMN 123
CWM RHONDDA 413, 501, 569

DAISY HILL 635
DARWALL'S 148th 9, 110, 342, 542
DAVOS 488
DEEP RIVER 538
DENNIS 393
DETROIT 382
DIADEM 100
DIADEMATA 317, 335
DISTRESS 351
DIVERNON 696
DIVINUM MYSTERIUM 181, 673
DIX 40, 236
DOVE OF PEACE 706
DOWN AMPNEY 330
DUDLEY 579
DUKE STREET 63, 341, 414
DUNCANNON 253
DUNDEE 65

EARTH AND ALL STARS 306, 642
EASTER HYMN 288
EASTVIEW 608
EBENEZER 398

EIN' FESTE BURG 507
EL CAMINO 624
EL NATHAN 407
ELLACOMBE 31, 267
ELLERS 385, 711
ENDLESS SONG 424
ENGELBERG 7, 553
ERMUNTRE DICH 202
ES IST EIN ROS' 190
EUCHARIST 690
EVANSTON NEW 707
EVENING HYMN 627
EVENTIDE 274, 521

FACE TO FACE 535
FAITHFULNESS 72
FESTAL SONG 231, 566, 590
FESTIVAL CANTICLE 315
FILLMORE 60
FINEST WHEAT 705
FINLANDIA 372, 451
FOLLOW 209
FOREST GREEN 540, 570
FOUNDATION 411

GABRIEL'S MESSAGE 169
GALILEE 345
GALLANT 567
GARDEN 300
GARU 309
GATES 165
GATHER US IN 649
GELOBT SEI GOTT 307
GENEVA 124 708
GENEVAN 42 155
GERMANY 591, 687
GIFT OF LOVE 397, 612, 682
GLORIA 188
GLORIA CUECA 195
GO DOWN, MOSES 618
GO, TELL IT 218
GOD BE WITH YOU 716
GOODNESS IS STRONGER 296
GORDON 468
GRATUS 720
GREATOREX 734
GREENBELT 632
GREENSLEEVES 184
GROSSER GOTT 138
GUITING POWER 336

HALELUYA! PELO TSO RONA 709
HALL 455

HALLELUJAH! WHAT A SAVIOR 301
HAMBURG 261
HANKEY 560
HANOVER 112, 531
HANSON PLACE 522
HAPPY DAY 368
HE LEADETH ME 499
HEAVEN 525
HENDON 466
HERZLICH TUT MICH VERLAGEN (PASSION CHORALE) 284, 371
HERZLIEBSTER JESU 262
HOLINESS 483
HOLY IS THE LORD 151
HOLY MANNA 644, 647
HOUGHTON 643
HOUSTON 248
HUDSON 258
HYFRYDOL 90, 149, 153, 320, 356
HYMN TO JOY 24, 59, 289, 667

I AM THINE 408
I WANT TO BE A CHRISTIAN 457
I WONDER AS I WANDER 225
I'M GONNA LIVE 574
IL EST NÉ 201
IN BABILONE 128, 423, 571
IN DULCI JUBILO 198
INTO MY HEART 485
IRBY 183
ISLA DEL ENCANTO 238
ISRAELI 619
IT IS WELL (VILLE DU HAVRE) 428
ITALIAN HYMN 148, 561
IVERSON 492

JACOB 418
JERUSALEM 539
JESU, MEINE FREUDE 431
JESUS LOVES ME 437
JESUS SAVES 554
JOY IN THE MORNING 533
JOYFUL SINGING 197
JOYFUL SONG 95
JOYOUS LIGHT 199
JUBILEE 329
JUDAS MACCABEUS 310
JUDSON 137
JÜNGST 200
JUXTAPOSITION 215

KELVINGROVE 350
KINDRED 602
KINGS OF ORIENT 233
KING'S WESTON 321, 555
KINGSFOLD 237, 242, 278, 346, 434
KIRKEN DEN ER ET 546
KORU 683
KREMSER 81, 726
KUM BA YAH 487, 606

LACQUIPARLE 26
LAMB OF GOD 281, 503
LANCASHIRE 298, 508
LAND OF REST 252, 738
LANDAS 406
LASST UNS ERFREUEN 23, 147, 322, 663
LAUDA ANIMA 82
LAUDES DOMINI 111, 332
LAUDS 133
LEAD ME 498
LEONI 16, 615
LET US BREAK BREAD 699
LIFT EVERY VOICE 729
LIKE A CHILD 162
LINSTEAD 39, 369, 698
LLANFAIR 295, 323
LLANGLOFFAN 626
LOBE DEN HERREN 71
LONDONDERRY AIR 433
LONESOME VALLEY 254
LORD OF THE DANCE 118
LORD OF THE YEARS 70
LYONS 2

MADRID 87
MAJESTAS 101
MANY NAMES 58
MARCHING TO ZION 390
MARION 113
MARTIN 512
MARTYRDOM 263
MARY'S CHILD 194
MARYTON 589
MATERNA 727
McKEE 600
MEAL OF LOVE 704
MEGERRAN 585
MEINEKE 733
MELITA 74
MENDELSSOHN 185
MERENGUE 739
MERLE'S TUNE 158, 545, 558
MERTON 416
MESSAGE 562
MIEIR 102
MIT FREUDEN ZART 25, 56
MODESTO 692
MOODY 353
MORECAMBE 132
MORNING SONG 604
MORNING STAR 37, 235
MOUNT AUBURN 516
MOWSLEY 246
MUNICH 241, 334, 670
MY SAVIOR'S LOVE 277

NATIONAL HYMN 728
NATOMAH 130
NCHEU 297
NEAR THE CROSS 479
NEED 476
NETTLETON 68, 93, 541, 577
NEUMARK (WER NUR DE LIEBEN GOTT) 234, 429
NEW BRITAIN 422
NEW DISCIPLES 364
NEW WORLD CAROL 217
NICAEA 136
NOEL 172, 388
NOËL NOUVELET 193, 311
NOW 700
NUN DANKET ALLE GOTT 14
NUN KOMM, DER HEIDEN HEILAND 168

O FILII ET FILIAE 313
O, HOW I LOVE JESUS 109
O PERFECT LOVE 610
O QUANTA QUALIA 75, 528
O-SO-SO 157
O WALY WALY 275
OASIS 432
OLD 100th 34, 661
OLD 113th 79
OLD RUGGED CROSS 260
OLIVET 419
OMNI DIE 135
ONSLOW SQUARE 13
OPEN MY EYES 480

PARKSTONE 367
PASSION CHORALE (HERZLICH TUT MICH VERLANGEN) 284, 371
PERSONENT HODIE 167, 204, 304
PESCADOR DE HOMBRES 347
PICARDY 232, 691
PLEADING SAVIOR 245, 383, 684
POLISH CAROL (W ZLOBIE LEZY) 221, 293
PORT JERVIS 550
POSADA 226
PRAYER OF ST. FRANCIS 587

PRECIOUS LORD 500
PROMISE 515
PROMISED LAND 519
PROMISED ONE 159
PUER NOBIS 144, 156, 244, 299
PURPOSE 564

QUAM DILECTA 387
QUEBEC 613
QUEM PASTORES LAUDAVERE 20
QUIET UNDERSTANDING 701

RADIANT CITY 620
RATHBUN 264
RATISBON 91
REDHEAD 272
REGENT SQUARE 99, 189, 318, 621
REJOICE, REJOICE 160
RENDEZ À DIEU 8, 239, 693
RENEWED 145
REPTON 412, 573
REST 470
RESURRECTION 447
REVIVE US AGAIN 463
RHOSYMEDRE 583
ROCKINGHAM 718
ROEDER 29
ROSAS 33
ROYAL OAK 30
RUSSIAN HYMN 517
RUSTINGTON 3, 104, 572, 622, 641

SAGINA 366
SALVATION 586
SALZBURG 6, 247
SAMANTHRA 532
SAMSON 445
SANDON 409
SARADAY 378
SCHUMANN 688
SHARPTHORNE 686
SHELDONIAN 331
SHOWALTER 496
SICILIAN MARINERS 208, 669, 748
SINE NOMINE 518, 529
SINGING LOVE 454
SIYAHAMBA 76
SLANE 27, 453, 469, 502
SOLID ROCK 405
SOMOS DEL SEÑOR 415
SOUTHWELL 386, 636
SPIRITUS VITAE 328
ST. AGNES 420, 607
ST. ANNE 84
ST. CATHERINE 530
ST. CHRISTOPHER 255
ST. CLEMENT 107
ST. COLUMBA 389
ST. DENIO 28, 48
ST. GEORGE'S, WINDSOR 243, 721
ST. GERTRUDE 509
ST. LEONARDS 464
ST. LOUIS 180
ST. MAGNUS 339
ST. MARGARET 446
ST. MICHAEL 381
ST. PETER 603
ST. THEODULPH 265
ST. THOMAS 11, 67, 549
STAND BY ME 495
STANLEY BEACH 616, 678
STAR-CHILD 223
STEAL AWAY 527
STILL, STILL, STILL 214
STILLE NACHT 186
STITELER 417
STRENGTH 514
STRENGTH AND STAY 394
STUTTGART 677
SUFFERER 280
SURRENDER 474
SURSUM CORDA 475
SUSSEX CAROL 222, 611
SWEET HOUR 478
SWING LOW 520
SYMPHONY 547

TABLESONG 617
TACK O GUD 725
TALLIS' CANON 715, 717, 747
TAULÉ 163
TEMPUS ADEST FLORIDUM 534
TENDERNESS 38
TERRA BEATA 21
THAT NAME 108
THAXTED 64
THE CALL 403
THE FIRST NOEL 229
THOMPSON 348
THREEFOLD GIFTS 401
THUMA MINA 713
TIDINGS 565
TO GOD BE THE GLORY 66, 142
TOKYO 597
TOPLADY 384
TORONTO 578
TOULON 77
TRENTHAM 461
TRINITY 139
TRURO 176, 268, 312
TRUST AND OBEY 443
TRUST IN JESUS 442
TRYGGARE KAN INGEN VARA 83
TWILIGHT 599, 629

UNE JEUNE PUCELLE 213
ÜTTINGEN 141

VENI CREATOR SPIRITUS 325
VENI EMMANUEL 154
VICAR 404
VICTORY 290
VILLE DU HAVRE (IT IS WELL) 428
VRUECHTEN 292, 308

W ZLOBIE LEZY (POLISH CAROL) 221, 293
WACHET AUF 164
WALK WITH ME 506
WALNUT 170
WAREHAM 623
WATERLIFE 680
WEBB 513
WEISSE FLAGGEN 645
WELLESLEY 61
WELWYN 582
WER NUR DEN LIEBEN GOTT (NEUMARK) 234, 429
WERE YOU THERE 283
WHITFIELD 594
WHITNEY 210
WHOLE WORLD 80
WIE LIEBLICH IST DER MAIEN 702, 724
WIE SCHÖN LEUCHTET 230
WINCHESTER NEW 250
WIR HATTEN GEBAUET 175
WOJTKIEWIECZ 89
WONDERFUL CHILD 219
WONDERFUL GRACE 362
WONDROUS LOVE 257
WOODLANDS 41
WOODWORTH 354
WORDS OF LIFE, 668
WROSLYN ROAD 276
WYCLIFF 681
WYE VALLEY 435
WYLDE GREEN 662

YE BANKS AND BRAES 628
YISRAEL V'ORAITA 124

Metrical Index

S.M (6.6.8.6.)
BOYLSTON 588
DENNIS 393
FESTAL SONG 231, 566, 590
SCHUMANN 688
SOUTHWELL 386, 636
ST. MICHAEL 381
ST. THOMAS 11, 67, 549
TRENTHAM 461

S.M. with Refrain
MARION 113

S.M.D.
DIADEMATA 317, 335
TERRA BEATA 21

C.M. (8.6.8.6.)
ARLINGTON 510
AZMON 96
CHRISTMAS 228
CRIMOND 86
DETROIT 382
DUNDEE 65
EVANSTON NEW 707
LAND OF REST 252, 738
MARTYRDOM 263
McKEE 600, 601
MORNING SONG 604
NEW BRITAIN 422
ST. AGNES 420, 607
ST. ANNE 84
ST. MAGNUS 339
ST. PETER 603

C.M. with Refrain
DUNCANNON 253
EL NATHAN 407
FINEST WHEAT 705
HUDSON 258
LANDAS 406
O, HOW I LOVE JESUS 109
PROMISED LAND 519

C.M. with Repeats
ANTIOCH 179
DIADEM 100

C.M.D.
A PURPLE ROBE 279
ALIDA'S TUNE 584
CAROL 191
ELLACOMBE 31
GRATUS 720
KINGSFOLD 237, 242, 278, 346, 434
MATERNA 727
NOEL 172, 388
SALVATION 586

L.M. (8.8.8.8.)
ALLELUIA 316
CANONBURY 32, 526, 593, 638
DISTRESS 351
DUKE STREET 63, 341, 414
GERMANY 591, 687
GIFT OF LOVE 397, 612, 682
HAMBURG 261
INTO MY HEART 485
JACOB 418
MARYTON 589
MOUNT AUBURN 516
OLD 100th 34, 661
PUER NOBIS 144, 156, 244, 299
ROCKINGHAM 718
TALLIS' CANON 715, 717, 747
TRURO 176, 268, 312
TRYGGARE KAN INGEN VARA 83
VENI CREATOR SPIRITUS 325
WAREHAM 623
WOODWORTH 354

L.M. with Alleluias
LASST UNS ERFREUEN 23, 147, 322, 663

L.M. with Refrain
HAPPY DAY 368
HE LEADETH ME 499
LAMB OF GOD 281
LINSTEAD 369, 698
SOLID ROCK 405
VENI EMMANUEL 154

L.M.D.
JERUSALEM 539
RADIANT CITY 620
SAGINA 366
SWEET HOUR 478

3.3.3.3.3.3.3.D.
LIKE A CHILD 162

3.6.9.8.3.6.
STILL, STILL, STILL 214

4.4.4.3.
THUMA MINA 713

4.5.4.5. with Refrain
STAR-CHILD 223

4.5.7.4.5.7. with Refrain
EARTH AND ALL STARS 642

4.5.8.4.5.7.
DAVOS 488

4.5.10.4.5.10. with Refrain
EARTH AND ALL STARS 306

5.4.5.4.D.
ADELAIDE 486

5.4.6.7.7.
ROEDER 29

5.5.5.4.D.
BUNESSAN 35, 425, 609, 679, 722
EVENING HYMN 627

5.5.5.5.D.
NEW DISCIPLES 364

5.5.5.6
STITELER 417

5.5.6.5.6.5.6.5. with Refrain
JUDAS MACCABEUS 310

5.5.7.4.4.7.
SICILIAN MARINERS 208

5.5.8.8. with Refrain
MANY NAMES 58

5.5.9.5.5.9.
KINDRED 602

5.5.10.D.
TENDERNESS 38

5.6.8.5.5.8.
CRUSADER'S HYMN 123

5.6.10.D.
TWILIGHT 599, 629

6.4.6.4. with Refrain
NEED 476

6.4.6.4.D.
BREAD OF LIFE 665

6.5.5.5.5.6.
WROSLYN ROAD 276

6.5.5.6.
O-SO-SO 157

6.5.6.5. with Refrain
CHRIST AROSE 294
NOËL NOUVELET 193

6.5.6.5.D.
HOLINESS 483
HOLY IS THE LORD 151
KING'S WESTON 321, 555

6.5.6.5.D. with Refrain
ST. GERTRUDE 509
WYE VALLEY 435

6.6.4.6.6.6.4.
AMERICA 731
ITALIAN HYMN 148, 561
OLIVET 419

6.6.5.5.6.6.6.4.
MAJESTAS 101

6.6.5.6.6.5.7.8.6.
JESU, MEINE FREUDE 431

6.6.6.D.
LAUDES DOMINI 332

6.6.6.6.
PARKSTONE 367

6.6.6.6. with Refrain
EASTVIEW 608

6.6.6.6.D.
MADRID 87

6.6.6.6.3.3.6.
SHARPTHORNE 686

6.6.6.6.4.4.8.
DARWALL'S 148th 9, 110

6.6.6.6.6. with Refrain
PERSONENT HODIE 167, 204, 304

6.6.6.6.6.6.
LAUDES DOMINI 111

6.6.6.6.8.8.
DARWALL'S 148th 342, 542

6.6.6.6.8.8.8.
RHOSYMEDRE 583

6.6.8.4.D.
LEONI 16, 615

6.6.8.8.6.6. with Refrain
MARCHING TO ZION 390

6.6.9.6.6.9.
PRECIOUS LORD 500

6.6.9.D. with Refrain
TRUST AND OBEY 443

6.7.6.7.
WHITNEY 210

6.7.6.7. with Refrain
VRUECHTEN 308

6.7.6.7.6.6.6.6.
NUN DANKET ALLE GOTT 14

6.7.6.8.D. with Refrain
ROSAS 33

6.6.11.D.
DOWN AMPNEY 330

6.6.11.6.6.11.D.
ASH GROVE 712

6.11.6.11. with Refrain
VRUECHTEN 292

7.5.7.5.D.
TOKYO 597

7.6.7.6.
MARY'S CHILD 194

7.6.7.6. with Refrain
NEAR THE CROSS 479
ROYAL OAK 30

7.6.7.6.D.
ANGEL'S STORY 458
AURELIA 544, 552
BECK 596
BRED DINA VIDA VINGAR 456
ELLACOMBE 267
HERZLICH TUT MICH VERLANGEN (PASSION CHORALE) 284, 371
LANCASHIRE 298, 508
LLANGLOFFAN 626
MEAL OF LOVE 704
MERLE'S TUNE 158, 545, 558

7.6.7.6.D.
MUNICH 241, 334, 670
PASSION CHORALE (HERZLICH TUT MICH VERLANGEN) 284, 371
ST. THEODULPH 265
TEMPUS ADEST FLORIDUM 534
WALNUT 170
WEBB 513
WIE LIEBLICH IST DER MAIEN 702, 724

7.6.7.6.D. with Refrain
HANKEY 560

7.6.7.6.6.6.4.4.6.
OASIS 432

7.6.7.6.6.6.7.6
ANDUJAR 206

7.6.7.6.6.7.6.
ES IST EIN ROS' 190

7.6.7.6.7.6.
ANNUNCIATION 171
WIR HATTEN GEBAUET 175

7.6.7.6.7.7.7.6.
AMSTERDAM 46
JESUS SAVES 554
KELVINGROVE 350

7.6.7.6.7.7. with Refrain
BEREDEN VÄG FÖR HERRAN 152

7.6.8.6.8.6.8.6.
ST. CHRISTOPHER 255

7.7.7.7.
LAUDS 133
NUN KOMM, DER HEIDEN HEILAND 168
THE CALL 403

7.7.7.7. with Alleluias
EASTER HYMN 288

LLANFAIR 295, 323

7.7.7.7. with Refrain
GLORIA 188
JESUS LOVES ME 437

7.7.7.7.D.
ABERYSTWYTH 333, 439
MENDELSSOHN 185
SALZBURG 6, 247
ST. GEORGE'S, WINDSOR 243, 721

7.7.7.7.7.
HENDON 466

7.7.7.7.7.7.
DIX 40, 236
RATISBON 91
REDHEAD 272
TOPLADY 384

7.7.7.8
HALLELUJAH! WHAT A SAVIOR 301

7.7.8.7. with Refrain
PORT JERVIS 550

7.7.11.8.
ONSLOW SQUARE 13

7.8.7.8.4.
MOWSLEY 246

7.8.7.8.7.7.
GROSSER GOTT 138

8.4.8.4.8.8.8.4.
AR HYD Y NOS 719, 723

8.5.8.5.7.9.
GUITING POWER 336

8.6.8.6.D.
FOREST GREEN 540, 570
GALLANT 567

8.6.8.6.6.
DOVE OF PEACE 706

8.6.8.6.6.6. with Refrain
WORDS OF LIFE 668

8.6.8.6.6.6.8.6.
CLEANSING FOUNTAIN 256

8.6.8.6.7.6.8.6.
ST. LOUIS 180

8.6.8.6.8.6.
BROTHER JAMES' AIR 73
CORONATION 106

8.6.8.6.8.8. with Refrain
UNE JEUNE PUCELLE 213

8.6.8.8.6.
REST 470

8.6.8.8.6.6.
REPTON 412, 573

8.7.8.5.
ST. LEONARDS 464

8.7.8.7.
ALL FOR JESUS 460
BARBARA ALLEN 150
CHARLESTOWN 625
GALILEE 345
MERTON 416
OMNI DIE 135
RATHBUN 264
RENEWED 145
ST. COLUMBA 389
STUTTGART 677
WELLESLEY 61
WYCLIFF 681

8.7.8.7. with Refrain
ENDLESS SONG 424
FACE TO FACE 535
GREENSLEEVES 184
HANSON PLACE 522
HEAVEN 525

8.7.8.7. with Refrain
MODESTO 692
MY SAVIOR'S LOVE 277
SURRENDER 474
TRUST IN JESUS 442

8.7.8.7.D.
ABBOT'S LEIGH 1, 536, 548, 592
ALL THE WAY 505
AUSTRIAN HYMN 17, 580, 598
BEACH SPRING 459, 477, 551, 575, 655, 695
BEECHER 358, 581
BLAENWERN 671
BRADBURY 440
CONVERSE 473
EBENEZER 398
HOLY MANNA 644, 647
HYFRYDOL 90, 149, 153, 320, 356
HYMN TO JOY 24, 59, 289, 667
IN BABILONE 128, 423, 571
JOYFUL SINGING 197
JOYOUS LIGHT 199
JUBILEE 329
MEGERRAN 585
NETTLETON 68, 93, 541, 577
PLEADING SAVIOR 245, 383, 684
POLISH CAROL (W ZLOBIE LEZY) 293
PROMISE 515
RUSTINGTON 3, 104, 572, 622, 641
TACK O GUD 725
W ZLOBIE LEZY (POLISH CAROL) 293
WEISSE FLAGGEN 645

8.7.8.7.4.7.
WYLDE GREEN 662

8.7.8.7.6.
BRIDEGROOM 327, 400

8.7.8.7.6.6.6.6.7.
EIN' FESTE BURG 507

8.7.8.7.7.7.
IRBY 183

8.7.8.7.7.7.8.8.
GENEVAN 42 155

8.7.8.7.8.7.
LAUDA ANIMA 82
PICARDY 232, 691
REGENT SQUARE 99, 189, 318, 621
SICILIAN MARINERS 669, 748
TRINITY 139

8.7.9.8.8.7.
BESANÇON 161

8.7.8.7.8.7.7.
CWM RHONDDA 413, 501, 569
DIVINUM MYSTERIUM 181, 673
W ZLOBIE LEZY (POLISH CAROL) 221

8.7.8.7.8.8.7.
MIT FREUDEN ZART 25, 56

8.7.8.7.8.8.7.7.
ERMUNTRE DICH 202

8.8.8. with Alleluias
GELOBT SEI GOTT 307
O FILII ET FILIAE 313
VICTORY 290

8.8.8.4.
THREEFOLD GIFTS 401

8.8.8.4.4.8.
DAISY HILL 635

8.8.8.5.
KUM BA YAH 487, 606

8.8.8.6. with Refrain
KINGS OF ORIENT 233

8.8.8.7.
QUEM PASTORES LAUDAVERE 20

8.8.8.8.
BOZELL 640
QUEBEC 613
WINCHESTER NEW 250

8.8.8.8. with Refrain
LINSTEAD 39

8.8.8.8.D.
LAMB OF GOD 503
YE BANKS AND BRAES 628

8.8.8.8.6.
ST. MARGARET 446

8.8.8.8.8.8.
ABINGDON 55
MELITA 74
OLD 113th 79
ST. CATHERINE 530
SUSSEX CAROL 222, 611

8.8.8.8.8.8.8.8.
KIRKEN DEN ER ET 546

8.8.8.12.
ISRAELI 619

8.8.9.8.8.8.8.4
OPEN MY EYES 480

8.9.10.7. with Refrain
GARDEN 300

9.8.9.5. with Refrain
YISRAEL V'ORAITA 124

9.8.9.8.
BEGINNINGS 355
GOD BE WITH YOU 716
O WALY WALY 275
SPIRITUS VITAE 328
ST. CLEMENT 107

9.8.9.8.D.
RENDEZ À DIEU 8, 239, 693

9.8.9.8.8.8.
NEUMARK (WER NUR DEN LIEBEN GOTT) 234, 429

9.9.9.7. with Refrain
CALYPSO CAROL 227

9.9.9.9.
KORU 683

9.9.9.9. with Refrain
MOODY 353

9.10.9.9. with Refrain
ASSURANCE 426

9.10.10.9.
AMSTEIN 36

10.4.10.4.10.10.
SANDON 409

10.6.10.6.8.8.8.6.
ALL IS WELL 462

10.7.10.7. with Refrain
I AM THINE 408

10.7.10.8. with Refrain
HOUSTON 248

10.8.8.7.7. with Refrain
MESSAGE 562

10.8.10.8. with Refrain
SWING LOW 520

10.9.10.9.
BUNESSAN 78

10.9.10.9. with Refrain
SHOWALTER 496

10.9.10.9.D.
BLOTT EN DAG 449

10.10. with Refrain
LET US BREAK BREAD 699

10.10.10. with Alleluias
ENGELBERG 7, 553
SINE NOMINE 518, 529

10.10.10.8.
ASSAM 344

10.10.10.10.
A VA DE 694
CRUCIFER 287
ELLERS 385, 711
EVENTIDE 274, 521
GREENBELT 632
HALL 455
MORECAMBE 132
NATIONAL HYMN 728
SHELDONIAN 331
SLANE 27, 453, 502
SURSUM CORDA 475
TOULON 77
WOODLANDS 41

10.10.10.10.10.
GENEVA 124 708

10.10.10.10.10.10.
FINLANDIA 451

10.10.11.11.
HANOVER 112, 531
LYONS 2
STANLEY BEACH 616, 678

10.10.12.10.
GABRIEL'S MESSAGE 169

10.11.11.6.
CHRISTE SANCTORUM 121, 524

10.11.11.12.
SLANE 469

11.7.11.7. with Refrain
THOMPSON 348

11.8.11.8.D.
SAMANTHRA 532

11.8.11.9. with Refrain
VILLE DU HAVRE (IT IS WELL) 428

11.10.10.11.
NOËL NOUVELET 311

11.10.11.9.
RUSSIAN HYMN 517

11.10.11.10.
LORD OF THE YEARS 70
MORNING STAR 37, 235
O PERFECT LOVE 610
O QUANTA QUALIA 75, 528
STRENGTH AND STAY 394
VICAR 404
WELWYN 582

11.10.11.10. with Refrain
FAITHFULNESS 72
TABLESONG 617
TIDINGS 565

11.10.11.10. with Coda
TORONTO 578

11.10.11.10.D.
LONDONDERRY AIR 433

11.10.11.10.11.10.
FINLANDIA 372

11.11. with Refrain
REVIVE US AGAIN 463

11.11.7.7.11.
STAND BY ME 495

11.11.10.8.8.
NCHEU 297

11.11.11.5
CHRISTE SANCTORUM 140
HERZLIEBSTER JESU 262
WOJTKIEWIECZ 89

11.11.11.6.
CHRISTE SANCTORUM 324

11.11.11.10.
STRENGTH 514

11.11.11.11.
ANNIVERSARY SONG 685
AU CLAIR DE LA LUNE 634
AWAY IN A MANGER 203
CRADLE SONG 205
FOUNDATION 411
GORDON 468
HOUGHTON 643
ST. DENIO 28, 48

11.11.11.11. with Refrain
TO GOD BE THE GLORY 66, 142

11.11.12.12.
TAULÉ 163

11.11.14.8.9.
SYMPHONY 547

11.12.12.10.
NICAEA 136

12.9.12.11.
SAMSON 445

12.9.12.12.9.
WONDROUS LOVE 257

12.10.12.10.
ÜTTINGEN 141

12.10.12.10.11.10.11.10.
JOYFUL SONG 95

12.11.12. with Refrain
EL CAMINO 624

12.11.12.11.
KREMSER 81, 726

12.11.12.11.D.
ASH GROVE 22

12.12. with Refrain
ISLA DEL ENCANTO 238
PROMISED ONE 159

12.12.12.
ACCLAMATIONS 672

13.13.13.11. with Refrain
ACKLEY 302

13.13.13.13.13.13.
THAXTED 64

14.12.12.14.
CONRAD 49

14.14.4.7.8.
LOBE DEN HERREN 71

14.14.14.14.
DUDLEY 579

15.15.15.6. with Refrain
BATTLE HYMN 730

Index of Authors, Composers and Sources

Ackley, Alfred H. (1887-1960) 302
Adam, Adolphe C. (1803-1856) 187
Adams, Stephen R. (1943-) 396
Adkins, Donna (1940-) 146
African Chewa hymn 297
African folk song 674
African Prayer Book, An 296
African-American 365
African-American melody 600
African-American spiritual 80, 209, 218, 219, 220, 249, 254, 280, 283 457, 481, 487, 506, 512, 520, 527, 537, 538, 574, 606, 618, 631, 699, 746
Ahnfelt, Oscar (1813-1882) 449
Ainger, Arthur C. (1841-1919) 564
Ainger, Geoffrey (1925-) 194
Airs sur les hymnes sacrez, 1623 313
Akers, Doris (1922-1995) 134, 498
Alcuin (8th c.) 418
Alexander, Cecil F. (1818-1895) 30, 183, 345
Alexander, James W. (1804-1859) 284
Alford, Henry (1810-1871) 721
Alford, Janie (1887-1986) 329
Alington, Cyril A. (1872-1955) 307
Allen, Chester G. (1838-1878) 95
Allen, David (1941-) 491, 568
Alte Catholische Geistliche Kirchengesänge, 1599 190
Altrogge, Mark (1950-) 53
Ambrose of Milan (4th c.) 144, 168
American melody 109, 252, 256, 519, 706, 730, 738
Anderson, Fred R. (1941-) 567
Angoni war song 297
Anonymous 109, 114, 119, 148, 203, 205, 305, 344, 415, 422, 450, 504, 606, 650
Appalachian carol 225
Appalachian folk hymn 257
Appalachian melody 225
Arne, Thomas A. (1710-1778) 510
Arthur, John W. (1922-1980) 315
Asimakoupoulos, Gregory E. (1952-) 682
Atkins, George (18th c.) 647
Atkinson, Frederick C. (1841-1897) 132
Augsburg Publishing House (1972) 694
Austrian carol 214
Austrian melody 214
Avery, Richard K. (1934-) 550

Babcock, Maltbie (1858-1901) 21
Bach, J.S. (1685-1750) 6, 164, 202, 230, 247, 284, 371, 431
Backstrom, Carl E. (1901-1984) 725
Bain, James L. (1840-1925) 73
Baker, Henry W. (1821-1877) 181, 613
Baker, Theodore (1851-1934) 81, 190
Baloche, Paul (1962-) 656
Barham-Gould, A. Cyril (1891-1953) 464
Baring-Gould, Sabine (1834-1924) 169, 509
Barnard, John (1948-) 336, 433
Barnby, Joseph (1838-1896) 111, 332, 610
Basque carol 169
Basque melody 169
Batastini, Robert (1942-) 697
Bateman, Christian H. (1813-1889) 87
Bates, Katharine L. (1859-1929) 727
Batstone, Bill (20th c.) 251
Batya, Naomi (1961-) 338
Baughen, Michael (1930-) 70, 101, 488, 492, 619
Bayly, Albert F. (1901-1984) 575, 645, 686, 722
Beaker (20th c.) 494
Beall, Mary Kay (1943-) 720
Beck, John Ness (1930-1986) 596
Bede, The Venerable (673-735) 322
Beethoven, Ludwig van (1770-1827) 24, 59, 289, 667
Bell, John L. (1949-) 282, 296, 350, 628
Benedicite, The 25
Bennard, George (1873-1958) 260
Benson, Louis F. (1855-1930) 242
Berg, Carolina Sandell (1832-1903) 83, 449, 456
Bernard of Clairvaux, (1091-1153) 284
Berthier, Jacques (1923-1994) 173, 174, 212, 240, 285, 286, 303, 399, 421, 448, 484, 697
Bianco da Siena (d. 1434) 330
Bible, Ken (1950-) 647
Blankenship, Mark (1943-) 137
Bliss, Philip P. (1838-1876) 301, 356, 428, 668
Bock, Fred (1939-1998) 547
Bode, John E. (1816-1874) 458
Bohemian Brethren's *Kirchengesänge*, Berlin, 1566 25, 56
Bonhöffer, Dietrich (1906-1945) 75
Borthwick, Jane L. (1813-1897) 451
Bourgeois, Louis (ca. 1510-1561) 8, 34, 155, 239, 661, 693
Bowring, John (1792-1872) 264
Bradbury, William B. (1816-1868) 354, 405, 437, 440, 478, 499
Brahms, Johannes (1833-1897) 547
Brazilian folk melody 15
Brazilian folk song 15
Breck, Carrie E. (1855-1934) 535
Bridges, Matthew (1800-1894) 317
Bridges, Robert (1844-1930) 262
Briggs, George W. (1875-1959) 667
Brokering, Herbert F. (1926-) 306, 642
Brooke, Stopford A. (1832-1916) 6
Brooks, Phillips (1835-1893) 180
Brooks, R.T. (1918-1985) 662
Brown, Scott Wesley (1952-) 436
Brubeck, Dave (1920-) 226
Brubeck, Iola (1923-) 226
Bryne, Mary E. (1880-1931) 502
Buchanan, Annabel Morris (1889-1983) 252
Budry, Edmond L. (1854-1932) 310
Bullock, Geoff (20th c.) 467
Burleigh, Harry T. (1866-1949) 600
Bush, AnnaMae Meyer (1947-) 739

Calvin, John (1509-1564) 77
Calvisius, Seth (1556-1615) 168
Cameron, Catherine (1927-) 644
Cameroon 402
Campbell, Thomas (1777-1844) 366
Cantica Laudis, 1850 688
Caribbean 5
Caribbean melody 5
Carlson, Richard K. (1956-) 145
Carter, John (1930-) 165, 378, 444
Carter, Sydney (1915-) 118
Cartford, Gerhard (1923-) 15
Caswall, Edward (1814-1878) 111, 420
Cathey, Mary Jackson (1926-) 548, 747
Chambers, Brent (1948-) 12
Chandler, John (1806-1876) 156
Change, Constant (1964-) 98
Chapman, J. Wilbur (1859-1918) 90
Chapman, Morris (1938-) 361, 605

Chapman, Steven Curtis (1962-) 637
Chatfield, Allen W. (1808-1896) 386
Chávez-Melo, Skinner (1944-1992) 163, 347
Cherry, Constance (1953-) 566, 622
Chisholm, Thomas O. (1866-1960) 72
Chisum, John (1958-) 370
Christensen, Chris (1957-) 563
von Christierson, Frank (1900-1996) 475, 570, 681
Christian Lyre, The, 1830 245, 383, 684
Christmas Carols New and Old, 1871 184
Church Hymnal, The, 1894 235
Clarke, Harry D. (1888-1957) 485
Clarke, Jeremiah (ca. 1670-1707) 339
Clarkson, Margaret (1915-) 27, 78, 110, 142, 578, 586, 671
Clephane, Elizabeth C. (1830-1869) 255
Cloninger, Claire (1942-) 361, 383
Coates, Stephen (1952-) 227
Cober, Kenneth L. (1902-) 462
Coelho, Terrye (1952-) 143
Coffin, Charles (1676-1749) 156
Coffin, Henry S. (1877-1954) 154
Coleman, T. Brian (1920-) 432
Cole-Turner, Ronald S. (1948-) 677
Columbian Harmony, 1825 644, 647
Colvin, Tom (1925-2000) 130, 211, 273, 297, 309
Conkey, Ithamar (1815-1867) 264
Conty, Sophie (1961-) 338
Converse, Charles C. (1832-1918) 473
Coomes, Tommy (1946-) 646
Copes, V. Earle (1921-) 79, 404
Corbett-Wood, Sondra (1963-) 69
Corner, David Gregof (1585-1648) 135
Cortez, Jaime (1963-) 444
Cory, Julia C. (1882-1963) 726
Cosin, John (1594-1672) 325
Costen, Melva W. (b. 1933-) 481
Cowper, William (1731-1800) 65, 256
Cox, Frances (1812-1897) 56
Crawford, Mary Babcock (1909-) 21
Crocker, Elisabeth (1950-) 488
Croft, William (1678-1727) 84, 112, 531
Croly, George (1780-1860) 132
Cropper, Margaret (1886-1980) 634
Crosby, Fanny J. (1820-1915) 66, 95, 408, 426, 479, 505
Crotch, William (1775-1847) 381
Crouch, Andraé (1945-) 4, 363, 452, 523
Crüger, Johann (1598-1662) 14, 262, 431
Crum, J.M.C. (1872-1958) 311
Cull, Bob (1949-) 491
Cummings, William H. (1831-1915) 185
Cutts, Peter (1937-) 139, 327, 400, 516, 662

Damazio, Sharon (1953-) 340
Damon, Daniel Charles (1955-) 162, 417, 599, 629, 692
Damon's, William *Psalms*, 1579 386
Danish 744
Darwall, John (1731-1789) 9, 110, 342, 542
Dauermann, Stuart (1944-) 710
David's Psalmen, 1685 292, 308
Davis, Geron (1960-) 654
Davis, Katherine K. (1892-1980) 22
Daw, Carl P. Jr. (1944-) 25, 73, 107, 149, 170, 245, 247, 327, 381, 388, 423, 517, 539, 684, 691, 695
Dawn, Marva J. (1948-) 655
Dearman, Kirk (1952-) 651
Delavan, Macon (1932-1995) 52
Dempsey, Larry (1946-1995) 103
Dix, William C. (1837-1898) 184, 236, 320

Doan, Gilbert E. (1930-) 694
Doane, William H. (1832-1915) 66, 142, 408, 479
Doddridge, Philip (1702-1751) 368
Doerksen, Brian (20th c.) 374
Dorsey, Thomas A. (1899-1993) 500
Douglas, C. Winfred (1867-1944) 673, 708
Douglas, Robert F. (1941-) 125, 224
Doving, Carl (1867-1937) 546
Doxology 34
Draper, William H. (1855-1933) 23
Dresden 743
Duba, Arlo D. (1929-) 545
Duck, Ruth (1947-) 231, 551, 643
Dudley-Smith, Timothy (1926-) 9, 13, 41, 70, 101, 239, 274, 279, 324, 335, 346, 400, 412, 432, 433, 453, 488, 702
Duffield, George (1818-1888) 513
Duffner, Delores, OSB (20th c.) 577
Dufford, Bob, S.J. (1943-) 430
Dunstan, Sylvia G. (1955-1993) 99, 553
Dutch melody (18th c.) 128, 423, 571
Dwight, John S. (1813-1893) 187
Dwight, Timothy (1752-1817) 549
Dykes, John B. (1823-1876) 74, 75, 136, 394, 420, 607

Early American melody 584
Early Christian Liturgy 120
Edmunds, Lidie H. (19th c.) 406
Edwards, John David (1806-1885) 583
Edwards, Robert L. (1915-) 572
Edwards, Rusty (1955-) 93, 171, 552
Ehret, Walter (1918-) 214, 238
Elijah 380
Ellerton, John (1826-1893) 711
Elliott, Charlotte (1789-1871) 354
Ellor, James (1819-1899) 100
Elvey, George J. (1816-1893) 243, 317, 335, 721
Emerson, Luther O. (1820-1915) 723
Enchiridia, 1524 168
English carol 222, 229, 611
English folk tune 150
English melody, 21, 30, 172, 184, 237, 242, 275, 278, 346, 388, 397, 434, 540, 570, 612, 682
Escamilla, Roberto (1931-) 33, 415
Eslinger, Elise S. (1942-) 33, 415
Espinosa, Eddie (1953-) 373
Evans, David (1874-1948) 35, 87, 140, 626, 679
Evans, David (20th c.) 129
Evans, George K. (1917-) 214, 238
Everest, Charles W. (1814-1877) 351
Excell, Edwin O. (1851-1921) 422

Faber, Frederick W. (1814-1863) 61, 530
Farjeon, Eleanor (1881-1965) 35, 161
Farquharson, Walter (1936-) 28
Fawcett, John (1740-1817) 393, 748
Fay, Mike (20th c.) 646
Featherstone, William R. (1846-1873) 468
Fedak, Alfred V. (1953-) 364
Ferguson, Greg (20th c.) 639
Ferguson, John (1941-) 159
Fettke, Tom (1941-) 514, 563
Fillmore, James H. (1849-1936) 60
Fischer, William G. (1835-1912) 560
Fishel, Donald (1950-) 291
Fitts, Bob (1955-) 19
Foley, John B. (1939-) 689
Foreman, Mark (20th c.) 127
Forness, Norman O. (1936-) 590

Fosdick, Harry E. (1878-1969) 569
Foulkes, William H. (1877-1962) 455
Foundery Collection, 1742 46
Foundling Hospital Collection, The, 1796 17
Founds, Rick (1954-) 88
Francis, Samuel Trevor (1834-1925) 398
Franck, Johann (1618-1677) 431
Franz, Ignaz (1719-1790) 138
Franzen, Frans Mikael (1772-1847) 152
Frazier, Philip (1892-1964) 26
French carol 188, 193, 201, 213, 311
French melody 154, 161, 232, 313, 634, 691
Fritsch, Carolyn (20th c.) 124
Fry, Steve (1954-) 271
Funk's *Genuine Church Music*, 1832 411

Gabaraín, Cesareo (1936-1991) 347
Gabriel, Charles H. (1856-1932) 277
Gaelic melody 35, 78, 425, 609, 679, 722
Gaither, Gloria (1942-) 108, 125, 372, 447
Gaither, William J. (1936-) 108, 447
Gardiner's, William *Sacred Melodies*, 1815 2, 591, 687
Garrett, Les (1944-) 652
Gaunt, Alan (1935-) 369, 558
Gauntlett, Henry J. (1805-1876) 183, 677
Geistliche Kirchengesäng, 1599 190
Geistliche Kirchengesäng, Cologne, 1623 23, 147, 322, 663
Genevan Psalter, 1551 8, 34, 77, 155, 239, 381, 661, 693, 708
German 190
German carol 200
German folk tune 175
German melody 20, 198
Gertmenian, James (1947-) 250
Gesangbuch, Münster, 1677 123
Gesangbuch der H.W.K. Kofkapelle, 1784 31, 267
Ghana folk song 130, 273, 309
Giardini, Felice de (1716-1796) 148, 561
Gibson, Colin (1933-) 38, 276, 454
Gillard, Richard (1953-) 391
Gilmore, Joseph H. (1834-1918) 499
Gladden, Washington (1836-1918) 589
Gläser, Carl G. (1784-1829) 96
Gloria Patri 733, 734
Gordon, Adoniram J. (1836-1895) 468
Gordon, Nancy (1955-) 410
Goss, John (1800-1880) 82
Grant, Amy (1960-) 664
Grant, David (1833-1893) 86
Grant, Robert (1779-1838) 2
Greatorex, Henry W. (1813-1858) 734
Greatorex, Walter (1877-1949) 41
Greco, Eugene (1960-) 45
Greek hymn 107
Greek litany 379
Green, Fred Pratt (1903-2000) 1, 7, 37, 75, 121, 167, 202, 241, 275, 278, 332, 401, 413, 526, 531, 555, 573, 623, 627, 638, 672, 723
Green, Melody (1946-) 117
Greene, Buddy (20th c.) 192
Greiter, Matthaus (ca. 1500-1550) 79
Grindal, Gracia (1943 -) 171, 175, 456
Grotenhuis, Dale (1931-) 120, 392
Groves, Alexander (1842-1909) 665
Gruber, Franz (1787-1863) 186
Grundtvig, Nikolai F.S. (1783-1872) 546
Guarani Kyrie 377
Gurney, Dorothy F. (1858-1932) 610
Gustafson,Gerrit (1948-) 45
Gutiérrez-Achon, Raquel (1927-) 347

Haas, David (1957-) 627, 666
Hackett, Kevin R. (1956-) 309
Hammond, Mary J. (1878-1964) 328
Handel, George Frideric (1685-1759) 179, 228, 310
Hankey, A. Catherine (1834-1911) 560
Harding, James P. (1850-1911) 37, 235
Harkness, Georgia (1891-1974) 404
Harrah, Walt (1948-) 57, 62, 690
Harville, Jamie (1960-) 410
Hassler, Hans Leo (1564-1612) 284, 371
Hastings, Thomas (1784-1872) 384
Hatch, Edwin (1835-1889) 461
Hatton, John (ca. 1710-1793) 63, 341, 414
Haugen, Marty (1950-) 160, 199, 630, 649
Havergal, Frances R. (1836-1879) 435, 466, 593
Havergal, William H. (1793-1870) 91, 250
Hawks, Annie S. (1835-1918) 476
Haydn, Franz Joseph (1732-1809) 17, 580, 598
Haydn, Johann M. (1737-1806) 2
Hayford, Jack W. (1934-) 43
Head, Elizabeth Ann P. (1850-1936) 328
Hearn, Naida (1944-) 177
Heber, Reginald (1783-1826) 136, 235, 693
Hebrew melody 16, 615, 714
Hebrew *Yigdal* 16
Hedge, Frederick H. (1805-1890) 507
Heermann, Johann (1585-1647) 262
Helmore, Thomas (1811-1890) 154
Hemy, Henri F. (1818-1888) 530
Henry Ware, Jr. (1794-1843) 607
Herbert, George (1593-1633) 49, 403
Herklots, Rosamond E. (1905-1987) 382
Hernaman, Claudia F. (1838-1898) 252
Herring, Anne (1945-) 314
Hewitt, Eliza E. (1851-1920) 525
Hewitt, John H. (1801-1890) 258
Hicks, Roy Jr. (1943-) 115
Hillert, Richard (1923-) 315
Hine, Stuart K. (1899-1989) 51
Hintze, Jakob (1622-1702) 6, 247
Hispanic folk song 207
Hoare, Brian (1935-) 540
Hodges, Edward (1796-1867) 289
Hoffman, Elisha A. (1839-1929) 496
Holden, Oliver (1765-1844) 106
Holst, Gustav T. (1874-1934) 64, 167, 196, 204, 304
Holstein, Jane (1958-) 402, 456, 587
Hopkins, Edward J. (1818-1901) 385, 711
Hopkins, John H. Jr. (1820-1891) 233
Hopson, Hal H. (1933-) 5, 76, 147, 158, 197, 329, 397, 415, 545, 558, 584, 612, 682, 704, 741
How, William W. (1823-1897) 529, 670, 688
Howe, Julia Ward (1819-1910) 730
Hoyle, R. Birch (1875-1939) 310
Huber, Jane Parker (1926-) 24, 172, 334, 581
Hudson, Ralph E. (1843-1901) 258
Hughes, John (1873-1932) 413, 501, 569
Hull, Eleanor H. (1860-1935) 502
Hultman, John A. (1861-1942) 725
Hurd, David (1950-) 206
Husband, John J. (1760-1825) 463
Hussey, Jennie E. (1874-1958) 253
Hustad, Donald P. (1918-) 201, 225, 519, 537, 635, 714, 740
Hymnal 1933 372, 451

Hymns for the Young, 1836 440
Hytrek, Theophane (1915-1992) 430

Idle, Christopher (1938-) 3, 150, 234, 367, 418, 434, 445, 528, 534, 669
Iliff, David (1939-) 70
Indian folk tune 344
Irish hymn 502
Irish melody 27, 389, 433, 453, 469, 502
Irons, Herbert S. (1834-1905) 636
Irvine, Jessie S. (1836-1887) 86
Israeli folk song 174, 159
Israeli melody 619
Israeli round 714
Iverson, Daniel (1890-1977) 492

Jabusch, Willard F. (1930-) 159
Jackson, Jill (1913-1995) 614
Jackson, Robert (1842-1914) 461
Jackson, Thomas A. (1931-) 580
Jacob, Gordon (1895-1984) 73
Jamaican folk tune 39, 369, 698
Jean de Brébeuf (1593-1649) 213
Jernigan, Dennis L. (1959-) 427
John of Damascus (8th c.) 298
Johnson, David N. (1922-1987) 306, 642
Johnson, J. Rosamund (1873-1954) 729
Johnson, James Weldon (1871-1938) 729
Johnson, Linda Lee (1947-) 514
Johnson, Nelsie T. (1912-) 249, 746
Johnston, Julia H. (1849-1919) 353
Jolly, Hilary (1945-) 536
Joncas, Michael (1951-) 438
Jubilate Hymns, 1982 243, 289, 460, 718
Judah, Daniel ben (ca. 1400) 16
Jude, William H. (1851-1922) 345
Jüngst, Hugo (1853-1923) 200

Kaan, Fred (1929-) 204, 389, 416, 524, 596, 616, 621, 698, 715
Kaiser, Kurt (1934-) 270, 557
Katholisches Gesangbuch, 1774 138
Katholisches Gesangbuch, 1828 111
Kelly, Thomas (1769-1855) 339
Ken, Thomas (1637-1711) 34
Kendrick, Graham (1950-) 97, 259, 319, 357, 556
Kentucky Harmony, 1813 604
Kentucky Harmony, 1816 586
Kerr, Hugh T. (1872-1950) 409
Kethe, William (ca. 1530-1594) 661
Kilpatrick, Bob (1952-) 465
Kirkpatrick, William J. (1838-1921) 205, 253, 406, 442, 554
Kitchin, George W. (1827-1912) 287
Klein, Laurie (1950-) 85
Klug, Ronald A. (1939-) 89
Knapp, Phoebe P. (1839-1908) 426
Knapp, William (1698-1768) 623
Kocher, Conrad (1786-1872) 40, 236
Koizumi, Isao (1907-1992) 597
Kremser, Edward (1838-1914) 81, 726
Kreutz, Robert E. (1922-1996) 705
Kwillia, Billema (1925-) 694

Lafferty, Karen (1948-) 349
Landsberg, Max (1845-1928) 16
Lanier, H. Glen (1925-1978) 503
Lathbury, Mary A. (1841-1913) 665
Latin 154, 290, 303, 399, 420
Latin carol 198
Latin hymn 244, 295, 299
Latin American 737
Laufer, Calvin Weiss (1874-1938) 455
Leavitt's *The Christian Lyre*, 1830 245, 383, 684
Lee, Geonyong (1947-) 157
Lee, James V. (1892-1959) 608
Leech, Bryan Jeffery (1931-) 547, 579, 607, 687, 696,
Lemmel, Helen H. (1864-1961) 472
Liljestrand, Paul (1931-) 49
Lillenas, Haldor (1885-1959) 362
Lindeman, Ludvig M. (1812-1887) 546
Littledale, Richard Frederick (1833-1890) 330
Liturgy of St. James 232
Lloyd, Eva B. (1912-) 459
Lockwood, George (1946-) 33, 347, 415, 624
Longstaff, William D. (1822-1894) 483
Lovelace, Austin C. (1919-) 401, 532, 706
Lowry, Mark (20th c.) 192
Lowry, Robert (1826-1899) 294, 390, 424, 476, 505, 522
Luff, Alan (1928-) 542
Luther, Martin (1483-1546) 168, 507
Lutheran Book of Worship, 1978 230, 322
Lutkin, Peter C. (1858-1931) 749
Lvov, Alexis (1799-1870) 517
Lyon, Meyer (1751-1797) 16, 615
Lyra Davidica, 1708 288, 295
Lyte, Henry F. (1793-1847) 82, 521

MacAlmon, Terry (1955-) 660
Mackay, William P. (1839-1885) 463
Maker, Frederick C. (1844-1927) 255, 470
Malan, Henri A. César (1787-1864) 466
Malawi melody 211
Malotte, Albert Hay (1895-1964) 740
Manley, James K. (1940-) 326
Mann, Arthur H. (1850-1929) 458
Mann, Newton (1836-1926) 16
Manzano, Miguel (20th c.) 624
Marsh, Donald S. (1923-) 550
Marshall, Jane (1924-) 418, 583, 617, 640, 685
Marshall, Madeleine Forell (1946-) 163
Martínez, Raquel Mora (1940-) 33
Mason & Webb's *Cantica Laudis*, 1850 688
Mason, Lowell (1792-1872) 96, 179, 256, 261, 393, 419, 588
Matheson, George (1842-1906) 446
Matsikenyiri, Patrick (1937-) 659
McFarland, John Thomas (1851-1913) 203, 205
McGee, Bob (1944-) 178
McGranahan, James (1840-1907) 407
McHugh, Phill (1951-) 125, 568
McIntosh, Rigdon M. (1836-1899) 519
McSpadden, Gary (1943-) 98
Medema, Ken (1943-) 489, 543
Medley, Samuel (1738-1799) 414
Meineke, Christoph (1782-1850) 733
Melodia Sacra, 1815 228
Mendelssohn, Felix (1809-1847) 14, 185, 334, 380, 670
Messiter, Arthur H. (1834-1916) 113
Middleton, Jesse Edgar (1872-1960) 213
Mieir, Audrey (1916-1996) 102
Miles, C. Austin (1868-1946) 300
Miller, Edward (1731-1807) 718
Miller, Margaret D. (1927 -) 694
Miller, Sy (1908-1971) 614

Mills, Pauline Michael (1898-1992) 126
Milman, Henry H. (1791-1868) 268
Moen, Don (1950-) 45
Mohr, Jon (1955-) 497
Mohr, Joseph (1792-1848) 186
Molefe, S.C. (20th c.) 741
Monk, William H. (1823-1889) 40, 274, 290, 416, 521
Monsell, John Samuel Bewley (1811-1875) 724
Montgomery, James (1771-1854) 11, 189, 272
Moody, Dave (1948-) 92
Moore, William (19th c.) 647
Morgan, Reuben (1975-) 360
Mote, Edward (1797-1874) 405
Moultrie, Gerard (1829-1885) 232
Mountain, James (1844-1933) 435
Mowbray, David (1938-) 304, 608, 673
Moyer, J. Harold (1927-) 170
Mullins, Rich (20th c.) 658
Murray, James R. (1841-1905) 203
Murray, Shirley Erena (1931-) 38, 135, 217, 223, 276, 292, 394, 477, 518, 602, 609, 615, 617, 635, 641, 683
Muscogee (Creek) Indian 735
Musikalisches Handbuch, 1690 250

Nägeli, Johann G. (1773-1836) 393
Native American melody 26
Neale, John M. (1818-1866) 154, 181, 198, 265, 298, 299, 313
Neander, Joachim (1650-1680) 71
Nederlandtsch Gedenckclanck, 1626 81, 726
Neidlinger, William Harold (1900-) 224
Nelson, Greg (1948-) 568
Nelson, Jeff (20th c.) 436
Nelson, Marc (20th c.) 675
Nelson, Ronald A. (1927-) 477, 575
Netherlands folk hymn, 81
Neumark, Georg (1621-1681) 234, 429
Neuvermehrtes Gesangbuch, 1693 241, 334, 670
New Universal Psalmodist, 1770 11, 67, 549
Newbolt, Michael R. (1874-1956) 287
Newton, John (1725-1807) 422, 598
Nichol, H. Ernest (1862-1928 , 562
Nichols, Kevin (1929-) 371
Nicholson, Sydney H. (1875-1947) 287
Nicolai, Philipp (1556-1608) 164, 230
Niles, John Jacob (1892-1980) 225
Noel, Caroline Maria (1817-1877) 321
Noland, Rory (20th c.) 639
North, Frank Mason (1850-1935) 591
Norton, Christopher (1953-) 376
Norwegian melody 406
Nystrom, Martin (1956-) 471

Oakeley, Frederick (1802-1880) 114, 182
O'Carroll, Fintan (d. 1977) 736
O'Driscoll, Herbert (1928-) 141
Olearius, Johannes G. (1611-1684) 155
Olivar, J.A. (20th c.) 624
Olivers, Thomas (1725-1799) 16
Olson, Ernest W. (1870-1958) 83
Orr, J. Edwin (1912-1987) 385
O'Shields, Michael (1948-) 653
Oudaen's, J. *David's Psalmen*, 1685 292, 308
Owens, Jimmy (1930-) 44
Owens, Priscilla J. (1829-1907) 554
Owens-Collins, Jamie (1955-) 511
Oxenham, John (1852-1941) 600, 603

Palestrina, Giovanni Pierluigi da (1525-1594) 290
Palmer, Ray (1808-1887) 419
Paraguayan 377
Paris Antiphoner, 1681 75, 121, 140, 324, 524, 528
Paris, Twila (1958-) 122, 281, 337, 503
Parker, Alice (1925-) 150, 292
Parry, C. Hubert H. (1848-1918) 3, 104, 412, 539, 572, 573, 622, 641
Parry, Joseph (1841-1903) 333, 439
Patterson, Joy F. (1931-) 532, 571, 620, 632, 683
Patty, Sandi (1956-) 125
Pavlechko, Thomas (1962-) 620, 632
Peace, Albert L. (1844-1912) 446
Peacey, J.R. (1896-1971) 331, 708
Peacock, David (1949-) 367
Perronet, Edward (1726-1792) 100, 106
Perry, Michael (1942-1996) 20, 64, 158, 197, 227, 600, 636, 707
Peruvian melody 732
Peterson, John W. (1921-) 578
Pettman, Edgar (1865-1943) 169
Piae Cantiones, 1582 167, 204, 304, 534
Pierpoint, Folliott S. (1835-1917) 40
Plainsong 181, 325, 673
Plumptre, Edward H. (1821-1891) 113
Polish carol 221
Polish folk tune 221, 293
Pollard, Adelaide A. (1862-1934) 486
Polman, Bert (1945-) 739
Pope, Marion (20th c.) 157
Pope, Michael (20th c.) 559
Post, Marie J. (1919-) 60
Pote, Allen (1945-) 737
Pott, Francis (1832-1909) 290
Potter, Doreen (1925-1980) 39, 369, 698
Praetorius, Michael (1571-1621) 144, 156, 190, 244, 299, 303
Pratt, Andrew (1948-) 604
Price, Charles P. (1920-1999) 152
Prichard, Rowland H. (1811-1887) 90, 149, 153, 320, 356
Prudentius, Marcus Aurelius C. 181
Psalmodia Evangelica, 1789 176, 268, 312
Puerto Rican carol 238
Puerto Rican melody 238
Pulkingham, Betty (1928-) 703
Purday, Charles H. (1799-1885) 409

Quinn, James S.J. (1919-) 425

Radford, Jeffrey (1953-) 219
Rankin, Jeremiah E. (1828-1904) 716
Ravenscroft, Thomas (1592-1635) 65
Redhead, Richard (1820-1901) 272
Redner, Lewis H. (1831-1908) 180
Reed, Edith M.G. (1885-1933) 221
Reid, William W. Jr. (1923-) 626
Reimann, Heinrich (1850-1906) 25, 56
Reinagle, Alexander R. (1799-1877) 603
Renville, Joseph R. (19th c.) 26
Repository of Sacred Music, 1813 68, 93, 541, 577
Rheinhardt's, Johann H. *Choralbuch*, 1754 141
Richards, John (1939-) 128
Ridout, Daniel L. (1899-1982) 495
Rimbault, Edward F. (1816-1876) 368
Rinkart, Martin (1586-1649) 14
Rippon, John (1751-1836) 100, 106
Rippon's *Selection of Hymns*, 1787 411
Rist, Johann (1607-1667) 202

Robb, John Donald (1892-1989) 207
Roberts, Daniel C. (1841-1907) 728
Roberts, John (1822-1877) 48, 323
Robinson, Robert (1735-1790) 68
Rockstro, William Smith (1823-1895) 135
Röntgen, Julius (1855-1933) 128, 571
Root, George F. (1820-1895) 387
Rosas, Carlos (20th c.) 33
Rossetti, Christina (1830-1894) 196, 210
Routley, Erik (1917-1982) 8, 55, 524, 625, 686, 707
Rowan, William P. (1951-) 58
Rowlands, William P. (1860-1937) 671
Rowthorn, Jeffery (1934-) 32, 592
Rubin, Steffi Geiser (1950-) 710
Ruis, David (20th c.) 648
Runyan, William M. (1870-1957) 72
Rusbridge, A.E. (1917-1969) 221, 293
Russian Orthodox 379
Rutter, John (1945-) 742

Sacred Harp, The, 1844 459, 462, 477, 551, 575, 655, 695
Sadler, Gary (1954-) 370
Salley, Jerry (20th c.) 637
Sammis, John H. (1846-1919) 443
Sanchez, Pete Jr. (1948-) 47
Sanctus 738
Sandys', W. *Christmas Carols*, 1833 229
Sateren, Leland (1913-) 712
Saward, Michael (1932-) 336, 679
Schalk, Carl F. (1929-) 29, 616, 678, 700
von Schlegel, Katherina (18th c.) 451
Schlesische Volkslieder, 1842 123
Scholefield, Clement (1839-1904) 107
Scholtes, Peter (1938-) 595
Schop, Johann (1590-1664) 202
Schrader, Jack (1942-) 15, 26, 126, 187, 192, 209, 239, 245, 254, 383, 425, 450, 469, 502, 551, 602, 609, 655, 672, 674, 676, 695, 722,738
Schubert, Franz (1797-1828) 151, 745
Schulz-Widmar, Russell (1944-) 561, 613
Schumann, Robert A. (1810-1856) 32, 526, 593, 638
Schutmaat, Alvin (1921-1988) 624
Schutte, Daniel L. (1947-) 10, 559
Schütz, Johann J. (1640-1690) 56
Scott, Clara H. (1841-1897) 480
Scott-Gatty, Alfred (1847-1918) 582
Scottish melody 350, 628
Scottish Psalter, 1615 65
Scottish Psalter, 1650 86
Scriven, Joseph M. (1819-1886) 473
Scruggs, Randy (20th c.) 482
Sears, Edmund H. (1810-1876) 191
Seddon, James E. (1915-1983) 541
Seerveld, Calvin (1930-) 168
Selection of Hymns, 1787 411
Shaker melody 118
Shaw, Martin (1875-1958) 30, 161, 564
Sheppard, Franklin L. (1852-1930) 21
Sherwin, William F. (1826-1888) 665
Showalter, Anthony J. (1858-1924) 496
Shurtleff, Ernest W. (1862-1917) 508
Sibelius, Jean (1865-1957) 372, 451
Sicilian melody 208, 669, 748
Sinclair, Jerry (1943-1993) 316
Skillings, Otis (1935-) 395
Skoog, Andrew L. (1856-1934) 449
Sleeth, Natalie (1930-1992) 215, 515, 533
Smallwood, Richard (1948-) 498
Smart, Henry T. (1813-1879) 99, 189, 298, 318, 508, 621
Smith, Alfred Morton (1879-1971) 475
Smith, Deborah D. (1958-) 50
Smith, Elizabeth I. (1817-1898) 77
Smith, Gary Alan (1947-) 676, 689
Smith, H. Percy (1825-1898) 589
Smith, Henry (1952-) 359
Smith, Michael W. (1957-) 42, 50, 664
Smith, Robert (1780-1829) 263
Smith, Samuel F. (1808-1895) 731
Smith, Tedd (1927-) 701
Smith, Walter Chalmers (1824-1908) 48
Smith, William Farley (1941-) 512
Somma, Bob (20th c.) 251
Songs for Liturgy and More Hymns and Spiritual Songs, 1971 586
Sosa, Pablo (1933-) 195
South African 76, 269, 709, 713
Southern Harmony, 1835 257, 351, 532
Spaeth, Harriet Krauth (1845-1925) 190
Spafford, Horatio G. (1828-1888) 428
Spanish 739
Spanish melody 87, 415, 739
Sparrow-Simpson, William J. (1859-1952) 460
St. Francis of Assisi (1182-1226) 23
St. Patrick's Breastplate 425
St. Teresa of Jesus 421
Stainer, John (1840-1901) 229, 460, 681
Stanford, Charles V. (1852-1924) 7, 553
Stanton, Walter K. (1891-1978) 585
Starke, Stephen P. (1955-) 39
Stassen, Linda (1951-) 120
Stead, Louisa M.R. (1850-1917) 442
Stebbins, George C. (1846-1945) 483, 486
Stennett, Samuel (1727-1795) 519
Steurlein, Johann (1546-1613) 702, 724
Stone, Samuel J. (1839-1900) 544
Storm, August Ludvig (1862-1914) 725
Stowe, Everett M. (20th c.) 597
Stralsund Gesangbuch, 1665 71
Strasburger Kirchenamt, 1525 79
Struther, Jan (1901-1953) 469
Sullivan, Arthur S. (1842-1900) 172, 388, 509
Suppe, Gertrude C. (1911-) 347
Supplement to Kentucky Harmony, 1820 382
Supplement to Psalmody 718
Swedish folk tune 456
Swedish melody 83
Swenska Psalmboke, Then, 1697 152
Synesius of Cyrene (ca. 375-430) 386

Tabell, Roland (1934-) 441, 533, 579
Taizé Community 166, 173, 174, 212, 216, 240, 285, 286, 303, 421, 448, 484, 697
Talbot, John Michael (20th c.) 375, 633
Tallis, Thomas (ca. 1505-1585) 715, 717, 747
Tate, Nahum (1652-1715) 228
Taulé, Alberto (1932-) 163
Taylor, Cyril V. (1907-1991) 1, 246, 331, 536, 548, 592
Te Deum 138
Te Deum Laudamus 3
Temple, Sebastian (1928-1998) 587
Teschner, Melchior (1584-1635) 265
Theodulph of Orleans (ca. 760-821) 265
Thesaurus Musicus, 1744 731
Thomas, Eugene (1941-) 43, 80
Thomerson, Kathleen (1934-) 248
Thompson, John (1950-) 482

Thompson, Will L. (1847-1909) 348
Thomson, Mary A. (1834-1923) 565
Threlfall, Jennette (1821-1880) 267
Thring, Godfrey (1823-1903) 317
Thrupp, Dorothy A. (1779-1847) 440
Thum, Pam (1961-) 98
Thuma Mina 713
Tindley, Charles A. (1851-1933) 495
Tisserand, Jean (d. 1494) 313
Tochter Sion, 1741 645
Tomer, William G. (1833-1896) 716
Toolan, Suzanne (1927-) 703
Toplady, Augustus M. (1740-1778) 384
Tourjée, Lizzie S. (1858-1913) 61
Townend, Stuart (20th c.) 105
Towner, Daniel B. (1850-1919) 353, 443
Traditional 732
Tredinnick, Noël (1949-) 101, 279
Trier manuscript (15th c.) 144, 156, 244, 299
Troeger, Thomas H. (1945-) 237, 333
Troutbeck, John (1832-1899) 202
Tullar, Grant C. (1869-1950) 535
Tunney, Dick (1956-) 54
Tunney, Melodie (1960-) 54
Tuttle, Carl (1953-) 266
Tutu, Desmond (1931-) 296

United States Sacred Harmony, The, 1799 625
Utterbach, Clinton (20th c.) 18

Vajda, Jaroslav J. (1919-) 29, 429, 700, 719
Van Dyke, Henry (1852-1933) 59
VanDeVenter, Judson W. (1855-1939) 474
Vaughan Williams, Ralph (1872-1958) 20, 23, 149, 153, 222, 232, 237, 242, 278, 320, 321, 322, 330, 346, 403, 434, 518, 529, 540, 555, 570, 611, 663, 691
Veni Creator Spiritus 325
Virginia Harmony, 1831 422
Von Brethorst, Leona (1923-) 657
Vulpius, Melchior (1560-1615) 307

Wade, John F. (1711-1786) 114, 182
Wade's, John F. *Cantus Diversi*, 1751 114, 182
Walch, James (1837-1901) 565
Walford, William W. (1772-1850) 478
Walker, Christopher (1947-) 736
Walter, William H. (1825-1893) 231, 566, 590
Walton, James G. (1821-1905) 530
Walworth, Clarence A. (1820-1900) 138
Ward, Samuel A. (1848-1903) 727
Ware, Henry Jr. (1794-1843) 607
Warner, Anna B. (1820-1915) 437
Warren, George W. (1828-1902) 728
Warren, Norman (1934-) 445
Watts, Isaac (1674-1748) 31, 63, 67, 79, 84, 179, 258, 261, 263, 341, 390, 510
Weaver, Geoff (1943-) 269
Weaver, John (1937-) 36, 275, 409, 567
Webb, Benjamin (1819-1885) 244
Webb, Charles H. (1933-) 273, 614, 735
Webb, George J. (1803-1887) 513
Webster, Bradford Gray (1898-1991) 582
Weeden, Winfield S. (1847-1908) 474
Weissel, George (1590-1635) 176
Weissrock, John (20th c.) 559
Welsh folk tune 712
Welsh melody 22, 28, 48, 626, 719, 723
Werner's, J.G. *Choralbuch*, 1815 91
Wesley, Charles (1707-1788) 46, 91, 96, 112, 153, 185, 288, 295, 318, 323, 342, 358, 366, 439, 588, 718
Wesley, John (1703-1791) 79
Wesley, Samuel S. (1810-1876) 544, 552
Wesleyan Sacred Harp, 1854 368
Westendorf, Omer (1916-1998) 705, 712
Wetzel, Richard D. (1935-) 194
Weyman's *Melodia Sacra*, 1815 228
Whelpton, George (1847-1930) 490
White, B.F. (1800-1879) 459, 477, 551, 575, 655, 695
Whitfield, Frederick (1829-1904) 109
Whiting, William (1825-1878) 74
Whitney, Maurice C. (1909-1984) 210
Whittier, John G. (1807-1892) 470
Whittle, Daniel W. (1840-1901) 407
Wickham, John (20th c.) 169
Wilbur, Richard (1921-) 206
Wilkinson, Kate B. (1859-1928) 464
Willan, Healey (1880-1968) 325
Willard, Kelly (1956-) 493, 576
Williams', Aaron *New Universal Psalmodist*, 1770 11, 67, 549
Williams', Aaron *Supplement to Psalmody* 718
Williams, Peter (1722-1796) 501
Williams, Robert (1781-1821) 295, 323
Williams, Thomas J. (1869-1944) 398
Williams', Thomas *Psalmodia Evangelica*, 1789 176, 268, 312
Williams, William (1717-1791) 501
Willis, Richard S. (1819-1900) 191
Wilson, David G. (1940-) 13, 279
Wilson, Emily D. (1865-1942) 525
Wilson, Hugh (1764-1824) 263
Wilson, John W. (1905-1992) 133, 594
Wimber, John (1934-1997) 352
Winkworth, Catherine (1827-1878) 14, 71, 155, 164, 176, 230, 429, 431
Witt, Christian F. (1660-1716) 677
Wolcott, Samuel (1813-1886) 561
Wolfe, Lanny (1942-) 131
Wood, Dale (1934-) 89
Wood, James H. (1921-) 459
Woodward, George R. (1848-1934) 156, 244, 299, 308
Woollett, Barbara (1937-) 376, 663
Wordsworth, Christopher (1807-1885) 243, 289
Work, John W. (1872-1925) 218
Wren, Brian (1936-) 36, 55, 58, 104, 133, 139, 147, 165, 208, 246, 293, 312, 355, 364, 516, 584, 585, 594, 601, 611, 612, 678, 704, 706, 717
Wright, Priscilla (1928-) 392
Wyeth's, John *Repository of Sacred Music*, 1813 68, 93, 541, 577
Wyrtzen, Don (1942-) 116

Yamaguchi, Tokuo (20th c.) 597
Yardley, H. Francis (1911-1990) 140
Ylvisaker, John C. (1937-) 680
York, Terry W. (1949-) 137
Young, Carlton R. (1926-) 27, 217, 223, 355, 377, 453, 625, 643, 699
Young, John F. (1820-1885) 186

Zschech, Darlene (1965-) 94, 343
Zulu melody 76
Zundel, John (1815-1882) 358, 581

Topical Index

ADORATION
216 Adoramus Te (We Adore You)
23 All Creatures of Our God and King
106 All Hail the Power of Jesus' Name (CORONATION)
100 All Hail the Power of Jesus' Name (DIADEM)
321 At the Name of Jesus
87 Come, Christians, Join to Sing
148 Come, Thou Almighty King
67 Come, We That Love the Lord
123 Fairest Lord Jesus
143 Father, I Adore You
146 Glorify Thy Name
27 God of Creation, All-Powerful
569 God of Grace and God of Glory
3 God, We Praise You!
138 Holy God, We Praise Your Name
51 How Great Thou Art
85 I Love You, Lord
59 Joyful, Joyful, We Adore Thee
22 Let All Things Now Living
287 Lift High the Cross
358 Love Divine, All Loves Excelling
170 My Soul Proclaims with Wonder
8 New Songs of Celebration
14 Now Thank We All Our God
114 O Come, Let Us Adore Him
17 Praise the Lord! O Heavens, Adore Him
46 Praise the Lord Who Reigns Above
71 Praise to the Lord, the Almighty
342 Rejoice, the Lord Is King!
56 Sing Praise to God Who Reigns Above
126 Thou Art Worthy
110 We Come, O Christ, to You
726 We Praise You, O God
337 We Will Glorify
7 When in Our Music God Is Glorified
111 When Morning Gilds the Skies
116 Worthy Is the Lamb
112 You Servants of God

ADVENT
160 Awake! Awake, and Greet the New Morn
158 Blessed Be the God of Israel
202 Break Forth, O Beauteous Heavenly Light
153 Come, Thou Long-Expected Jesus
155 Comfort, Comfort Now My People
172 For Ages Women Hoped and Prayed
225 I Wonder as I Wander
170 My Soul Proclaims with Wonder
154 O Come, O Come, Emmanuel
208 Oh, How Joyfully
156 On Jordan's Bank the Baptist's Cry
161 People, Look East
223 Star-Child
41 Tell Out, My Soul
164 Wake, Awake, for Night Is Flying
175 We Light the Advent Candles

ADVERSITY
421 Nothing Can Trouble (Nada te Turbe)
638 O Christ, the Healer, We Have Come

AGING
617 A Place at the Table
680 Borning Cry
518 Give Thanks for Life
409 God of Our Life
597 Here, O Lord, Your Servants Gather
608 Lord of Our Growing Years
433 O Christ the Same
503 O God, Your Constant Care and Love
500 Precious Lord, Take My Hand
495 Stand by Me
558 The World Is Full of Stories
632 When Aimless Violence Takes Those We Love

ALL SAINTS' DAY
39 All You Works of God, Bless the Lord!
306 Alleluia! Jesus Is Risen!
517 Christ the Victorious
530 Faith of Our Fathers
497 Find Us Faithful
529 For All the Saints
518 Give Thanks for Life
138 Holy God, We Praise Your Name
136 Holy, Holy, Holy! Lord God Almighty!
526 How Blest Are They
434 If Christ Had Not Been Raised from Death
524 Lord of the Living
531 Rejoice in God's Saints
113 Rejoice, Ye Pure in Heart
590 Rise Up, O Saints of God!
522 Shall We Gather at the River
542 They Did Not Build in Vain

ANNIVERSARIES
609 Come to a Wedding
579 This Is a Time to Remember

ARTS & SCIENCES
643 Colorful Creator
723 For the Fruit of All Creation
641 For the Music of Creation
37 God in His Love for Us
644 God, Who Stretched the Spangled Heavens
678 In Water We Grow
599 Shadow and Substance
577 Sing a New Church
141 Sing of a God in Majestic Divinity
36 Thank You, God, for Water, Soil, and Air
413 When Our Confidence Is Shaken
645 When the Morning Stars Together

ASCENSION
322 A Hymn of Glory Let Us Sing!
289 Alleluia, Alleluia! Hearts to Heaven
320 Alleluia, Sing to Jesus!
105 Beautiful Savior
324 Christ High Ascended
335 Christ the Eternal Lord
517 Christ the Victorious
336 Christ Triumphant, Ever Reigning
91 Christ, Whose Glory Fills the Skies
119 Come into His Presence
317 Crown Him with Many Crowns
307 Good Christians All, Rejoice
323 Hail the Day That Sees Him Rise
301 Hallelujah! What a Savior!
122 He Is Exalted
43 Majesty
150 My Lord of Light
244 O Love, How Deep, How Broad
339 The Head That Once Was Crowned

ASPIRATION
460 All for Jesus!
471 As the Deer
502 Be Thou My Vision
461 Breathe on Me, Breath of God
418 Eternal Light, Shine in My Heart
499 He Leadeth Me
476 I Need Thee Every Hour
474 I Surrender All
248 I Want to Walk as a Child of the Light
345 Jesus Calls Us o'er the Tumult
431 Jesus, Priceless Treasure
504 Just a Closer Walk with Thee
465 Lord, Be Glorified
457 Lord, I Want to Be a Christian
469 Lord of All Hopefulness
328 O Breath of Life
446 O Love That Will Not Let Me Go
589 O Master, Let Me Walk with Thee
480 Open My Eyes, That I May See
132 Spirit of God, Descend upon My Heart
492 Spirit of the Living God
343 The Potter's Hand
467 The Power of Your Love
133 There's a Spirit in the Air
333 Wind Who Makes All Winds That Blow

ASSURANCE
619 Because He Died and Is Risen
426 Blessed Assurance
425 Christ Beside Me
449 Day by Day
411 How Firm a Foundation
414 I Know That My Redeemer Lives!

441 Trust in the Lord
428 When Peace Like a River

ATONEMENT
258 At the Cross
255 Beneath the Cross of Jesus
317 Crown Him with Many Crowns
301 Hallelujah! What a Savior!
51 How Great Thou Art
251 I Come to the Cross
253 Lead Me to Calvary
150 My Lord of Light
277 My Savior's Love
368 O Happy Day
284 O Sacred Head, Now Wounded
384 Rock of Ages
260 The Old Rugged Cross
66 To God Be the Glory
110 We Come, O Christ, to You
257 What Wondrous Love Is This

BAPTISM
231 Arise, Your Light Is Come!!
679 Baptized in Water
680 Borning Cry
677 Child of Blessing, Child of Promise
676 Come, Be Baptized
649 Gather Us In
553 Go to the World!
678 In Water We Grow
683 Little One, Born to Bring
681 Lord, We Bring to You Our Children
135 Loving Spirit
140 Praise and Thanksgiving Be to God
577 Sing a New Church
682 The Fruit of Love
456 Thy Holy Wings
360 What the Lord Has Done in Me
241 When Jesus Came to Jordan
239 When John Baptized by Jordan's River

CANON/ROUND
747 Go with Us, Lord
735 Hallelujah (Heleluyan)
338 King of Kings
650 Rejoice in the Lord Always
714 Shalom, My Friends
427 You Are My All in All

CARE OF CREATION
28 For Beauty of Meadows
40 For the Beauty of the Earth
723 For the Fruit of All Creation
37 God in His Love for Us
36 Thank You, God, for Water, Soil, and Air
21 This Is My Father's World
38 Touch the Earth Lightly
583 You Call Us, Lord

CHILD DEDICATION
680 Borning Cry
83 Children of the Heavenly Father
80 He's Got the Whole World in His Hands
683 Little One, Born to Bring
681 Lord, We Bring to You Our Children
135 Loving Spirit
682 The Fruit of Love
456 Thy Holy Wings

CHILDREN
680 Borning Cry
677 Child of Blessing, Child of Promise
83 Children of the Heavenly Father
719 Go, My Children, with My Blessing
1 God Is Here!
607 Happy the Home When God Is There
267 Hosanna, Loud Hosanna
437 Jesus Loves Me
162 like a child
489 Lord, Listen to Your Children Praying
681 Lord, We Bring to You Our Children
629 Strong, Gentle Children
682 The Fruit of Love
456 Thy Holy Wings
567 With Welcome Heart We Greet You, Lord

CHRIST THE KING
322 A Hymn of Glory Let Us Sing!
92 All Hail King Jesus
106 All Hail the Power of Jesus' Name (CORONATION)
100 All Hail the Power of Jesus' Name (DIADEM)
289 Alleluia, Alleluia! Hearts to Heaven
320 Alleluia, Sing to Jesus!
321 At the Name of Jesus
324 Christ High-Ascended
335 Christ the Eternal Lord
517 Christ the Victorious
336 Christ Triumphant, Ever Reigning
317 Crown Him with Many Crowns
123 Fairest Lord Jesus
305 He Is Lord
62 In the Lord Alone
341 Jesus Shall Reign
338 King of Kings
88 Lord, I Lift Your Name on High
43 Majesty
101 Name of All Majesty
400 Not for Tongues of Heaven's Angels
433 O Christ the Same
656 Open the Eyes of My Heart
95 Praise Him! Praise Him!
342 Rejoice, the Lord Is King!
113 Rejoice, Ye Pure in Heart
523 Soon and Very Soon
339 The Head That Once Was Crowned
159 The King of Glory Comes
337 We Will Glorify

CHRISTIAN COMMUNITY
393 Blest Be the Tie That Binds
546 Built on the Rock
571 Christ, You Call Us All to Service
615 Community of Christ

CHRISTMAS
206 A Stable Lamp Is Lighted
216 Adoramus Te (We Adore You)
163 All Earth Is Hopeful (Toda la Tierra)
249 Amen, Amen
189 Angels, from the Realms of Glory
188 Angels We Have Heard on High
236 As with Gladness
160 Awake! Awake, and Greet the New Morn
205 Away in a Manger (Kirkpatrick)
203 Away in a Manger (Murray)
194 Born in the Night, Mary's Child
235 Brightest and Best of the Stars
199 Carol at the Manger
197 Come and Hear the Joyful Singing
172 For Ages Women Hoped and Prayed
238 From a Distant Home (De Tierra Lejana Venimos)
240 Gloria, Gloria
195 Gloria, Gloria, Gloria
218 Go, Tell It on the Mountain
226 God's Love Made Visible!
198 Good Christian Friends, Rejoice
185 Hark! The Herald Angels Sing
201 He Is Born
104 Hidden Christ, Alive for Ever
225 I Wonder as I Wander
196 In the Bleak Midwinter
221 Infant Holy, Infant Lowly
191 It Came upon the Midnight Clear
219 Jesus, Oh, What a Wonderful Child
179 Joy to the World!
232 Let All Mortal Flesh Keep Silence
162 like a child
190 Lo, How a Rose E'er Blooming
167 Long Ago, Prophets Knew
118 Lord of the Dance
210 Love Came Down at Christmas
192 Mary, Did You Know?
220 Mary Had a Baby
97 Meekness and Majesty
170 My Soul Proclaims with Wonder
217 No Obvious Angels
182 O Come, All Ye Faithful
114 O Come, Let Us Adore Him
187 O Holy Night
180 O Little Town of Bethlehem
242 O Sing a Song of Bethlehem
181 Of the Father's Love Begotten
208 Oh, How Joyfully

207 Oh, Sleep Now, Holy Baby (A La Ru)
222 On Christmas Night All Christians Sing
183 Once in Royal David's City
212 Raise a Song of Gladness (Jubilate Deo)
209 Rise Up, Shepherd, and Follow
227 See Him Lying on a Bed of Straw
186 Silent Night! Holy Night!
193 Sing We Now of Christmas
223 Star-Child
214 Still, Still, Still
211 That Boy-Child of Mary
169 The Angel Gabriel from Heaven Came
224 The Birthday of a King
229 The First Noel
237 The Hands That First Held Mary's Child
171 To a Maid Whose Name Was Mary
213 'Twas in the Moon of Wintertime
540 Two Thousand Years Since Bethlehem
215 Were You There on That Christmas Night
184 What Child Is This
165 When God Is a Child
200 While by the Sheep
228 While Shepherds Watched Their Flocks

CHURCH - FELLOWSHIP
393 Blest Be the Tie That Binds
443 Trust and Obey
702 We Come as Guests Invited

CHURCH - FINAL VICTORY
106 All Hail the Power of Jesus' Name (CORONATION)
100 All Hail the Power of Jesus' Name (DIADEM)
447 Because He Lives
548 Come, Great God of All the Ages
529 For All the Saints
569 God of Grace and God of Glory
515 Hymn of Promise
79 I'll Praise My Maker While I've Breath
445 In the Day of Need
90 Jesus! What a Friend for Sinners!
508 Lead On, O King Eternal
519 On Jordan's Stormy Banks I Stand
523 Soon and Very Soon
544 The Church's One Foundation
579 This Is a Time to Remember
525 When We All Get to Heaven
622 When Will People Cease Their Fighting?

CHURCH - HERITAGE
546 Built on the Rock
541 Church of God, Elect and Glorious
27 God of Creation, All-Powerful
604 Great God, as We Are Gathering
332 Let Every Christian Pray
577 Sing a New Church
544 The Church's One Foundation
682 The Fruit of Love
580 We Are Called to Be God's People
547 We Are God's People
555 When the Church of Jesus

CHURCH - LIFE TOGETHER
695 As We Gather at Your Table
606 As Your Family, Lord, Meet Us Here
393 Blest Be the Tie That Binds
581 Called as Partners in Christ's Service
696 Come, Share the Lord
392 Fear Not, Rejoice and Be Glad
716 God Be with You
409 God of Our Life
604 Great God, as We Are Gathering
596 Help Us Accept Each Other
559 Here I Am, Lord
327 Like the Murmur of the Dove's Song
400 Not for Tongues of Heaven's Angels
689 One Bread, One Body
682 The Fruit of Love
701 There's a Quiet Understanding
595 They'll Know We Are Christians
580 We Are Called to Be God's People
547 We Are God's People
550 We Are the Church
647 We Have Come to Join in Worship
602 Who Is My Mother, Who Is My Brother?
691 With the Body That Was Broken

CHURCH – MINISTRY
551 As a Fire Is Meant for Burning
581 Called as Partners in Christ's Service
561 Christ for the World! We Sing
584 Come, Celebrate the Call of God
615 Community of Christ
475 Eternal Spirit of the Living Christ
640 From Miles Around
708 Go Forth for God
149 God the Spirit, Guide and Guardian
573 How Clear Is Our Vocation, Lord
549 I Love Your Kingdom, Lord
634 Jesus' Hands Were Kind Hands
592 Lord, You Give the Great Commission
576 Make Me a Servant
565 O Christians, Haste
509 Onward, Christian Soldiers
586 Our Cities Cry to You, O God
531 Rejoice in God's Saints
462 Renew Your Church
590 Rise Up, O Saints of God!
455 Take Thou Our Minds, Dear Lord
41 Tell Out, My Soul
623 The Church of Christ in Every Age
350 The Summons
552 We All Are One in Mission
580 We Are Called to Be God's People
547 We Are God's People
594 We Are Your People
704 We Meet as Friends at Table
555 When the Church of Jesus
591 Where Cross the Crowded Ways of Life
391 Will You Let Me Be Your Servant
583 You Call Us, Lord

CHURCH - NATURE
546 Built on the Rock
541 Church of God, Elect and Glorious
569 God of Grace and God of Glory
549 I Love Your Kingdom, Lord
603 In Christ There Is No East or West (Oxenham)
600 In Christ There Is No East or West (Perry)
332 Let Every Christian Pray
287 Lift High the Cross
576 Make Me a Servant
670 O Word of God Incarnate
544 The Church's One Foundation
579 This Is a Time to Remember
580 We Are Called to Be God's People
547 We Are God's People
555 When the Church of Jesus

CHURCH - RENEWAL
1 God Is Here!
409 God of Our Life
669 Jesus, Come, for We Invite You
465 Lord, Be Glorified
328 O Breath of Life
371 Our Father, We Have Wandered
462 Renew Your Church
463 Revive Us Again
385 Search Me, O God
492 Spirit of the Living God
134 Sweet, Sweet Spirit
555 When the Church of Jesus
333 Wind Who Makes All Winds That Blow

CHURCH - UNITY
551 As a Fire Is Meant for Burning
611 As Man and Woman We Were Made
695 As We Gather at Your Table
393 Blest Be the Tie That Binds
581 Called as Partners in Christ's Service
276 Christ, Let Us Come with You
696 Come, Share the Lord
331 Filled with the Spirit's Power
572 God, Whose Giving Knows No Ending

604 Great God, as We Are Gathering
596 Help Us Accept Each Other
597 Here, O Lord, Your Servants Gather
706 I Come with Joy
549 I Love Your Kingdom, Lord
603 In Christ There Is No East or West (Oxenham)
600 In Christ There Is No East or West (Perry)
327 Like the Murmur of the Dove's Song
638 O Christ, the Healer, We Have Come
689 One Bread, One Body
124 Open Your Hearts
389 Put Peace into Each Other's Hands
395 The Bond of Love
544 The Church's One Foundation
701 There's a Quiet Understanding
595 They'll Know We Are Christians
552 We All Are One in Mission
580 We Are Called to Be God's People
547 We Are God's People
594 We Are Your People
704 We Meet as Friends at Table
602 Who Is My Mother, Who Is My Brother?

CHURCH - WORSHIP

646 As We Gather
40 For the Beauty of the Earth
649 Gather Us In
1 God Is Here!
2 O Worship the King
310 Thine Is the Glory
7 When in Our Music God Is Glorified
555 When the Church of Jesus

CITIES

625 All Who Love and Serve Your City
727 America, the Beautiful
644 God, Who Stretched the Spangled Heavens
627 Now It Is Evening
582 O Jesus Christ, May Grateful Hymns Be Rising
620 O Lord, You Gave Your Servant John
586 Our Cities Cry to You, O God
591 Where Cross the Crowded Ways of Life

COMFORT

521 Abide with Me
505 All the Way My Savior Leads Me
275 An Upper Room Did Our Lord Prepare
635 And Jesus Said
611 As Man and Woman We Were Made
432 As Water to the Thirsty
430 Be Not Afraid
451 Be Still, My Soul
666 Blest Are They
393 Blest Be the Tie That Binds
693 Bread of the World
380 Cast Thy Burden upon the Lord
325 Come, Holy Spirit, Our Souls Inspire
449 Day by Day
418 Eternal Light, Shine in My Heart
436 Grace Alone
516 Grief of Ending, Wordless Sorrow
499 He Leadeth Me
445 In the Day of Need
439 Jesus, Lover of My Soul
90 Jesus! What a Friend for Sinners!
683 Little One, Born to Bring
524 Lord of the Living
433 O Christ the Same
589 O Master, Let Me Walk with Thee
438 On Eagle's Wings
725 Thanks to God for My Redeemer
443 Trust and Obey
473 What a Friend We Have in Jesus
632 When Aimless Violence Takes Those We Love
428 When Peace Like a River
624 When the Poor Ones (Cuando el Pobre)
396 Where the Spirit of the Lord Is

COMMISSIONING

584 Come, Celebrate the Call of God
497 Find Us Faithful
592 Lord, You Give the Great Commission
578 So Send I You
492 Spirit of the Living God

COMMITMENT

588 A Charge to Keep I Have
460 All for Jesus!
510 Am I a Soldier of the Cross
459 Come, All Christians, Be Committed
684 For the Life That You Have Given
394 God of All Time
559 Here I Am, Lord
408 I Am Thine, O Lord
251 I Come to the Cross
344 I Have Decided to Follow Jesus
474 I Surrender All
574 I'm Gonna Live So God Can Use Me
357 Knowing You
253 Lead Me to Calvary
614 Let There Be Peace on Earth
457 Lord, I Want to Be a Christian
464 May the Mind of Christ, My Savior
468 My Jesus, I Love Thee
492 Spirit of the Living God
466 Take My Life and Let It Be
455 Take Thou Our Minds, Dear Lord
343 The Potter's Hand
467 The Power of Your Love
350 The Summons
443 Trust and Obey
580 We Are Called to Be God's People
110 We Come, O Christ, to You
566 Your Servant Comes This Hour

COMMUNION

617 A Place at the Table
275 An Upper Room Did Our Lord Prepare
274 An Upper Room with Evening Lamps
695 As We Gather at Your Table
606 As Your Family, Lord, Meet Us Here
693 Bread of the World
665 Break Now the Bread of Life
276 Christ, Let Us Come with You
655 Come Away from Rush and Hurry
694 Come, Let Us Eat
403 Come, My Way, My Truth, My Life
696 Come, Share the Lord
697 Eat This Bread
692 Eat This Bread and Never Hunger
649 Gather Us In
1 God Is Here!
404 Hope of the World
703 I Am the Bread of Life
706 I Come with Joy
669 Jesus, Come, for We Invite You
699 Let Us Break Bread Together
715 Now Let Us from This Table Rise
700 Now the Silence
689 One Bread, One Body
389 Put Peace into Each Other's Hands
577 Sing a New Church
133 There's a Spirit in the Air
315 This Is the Feast of Victory
702 We Come as Guests Invited
704 We Meet as Friends at Table
690 We Remember You
707 We Thank You, God, for Feeding Us
602 Who Is My Mother, Who Is My Brother?
691 With the Body That Was Broken
705 You Satisfy the Hungry Heart

COMPASSION

570 As Saints of Old Their First-fruits Brought
615 Community of Christ
630 Healer of Our Every Ill
372 I Then Shall Live
576 Make Me a Servant
400 Not for Tongues of Heaven's Angels
624 When the Poor Ones (Cuando el Pobre)

CONFESSION

373 Change My Heart, O God

68 Come, Thou Fount of Every Blessing
378 Create in Me a Clean Heart, O God
470 Dear Lord and Father of Mankind
569 God of Grace and God of Glory
416 God! When Human Bonds Are Broken
353 Grace Greater than Our Sin
486 Have Thine Own Way, Lord!
636 Heal Me, Hands of Jesus
370 Healing Grace
476 I Need Thee Every Hour
285 Jesus, Remember Me
504 Just a Closer Walk with Thee
354 Just As I Am
379 Kyrie
377 Kyrie Eleison (Ore Poriaju Vereko)
386 Lord Jesus, Think on Me
419 My Faith Looks Up to Thee
328 O Breath of Life
284 O Sacred Head, Now Wounded
371 Our Father, We Have Wandered
374 Refiner's Fire
385 Search Me, O God
495 Stand by Me
467 The Power of Your Love
628 We Cannot Measure How You Heal
555 When the Church of Jesus

CONFIRMATION
231 Arise, Your Light Is Come!!
426 Blessed Assurance
680 Borning Cry
497 Find Us Faithful
559 Here I Am, Lord
675 I Believe in Jesus
589 O Master, Let Me Walk with Thee

CONFLICT - SPIRITUAL
507 A Mighty Fortress Is Our God
510 Am I a Soldier of the Cross
514 Be Strong in the Lord
529 For All the Saints
569 God of Grace and God of Glory
637 His Strength Is Perfect
506 I Want Jesus to Walk with Me
504 Just a Closer Walk with Thee
252 Lord, Who Throughout These Forty Days
458 O Jesus, I Have Promised
509 Onward, Christian Soldiers
578 So Send I You
513 Stand Up, Stand Up for Jesus
511 The Battle Belongs to the Lord
544 The Church's One Foundation
81 We Gather Together
726 We Praise You, O God

CONSECRATION
263 Alas! and Did My Savior Bleed
258 At the Cross
677 Child of Blessing, Child of Promise

459 Come, All Christians, Be Committed
655 Come Away from Rush and Hurry
559 Here I Am, Lord
404 Hope of the World
408 I Am Thine, O Lord
344 I Have Decided to Follow Jesus
474 I Surrender All
357 Knowing You
70 Lord, for the Years
446 O Love That Will Not Let Me Go
482 Sanctuary
385 Search Me, O God
713 Send Me, Jesus
492 Spirit of the Living God
466 Take My Life and Let It Be
455 Take Thou Our Minds, Dear Lord
605 The Family Prayer Song
343 The Potter's Hand
350 The Summons
443 Trust and Obey
580 We Are Called to Be God's People
685 What Gift Can We Bring
261 When I Survey the Wondrous Cross
566 Your Servant Comes This Hour

COURAGE
510 Am I a Soldier of the Cross
514 Be Strong in the Lord
529 For All the Saints
569 God of Grace and God of Glory
531 Rejoice in God's Saints
711 Savior, Again to Your Dear Name
351 "Take Up Your Cross," the Savior Said
73 The Lord My Shepherd Guards Me Well
133 There's a Spirit in the Air
166 Wait for the Lord
580 We Are Called to Be God's People
632 When Aimless Violence Takes Those We Love

CREATION
23 All Creatures of Our God and King
30 All Things Bright and Beautiful
39 All You Works of God, Bless the Lord!
9 Come, Let Us Praise the Lord
32 Creating God, Your Fingers Trace
642 Earth and All Stars
123 Fairest Lord Jesus
28 For Beauty of Meadows
40 For the Beauty of the Earth
723 For the Fruit of All Creation
641 For the Music of Creation
37 God in His Love for Us
27 God of Creation, All-Powerful
29 God of the Sparrow
644 God, Who Stretched the Spangled Heavens
24 God, You Spin the Whirling Planets

55 Great God, Your Love Has Called Us Here
80 He's Got the Whole World in His Hands
559 Here I Am, Lord
51 How Great Thou Art
31 I Sing the Almighty Power of God
59 Joyful, Joyful, We Adore Thee
25 Let All Creation Bless the Lord
22 Let All Things Now Living
6 Let the Whole Creation Cry
33 Let's Sing unto the Lord (Cantemos al Señor)
722 Praise and Thanksgiving
17 Praise the Lord! O Heavens, Adore Him
46 Praise the Lord Who Reigns Above
71 Praise to the Lord, the Almighty
599 Shadow and Substance
724 Sing to the Lord of Harvest
128 Spirit, Working in Creation
36 Thank You, God, for Water, Soil, and Air
710 The Trees of the Field
21 This Is My Father's World
720 With Grateful Heart I Thank You, Lord

CROSS
259 Amazing Love
451 Be Still, My Soul
272 Go to Dark Gethsemane
344 I Have Decided to Follow Jesus
264 In the Cross of Christ I Glory
253 Lead Me to Calvary
479 Near the Cross
446 O Love That Will Not Let Me Go
531 Rejoice in God's Saints
578 So Send I You
351 "Take Up Your Cross," the Savior Said
250 Throughout These Lenten Days and Nights

DEDICATION - BUILDING
548 Come, Great God of All the Ages
1 God Is Here!
542 They Did Not Build in Vain
579 This Is a Time to Remember

DEDICATION - INSTRUMENTS
7 When in Our Music God Is Glorified
645 When the Morning Stars Together

DISCIPLESHIP
615 Community of Christ
344 I Have Decided to Follow Jesus
345 Jesus Calls Us o'er the Tumult
592 Lord, You Give the Great Commission
347 Lord, You Have Come to the Lakeshore (Tú Has Venido a la Orilla)

589 O Master, Let Me Walk with Thee
349 Seek Ye First
351 "Take Up Your Cross," the Savior Said
682 The Fruit of Love

EASTER
585 A Prophet-Woman Broke a Jar
291 Alleluia No. 1
289 Alleluia, Alleluia! Hearts to Heaven
306 Alleluia! Jesus Is Risen!
249 Amen, Amen
105 Beautiful Savior
619 Because He Died and Is Risen
447 Because He Lives
292 Because You Live, O Christ
294 Christ Arose!
324 Christ High-Ascended
312 Christ Is Alive!
369 Christ Is God's Never Changing 'Yes!'
293 Christ Is Risen! Shout Hosanna!
309 Christ the Lord Is Risen!
288 Christ the Lord Is Risen Today
336 Christ Triumphant, Ever Reigning
314 Easter Song
475 Eternal Spirit of the Living Christ
307 Good Christians All, Rejoice
296 Goodness Is Stronger than Evil
305 He Is Lord
302 He Lives
297 His Battle Ended There
414 I Know That My Redeemer Lives!
653 I Will Call upon the Lord
434 If Christ Had Not Been Raised from Death
300 In the Garden
295 Jesus Christ Is Risen Today
254 Jesus Walked This Lonesome Valley
303 Jubilate Deo (In the Lord Rejoicing!)
118 Lord of the Dance
311 Now the Green Blade Rises
313 O Sons and Daughters, Let Us Sing!
304 Shout for Joy, Loud and Long
141 Sing of a God in Majestic Divinity
299 That Easter Day with Joy Was Bright
298 The Day of Resurrection!
290 The Strife Is O'er
310 Thine Is the Glory
355 This Is a Day of New Beginnings
308 This Joyful Eastertide
540 Two Thousand Years Since Bethlehem
364 Woman in the Night

ENCOURAGEMENT
432 As Water to the Thirsty
160 Awake! Awake, and Greet the New Morn
666 Blest Are They
75 By Gracious Powers
418 Eternal Light, Shine in My Heart
708 Go Forth for God
716 God Be with You
445 In the Day of Need
496 Leaning on the Everlasting Arms
524 Lord of the Living
400 Not for Tongues of Heaven's Angels
438 On Eagle's Wings
473 What a Friend We Have in Jesus
428 When Peace Like a River
391 Will You Let Me Be Your Servant

EPIPHANY
189 Angels, from the Realms of Glory
188 Angels We Have Heard on High
236 As with Gladness
235 Brightest and Best of the Stars
238 From a Distant Home (De Tierra Lejana Venimos)
226 God's Love Made Visible!
104 Hidden Christ, Alive for Ever
244 O Love, How Deep, How Broad
156 On Jordan's Bank the Baptist's Cry
247 Sing of God Made Manifest
243 Songs of Thankfulness and Praise
213 'Twas in the Moon of Wintertime
233 We Three Kings of Orient Are
165 When God Is a Child
234 Wise Men, They Came to Look for Wisdom

ETERNAL LIFE
507 A Mighty Fortress Is Our God
521 Abide with Me
451 Be Still, My Soul
447 Because He Lives
461 Breathe on Me, Breath of God
453 Christ Be My Leader
517 Christ the Victorious
148 Come, Thou Almighty King
418 Eternal Light, Shine in My Heart
535 Face to Face
529 For All the Saints
526 How Blest Are They
703 I Am the Bread of Life
79 I'll Praise My Maker While I've Breath
587 Make Me a Channel of Your Peace
26 Many and Great
446 O Love That Will Not Let Me Go
519 On Jordan's Stormy Banks I Stand
523 Soon and Very Soon
298 The Day of Resurrection!

EVANGELISM
588 A Charge to Keep I Have
581 Called as Partners in Christ's Service
561 Christ for the World! We Sing
459 Come, All Christians, Be Committed
601 Dear Christ, Uplifted from the Earth
692 Eat This Bread and Never Hunger
382 "Forgive Our Sins as We Forgive"
218 Go, Tell It on the Mountain
564 God Is Working His Purpose Out
572 God, Whose Giving Knows No Ending
436 Grace Alone
559 Here I Am, Lord
560 I Love to Tell the Story
356 I Will Sing of My Redeemer
698 Let Us Talents and Tongues Employ
593 Lord, Speak to Me
592 Lord, You Give the Great Commission
587 Make Me a Channel of Your Peace
586 Our Cities Cry to You, O God
557 Pass It On
568 People Need the Lord
722 Praise and Thanksgiving
713 Send Me, Jesus
712 Sent Forth by God's Blessing
319 Shine, Jesus, Shine
133 There's a Spirit in the Air
595 They'll Know We Are Christians
66 To God Be the Glory
552 We All Are One in Mission
550 We Are the Church
554 We Have Heard the Joyful Sound
390 We're Marching to Zion
562 We've a Story to Tell to the Nations
112 You Servants of God

EVENING
521 Abide with Me
502 Be Thou My Vision
453 Christ Be My Leader
425 Christ Beside Me
477 Come and Find the Quiet Center
412 He Comes to Us As One Unknown
633 Healer of My Soul
488 I Lift My Eyes to the Quiet Hills
20 Like a Mighty River Flowing
469 Lord of All Hopefulness
627 Now It Is Evening
107 O Light Whose Splendor Thrills
456 Thy Holy Wings

FAITH
493 Cares Chorus
530 Faith of Our Fathers
596 Help Us Accept Each Other
407 I Know Whom I Have Believed
496 Leaning on the Everlasting Arms
406 My Faith Has Found a Resting Place
419 My Faith Looks Up to Thee
400 Not for Tongues of Heaven's Angels
417 Not with Naked Eye
64 O God Beyond All Praising

FAITHFULNESS
606 As Your Family, Lord, Meet Us Here
497 Find Us Faithful
518 Give Thanks for Life
416 God! When Human Bonds Are Broken
72 Great Is Thy Faithfulness
748 Lord, Dismiss Us with Your Blessing
371 Our Father, We Have Wandered

FELLOWSHIP
393 Blest Be the Tie That Binds
696 Come, Share the Lord
603 In Christ There Is No East or West (Oxenham)
600 In Christ There Is No East or West (Perry)
544 The Church's One Foundation
701 There's a Quiet Understanding
443 Trust and Obey
580 We Are Called to Be God's People
702 We Come as Guests Invited

FOLLOWING & SERVING
588 A Charge to Keep I Have
460 All for Jesus!
661 All People That on Earth Do Dwell
625 All Who Love and Serve Your City
453 Christ Be My Leader
276 Christ, Let Us Come with You
571 Christ, You Call Us All to Service
459 Come, All Christians, Be Committed
584 Come, Celebrate the Call of God
615 Community of Christ
475 Eternal Spirit of the Living Christ
497 Find Us Faithful
684 For the Life That You Have Given
556 Go Forth in His Name
553 Go to the World!
569 God of Grace and God of Glory
644 God, Who Stretched the Spangled Heavens
499 He Leadeth Me
596 Help Us Accept Each Other
344 I Have Decided to Follow Jesus
372 I Then Shall Live
574 I'm Gonna Live So God Can Use Me
345 Jesus Calls Us o'er the Tumult
498 Lead Me, Guide Me
671 Lord, We Hear Your Word
592 Lord, You Give the Great Commission
347 Lord, You Have Come to the Lakeshore (Tú Has Venido a la Orilla)
587 Make Me a Channel of Your Peace
576 Make Me a Servant
64 O God Beyond All Praising
388 O God in Whom All Life Begins
458 O Jesus, I Have Promised
589 O Master, Let Me Walk with Thee
440 Savior, Like a Shepherd Lead Us
494 Step by Step
351 "Take Up Your Cross," the Savior Said
623 The Church of Christ in Every Age
350 The Summons
686 What Does the Lord Require
624 When the Poor Ones (Cuando el Pobre)
591 Where Cross the Crowded Ways of Life
391 Will You Let Me Be Your Servant
583 You Call Us, Lord
112 You Servants of God
648 You're Worthy of My Praise

FORGIVENESS
259 Amazing Love
447 Because He Lives
373 Change My Heart, O God
696 Come, Share the Lord
378 Create in Me a Clean Heart, O God
475 Eternal Spirit of the Living Christ
382 "Forgive Our Sins as We Forgive"
416 God! When Human Bonds Are Broken
353 Grace Greater than Our Sin
370 Healing Grace
596 Help Us Accept Each Other
376 How Long, O Lord
372 I Then Shall Live
354 Just As I Am
386 Lord Jesus, Think on Me
587 Make Me a Channel of Your Peace
419 My Faith Looks Up to Thee
277 My Savior's Love
374 Refiner's Fire
385 Search Me, O God
495 Stand by Me

FREEDOM & LIBERATION
366 And Can It Be
158 Blessed Be the God of Israel
621 For the Healing of the Nations
618 Go Down, Moses
533 Joy in the Morning
729 Lift Every Voice and Sing
731 My Country, 'Tis of Thee
512 We Shall Overcome
360 What the Lord Has Done in Me
257 What Wondrous Love Is This
555 When the Church of Jesus
622 When Will People Cease Their Fighting?
591 Where Cross the Crowded Ways of Life
234 Wise Men, They Came to Look for Wisdom
364 Woman in the Night
362 Wonderful Grace of Jesus

FUNERAL & MEMORIAL
521 Abide with Me
505 All the Way My Savior Leads Me
451 Be Still, My Soul
83 Children of the Heavenly Father
453 Christ Be My Leader
535 Face to Face
529 For All the Saints
518 Give Thanks for Life
409 God of Our Life
516 Grief of Ending, Wordless Sorrow
526 How Blest Are They
515 Hymn of Promise
434 If Christ Had Not Been Raised from Death
524 Lord of the Living
500 Precious Lord, Take My Hand
384 Rock of Ages
522 Shall We Gather at the River
495 Stand by Me
520 Swing Low, Sweet Chariot
725 Thanks to God for My Redeemer
632 When Aimless Violence Takes Those We Love
428 When Peace Like a River
415 When We Are Living (Pues Si Vivimos)

GATHERING
661 All People That on Earth Do Dwell
646 As We Gather
606 As Your Family, Lord, Meet Us Here
655 Come Away from Rush and Hurry
87 Come, Christians, Join to Sing
119 Come into His Presence
9 Come, Let Us Praise the Lord
67 Come, We That Love the Lord
649 Gather Us In
1 God Is Here!
604 Great God, as We Are Gathering
55 Great God, Your Love Has Called Us Here
597 Here, O Lord, Your Servants Gather
545 How Lovely, Lord, How Lovely
659 Jesus, We Are Here (Jesu Tawa Pano)
332 Let Every Christian Pray
33 Let's Sing unto the Lord (Cantemos al Señor)
388 O God in Whom All Life Begins
71 Praise to the Lord, the Almighty
128 Spirit, Working in Creation
134 Sweet, Sweet Spirit
387 The Lord Is in His Holy Temple
701 There's a Quiet Understanding
355 This Is a Day of New Beginnings
652 This Is the Day
651 We Bring the Sacrifice of Praise
81 We Gather Together
647 We Have Come to Join in Worship
685 What Gift Can We Bring

111 When Morning Gilds the Skies
567 With Welcome Heart We Greet You, Lord
613 Your Love, O God, Has Called Us

GOD - CREATOR
23 All Creatures of Our God and King
30 All Things Bright and Beautiful
12 Be Exalted, O God
643 Colorful Creator
9 Come, Let Us Praise the Lord
32 Creating God, Your Fingers Trace
642 Earth and All Stars
74 Eternal Father, Strong to Save
123 Fairest Lord Jesus
28 For Beauty of Meadows
723 For the Fruit of All Creation
63 Give to Our God Immortal Praise
145 Glory Be to God, Creator
37 God in His Love for Us
139 God Is One, Unique and Holy
27 God of Creation, All-Powerful
78 God of the Ages, History's Maker
728 God of the Ages, Whose Almighty Hand
29 God of the Sparrow
149 God the Spirit, Guide and Guardian
3 God, We Praise You!
644 God, Who Stretched the Spangled Heavens
24 God, You Spin the Whirling Planets
80 He's Got the Whole World in His Hands
559 Here I Am, Lord
51 How Great Thou Art
31 I Sing the Almighty Power of God
79 I'll Praise My Maker While I've Breath
25 Let All Creation Bless the Lord
22 Let All Things Now Living
33 Let's Sing unto the Lord (Cantemos al Señor)
20 Like a Mighty River Flowing
26 Many and Great
17 Praise the Lord! O Heavens, Adore Him
71 Praise to the Lord, the Almighty
36 Thank You, God, for Water, Soil, and Air
21 This Is My Father's World
652 This Is the Day

GOD - FAITHFULNESS
507 A Mighty Fortress Is Our God
451 Be Still, My Soul
4 Bless His Holy Name
75 By Gracious Powers
380 Cast Thy Burden upon the Lord
83 Children of the Heavenly Father
27 God of Creation, All-Powerful
663 God's Holy Ways Are Just and True
50 Great Is the Lord
72 Great Is Thy Faithfulness
411 How Firm a Foundation
407 I Know Whom I Have Believed
60 I Will Sing of the Mercies
429 If You Will Trust in God to Guide You
435 Like a River Glorious
84 O God, Our Help in Ages Past
503 O God, Your Constant Care and Love
2 O Worship the King
438 On Eagle's Wings
82 Praise, My Soul, the King of Heaven
478 Sweet Hour of Prayer
76 We Are Singing, for the Lord Is Our Light

GOD - FATHER
322 A Hymn of Glory Let Us Sing!
505 All the Way My Savior Leads Me
83 Children of the Heavenly Father
121 Christ Is the World's Light
541 Church of God, Elect and Glorious
148 Come, Thou Almighty King
449 Day by Day
470 Dear Lord and Father of Mankind
74 Eternal Father, Strong to Save
146 Glorify Thy Name
667 God Has Spoken by the Prophets
72 Great Is Thy Faithfulness
48 Immortal, Invisible, God Only Wise
371 Our Father, We Have Wandered
82 Praise, My Soul, the King of Heaven
142 Sing Praise to the Father
682 The Fruit of Love
117 There Is a Redeemer
57 Think About His Love
21 This Is My Father's World
137 Worthy of Worship

GOD - GLORY
12 Be Exalted, O God
129 Be Still, for the Spirit of the Lord
148 Come, Thou Almighty King
667 God Has Spoken by the Prophets
564 God Is Working His Purpose Out
569 God of Grace and God of Glory
50 Great Is the Lord
48 Immortal, Invisible, God Only Wise
6 Let the Whole Creation Cry
45 Mighty Is Our God
363 My Tribute
46 Praise the Lord Who Reigns Above
10 Sing a New Song
141 Sing of a God in Majestic Divinity
56 Sing Praise to God Who Reigns Above
66 To God Be the Glory

GOD - GRACE
521 Abide with Me
422 Amazing Grace!
63 Give to Our God Immortal Praise
598 Glorious Things of Thee Are Spoken
569 God of Grace and God of Glory
663 God's Holy Ways Are Just and True
353 Grace Greater than Our Sin
77 I Greet Thee, Who My Sure Redeemer Art
608 Lord of Our Growing Years
8 New Songs of Celebration
82 Praise, My Soul, the King of Heaven
462 Renew Your Church
57 Think About His Love
583 You Call Us, Lord
613 Your Love, O God, Has Called Us

GOD - GUIDE
505 All the Way My Savior Leads Me
451 Be Still, My Soul
514 Be Strong in the Lord
63 Give to Our God Immortal Praise
716 God Be with You
65 God Moves in a Mysterious Way
409 God of Our Life
78 God of the Ages, History's Maker
728 God of the Ages, Whose Almighty Hand
149 God the Spirit, Guide and Guardian
501 Guide Me, O Thou Great Jehovah
499 He Leadeth Me
429 If You Will Trust in God to Guide You
498 Lead Me, Guide Me
70 Lord, for the Years
84 O God, Our Help in Ages Past
500 Precious Lord, Take My Hand
494 Step by Step
441 Trust in the Lord
81 We Gather Together
726 We Praise You, O God
333 Wind Who Makes All Winds That Blow

GOD - HOLINESS
129 Be Still, for the Spirit of the Lord
4 Bless His Holy Name
369 Christ Is God's Never Changing 'Yes!'
139 God Is One, Unique and Holy
50 Great Is the Lord
138 Holy God, We Praise Your Name
151 Holy Is the Lord
739 "Holy, Holy, Holy" ("Santo, Santo, Santo")
738 Holy, Holy, Holy Lord
136 Holy, Holy, Holy! Lord God Almighty!
6 Let the Whole Creation Cry
656 Open the Eyes of My Heart
737 Santo, Santo, Santo
16 The God of Abraham Praise

GOD - IMAGE
617 A Place at the Table

611 As Man and Woman We Were Made
643 Colorful Creator
28 For Beauty of Meadows
644 God, Who Stretched the Spangled Heavens
24 God, You Spin the Whirling Planets
55 Great God, Your Love Has Called Us Here
48 Immortal, Invisible, God Only Wise
381 Restore in Us, O God
599 Shadow and Substance

GOD - KING
471 As the Deer
658 Awesome God
19 Blessed Be the Lord God Almighty
148 Come, Thou Almighty King
67 Come, We That Love the Lord
78 God of the Ages, History's Maker
77 I Greet Thee, Who My Sure Redeemer Art
176 Lift Up Your Heads, O Mighty Gates
137 Worthy of Worship

GOD - LOVE
585 A Prophet-Woman Broke a Jar
259 Amazing Love
366 And Can It Be
258 At the Cross
9 Come, Let Us Praise the Lord
68 Come, Thou Fount of Every Blessing
518 Give Thanks for Life
58 God of Many Names
29 God of the Sparrow
663 God's Holy Ways Are Just and True
226 God's Love Made Visible!
55 Great God, Your Love Has Called Us Here
59 Joyful, Joyful, We Adore Thee
70 Lord, for the Years
358 Love Divine, All Loves Excelling
446 O Love That Will Not Let Me Go
181 Of the Father's Love Begotten
124 Open Your Hearts
371 Our Father, We Have Wandered
557 Pass It On
46 Praise the Lord Who Reigns Above
444 Rain Down
13 Sing a New Song to the Lord
56 Sing Praise to God Who Reigns Above
11 Stand Up and Bless the Lord
16 The God of Abraham Praise
61 There's a Wideness in God's Mercy
57 Think About His Love
38 Touch the Earth Lightly
399 Ubi Caritas et Amor (Where True Charity and Love Abide)
613 Your Love, O God, Has Called Us

GOD - MAJESTY
148 Come, Thou Almighty King
65 God Moves in a Mysterious Way
50 Great Is the Lord
51 How Great Thou Art
42 How Majestic Is Your Name
31 I Sing the Almighty Power of God
53 I Stand in Awe
508 Lead On, O King Eternal
49 Let All the World
43 Majesty
97 Meekness and Majesty
94 Shout to the Lord

GOD - MYSTERY
138 Holy God, We Praise Your Name
515 Hymn of Promise
53 I Stand in Awe
48 Immortal, Invisible, God Only Wise
97 Meekness and Majesty
417 Not with Naked Eye
700 Now the Silence
599 Shadow and Substance
141 Sing of a God in Majestic Divinity
413 When Our Confidence Is Shaken
705 You Satisfy the Hungry Heart

GOD - NAMES
92 All Hail King Jesus
661 All People That on Earth Do Dwell
320 Alleluia, Sing to Jesus!
105 Beautiful Savior
4 Bless His Holy Name
9 Come, Let Us Praise the Lord
148 Come, Thou Almighty King
32 Creating God, Your Fingers Trace
340 Crown Him King of Kings
178 Emmanuel, Emmanuel
28 For Beauty of Meadows
146 Glorify Thy Name
145 Glory Be to God, Creator
27 God of Creation, All-Powerful
58 God of Many Names
149 God the Spirit, Guide and Guardian
138 Holy God, We Praise Your Name
42 How Majestic Is Your Name
338 King of Kings
8 New Songs of Celebration
11 Stand Up and Bless the Lord
16 The God of Abraham Praise
673 We Believe in God Almighty

GOD - POWER
507 A Mighty Fortress Is Our God
658 Awesome God
4 Bless His Holy Name
75 By Gracious Powers
32 Creating God, Your Fingers Trace
642 Earth and All Stars
27 God of Creation, All-Powerful
569 God of Grace and God of Glory
80 He's Got the Whole World in His Hands

31 I Sing the Almighty Power of God
48 Immortal, Invisible, God Only Wise
26 Many and Great
17 Praise the Lord! O Heavens, Adore Him
46 Praise the Lord Who Reigns Above
511 The Battle Belongs to the Lord

GOD - PRESENCE
521 Abide with Me
432 As Water to the Thirsty
430 Be Not Afraid
129 Be Still, for the Spirit of the Lord
502 Be Thou My Vision
75 By Gracious Powers
477 Come and Find the Quiet Center
718 Forth In Your Name
649 Gather Us In
598 Glorious Things of Thee Are Spoken
747 Go with Us, Lord
716 God Be with You
58 God of Many Names
78 God of the Ages, History's Maker
29 God of the Sparrow
678 In Water We Grow
469 Lord of All Hopefulness
135 Loving Spirit
417 Not with Naked Eye
438 On Eagle's Wings
131 Surely the Presence
624 When the Poor Ones (Cuando el Pobre)

GOD - PROVIDENCE
83 Children of the Heavenly Father
449 Day by Day
37 God in His Love for Us
564 God Is Working His Purpose Out
65 God Moves in a Mysterious Way
394 God of All Time
27 God of Creation, All-Powerful
78 God of the Ages, History's Maker
24 God, You Spin the Whirling Planets
663 God's Holy Ways Are Just and True
436 Grace Alone
486 Have Thine Own Way, Lord!
545 How Lovely, Lord, How Lovely
77 I Greet Thee, Who My Sure Redeemer Art
488 I Lift My Eyes to the Quiet Hills
31 I Sing the Almighty Power of God
435 Like a River Glorious
84 O God, Our Help in Ages Past
71 Praise to the Lord, the Almighty
495 Stand by Me
21 This Is My Father's World
81 We Gather Together

GOD - REIGN
658 Awesome God
502 Be Thou My Vision

19 Blessed Be the Lord God Almighty
121 Christ Is the World's Light
9 Come, Let Us Praise the Lord
667 God Has Spoken by the Prophets
564 God Is Working His Purpose Out
3 God, We Praise You!
226 God's Love Made Visible!
138 Holy God, We Praise Your Name
508 Lead On, O King Eternal
49 Let All the World
26 Many and Great
45 Mighty Is Our God
730 Mine Eyes Have Seen the Glory
46 Praise the Lord Who Reigns Above
71 Praise to the Lord, the Almighty
56 Sing Praise to God Who Reigns Above
16 The God of Abraham Praise
337 We Will Glorify
52 You Are My God

GOD - WISDOM

658 Awesome God
502 Be Thou My Vision
418 Eternal Light, Shine in My Heart
149 God the Spirit, Guide and Guardian
31 I Sing the Almighty Power of God
53 I Stand in Awe
69 I Worship You, Almighty God
48 Immortal, Invisible, God Only Wise

GOING FORTH

274 An Upper Room with Evening Lamps
459 Come, All Christians, Be Committed
718 Forth In Your Name
708 Go Forth for God
556 Go Forth in His Name
719 Go, My Children, with My Blessing
717 Go Now in Peace
218 Go, Tell It on the Mountain
747 Go with Us, Lord
716 God Be with You
436 Grace Alone
604 Great God, as We Are Gathering
709 Hallelujah! We Sing Your Praises
639 He Is Able
706 I Come with Joy
344 I Have Decided to Follow Jesus
508 Lead On, O King Eternal
748 Lord, Dismiss Us with Your Blessing
671 Lord, We Hear Your Word
575 Lord, Whose Love Through Humble Service
715 Now Let Us from This Table Rise
388 O God in Whom All Life Begins
401 Of All the Spirit's Gifts to Me
711 Savior, Again to Your Dear Name
712 Sent Forth by God's Blessing
714 Shalom, My Friends
749 The Lord Bless You and Keep You
710 The Trees of the Field
652 This Is the Day
674 What a Mighty God
567 With Welcome Heart We Greet You, Lord
583 You Call Us, Lord
566 Your Servant Comes This Hour

GOOD FRIDAY

279 A Purple Robe
262 Ah, Holy Jesus
263 Alas! and Did My Savior Bleed
259 Amazing Love
249 Amen, Amen
258 At the Cross
282 Behold the Lamb of God
255 Beneath the Cross of Jesus
301 Hallelujah! What a Savior!
280 He Never Said a Mumbalin' Word
408 I Am Thine, O Lord
264 In the Cross of Christ I Glory
254 Jesus Walked This Lonesome Valley
281 Lamb of God
253 Lead Me to Calvary
386 Lord Jesus, Think on Me
419 My Faith Looks Up to Thee
277 My Savior's Love
284 O Sacred Head, Now Wounded
286 Stay with Me
260 The Old Rugged Cross
250 Throughout These Lenten Days and Nights
278 To Mock Your Reign
283 Were You There
257 What Wondrous Love Is This
261 When I Survey the Wondrous Cross
413 When Our Confidence Is Shaken

GRACE THROUGH FAITH

422 Amazing Grace!
258 At the Cross
436 Grace Alone
406 My Faith Has Found a Resting Place
690 We Remember You
362 Wonderful Grace of Jesus

GRIEF

521 Abide with Me
451 Be Still, My Soul
91 Christ, Whose Glory Fills the Skies
416 God! When Human Bonds Are Broken
516 Grief of Ending, Wordless Sorrow
411 How Firm a Foundation
How Long, O Lord
345 Jesus Calls Us o'er the Tumult
524 Lord of the Living
575 Lord, Whose Love Through Humble Service
419 My Faith Looks Up to Thee
443 Trust and Obey
473 What a Friend We Have in Jesus
632 When Aimless Violence Takes Those We Love

GUIDANCE

505 All the Way My Savior Leads Me
422 Amazing Grace!
430 Be Not Afraid
451 Be Still, My Soul
514 Be Strong in the Lord
502 Be Thou My Vision
158 Blessed Be the God of Israel
680 Borning Cry
276 Christ, Let Us Come with You
548 Come, Great God of All the Ages
127 Come, Holy Spirit
329 Come, O Spirit, Dwell Among Us
392 Fear Not, Rejoice and Be Glad
410 Firm Foundation
747 Go with Us, Lord
716 God Be with You
65 God Moves in a Mysterious Way
409 God of Our Life
78 God of the Ages, History's Maker
728 God of the Ages, Whose Almighty Hand
130 God Sends Us the Spirit
149 God the Spirit, Guide and Guardian
501 Guide Me, O Thou Great Jehovah
499 He Leadeth Me
429 If You Will Trust in God to Guide You
669 Jesus, Come, for We Invite You
90 Jesus! What a Friend for Sinners!
504 Just a Closer Walk with Thee
498 Lead Me, Guide Me
508 Lead On, O King Eternal
22 Let All Things Now Living
729 Lift Every Voice and Sing
176 Lift Up Your Heads, O Mighty Gates
162 like a child
748 Lord, Dismiss Us with Your Blessing
419 My Faith Looks Up to Thee
500 Precious Lord, Take My Hand
713 Send Me, Jesus
494 Step by Step
483 Take Time to Be Holy
682 The Fruit of Love
73 The Lord My Shepherd Guards Me Well
343 The Potter's Hand
664 Thy Word
441 Trust in the Lord
81 We Gather Together
726 We Praise You, O God
333 Wind Who Makes All Winds That Blow

HARVEST

570 As Saints of Old Their First-fruits Brought
721 Come, Ye Thankful People, Come

392 Fear Not, Rejoice and Be Glad
723 For the Fruit of All Creation
37 God in His Love for Us
564 God Is Working His Purpose Out
72 Great Is Thy Faithfulness
722 Praise and Thanksgiving
724 Sing to the Lord of Harvest
688 We Give Thee but Thine Own

HEALING

432 As Water to the Thirsty
447 Because He Lives
561 Christ for the World! We Sing
312 Christ Is Alive!
621 For the Healing of the Nations
640 From Miles Around
394 God of All Time
728 God of the Ages, Whose Almighty Hand
416 God! When Human Bonds Are Broken
572 God, Whose Giving Knows No Ending
486 Have Thine Own Way, Lord!
636 Heal Me, Hands of Jesus
633 Healer of My Soul
630 Healer of Our Every Ill
573 How Clear Is Our Vocation, Lord
675 I Believe in Jesus
383 If My People's Hearts Are Humbled
634 Jesus' Hands Were Kind Hands
439 Jesus, Lover of My Soul
361 Jesus, Your Name
575 Lord, Whose Love Through Humble Service
406 My Faith Has Found a Resting Place
479 Near the Cross
638 O Christ, the Healer, We Have Come
93 Praise the One Who Breaks the Darkness
563 Song for the Nations
629 Strong, Gentle Children
631 There Is a Balm in Gilead
61 There's a Wideness in God's Mercy
442 'Tis So Sweet to Trust in Jesus
628 We Cannot Measure How You Heal
413 When Our Confidence Is Shaken
591 Where Cross the Crowded Ways of Life
364 Woman in the Night

HEAVEN

322 A Hymn of Glory Let Us Sing!
521 Abide with Me
505 All the Way My Savior Leads Me
306 Alleluia! Jesus Is Risen!
422 Amazing Grace!
635 And Jesus Said
695 As We Gather at Your Table
451 Be Still, My Soul
502 Be Thou My Vision
447 Because He Lives
158 Blessed Be the God of Israel
393 Blest Be the Tie That Binds
91 Christ, Whose Glory Fills the Skies
696 Come, Share the Lord
449 Day by Day
538 Deep River
418 Eternal Light, Shine in My Heart
535 Face to Face
529 For All the Saints
717 Go Now in Peace
409 God of Our Life
501 Guide Me, O Thou Great Jehovah
323 Hail the Day That Sees Him Rise
301 Hallelujah! What a Savior!
528 Here from All Nations
549 I Love Your Kingdom, Lord
504 Just a Closer Walk with Thee
468 My Jesus, I Love Thee
346 O Come to Me, the Master Said
519 On Jordan's Stormy Banks I Stand
500 Precious Lord, Take My Hand
711 Savior, Again to Your Dear Name
522 Shall We Gather at the River
348 Softly and Tenderly
523 Soon and Very Soon
527 Steal Away
117 There Is a Redeemer
525 When We All Get to Heaven

HERITAGE

727 America, the Beautiful
695 As We Gather at Your Table
530 Faith of Our Fathers
564 God Is Working His Purpose Out
394 God of All Time
623 The Church of Christ in Every Age
16 The God of Abraham Praise
558 The World Is Full of Stories
594 We Are Your People
726 We Praise You, O God

HOLY SPIRIT

129 Be Still, for the Spirit of the Lord
461 Breathe on Me, Breath of God
477 Come and Find the Quiet Center
330 Come Down, O Love Divine
127 Come, Holy Spirit
325 Come, Holy Spirit, Our Souls Inspire
329 Come, O Spirit, Dwell Among Us
475 Eternal Spirit of the Living Christ
481 Every Time I Feel the Spirit
331 Filled with the Spirit's Power
130 God Sends Us the Spirit
149 God the Spirit, Guide and Guardian
327 Like the Murmur of the Dove's Song
135 Loving Spirit
328 O Breath of Life
401 Of All the Spirit's Gifts to Me
480 Open My Eyes, That I May See
385 Search Me, O God
132 Spirit of God, Descend upon My Heart
492 Spirit of the Living God
352 Spirit Song
326 Spirit, Spirit of Gentleness
128 Spirit, Working in Creation
134 Sweet, Sweet Spirit
701 There's a Quiet Understanding
133 There's a Spirit in the Air
673 We Believe in God Almighty
396 Where the Spirit of the Lord Is
333 Wind Who Makes All Winds That Blow

HOME & FAMILY

611 As Man and Woman We Were Made
609 Come to a Wedding
497 Find Us Faithful
607 Happy the Home When God Is There
596 Help Us Accept Each Other
465 Lord, Be Glorified
469 Lord of All Hopefulness
681 Lord, We Bring to You Our Children
610 O Perfect Love
725 Thanks to God for My Redeemer
605 The Family Prayer Song
682 The Fruit of Love
612 When Love Is Found
602 Who Is My Mother, Who Is My Brother?
720 With Grateful Heart I Thank You, Lord
613 Your Love, O God, Has Called Us

HOPE

635 And Jesus Said
430 Be Not Afraid
447 Because He Lives
666 Blest Are They
561 Christ for the World! We Sing
153 Come, Thou Long-Expected Jesus
418 Eternal Light, Shine in My Heart
410 Firm Foundation
717 Go Now in Peace
3 God, We Praise You!
436 Grace Alone
516 Grief of Ending, Wordless Sorrow
630 Healer of Our Every Ill
596 Help Us Accept Each Other
597 Here, O Lord, Your Servants Gather
404 Hope of the World
424 How Can I Keep from Singing?
77 I Greet Thee, Who My Sure Redeemer Art
434 If Christ Had Not Been Raised from Death
429 If You Will Trust in God to Guide You
125 In the Name of the Lord
420 Jesus, the Very Thought of Thee
729 Lift Every Voice and Sing
469 Lord of All Hopefulness
587 Make Me a Channel of Your Peace

405 My Hope Is Built on Nothing Less
479 Near the Cross
400 Not for Tongues of Heaven's Angels
484 O Lord, Hear My Prayer
589 O Master, Let Me Walk with Thee
161 People, Look East
174 Prepare the Way of the Lord
444 Rain Down
522 Shall We Gather at the River
725 Thanks to God for My Redeemer
355 This Is a Day of New Beginnings
672 This Is the Threefold Truth
673 We Believe in God Almighty
616 We Meet You, O Christ
165 When God Is a Child

HUNGER
596 Help Us Accept Each Other
528 Here from All Nations
372 I Then Shall Live
575 Lord, Whose Love Through Humble Service
620 O Lord, You Gave Your Servant John
623 The Church of Christ in Every Age
73 The Lord My Shepherd Guards Me Well
133 There's a Spirit in the Air
38 Touch the Earth Lightly
704 We Meet as Friends at Table
555 When the Church of Jesus
415 When We Are Living (Pues Si Vivimos)
705 You Satisfy the Hungry Heart

INCARNATION
330 Come Down, O Love Divine
153 Come, Thou Long-Expected Jesus
172 For Ages Women Hoped and Prayed
226 God's Love Made Visible!
185 Hark! The Herald Angels Sing
402 He Came Down
412 He Comes to Us As One Unknown
162 like a child
97 Meekness and Majesty
670 O Word of God Incarnate
181 Of the Father's Love Begotten
227 See Him Lying on a Bed of Straw
141 Sing of a God in Majestic Divinity
247 Sing of God Made Manifest
223 Star-Child

INVITATION
676 Come, Be Baptized
485 Into My Heart
354 Just As I Am
348 Softly and Tenderly
472 Turn Your Eyes upon Jesus

JESUS CHRIST - ASCENSION
322 A Hymn of Glory Let Us Sing!
320 Alleluia, Sing to Jesus!
105 Beautiful Savior
324 Christ High-Ascended
317 Crown Him with Many Crowns
323 Hail the Day That Sees Him Rise
301 Hallelujah! What a Savior!
88 Lord, I Lift Your Name on High
43 Majesty
150 My Lord of Light
244 O Love, How Deep, How Broad
656 Open the Eyes of My Heart
463 Revive Us Again
339 The Head That Once Was Crowned
673 We Believe in God Almighty

JESUS CHRIST - BAPTISM
243 Songs of Thankfulness and Praise
241 When Jesus Came to Jordan
239 When John Baptized by Jordan's River

JESUS CHRIST – BIRTH
206 A Stable Lamp Is Lighted
216 Adoramus Te (We Adore You)
163 All Earth Is Hopeful (Toda la Tierra)
249 Amen, Amen
189 Angels, from the Realms of Glory
188 Angels We Have Heard on High
160 Awake! Awake, and Greet the New Morn
205 Away in a Manger (Kirkpatrick)
203 Away in a Manger (Murray)
194 Born in the Night, Mary's Child
202 Break Forth, O Beauteous Heavenly Light
235 Brightest and Best of the Stars
199 Carol at the Manger
197 Come and Hear the Joyful Singing
153 Come, Thou Long-Expected Jesus
172 For Ages Women Hoped and Prayed
238 From a Distant Home (De Tierra Lejana Venimos)
240 Gloria, Gloria
195 Gloria, Gloria, Gloria
218 Go, Tell It on the Mountain
226 God's Love Made Visible!
198 Good Christian Friends, Rejoice
185 Hark! The Herald Angels Sing
201 He Is Born
104 Hidden Christ, Alive for Ever
225 I Wonder as I Wander
196 In the Bleak Midwinter
221 Infant Holy, Infant Lowly
191 It Came upon the Midnight Clear
219 Jesus, Oh, What a Wonderful Child
179 Joy to the World!
232 Let All Mortal Flesh Keep Silence
162 like a child
190 Lo, How a Rose E'er Blooming
167 Long Ago, Prophets Knew
88 Lord, I Lift Your Name on High
118 Lord of the Dance
210 Love Came Down at Christmas
192 Mary, Did You Know?
220 Mary Had a Baby
97 Meekness and Majesty
730 Mine Eyes Have Seen the Glory
170 My Soul Proclaims with Wonder
217 No Obvious Angels
182 O Come, All Ye Faithful
187 O Holy Night
180 O Little Town of Bethlehem
242 O Sing a Song of Bethlehem
181 Of the Father's Love Begotten
208 Oh, How Joyfully
207 Oh, Sleep Now, Holy Baby (A La Ru)
222 On Christmas Night All Christians Sing
183 Once in Royal David's City
212 Raise a Song of Gladness (Jubilate Deo)
209 Rise Up, Shepherd, and Follow
227 See Him Lying on a Bed of Straw
186 Silent Night! Holy Night!
193 Sing We Now of Christmas
223 Star-Child
214 Still, Still, Still
211 That Boy-Child of Mary
169 The Angel Gabriel from Heaven Came
224 The Birthday of a King
229 The First Noel
237 The Hands That First Held Mary's Child
171 To a Maid Whose Name Was Mary
213 'Twas in the Moon of Wintertime
540 Two Thousand Years Since Bethlehem
673 We Believe in God Almighty
616 We Meet You, O Christ
233 We Three Kings of Orient Are
215 Were You There on That Christmas Night
184 What Child Is This
165 When God Is a Child
200 While by the Sheep
228 While Shepherds Watched Their Flocks
364 Woman in the Night

JESUS CHRIST – BLOOD
259 Amazing Love
366 And Can It Be
679 Baptized in Water
426 Blessed Assurance
68 Come, Thou Fount of Every Blessing
353 Grace Greater than Our Sin
528 Here from All Nations
51 How Great Thou Art
356 I Will Sing of My Redeemer
354 Just As I Am
281 Lamb of God
405 My Hope Is Built on Nothing Less
363 My Tribute
109 O, How I Love Jesus

384 Rock of Ages
623 The Church of Christ in Every Age
544 The Church's One Foundation
229 The First Noel
260 The Old Rugged Cross
256 There Is a Fountain Filled with Blood
61 There's a Wideness in God's Mercy
315 This Is the Feast of Victory
442 'Tis So Sweet to Trust in Jesus
261 When I Survey the Wondrous Cross

JESUS CHRIST - CROSS

279 A Purple Robe
521 Abide with Me
262 Ah, Holy Jesus
263 Alas! and Did My Savior Bleed
291 Alleluia No. 1
275 An Upper Room Did Our Lord Prepare
274 An Upper Room with Evening Lamps
258 At the Cross
619 Because He Died and Is Risen
255 Beneath the Cross of Jesus
194 Born in the Night, Mary's Child
312 Christ Is Alive!
655 Come Away from Rush and Hurry
382 "Forgive Our Sins as We Forgive"
272 Go to Dark Gethsemane
553 Go to the World!
29 God of the Sparrow
3 God, We Praise You!
572 God, Whose Giving Knows No Ending
454 He Came Singing Love
280 He Never Said a Mumbalin' Word
597 Here, O Lord, Your Servants Gather
404 Hope of the World
573 How Clear Is Our Vocation, Lord
51 How Great Thou Art
408 I Am Thine, O Lord
675 I Believe in Jesus
251 I Come to the Cross
344 I Have Decided to Follow Jesus
356 I Will Sing of My Redeemer
600 In Christ There Is No East or West (Perry)
264 In the Cross of Christ I Glory
295 Jesus Christ Is Risen Today
254 Jesus Walked This Lonesome Valley
508 Lead On, O King Eternal
287 Lift High the Cross
88 Lord, I Lift Your Name on High
575 Lord, Whose Love Through Humble Service
97 Meekness and Majesty
101 Name of All Majesty
479 Near the Cross
367 Now Let Us Learn of Christ
244 O Love, How Deep, How Broad
284 O Sacred Head, Now Wounded
242 O Sing a Song of Bethlehem
509 Onward, Christian Soldiers
113 Rejoice, Ye Pure in Heart
384 Rock of Ages
304 Shout for Joy, Loud and Long
351 "Take Up Your Cross," the Savior Said
237 The Hands That First Held Mary's Child
339 The Head That Once Was Crowned
260 The Old Rugged Cross
552 We All Are One in Mission
628 We Cannot Measure How You Heal
616 We Meet You, O Christ
690 We Remember You
283 Were You There
360 What the Lord Has Done in Me
261 When I Survey the Wondrous Cross
241 When Jesus Came to Jordan
413 When Our Confidence Is Shaken
364 Woman in the Night

JESUS CHRIST – DEATH

206 A Stable Lamp Is Lighted
262 Ah, Holy Jesus
259 Amazing Love
249 Amen, Amen
255 Beneath the Cross of Jesus
142 Sing Praise to the Father
662 Thanks to God Whose Word Was Spoken
544 The Church's One Foundation
672 This Is the Threefold Truth
283 Were You There
261 When I Survey the Wondrous Cross

JESUS CHRIST - FRIEND

320 Alleluia, Sing to Jesus!
635 And Jesus Said
425 Christ Beside Me
276 Christ, Let Us Come with You
601 Dear Christ, Uplifted from the Earth
55 Great God, Your Love Has Called Us Here
669 Jesus, Come, for We Invite You
431 Jesus, Priceless Treasure
90 Jesus! What a Friend for Sinners!
162 like a child
347 Lord, You Have Come to the Lakeshore (Tú Has Venido a la Orilla)
346 O Come to Me, the Master Said
458 O Jesus, I Have Promised
440 Savior, Like a Shepherd Lead Us
365 Thank You, Lord
442 'Tis So Sweet to Trust in Jesus
702 We Come as Guests Invited
473 What a Friend We Have in Jesus

JESUS CHRIST - KING

322 A Hymn of Glory Let Us Sing!
265 All Glory, Laud and Honor
92 All Hail King Jesus
106 All Hail the Power of Jesus' Name (CORONATION)
100 All Hail the Power of Jesus' Name (DIADEM)
289 Alleluia, Alleluia! Hearts to Heaven
291 Alleluia No. 1
319 Alleluia, Sing to Jesus!
321 At the Name of Jesus
502 Be Thou My Vision
105 Beautiful Savior
425 Christ Beside Me
324 Christ High-Ascended
87 Come, Christians, Join to Sing
9 Come, Let Us Praise the Lord
148 Come, Thou Almighty King
340 Crown Him King of Kings
317 Crown Him with Many Crowns
3 God, We Praise You!
323 Hail the Day That Sees Him Rise
301 Hallelujah! What a Savior!
122 He Is Exalted
305 He Is Lord
102 His Name Is Wonderful
266 Hosanna (Tuttle)
267 Hosanna, Loud Hosanna
77 I Greet Thee, Who My Sure Redeemer Art
414 I Know That My Redeemer Lives!
62 In the Lord Alone
318 Jesus Comes with Clouds Descending
341 Jesus Shall Reign
179 Joy to the World!
338 King of Kings
253 Lead Me to Calvary
508 Lead On, O King Eternal
232 Let All Mortal Flesh Keep Silence
287 Lift High the Cross
271 Lift Up Your Heads
176 Lift Up Your Heads, O Mighty Gates
88 Lord, I Lift Your Name on High
43 Majesty
97 Meekness and Majesty
101 Name of All Majesty
433 O Christ the Same
96 O for a Thousand Tongues to Sing
64 O God Beyond All Praising
181 Of the Father's Love Begotten
156 On Jordan's Bank the Baptist's Cry
509 Onward, Christian Soldiers
82 Praise, My Soul, the King of Heaven
152 Prepare the Way, O Zion
342 Rejoice, the Lord Is King!
113 Rejoice, Ye Pure in Heart
523 Soon and Very Soon
466 Take My Life and Let It Be
455 Take Thou Our Minds, Dear Lord
224 The Birthday of a King
339 The Head That Once Was Crowned

159 The King of Glory Comes
117 There Is a Redeemer
21 This Is My Father's World
278 To Mock Your Reign
213 'Twas in the Moon of Wintertime
110 We Come, O Christ, to You
337 We Will Glorify
184 What Child Is This
534 When the King Shall Come Again
234 Wise Men, They Came to Look for Wisdom
648 You're Worthy of My Praise

JESUS CHRIST - LAMB OF GOD
317 Crown Him with Many Crowns
103 Glory to the Lamb
98 Hallelujah! Praise the Lamb!
248 I Want to Walk as a Child of the Light
431 Jesus, Priceless Treasure
354 Just As I Am
281 Lamb of God
419 My Faith Looks Up to Thee
479 Near the Cross
260 The Old Rugged Cross
256 There Is a Fountain Filled with Blood
117 There Is a Redeemer
250 Throughout These Lenten Days and Nights
690 We Remember You
337 We Will Glorify
360 What the Lord Has Done in Me
257 What Wondrous Love Is This
116 Worthy Is the Lamb
427 You Are My All in All
99 You, Lord, Are Both Lamb and Shepherd

JESUS CHRIST - LIFE & MINISTRY
249 Amen, Amen
402 He Came Down
597 Here, O Lord, Your Servants Gather
669 Jesus, Come, for We Invite You
634 Jesus' Hands Were Kind Hands
361 Jesus, Your Name
118 Lord of the Dance
575 Lord, Whose Love Through Humble Service
347 Lord, You Have Come to the Lakeshore (Tú Has Venido a la Orilla)
192 Mary, Did You Know?
244 O Love, How Deep, How Broad
230 O Morning Star, How Fair and Bright!
242 O Sing a Song of Bethlehem
183 Once in Royal David's City
141 Sing of a God in Majestic Divinity
128 Spirit, Working in Creation
662 Thanks to God Whose Word Was Spoken
237 The Hands That First Held Mary's Child
250 Throughout These Lenten Days and Nights
540 Two Thousand Years Since Bethlehem
673 We Believe in God Almighty
360 What the Lord Has Done in Me
241 When Jesus Came to Jordan
364 Woman in the Night

JESUS CHRIST - LIGHT
231 Arise, Your Light Is Come
551 As a Fire Is Meant for Burning
160 Awake! Awake, and Greet the New Morn
502 Be Thou My Vision
202 Break Forth, O Beauteous Heavenly Light
121 Christ Is the World's Light
91 Christ, Whose Glory Fills the Skies
264 In the Cross of Christ I Glory
150 My Lord of Light
107 O Light Whose Splendor Thrills
144 O Splendor of God's Glory Bright
670 O Word of God Incarnate
93 Praise the One Who Breaks the Darkness
319 Shine, Jesus, Shine
299 That Easter Day with Joy Was Bright
536 Through the Darkness of the Ages
472 Turn Your Eyes upon Jesus
76 We Are Singing, for the Lord Is Our Light
175 We Light the Advent Candles
562 We've a Story to Tell to the Nations
111 When Morning Gilds the Skies

JESUS CHRIST - LORDSHIP
106 All Hail the Power of Jesus' Name (CORONATION)
100 All Hail the Power of Jesus' Name (DIADEM)
294 Christ Arose!
309 Christ the Lord Is Risen!
119 Come into His Presence
340 Crown Him King of Kings
317 Crown Him with Many Crowns
556 Go Forth in His Name
305 He Is Lord
102 His Name Is Wonderful
267 Hosanna, Loud Hosanna
573 How Clear Is Our Vocation, Lord
669 Jesus, Come, for We Invite You
341 Jesus Shall Reign
338 King of Kings
101 Name of All Majesty
458 O Jesus, I Have Promised
298 The Day of Resurrection!
339 The Head That Once Was Crowned
315 This Is the Feast of Victory
552 We All Are One in Mission
702 We Come as Guests Invited
337 We Will Glorify

JESUS CHRIST - LOVE
262 Ah, Holy Jesus
505 All the Way My Savior Leads Me
259 Amazing Love
366 And Can It Be
454 He Came Singing Love
560 I Love to Tell the Story
356 I Will Sing of My Redeemer
273 Jesu, Jesu, Fill Us with Your Love
439 Jesus, Lover of My Soul
437 Jesus Loves Me
420 Jesus, the Very Thought of Thee
90 Jesus! What a Friend for Sinners!
253 Lead Me to Calvary
358 Love Divine, All Loves Excelling
464 May the Mind of Christ, My Savior
419 My Faith Looks Up to Thee
277 My Savior's Love
367 Now Let Us Learn of Christ
328 O Breath of Life
270 O How He Loves You and Me
109 O, How I Love Jesus
244 O Love, How Deep, How Broad
398 O the Deep, Deep Love of Jesus
440 Savior, Like a Shepherd Lead Us
352 Spirit Song
682 The Fruit of Love
261 When I Survey the Wondrous Cross

JESUS CHRIST - MAJESTY
322 A Hymn of Glory Let Us Sing!
106 All Hail the Power of Jesus' Name (CORONATION)
100 All Hail the Power of Jesus' Name (DIADEM)
105 Beautiful Savior
318 Jesus Comes with Clouds Descending
271 Lift Up Your Heads
43 Majesty
97 Meekness and Majesty
101 Name of All Majesty
82 Praise, My Soul, the King of Heaven
268 Ride On, Ride On in Majesty!
94 Shout to the Lord
337 We Will Glorify

JESUS CHRIST - NAME
106 All Hail the Power of Jesus' Name (CORONATION)
100 All Hail the Power of Jesus' Name (DIADEM)
321 At the Name of Jesus
105 Beautiful Savior
178 Emmanuel, Emmanuel
123 Fairest Lord Jesus
146 Glorify Thy Name
102 His Name Is Wonderful
675 I Believe in Jesus
125 In the Name of the Lord
177 Jesus, Name Above All Names
420 Jesus, the Very Thought of Thee
361 Jesus, Your Name
115 Praise the Name of Jesus
710 Savior, Again to Your Dear Name
108 There's Something About That Name
110 We Come, O Christ, to You

JESUS CHRIST - PASSION

585 A Prophet-Woman Broke a Jar
279 A Purple Robe
262 Ah, Holy Jesus
263 Alas! and Did My Savior Bleed
265 All Glory, Laud and Honor
366 And Can It Be
258 At the Cross
255 Beneath the Cross of Jesus
121 Christ Is the World's Light
317 Crown Him with Many Crowns
238 From a Distant Home (De Tierra Lejana Venimos)
272 Go to Dark Gethsemane
301 Hallelujah! What a Savior!
280 He Never Said a Mumbalin' Word
297 His Battle Ended There
356 I Will Sing of My Redeemer
254 Jesus Walked This Lonesome Valley
357 Knowing You
253 Lead Me to Calvary
252 Lord, Who Throughout These Forty Days
468 My Jesus, I Love Thee
150 My Lord of Light
277 My Savior's Love
244 O Love, How Deep, How Broad
284 O Sacred Head, Now Wounded
95 Praise Him! Praise Him!
384 Rock of Ages
286 Stay with Me
260 The Old Rugged Cross
250 Throughout These Lenten Days and Nights
278 To Mock Your Reign
702 We Come as Guests Invited
283 Were You There
360 What the Lord Has Done in Me
261 When I Survey the Wondrous Cross
364 Woman in the Night

JESUS CHRIST - PRESENCE

459 All for Jesus!
274 An Upper Room with Evening Lamps
635 And Jesus Said
430 Be Not Afraid
425 Christ Beside Me
412 He Comes to Us As One Unknown
302 He Lives
476 I Need Thee Every Hour
506 I Want Jesus to Walk with Me
300 In the Garden
134 Sweet, Sweet Spirit

JESUS CHRIST - REDEEMER

320 Alleluia, Sing to Jesus!
282 Behold the Lamb of God
317 Crown Him with Many Crowns
77 I Greet Thee, Who My Sure Redeemer Art
414 I Know That My Redeemer Lives!
356 I Will Sing of My Redeemer
177 Jesus, Name Above All Names
468 My Jesus, I Love Thee
95 Praise Him! Praise Him!
725 Thanks to God for My Redeemer
117 There Is a Redeemer

JESUS CHRIST - REIGN

322 A Hymn of Glory Let Us Sing!
279 A Purple Robe
106 All Hail the Power of Jesus' Name (CORONATION)
100 All Hail the Power of Jesus' Name (DIADEM)
289 Alleluia, Alleluia! Hearts to Heaven
320 Alleluia, Sing to Jesus!
321 At the Name of Jesus
502 Be Thou My Vision
105 Beautiful Savior
453 Christ Be My Leader
324 Christ High-Ascended
121 Christ Is the World's Light
340 Crown Him King of Kings
317 Crown Him with Many Crowns
123 Fairest Lord Jesus
556 Go Forth in His Name
3 God, We Praise You!
323 Hail the Day That Sees Him Rise
122He Is Exalted
104 Hidden Christ, Alive for Ever
404 Hope of the World
414 I Know That My Redeemer Lives!
318 Jesus Comes with Clouds Descending
341 Jesus Shall Reign
179 Joy to the World!
70 Lord, for the Years
101 Name of All Majesty
400 Not for Tongues of Heaven's Angels
342 Rejoice, the Lord Is King!
268 Ride On, Ride On in Majesty!
315 This Is the Feast of Victory
278 To Mock Your Reign
337 We Will Glorify
112 You Servants of God

JESUS CHRIST - RESURRECTION

322 A Hymn of Glory Let Us Sing!
585 A Prophet-Woman Broke a Jar
289 Alleluia, Alleluia! Hearts to Heaven
306 Alleluia! Jesus Is Risen!
291 Alleluia No. 1
249 Amen, Amen
105 Beautiful Savior
619 Because He Died and Is Risen
447 Because He Lives
292 Because You Live, O Christ
294 Christ Arose!
324 Christ High-Ascended
312 Christ Is Alive!
369 Christ Is God's Never Changing 'Yes!'
293 Christ Is Risen! Shout Hosanna!
309 Christ the Lord Is Risen!
288 Christ the Lord Is Risen Today
336 Christ Triumphant, Ever Reigning
314 Easter Song
331 Filled with the Spirit's Power
454 He Came Singing Love
305 He Is Lord
302 He Lives
297 His Battle Ended There
404 Hope of the World
414 I Know That My Redeemer Lives!
434 If Christ Had Not Been Raised from Death
300 In the Garden
295 Jesus Christ Is Risen Today
254 Jesus Walked This Lonesome Valley
303 Jubilate Deo (In the Lord Rejoicing!)
698 Let Us Talents and Tongues Employ
88 Lord, I Lift Your Name on High
524 Lord of the Living
311 Now the Green Blade Rises
242 O Sing a Song of Bethlehem
313 O Sons and Daughters, Let Us Sing!
334 On Pentecost They Gathered
590 Rise Up, O Saints of God!
304 Shout for Joy, Loud and Long
10 Sing a New Song
120 Sing Alleluia to the Lord
141 Sing of a God in Majestic Divinity
299 That Easter Day with Joy Was Bright
298 The Day of Resurrection!
159 The King of Glory Comes
290 The Strife Is O'er
310 Thine Is the Glory
355 This Is a Day of New Beginnings
672 This Is the Threefold Truth
308 This Joyful Eastertide
673 We Believe in God Almighty

JESUS CHRIST – RETURN (See SECOND COMING)

JESUS CHRIST - SAVIOR

316 Alleluia
282 Behold the Lamb of God
426 Blessed Assurance
194 Born in the Night, Mary's Child
294 Christ Arose!
453 Christ Be My Leader
601 Dear Christ, Uplifted from the Earth
123 Fairest Lord Jesus
359 Give Thanks
302 He Lives
414 I Know That My Redeemer Lives!
474 I Surrender All
177 Jesus, Name Above All Names
420 Jesus, the Very Thought of Thee
659 Jesus, We Are Here (Jesu Tawa Pano)
90 Jesus! What a Friend for Sinners!

406 My Faith Has Found a Resting Place
468 My Jesus, I Love Thee
363 My Tribute
101 Name of All Majesty
433 O Christ the Same
368 O Happy Day
109 O, How I Love Jesus
284 O Sacred Head, Now Wounded
95 Praise Him! Praise Him!
93 Praise the One Who Breaks the Darkness
384 Rock of Ages
227 See Him Lying on a Bed of Straw
442 'Tis So Sweet to Trust in Jesus
66 To God Be the Glory
110 We Come, O Christ, to You
554 We Have Heard the Joyful Sound
562 We've a Story to Tell to the Nations
473 What a Friend We Have in Jesus
360 What the Lord Has Done in Me
241 When Jesus Came to Jordan
239 When John Baptized by Jordan's River

JESUS CHRIST - SHEPHERD

505 All the Way My Savior Leads Me
635 And Jesus Said
9 Come, Let Us Praise the Lord
1 God Is Here!
149 God the Spirit, Guide and Guardian
633 Healer of My Soul
102 His Name Is Wonderful
637 His Strength Is Perfect
488 I Lift My Eyes to the Quiet Hills
281 Lamb of God
440 Savior, Like a Shepherd Lead Us
352 Spirit Song
73 The Lord My Shepherd Guards Me Well
86 The Lord's My Shepherd, I'll Not Want
99 You, Lord, Are Both Lamb and Shepherd
705 You Satisfy the Hungry Heart

JESUS CHRIST - SUFFERING

255 Beneath the Cross of Jesus
272 Go to Dark Gethsemane
97 Meekness and Majesty
93 Praise the One Who Breaks the Darkness
540 Two Thousand Years Since Bethlehem

JESUS CHRIST - TEACHING

453 Christ Be My Leader
667 God Has Spoken by the Prophets
597 Here, O Lord, Your Servants Gather
593 Lord, Speak to Me
244 O Love, How Deep, How Broad

JESUS CHRIST - TEMPTATION

241 When Jesus Came to Jordan

JESUS CHRIST - TRANSFIGURATION

246 Jesus on the Mountain Peak
247 Sing of God Made Manifest
245 We Have Come at Christ's Own Bidding
99 You, Lord, Are Both Lamb and Shepherd

JOY

236 As with Gladness
426 Blessed Assurance
67 Come, We That Love the Lord
40 For the Beauty of the Earth
709 Hallelujah! We Sing Your Praises
657 He Has Made Me Glad
424 How Can I Keep from Singing?
706 I Come with Joy
414 I Know That My Redeemer Lives!
372 I Then Shall Live
300 In the Garden
345 Jesus Calls Us o'er the Tumult
420 Jesus, the Very Thought of Thee
533 Joy in the Morning
179 Joy to the World!
59 Joyful, Joyful, We Adore Thee
496 Leaning on the Everlasting Arms
54 Let There Be Praise
435 Like a River Glorious
671 Lord, We Hear Your Word
446 O Love That Will Not Let Me Go
610 O Perfect Love
401 Of All the Spirit's Gifts to Me
208 Oh, How Joyfully
212 Raise a Song of Gladness (Jubilate Deo)
10 Sing a New Song
710 The Trees of the Field
651 We Bring the Sacrifice of Praise

JUSTICE & PEACE

617 A Place at the Table
163 All Earth Is Hopeful (Toda la Tierra)
625 All Who Love and Serve Your City
231 Arise, Your Light Is Come!!
619 Because He Died and Is Risen
158 Blessed Be the God of Israel
581 Called as Partners in Christ's Service
561 Christ for the World! We Sing
312 Christ Is Alive!
571 Christ, You Call Us All to Service
615 Community of Christ
621 For the Healing of the Nations
37 God in His Love for Us
569 God of Grace and God of Glory
644 God, Who Stretched the Spangled Heavens
24 God, You Spin the Whirling Planets
663 God's Holy Ways Are Just and True
596 Help Us Accept Each Other
600 In Christ There Is No East or West (Perry)
532 Isaiah the Prophet Has Written of Old
533 Joy in the Morning
575 Lord, Whose Love Through Humble Service
592 Lord, You Give the Great Commission
587 Make Me a Channel of Your Peace
170 My Soul Proclaims with Wonder
217 No Obvious Angels
539 O Day of Peace
626 O God of Every Nation
620 O Lord, You Gave Your Servant John
586 Our Cities Cry to You, O God
152 Prepare the Way, O Zion
389 Put Peace into Each Other's Hands
531 Rejoice in God's Saints
462 Renew Your Church
590 Rise Up, O Saints of God!
577 Sing a New Church
13 Sing a New Song to the Lord
56 Sing Praise to God Who Reigns Above
41 Tell Out, My Soul
623 The Church of Christ in Every Age
61 There's a Wideness in God's Mercy
21 This Is My Father's World
552 We All Are One in Mission
512 We Shall Overcome
686 What Does the Lord Require
555 When the Church of Jesus
624 When the Poor Ones (Cuando el Pobre)
622 When Will People Cease Their Fighting?
591 Where Cross the Crowded Ways of Life

KINGDOM OF GOD

507 A Mighty Fortress Is Our God
430 Be Not Afraid
666 Blest Are They
581 Called as Partners in Christ's Service
571 Christ, You Call Us All to Service
548 Come, Great God of All the Ages
708 Go Forth for God
564 God Is Working His Purpose Out
27 God of Creation, All-Powerful
569 God of Grace and God of Glory
528 Here from All Nations
597 Here, O Lord, Your Servants Gather
549 I Love Your Kingdom, Lord
372 I Then Shall Live
532 Isaiah the Prophet Has Written of Old
318 Jesus Comes with Clouds Descending
285 Jesus, Remember Me

179 Joy to the World!
508 Lead On, O King Eternal
730 Mine Eyes Have Seen the Glory
539 O Day of Peace
626 O God of Every Nation
620 O Lord, You Gave Your Servant John
2 O Worship the King
509 Onward, Christian Soldiers
586 Our Cities Cry to You, O God
46 Praise the Lord Who Reigns Above
152 Prepare the Way, O Zion
342 Rejoice, the Lord Is King!
462 Renew Your Church
168 Savior of the Nations, Come
349 Seek Ye First
712 Sent Forth by God's Blessing
13 Sing a New Song to the Lord
455 Take Thou Our Minds, Dear Lord
159 The King of Glory Comes
740 The Lord's Prayer
21 This Is My Father's World
547 We Are God's People
512 We Shall Overcome
562 We've a Story to Tell to the Nations
686 What Does the Lord Require
555 When the Church of Jesus
534 When the King Shall Come Again
622 When Will People Cease Their Fighting?
591 Where Cross the Crowded Ways of Life
112 You Servants of God

LABOR & LEISURE

625 All Who Love and Serve Your City
459 Come, All Christians, Be Committed
642 Earth and All Stars
723 For the Fruit of All Creation
684 For the Life That You Have Given
718 Forth In Your Name
572 God, Whose Giving Knows No Ending
573 How Clear Is Our Vocation, Lord
469 Lord of All Hopefulness
433 O Christ the Same
626 O God of Every Nation
712 Sent Forth by God's Blessing
237 The Hands That First Held Mary's Child
133 There's a Spirit in the Air
686 What Does the Lord Require
525 When We All Get to Heaven
720 With Grateful Heart I Thank You, Lord

LENT

376 How Long, O Lord
252 Lord, Who Throughout These Forty Days
250 Throughout These Lenten Days and Nights

LORD'S SUPPER

617 A Place at the Table
275 An Upper Room Did Our Lord Prepare
274 An Upper Room with Evening Lamps
611 As Man and Woman We Were Made
695 As We Gather at Your Table
606 As Your Family, Lord, Meet Us Here
693 Bread of the World
665 Break Now the Bread of Life
274 Christ, Let Us Come with You
655 Come Away from Rush and Hurry
694 Come, Let Us Eat
403 Come, My Way, My Truth, My Life
696 Come, Share the Lord
697 Eat This Bread
692 Eat This Bread and Never Hunger
649 Gather Us In
1 God Is Here!
394 God of All Time
55 Great God, Your Love Has Called Us Here
404 Hope of the World
703 I Am the Bread of Life
706 I Come with Joy
669 Jesus, Come, for We Invite You
699 Let Us Break Bread Together
698 Let Us Talents and Tongues Employ
627 Now It Is Evening
715 Now Let Us from This Table Rise
700 Now the Silence
346 O Come to Me, the Master Said
689 One Bread, One Body
389 Put Peace into Each Other's Hands
577 Sing a New Church
120 Sing Alleluia to the Lord
544 The Church's One Foundation
701 There's a Quiet Understanding
133 There's a Spirit in the Air
355 This Is a Day of New Beginnings
315 This Is the Feast of Victory
672 This Is the Threefold Truth
673 We Believe in God Almighty
702 We Come as Guests Invited
704 We Meet as Friends at Table
690 We Remember You
707 We Thank You, God, for Feeding Us
612 When Love Is Found
691 With the Body That Was Broken
705 You Satisfy the Hungry Heart

LOVE

471 As the Deer
451 Be Still, My Soul
728 God of the Ages, Whose Almighty Hand
226 God's Love Made Visible!
296 Goodness Is Stronger than Evil
399 Ubi Caritas et Amor (Where True Charity and Love Abide)
391 Will You Let Me Be Your Servant

LOVE FOR CHRIST

357 Knowing You
468 My Jesus, I Love Thee
400 Not for Tongues of Heaven's Angels
367 Now Let Us Learn of Christ
109 O, How I Love Jesus
401 Of All the Spirit's Gifts to Me
491 Open Our Eyes
365 Thank You, Lord

LOVE FOR OTHERS

551 As a Fire Is Meant for Burning
393 Blest Be the Tie That Binds
541 Church of God, Elect and Glorious
609 Come to a Wedding
40 For the Beauty of the Earth
640 From Miles Around
394 God of All Time
572 God, Whose Giving Knows No Ending
454 He Came Singing Love
630 Healer of Our Every Ill
596 Help Us Accept Each Other
559 Here I Am, Lord
706 I Come with Joy
372 I Then Shall Live
273 Jesu, Jesu, Fill Us with Your Love
59 Joyful, Joyful, We Adore Thee
489 Lord, Listen to Your Children Praying
210 Love Came Down at Christmas
576 Make Me a Servant
400 Not for Tongues of Heaven's Angels
367 Now Let Us Learn of Christ
589 O Master, Let Me Walk with Thee
401 Of All the Spirit's Gifts to Me
531 Rejoice in God's Saints
462 Renew Your Church
395 The Bond of Love
397 The Gift of Love
595 They'll Know We Are Christians
647 We Have Come to Join in Worship
704 We Meet as Friends at Table
612 When Love Is Found
602 Who Is My Mother, Who Is My Brother?
391 Will You Let Me Be Your Servant
705 You Satisfy the Hungry Heart

MARRIAGE

611 As Man and Woman We Were Made
680 Borning Cry
609 Come to a Wedding
612 When Love Is Found
613 Your Love, O God, Has Called Us

MAUNDY THURSDAY

276 Christ, Let Us Come with You
403 Come, My Way, My Truth, My Life

697 Eat This Bread
272 Go to Dark Gethsemane
273 Jesu, Jesu, Fill Us with Your Love
699 Let Us Break Bread Together

MERCY

617 A Place at the Table
279 A Purple Robe
505 All the Way My Savior Leads Me
366 And Can It Be
426 Blessed Assurance
158 Blessed Be the God of Israel
380 Cast Thy Burden upon the Lord
655 Come Away from Rush and Hurry
68 Come, Thou Fount of Every Blessing
449 Day by Day
409 God of Our Life
50 Great Is the Lord
72 Great Is Thy Faithfulness
528 Here from All Nations
376 How Long, O Lord
60 I Will Sing of the Mercies
377 Kyrie Eleison (Ore Poriaju Vereko)
699 Let Us Break Bread Together
375 Lord, Have Mercy
575 Lord, Whose Love Through Humble Service
479 Near the Cross
444 Rain Down
440 Savior, Like a Shepherd Lead Us
41 Tell Out, My Soul
86 The Lord's My Shepherd, I'll Not Want
61 There's a Wideness in God's Mercy
686 What Does the Lord Require

MISSION

588 A Charge to Keep I Have
551 As a Fire Is Meant for Burning
581 Called as Partners in Christ's Service
561 Christ for the World! We Sing
324 Christ High-Ascended
335 Christ the Eternal Lord
459 Come, All Christians, Be Committed
548 Come, Great God of All the Ages
9 Come, Let Us Praise the Lord
329 Come, O Spirit, Dwell Among Us
67 Come, We That Love the Lord
615 Community of Christ
601 Dear Christ, Uplifted from the Earth
204 Down to Earth, as a Dove
123 Fairest Lord Jesus
331 Filled with the Spirit's Power
621 For the Healing of the Nations
640 From Miles Around
708 Go Forth for God
556 Go Forth in His Name
553 Go to the World!
564 God Is Working His Purpose Out
130 God Sends Us the Spirit
572 God, Whose Giving Knows No Ending
24 God, You Spin the Whirling Planets
436 Grace Alone
559 Here I Am, Lord
404 Hope of the World
560 I Love to Tell the Story
372 I Then Shall Live
698 Let Us Talents and Tongues Employ
593 Lord, Speak to Me
575 Lord, Whose Love Through Humble Service
592 Lord, You Give the Great Commission
565 O Christians, Haste
96 O for a Thousand Tongues to Sing
368 O Happy Day
398 O the Deep, Deep Love of Jesus
670 O Word of God Incarnate
586 Our Cities Cry to You, O God
557 Pass It On
568 People Need the Lord
722 Praise and Thanksgiving
531 Rejoice in God's Saints
89 Rise, Shine, You People!
713 Send Me, Jesus
712 Sent Forth by God's Blessing
319 Shine, Jesus, Shine
724 Sing to the Lord of Harvest
578 So Send I You
563 Song for the Nations
623 The Church of Christ in Every Age
133 There's a Spirit in the Air
552 We All Are One in Mission
580 We Are Called to Be God's People
550 We Are the Church
554 We Have Heard the Joyful Sound
707 We Thank You, God, for Feeding Us
390 We're Marching to Zion
562 We've a Story to Tell to the Nations
602 Who Is My Mother, Who Is My Brother?
362 Wonderful Grace of Jesus
668 Wonderful Words of Life
112 You Servants of God
566 Your Servant Comes This Hour

MORNING

23 All Creatures of Our God and King
30 All Things Bright and Beautiful
502 Be Thou My Vision
477 Come and Find the Quiet Center
649 Gather Us In
409 God of Our Life
78 God of the Ages, History's Maker
72 Great Is Thy Faithfulness
633 Healer of My Soul
136 Holy, Holy, Holy! Lord God Almighty!
33 Let's Sing unto the Lord (Cantemos al Señor)
20 Like a Mighty River Flowing
469 Lord of All Hopefulness
35 Morning Has Broken
537 My Lord! What a Morning
144 O Splendor of God's Glory Bright
56 Sing Praise to God Who Reigns Above
494 Step by Step
544 The Church's One Foundation
355 This Is a Day of New Beginnings
111 When Morning Gilds the Skies
567 With Welcome Heart We Greet You, Lord

MULTI-CULTURAL SONGS

163 All Earth Is Hopeful (Toda la Tierra)
741 Amen, Sing Praises to the Lord! (Amen, Siakudumisa!)
309 Christ the Lord Is Risen!
694 Come, Let Us Eat
157 Come Now, O Prince of Peace (O-so-so)
238 From a Distant Home (De Tierra Lejana Venimos)
195 Gloria, Gloria, Gloria
732 Glory to God, Glory in the Highest
130 God Sends Us the Spirit
5 Halle, Halle, Hallelujah
735 Hallelujah (Heleluyan)
709 Hallelujah! We Sing Your Praises
402 He Came Down
597 Here, O Lord, Your Servants Gather
297 His Battle Ended There
739 "Holy, Holy, Holy" ("Santo, Santo, Santo")
273 Jesu, Jesu, Fill Us with Your Love
659 Jesus, We Are Here (Jesu Tawa Pano)
377 Kyrie Eleison (Ore Poriaju Vereko)
33 Let's Sing unto the Lord (Cantemos al Señor)
347 Lord, You Have Come to the Lakeshore (Tú Has Venido a la Orilla)
26 Many and Great
421 Nothing Can Trouble (Nada te Turbe)
15 O, Sing to the Lord (Cantad al Señor)
207 Oh, Sleep Now, Holy Baby (A La Ru)
124 Open Your Hearts
269 Sanna, Sannanina
737 Santo, Santo, Santo (Holy, Holy, Holy)
713 Send Me Jesus
714 Shalom, My Friends (Shalom Chaverim)
211 That Boy-Child of Mary
159 The King of Glory Comes
399 Ubi Caritas et Amor (Where True Charity and Love Abide)
76 We Are Singing, for the Lord Is Our Light (Siyahamba)
674 What a Mighty God

624 When the Poor Ones (Cuando el Pobre)
415 When We Are Living (Pues Si Vivimos)

MUSIC & SINGING
322 A Hymn of Glory Let Us Sing!
23 All Creatures of Our God and King
92 All Hail King Jesus
289 Alleluia, Alleluia! Hearts to Heaven
320 Alleluia, Sing to Jesus!
741 Amen, Sing Praises to the Lord!
561 Christ for the World! We Sing
87 Come, Christians, Join to Sing
119 Come into His Presence
9 Come, Let Us Praise the Lord
68 Come, Thou Fount of Every Blessing
641 For the Music of Creation
3 God, We Praise You!
5 Halle, Halle, Hallelujah
709 Hallelujah! We Sing Your Praises
454 He Came Singing Love
424 How Can I Keep from Singing?
660 I Sing Praises
356 I Will Sing of My Redeemer
60 I Will Sing of the Mercies
33 Let's Sing unto the Lord (Cantemos al Señor)
729 Lift Every Voice and Sing
8 New Songs of Celebration
96 O for a Thousand Tongues to Sing
582 O Jesus Christ, May Grateful Hymns Be Rising
242 O Sing a Song of Bethlehem
313 O Sons and Daughters, Let Us Sing!
577 Sing a New Church
10 Sing a New Song
13 Sing a New Song to the Lord
120 Sing Alleluia to the Lord
141 Sing of a God in Majestic Divinity
247 Sing of God Made Manifest
56 Sing Praise to God Who Reigns Above
142 Sing Praise to the Father
724 Sing to the Lord of Harvest
193 Sing We Now of Christmas
563 Song for the Nations
76 We Are Singing, for the Lord Is Our Light
7 When in Our Music God Is Glorified
111 When Morning Gilds the Skies
645 When the Morning Stars Together
525 When We All Get to Heaven

NATION
727 America, the Beautiful
728 God of the Ages, Whose Almighty Hand
383 If My People's Hearts Are Humbled
730 Mine Eyes Have Seen the Glory
731 My Country, 'Tis of Thee
626 O God of Every Nation
159 The King of Glory Comes

NATURE
23 All Creatures of Our God and King
30 All Things Bright and Beautiful
39 All You Works of God, Bless the Lord!
9 Come, Let Us Praise the Lord
642 Earth and All Stars
123 Fairest Lord Jesus
28 For Beauty of Meadows
40 For the Beauty of the Earth
723 For the Fruit of All Creation
37 God in His Love for Us
72 Great Is Thy Faithfulness
51 How Great Thou Art
515 Hymn of Promise
488 I Lift My Eyes to the Quiet Hills
31 I Sing the Almighty Power of God
59 Joyful, Joyful, We Adore Thee
22 Let All Things Now Living
6 Let the Whole Creation Cry
35 Morning Has Broken
8 New Songs of Celebration
557 Pass It On
17 Praise the Lord! O Heavens, Adore Him
13 Sing a New Song to the Lord
724 Sing to the Lord of Harvest
243 Songs of Thankfulness and Praise
36 Thank You, God, for Water, Soil, and Air
725 Thanks to God for My Redeemer
710 The Trees of the Field
21 This Is My Father's World
534 When the King Shall Come Again
720 With Grateful Heart I Thank You, Lord

NEW LIFE IN CHRIST
258 At the Cross
202 Break Forth, O Beauteous Heavenly Light
373 Change My Heart, O God
314 Easter Song
649 Gather Us In
27 God of Creation, All-Powerful
55 Great God, Your Love Has Called Us Here
372 I Then Shall Live
678 In Water We Grow
287 Lift High the Cross
368 O Happy Day
142 Sing Praise to the Father
682 The Fruit of Love
355 This Is a Day of New Beginnings
540 Two Thousand Years Since Bethlehem
239 When John Baptized by Jordan's River

NEW YEAR
564 God Is Working His Purpose Out
409 God of Our Life
728 God of the Ages, Whose Almighty Hand
579 This Is a Time to Remember

OBEDIENCE
551 As a Fire Is Meant for Burning
684 For the Life That You Have Given
382 "Forgive Our Sins as We Forgive"
78 God of the Ages, History's Maker
573 How Clear Is Our Vocation, Lord
372 I Then Shall Live
574 I'm Gonna Live So God Can Use Me
429 If You Will Trust in God to Guide You
345 Jesus Calls Us o'er the Tumult
659 Jesus, We Are Here (Jesu Tawa Pano)
748 Lord, Dismiss Us with Your Blessing
671 Lord, We Hear Your Word
715 Now Let Us from This Table Rise
388 O God in Whom All Life Begins
483 Take Time to Be Holy
169 The Angel Gabriel from Heaven Came
623 The Church of Christ in Every Age
443 Trust and Obey
580 We Are Called to Be God's People
547 We Are God's People
686 What Does the Lord Require

OFFERING
687 All Things Are Yours!
570 As Saints of Old Their First-fruits Brought
236 As with Gladness
235 Brightest and Best of the Stars
459 Come, All Christians, Be Committed
684 For the Life That You Have Given
718 Forth In Your Name
1 God Is Here!
572 God, Whose Giving Knows No Ending
559 Here I Am, Lord
196 In the Bleak Midwinter
253 Lead Me to Calvary
565 O Christians, Haste
270 O How He Loves You and Me
577 Sing a New Church
724 Sing to the Lord of Harvest
466 Take My Life and Let It Be
579 This Is a Time to Remember
547 We Are God's People
651 We Bring the Sacrifice of Praise
688 We Give Thee but Thine Own
726 We Praise You, O God
686 What Does the Lord Require
685 What Gift Can We Bring
261 When I Survey the Wondrous Cross

555 When the Church of Jesus
415 When We Are Living (Pues Si Vivimos)
583 You Call Us, Lord

ORDINATION
588 A Charge to Keep I Have
584 Come, Celebrate the Call of God
149 God the Spirit, Guide and Guardian

PALM SUNDAY
206 A Stable Lamp Is Lighted
92 All Hail King Jesus
158 Blessed Be the God of Israel
266 Hosanna (Tuttle)
267 Hosanna, Loud Hosanna
125 In the Name of the Lord
22 Let All Things Now Living
271 Lift Up Your Heads
176 Lift Up Your Heads, O Mighty Gates
152 Prepare the Way, O Zion
268 Ride On, Ride On in Majesty!
159 The King of Glory Comes

PARDON (See FORGIVENESS)

PEACE - INNER
432 As Water to the Thirsty
477 Come and Find the Quiet Center
655 Come Away from Rush and Hurry
470 Dear Lord and Father of Mankind
717 Go Now in Peace
424 How Can I Keep from Singing?
476 I Need Thee Every Hour
533 Joy in the Morning
435 Like a River Glorious
446 O Love That Will Not Let Me Go
589 O Master, Let Me Walk with Thee
428 When Peace Like a River
396 Where the Spirit of the Lord Is

PEACE ON EARTH
157 Come Now, O Prince of Peace (O-so-so)
615 Community of Christ
614 Let There Be Peace on Earth
587 Make Me a Channel of Your Peace
539 O Day of Peace
389 Put Peace into Each Other's Hands
512 We Shall Overcome
622 When Will People Cease Their Fighting?

PENITENCE
373 Change My Heart, O God
155 Comfort, Comfort Now My People
378 Create in Me a Clean Heart, O God
416 God! When Human Bonds Are Broken
636 Heal Me, Hands of Jesus
370 Healing Grace
474 I Surrender All
383 If My People's Hearts Are Humbled
379 Kyrie
377 Kyrie Eleison (Ore Poriaju Vereko)
386 Lord Jesus, Think on Me
252 Lord, Who Throughout These Forty Days
468 My Jesus, I Love Thee
371 Our Father, We Have Wandered
374 Refiner's Fire
495 Stand by Me
628 We Cannot Measure How You Heal
239 When John Baptized by Jordan's River

PENTECOST
585 A Prophet-Woman Broke a Jar
461 Breathe on Me, Breath of God
543 Come Build a Church
330 Come Down, O Love Divine
127 Come, Holy Spirit
325 Come, Holy Spirit, Our Souls Inspire
329 Come, O Spirit, Dwell Among Us
475 Eternal Spirit of the Living Christ
392 Fear Not, Rejoice and Be Glad
331 Filled with the Spirit's Power
1 God Is Here!
130 God Sends Us the Spirit
149 God the Spirit, Guide and Guardian
528 Here from All Nations
332 Let Every Christian Pray
327 Like the Murmur of the Dove's Song
489 Lord, Listen to Your Children Praying
328 O Breath of Life
334 On Pentecost They Gathered
656 Open the Eyes of My Heart
463 Revive Us Again
713 Send Me, Jesus
132 Spirit of God, Descend upon My Heart
492 Spirit of the Living God
326 Spirit, Spirit of Gentleness
128 Spirit, Working in Creation
134 Sweet, Sweet Spirit
542 They Did Not Build in Vain
540 Two Thousand Years Since Bethlehem
550 We Are the Church
647 We Have Come to Join in Worship
333 Wind Who Makes All Winds That Blow

PILGRIMAGE
422 Amazing Grace!
432 As Water to the Thirsty
158 Blessed Be the God of Israel
680 Borning Cry
449 Day by Day
618 Go Down, Moses
409 God of Our Life
728 God of the Ages, Whose Almighty Hand
501 Guide Me, O Thou Great Jehovah
506 I Want Jesus to Walk with Me
225 I Wonder as I Wander
508 Lead On, O King Eternal
496 Leaning on the Everlasting Arms
22 Let All Things Now Living
729 Lift Every Voice and Sing
748 Lord, Dismiss Us with Your Blessing
608 Lord of Our Growing Years
575 Lord, Whose Love Through Humble Service
715 Now Let Us from This Table Rise
14 Now Thank We All Our God
84 O God, Our Help in Ages Past
503 O God, Your Constant Care and Love
519 On Jordan's Stormy Banks I Stand
500 Precious Lord, Take My Hand
522 Shall We Gather at the River
495 Stand by Me
511 The Battle Belongs to the Lord
558 The World Is Full of Stories
452 Through It All
536 Through the Darkness of the Ages
443 Trust and Obey
390 We're Marching to Zion
612 When Love Is Found
525 When We All Get to Heaven
391 Will You Let Me Be Your Servant
234 Wise Men, They Came to Look for Wisdom

PRAISE OF GOD
30 All Things Bright and Beautiful
471 As the Deer
658 Awesome God
19 Blessed Be the Lord God Almighty
197 Come and Hear the Joyful Singing
9 Come, Let Us Praise the Lord
148 Come, Thou Almighty King
32 Creating God, Your Fingers Trace
44 Doxology (Owens)
642 Earth and All Stars
40 For the Beauty of the Earth
63 Give to Our God Immortal Praise
240 Gloria, Gloria
195 Gloria, Gloria, Gloria
145 Glory Be to God, Creator
734 Glory Be to the Father (GREATOREX)
733 Glory Be to the Father (MEINEKE)
732 Glory to God, Glory in the Highest
139 God Is One, Unique and Holy
27 God of Creation, All-Powerful
3 God, We Praise You!
663 God's Holy Ways Are Just and True

226 God's Love Made Visible!
50 Great Is the Lord
5 Halle, Halle, Hallelujah
735 Hallelujah (Heleluyan)
528 Here from All Nations
138 Holy God, We Praise Your Name
739 "Holy, Holy, Holy" ("Santo, Santo, Santo")
738 Holy, Holy, Holy Lord
151 Holy Is the Lord
51 How Great Thou Art
42 How Majestic Is Your Name
660 I Sing Praises
53 I Stand in Awe
69 I Worship You, Almighty God
79 I'll Praise My Maker While I've Breath
48 Immortal, Invisible, God Only Wise
62 In the Lord Alone
59 Joyful, Joyful, We Adore Thee
25 Let All Creation Bless the Lord
49 Let All the World
22 Let All Things Now Living
6 Let the Whole Creation Cry
54 Let There Be Praise
699 Let Us Break Bread Together
33 Let's Sing unto the Lord (Cantemos al Señor)
435 Like a River Glorious
173 Magnificat (Sing Out, My Soul)
45 Mighty Is Our God
170 My Soul Proclaims with Wonder
363 My Tribute
8 New Songs of Celebration
96 O for a Thousand Tongues to Sing
64 O God Beyond All Praising
84 O God, Our Help in Ages Past
503 O God, Your Constant Care and Love
144 O Splendor of God's Glory Bright
140 Praise and Thanksgiving Be to God
34 Praise God from Whom All Blessings Flow (Old 100th)
147 Praise God from Whom All Blessings Flow (Wren)
46 Praise the Lord Who Reigns Above
71 Praise to the Lord, the Almighty
650 Rejoice in the Lord Always
737 Santo, Santo, Santo
577 Sing a New Church
56 Sing Praise to God Who Reigns Above
423 Surely It Is God Who Saves Me
41 Tell Out, My Soul
16 The God of Abraham Praise
652 This Is the Day
315 This Is the Feast of Victory
126 Thou Art Worthy
66 To God Be the Glory
651 We Bring the Sacrifice of Praise
47 We Exalt Thee
726 We Praise You, O God
674 What a Mighty God
691 With the Body That Was Broken
137 Worthy of Worship
52 You Are My God

PRAISE TO CHRIST

460 All for Jesus!
265 All Glory, Laud and Honor
505 All the Way My Savior Leads Me
316 Alleluia
291 Alleluia No. 1
366 And Can It Be
611 As Man and Woman We Were Made
321 At the Name of Jesus
105 Beautiful Savior
426 Blessed Assurance
453 Christ Be My Leader
369 Christ Is God's Never Changing 'Yes!'
335 Christ the Eternal Lord
288 Christ the Lord Is Risen Today
517 Christ the Victorious
336 Christ Triumphant, Ever Reigning
197 Come and Hear the Joyful Singing
87 Come, Christians, Join to Sing
119 Come into His Presence
148 Come, Thou Almighty King
153 Come, Thou Long-Expected Jesus
340 Crown Him King of Kings
314 Easter Song
123 Fairest Lord Jesus
238 From a Distant Home (De Tierra Lejana Venimos)
103 Glory to the Lamb
436 Grace Alone
98 Hallelujah! Praise the Lamb!
301 Hallelujah! What a Savior!
454 He Came Singing Love
639 He Is Able
201 He Is Born
122 He Is Exalted
528 Here from All Nations
597 Here, O Lord, Your Servants Gather
104 Hidden Christ, Alive for Ever
102 His Name Is Wonderful
654 Holy Ground
404 Hope of the World
267 Hosanna, Loud Hosanna
675 I Believe in Jesus
85 I Love You, Lord
125 In the Name of the Lord
431 Jesus, Priceless Treasure
341 Jesus Shall Reign
420 Jesus, the Very Thought of Thee
659 Jesus, We Are Here (Jesu Tawa Pano)
338 King of Kings
88 Lord, I Lift Your Name on High
358 Love Divine, All Loves Excelling
43 Majesty
97 Meekness and Majesty
468 My Jesus, I Love Thee
150 My Lord of Light
101 Name of All Majesty
114 O Come, Let Us Adore Him
96 O for a Thousand Tongues to Sing
270 O How He Loves You and Me
109 O, How I Love Jesus
582 O Jesus Christ, May Grateful Hymns Be Rising
230 O Morning Star, How Fair and Bright!
15 O, Sing to the Lord (Cantad al Señor)
313 O Sons and Daughters, Let Us Sing!
95 Praise Him! Praise Him!
115 Praise the Name of Jesus
93 Praise the One Who Breaks the Darkness
82 Praise, My Soul, the King of Heaven
94 Shout to the Lord
299 That Easter Day with Joy Was Bright
544 The Church's One Foundation
73 The Lord My Shepherd Guards Me Well
108 There's Something About That Name
126 Thou Art Worthy
472 Turn Your Eyes upon Jesus
110 We Come, O Christ, to You
337 We Will Glorify
360 What the Lord Has Done in Me
111 When Morning Gilds the Skies
415 When We Are Living (Pues Si Vivimos)
116 Worthy Is the Lamb
427 You Are My All in All
99 You, Lord, Are Both Lamb and Shepherd
648 You're Worthy of My Praise

PRAYER

450 Be Still and Know
502 Be Thou My Vision
393 Blest Be the Tie That Binds
493 Cares Chorus
380 Cast Thy Burden upon the Lord
470 Dear Lord and Father of Mankind
74 Eternal Father, Strong to Save
475 Eternal Spirit of the Living Christ
481 Every Time I Feel the Spirit
684 For the Life That You Have Given
436 Grace Alone
370 Healing Grace
490 Hear Our Prayer, O Lord
376 How Long, O Lord
408 I Am Thine, O Lord
488 I Lift My Eyes to the Quiet Hills
549 I Love Your Kingdom, Lord
574 I'm Gonna Live So God Can Use Me
383 If My People's Hearts Are Humbled
429 If You Will Trust in God to Guide You
445 In the Day of Need
487 Kum Ba Yah
332 Let Every Christian Pray
327 Like the Murmur of the Dove's Song

489 Lord, Listen to Your Children Praying
419 My Faith Looks Up to Thee
700 Now the Silence
484 O Lord, Hear My Prayer
480 Open My Eyes, That I May See
462 Renew Your Church
440 Savior, Like a Shepherd Lead Us
349 Seek Ye First
132 Spirit of God, Descend upon My Heart
286 Stay with Me
478 Sweet Hour of Prayer
483 Take Time to Be Holy
605 The Family Prayer Song
740 The Lord's Prayer
350 The Summons
472 Turn Your Eyes upon Jesus
628 We Cannot Measure How You Heal
704 We Meet as Friends at Table
473 What a Friend We Have in Jesus
413 When Our Confidence Is Shaken
555 When the Church of Jesus
583 You Call Us, Lord
566 Your Servant Comes This Hour

PROCLAMATION

30 All Things Bright and Beautiful
291 Alleluia No. 1
695 As We Gather at Your Table
665 Break Now the Bread of Life
581 Called as Partners in Christ's Service
667 God Has Spoken by the Prophets
1 God Is Here!
564 God Is Working His Purpose Out
663 God's Holy Ways Are Just and True
560 I Love to Tell the Story
6 Let the Whole Creation Cry
593 Lord, Speak to Me
592 Lord, You Give the Great Commission
565 O Christians, Haste
670 O Word of God Incarnate
480 Open My Eyes, That I May See
462 Renew Your Church
319 Shine, Jesus, Shine
13 Sing a New Song to the Lord
578 So Send I You
41 Tell Out, My Soul
580 We Are Called to Be God's People
673 We Believe in God Almighty
554 We Have Heard the Joyful Sound
390 We're Marching to Zion
562 We've a Story to Tell to the Nations
668 Wonderful Words of Life
112 You Servants of God

PROMISE & HOPE

422 Amazing Grace!
430 Be Not Afraid
153 Come, Thou Long-Expected Jesus
155 Comfort, Comfort Now My People
449 Day by Day
535 Face to Face
499 He Leadeth Me
411 How Firm a Foundation
515 Hymn of Promise
429 If You Will Trust in God to Guide You
435 Like a River Glorious
405 My Hope Is Built on Nothing Less
458 O Jesus, I Have Promised
579 This Is a Time to Remember
672 This Is the Threefold Truth

PROVIDENCE

32 Creating God, Your Fingers Trace
421 Nothing Can Trouble (Nada te Turbe)
503 O God, Your Constant Care and Love
438 On Eagle's Wings
444 Rain Down

RECONCILIATION

259 Amazing Love
157 Come Now, O Prince of Peace (O-so-so)
382 "Forgive Our Sins as We Forgive"
416 God! When Human Bonds Are Broken
600 In Christ There Is No East or West (Perry)
533 Joy in the Morning
700 Now the Silence
628 We Cannot Measure How You Heal
512 We Shall Overcome
602 Who Is My Mother, Who Is My Brother?
691 With the Body That Was Broken

REDEMPTION

279 A Purple Robe
263 Alas! and Did My Savior Bleed
259 Amazing Love
366 And Can It Be
426 Blessed Assurance
158 Blessed Be the God of Israel
121 Christ Is the World's Light
317 Crown Him with Many Crowns
251 I Come to the Cross
407 I Know Whom I Have Believed
356 I Will Sing of My Redeemer
256 There Is a Fountain Filled with Blood
66 To God Be the Glory
110 We Come, O Christ, to You
726 We Praise You, O God
360 What the Lord Has Done in Me

RENEWAL

551 As a Fire Is Meant for Burning
461 Breathe on Me, Breath of God
373 Change My Heart, O God
378 Create in Me a Clean Heart, O God
1 God Is Here!
596 Help Us Accept Each Other
573 How Clear Is Our Vocation, Lord
488 I Lift My Eyes to the Quiet Hills
669 Jesus, Come, for We Invite You
327 Like the Murmur of the Dove's Song
715 Now Let Us from This Table Rise
311 Now the Green Blade Rises
328 O Breath of Life
371 Our Father, We Have Wandered
374 Refiner's Fire
462 Renew Your Church
381 Restore in Us, O God
492 Spirit of the Living God
326 Spirit, Spirit of Gentleness
134 Sweet, Sweet Spirit
86 The Lord's My Shepherd, I'll Not Want
540 Two Thousand Years Since Bethlehem

REST

505 All the Way My Savior Leads Me
430 Be Not Afraid
426 Blessed Assurance
546 Built on the Rock
425 Christ Beside Me
517 Christ the Victorious
655 Come Away from Rush and Hurry
694 Come, Let Us Eat
9 Come, Let Us Praise the Lord
470 Dear Lord and Father of Mankind
538 Deep River
633 Healer of My Soul
545 How Lovely, Lord, How Lovely
488 I Lift My Eyes to the Quiet Hills
420 Jesus, the Very Thought of Thee
435 Like a River Glorious
386 Lord Jesus, Think on Me
469 Lord of All Hopefulness
479 Near the Cross
433 O Christ the Same
519 On Jordan's Stormy Banks I Stand
711 Savior, Again to Your Dear Name
348 Softly and Tenderly
456 Thy Holy Wings
442 'Tis So Sweet to Trust in Jesus
110 We Come, O Christ, to You
685 What Gift Can We Bring
567 With Welcome Heart We Greet You, Lord
446 O Love That Will Not Let Me Go

SECOND COMING OF CHRIST

92 All Hail King Jesus
625 All Who Love and Serve Your City
321 At the Name of Jesus
160 Awake! Awake, and Greet the New Morn
312 Christ Is Alive!
91 Christ, Whose Glory Fills the Skies
696 Come, Share the Lord
418 Eternal Light, Shine in My Heart
556 Go Forth in His Name
301 Hallelujah! What a Savior!

51 How Great Thou Art
318 Jesus Comes with Clouds Descending
533 Joy in the Morning
271 Lift Up Your Heads
176 Lift Up Your Heads, O Mighty Gates
162 like a child
167 Long Ago, Prophets Knew
730 Mine Eyes Have Seen the Glory
537 My Lord! What a Morning
400 Not for Tongues of Heaven's Angels
620 O Lord, You Gave Your Servant John
156 On Jordan's Bank the Baptist's Cry
586 Our Cities Cry to You, O God
161 People, Look East
152 Prepare the Way, O Zion
342 Rejoice, the Lord Is King!
168 Savior of the Nations, Come
523 Soon and Very Soon
159 The King of Glory Comes
672 This Is the Threefold Truth
536 Through the Darkness of the Ages
250 Throughout These Lenten Days and Nights
166 Wait for the Lord
164 Wake, Awake, for Night Is Flying
175 We Light the Advent Candles
428 When Peace Like a River
534 When the King Shall Come Again
622 When Will People Cease Their Fighting?

SERVICE MUSIC - ACCLAMATION
675 I Believe in Jesus
672 This Is the Threefold Truth

SERVICE MUSIC - ALLELUIA
316 Alleluia
736 Celtic Alleluia
307 Good Christians All, Rejoice
5 Halle, Halle, Hallelujah
735 Hallelujah (Heleluyan)
212 Raise a Song of Gladness (Jubilate Deo)

SERVICE MUSIC - AMEN
742 Amen (Rutter)
743-746 Amens
249 Amen, Amen
741 Amen, Sing Praises to the Lord!
732 Glory to God, Glory in the Highest

SERVICE MUSIC - BENEDICTION
747 Go with Us, Lord
716 God Be with You
748 Lord, Dismiss Us with Your Blessing
712 Sent Forth by God's Blessing
749 The Lord Bless You and Keep You

SERVICE MUSIC - CALL TO WORSHIP
387 The Lord Is in His Holy Temple
652 This Is the Day

SERVICE MUSIC - CREED
675 I Believe in Jesus
672 This Is the Threefold Truth
673 We Believe in God Almighty

SERVICE MUSIC - DOXOLOGY
44 Doxology (Owens)
34 Praise God from Whom All Blessings Flow (Old 100th)
147 Praise God from Whom All Blessings Flow (Wren)

SERVICE MUSIC - GLORIA PATRI
240 Gloria, Gloria
734 Glory Be to the Father (GREATOREX)
733 Glory Be to the Father (MEINEKE)
732 Glory to God, Glory in the Highest

SERVICE MUSIC - KYRIE
379 Kyrie
377 Kyrie Eleison (Ore Poriaju Vereko)
375 Lord, Have Mercy

SERVICE MUSIC - PRAYER RESPONSE
490 Hear Our Prayer, O Lord
285 Jesus, Remember Me
487 Kum Ba Yah
423 Surely It Is God Who Saves Me
740 The Lord's Prayer

SERVICE MUSIC – SANCTUS
739 "Holy, Holy, Holy" ("Santo, Santo, Santo")
738 Holy, Holy, Holy Lord
737 Santo, Santo, Santo

SIN
262 Ah, Holy Jesus
263 Alas! and Did My Savior Bleed
353 Grace Greater than Our Sin
374 Refiner's Fire
385 Search Me, O God
256 There Is a Fountain Filled with Blood
428 When Peace Like a River

SORROW
451 Be Still, My Soul
411 How Firm a Foundation
345 Jesus Calls Us o'er the Tumult

SPIRITUALS
249 Amen, Amen
538 Deep River
481 Every Time I Feel the Spirit
618 Go Down, Moses
218 Go, Tell It on the Mountain
280 He Never Said a Mumbalin' Word
80 He's Got the Whole World in His Hands
506 I Want Jesus to Walk with Me
574 I'm Gonna Live So God Can Use Me
254 Jesus Walked This Lonesome Valley
487 Kum Ba Yah
457 Lord, I Want to Be a Christian
220 Mary Had a Baby
537 My Lord! What a Morning
209 Rise Up, Shepherd, and Follow
527 Steal Away
520 Swing Low, Sweet Chariot
365 Thank You, Lord
631 There Is a Balm in Gilead
512 We Shall Overcome
283 Were You There

STEWARDSHIP
588 A Charge to Keep I Have
687 All Things Are Yours!
570 As Saints of Old Their First-fruits Brought
236 As with Gladness
235 Brightest and Best of the Stars
459 Come, All Christians, Be Committed
28 For Beauty of Meadows
723 For the Fruit of All Creation
684 For the Life That You Have Given
718 Forth In Your Name
37 God in His Love for Us
1 God Is Here!
572 God, Whose Giving Knows No Ending
565 O Christians, Haste
577 Sing a New Church
724 Sing to the Lord of Harvest
466 Take My Life and Let It Be
397 The Gift of Love
579 This Is a Time to Remember
472 Turn Your Eyes upon Jesus
547 We Are God's People
688 We Give Thee but Thine Own
726 We Praise You, O God
686 What Does the Lord Require
685 What Gift Can We Bring
261 When I Survey the Wondrous Cross
555 When the Church of Jesus
415 When We Are Living (Pues Si Vivimos)

SUFFERING
430 Be Not Afraid
451 Be Still, My Soul
693 Bread of the World
75 By Gracious Powers
155 Comfort, Comfort Now My People
449 Day by Day
717 Go Now in Peace
416 God! When Human Bonds Are Broken
636 Heal Me, Hands of Jesus
630 Healer of Our Every Ill

476 I Need Thee Every Hour
506 I Want Jesus to Walk with Me
383 If My People's Hearts Are Humbled
435 Like a River Glorious
419 My Faith Looks Up to Thee
638 O Christ, the Healer, We Have Come
433 O Christ the Same
109 O, How I Love Jesus
495 Stand by Me
278 To Mock Your Reign
443 Trust and Obey
473 What a Friend We Have in Jesus
632 When Aimless Violence Takes Those We Love
612 When Love Is Found
413 When Our Confidence Is Shaken
428 When Peace Like a River
415 When We Are Living (Pues Si Vivimos)
396 Where the Spirit of the Lord Is

SURRENDER
263 Alas! and Did My Savior Bleed
502 Be Thou My Vision
474 I Surrender All
486 Have Thine Own Way, Lord!
464 May the Mind of Christ, My Savior
385 Search Me, O God

TAIZÉ SONGS
216 Adoramus Te (We Adore You)
697 Eat This Bread
240 Gloria, Gloria
448 In the Lord I'll Be Ever Thankful
285 Jesus, Remember Me
303 Jubilate Deo (In the Lord Rejoicing!)
173 Magnificat (Sing Out, My Soul)
421 Nothing Can Trouble (Nada te Turbe)
484 O Lord, Hear My Prayer
174 Prepare the Way of the Lord
212 Raise a Song of Gladness (Jubilate Deo)
286 Stay with Me
399 Ubi Caritas et Amor (Where True Charity and Love Abide)
166 Wait for the Lord

TEMPTATION
521 Abide with Me
505 All the Way My Savior Leads Me
68 Come, Thou Fount of Every Blessing
449 Day by Day
633 Healer of My Soul
637 His Strength Is Perfect
476 I Need Thee Every Hour
506 I Want Jesus to Walk with Me
90 Jesus! What a Friend for Sinners!
504 Just a Closer Walk with Thee
386 Lord Jesus, Think on Me
252 Lord, Who Throughout These Forty Days
711 Savior, Again to Your Dear Name
132 Spirit of God, Descend upon My Heart
478 Sweet Hour of Prayer
473 What a Friend We Have in Jesus

THANKSGIVING & GRATITUDE
291 Alleluia No. 1
570 As Saints of Old Their First-fruits Brought
643 Colorful Creator
721 Come, Ye Thankful People, Come
44 Doxology (Owens)
40 For the Beauty of the Earth
723 For the Fruit of All Creation
359 Give Thanks
518 Give Thanks for Life
728 God of the Ages, Whose Almighty Hand
29 God of the Sparrow
572 God, Whose Giving Knows No Ending
72 Great Is Thy Faithfulness
60 I Will Sing of the Mercies
448 In the Lord I'll Be Ever Thankful
22 Let All Things Now Living
748 Lord, Dismiss Us with Your Blessing
363 My Tribute
14 Now Thank We All Our God
433 O Christ the Same
722 Praise and Thanksgiving
140 Praise and Thanksgiving Be to God
34 Praise God from Whom All Blessings Flow (Old 100th)
342 Rejoice, the Lord Is King!
482 Sanctuary
724 Sing to the Lord of Harvest
243 Songs of Thankfulness and Praise
36 Thank You, God, for Water, Soil, and Air
365 Thank You, Lord
725 Thanks to God for My Redeemer
662 Thanks to God Whose Word Was Spoken
117 There Is a Redeemer
701 There's a Quiet Understanding
651 We Bring the Sacrifice of Praise
702 We Come as Guests Invited
81 We Gather Together
688 We Give Thee but Thine Own
726 We Praise You, O God
690 We Remember You
685 What Gift Can We Bring
720 With Grateful Heart I Thank You, Lord
567 With Welcome Heart We Greet You, Lord
705 You Satisfy the Hungry Heart
112 You Servants of God

TRINITY
322 A Hymn of Glory Let Us Sing!
23 All Creatures of Our God and King
39 All You Works of God, Bless the Lord!
289 Alleluia, Alleluia! Hearts to Heaven
121 Christ Is the World's Light
197 Come and Hear the Joyful Singing
676 Come, Be Baptized
325 Come, Holy Spirit, Our Souls Inspire
148 Come, Thou Almighty King
44 Doxology (Owens)
74 Eternal Father, Strong to Save
143 Father, I Adore You
529 For All the Saints
146 Glorify Thy Name
145 Glory Be to God, Creator
734 Glory Be to the Father (GREATOREX)
733 Glory Be to the Father (MEINEKE)
719 Go, My Children, with My Blessing
717 Go Now in Peace
667 God Has Spoken by the Prophets
1 God Is Here!
139 God Is One, Unique and Holy
58 God of Many Names
3 God, We Praise You!
138 Holy God, We Praise Your Name
136 Holy, Holy, Holy! Lord God Almighty!
151 Holy Is the Lord
295 Jesus Christ Is Risen Today
150 My Lord of Light
107 O Light Whose Splendor Thrills
244 O Love, How Deep, How Broad
144 O Splendor of God's Glory Bright
181 Of the Father's Love Begotten
156 On Jordan's Bank the Baptist's Cry
140 Praise and Thanksgiving Be to God
34 Praise God from Whom All Blessings Flow (Old 100th)
147 Praise God from Whom All Blessings Flow (Wren)
381 Restore in Us, O God
89 Rise, Shine, You People!
168 Savior of the Nations, Come
141 Sing of a God in Majestic Divinity
142 Sing Praise to the Father
128 Spirit, Working in Creation
662 Thanks to God Whose Word Was Spoken
544 The Church's One Foundation
682 The Fruit of Love
117 There Is a Redeemer
542 They Did Not Build in Vain
595 They'll Know We Are Christians
355 This Is a Day of New Beginnings
673 We Believe in God Almighty

TRUST
588 A Charge to Keep I Have
450 Be Still and Know
493 Cares Chorus
453 Christ Be My Leader
425 Christ Beside Me

449 Day by Day
470 Dear Lord and Father of Mankind
27 God of Creation, All-Powerful
409 God of Our Life
80 He's Got the Whole World in His Hands
526 How Blest Are They
376 How Long, O Lord
429 If You Will Trust in God to Guide You
439 Jesus, Lover of My Soul
435 Like a River Glorious
683 Little One, Born to Bring
406 My Faith Has Found a Resting Place
405 My Hope Is Built on Nothing Less
479 Near the Cross
417 Not with Naked Eye
64 O God Beyond All Praising
589 O Master, Let Me Walk with Thee
115 Praise the Name of Jesus
132 Spirit of God, Descend upon My Heart
513 Stand Up, Stand Up for Jesus
423 Surely It Is God Who Saves Me
483 Take Time to Be Holy
452 Through It All
443 Trust and Obey
441 Trust in the Lord
166 Wait for the Lord
685 What Gift Can We Bring
525 When We All Get to Heaven
648 You're Worthy of My Praise

UNITY
617 A Place at the Table
551 As a Fire Is Meant for Burning
695 As We Gather at Your Table
581 Called as Partners in Christ's Service
561 Christ for the World! We Sing
121 Christ Is the World's Light
157 Come Now, O Prince of Peace (O-so-so)
696 Come, Share the Lord
32 Creating God, Your Fingers Trace
331 Filled with the Spirit's Power
621 For the Healing of the Nations
641 For the Music of Creation
572 God, Whose Giving Knows No Ending
607 Happy the Home When God Is There
596 Help Us Accept Each Other
528 Here from All Nations
706 I Come with Joy
600 In Christ There Is No East or West (Perry)
59 Joyful, Joyful, We Adore Thee
614 Let There Be Peace on Earth
698 Let Us Talents and Tongues Employ
327 Like the Murmur of the Dove's Song
610 O Perfect Love
689 One Bread, One Body
124 Open Your Hearts
722 Praise and Thanksgiving
389 Put Peace into Each Other's Hands
577 Sing a New Church
492 Spirit of the Living God
395 The Bond of Love
229 The First Noel
701 There's a Quiet Understanding
595 They'll Know We Are Christians
38 Touch the Earth Lightly
552 We All Are One in Mission
580 We Are Called to Be God's People
547 We Are God's People
512 We Shall Overcome
622 When Will People Cease Their Fighting?

WEDDINGS (See also: LOVE)
609 Come to a Wedding
669 Jesus, Come, for We Invite You
610 O Perfect Love
612 When Love Is Found
613 Your Love, O God, Has Called Us

WITNESS
510 Am I a Soldier of the Cross
695 As We Gather at Your Table
426 Blessed Assurance
324 Christ High-Ascended
459 Come, All Christians, Be Committed
9 Come, Let Us Praise the Lord
497 Find Us Faithful
529 For All the Saints
24 God, You Spin the Whirling Planets
436 Grace Alone
407 I Know Whom I Have Believed
560 I Love to Tell the Story
60 I Will Sing of the Mercies
327 Like the Murmur of the Dove's Song
592 Lord, You Give the Great Commission
405 My Hope Is Built on Nothing Less
368 O Happy Day
589 O Master, Let Me Walk with Thee
56 Sing Praise to God Who Reigns Above
578 So Send I You
128 Spirit, Working in Creation
466 Take My Life and Let It Be
483 Take Time to Be Holy
558 The World Is Full of Stories
133 There's a Spirit in the Air
580 We Are Called to Be God's People
554 We Have Heard the Joyful Sound
390 We're Marching to Zion
562 We've a Story to Tell to the Nations
720 With Grateful Heart I Thank You, Lord
364 Woman in the Night
362 Wonderful Grace of Jesus
668 Wonderful Words of Life

WORD & TEACHING
695 As We Gather at Your Table
619 Because He Died and Is Risen
666 Blest Are They
693 Bread of the World
665 Break Now the Bread of Life
546 Built on the Rock
459 Come, All Christians, Be Committed
449 Day by Day
418 Eternal Light, Shine in My Heart
410 Firm Foundation
382 "Forgive Our Sins as We Forgive"
27 God of Creation, All-Powerful
728 God of the Ages, Whose Almighty Hand
607 Happy the Home When God Is There
596 Help Us Accept Each Other
411 How Firm a Foundation
545 How Lovely, Lord, How Lovely
42 How Majestic Is Your Name
703 I Am the Bread of Life
488 I Lift My Eyes to the Quiet Hills
560 I Love to Tell the Story
532 Isaiah the Prophet Has Written of Old
437 Jesus Loves Me
246 Jesus on the Mountain Peak
681 Lord, We Bring to You Our Children
671 Lord, We Hear Your Word
464 May the Mind of Christ, My Savior
406 My Faith Has Found a Resting Place
433 O Christ the Same
462 Renew Your Church
349 Seek Ye First
41 Tell Out, My Soul
662 Thanks to God Whose Word Was Spoken
579 This Is a Time to Remember
452 Through It All
664 Thy Word
441 Trust in the Lord
547 We Are God's People
562 We've a Story to Tell to the Nations
668 Wonderful Words of Life
566 Your Servant Comes This Hour

Alphabetical Index

Cross-referenced common titles and first lines are in italics.

588 A Charge to Keep I Have
322 A Hymn of Glory Let Us Sing!
207 *A La Ru*
507 A Mighty Fortress Is Our God
617 A Place at the Table
585 A Prophet-Woman Broke a Jar
279 A Purple Robe
206 A Stable Lamp Is Lighted
521 Abide with Me
216 Adoramus Te
262 Ah, Holy Jesus
263 Alas! and Did My Savior Bleed (MARTYRDOM)
258 *Alas! and Did My Savior Bleed (HUDSON)*
23 All Creatures of Our God and King
163 All Earth Is Hopeful
460 All for Jesus!
265 All Glory, Laud and Honor
92 All Hail King Jesus!
106 All Hail the Power of Jesus' Name! (CORONATION)
100 All Hail the Power of Jesus' Name! (DIADEM)
357 *All I Once Held Dear*
661 All People That on Earth Do Dwell
505 All the Way My Savior Leads Me
687 All Things Are Yours!
30 All Things Bright and Beautiful
474 *All to Jesus I Surrender*
625 All Who Love and Serve Your City
39 All You Works of God, Bless the Lord!
316 Alleluia
291 *Alleluia, Alleluia! Give Thanks*
289 Alleluia, Alleluia! Hearts to Heaven
306 Alleluia! Jesus Is Risen!
291 Alleluia No. 1
320 Alleluia, Sing to Jesus!
510 Am I a Soldier of the Cross
422 Amazing Grace!
259 Amazing Love
249 Amen, Amen
744 Amen (Danish)
743 Amen (Dresden)
746 Amen (Johnson)
742 Amen (Rutter)
745 Amen (Schubert)
741 Amen, Sing Praises to the Lord!
741 *Amen, Siakudumisa!*
727 America, the Beautiful
275 An Upper Room Did Our Lord Prepare
274 An Upper Room with Evening Lamps
366 And Can It Be
635 And Jesus Said
189 Angels, from the Realms of Glory
188 Angels We Have Heard on High
231 Arise, Your Light Is Come!
551 As a Fire Is Meant for Burning
611 As Man and Woman We Were Made
570 As Saints of Old Their First-fruits Brought
471 As the Deer
432 As Water to the Thirsty
646 As We Gather
695 As We Gather at Your Table
236 As with Gladness
606 As Your Family, Lord, Meet Us Here
258 At the Cross
321 At the Name of Jesus
160 Awake! Awake, and Greet the New Morn
205 Away in a Manger (Kirkpatrick)
203 Away in a Manger (Murray)
658 Awesome God
679 Baptized in Water
730 *Battle Hymn of the Republic*
12 Be Exalted, O God
430 Be Not Afraid
450 Be Still and Know
129 Be Still, for the Spirit of the Lord
451 Be Still, My Soul
514 Be Strong in the Lord
502 Be Thou My Vision
105 Beautiful Savior
619 Because He Died and Is Risen
447 Because He Lives
292 Because You Live, O Christ
282 Behold the Lamb of God
255 Beneath the Cross of Jesus
4 Bless His Holy Name
4 *Bless the Lord, O My Soul*
426 Blessed Assurance
158 Blessed Be the God of Israel
19 Blessed Be the Lord God Almighty
18 *Blessed Be the Name of the Lord*
666 Blest Are They
393 Blest Be the Tie That Binds
194 Born in the Night, Mary's Child
680 Borning Cry
693 Bread of the World

202 Break Forth, O Beauteous Heavenly Light
665 Break Now the Bread of Life
461 Breathe on Me, Breath of God
235 Brightest and Best of the Stars
546 Built on the Rock
75 By Gracious Powers
581 Called as Partners in Christ's Service
15 *Cantad al Señor*
33 *Cantemos al Señor*
493 Cares Chorus
199 Carol at the Manger
380 Cast Thy Burden upon the Lord
736 Celtic Alleluia
373 Change My Heart, O God
677 Child of Blessing, Child of Promise
83 Children of the Heavenly Father
294 Christ Arose!
453 Christ Be My Leader
425 Christ Beside Me
561 Christ for the World! We Sing
324 Christ High-Ascended
312 Christ Is Alive!
369 Christ Is God's Never Changing 'Yes!'
293 Christ Is Risen! Shout Hosanna!
121 Christ Is the World's Light
276 Christ, Let Us Come with You
335 Christ the Eternal Lord
309 Christ the Lord Is Risen!
288 Christ the Lord Is Risen Today
517 Christ the Victorious
336 Christ Triumphant, Ever Reigning
91 Christ, Whose Glory Fills the Skies
571 Christ, You Call Us All to Service
541 Church of God, Elect and Glorious
643 Colorful Creator
459 Come, All Christians, Be Committed
605 *Come and Fill Our Homes with Your Presence*
477 Come and Find the Quiet Center
197 Come and Hear the Joyful Singing
676 *Come As a Child*
655 Come Away from Rush and Hurry
676 Come, Be Baptized
543 Come Build a Church
584 Come, Celebrate the Call of God
87 Come, Christians, Join to Sing
330 Come Down, O Love Divine
548 Come, Great God of All the Ages
127 Come, Holy Spirit
325 Come, Holy Spirit, Our Souls Inspire
119 Come into His Presence
694 Come, Let Us Eat
9 Come, Let Us Praise the Lord
403 Come, My Way, My Truth, My Life
157 Come Now, O Prince of Peace
329 Come, O Spirit, Dwell Among Us
696 Come, Share the Lord
148 Come, Thou Almighty King
68 Come, Thou Fount of Every Blessing
153 Come, Thou Long-Expected Jesus
609 Come to a Wedding
67 Come, We That Love the Lord
390 *Come, We That Love the Lord*
721 Come, Ye Thankful People, Come
155 Comfort, Comfort Now My People
615 Community of Christ
378 Create in Me a Clean Heart, O God
32 Creating God, Your Fingers Trace
340 Crown Him King of Kings
317 Crown Him with Many Crowns
624 *Cuando el Pobre*
449 Day by Day
238 *De Tierra Lejana Venimos*
601 Dear Christ, Uplifted from the Earth
470 Dear Lord and Father of Mankind
538 Deep River
204 Down to Earth, as a Dove
34 *Doxology (OLD 100th)*
44 Doxology (Owens)
147 *Doxology (Wren)*
408 *Draw Me Nearer*
642 Earth and All Stars
314 Easter Song
697 Eat This Bread
692 Eat This Bread and Never Hunger
178 Emmanuel, Emmanuel
74 Eternal Father, Strong to Save
418 Eternal Light, Shine in My Heart
475 Eternal Spirit of the Living Christ
436 *Every Promise We Can Make*
481 Every Time I Feel the Spirit
535 Face to Face
123 Fairest Lord Jesus
530 Faith of Our Fathers
143 Father, I Adore You
146 *Father, We Love You*
392 Fear Not, Rejoice and Be Glad
331 Filled with the Spirit's Power
497 Find Us Faithful
410 Firm Foundation
172 For Ages Women Hoped and Prayed
529 For All the Saints
28 For Beauty of Meadows
617 *For Everyone Born, A Place at the Table*
40 For the Beauty of the Earth

723 For the Fruit of All Creation
621 For the Healing of the Nations
684 For the Life That You Have Given
641 For the Music of Creation
47 *For Thou, O Lord, Art High*
382 "Forgive Our Sins as We Forgive"
718 Forth in Your Name
238 From a Distant Home
640 From Miles Around
649 Gather Us In
705 *Gift of Finest Wheat*
359 Give Thanks
518 Give Thanks for Life
63 Give to Our God Immortal Praise
240 Gloria, Gloria
195 Gloria, Gloria, Gloria
146 Glorify Thy Name
598 Glorious Things of Thee Are Spoken
145 Glory Be to God, Creator
734 Glory Be to the Father (GREATOREX)
733 Glory Be to the Father (MEINEKE)
240 *Glory to God*
732 Glory to God, Glory in the Highest
103 Glory to the Lamb
618 Go Down, Moses
708 Go Forth for God
556 Go Forth in His Name
719 Go, My Children, with My Blessing
717 Go Now in Peace
218 Go, Tell It on the Mountain
272 Go to Dark Gethsemane
553 Go to the World!
747 Go with Us, Lord
716 God Be with You
667 God Has Spoken by the Prophets
37 God in His Love for Us
1 God Is Here!
139 God Is One, Unique and Holy
564 God Is Working His Purpose Out
65 God Moves in a Mysterious Way
394 God of All Time
27 God of Creation, All-Powerful
569 God of Grace and God of Glory
58 God of Many Names
409 God of Our Life
78 God of the Ages, History's Maker
728 God of the Ages, Whose Almighty Hand
29 God of the Sparrow
130 God Sends Us the Spirit
447 *God Sent His Son, They Called Him Jesus*
149 God the Spirit, Guide and Guardian
3 God, We Praise You!
416 God! When Human Bonds Are Broken
644 God, Who Stretched the Spangled Heavens
572 God, Whose Giving Knows No Ending
24 God, You Spin the Whirling Planets
663 God's Holy Ways Are Just and True
226 God's Love Made Visible!
198 Good Christian Friends, Rejoice
307 Good Christians All, Rejoice
296 Goodness Is Stronger than Evil
436 Grace Alone
353 Grace Greater than Our Sin
604 Great God, as We Are Gathering
55 Great God, Your Love Has Called Us Here
50 Great Is the Lord
72 Great Is Thy Faithfulness
516 Grief of Ending, Wordless Sorrow
501 Guide Me, O Thou Great Jehovah
323 Hail the Day That Sees Him Rise
5 Halle, Halle, Hallelujah
735 Hallelujah
98 Hallelujah! Praise the Lamb!
709 Hallelujah! We Sing Your Praises
301 Hallelujah! What a Savior!
607 Happy the Home When God Is There
185 Hark! the Herald Angels Sing
486 Have Thine Own Way, Lord!
402 He Came Down
454 He Came Singing Love
412 He Comes to Us As One Unknown
657 He Has Made Me Glad
639 He Is Able
201 He Is Born
122 He Is Exalted
305 He Is Lord
499 He Leadeth Me
302 He Lives
280 He Never Said a Mumbalin' Word
80 He's Got the Whole World in His Hands
636 Heal Me, Hands of Jesus
633 Healer of My Soul
630 Healer of Our Every Ill
370 Healing Grace
490 Hear Our Prayer, O Lord
314 *Hear the Bells Ringing*
735 *Heleluyan*
596 Help Us Accept Each Other
528 Here from All Nations
559 Here I Am, Lord

649 *Here in This Place*
597 Here, O Lord, Your Servants Gather
104 Hidden Christ, Alive for Ever
297 His Battle Ended There
102 His Name Is Wonderful
637 His Strength Is Perfect
199 *Holy Child Within the Manger*
138 Holy God, We Praise Your Name
654 Holy Ground
739 "Holy, Holy, Holy"
737 *Holy, Holy, Holy*
738 Holy, Holy, Holy Lord
136 Holy, Holy, Holy! Lord God Almighty!
151 Holy Is the Lord
165 *Hope Is a Star*
404 Hope of the World
266 Hosanna (Tuttle)
269 *Hosanna (South African)*
267 Hosanna, Loud Hosanna
526 How Blest Are They
424 How Can I Keep from Singing?
363 *How Can I Say Thanks*
573 How Clear Is Our Vocation, Lord
411 How Firm a Foundation
51 How Great Thou Art
376 How Long, O Lord
545 How Lovely, Lord, How Lovely
42 How Majestic Is Your Name
107 *Hymn of Light*
515 Hymn of Promise
519 *I Am Bound for the Promised Land*
703 I Am the Bread of Life
550 *I Am the Church!*
408 I Am Thine, O Lord
504 *I Am Weak, but Thou Art Strong*
675 I Believe in Jesus
493 *I Cast All My Cares upon You*
251 I Come to the Cross
300 *I Come to the Garden Alone*
706 I Come with Joy
118 *I Danced in the Morning*
47 *I Exalt Thee*
77 I Greet Thee, Who My Sure Redeemer Art
344 I Have Decided to Follow Jesus
407 *I Know Not Why God's Wondrous Grace*
414 I Know That My Redeemer Lives!
407 I Know Whom I Have Believed
488 I Lift My Eyes to the Quiet Hills
560 I Love to Tell the Story
85 I Love You, Lord
549 I Love Your Kingdom, Lord
476 I Need Thee Every Hour
302 *I Serve a Risen Savior*
660 I Sing Praises
31 I Sing the Almighty Power of God
277 *I Stand Amazed in the Presence*
53 I Stand in Awe
474 I Surrender All
720 *I Thank You, Lord, for Each New Day*
559 *I, the Lord of Sea and Sky*
372 I Then Shall Live
506 I Want Jesus to Walk with Me
248 I Want to Walk as a Child of the Light
680 *I Was There to Hear Your Borning Cry*
653 I Will Call upon the Lord
657 *I Will Enter His Gates*
356 I Will Sing of My Redeemer
60 I Will Sing of the Mercies
648 *I Will Worship with All of My Heart*
225 I Wonder as I Wander
69 I Worship You, Almighty God
79 I'll Praise My Maker While I've Breath
574 I'm Gonna Live So God Can Use Me
434 If Christ Had Not Been Raised from Death
383 If My People's Hearts Are Humbled
429 If You Will Trust in God to Guide You
48 Immortal, Invisible, God Only Wise
603 In Christ There Is No East or West (Oxenham)
600 In Christ There Is No East or West (Perry)
511 *In Heavenly Armor We'll Enter the Land*
465 *In My Life, Lord*
196 In the Bleak Midwinter
515 *In the Bulb There Is a Flower*
264 In the Cross of Christ I Glory
445 In the Day of Need
300 In the Garden
224 *In the Little Village of Bethlehem*
62 In the Lord Alone
448 In the Lord I'll Be Ever Thankful
303 *In the Lord Rejoicing!*
125 In the Name of the Lord
678 In Water We Grow
221 Infant Holy, Infant Lowly
485 Into My Heart
532 Isaiah the Prophet Has Written of Old
191 It Came upon the Midnight Clear
428 *It Is Well with My Soul*
557 *It Only Takes a Spark*
273 Jesu, Jesu, Fill Us with Your Love
659 *Jesu Tawa Pano*

108 *Jesus, Jesus, Jesus*
345 Jesus Calls Us o'er the Tumult
295 Jesus Christ Is Risen Today
669 Jesus, Come, for We Invite You
318 Jesus Comes with Clouds Descending
634 Jesus' Hands Were Kind Hands
479 *Jesus, Keep Me Near the Cross*
439 Jesus, Lover of My Soul
437 Jesus Loves Me
177 Jesus, Name Above All Names
219 Jesus, Oh, What a Wonderful Child
246 Jesus on the Mountain Peak
431 Jesus, Priceless Treasure
285 Jesus, Remember Me
554 *Jesus Saves!*
341 Jesus Shall Reign
420 Jesus, the Very Thought of Thee
254 Jesus Walked This Lonesome Valley
659 Jesus, We Are Here
90 Jesus! What a Friend for Sinners!
361 Jesus, Your Name
410 *Jesus, You're My Firm Foundation*
533 Joy in the Morning
179 Joy to the World!
59 Joyful, Joyful, We Adore Thee
303 Jubilate Deo (In the Lord Rejoicing!)
212 *Jubilate Deo (Raise a Song of Gladness)*
504 Just a Closer Walk with Thee
354 Just As I Am
338 King of Kings
253 *King of My Life, I Crown Thee Now*
273 *Kneels at the Feet of His Friends*
357 Knowing You
487 Kum Ba Yah
379 Kyrie
377 Kyrie Eleison
281 Lamb of God
498 Lead Me, Guide Me
253 Lead Me to Calvary
508 Lead On, O King Eternal
496 Leaning on the Everlasting Arms
25 Let All Creation Bless the Lord
232 Let All Mortal Flesh Keep Silence
49 Let All the World
22 Let All Things Now Living
332 Let Every Christian Pray
360 *Let the Weak Say, "I Am Strong"*
6 Let the Whole Creation Cry
614 Let There Be Peace on Earth
54 Let There Be Praise
699 Let Us Break Bread Together
698 Let Us Talents and Tongues Employ
33 Let's Sing unto the Lord
729 Lift Every Voice and Sing
287 Lift High the Cross
271 Lift Up Your Heads
176 Lift Up Your Heads, O Mighty Gates
120 *Lift Up Your Hearts unto the Lord*
162 like a child
20 Like a Mighty River Flowing
435 Like a River Glorious
327 Like the Murmur of the Dove's Song
683 Little One, Born to Bring
190 Lo, How a Rose E'er Blooming
167 Long Ago, Prophets Knew
465 Lord, Be Glorified
748 Lord, Dismiss Us with Your Blessing
70 Lord, for the Years
375 Lord, Have Mercy
467 *Lord, I Come to You*
88 Lord, I Lift Your Name on High
457 Lord, I Want to Be a Christian
386 Lord Jesus, Think on Me
489 Lord, Listen to Your Children Praying
469 Lord of All Hopefulness
608 Lord of Our Growing Years
118 Lord of the Dance
524 Lord of the Living
482 *Lord, Prepare Me to Be a Sanctuary*
593 Lord, Speak to Me
319 *Lord, the Light of Your Love*
681 Lord, We Bring to You Our Children
671 Lord, We Hear Your Word
252 Lord, Who Throughout These Forty Days
575 Lord, Whose Love Through Humble Service
592 Lord, You Give the Great Commission
379 *Lord, Have Mercy*
347 Lord, You Have Come to the Lakeshore
210 Love Came Down at Christmas
358 Love Divine, All Loves Excelling
135 Loving Spirit
294 *Low in the Grave He Lay*
173 Magnificat
43 Majesty
587 Make Me a Channel of Your Peace
576 Make Me a Servant
301 *"Man of Sorrows" What a Name*
26 Many and Great
353 *Marvelous Grace of Our Loving Lord*
192 Mary, Did You Know?
220 Mary Had a Baby
400 *May Love Be Ours*
464 May the Mind of Christ, My Savior
563 *May We Be a Shining Light*

97 Meekness and Majesty
370 *Merciful God and Father*
45 Mighty Is Our God
730 Mine Eyes Have Seen the Glory
35 Morning Has Broken
731 My Country, 'Tis of Thee
406 My Faith Has Found a Resting Place
419 My Faith Looks Up to Thee
405 My Hope Is Built on Nothing Less
468 My Jesus, I Love Thee
94 *My Jesus, My Savior, Lord There Is None Like You*
424 *My Life Flows on in Endless Song*
150 My Lord of Light
537 My Lord! What a Morning
259 *My Lord, What Love Is This*
277 My Savior's Love
170 My Soul Proclaims with Wonder
363 My Tribute
421 *Nada te Turbe*
101 Name of All Majesty
479 Near the Cross
8 New Songs of Celebration
217 No Obvious Angels
400 Not for Tongues of Heaven's Angels
417 Not with Naked Eye
421 Nothing Can Trouble
627 Now It Is Evening
715 Now Let Us from This Table Rise
367 Now Let Us Learn of Christ
14 Now Thank We All Our God
311 Now the Green Blade Rises
700 Now the Silence
727 *O Beautiful for Spacious Skies*
328 O Breath of Life
638 O Christ, the Healer, We Have Come
433 O Christ the Same
565 O Christians, Haste
182 O Come, All Ye Faithful
114 O Come, Let Us Adore Him
154 O Come, O Come, Emmanuel
346 O Come to Me, the Master Said
539 O Day of Peace
96 O for a Thousand Tongues to Sing
64 O God Beyond All Praising
388 O God in Whom All Life Begins
626 O God of Every Nation
84 O God, Our Help in Ages Past
494 *O God, You Are My God*
503 O God, Your Constant Care and Love
368 O Happy Day
187 O Holy Night
270 O How He Loves You and Me
109 O, How I Love Jesus
582 O Jesus Christ, May Grateful Hymns Be Rising
458 O Jesus, I Have Promised
352 *O Let the Son of God Enfold You*
107 O Light Whose Splendor Thrills
180 O Little Town of Bethlehem
377 *O Lord, Have Mercy*
484 O Lord, Hear My Prayer
51 *O Lord My God, When I in Awesome Wonder*
42 *O Lord, Our Lord, How Majestic Is Your Name*
620 O Lord, You Gave Your Servant John
244 O Love, How Deep, How Broad
446 O Love That Will Not Let Me Go
589 O Master, Let Me Walk with Thee
497 *O May All Who Come Behind Us*
230 O Morning Star, How Fair and Bright!
610 O Perfect Love
284 O Sacred Head, Now Wounded
242 O Sing a Song of Bethlehem
15 O, Sing to the Lord
313 O Sons and Daughters, Let Us Sing!
144 O Splendor of God's Glory Bright
398 O the Deep, Deep Love of Jesus
670 O Word of God Incarnate
2 O Worship the King
401 Of All the Spirit's Gifts to Me
181 Of the Father's Love Begotten
208 Oh, How Joyfully
207 Oh, Sleep Now, Holy Baby
260 *On a Hill Far Away*
222 On Christmas Night All Christians Sing
438 On Eagle's Wings
156 On Jordan's Bank the Baptist's Cry
519 On Jordan's Stormy Banks I Stand
334 On Pentecost They Gathered
183 Once in Royal David's City
689 One Bread, One Body
509 Onward, Christian Soldiers
480 Open My Eyes, That I May See
491 Open Our Eyes
656 Open the Eyes of My Heart
124 Open Your Hearts
377 *Oré Poriajú Verekó*
157 *O-so-so*
586 Our Cities Cry to You, O God
371 Our Father, We Have Wandered
740 *Our Father, Who Art in Heaven*
90 *Our Great Savior*
658 *Our God Is an Awesome God*
557 Pass It On

161 People, Look East
568 People Need the Lord
722 Praise and Thanksgiving
140 Praise and Thanksgiving Be to God
34 Praise God from Whom All Blessings Flow (OLD 100th)
44 *Praise God from Whom All Blessings Flow (Owens)*
147 Praise God From Whom All Blessings Flow (Wren)
95 Praise Him! Praise Him!
82 Praise, My Soul, the King of Heaven
17 Praise the Lord! O Heavens, Adore Him
46 Praise the Lord Who Reigns Above
115 Praise the Name of Jesus
93 Praise the One Who Breaks the Darkness
71 Praise to the Lord, the Almighty
587 *Prayer of St. Francis*
500 Precious Lord, Take My Hand
152 Prepare the Way, O Zion
174 Prepare the Way of the Lord
415 *Pues Si Vivimos*
374 *Purify My Heart*
389 Put Peace into Each Other's Hands
444 Rain Down
212 Raise a Song of Gladness
374 Refiner's Fire
531 Rejoice in God's Saints
650 Rejoice in the Lord Always
342 Rejoice, the Lord Is King!
113 Rejoice, Ye Pure in Heart
462 Renew Your Church
381 Restore in Us, O God
463 Revive Us Again
268 Ride On, Ride On in Majesty!
89 Rise, Shine, You People!
590 Rise Up, O Saints of God!
209 Rise Up, Shepherd, and Follow
384 Rock of Ages
482 Sanctuary
269 Sanna, Sannanina
739 *"Santo, Santo, Santo"*
737 Santo, Santo, Santo
711 Savior, Again to Your Dear Name
440 Savior, Like a Shepherd Lead Us
168 Savior of the Nations, Come
385 Search Me, O God
227 See Him Lying on a Bed of Straw
249 *See the Little Baby Lying in a Manger*
349 Seek Ye First
713 Send Me, Jesus
712 Sent Forth by God's Blessing
599 Shadow and Substance
522 Shall We Gather at the River
714 *Shalom Chaverim*
714 Shalom, My Friends
319 Shine, Jesus, Shine
304 Shout for Joy, Loud and Long
94 Shout to the Lord
186 Silent Night! Holy Night!
577 Sing a New Church
10 Sing a New Song
13 Sing a New Song to the Lord
120 Sing Alleluia to the Lord
141 Sing of a God in Majestic Divinity
247 Sing of God Made Manifest
173 *Sing Out, My Soul*
56 Sing Praise to God Who Reigns Above
142 Sing Praise to the Father
525 *Sing the Wondrous Love of Jesus*
668 *Sing Them Over Again to Me*
724 Sing to the Lord of Harvest
193 Sing We Now of Christmas
76 *Siyahamba*
578 So Send I You
348 Softly and Tenderly
563 Song for the Nations
243 Songs of Thankfulness and Praise
523 Soon and Very Soon
132 Spirit of God, Descend upon My Heart
492 Spirit of the Living God
352 Spirit Song
326 Spirit, Spirit of Gentleness
128 Spirit, Working in Creation
130 *Spirit-Friend*
495 Stand by Me
11 Stand Up and Bless the Lord
513 Stand Up, Stand Up for Jesus
223 Star-Child
286 Stay with Me
527 Steal Away
494 Step by Step
214 Still, Still, Still
629 Strong, Gentle Children
577 *Summoned by the God Who Made Us*
423 Surely It Is God Who Saves Me
131 Surely the Presence
478 Sweet Hour of Prayer
134 Sweet, Sweet Spirit
520 Swing Low, Sweet Chariot
343 *Take Me, Mold Me, Use Me*
466 Take My Life and Let It Be
455 Take Thou Our Minds, Dear Lord
483 Take Time to Be Holy
351 "Take Up Your Cross," the Savior Said

41 Tell Out, My Soul
36 Thank You, God, for Water, Soil, and Air
365 Thank You, Lord
725 Thanks to God for My Redeemer
662 Thanks to God Whose Word Was Spoken
211 That Boy-Child of Mary
299 That Easter Day with Joy Was Bright
169 The Angel Gabriel from Heaven Came
511 The Battle Belongs to the Lord
224 The Birthday of a King
395 The Bond of Love
623 The Church of Christ in Every Age
544 The Church's One Foundation
298 The Day of Resurrection!
605 The Family Prayer Song
229 The First Noel
682 The Fruit of Love
397 The Gift of Love
16 The God of Abraham Praise
237 The Hands That First Held Mary's Child
339 The Head That Once Was Crowned
159 The King of Glory Comes
749 The Lord Bless You and Keep You
387 The Lord Is in His Holy Temple
73 The Lord My Shepherd Guards Me Well
86 The Lord's My Shepherd, I'll Not Want
740 The Lord's Prayer
18 The Name of the Lord
260 The Old Rugged Cross
343 The Potter's Hand
467 The Power of Your Love
391 *The Servant Song*
405 *The Solid Rock*
290 The Strife Is O'er
350 The Summons
710 The Trees of the Field
558 The World Is Full of Stories
631 There Is a Balm in Gilead
256 There Is a Fountain Filled with Blood
109 *There Is a Name I Love to Hear*
117 There Is a Redeemer
125 *There Is Strength in the Name of the Lord*
533 *There'll Be Joy in the Morning*
701 There's a Quiet Understanding
133 There's a Spirit in the Air
209 *There's a Star in the East on Christmas Morn*
134 *There's a Sweet, Sweet Spirit in This Place*
61 There's a Wideness in God's Mercy
108 There's Something About That Name
280 *They Crucified My Lord*
542 They Did Not Build in Vain
595 They'll Know We Are Christians
310 Thine Is the Glory
57 Think About His Love
355 This Is a Day of New Beginnings
579 This Is a Time to Remember
21 This Is My Father's World
652 This Is the Day
315 This Is the Feast of Victory
672 This Is the Threefold Truth
308 This Joyful Eastertide
126 Thou Art Worthy
397 *Though I May Speak with Bravest Fire*
452 Through It All
536 Through the Darkness of the Ages
250 Throughout These Lenten Days and Nights
456 Thy Holy Wings
664 Thy Word
442 'Tis So Sweet to Trust in Jesus
171 To a Maid Whose Name Was Mary
66 To God Be the Glory
363 *To God Be the Glory*
278 To Mock Your Reign
163 *Toda la Tierra*
38 Touch the Earth Lightly
443 Trust and Obey
441 Trust in the Lord
347 *Tú Has Venido a la Orilla*
472 Turn Your Eyes upon Jesus
213 'Twas in the Moon of Wintertime
540 Two Thousand Years Since Bethlehem
399 Ubi Caritas et Amor
166 Wait for the Lord
164 Wake, Awake, for Night Is Flying
216 *We Adore You*
552 We All Are One in Mission
580 We Are Called to Be God's People
547 We Are God's People
556 *We Are His Children*
395 *We Are One in the Bond of Love*
595 *We Are One in the Spirit*
76 We Are Singing, for the Lord Is Our Light
654 *We Are Standing on Holy Ground*
550 We Are the Church
594 We Are Your People
673 We Believe in God Almighty
651 We Bring the Sacrifice of Praise
628 We Cannot Measure How You Heal

702 We Come as Guests Invited
110 We Come, O Christ, to You
47 We Exalt Thee
696 *We Gather Here in Jesus' Name*
81 We Gather Together
688 We Give Thee but Thine Own
245 We Have Come at Christ's Own Bidding
647 We Have Come to Join in Worship
554 We Have Heard the Joyful Sound
175 We Light the Advent Candles
704 We Meet as Friends at Table
616 We Meet You, O Christ
463 *We Praise Thee, O God*
726 We Praise You, O God
690 We Remember You
512 We Shall Overcome
707 We Thank You, God, for Feeding Us
233 We Three Kings of Orient Are
337 We Will Glorify
390 We're Marching to Zion
562 We've a Story to Tell to the Nations
283 Were You There
215 Were You There on That Christmas Night
496 *What a Fellowship, What a Joy Divine*
473 What a Friend We Have in Jesus
674 What a Mighty God
184 What Child Is This
686 What Does the Lord Require
685 What Gift Can We Bring
360 What the Lord Has Done in Me
257 What Wondrous Love Is This
632 When Aimless Violence Takes Those We Love
165 When God Is a Child
261 When I Survey the Wondrous Cross
7 When in Our Music God Is Glorified
618 *When Israel Was in Egypt's Land*
241 When Jesus Came to Jordan
239 When John Baptized by Jordan's River
612 When Love Is Found
111 When Morning Gilds the Skies
413 When Our Confidence Is Shaken
428 When Peace Like a River
555 When the Church of Jesus
534 When the King Shall Come Again
645 When the Morning Stars Together
624 When the Poor Ones
495 *When the Storms of Life Are Raging*
525 When We All Get to Heaven
415 When We Are Living
443 *When We Walk with the Lord*
622 When Will People Cease Their Fighting?
591 Where Cross the Crowded Ways of Life
396 Where the Spirit of the Lord Is
399 *Where True Charity and Love Abide*
200 While by the Sheep
228 While Shepherds Watched Their Flocks
602 Who Is My Mother, Who Is My Brother?
350 *Will You Come and Follow Me*
391 Will You Let Me Be Your Servant
333 Wind Who Makes All Winds That Blow
234 Wise Men, They Came to Look for Wisdom
720 With Grateful Heart I Thank You, Lord
691 With the Body That Was Broken
567 With Welcome Heart We Greet You, Lord
364 Woman in the Night
362 Wonderful Grace of Jesus
668 Wonderful Words of Life
116 Worthy Is the Lamb
137 Worthy of Worship
53 *You Are Beautiful Beyond Description*
427 You Are My All in All
52 You Are My God
427 *You Are My Strength When I Am Weak*
583 You Call Us, Lord
99 You, Lord, Are Both Lamb and Shepherd
705 You Satisfy the Hungry Heart
112 You Servants of God
430 *You Shall Cross the Barren Desert*
710 *You Shall Go Out with Joy*
438 *You Who Dwell in the Shelter of the Lord*
648 You're Worthy of My Praise
613 Your Love, O God, Has Called Us
281 *Your Only Son, No Sin to Hide*
566 Your Servant Comes This Hour